MACROECONOMICS

CANADA IN THE GLOBAL ENVIRONMENT

EIGHTH EDITION

The moment you know

It's that inspired moment when something makes perfect sense. **MyEconLab for Parkin and Bade,** *Economics: Canada in the Global Environment,* **Eighth Edition**

MyEconLab is a dynamic online tool that helps you reach that moment, time and again.

- Chapter tests generate your personal study plan and an assignment tool lets your instructor guide your learning toward those moments of true understanding.

- Practise problems directly from the textbook's Review Quiz and end-of-chapter Problems and Applications in your personal Study Plan with links to online learning resources.

- "Help-Me-Solve-This" breaks down a problem and guides you through the steps to solve it.

- Links to the eText guide you to revisit a concept or explanation when needed.

- Animated graphs with audio explanations reinforce your reading.

- The graphing tool enables you to build and manipulate graphs to understand how concepts, numbers, and graphs connect.

- Unlimited Practice: Hundreds of practice questions ensure that you get as much practice as you need, and as you work on each exercise, instant feedback helps you understand and apply the concepts.

Study on the Go

Scan the QR code at the end of each chapter to link to resources you can use on your smart-phone. Study on the Go provides a convenient and unprecedented integration between text and online content:

- Glossary flashcards
- Audio summaries
- Quizzes to make the most of your time when you're on the move

MICHAEL PARKIN   ROBIN BADE

MACROECONOMICS

CANADA IN THE GLOBAL ENVIRONMENT

EIGHTH EDITION

PEARSON

Toronto

Vice-President, Editorial Director: Gary Bennett
Editor-in-Chief: Nicole Lukach
Acquisitions Editor: Claudine O'Donnell
Senior Marketing Manager: Leigh-Anne Graham
Developmental Editor: Karen Townsend
Lead Project Manager: Söğüt Y. Güleç
Manufacturing Manager: Susan Johnson
Production Editor: Leanne Rancourt
Copy Editor: Trish O'Reilly

Proofreader: Sally Glover
Compositor: Nelson Gonzalez
Technical Illustrator: Richard Parkin
Permissions Researcher: Rema Celio
Photo Researchers: Rema Celio and Dominic Farrell
Art Director: Julia Hall
Cover and Interior Designer: Anthony Leung
Cover Image: Getty Images

Credits and acknowledgments of material borrowed from other sources and reproduced, with permission, in this textbook appear on the appropriate page within the text and on p. C-1.

Statistics Canada information is used with the permission of the Minister of Industry, as Minister responsible for Statistics Canada. Information on the availability of the wide range of data from Statistics Canada can be obtained from Statistics Canada's Regional Offices, its World Wide Web site at www.statcan.gc.ca, and its toll-free access number 1-800-263-1136.

If you purchased this book outside the United States or Canada, you should be aware that it has been imported without the approval of the publisher or the author.

10 9 8 7 6 5 4 3 2 [CKV]

Library and Archives Canada Cataloguing in Publication

Parkin, Michael, 1939–
    Macroeconomics : Canada in the global environment / Michael Parkin, Robin Bade. — 8th ed.

Includes index.
ISBN 978-0-321-77810-9

    1. Macroeconomics—Textbooks. 2. Canada—Economic conditions—
1991– —Textbooks. I. Bade, Robin II. Title.

HB172.5.P363 2013   339   C2011-906096-5

ISBN 978-0-321-77810-9

TO

OUR STUDENTS

Michael Parkin

received his training as an economist at the Universities of Leicester and Essex in England. He is Professor Emeritus in the Department of Economics at the University of Western Ontario, Canada. Professor Parkin has held faculty appointments at Brown University, the University of Manchester, the University of Essex, and Bond University. He is a past president of the Canadian Economics Association and has served on the editorial boards of the *American Economic Review* and the *Journal of Monetary Economics* and as managing editor of the *Canadian Journal of Economics*. Professor Parkin's research on macroeconomics, monetary economics, and international economics has resulted in over 160 publications in journals and edited volumes, including the *American Economic Review*, the *Journal of Political Economy*, the *Review of Economic Studies*, the *Journal of Monetary Economics*, and the *Journal of Money, Credit and Banking*. He became most visible to the public with his work on inflation that discredited the use of wage and price controls. Michael Parkin also spearheaded the movement towards European monetary union.

Robin Bade

earned degrees in mathematics and economics at the University of Queensland and her Ph.D. at the Australian National University. She has held faculty appointments at the University of Edinburgh in Scotland, at Bond University in Australia, and at the Universities of Manitoba, Toronto, and Western Ontario in Canada. Her research on international capital flows appears in the *International Economic Review* and the *Economic Record*.

Professor Parkin and Dr. Bade are the joint authors of *Foundations of Economics* (Addison Wesley), *Modern Macroeconomics* (Pearson Education Canada), an intermediate text, and have collabrated on many research and textbook writing projects. They are both experienced and dedicated teachers of introductory economics.

BRIEF CONTENTS

PART 1
INTRODUCTION 1
CHAPTER 1 What Is Economics? 1
CHAPTER 2 The Economic Problem 29

PART 2
HOW MARKETS WORK 55
CHAPTER 3 Demand and Supply 55

PART 7
MONITORING MACROECONOMIC PERFORMANCE 467
CHAPTER 20 Measuring GDP and Economic Growth 467
CHAPTER 21 Monitoring Jobs and Inflation 491

PART 8
MACROECONOMIC TRENDS 517
CHAPTER 22 Economic Growth 517
CHAPTER 23 Finance, Saving, and Investment 543

CHAPTER 24 Money, the Price Level, and Inflation 567
CHAPTER 25 The Exchange Rate and the Balance of Payments 593

PART 9
MACROECONOMIC FLUCTUATIONS 623
CHAPTER 26 Aggregate Supply and Aggregate Demand 623
CHAPTER 27 Expenditure Multipliers: The Keynesian Model 647
CHAPTER 28 Canadian Inflation, Unemployment, and Business Cycle 677

PART 10
MACROECONOMIC POLICY 703
CHAPTER 29 Fiscal Policy 703
CHAPTER 30 Monetary Policy 727
CHAPTER 31 International Trade Policy 751

PREFACE

The future is always uncertain. But at some times, and now is one such time, the range of possible futures is enormous. The major sources of this great uncertainty are economic policy and global macroeconomic forces. There is uncertainty about the way in which international trade policy will evolve as protectionism and trade agreements clash for centre stage. There is uncertainty about exchange rate policy as competitive devaluation rears its head. There is extraordinary uncertainty about monetary policy with the Bank of Canada holding interest rates at historical lows in an attempt to stimulate a flagging economy. And there is uncertainty about fiscal policy as federal and provincial budget deficits seem ever harder to control. In the global economy, the European debt crisis is the dominant source of uncertainty. But whether or when economic growth in China and India will slow and dampen the growth of the rest of the world is a big unknown.

Since the global financial crisis of August 2007 moved economics from the business report to the front page, justified fear has gripped producers, consumers, financial institutions, and governments.

Even the *idea* that the market is an efficient mechanism for allocating scarce resources came into question as some political leaders trumpeted the end of capitalism and the dawn of a new economic order in which tighter regulation reigned in unfettered greed.

Rarely do teachers of economics have such a rich feast on which to draw. And rarely are the principles of economics more surely needed to provide the solid foundation on which to think about economic events and navigate the turbulence of economic life.

Although thinking like an economist can bring a clearer perspective to and deeper understanding of today's events, students don't find the economic way of thinking easy or natural. *Macroeconomics* seeks to put clarity and understanding in the grasp of the student through its careful and vivid exploration of the tension between self-interest and the social interest, the role and power of incentives—of opportunity cost and marginal benefit—and demonstrating the possibility that markets supplemented by other mechanisms might allocate resources efficiently.

Parkin and Bade students begin to think about issues the way real economists do and learn how to explore difficult policy problems and make more-informed decisions in their own economic lives.

◆ The Eighth Edition Revision

Simpler where possible, stripped of some technical detail, more copiously illustrated with well-chosen photographs, reinforced with improved chapter summaries and problem sets, and even more tightly integrated with MyEconLab: These are the hallmarks of this eighth edition of *Macroeconomics: Canada in the Global Environment*.

This comprehensive revision also incorporates and responds to the detailed suggestions for improvements made by reviewers and users, both in the broad architecture of the text and in each chapter.

The revision builds on the improvements achieved in previous editions and retains its thorough and detailed presentation of the principles of economics, its emphasis on real-world examples and applications, its development of critical thinking skills, its diagrams renowned for pedagogy and precision, and its path-breaking technology.

Most chapters have been fine-tuned to achieve even greater clarity and to present the material in a more straightforward, visual, and intuitive way. Some chapters have been thoroughly reworked to cover new issues, particularly those that involve current policy problems. These changes are aimed at better enabling students to learn how to use the economic toolkit to analyze their own decisions and understand the events and issues they are confronted with in the media and at the ballot box.

Current issues organize each chapter. News stories about today's major economic events tie each chapter together, from new briefer chapter-opening questions to end-of-chapter problems and online practice. Each chapter includes a discussion of a critical issue of our time to demonstrate how economic theory can be applied to explore a particular debate or question. Among the many issues covered are

- The gains from trade, globalization, and protectionism in Chapters 2 and 31
- How ethanol competes with food and drives its price up in Chapter 2
- The fluctuating price of coffee in Chapter 3
- Recession and unemployment in Chapters 21, 26, and 28
- Currency fluctuations and the managed Chinese yuan in Chapter 25
- Fiscal stimulus and the debate about the fiscal stimulus multipliers in Chapter 29
- Monetary stimulus in Chapter 30

Real-world examples and applications appear in the body of each chapter and in the end-of-chapter problems and applications, which are available in MyEconLab for assignment as homework, quizzes, or tests.

A selection of questions that appear daily in MyEconLab in *Economics in the News* are also available for assignment as homework, quizzes, or tests.

Highpoints of the Revision

All the chapters have been updated to incorporate data through the second quarter of 2011 (later for some variables) and the news and policy situation through the fall of 2011. Beyond these general updates, the macro chapters feature the following eight notable revisions:

1. *Measuring GDP and Economic Growth* (Chapter 20): We have revised the section on cross-country comparisons and the limitations of GDP to make the material clearer and added photo illustrations of purchasing power parity and of items omitted from GDP. A new appendix to this chapter explains the graphing of time-series data and the use of a ratio scale to reveal trends. The Mathematical Note on chain linking has been simplified.

2. *Monitoring Jobs and Inflation* (Chapter 21): This chapter now includes a discussion and illustration of the duration of unemployment spells. We have rewritten the section on full employment and the influences on the natural unemployment rate. The coverage of the price level has been expanded to define and explain the costs of deflation as well as inflation.

3. *Economic Growth* (Chapter 22): We have simplified this chapter by omitting the technical details on growth accounting and replacing them with an intuitive discussion of the crucial role of human capital and intellectual property rights. We illustrate the role played by these key factors in Britain's Industrial Revolution. We have made the chapter more relevant and empirical by including a summary of the correlations between the growth rate and the positive and negative influences on it.

4. *Money, the Price Level, and Inflation* (Chapter 24): This chapter compares the Bank of Canada's response to the global financial crisis with the U.S. Federal Reserve's extraordinary injection of mone-

tary base following the financial panic of 2008. We have redrawn the line between this chapter, the "money and banking" chapter, and the later "monetary policy" chapter by including in this chapter a complete explanation of how an open-market operation works. We have also provided clearer and more thorough explanations of the money multiplier and money market equilibrium in the short and the long run and in the transition to the long run.

5. *The Exchange Rate and the Balance of Payments* (Chapter 25): We have revised this chapter to better explain the distinction between the fundamentals and the role of expectations. We have also included an explanation of how arbitrage works in the foreign exchange market and the temporary and risky nature of seeking to profit from the so-called "carry trade."

6. *Aggregate Supply and Aggregate Demand* (Chapter 26): We have revised the section of this chapter that explains the use of the *AS-AD* model to understand growth and inflation trends and business cycle fluctuations. We have closely tied these explanations to the Canadian data on growth, inflation, and the business cycle with an emphasis on the most recent business cycle.

7. *Fiscal Policy* (Chapter 29): The topic of this chapter is front-page news almost every day and is likely to remain so. The revision describes the budget deficit and the accumulating debt and explains the consequences of the uncertainty they engender. A thoroughly revised section examines the fiscal stimulus measures taken over the past year, channels through which the stimulus works, its unwanted side effects, its potentially limited power, and its shortcomings. The controversy about and range of views on the size of the fiscal stimulus multiplier is examined.

8. *Monetary Policy* (Chapter 30): This chapter describes and explains the monetary policy responses to the 2008–2009 recession and the persistent headwinds of 2010 and 2011. It also contains an improved description of the Bank of Canada's decision-making process. Technical details about alternative monetary policy strategies have been replaced with a shorter and more focused discussion of this topic and the need to bring clarity and predictability to monetary policy to anchor inflation expectations.

◆ Features to Enhance Teaching and Learning

Reading Between the Lines

This Parkin and Bade hallmark helps students think like economists by connecting chapter tools and concepts to the world around them. In *Reading Between the Lines*, which appears at the end of each chapter, students apply the tools they have just learned by analyzing an article from a newspaper or news Web site. Each article sheds additional light on the questions first raised in the Chapter Opener. Questions about the article also appear with the end-of-chapter problems and applications.

READING BETWEEN THE LINES

Demand and Supply: The Price of Coffee

Coffee Surges on Poor Colombian Harvests
FT.com
July 30, 2010

Coffee prices hit a 12-year high on Friday on the back of low supplies of premium Arabica coffee from Colombia after a string of poor crops in the Latin American country.

The strong fundamental picture has also encouraged hedge funds to reverse their previous bearish views on coffee prices.

In New York, ICE September Arabica coffee jumped 3.2 percent to 178.75 cents per pound, the highest since February 1998. It traded later at 177.25 cents, up 6.8 percent on the week.

The London-based International Coffee Organization on Friday warned that the "current tight demand and supply situation" was "likely to persist in the near to medium term."

Coffee industry executives believe prices could rise towards 200 cents per pound in New York before the arrival of the new Brazilian crop later this year.

"Until October it is going to be tight on high quality coffee," said a senior executive at one of Europe's largest coffee roasters. He said: "The industry has been surprised by the scarcity of high quality beans."

Colombia coffee production, key for supplies of premium beans, last year plunged to a 33-year low of 7.8m bags, each of 60kg, down nearly a third from 11.1m bags in 2008, tightening supplies worldwide. ...

Excerpted from "Coffee Surges on Poor Colombian Harvests" by Javier Blas. *Financial Times*, July 30, 2010. Reprinted with permission.

ESSENCE OF THE STORY

■ The price of premium Arabica coffee increased by 3.2 percent to almost 180 cents per pound in July 2010, the highest price since February 1998.

■ A sequence of poor crops in Colombia cut the production of premium Arabica coffee to a 33-year low of 7.8 million 60kilogram bags, down from 11.1 million bags in 2008.

■ The International Coffee Organization said that the

ECONOMIC ANALYSIS

■ This news article reports two sources of changes in supply and demand that changed the price of coffee.

■ The first source of change is the sequence of poor harvests in Colombia. These events decreased the world supply of Arabica coffee. (Arabica is the type that Starbucks uses.)

■ Before the reported events, the world production of Arabica was 120 million bags per year and its price was 174 cents per pound.

■ The decrease in the Colombian harvest decreased world production to about 116 million bags, which is about 3 percent of world production.

■ Figure 1 shows the situation before the poor Colombia harvests and the effects of those poor harvests. The demand curve is *D* and initially, the supply curve was S_0. The market equilibrium is at 120 million bags per year and a price of 174 cents per pound.

Figure 1 The Effects of the Colombian Crop

Economics in the News

32. After you have studied *Reading Between the Lines* on pp. 74–75, answer the following questions.
   a. What happened to the price of coffee in 2010?
   b. What substitutions do you expect might have been made to decrease the quantity of coffee demanded?
   c. What influenced the demand for coffee in 2010 and what influenced the quantity of coffee demanded?

Diagrams That Show the Action

Through the past seven editions, this book has set new standards of clarity in its diagrams; the eighth edition continues to uphold this tradition. Our goal has always been to show "where the economic action is." The diagrams in this book continue to generate an enormously positive response, which confirms our view that graphical analysis is the most powerful tool available for teaching and learning economics.

Because many students find graphs hard to work with, we have developed the entire art program with the study and review needs of the student in mind.

The diagrams feature
- Original curves consistently shown in blue
- Shifted curves, equilibrium points, and other important features highlighted in red
- Colour-blended arrows to suggest movement
- Graphs paired with data tables
- Diagrams labelled with boxed notes
- Extended captions that make each diagram and its caption a self-contained object for study and review

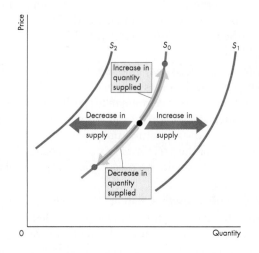

Chapter Objectives

Each chapter begins with a list of learning objectives, which enables students to see exactly where the chapter is going and to set their goals before they embark on their detailed study.

Chapter Openers

Each chapter opens with a carefully chosen photograph, question, and student-friendly vignette designed to give the student a quick sense of what the chapter is about and how it connects with their own economic world and experience. The chapter-opening story is woven into the body of the chapter and explored further in the *Reading Between the Lines* feature that ends the chapter.

Economics in Action Boxes

This new feature uses boxes within the chapter to address current events and economic occurrences that highlight and amplify the topics covered in the chapter. Instead of simply reporting the current events, the material in the boxes applies the event to an economics lesson, enabling students to see how economics plays a part in the world around them as they read through the chapter.

Some of the many issues covered in these boxes include the global market for crude oil, the best affordable choice of movies and DVDs, the cost of selling a pair of shoes, how Apple doesn't make the iPhone, the trends and cycles in real GDP and the price level, and the size of the fiscal stimulus multiplier. A complete list can be found on the inside back cover.

Economics in Action
The Global Market for Crude Oil

The demand and supply model provides insights into all competitive markets. Here, we'll apply what you've learned about the effects of an increase in demand to the global market for crude oil.

Crude oil is like the life-blood of the global economy. It is used to fuel our cars, airplanes, trains, and buses, to generate electricity, and to produce a wide range of plastics. When the price of crude oil rises, the costs of transportation, power, and materials all increase.

In 2001, the price of a barrel of oil was $20 (using the value of money in 2010). In 2008, before the global financial crisis ended a long period of economic expansion, the price peaked at $127 a barrel.

While the price of oil was rising, the quantity of oil produced and consumed also increased. In 2001, the world produced 65 million barrels of oil a day. By 2008, that quantity was 72 million barrels.

Who or what has been raising the price of oil? Is it the action of greedy oil producers? Oil producers might be greedy, and some of them might be big enough to withhold supply and raise the price, but it wouldn't be in their self-interest to do so. The higher price would bring forth a greater quantity supplied from other producers and the profit of the producer limiting supply would fall.

Oil producers could try to cooperate and jointly withhold supply. The Organization of Petroleum Exporting Countries, OPEC, is such a group of producers. But OPEC doesn't control the *world* supply and its members' self-interest is to produce the quantities that give them the maximum attainable profit.

So even though the global oil market has some big players, they don't fix the price. Instead, the actions of thousands of buyers and sellers and the forces of demand and supply determine the price of oil.

So how have demand and supply changed?

Because both the price and the quantity have increased, the demand for oil must have increased. Supply might have changed, too, but here we'll suppose that supply has remained the same.

The global demand for oil has increased for one major reason: World income has increased. The increase has been particularly large in the emerging economies of Brazil, China, and India. Increased world income has increased the demand for oil-using goods such as electricity, gasoline, and plastics, which in turn has increased the demand for oil.

The figure illustrates the effects of the increase in demand on the global oil market. The supply of oil remained constant along supply curve S. The demand for oil in 2001 was D_{2001}, so in 2001 the price was $20 a barrel and the quantity was 65 million barrels per day. The demand for oil increased and by 2008 it had reached D_{2008}. The price of oil increased to $127 a barrel and the quantity increased to 72 million barrels a day. The increase in the quantity is an *increase in the quantity supplied*, not an increase in supply.

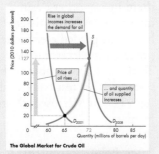

The Global Market for Crude Oil

Key Terms

Highlighted terms simplify the student's task of learning the vocabulary of economics. Each highlighted term appears in an end-of-chapter list with its page number, in an end-of-book glossary with its page number, boldfaced in the index, and in MyEconLab in the interactive glossary and flashcards.

End-of-Chapter Summary

Each chapter closes with a concise summary organized by major topics and list of key terms with page references. These learning tools provide students with a summary for review and exam preparation.

In-Text Review Quizzes and End-of-Chapter Problems and Applications

A review quiz at the end of each major section enables students to determine whether a topic needs further study before moving on, and problems and applications at the end of each chapter provide an opportunity to practice and apply the topics of the chapter.

All the review quizzes and end-of-chapter problems and applications are in the MyEconLab study plan (shown below), where students can work them and receive instant feedback and explanations.

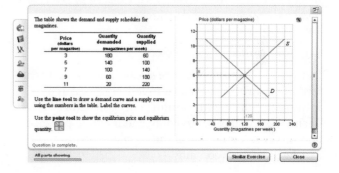

Interviews with Economists

Each major part of the text closes with a summary feature that includes an interview with a leading economist whose research and expertise correlates to what the student has just learned. These interviews explore the background, education, and research that these prominent economists have conducted, as well as advice for those who want to continue the study of economics.

For the Instructor

This book enables you to focus on the economic way of thinking and choose your own course structure in your principles course.

Focus on the Economic Way of Thinking

As an instructor, you know how hard it is to encourage a student to think like an economist. But that is your goal. Consistent with this goal, the text focuses on and repeatedly uses the central ideas of choice; tradeoff; opportunity cost; the margin; incentives; the gains from voluntary exchange; the forces of demand, supply, and equilibrium; the pursuit of economic rent; the tension between self-interest and the social interest; and the scope and limitations of government actions.

Flexible Structure

You have preferences for how you want to teach your course. We have organized this book to enable you to do so. The flexibility chart on p. xix illustrate the book's flexibility. By following the arrows through the charts you can select the path that best fits your preference for course structure. Whether you want to teach a traditional course that blends theory and policy, or one that takes a fast-track through either theory or policy issues, *Macroeconomics: Canada in the Global Environment* gives you the choice.

Supplemental Resources

Instructor's Manual We have streamlined and reorganized the Instructor's Manual to reflect the focus and intuition of the eighth edition. The Instructor's Manual integrates the teaching and learning package and serves as a guide to all the supplements.

Each chapter contains

- A chapter overview
- A list of what's new in the eighth edition
- Ready-to-use lecture notes

A new user can walk into a classroom armed to deliver a polished lecture. The lecture notes provide an outline of the chapter; concise statements of key material; alternative tables and figures; key terms and definitions; boxes that highlight key concepts, provide an interesting anecdote, or suggest how to handle a difficult idea; and additional discussion questions. The PowerPoint® lecture notes incorporate the chapter outlines and teaching suggestions.

Solutions Manual For ease of use and instructor reference, a comprehensive Solutions Manual provides instructors with detailed solutions to the Review Quizzes and the end-of-chapter Study Plan Problems and Applications as well as Additional Problems and Applications. The Solutions Manual is available electronically on the Instructor's Resource Centre DVD (IRDVD), in the Instructor's Resources section of MyEconLab, and on the Instructor's Resource Centre.

Test Bank The eighth edition test bank (Test Item File), with more than 3,000 multiple-choice questions, has been prepared by Jeannie Gillmore of the University of Western Ontario. Jeannie has reviewed and edited all existing questions to ensure their clarity and consistency with the eighth edition and incorporated new questions. The new questions follow the style and format of the end-of-chapter text problems and provide the instructor with a whole new set of testing opportunities and/or homework assignments. Test Item File questions are available in MyEconLab for instructors to use in a test, quiz, or as homework.

TestGen Pearson TestGen enables instructors to view and edit test bank questions, generate tests, and print them in a variety of formats. Powerful search and sort functions make it easy to locate questions and arrange them in any order desired. TestGen also enables instructors to administer tests on a local area network, have tests graded electronically, and have the results prepared in electronic or printed reports. Pearson TestGen is compatible with Windows® or Macintosh® systems. This test bank is also available as a Test Item File in Microsoft Word® and Adobe Acrobat® formats.

PowerPoint® Resources Robin Bade has developed the full-colour Microsoft PowerPoint Lecture Presentation for each chapter, which includes the figures and tables from the text, animated graphs, and speaking notes. The lecture notes in the Instructor's Manual and the slide outlines are correlated, and the speaking notes are based on the Instructor's Manual teaching suggestions.

A separate set of PowerPoint files containing large-scale versions of all the text's figures (most of them animated) and tables are also available. The presentations can be used electronically in the classroom or printed to create hard-copy transparency masters. This item is available for Macintosh and Windows.

Clicker-Ready PowerPoint Resources (PRS Questions) Each chapter of the text includes 10 multiple-choice questions that test important concepts. Instructors can use these questions as in-class assignments or review quizzes.

Instructor's Resource Centre DVD (IRDVD) Fully compatible with Windows and Macintosh, this IRDVD contains files of every instructor supplement. Files included are Adobe PDF files of the Instructor's Manual, Test Item File, and Solutions Manual; PowerPoint resources; clicker-ready resources; and the TestGen. Add this useful resource to your exam copy bookbag or locate your local Pearson Canada sales representative at http://catalogue.pearsoned.ca/educator to request a copy of the IRDVD.

Instructors can download supplements from a secure, instructor-only source via the Pearson Canada Higher Education Instructor Resource Centre Web page (www.pearsonhighered.com/irc).

Economics Videos and Assignable Questions Featuring abcNEWS Economics videos featuring ABC News enliven your course with short news clips featuring real-world issues. These videos, available in MyEconLab, feature news footage and commentary by economists. Questions for each video clip are available for assignment in MyEconLab.

CourseSmart CourseSmart goes beyond traditional expectations—providing instant, online access to the textbooks and course materials you need at a lower cost for students. And even as students save money, you can save time and hassle with a digital eTextbook that allows you to search for the most relevant content at the very moment you need it. Whether it's evaluating textbooks or creating lecture notes to help students with difficult concepts, CourseSmart can make life a little easier. See how when you visit www.coursesmart.com/instructors.

Technology Specialists Pearson's Technology Specialists work with faculty and campus course designers to ensure that Pearson technology products, assessment tools, and online course materials are tailored to meet your specific needs. This highly qualified team is dedicated to helping schools take full advantage of a wide range of educational resources by assisting in the integration of a variety of instructional materials and media formats. Your local Pearson Canada sales representative can provide you with more details on this service program.

For the Student

Study Guide

The eighth edition Study Guide by Avi Cohen of York University and Harvey King of the University of Regina is carefully coordinated with the text, MyEconLab, and the Test Item File. Each chapter of the Study Guide contains key concepts, helpful hints, true/false/uncertain questions, multiple-choice questions, and short-answer questions. Each Part Wrapup contains questions that go across chapters, which gives students an opportunity to test their cumulative understanding and to work a sample midterm test.

Study on the Go

Pearson's Study on the Go is an unprecedented mobile integration between text and online content. Students link to Study on the Go content directly from their smartphones, allowing them to study whenever and wherever they wish! Go to one of the sites below to see how you can download an app to your smartphone for free. Once the app is installed, scan the QR code on the summary page of each chapter to link to Study on the Go content, which includes the popular study tools: glossary, flashcards, audio summaries, and multiple-choice quizzes.

ScanLife: http://getscanlife.com
NeoReader: http://get.neoreader.com
QuickMark: www.quickmark.com.tw

PowerPoint Lecture Notes

Robin Bade has developed the full-colour Microsoft PowerPoint Lecture Notes for each chapter, which include animated versions of the textbook figures. Take these notes to class and edit them to create your own personal summary for review.

CourseSmart

CourseSmart goes beyond traditional expectations—providing instant, online access to the textbooks and course materials you need at an average saving of 60 percent. With instant access from any computer and the ability to search your text, you'll find the content you need quickly, no matter where you are. And with online tools such as highlighting and note-taking, you can save time and study efficiently. See all the benefits at www.coursesmart.com/students.

◆ MyEconLab

MyEconLab's powerful assessment and tutorial system works hand-in-hand with *Macroeconomics: Canada in the Global Enviroment*. With comprehensive homework, quiz, test, and tutorial options, instructors can manage all assessment needs in one program.

- All of the Review Quiz questions and end-of-chapter Problems and Applications are assignable and automatically graded.
- Students can work the Review Quiz questions and end-of-chapter Study Plan Problems and Applications as part of the MyEconLab Study Plan.
- Instructors can assign the end-of-chapter Additional Problems and Applications as auto-graded assignments. These Problems and Applications are not available to students in MyEconLab unless assigned by the instructor.
- Many of the problems and applications are algorithmic, draw-graph, and numerical exercises.
- Test Item File questions are available for assignment as homework.
- The Custom Exercise Builder gives instructors the flexibility of creating their own problems for assignment.
- The powerful Gradebook records each student's performance and time spent on Tests, the Study Plan, and Homework and generates reports by student or by chapter.
- *Economics in the News* is a turn-key solution to bringing daily news into the classroom. Updated weekly during the academic year, we upload two relevant articles (one micro, one macro) and provide links for further information and questions that may be assigned for homework or for classroom discussion.

Experiments in MyEconLab

Experiments are a fun and engaging way to promote active learning and mastery of important economic concepts. Pearson's Experiments program is flexible and easy for instructors and students to use.

- Single-player experiments allow your students to play against virtual players from anywhere at any time with an Internet connection.
- Multiplayer experiments allow you to assign and manage a real-time experiment with your class.
- Pre- and post-questions for each experiment are available for assignment in MyEconLab.

MyEconLab Also Includes

- Enhanced Pearson eText, available within the online course materials and offline via an iPad app, allows instructors and students to highlight, bookmark, and take notes.
- Advanced Communication Tools enable students and instructors communication through email, discussion board, chat, and ClassLive.
- Customization options provide new and enhanced ways to share documents, add content, and rename menu items.
- Prebuilt courses offer a turn-key way for instructors to create a course that includes pre-built assignments distributed by chapter.
- Temporary Access for students who are awaiting financial aid provides a 17-day grace period of temporary access.
- A comprehensive suite of ABC News videos, which address current topics such as education, energy, U.S. Federal Reserve policy, and business cycles, is available for classroom use. Video-specific exercises are available for instructor assignment.

Robin and Michael, assisted by Jeannie Gillmore and Laurel Davies, author and oversee all of the MyEconLab content for *Economics*. Our peerless MyEconLab team has worked hard to ensure that it is tightly integrated with the book's content and vision. A more detailed walk-through of the student benefits and features of MyEconLab can be found on the inside front cover. Visit www.myeconlab.com for more information and an online demonstration of instructor and student features.

◆ Acknowledgments

We thank our current and former colleagues and friends at the University of Western Ontario who have taught us so much. They are Jim Davies, Jeremy Greenwood, Ig Horstmann, Peter Howitt, Greg Huffman, David Laidler, Phil Reny, Chris Robinson, John Whalley, and Ron Wonnacott. We also thank Doug McTaggart and Christopher Findlay, co-authors of the Australian edition, and Melanie Powell and Kent Matthews, co-authors of the European edition. Suggestions arising from their adaptations of earlier editions have been helpful to us in preparing this edition.

We thank the several thousand students whom we have been privileged to teach. The instant response that comes from the look of puzzlement or enlightenment has taught us how to teach economics.

It is a special joy to thank the many outstanding editors, media specialists, and others at Pearson Canada who contributed to the concerted publishing effort that brought this edition to completion. Allan Reynolds, President and CEO; Steve O'Hearn, President Higher Education; Gary Bennett, Vice-President and Editorial Director for Higher Education; and Nicole Lukach, Editor-in-Chief Business and Economics have provided outstanding corporate direction. They have built a culture that brings out the best in its editors and authors.

Claudine O'Donnell, Acquisitions Editor for Economics and our sponsoring editor, played a major role in shaping this revision and the many outstanding supplements that accompany it. Claudine brings intelligence and insight to her work and is Canada's pre-eminent economics editor. Karen Townsend, Developmental Editor, managed the supplements' authors and reviewers. Victoria Naik, Media Content Developer, ensured that all our media assets were correctly assembled. Leigh-Anne Graham provided inspired marketing strategy and direction.

Our Production Editor, Leanne Rancourt, under the direction of Sögüt Güleç, Lead Project Manager, again kept her eye to the production process and its contributors. Trish O'Reilly, Sally Glover, and Kit Pasula provided a careful, consistent copy edit, proofread, and accuracy check. Anthony Leung designed the cover and package and yet again surpassed the challenge of ensuring that we meet the highest design standards.

We thank our talented eighth edition supplements authors and contributors—Avi Cohen, Laurel Davies, Jeannie Gillmore, and Harvey King.

We thank the many exceptional reviewers who have shared their insights through the various editions of this book. Their contribution has been invaluable.

We thank the people who work directly with us. Jeannie Gillmore provided outstanding research assistance on many topics, including the *Reading Between the Lines* news articles. Richard Parkin created the electronic art files and offered many ideas that improved the figures in this book. And Laurel Davies managed an ever-growing and ever more complex MyEconLab database.

Classroom experience will test the value of this book. We would appreciate hearing from instructors and students about how we can continue to improve it in future editions.

Michael Parkin
Robin Bade
London, Ontario, Canada
michael.parkin@uwo.ca
robin@econ100.com

 **Reviewers**

Syed Ahmed, Red Deer Community College
Ather H. Akbari, Saint Mary's University
Doug Allen, Simon Fraser University
Benjamin Amoah, University of Guelph
Torben Andersen, Red Deer College
Terri Anderson, Fanshawe College
Syed Ashan, Concordia University
Fred Aswani, McMaster University
Iris Au, University of Toronto, Scarborough
Keith Baxter, Bishop's University
Andy Baziliauskas, University of Winnipeg
Dick Beason, University of Alberta
Karl Bennett, University of Waterloo
Ronald Bodkin, University of Ottawa
Caroline Boivin, Concordia University
Paul Booth, University of Alberta
John Boyd, University of British Columbia
John Brander, University of New Brunswick
Larry Brown, Selkirk College
Sam Bucovetsky, York University
Bogdan Buduru, Concordia University
Lutz-Alexander Busch, University of Waterloo
Beverly J. Cameron, University of Manitoba
Norman Cameron, University of Manitoba
Emanuel Carvalho, University of Waterloo
Francois Casas, University of Toronto
Alan Tak Yan Chan, Atlantic Baptist University
Robert Cherneff, University of Victoria
Jason Childs, University of New Brunswick, Saint John
Saud Choudhry, Trent University
Louis Christofides, University of Guelph
Kam Hon Chu, Memorial University of Newfoundland
George Churchman, University of Manitoba
Avi J. Cohen, York University
Constantin Colonescu, Grant MacEwan University
Ryan A. Compton, University of Manitoba
Marilyn Cottrell, Brock University
Rosilyn Coulson, Douglas College
Brian Coulter, University College of the Fraser Valley
Stanya Cunningham, Concordia University College of Alberta
Douglas Curtis, Trent University
Garth Davies, Olds College
Ajit Dayanandan, University of Northern British Columbia
Carol Derksen, Red River College
David Desjardins, John Abbott College
Vaughan Dickson, University of New Brunswick (Fredericton)
Livio Di Matteo, Lakehead University
Mohammed Dore, Brock University
Torben Drewes, Trent University

Byron Eastman, Laurentian University

Fahira Eston, Humber College

Sigrid Ewender, Kwantlen Polytechnic University

Brian Ferguson, University of Guelph

Len Fitzpatrick, Carleton University

Peter Fortura, Algonquin College

Oliver Franke, Athabasca University

Bruno Fullone, George Brown College

Donald Garrie, Georgian College

Philippe Ghayad, Dawson College and Concordia University

David Gray, University of Ottawa

Sandra Hadersbeck, Okanagan College

Rod Hill, University of New Brunswick

Eric Kam, Ryerson University

Susan Kamp, University of Alberta

Cevat Burc Kayahan, University of Guelph

Peter Kennedy, Simon Fraser University

Harvey King, University of Regina

Patricia Koss, Concordia University

Robert Kunimoto, Mt. Royal University

David Johnson, Wilfrid Laurier University

Cliff Jutlah, York University, Glendon Campus

Michael G. Lanyi, University of Lethbridge

Eva Lau, University of Waterloo

Gordon Lee, University of Alberta

Byron Lew, Trent University

Anastasia M. Lintner, University of Guelph

Scott Lynch, Memorial University

Dan MacKay, SIAST

Leigh MacDonald, University of Western Ontario

Keith MacKinnon, York University

Mohammad Mahbobi, Thompson Rivers University

S. Manchouri, University of Alberta

Christian Marfels, Dalhousie University

Raimo Martalla, Malaspina University College

Perry Martens, University of Regina

Roberto Martínez-Espíneira, St. Francis Xavier University

Dennis McGuire, Okanagan University College

Rob Moir, University of New Brunswick, Saint John

Saeed Moshiri, University of Manitoba

Joseph Muldoon, Trent University

David Murrell, University of New Brunswick, Fredericton

Robin Neill, Carleton University

A. Gyasi Nimarko, Vanier College

Sonia Novkovic, Saint Mary's University

John O'Brien, Concordia University

Arne Paus-Jenssen, University of Saskatchewan

Andrea Podhorsky, York University

Derek Pyne, Memorial University of Newfoundland

Stephen Rakoczy, Humber College

Don Reddick, Kwantlen University College

June Riley, John Abbott College

E. Riser, Memorial University

Roberta Robb, Brock University

Nick Rowe, Carleton University

Michael Rushton, University of Regina

Balbir Sahni, Concordia University

Brian Scarfe, University of Regina

Marlyce Searcy, SIAST Palliser

Jim Sentance, University of Prince Edward Island

Lance Shandler, Kwantlen University College

Stan Shedd, University of Calgary

Chandan Shirvaikar, Red Deer College

Peter Sinclair, Wilfrid Laurier University

Ian Skaith, Fanshawe College

Scott Skjei, Acadia University

Judith Skuce, Georgian College

George Slasor, University of Toronto

Norman Smith, Georgian College

Bert Somers, John Abbott College

Lewis Soroka, Brock University

Glen Stirling, University of Western Ontario

Brennan Thompson, Ryerson University

Irene Trela, University of Western Ontario

Russell Uhler, University of British Columbia

Brian VanBlarcom, Acadia University

Marianne Vigneault, Bishop's University

Jane Waples, Memorial University of Newfoundland

Tony Ward, Brock University

Bruce Wilkinson, University of Alberta

Christopher Willmore, University of Victoria

Andrew Wong, Grant MacEwan University

Peter Wylie, University of British Columbia, Okanagan

Arthur Younger, Humber College Institute of Technology and Advanced Learning

Ayoub Yousefi, University of Western Ontario

Weiqiu Yu, University of New Brunswick, Fredericton

Flexibility

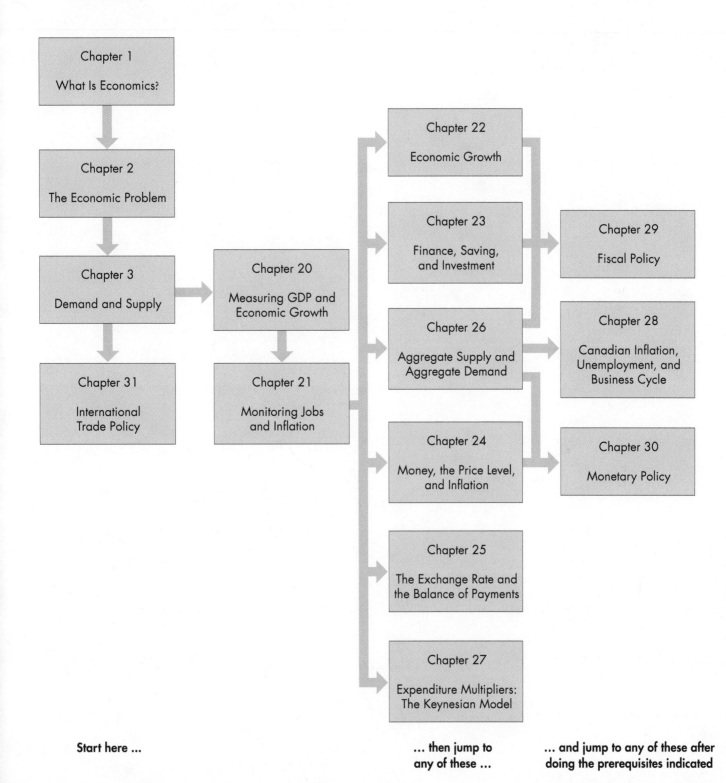

Start here ...   **... then jump to**   **... and jump to any of these after**
                                       any of these ...   **doing the prerequisites indicated**

TABLE OF CONTENTS

PART ONE
INTRODUCTION 1

CHAPTER 1 ◆ What Is Economics? 1

Definition of Economics 2

Two Big Economic Questions 3
What, How, and For Whom? 3
Can the Pursuit of Self-Interest Promote the Social
Interest? 5

The Economic Way of Thinking 8
A Choice Is a Tradeoff 8
Making a Rational Choice 8
Benefit: What You Gain 8
Cost: What You *Must* Give Up 8
How Much? Choosing at the Margin 9
Choices Respond to Incentives 9

Economics as Social Science and Policy Tool 10
Economist as Social Scientist 10
Economist as Policy Adviser 10

Summary (Key Points and Key Terms) and
Problems and Applications appear at the end of
each chapter.

Appendix Graphs in Economics 13

Graphing Data 13
Scatter Diagrams 14

Graphs Used in Economic Models 16
Variables That Move in the Same Direction 16
Variables That Move in Opposite Directions 17
Variables That Have a Maximum or a
Minimum 18
Variables That Are Unrelated 19

The Slope of a Relationship 20
The Slope of a Straight Line 20
The Slope of a Curved Line 21

**Graphing Relationships Among More Than
Two Variables** 22
Ceteris Paribus 22
When Other Things Change 23

MATHEMATICAL NOTE
Equations of Straight Lines 24

CHAPTER 2 ◆ The Economic Problem 29

Production Possibilities and Opportunity Cost 30
Production Possibilities Frontier 30
Production Efficiency 31
Tradeoff Along the *PPF* 31
Opportunity Cost 31

Using Resources Efficiently 33
The *PPF* and Marginal Cost 33
Preferences and Marginal Benefit 34
Allocative Efficiency 35

Economic Growth 36
The Cost of Economic Growth 36
A Nation's Economic Growth 37

Gains from Trade 38
Comparative Advantage and Absolute
  Advantage 38
Achieving the Gains from Trade 39

Economic Coordination 41
Firms 41
Markets 42
Property Rights 42
Money 42
Circular Flows Through Markets 42
Coordinating Decisions 42

READING BETWEEN THE LINES
The Rising Opportunity Cost of Food 44

PART ONE WRAP-UP ◆

Understanding the Scope of Economics
Your Economic Revolution 83

Talking with
Jagdish Bhagwati 84

**PART 2
HOW MARKETS WORK** 55

CHAPTER 3 ◆ Demand and Supply 55

Markets and Prices 56

Demand 57
The Law of Demand 57
Demand Curve and Demand Schedule 57
A Change in Demand 58
A Change in the Quantity Demanded Versus a
  Change in Demand 60

Supply 62
The Law of Supply 62
Supply Curve and Supply Schedule 62
A Change in Supply 63
A Change in the Quantity Supplied Versus a
  Change in Supply 64

Market Equilibrium 66
Price as a Regulator 66
Price Adjustments 67

Predicting Changes in Price and Quantity 68
An Increase in Demand 68
A Decrease in Demand 68
An Increase in Supply 70
A Decrease in Supply 70
All the Possible Changes in Demand and
  Supply 72

READING BETWEEN THE LINES
Demand and Supply: The Price of Coffee 74

MATHEMATICAL NOTE
Demand, Supply, and Equilibrium 76

PART TWO WRAP-UP ◆

Understanding How Markets Work
The Amazing Market 83

Talking With
Susan Athey 84

PART 7

MONITORING MACROECONOMIC PERFORMANCE 467

CHAPTER 20 ◆ Measuring GDP and Economic Growth 467

Gross Domestic Product 468
GDP Defined 468
GDP and the Circular Flow of Expenditure and Income 469
Why Is Domestic Product "Gross"? 470

Measuring Canada's GDP 471
The Expenditure Approach 471
The Income Approach 472
Nominal GDP and Real GDP 473
Calculating Real GDP 473

The Uses and Limitations of Real GDP 474
The Standard of Living Over Time 474
The Standard of Living Across Countries 476
Limitations of Real GDP 477

READING BETWEEN THE LINES
Real GDP Forecasts in the Uncertain Economy of 2011 480

Appendix Graphs in Macroeconomics 482

The Time-Series Graph 482
Making a Time-Series Graph 482
Reading a Time-Series Graph 482
Ratio Scale Reveals Trend 483
A Time-Series with a Trend 483
Using a Ratio Scale 483

MATHEMATICAL NOTE
Chained-Dollar Real GDP 484

CHAPTER 21 ◆ Monitoring Jobs and Inflation 491

Employment and Unemployment 492
Why Unemployment Is a Problem 492
Labour Force Survey 493
Four Labour Market Indicators 493
Other Definitions of Unemployment 495
Most Costly Unemployment 496

Unemployment and Full Employment 497
Frictional Unemployment 497
Structural Unemployment 497
Cyclical Unemployment 497
"Natural" Unemployment 497
Real GDP and Unemployment Over the Cycle 498
The Trend in the Natural Unemployment Rate 499

The Price Level, Inflation, and Deflation 500
Why Inflation and Deflation Are Problems 500
The Consumer Price Index 501
Reading the CPI Numbers 501
Constructing the CPI 501
Measuring the Inflation Rate 502
Distinguishing High Inflation from a High Price Level 503
The Biased CPI 503
The Magnitude of the Bias 504
Some Consequences of the Bias 504
Alternative Price Indexes 504
Core Inflation 504
The Real Variables in Macroeconomics 505

READING BETWEEN THE LINES
Jobs Growth Lags Recovery 506

PART SEVEN WRAP-UP ◆

Monitoring Macroeconomic Performance
The Big Picture 513

Talking With
Peter Howitt 514

PART 8
MACROECONOMIC TRENDS 517

CHAPTER 22 ◆ Economic Growth   517

The Basics of Economic Growth   518
Calculating Growth Rates   518
The Magic of Sustained Growth   518
Applying the Rule of 70   519

Economic Growth Trends   520
Growth in the Canadian Economy   520
Real GDP Growth in the World Economy   521

How Potential GDP Grows   523
What Determines Potential GDP?   523
What Makes Potential GDP Grow?   525

Why Labour Productivity Grows   528
Preconditions for Labour Productivity
    Growth   528
Physical Capital Growth   529
Human Capital Growth   529
Technological Advances   529

Growth Theories, Evidence, and Policies   531
Classical Growth Theory   531
Neoclassical Growth Theory   531
New Growth Theory   532
New Growth Theory Versus Malthusian
    Theory   534
Sorting Out the Theories   534
The Empirical Evidence on the Causes of
    Economic Growth   534
Policies for Achieving Faster Growth   534

READING BETWEEN THE LINES
Economic Growth in China   536

CHAPTER 23 ◆ Finance, Saving, and
                      Investment   543

Financial Institutions and Financial
Markets   544
Finance and Money   544
Physical Capital and Financial Capital   544
Capital and Investment   544
Wealth and Saving   544
Financial Capital Markets   545
Financial Institutions   546
Insolvency and Illiquidity   547
Interest Rates and Asset Prices   548

The Loanable Funds Market   548
Funds that Finance Investment   548
The Real Interest Rate   549
The Demand for Loanable Funds   550
The Supply of Loanable Funds   551
Equilibrium in the Loanable Funds Market   552
Changes in Demand and Supply   552

Government in the Loanable Funds Market   555
A Government Budget Surplus   555
A Government Budget Deficit   555

The Global Loanable Funds Market   557
International Capital Mobility   557
International Borrowing and Lending   557
Demand and Supply in the Global and
    National Markets   557

READING BETWEEN THE LINES
Euro Crisis and the Global Market   560

CHAPTER 24 ◆ Money, the Price Level, and
                    Inflation 567

What Is Money? 568
Medium of Exchange 568
Unit of Account 568
Store of Value 569
Money in Canada Today 569

The Banking System 571
Depository Institutions 571
The Bank of Canada 572

How Banks Create Money 575
Creating Deposits by Making Loans 575
The Money Creation Process 576
The Money Multiplier 577

The Money Market 578
The Influences on Money Holding 578
The Demand for Money 579
Shifts in the Demand for Money Curve 579
Money Market Equilibrium 580

The Quantity Theory of Money 582

READING BETWEEN THE LINES
Can More Money Keep a Recovery Going? 584

MATHEMATICAL NOTE
The Money Multiplier 586

CHAPTER 25 ◆ The Exchange Rate and the
Balance of Payments 593

The Foreign Exchange Market 594
Trading Currencies 594
Exchange Rates 594
Questions About the Canadian Dollar Exchange
Rate 594
An Exchange Rate Is a Price 594
The Demand for One Money Is the Supply of
Another Money 595
Demand in the Foreign Exchange Market 595
Demand Curve for Canadian Dollars 596
Supply in the Foreign Exchange Market 597
Supply Curve for Canadian Dollars 597
Market Equilibrium 598

Exchange Rate Fluctuations 599
A Change in Demand for Canadian Dollars 599
A Change in Supply of Canadian Dollars 600
Changes in the Exchange Rate 600
Fundamentals, Expectations, and Arbitrage 602
The Real Exchange Rate 603

Exchange Rate Policy 604
Flexible Exchange Rate 604
Fixed Exchange Rate 604
Crawling Peg 605

Financing International Trade 607
Balance of Payments Accounts 607
Borrowers and Lenders 609
Debtors and Creditors 609
Is U.S. International Borrowing a Problem? 609
Current Account Balance 610
Net Exports 610
Where Is the Exchange Rate? 611

READING BETWEEN THE LINES
China's Exchange Rate Policy 612

PART EIGHT **WRAP-UP ◆**

Understanding Macroeconomic Trends
Expanding the Frontier 619

Talking With
Xavier Sala-i-Martin 620

PART 9
MACROECONOMIC FLUCTUATIONS 623

CHAPTER 26 ◆ Aggregate Supply and Aggregate Demand 623

Aggregate Supply 624
  Quantity Supplied and Supply 624
  Long-Run Aggregate Supply 624
  Short-Run Aggregate Supply 625
  Changes in Aggregate Supply 626

Aggregate Demand 628
  The Aggregate Demand Curve 628
  Changes in Aggregate Demand 629

Explaining Macroeconomic Trends and Fluctuations 632
  Short-Run Macroeconomic Equilibrium 632
  Long-Run Macroeconomic Equilibrium 632
  Economic Growth and Inflation in the AS-AD Model 633
  The Business Cycle in the AS-AD Model 634
  Fluctuations in Aggregate Demand 636
  Fluctuations in Aggregate Supply 637

Macroeconomic Schools of Thought 638
  The Classical View 638
  The Keynesian View 638
  The Monetarist View 639
  The Way Ahead 639

READING BETWEEN THE LINES
  Aggregate Supply and Aggregate Demand in Action 640

CHAPTER 27 ◆ Expenditure Multipliers: The Keynesian Model 647

Fixed Prices and Expenditure Plans 648
  Expenditure Plans 648
  Consumption and Saving Plans 648
  Marginal Propensities to Consume and Save 650
  Slopes and Marginal Propensities 650
  Consumption as a Function of Real GDP 651
  Import Function 651

Real GDP with a Fixed Price Level 652
  Aggregate Planned Expenditure 652
  Actual Expenditure, Planned Expenditure, and Real GDP 653
  Equilibrium Expenditure 654
  Convergence to Equilibrium 655

The Multiplier 656
  The Basic Idea of the Multiplier 656
  The Multiplier Effect 656
  Why Is the Multiplier Greater Than 1? 657
  The Size of the Multiplier 657
  The Multiplier and the Slope of the AE Curve 658
  Imports and Income Taxes 659
  The Multiplier Process 659
  Business Cycle Turning Points 660

The Multiplier and the Price Level 661
  Adjusting Quantities and Prices 661
  Aggregate Expenditure and Aggregate Demand 661
  Deriving the Aggregate Demand Curve 661
  Changes in Aggregate Expenditure and Aggregate Demand 662
  Equilibrium Real GDP and the Price Level 663

READING BETWEEN THE LINES
  Inventory Investment in a 2011 Contraction 666

MATHEMATICAL NOTE
The Algebra of the Keynesian Model 668

CHAPTER 28 ◆ **Canadian Inflation, Unemployment, and Business Cycle**   677

Inflation Cycles   678
Demand-Pull Inflation   678
Cost-Push Inflation   680
Expected Inflation   682
Forecasting Inflation   683
Inflation and the Business Cycle   683

Inflation and Unemployment: The Phillips Curve   684
The Short-Run Phillips Curve   684
The Long-Run Phillips Curve   685
Changes in the Natural Unemployment Rate   685

The Business Cycle   687
Mainstream Business Cycle Theory   687
Real Business Cycle Theory   688

READING BETWEEN THE LINES
Labour Markets in Slow Recovery   692

PART NINE **WRAP-UP** ◆

Understanding Macroeconomic Fluctuations
Boom and Bust   699

Talking With
Ricardo J. Caballero   700

PART 10
MACROECONOMIC POLICY   703

CHAPTER 29 ◆ **Fiscal Policy**   703

The Federal Budget   704
Budget Making   704
Highlights of the 2011 Budget   704
The Budget in Historical Perspective   705

Supply-Side Effects of Fiscal Policy   710
Full Employment and Potential GDP   710
The Effects of the Income Tax   710
Taxes on Expenditure and the Tax Wedge   711
Taxes and the Incentive to Save and Invest   712
Tax Revenues and the Laffer Curve   713
The Supply-Side Debate   713

Fiscal Stimulus   714
Automatic Fiscal Policy and Cyclical and Structural Budget Balances   714
Discretionary Fiscal Stimulus   715

READING BETWEEN THE LINES
Harper's Fiscal Policy   720

CHAPTER 30 ◆ Monetary Policy 727

Monetary Policy Objectives and Framework 728
Monetary Policy Objective 728
Responsibility for Monetary Policy 729

The Conduct of Monetary Policy 730
The Monetary Policy Instrument 730
The Bank's Interest Rate Decision 731
Hitting the Overnight Rate Target 731

Monetary Policy Transmission 733
Quick Overview 733
Interest Rate Changes 733
Exchange Rate Fluctuations 734
Money and Bank Loans 735
The Long-Term Real Interest Rate 735
Expenditure Plans 735
The Change in Aggregate Demand, Real GDP, and the Price Level 736
The Bank of Canada Fights Recession 736
The Bank of Canada Fights Inflation 738
Loose Links and Long and Variable Lags 739

Extraordinary Monetary Stimulus 741
The Key Elements of the Crisis 741
The Policy Actions 742
Painfully Slow Recovery 742
Policy Strategies and Clarity 742

READING BETWEEN THE LINES
The Bank of Canada Fights Recession in 2011 744

CHAPTER 31 ◆ International Trade Policy 751

How Global Markets Work 752
International Trade Today 752
What Drives International Trade? 752
Why Canada Imports T-Shirts 753
Why Canada Exports Regional Jets 754
Winners and Losers from International Trade 755

International Trade Restrictions 756
Tariffs 756
Import Quotas 758
Other Import Barriers 760
Export Subsidies 760

The Case Against Protection 761
The Infant-Industry Argument 761
The Dumping Argument 761
Saves Jobs 762
Allows Us to Compete with Cheap Foreign Labour 762
Penalizes Lax Environmental Standards 762
Prevents Rich Countries from Exploiting Developing Countries 763
Offshore Outsourcing 763
Avoiding Trade Wars 764
Why Is International Trade Restricted? 764
Compensating Losers 765

READING BETWEEN THE LINES
A Tariff on Ski Jackets 766

PART TEN WRAP-UP ◆

Understanding Macroeconomic Policy
Tradeoffs and Free Lunches 773
Talking With
Pierre Siklos 774

Glossary G-1
Index I-1
Credits C-1

MACROECONOMICS

CANADA IN THE GLOBAL ENVIRONMENT

EIGHTH EDITION

CHAPTER
1

What Is Economics?

After studying this chapter, you will be able to

◆ Define economics and distinguish between microeconomics and macroeconomics

◆ Explain the two big questions of economics

◆ Explain the key ideas that define the economic way of thinking

◆ Explain how economists go about their work as social scientists and policy advisers

You are studying economics at a time of enormous challenge and change. Every day, new businesses are born and old ones die; new jobs are created and old ones disappear. Nations, businesses, and individuals must find ways of coping with economic change.

Your life will be shaped by the challenges that *you* face and the opportunities that *you* create. But to face those challenges and seize the opportunities they present, you must understand the powerful forces at play. The economics that you're about to learn will become your most reliable guide. This chapter gets you started. It describes the questions that economists try to answer and the ways in which they think as they search for the answers.

◆ Definition of Economics

A fundamental fact dominates our lives: We want more than we can get. Our inability to get everything we want is called **scarcity**. Scarcity is universal. It confronts all living things. Even parrots face scarcity!

Not only do I want a cracker—we all want a cracker!

© Frank Modell/The New Yorker Collection/www.cartoonbank.com

Think about the things that *you* want and the scarcity that *you* face. You want to live a long and healthy life. You want to go to a good school, college, or university. You want to live in a well-equipped, spacious, and comfortable home. You want the latest smart phone and a faster Internet connection for your laptop or iPad. You want some sports and recreational gear—perhaps some new skates or skis, or a new bike. And you want more time, much more than is available, to go to class, do your homework, play sports and games, read novels, go to the movies, listen to music, travel, and hang out with your friends.

What you can afford to buy is limited by your income and by the prices you must pay. And your time is limited by the fact that your day has 24 hours.

You want some other things that only governments provide. You want to live in a peaceful and secure world and safe neighbourhood and enjoy the benefits of clean air, lakes, and rivers.

What governments can afford is limited by the taxes they collect. Taxes lower people's incomes and compete with the other things they want to buy.

What everyone can get—what *society* can get—is limited by the productive resources available. These resources are the gifts of nature, human labour and ingenuity, and all the previously produced tools and equipment.

Because we can't get everything we want, we must make *choices*. You can't afford *both* a laptop *and* an iPhone, so you must *choose* which one to buy. You can't spend tonight *both* studying for your next test *and* going to the movies, so again, you must *choose* which one to do. Governments can't spend a tax dollar on *both* national defence *and* environmental protection, so they must *choose* how to spend that dollar.

Your choices must somehow be made consistent with the choices of others. If you choose to buy a laptop, someone else must choose to sell it. Incentives reconcile choices. An **incentive** is a reward that encourages an action or a penalty that discourages one. Prices act as incentives. If the price of a laptop is too high, more will be offered for sale than people want to buy. And if the price is too low, fewer will be offered for sale than people want to buy. But there is a price at which choices to buy and sell are consistent.

Economics is the social science that studies the *choices* that individuals, businesses, governments, and entire societies make as they cope with *scarcity* and the *incentives* that influence and reconcile those choices.

The subject has two parts:

■ Microeconomics
■ Macroeconomics

Microeconomics is the study of the choices that individuals and businesses make, the way these choices interact in markets, and the influence of governments. Some examples of microeconomic questions are: Why are people downloading more movies? How would a tax on e-commerce affect eBay?

Macroeconomics is the study of the performance of the national economy and the global economy. Some examples of macroeconomic questions are: Why is the Canadian unemployment rate so high? Can the Bank of Canada make our economy expand by cutting interest rates?

◆ REVIEW QUIZ

1 List some examples of the scarcity that you face.
2 Find examples of scarcity in today's headlines.
3 Find an illustration of the distinction between microeconomics and macroeconomics in today's headlines.

You can work these questions in Study Plan 1.1 and get instant feedback.

───────────── MyEconLab ◆

◈ Two Big Economic Questions

Two big questions summarize the scope of economics:

- How do choices end up determining *what, how,* and *for whom* goods and services are produced?
- Can the choices that people make in the pursuit of their own *self-interest* also promote the broader *social interest*?

What, How, and For Whom?

Goods and services are the objects that people value and produce to satisfy human wants. *Goods* are physical objects such as cell phones and automobiles. *Services* are tasks performed for people such as cellphone service and auto-repair service.

What? What we produce varies across countries and changes over time. In Canada today, agriculture accounts for 2 percent of total production, manufactured goods for 20 percent, and services (retail and wholesale trade, health care, and education are the biggest ones) for 78 percent. In contrast, in China today, agriculture accounts for 10 percent of total production, manufactured goods for 46 percent, and services for 44 percent. Figure 1.1 shows these numbers and also the percentages for Brazil, which fall between those for Canada and China.

What determines these patterns of production? How do choices end up determining the quantities of cell phones, automobiles, cellphone service, auto-repair service, and the millions of other items that are produced in Canada and around the world?

How? Goods and services are produced by using productive resources that economists call **factors of production**. Factors of production are grouped into four categories:

- Land
- Labour
- Capital
- Entrepreneurship

Land The "gifts of nature" that we use to produce goods and services are called **land**. In economics, land is what in everyday language we call *natural resources*. It includes land in the everyday sense together with minerals, oil, gas, coal, water, air, forests, and fish.

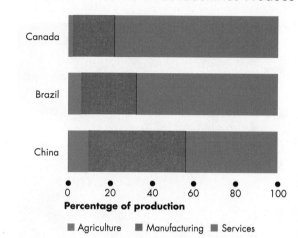

FIGURE 1.1 What Three Countries Produce

Percentage of production

■ Agriculture ■ Manufacturing ■ Services

Agriculture and manufacturing are small percentages of production in rich countries such as Canada and large percentages of production in poorer countries such as China. Most of what is produced in Canada is services. The percentages for Brazil lie between those for Canada and China.

Source of data: Central Intelligence Agency, CIA Factbook 2011.

MyEconLab animation ◈

Our land surface and water resources are renewable and some of our mineral resources can be recycled. But the resources that we use to create energy are nonrenewable—they can be used only once.

Labour The work time and work effort that people devote to producing goods and services is called **labour**. Labour includes the physical and mental efforts of all the people who work on farms and construction sites and in factories, shops, and offices.

The *quality* of labour depends on **human capital**, which is the knowledge and skill that people obtain from education, on-the-job training, and work experience. You are building your own human capital right now as you work on your economics course, and your human capital will continue to grow as you gain work experience.

Human capital expands over time. Today, 93 percent of the adult population of Canada have completed high school and 23 percent have a university degree and a further 40 percent have some postsecondary education. Figure 1.2 shows these measures of human capital in Canada since 1975.

FIGURE 1.2 A Measure of Human Capital

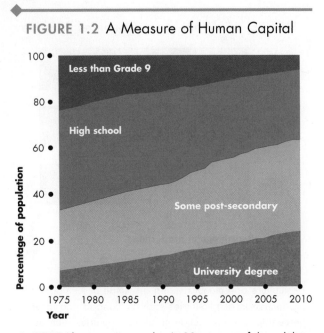

In 2009 (the most recent data), 23 percent of the adult population had a university degree. A further 40 percent had some post-secondary education, and 93 percent had completed high school.

Source of data: Statistics Canada.

━━━━━━━━━━━━━━━ MyEconLab (animation) ◆

Capital The tools, instruments, machines, buildings, and other constructions that businesses use to produce goods and services are called **capital**.

In everyday language, we talk about money, stocks, and bonds as being "capital." These items are *financial* capital. Financial capital plays an important role in enabling businesses to borrow the funds that they use to buy physical capital. But because financial capital is not used to produce goods and services, it is not a productive resource.

Entrepreneurship The human resource that organizes labour, land, and capital is called **entrepreneurship**. Entrepreneurs come up with new ideas about what and how to produce, make business decisions, and bear the risks that arise from these decisions.

What determines the quantities of factors of production that are used to produce goods and services?

For Whom? Who consumes the goods and services that are produced depends on the incomes that people earn. People with large incomes can buy a wide range of goods and services. People with small incomes have fewer options and can afford a smaller range of goods and services.

People earn their incomes by selling the services of the factors of production they own:

- Land earns **rent**.
- Labour earns **wages**.
- Capital earns **interest**.
- Entrepreneurship earns **profit**.

Which factor of production earns the most income? The answer is labour. Wages and fringe benefits are around 70 percent of total income. Land, capital, and entrepreneurship share the rest. These percentages have been remarkably constant over time.

Knowing how income is shared among the factors of production doesn't tell us how it is shared among individuals. And the distribution of income among individuals is extremely unequal. You know of some people who earn very large incomes: Mike Lazaridis of RIM, the maker of the BlackBerry, earned $4.6 million in 2010 and he was only 437th on *Forbes* World's Richest People list.

You know of even more people who earn very small incomes. Servers at Tim Horton's earn about $9 an hour; checkout clerks, cleaners, and textile and leather workers all earn less than $10 an hour.

You probably know about other persistent differences in incomes. Men, on average, earn more than women; whites earn more than minorities; college graduates earn more than high-school graduates.

We can get a good sense of who consumes the goods and services produced by looking at the percentages of total income earned by different groups of people. The 20 percent of people with the lowest incomes earn about 5 percent of total income, while the richest 20 percent earn close to 50 percent of total income. So on average, people in the richest 20 percent earn more than 10 times the incomes of those in the poorest 20 percent.

Why is the distribution of income so unequal? Why do women and minorities earn less than white males?

Economics provides some answers to all these questions about what, how, and for whom goods and services are produced and much of the rest of this book will help you to understand those answers.

We're now going to look at the second big question of economics: Can the pursuit of self-interest promote the social interest? This question is a difficult one both to appreciate and to answer.

Can the Pursuit of Self-Interest Promote the Social Interest?

Every day, you and 33 million other Canadians, along with 7 billion people in the rest of the world, make economic choices that result in *what, how,* and *for whom* goods and services are produced.

Self-Interest A choice is in your **self-interest** if you think that choice is the best one available for you. You make most of your choices in your self-interest. You use your time and other resources in the ways that make the most sense to you, and you don't think too much about how your choices affect other people. You order a home delivery pizza because you're hungry and want to eat. You don't order it thinking that the delivery person needs an income. And when the pizza delivery person shows up at your door, he's not doing you a favour. He's pursuing his self-interest and hoping for a good tip.

Social Interest A choice is in the **social interest** if it leads to an outcome that is the best for society as a whole. The social interest has two dimensions: efficiency and equity (or fairness). What is best for society is an efficient and fair use of resources.

Economists say that **efficiency** is achieved when the available resources are used to produce goods and services at the lowest possible cost and in the quantities that give the greatest possible value or benefit. We will make the concept of efficiency precise and clear in Chapter 2. For now, just think of efficiency as a situation in which resources are put to their best possible use.

Equity or fairness doesn't have a crisp definition. Reasonable people, both economists and others, have a variety of views about what is fair. There is always room for disagreement and a need to be careful and clear about the notion of fairness being used.

The Big Question Can we organize our economic lives so that when each one of us makes choices that are in our self-interest, we promote the social interest? Can trading in free markets achieve the social interest? Do we need government action to achieve the social interest? Do we need international cooperation and treaties to achieve the global social interest?

Questions about the social interest are hard ones to answer and they generate discussion, debate, and disagreement. Let's put a bit of flesh on these questions with four examples.

The examples are

- Globalization
- The information-age economy
- Climate change
- Economic instability

Globalization The term *globalization* means the expansion of international trade, borrowing and lending, and investment.

Globalization is in the self-interest of those consumers who buy low-cost goods and services produced in other countries; and it is in the self-interest of the multinational firms that produce in low-cost regions and sell in high-price regions. But is globalization in the self-interest of the low-wage worker in Malaysia who sews your new running shoes and the displaced shoemaker in Toronto? Is it in the social interest?

Economics in Action
Life in a Small and Ever-Shrinking World

When Nike produces sports shoes, people in Malaysia get work; and when China buys new regional jets, Canadians who work at Bombardier in Toronto build them. While globalization brings expanded production and job opportunities for some workers, it destroys many Canadian jobs. Workers in manufacturing industries must learn new skills, take service jobs—which are often lower paid—or retire earlier than previously planned.

The Information-Age Economy The technological change of the past 40 years has been called the *Information Revolution.*

The information revolution has clearly served your self-interest: It has provided your cell phone, laptop, loads of handy applications, and the Internet. It has also served the self-interest of Bill Gates of Microsoft and Gordon Moore of Intel, both of whom have seen their wealth soar.

But did the information revolution best serve the social interest? Did Microsoft produce the best possible Windows operating system and sell it at a price that was in the social interest? Did Intel make the right quality of chips and sell them in the right quantities for the right prices? Or was the quality too low and the price too high? Would the social interest have been better served if Microsoft and Intel had faced competition from other firms?

Economics in Action
Chips and Windows

Gordon Moore, who founded the chip-maker Intel, and Bill Gates, a co-founder of Microsoft, held privileged positions in the *Information Revolution.*

For many years, Intel chips were the only available chips and Windows was the only available operating system for the original IBM PC and its clones. The PC and Apple's Mac competed, but the PC had a huge market share.

An absence of competition gave Intel and Microsoft the power and ability to sell their products at prices far above the cost of production. If the prices of chips and Windows had been lower, many more people would have been able to afford a computer and would have chosen to buy one.

Climate Change Climate change is a huge political issue today. Every serious political leader is acutely aware of the problem and of the popularity of having proposals that might lower carbon emissions.

Every day, when you make self-interested choices to use electricity and gasoline, you contribute to carbon emissions; you leave your carbon footprint. You can lessen your carbon footprint by walking, riding a bike, taking a cold shower, or planting a tree.

But can each one of us be relied upon to make decisions that affect the Earth's carbon-dioxide concentration in the social interest? Must governments change the incentives we face so that our self-interested choices are also in the social interest? How can governments change incentives? How can we encourage the use of wind and solar power to replace the burning of fossil fuels that brings climate change?

Economics in Action
Greenhouse Gas Emissions

Burning fossil fuels to generate electricity and to power airplanes, automobiles, and trucks pours a staggering 28 billions tonnes (4 tonnes per person) of carbon dioxide into the atmosphere each year.

Two-thirds of the world's carbon emissions comes from the United States, China, the European Union, Russia, and India. The fastest growing emissions are coming from India and China.

The amount of global warming caused by economic activity and its effects are uncertain, but the emissions continue to grow and pose huge risks.

Economic Instability The years between 1993 and 2007 were a period of remarkable economic stability, so much so that they've been called the *Great Moderation*. During those years, the Canadian and global economies were on a roll. Incomes in Canada increased by 30 percent and incomes in China tripled.

Economics in Action
A Credit Crunch

Flush with funds and offering record low interest rates, U.S. banks went on a lending spree to home buyers. Rapidly rising home prices made home owners feel well off and they were happy to borrow and spend. Home loans were bundled into securities that were sold and resold to banks around the world.

In 2006, as interest rates began to rise and the rate of rise in home prices slowed, borrowers defaulted on their loans. What started as a trickle became a flood. As more people defaulted, banks took losses that totalled billions of dollars by mid-2007.

Global credit markets stopped working, and people began to fear a prolonged slowdown in economic activity. Some even feared the return of the economic trauma of the *Great Depression* of the 1930s. The U.S. Federal Reserve and the Bank of Canada, determined to avoid a catastrophe, started lending on a very large scale to troubled banks.

The Bank of Canada avoided a catastrophe, but many people did lose their jobs and some were forced to sell their homes.

There was a short-lived financial crisis in some Asian economies in 1997 but nothing serious enough to upset sustained global income growth.

But in August 2007, a period of financial stress began. A bank in France was the first to feel the pain that soon would grip the entire global financial system.

Banks take in people's deposits and get more funds by borrowing from each other and from other firms. Banks use these funds to make loans. All the banks' choices to borrow and lend and the choices of people and businesses to lend to and borrow from banks are made in self-interest. But does this lending and borrowing serve the social interest? Is there too much borrowing and lending that needs to be reined in, or is there too little and a need to stimulate more?

When the banks got into trouble in 2008, they received bailout loans from governments and central banks such as the U.S. Federal Reserve and the Bank of Canada. Did the bailout of troubled banks in the global financial crisis serve the social interest?

Banks weren't the only recipients of public funds. General Motors was saved by U.S. and Canadian government bailouts. GM makes its decisions in its self-interest. Did the bailouts of GM serve the social interest?

REVIEW QUIZ

1 Describe the broad facts about *what*, *how*, and *for whom* goods and services are produced.
2 Use headlines from the recent news to illustrate the potential for conflict between self-interest and the social interest.

You can work these questions in Study Plan 1.2 and get instant feedback.

——————————— MyEconLab ◆

We've looked at four topics and asked many questions that illustrate the big question: Can choices made in the pursuit of self-interest also promote the social interest? We've asked questions but not answered them because we've not yet explained the economic principles needed to do so.

By working through this book, you will discover the economic principles that help economists figure out when the social interest is being served, when it is not, and what might be done when it is not being served. We will return to each of the unanswered questions in future chapters.

◆ The Economic Way of Thinking

The questions that economics tries to answer tell us about the *scope of economics,* but they don't tell us how economists *think* and go about seeking answers to these questions. You're now going to see how economists go about their work.

We're going to look at six key ideas that define the *economic way of thinking.* These ideas are

- A choice is a *tradeoff.*
- People make *rational choices* by comparing *benefits* and *costs.*
- *Benefit* is what you gain from something.
- *Cost* is what you *must give up* to get something.
- Most choices are "*how-much*" choices made at the *margin.*
- Choices respond to *incentives.*

A Choice Is a Tradeoff

Because we face scarcity, we must make choices. And when we make a choice, we select from the available alternatives. For example, you can spend Saturday night studying for your next economics test or having fun with your friends, but you can't do both of these activities at the same time. You must choose how much time to devote to each. Whatever choice you make, you could have chosen something else.

You can think about your choices as tradeoffs. A **tradeoff** is an exchange—giving up one thing to get something else. When you choose how to spend your Saturday night, you face a tradeoff between studying and hanging out with your friends.

Making a Rational Choice

Economists view the choices that people make as rational. A **rational choice** is one that compares costs and benefits and achieves the greatest benefit over cost for the person making the choice.

Only the wants of the person making a choice are relevant to determine its rationality. For example, you might like your coffee black and strong but your friend prefers his milky and sweet. So it is rational for you to choose espresso and for your friend to choose cappuccino.

The idea of rational choice provides an answer to the first question: *What* goods and services will be

produced and in what quantities? The answer is those that people rationally choose to buy!

But how do people choose rationally? Why do more people choose a BlackBerry rather than an iPhone? Why don't CNR and CPR build high-speed tracks so that VIA Rail can run Bombardier's super-fast trains like those used in Europe? The answers turn on comparing benefits and costs.

Benefit: What You Gain

The **benefit** of something is the gain or pleasure that it brings and is determined by **preferences**—by what a person likes and dislikes and the intensity of those feelings. If you get a huge kick out of "Guitar Hero," that video game brings you a large benefit. And if you have little interest in listening to Yo Yo Ma playing a Vivaldi cello concerto, that activity brings you a small benefit.

Some benefits are large and easy to identify, such as the benefit that you get from being in school: A big piece of that benefit is the goods and services that you will be able to enjoy with the boost to your earning power when you graduate. Some benefits are small, such as the benefit you get from a slice of pizza.

Economists measure benefit as the most that a person is *willing to give up* to get something. You are willing to give up a lot to be in school. But you would give up only an iTunes download for a slice of pizza.

Cost: What You *Must* Give Up

The **opportunity cost** of something is the highest-valued alternative that must be given up to get it.

To make the idea of opportunity cost concrete, think about *your* opportunity cost of being in school. It has two components: the things you can't afford to buy and the things you can't do with your time.

Start with the things you can't afford to buy. You've spent all your income on tuition, residence fees, books, and a laptop. If you weren't in school, you would have spent this money on tickets to ball games and movies and all the other things that you enjoy. But that's only the start of your opportunity cost. You've also given up the opportunity to get a job. Suppose that the best job you could get if you weren't in school is working at the Royal Bank of Canada as a teller and earning $25,000 a year. Another part of your opportunity cost of being in school is all the things that you could buy with the extra $25,000 you would have had.

As you well know, being a student eats up many hours in class time, doing homework assignments, preparing for tests, and so on. To do all these school activities, you must give up many hours of what would otherwise be leisure time spent with your friends.

So the opportunity cost of being in school is all the good things that you can't afford and don't have the spare time to enjoy. You might want to put a dollar value on that cost or you might just list all the items that make up the opportunity cost.

The examples of opportunity cost that we've just considered are all-or-nothing costs—you're either in school or not in school. Most situations are not like this one. They involve choosing *how much* of an activity to do.

How Much? Choosing at the Margin

You can allocate the next hour between studying and instant messaging your friends, but the choice is not all or nothing. You must decide how many minutes to allocate to each activity. To make this decision, you compare the benefit of a little bit more study time with its cost—you make your choice at the **margin**.

The benefit that arises from an increase in an activity is called **marginal benefit**. For example, your marginal benefit from one more night of study before a test is the boost it gives to your grade. Your marginal benefit doesn't include the grade you're already achieving without that extra night of work.

The *opportunity cost* of an *increase* in an activity is called **marginal cost**. For you, the marginal cost of studying one more night is the cost of not spending that night on your favourite leisure activity.

To make your decisions, you compare marginal benefit and marginal cost. If the marginal benefit from an extra night of study exceeds its marginal cost, you study the extra night. If the marginal cost exceeds the marginal benefit, you don't study the extra night.

Choices Respond to Incentives

Economists take human nature as given and view people as acting in their self-interest. All people— you, other consumers, producers, politicians, and public servants—pursue their self-interest.

Self-interested actions are not necessarily *selfish* actions. You might decide to use your resources in ways that bring pleasure to others as well as to yourself. But a self-interested act gets the most benefit for *you* based on *your* view about benefit.

The central idea of economics is that we can predict the self-interested choices that people make by looking at the *incentives* they face. People undertake those activities for which marginal benefit exceeds marginal cost; and they reject options for which marginal cost exceeds marginal benefit.

For example, your economics instructor gives you a problem set and tells you these problems will be on the next test. Your marginal benefit from working these problems is large, so you diligently work them. In contrast, your math instructor gives you a problem set on a topic that she says will never be on a test. You get little marginal benefit from working these problems, so you decide to skip most of them.

Economists see incentives as the key to reconciling self-interest and social interest. When our choices are *not* in the social interest, it is because of the incentives we face. One of the challenges for economists is to figure out the incentives that result in self-interested choices being in the social interest.

Economists emphasize the crucial role that institutions play in influencing the incentives that people face as they pursue their self-interest. Laws that protect private property and markets that enable voluntary exchange are the fundamental institutions. You will learn as you progress with your study of economics that where these institutions exist, self-interest can indeed promote the social interest.

REVIEW QUIZ

1 Explain the idea of a tradeoff and think of three tradeoffs that you have made today.
2 Explain what economists mean by rational choice and think of three choices that you've made today that are rational.
3 Explain why opportunity cost is the best forgone alternative and provide examples of some opportunity costs that you have faced today.
4 Explain what it means to choose at the margin and illustrate with three choices at the margin that you have made today.
5 Explain why choices respond to incentives and think of three incentives to which you have responded today.

You can work these questions in Study Plan 1.3 and get instant feedback.

MyEconLab ◆

◆ Economics as Social Science and Policy Tool

Economics is both a social science and a toolkit for advising on policy decisions.

Economist as Social Scientist

As social scientists, economists seek to discover how the economic world works. In pursuit of this goal, like all scientists, economists distinguish between positive and normative statements.

Positive Statements A *positive* statement is about what *is*. It says what is currently believed about the way the world operates. A positive statement might be right or wrong, but we can test it by checking it against the facts. "Our planet is warming because of the amount of coal that we're burning" is a positive statement. We can test whether it is right or wrong.

A central task of economists is to test positive statements about how the economic world works and to weed out those that are wrong. Economics first got off the ground in the late 1700s, so it is a young science compared with, for example, physics, and much remains to be discovered.

Normative Statements A *normative* statement is about what *ought to be*. It depends on values and cannot be tested. Policy goals are normative statements. For example, "We ought to cut our use of coal by 50 percent" is a normative policy statement. You may agree or disagree with it, but you can't test it. It doesn't assert a fact that can be checked.

Unscrambling Cause and Effect Economists are particularly interested in positive statements about cause and effect. Are computers getting cheaper because people are buying them in greater quantities? Or are people buying computers in greater quantities because they are getting cheaper? Or is some third factor causing both the price of a computer to fall and the quantity of computers bought to increase?

To answer such questions, economists create and test economic models. An **economic model** is a description of some aspect of the economic world that includes only those features that are needed for the purpose at hand. For example, an economic model of a cellphone network might include features such as the prices of calls, the number of cellphone users, and the volume of calls. But the model would ignore cellphone colours and ringtones.

A model is tested by comparing its predictions with the facts. But testing an economic model is difficult because we observe the outcomes of the simultaneous change of many factors. To cope with this problem, economists look for natural experiments (situations in the ordinary course of economic life in which the one factor of interest is different and other things are equal or similar); conduct statistical investigations to find correlations; and perform economic experiments by putting people in decision-making situations and varying the influence of one factor at a time to discover how they respond.

Economist as Policy Adviser

Economics is useful. It is a toolkit for advising governments and businesses and for making personal decisions. Some of the most famous economists work partly as policy advisers.

For example, Jagdish Bhagwati of Columbia University, whom you will meet on pp. 52–54, has advised governments and international organizations on trade and economic development issues. And leading Canadian economists David Laidler of the University of Western Ontario and Christopher Ragan of McGill University have spent time advising the Bank of Canada and the Department of Finance.

All the policy questions on which economists provide advice involve a blend of the positive and the normative. Economics can't help with the normative part—the policy goal. But for a given goal, economics provides a method of evaluating alternative solutions—comparing marginal benefits and marginal costs and finding the solution that makes the best use of the available resources.

◆ REVIEW QUIZ

1 Distinguish between a positive statement and a normative statement and provide examples.
2 What is a model? Can you think of a model that you might use in your everyday life?
3 How do economists try to disentangle cause and effect?
4 How is economics used as a policy tool?

You can work these questions in Study Plan 1.4 and get instant feedback.

—————————————— MyEconLab ◆

SUMMARY

Key Points

Definition of Economics (p. 2)

- All economic questions arise from scarcity—from the fact that wants exceed the resources available to satisfy them.
- Economics is the social science that studies the choices that people make as they cope with scarcity.
- The subject divides into microeconomics and macroeconomics.

Working Problem 1 will give you a better understanding of the definition of economics.

Two Big Economic Questions (pp. 3–7)

- Two big questions summarize the scope of economics:

   1. How do choices end up determining *what, how,* and *for whom* goods and services are produced?

   2. When do choices made in the pursuit of *self-interest* also promote the *social interest*?

Working Problems 2 and 3 will give you a better understanding of the two big questions of economics.

The Economic Way of Thinking (pp. 8–9)

- Every choice is a tradeoff—exchanging more of something for less of something else.
- People make rational choices by comparing benefit and cost.
- Benefit is the gain you get from something.
- Cost—*opportunity cost*—is what you must give up to get something.
- Most choices are made at the *margin* by comparing marginal benefit and marginal cost.
- Choices respond to incentives.

Working Problems 4 and 5 will give you a better understanding of the economic way of thinking.

Economics as Social Science and Policy Tool (p. 10)

- Economists distinguish between positive statements—what is—and normative statements—what ought to be.
- To explain the economic world, economists create and test economic models.
- Economics is a toolkit used to provide advice on government, business, and personal economic decisions.

Working Problem 6 will give you a better understanding of economics as social science and policy tool.

Key Terms

Benefit, 8
Capital, 4
Economic model, 10
Economics, 2
Efficiency, 5
Entrepreneurship, 4
Factors of production, 3
Goods and services, 3
Human capital, 3
Incentive, 2
Interest, 4
Labour, 3
Land, 3
Macroeconomics, 2

Margin, 9
Marginal benefit, 9
Marginal cost, 9
Microeconomics, 2
Opportunity cost, 8
Preferences, 8
Profit, 4
Rational choice, 8
Rent, 4
Scarcity, 2
Self-interest, 5
Social interest, 5
Tradeoff, 8
Wages, 4

SCAN THIS

STUDY PLAN PROBLEMS AND APPLICATIONS

MyEconLab ◆ You can work Problems 1 to 6 in Chapter 1 Study Plan and get instant feedback.

Definition of Economics (Study Plan 1.1)

1. Apple Inc. decides to make iTunes freely available in unlimited quantities.
   a. Does Apple's decision change the incentives that people face?
   b. Is Apple's decision an example of a microeconomic or a macroeconomic issue?

Two Big Economic Questions (Study Plan 1.2)

2. Which of the following pairs does not match?
   a. Labour and wages
   b. Land and rent
   c. Entrepreneurship and profit
   d. Capital and profit

3. Explain how the following news headlines concern self-interest and the social interest.
   a. Starbucks Expands in China
   b. McDonald's Moves into Salads
   c. Food Must Be Labelled with Nutrition Data

The Economic Way of Thinking (Study Plan 1.3)

4. The night before an economics test, you decide to go to the movies instead of staying home and working your MyEconLab Study Plan. You get 50 percent on your test compared with the 70 percent that you normally score.
   a. Did you face a tradeoff?
   b. What was the opportunity cost of your evening at the movies?

5. **Costs Soar for London Olympics**
   The regeneration of East London, the site of the 2012 Olympic Games, is set to add extra £1.5 billion to taxpayers' bill.

   Source: *The Times*, London, July 6, 2006

   Is the cost of regenerating East London an opportunity cost of hosting the 2012 Olympic Games? Explain why or why not.

Economics as Social Science and Policy Tool
(Study Plan 1.4)

6. Which of the following statements is positive, which is normative, and which can be tested?
   a. Russia to lift grain export ban.
   b. China is the largest trading partner of Canada.
   c. The federal government should increase the production of biofuels.

ADDITIONAL PROBLEMS AND APPLICATIONS

MyEconLab ◆ You can work these problems in MyEconLab if assigned by your instructor.

Definition of Economics

7. **Hundreds Line up for 5 p.m. Ticket Giveaway**
   By noon, hundreds of Eminem fans had lined up for a chance to score free tickets to the concert.

   Source: *Detroit Free Press*, May 18, 2009

   When Eminem gave away tickets, what was free and what was scarce? Explain your answer.

Two Big Economic Questions

8. How does the creation of a successful movie influence *what*, *how*, and *for whom* goods and services are produced?

9. How does a successful movie illustrate self-interested choices that are also in the social interest?

The Economic Way of Thinking

10. Last fall, Costco opened its gas bar at a busy intersection just off Highway 401 in Toronto. Since then the neighbourhood has been swamped with cars, as drivers come from far and away for discounts of 10 cents a litre.
    a. What is the opportunity cost of a litre of gas? Explain.
    b. To control the crowd, Costco hires traffic police. What is the tradeoff that Costco faces?

11. What might be an incentive for you to take a class in summer school? List some of the benefits and costs involved in your decision. Would your choice be rational?

Economics as Social Science and Policy Tool

12. Look at today's *Financial Post*. What is the leading economic news story? With which of the big economic questions does it deal and what tradeoffs does it discuss or imply?

13. Provide two microeconomic statements and two macroeconomic statements. Classify your statements as positive or normative. Explain why.

APPENDIX

Graphs in Economics

After studying this appendix,
you will be able to

◆ Make and interpret a scatter diagram
◆ Identify linear and nonlinear relationships and
   relationships that have a maximum and a minimum
◆ Define and calculate the slope of a line
◆ Graph relationships among more than two
   variables

Graphing Data

A graph represents a quantity as a distance on a line.
In Fig. A1.1, a distance on the horizontal line represents temperature, measured in degrees Celsius. A
movement from left to right shows an increase in
temperature. The point 0 represents zero degrees
Celsius. To the right of 0, the temperature is positive. To the left of 0, the temperature is negative (as
indicated by the minus sign). A distance on the vertical line represents height, measured in thousands of
metres. The point 0 represents sea level. Points above
0 represent metres above sea level. Points below 0
represent metres below sea level (indicated by a
minus sign).

In Fig. A1.1, the two scale lines are perpendicu-
lar to each other and are called *axes*. The vertical line is
the *y*-axis, and the horizontal line is the *x*-axis. Each
axis has a zero point, which is shared by the two axes
and called the *origin*.

To make a two-variable graph, we need two pieces
of information: the value of the variable *x* and the
value of the variable *y*. For example, off the coast of
British Columbia, the temperature is 10 degrees—the
value of *x*. A fishing boat is located at 0 metres above
sea level—the value of *y*. These two bits of information appear as point *A* in Fig. A1.1. A climber at the
top of Mount McKinley on a cold day is 6,194 metres
above sea level in a zero-degree gale. These two pieces
of information appear as point *B*. On a warmer day, a
climber might be at the peak of Mt. McKinley when
the temperature is 10 degrees, at point *C*.

We can draw two lines, called *coordinates*, from
point *C*. One, called the *x*-coordinate, runs from

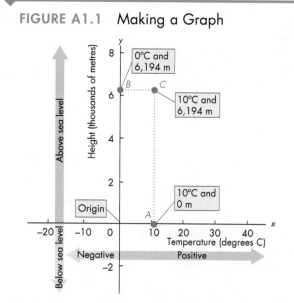

FIGURE A1.1   Making a Graph

Graphs have axes that measure quantities as distances.
Here, the horizontal axis (*x*-axis) measures temperature,
and the vertical axis (*y*-axis) measures height. Point *A*
represents a fishing boat at sea level (0 on the *y*-axis) on
a day when the temperature is 10°C. Point *B* represents a
climber at the top of Mt. McKinley, 6,194 metres above
sea level in a zero-degree gale. Point *C* represents a
climber at the top of Mt. McKinley, 6,194 metres above
sea level, at a temperature of 10°C.

━━━━━━ MyEconLab   animation   ◆

C to the vertical axis. This line is called "the
x-coordinate" because its length is the same as the
value marked off on the *x*-axis. The other, called the
y-coordinate, runs from *C* to the horizontal axis.
This line is called "the *y*-coordinate" because its
length is the same as the value marked off on the
y-axis.

We describe a point on a graph by the values of
its *x*-coordinate and its *y*-coordinate. For example, at
point *C*, *x* is 10 degrees and *y* is 6,194 metres.

A graph like that in Fig. A1.1 can be made using
any quantitative data on two variables. The graph
can show just a few points, like Fig. A1.1, or many
points. Before we look at graphs with many points,
let's reinforce what you've just learned by looking at
two graphs made with economic data.

Economists measure variables that describe *what,
how*, and *for whom* goods and services are produced.
These variables are quantities produced and prices.
Figure A1.2 shows two examples of economic graphs.

FIGURE A1.2 Two Graphs of Economic Data

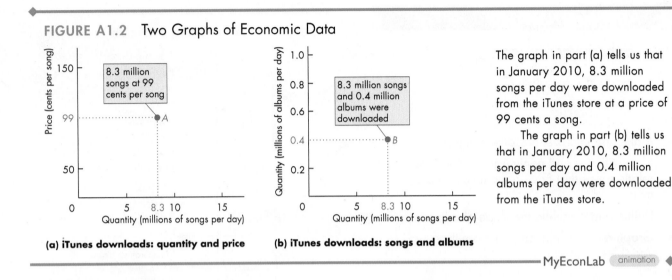

(a) iTunes downloads: quantity and price

(b) iTunes downloads: songs and albums

The graph in part (a) tells us that in January 2010, 8.3 million songs per day were downloaded from the iTunes store at a price of 99 cents a song.

The graph in part (b) tells us that in January 2010, 8.3 million songs per day and 0.4 million albums per day were downloaded from the iTunes store.

MyEconLab animation

Figure A1.2(a) is a graph about iTunes song downloads in January 2010. The *x*-axis measures the quantity of songs downloaded per day and the *y*-axis measures the price of a song. Point *A* tells us what the quantity and price were. You can "read" this graph as telling you that in January 2010, 8.3 million songs a day were downloaded at a price of 99¢ per song.

Figure A1.2(b) is a graph about iTunes song and album downloads in January 2010. The *x*-axis measures the quantity of songs downloaded per day and the *y*-axis measures the quantity of albums downloaded per day. Point *B* tells us what these quantities were. You can "read" this graph as telling you that in January 2010, 8.3 million songs and 0.4 million albums a day were downloaded.

The three graphs that you've just seen tell you how to make a graph and how to read a data point on a graph, but they don't improve on the raw data. Graphs become interesting and revealing when they contain a number of data points because then you can visualize the data.

Economists create graphs based on the principles in Figs. A1.1 and A1.2 to reveal, describe, and visualize the relationships among variables. We're now going to look at some examples. These graphs are called scatter diagrams.

Scatter Diagrams

A **scatter diagram** is a graph that plots the value of one variable against the value of another variable for a number of different values of each variable. Such a graph reveals whether a relationship exists between two variables and describes their relationship.

Movies and DVDs The table in Fig. A1.3 shows some data on two variables: the number of tickets sold at the box office and the number of DVDs sold for eight of the most popular movies in 2009.

What is the relationship between these two variables? Does a big box office success generate a large volume of DVD sales? Or does a box office success mean that fewer DVDs are sold?

We can answer these questions by making a scatter diagram. We do so by graphing the data in the table. In the graph in Fig. A1.3, each point shows the number of box office tickets sold (the *x* variable) and the number of DVDs sold (the *y* variable) of one of the movies. There are eight movies, so there are eight points "scattered" within the graph.

The point labelled *A* tells us that *Star Trek* sold 34 million tickets at the box office and 6 million DVDs. The points in the graph form a pattern, which reveals that larger box office sales are associated with larger DVD sales. But the points also tell us that this association is weak. You can't predict DVD sales with any confidence by knowing only the number of tickets sold at the box office.

Two Economic Examples Figure A1.4 shows two scatter diagrams of economic variables. Part (a) shows the relationship between income and expenditure in Canada from 2001 to 2010. Each point represents income and expenditure in a given year. For example, point *A* shows that in 2006, income was $26,000 and expenditure was $24,000. This graph shows that as income increases, so does expenditure, and the relationship is a close one.

FIGURE A1.3   Scatter Diagram

Movie	Tickets	DVDs
	(millions)	
Twilight	38	10
Transformers: Revenge of the Fallen	54	9
Up	39	8
Harry Potter and the Half-Blood Prince	40	7
Star Trek	34	6
The Hangover	37	6
Ice Age: Dawn of the Dinosaurs	26	5
The Proposal	22	5

The table lists the number of tickets sold at the box office and the number of DVDs sold for eight popular movies. The scatter diagram reveals the relationship between these two variables. Each point shows the values of the two variables for a specific movie. For example, point A shows the point for *Star Trek*, which sold 34 million tickets at the box office and 6 million DVDs. The pattern formed by the points shows that there is a tendency for large box office sales to bring greater DVD sales. But you couldn't predict how many DVDs a movie would sell just by knowing its box office sales.

Figure A1.4(b) shows a scatter diagram of Canadian unemployment and inflation from 2000 to 2010. In 2005, the unemployment rate was 7 percent and the inflation rate was 1.6 percent at point *B*. The data here show a loose negative relationship between the two variables. Higher unemployment is loosely associated with lower inflation.

You can see that a scatter diagram conveys a wealth of information, and it does so in much less space than we have used to describe only some of its features. But you do have to "read" the graph to obtain all this information.

FIGURE A1.4   Two Economic Scatter Diagrams

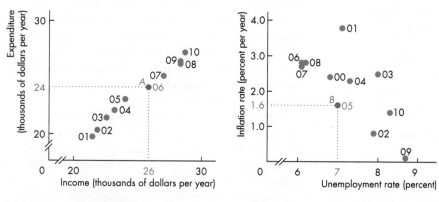

(a) Income and expenditure

(b) Unemployment and inflation

The scatter diagram in part (a) shows the relationship between income and expenditure from 2001 to 2010. Point A shows that in 2006, income was $26,000 on the x-axis and expenditure was $24,000 on the y-axis. This graph shows that as income increases, so does expenditure, and the relationship is a close one.

The scatter diagram in part (b) shows a loose negative relationship between unemployment and inflation in Canada during the 2000s.

Breaks in the Axes The graph in Fig. A1.4(a) has breaks in its axes, as shown by the small gaps. The breaks indicate that there are jumps from the origin, 0, to the first values recorded.

The breaks are used because the lowest values of income and expenditure exceed $18,000. If we made this graph with no breaks in its axes, there would be a lot of empty space, all the points would be crowded into the top right corner, and it would be difficult to see whether a relationship exists between these two variables. By breaking the axes, we are able to bring the relationship into view.

Putting a break in one or both axes is like using a zoom lens to bring the relationship into the centre of the graph and magnify it so that the relationship fills the graph.

Misleading Graphs Breaks can be used to highlight a relationship, but they can also be used to mislead—to make a graph that lies. The most common way of making a graph lie is to put a break in the axis and either to stretch or compress the scale. For example, suppose that in Fig. A1.4(a), the *y*-axis that measures expenditure ran from zero to $30,000 while the *x*-axis was the same as the one shown. The graph would now create the impression that despite a huge increase in income, expenditure had barely changed.

To avoid being misled, it is a good idea to get into the habit of always looking closely at the values and the labels on the axes of a graph before you start to interpret it.

Correlation and Causation A scatter diagram that shows a clear relationship between two variables, such as the one in Fig. A1.4(a), tells us that the two variables have a high correlation. When a high correlation is present, we can predict the value of one variable from the value of the other variable. But correlation does not imply causation.

Sometimes a high correlation is a coincidence, but sometimes it does arise from a causal relationship. It is likely, for example, that rising income causes rising expenditure (Fig. A1.4a) and that a high unemployment rate makes for a slack economy in which prices don't rise quickly, so the inflation rate is low (Fig. A1.4b).

You've now seen how we can use graphs in economics to show economic data and to reveal relationships. Next, we'll learn how economists use graphs to construct and display economic models.

Graphs Used in Economic Models

The graphs used in economics are not always designed to show real-world data. Often they are used to show general relationships among the variables in an economic model.

An *economic model* is a stripped-down, simplified description of an economy or of a component of an economy such as a business or a household. It consists of statements about economic behaviour that can be expressed as equations or as curves in a graph. Economists use models to explore the effects of different policies or other influences on the economy in ways that are similar to the use of model airplanes in wind tunnels and models of the climate.

You will encounter many different kinds of graphs in economic models, but there are some repeating patterns. Once you've learned to recognize these patterns, you will instantly understand the meaning of a graph. Here, we'll look at the different types of curves that are used in economic models, and we'll see some everyday examples of each type of curve. The patterns to look for in graphs are the following four cases:

- Variables that move in the same direction
- Variables that move in opposite directions
- Variables that have a maximum or a minimum
- Variables that are unrelated

Let's look at these four cases.

Variables That Move in the Same Direction

Figure A1.5 shows graphs of the relationships between two variables that move up and down together. A relationship between two variables that move in the same direction is called a **positive relationship** or a **direct relationship**. A line that slopes upward shows such a relationship.

Figure A1.5 shows three types of relationships: one that has a straight line and two that have curved lines. All the lines in these three graphs are called curves. Any line on a graph—no matter whether it is straight or curved—is called a *curve*.

A relationship shown by a straight line is called a **linear relationship**. Figure A1.5(a) shows a linear relationship between the number of kilometres travelled in 5 hours and speed. For example, point *A* shows that we will travel 200 kilometres in 5 hours if our speed is 40 kilometres an hour. If we double our speed to 80 kilometres an hour, we will travel 400 kilometres in 5 hours.

Figure A1.5(b) shows the relationship between distance sprinted and recovery time (the time it takes the heart rate to return to its normal resting rate). This relationship is an upward-sloping one that starts out quite flat but then becomes steeper as we move along the curve away from the origin. The reason this curve becomes steeper is that the additional recovery time needed from sprinting an additional 100 metres increases. It takes less than 5 minutes to recover from sprinting 100 metres but more than 10 minutes to recover from 200 metres.

Figure A1.5(c) shows the relationship between the number of problems worked by a student and the amount of study time. This relationship is an upward-sloping one that starts out quite steep and becomes flatter as we move along the curve away from the origin. Study time becomes less productive as the student spends more hours studying and becomes more tired.

Variables That Move in Opposite Directions

Some variables move in opposite directions. Figure A1.6 shows relationships between such variables. When variables move in opposite directions there is a **negative relationship** or an **inverse relationship.**

Figure A1.6(a) shows the relationship between the hours spent playing squash and the hours spent playing tennis when the total time available is 5 hours. One extra hour spent playing tennis means one hour less spent playing squash and vice versa. This relationship is negative and linear.

Figure A1.6(b) shows the relationship between the cost per kilometre travelled and the length of a journey. The longer the journey, the lower is the cost per kilometre. But as the journey length increases, even though the cost per kilometre decreases, the fall in the cost is smaller the longer the journey. This feature of the relationship is shown by the fact that the curve slopes downward, starting out steep at a short journey length and then becoming flatter as the journey length increases. This relationship arises because some of the costs are fixed, such as auto insurance, and the fixed costs are spread over a longer journey.

FIGURE A1.5   Positive (Direct) Relationships

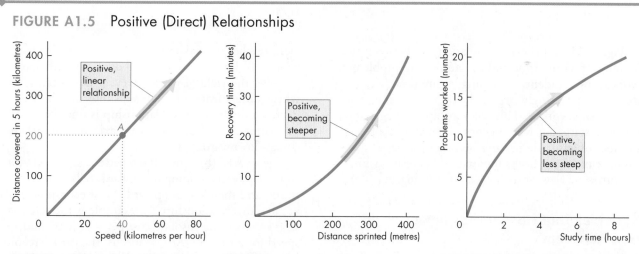

(a) Positive, linear relationship   **(b) Positive, becoming steeper**   **(c) Positive, becoming less steep**

Each part shows a positive (direct) relationship between two variables. That is, as the value of the variable measured on the *x*-axis increases, so does the value of the variable measured on the *y*-axis. Part (a) shows a linear positive relationship—as the two variables increase together, we move along a straight line.

Part (b) shows a positive relationship such that as the two variables increase together, we move along a curve that becomes steeper.

Part (c) shows a positive relationship such that as the two variables increase together, we move along a curve that becomes flatter.

FIGURE A1.6   Negative (Inverse) Relationships

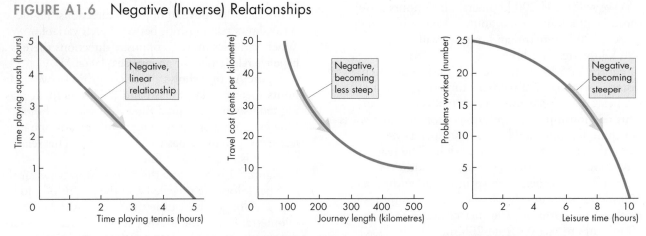

(a) Negative, linear relationship   **(b) Negative, becoming less steep**   **(c) Negative, becoming steeper**

Each part shows a negative (inverse) relationship between two variables. Part (a) shows a linear negative relationship. The total time spent playing tennis and squash is 5 hours. As the time spent playing tennis increases, the time spent playing squash decreases, and we move along a straight line.

Part (b) shows a negative relationship such that as the journey length increases, the travel cost decreases as we move along a curve that becomes less steep.

Part (c) shows a negative relationship such that as leisure time increases, the number of problems worked decreases as we move along a curve that becomes steeper.

Figure A1.6(c) shows the relationship between the amount of leisure time and the number of problems worked by a student. Increasing leisure time produces an increasingly large reduction in the number of problems worked. This relationship is a negative one that starts out with a gentle slope at a small number of leisure hours and becomes steeper as the number of leisure hours increases. This relationship is a different view of the idea shown in Fig. A1.5(c).

Variables That Have a Maximum or a Minimum

Many relationships in economic models have a maximum or a minimum. For example, firms try to make the maximum possible profit and to produce at the lowest possible cost. Figure A1.7 shows relationships that have a maximum or a minimum.

Figure A1.7(a) shows the relationship between rainfall and wheat yield. When there is no rainfall, wheat will not grow, so the yield is zero. As the rainfall increases up to 10 days a month, the wheat yield increases. With 10 rainy days a month, the wheat

yield reaches its maximum at 2 tonnes per hectare (point *A*). Rain in excess of 10 days a month starts to lower the yield of wheat. If every day is rainy, the wheat suffers from a lack of sunshine and the yield decreases to zero. This relationship is one that starts out sloping upward, reaches a maximum, and then slopes downward.

Figure A1.7(b) shows the reverse case—a relationship that begins sloping downward, falls to a minimum, and then slopes upward. Most economic costs are like this relationship. An example is the relationship between the gasoline cost per kilometre and speed for a car trip. At low speeds, the car is creeping in a traffic snarl-up. The number of kilometres per litre is low, so the gasoline cost per kilometre is high. At high speeds, the car is travelling faster than its efficient speed, using a large quantity of gasoline, and again the number of kilometres per litre is low and the gasoline cost per kilometre is high. At a speed of 100 kilometres an hour, the gasoline cost per kilometre is at its minimum (point *B*). This relationship is one that starts out sloping downward, reaches a minimum, and then slopes upward.

FIGURE A1.7   Maximum and Minimum Points

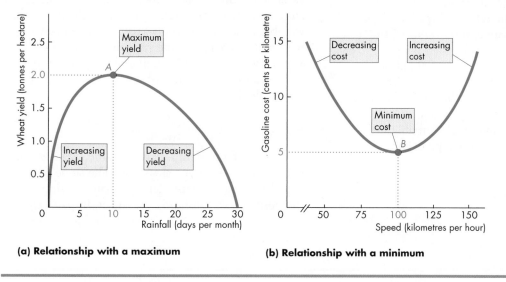

(a) Relationship with a maximum

(b) Relationship with a minimum

Part (a) shows a relationship that has a maximum point, *A*. The curve slopes upward as it rises to its maximum point, is flat at its maximum, and then slopes downward.

Part (b) shows a relationship with a minimum point, *B*. The curve slopes downward as it falls to its minimum, is flat at its minimum, and then slopes upward.

MyEconLab   animation

Variables That Are Unrelated

There are many situations in which no matter what happens to the value of one variable, the other variable remains constant. Sometimes we want to show the independence between two variables in a graph. Figure A1.8 shows two ways of achieving this.

In describing the graphs in Fig. A1.5 through Fig. A1.7, we have talked about curves that slope upward or downward, and curves that become less steep or steeper. Let's spend a little time discussing exactly what we mean by *slope* and how we measure the slope of a curve.

FIGURE A1.8   Variables That Are Unrelated

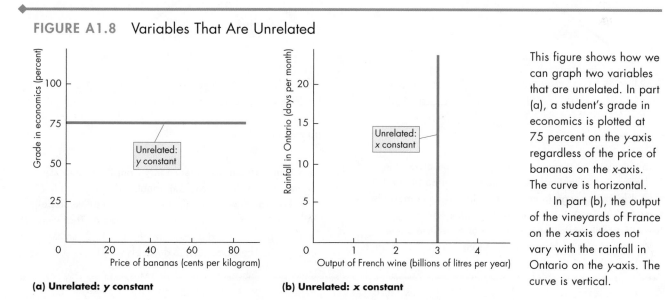

(a) Unrelated: *y* constant

(b) Unrelated: *x* constant

This figure shows how we can graph two variables that are unrelated. In part (a), a student's grade in economics is plotted at 75 percent on the *y*-axis regardless of the price of bananas on the *x*-axis. The curve is horizontal.

In part (b), the output of the vineyards of France on the *x*-axis does not vary with the rainfall in Ontario on the *y*-axis. The curve is vertical.

MyEconLab   animation

◆ The Slope of a Relationship

We can measure the influence of one variable on another by the slope of the relationship. The **slope** of a relationship is the change in the value of the variable measured on the y-axis divided by the change in the value of the variable measured on the x-axis. We use the Greek letter Δ (*delta*) to represent "change in." Thus Δy means the change in the value of the variable measured on the y-axis, and Δx means the change in the value of the variable measured on the x-axis. Therefore the slope of the relationship is

$$\text{Slope} = \frac{\Delta y}{\Delta x}.$$

If a large change in the variable measured on the y-axis (Δy) is associated with a small change in the variable measured on the x-axis (Δx), the slope is large and the curve is steep. If a small change in the variable measured on the y-axis (Δy) is associated with a large change in the variable measured on the x-axis (Δx), the slope is small and the curve is flat.

We can make the idea of slope clearer by doing some calculations.

The Slope of a Straight Line

The slope of a straight line is the same regardless of where on the line you calculate it. The slope of a straight line is constant. Let's calculate the slope of the positive relationship in Fig. A1.9. In part (a),

---

FIGURE A1.9   The Slope of a Straight Line

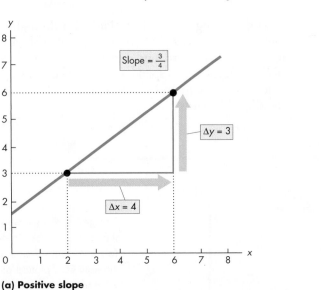

(a) Positive slope

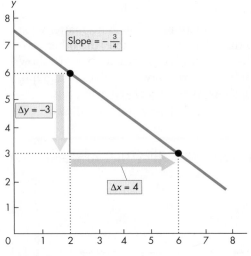

(b) Negative slope

To calculate the slope of a straight line, we divide the change in the value of the variable measured on the y-axis (Δy) by the change in the value of the variable measured on the x-axis (Δx) as we move along the line.

Part (a) shows the calculation of a positive slope. When x increases from 2 to 6, Δx equals 4. That change

in x brings about an increase in y from 3 to 6, so Δy equals 3. The slope (Δy/Δx) equals 3/4.

Part (b) shows the calculation of a negative slope. When x increases from 2 to 6, Δx equals 4. That increase in x brings about a decrease in y from 6 to 3, so Δy equals –3. The slope (Δy/Δx) equals –3/4.

when *x* increases from 2 to 6, *y* increases from 3 to 6. The change in *x* is +4—that is, Δx is 4. The change in *y* is +3—that is, Δy is 3. The slope of that line is

$$\frac{\Delta y}{\Delta x} = \frac{3}{4}.$$

In part (b), when *x* increases from 2 to 6, *y* decreases from 6 to 3. The change in *y* is *minus* 3—that is, *y* is −3. The change in *x* is *plus* 4—that is, Δx is 4. The slope of the curve is

$$\frac{\Delta y}{\Delta x} = \frac{-3}{4}.$$

Notice that the two slopes have the same magnitude (3/4), but the slope of the line in part (a) is positive (+3/+4 = 3/4) while that in part (b) is negative (−3/+4 = −3/4). The slope of a positive relationship is positive; the slope of a negative relationship is negative.

The Slope of a Curved Line

The slope of a curved line is trickier. The slope of a curved line is not constant, so the slope depends on where on the curved line we calculate it. There are two ways to calculate the slope of a curved line: You can calculate the slope at a point, or you can calculate the slope across an arc of the curve. Let's look at the two alternatives.

Slope at a Point To calculate the slope at a point on a curve, you need to construct a straight line that has the same slope as the curve at the point in question. Figure A1.10 shows how this is done. Suppose you want to calculate the slope of the curve at point *A*. Place a ruler on the graph so that the ruler touches point *A* and no other point on the curve, then draw a straight line along the edge of the ruler. The straight red line is this line, and it is the tangent to the curve at point *A*. If the ruler touches the curve only at point *A*, then the slope of the curve at point *A* must be the same as the slope of the edge of the ruler. If the curve and the ruler do not have the same slope, the line along the edge of the ruler will cut the curve instead of just touching it.

Now that you have found a straight line with the same slope as the curve at point *A*, you can calculate the slope of the curve at point *A* by calculating the slope of the straight line. Along the straight line, as *x*

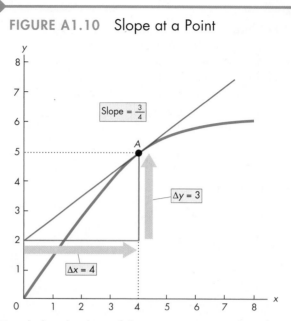

FIGURE A1.10   Slope at a Point

To calculate the slope of the curve at point *A*, draw the red line that just touches the curve at *A*—the tangent. The slope of this straight line is calculated by dividing the change in *y* by the change in *x* along the red line. When *x* increases from 0 to 4, Δx equals 4. That change in *x* is associated with an increase in *y* from 2 to 5, so Δy equals 3. The slope of the red line is 3/4, so the slope of the curve at point *A* is 3/4.

MyEconLab   animation

increases from 0 to 4 (Δx is 4) *y* increases from 2 to 5 (Δy is 3). Therefore the slope of the straight line is

$$\frac{\Delta y}{\Delta x} = \frac{3}{4}.$$

So the slope of the curve at point *A* is 3/4.

Slope Across an Arc An arc of a curve is a piece of a curve. Figure A1.11 shows the same curve as in Fig. A1.10, but instead of calculating the slope at point *A*, we are now going to calculate the slope across the arc from point *B* to point *C*. You can see that the slope of the curve at point *B* is greater than at point *C*. When we calculate the slope across an arc, we are calculating the average slope between two points. As we move along the arc from *B* to *C*, *x* increases from 3 to 5 and *y* increases from 4.0 to 5.5. The change in *x* is 2 (Δx is 2), and the change in *y* is 1.5 (Δy is 1.5).

FIGURE A1.11   Slope Across an Arc

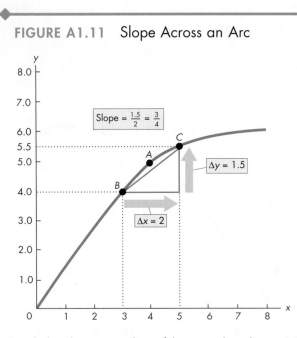

Slope $= \dfrac{1.5}{2} = \dfrac{3}{4}$

$\Delta y = 1.5$

$\Delta x = 2$

To calculate the average slope of the curve along the arc *BC*, draw a straight line from point *B* to point *C*. The slope of the line *BC* is calculated by dividing the change in *y* by the change in *x*. In moving from *B* to *C*, the increase in *x* is 2 (Δx equals 2) and the change in *y* is 1.5 (Δy equals 1.5). The slope of the line *BC* is 1.5 divided by 2, or 3/4. So the slope of the curve across the arc *BC* is 3/4.

——————————————— MyEconLab (animation) ◆

Therefore the slope is

$$\frac{\Delta y}{\Delta x} = \frac{1.5}{2} = \frac{3}{4}.$$

So the slope of the curve across the arc *BC* is 3/4.

This calculation gives us the slope of the curve between points *B* and *C*. The actual slope calculated is the slope of the straight red line from *B* to *C*. This slope approximates the average slope of the curve along the arc *BC*. In this particular example, the slope across the arc *BC* is identical to the slope of the curve at point *A*, but the calculation of the slope of a curve does not always work out so neatly. You might have fun constructing some more examples and a few counter examples.

You now know how to make and interpret a graph. So far, we've limited our attention to graphs of two variables. We're now going to learn how to graph more than two variables.

Graphing Relationships Among More Than Two Variables

We have seen that we can graph the relationship between two variables as a point formed by the *x*- and *y*-coordinates in a two-dimensional graph. You might be thinking that although a two-dimensional graph is informative, most of the things in which you are likely to be interested involve relationships among many variables, not just two. For example, the amount of ice cream consumed depends on the price of ice cream and the temperature. If ice cream is expensive and the temperature is low, people eat much less ice cream than when ice cream is inexpensive and the temperature is high. For any given price of ice cream, the quantity consumed varies with the temperature; and for any given temperature, the quantity of ice cream consumed varies with its price.

Figure A1.12 shows a relationship among three variables. The table shows the number of litres of ice cream consumed each day at two different temperatures and at a number of different prices of ice cream. How can we graph these numbers?

To graph a relationship that involves more than two variables, we use the *ceteris paribus* assumption.

Ceteris Paribus

Ceteris paribus (often shortened to *cet par*) means "if all other relevant things remain the same." To isolate the relationship of interest in a laboratory experiment, a scientist holds everything constant except for the variable whose effect is being studied. Economists use the same method to graph a relationship that has more than two variables.

Figure A1.12 shows an example. There, you can see what happens to the quantity of ice cream consumed when the price of ice cream varies but the temperature is held constant.

The curve labelled 21°C shows the relationship between ice cream consumption and the price of ice cream if the temperature remains at 21°C. The numbers used to plot that curve are those in the first two columns of the table. For example, if the temperature is 21°C, 10 litres of ice cream are consumed when the price is $2.75 a scoop and 18 litres are consumed when the price is $2.25 a scoop.

The curve labelled 32°C shows the relationship between ice cream consumption and the price of ice cream if the temperature remains at 32°C. The

FIGURE A1.12   Graphing a Relationship Among Three Variables

Price (dollars per scoop)	Ice cream consumption (litres per day)	
	21°C	32°C
2.00	25	50
2.25	18	36
2.50	13	26
2.75	**10**	**20**
3.00	7	14
3.25	5	10
3.50	3	6

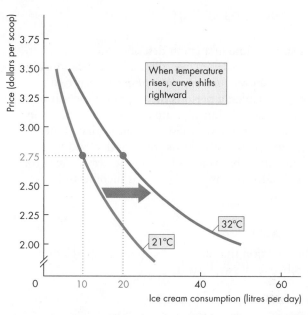

Ice cream consumption depends on its price and the temperature. The table tells us how many litres of ice cream are consumed each day at different prices and two different temperatures. For example, if the price is $2.75 a scoop and the temperature is 21°C, 10 litres of ice cream are consumed.

To graph a relationship among three variables, the value of one variable is held constant. The graph shows the relationship between price and consumption when temperature is held constant. One curve holds temperature at 21°C and the other holds it at 32°C.

A change in the price of ice cream brings a movement along one of the curves—along the blue curve at 21°C and along the red curve at 32°C.

When the temperature *rises* from 21°C to 32°C, the curve that shows the relationship between consumption and price *shifts* rightward from the blue curve to the red curve.

MyEconLab animation

numbers used to plot that curve are those in the first and third columns of the table. For example, if the temperature is 32°C, 20 litres are consumed when the price is $2.75 a scoop and 36 litres are consumed when the price is $2.25 a scoop.

When the price of ice cream changes but the temperature is constant, you can think of what happens in the graph as a movement along one of the curves. At 21°C there is a movement along the blue curve; at 32°C there is a movement along the red curve.

When Other Things Change

The temperature is held constant along each of the curves in Fig. A1.12, but in reality the temperature changes. When that event occurs, you can think of

what happens in the graph as a shift of the curve. When the temperature rises from 21°C to 32°C, the curve that shows the relationship between ice cream consumption and the price of ice cream shifts rightward from the blue curve to the red curve.

You will encounter these ideas of movements along and shifts of curves at many points in your study of economics. Think carefully about what you've just learned and make up some examples (with assumed numbers) about other relationships.

With what you have learned about graphs, you can move forward with your study of economics. There are no graphs in this book that are more complicated than those that have been explained in this appendix.

◆ MATHEMATICAL NOTE

Equations of Straight Lines

If a straight line in a graph describes the relationship between two variables, we call it a linear relationship. Figure 1 shows a *linear relationship* between two economic variables: a person's income and expenditure.

All linear relationships are described by the same general equation. We call the quantity that is measured on the horizontal axis (or *x*-axis) *x,* and we call the quantity that is measured on the vertical axis (or *y*-axis) *y.* In the case of Fig. 1, *x* is income and *y* is expenditure.

A Linear Equation

The equation that describes a straight-line relationship between *x* and *y* is

$$y = a + bx.$$

In this equation, *a* and *b* are fixed numbers and they are called *constants.* The values of *x* and *y* vary, so these numbers are called *variables.* Because the equation describes a straight line, the equation is called a linear equation.

The equation tells us that when the value of *x* is zero, the value of *y* is *a.* We call the constant *a* the *y*-axis intercept. The reason is that on the graph the straight line hits the *y*-axis at a value equal to *a.* Figure 1 illustrates the *y*-axis intercept.

For positive values of *x*, the value of *y* exceeds *a.* The constant *b* tells us by how much *y* increases above *a* as *x* increases. The constant *b* is the slope of the line.

Slope of Line

As we explain in the chapter, the slope of a relationship is the change in the value of *y* divided by the change in the value of *x.* We use the Greek letter Δ (delta) to represent "change in." So Δy means the change in the value of the variable measured on the *y*-axis, and Δx means the change in the value of the variable measured on the *x*-axis. Therefore the slope of the relationship is

$$\text{Slope} = \frac{\Delta y}{\Delta x}.$$

To see why the slope is *b*, suppose that initially the value of *x* is x_1, or \$200 in Fig. 2. The corresponding value of *y* is y_1, also \$200 in Fig. 2. The equation of the line tells us that

$$y_1 = a + bx_1. \tag{1}$$

Now the value of Δx increases by *x* to $x_1 + \Delta x$ (or \$400 in Fig. 2). And the value of *y* increases by Δy to $y_1 + \Delta y$ (or \$300 in Fig. 2).

The equation of the line now tells us that

$$y_1 + \Delta y = a + b(x_1 + \Delta x). \tag{2}$$

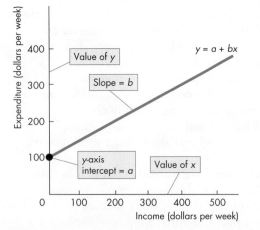

Figure 1 Linear relationship

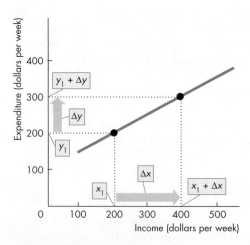

Figure 2 Calculating slope

To calculate the slope of the line, subtract equation (1) from equation (2) to obtain

$$\Delta y = b\Delta x \qquad (3)$$

and now divide equation (3) by x to obtain

$$\Delta y/\Delta x = b.$$

So the slope of the line is b.

Position of Line

The y-axis intercept determines the position of the line on the graph. Figure 3 illustrates the relationship between the y-axis intercept and the position of the line. In this graph, the y-axis measures saving and the x-axis measures income.

When the y-axis intercept, a, is positive, the line hits the y-axis at a positive value of y—as the blue line does. Its y-axis intercept is 100. When the y-axis intercept, a, is zero, the line hits the y-axis at the origin—as the purple line does. Its y-axis intercept is 0. When the y-axis intercept, a, is negative, the line hits the y-axis at a negative value of y—as the red line does. Its y-axis intercept is −100.

As the equations of the three lines show, the value of the y-axis intercept does not influence the slope of the line. All three lines have a slope equal to 0.5.

Positive Relationships

Figure 1 shows a positive relationship—the two variables x and y move in the same direction. All positive relationships have a slope that is positive. In the equation of the line, the constant b is positive. In this example, the y-axis intercept, a, is 100. The slope b equals $\Delta y/\Delta x$, which in Fig. 2 is 100/200 or 0.5. The equation of the line is

$$y = 100 + 0.5x.$$

Negative Relationships

Figure 4 shows a negative relationship—the two variables x and y move in opposite directions. All negative relationships have a slope that is negative. In the equation of the line, the constant b is negative. In the example in Fig. 4, the y-axis intercept, a, is 30. The slope, b, equals $\Delta y/\Delta x$, which is −20/2 or −10. The equation of the line is

$$y = 30 + (-10)x$$

or

$$y = 30 - 10x.$$

Example

A straight line has a y-axis intercept of 50 and a slope of 2. What is the equation of this line?

The equation of a straight line is

$$y = a + bx$$

where a is the y-axis intercept and b is the slope.

So the equation is

$$y = 50 + 2x.$$

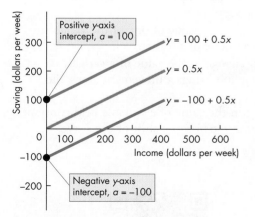

Figure 3 The y-axis intercept

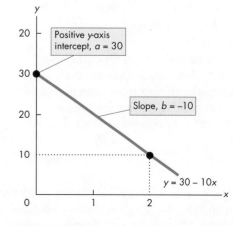

Figure 4 Negative relationship

REVIEW QUIZ

1 Explain how we "read" the three graphs in Figs. A1.1 and A1.2.
2 Explain what scatter diagrams show and why we use them.
3 Explain how we "read" the three scatter diagrams in Figs. A1.3 and A1.4.
4 Draw a graph to show the relationship between two variables that move in the same direction.
5 Draw a graph to show the relationship between two variables that move in opposite directions.
6 Draw a graph to show the relationship between two variables that have a maximum and a minimum.
7 Which of the relationships in Questions 4 and 5 is a positive relationship and which is a negative relationship?
8 What are the two ways of calculating the slope of a curved line?
9 How do we graph a relationship among more than two variables?
10 Explain what change will bring a *movement along* a curve.
11 Explain what change will bring a *shift* of a curve.

You can work these questions in Study Plan 1.A and get instant feedback.

— MyEconLab ◆

SUMMARY

Key Points

Graphing Data (pp. 13–16)

■ A graph is made by plotting the values of two variables *x* and *y* at a point that corresponds to their values measured along the *x*-axis and the *y*-axis.
■ A scatter diagram is a graph that plots the values of two variables for a number of different values of each.
■ A scatter diagram shows the relationship between the two variables. It shows whether they are positively related, negatively related, or unrelated.

Graphs Used in Economic Models (pp. 16–19)

■ Graphs are used to show relationships among variables in economic models.
■ Relationships can be positive (an upward-sloping curve), negative (a downward-sloping curve), positive and then negative (have a maximum point), negative and then positive (have a minimum point), or unrelated (a horizontal or vertical curve).

The Slope of a Relationship (pp. 20–22)

■ The slope of a relationship is calculated as the change in the value of the variable measured on the *y*-axis divided by the change in the value of the variable measured on the *x*-axis—that is, $\Delta y/\Delta x$.
■ A straight line has a constant slope.
■ A curved line has a varying slope. To calculate the slope of a curved line, we calculate the slope at a point or across an arc.

Graphing Relationships Among More Than Two Variables (pp. 22–23)

■ To graph a relationship among more than two variables, we hold constant the values of all the variables except two.
■ We then plot the value of one of the variables against the value of another.
■ A *cet par* change in the value of a variable on an axis of a graph brings a movement along the curve.
■ A change in the value of a variable held constant along the curve brings a shift of the curve.

Key Terms

Ceteris paribus, 22
Direct relationship, 16
Inverse relationship, 17
Linear relationship, 16
Negative relationship, 17
Positive relationship, 16
Scatter diagram, 14
Slope, 20

SCAN THIS

STUDY PLAN PROBLEMS AND APPLICATIONS

MyEconLab ◆ You can work Problems 1 to 11 in Chapter 1A Study Plan and get instant feedback.

Use the following spreadsheet to work Problems 1 to 3. The spreadsheet provides the economic data: Column A is the year, column B is the inflation rate, column C is the interest rate, column D is the growth rate, and column E is the unemployment rate.

	A	B	C	D	E
1	2000	2.4	4.3	5.7	6.8
2	2001	3.8	3.5	3.1	7.1
3	2002	0.8	2.4	2.1	7.9
4	2003	2.5	2.5	2.7	8.0
5	2004	2.3	1.8	1.8	7.3
6	2005	1.6	2.1	3.3	7.0
7	2006	2.8	2.8	3.9	6.1
8	2007	2.7	2.9	1.5	6.1
9	2008	2.8	2.1	1.7	6.2
10	2009	0.1	0.8	-2.5	8.7
11	2010	1.4	1.0	2.2	8.3

1. Draw a scatter diagram of the inflation rate and the interest rate. Describe the relationship.

2. Draw a scatter diagram of the growth rate and the unemployment rate. Describe the relationship.

3. Draw a scatter diagram of the interest rate and the unemployment rate. Describe the relationship.

Use the following news clip to work Problems 4 to 6.

***Clash of the Titans* Tops Box Office With Sales of $61.2 Million:**

Movie	Theatres (number)	Revenue (dollars per theatre)
Clash of the Titans	3,777	16,213
Tyler Perry's Why Did I Get Married	2,155	13,591
How To Train Your Dragon	4,060	7,145
The Last Song	2,673	5,989

Source: Bloomberg.com, April 5, 2010

4. Draw a graph of the relationship between the revenue per theatre on the *y*-axis and the number of theatres on the *x*-axis. Describe the relationship.

5. Calculate the slope of the relationship between 4,060 and 2,673 theatres.

6. Calculate the slope of the relationship between 2,155 and 4,060 theatres.

7. Calculate the slope of the following relationship.

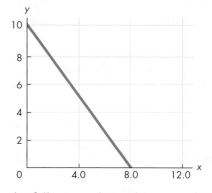

Use the following relationship to work Problems 8 and 9.

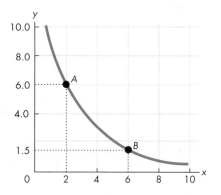

8. Calculate the slope of the relationship at point *A* and at point *B*.

9. Calculate the slope across the arc *AB*.

Use the following table to work Problems 10 and 11. The table gives the price of a balloon ride, the temperature, and the number of rides a day.

Price (dollars per ride)	Balloon rides (number per day)		
	10°C	20°C	30°C
5	32	40	50
10	27	32	40
15	18	27	32

10. Draw a graph to show the relationship between the price and the number of rides, when the temperature is 20°C. Describe this relationship.

11. What happens in the graph in Problem 10 if the temperature rises to 30°C?

ADDITIONAL ASSIGNABLE PROBLEMS AND APPLICATIONS

MyEconLab ◆ You can work these problems in MyEconLab if assigned by your instructor.

Use the following spreadsheet to work Problems 12 to 14. The spreadsheet provides data on oil and gasoline: Column A is the year, column B is the price of oil (dollars per barrel), column C is the price of gasoline (cents per litre), column D is quantity of crude oil produced, and column E is the quantity of gasoline refined (both in millions of barrels per day).

	A	B	C	D	E
1	1999	24	29	5.9	8.1
2	2000	30	38	5.8	8.2
3	2001	17	37	5.8	8.3
4	2002	24	35	5.7	8.4
5	2003	27	40	5.7	8.5
6	2004	37	47	5.4	8.7
7	2005	49	58	5.2	8.7
8	2006	56	65	5.1	8.9
9	2007	86	71	5.1	9.0
10	2008	43	82	5.0	8.9
11	2009	76	60	4.9	8.9

12. Draw a scatter diagram of the price of oil and the quantity of crude oil produced. Describe the relationship.
13. Draw a scatter diagram of the price of gasoline and the quantity of gasoline refined. Describe the relationship.
14. Draw a scatter diagram of the quantity of crude oil produced and the quantity of gasoline refined. Describe the relationship.

Use the following data to work Problems 15 to 17. Draw a graph that shows the relationship between the two variables x and y:

x	0	1	2	3	4	5
y	25	24	22	18	12	0

15. a. Is the relationship between the two variables positive or negative?
    b. Does the slope of the relationship become steeper or flatter as the value of x increases?
    c. Think of some economic relationships that might be similar to this one.
16. Calculate the slope of the relationship between the two variables when x equals 3.
17. Calculate the slope of the relationship across the arc as x increases from 4 to 5.

18. Calculate the slope of the curve at point A.

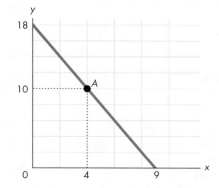

Use the following curve to work Problems 19 and 20.

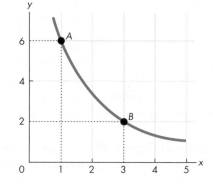

19. Calculate the slope at point A and at point B.
20. Calculate the slope across the arc AB.

Use the following table to work Problems 21 to 23. The table gives the price of an umbrella, the number purchased, and rainfall in millimetres (mm).

Price (dollars per umbrella)	Umbrellas purchased (number per day)		
	0 mm	200 mm	400 mm
20	4	7	8
30	2	4	7
40	1	2	4

21. Draw a graph to show the relationship between the price and the number of umbrellas purchased, holding the amount of rainfall constant at 200 mm. Describe this relationship.
22. What happens in the graph in Problem 21 if the price rises and rainfall is constant?
23. What happens in the graph in Problem 21 if the rainfall increases from 200 mm to 400 mm?

Grown
for
Biofuel

The Economic Problem

After studying this chapter, you will be able to

◆ Define the production possibilities frontier and use it to calculate opportunity cost

◆ Distinguish between production possibilities and preferences and define efficiency

◆ Explain how current production choices expand future production possibilities

◆ Explain how specialization and trade expand production possibilities

◆ Describe the economic institutions that coordinate decisions

Why does food cost much more today than it did a few years ago? One reason is that we're using corn to produce biofuel–ethanol. Another is that droughts have cut global grain production.

In this chapter, you will study an *economic model*—the production possibilities frontier—that explains how ethanol and drought raise the cost of producing food; that makes clear what it means to say that production is efficient or inefficient; that shows how we expand our production possibilities and how we gain by trading with others.

At the end of the chapter, in *Reading Between the Lines*, we return to explaining how producing ethanol has raised the cost of food.

Production Possibilities and Opportunity Cost

Every working day, in mines, factories, shops, and offices and on farms and construction sites across Canada, 17 million people produce a vast variety of goods and services valued at $5 billion. But the quantities of goods and services that we can produce are limited both by our available resources and by technology. And if we want to increase our production of one good, we must decrease our production of something else—we face a tradeoff. You are going to learn about the production possibilities frontier, which describes the limit to what we can produce and provides a neat way of thinking about and illustrating the idea of a tradeoff.

The **production possibilities frontier** (*PPF*) is the boundary between those combinations of goods and services that can be produced and those that cannot. To illustrate the *PPF*, we focus on two goods at a time and hold the quantities produced of all the other goods and services constant. That is, we look at a *model* economy in which everything remains the same except for the production of the two goods we are considering.

Let's look at the production possibilities frontier for cola and pizza, which represent *any* pair of goods or services.

Production Possibilities Frontier

The *production possibilities frontier* for cola and pizza shows the limits to the production of these two goods, given the total resources and technology available to produce them. Figure 2.1 shows this production possibilities frontier. The table lists some combinations of the quantities of pizza and cola that can be produced in a month given the resources available. The figure graphs these combinations. The *x*-axis shows the quantity of pizzas produced, and the *y*-axis shows the quantity of cola produced.

The *PPF* illustrates *scarcity* because we cannot attain the points outside the frontier. These points describe wants that can't be satisfied. We can produce at any point *inside* the *PPF* or *on* the *PPF*. These points are attainable. Suppose that in a typical month, we produce 4 million pizzas and 5 million cans of cola. Figure 2.1 shows this combination as point *E* and as possibility *E* in the table. The figure

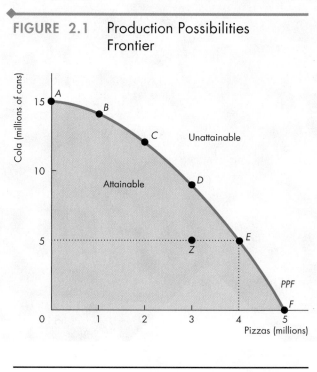

FIGURE 2.1   Production Possibilities Frontier

Possibility	Pizzas (millions)		Cola (millions of cans)
A	0	and	15
B	1	and	14
C	2	and	12
D	3	and	9
E	4	and	5
F	5	and	0

The table lists six production possibilities for cola and pizzas. Row *A* tells us that if we produce no pizzas, the maximum quantity of cola we can produce is 15 million cans. Points *A*, *B*, *C*, *D*, *E*, and *F* in the figure represent the rows of the table. The curve passing through these points is the production possibilities frontier (*PPF*).

The *PPF* separates the attainable from the unattainable. Production is possible at any point *inside* the orange area or *on* the frontier. Points outside the frontier are unattainable. Points inside the frontier, such as point *Z*, are inefficient because resources are wasted or misallocated. At such points, it is possible to use the available resources to produce more of either or both goods.

MyEconLab   animation

also shows other production possibilities. For example, we might stop producing pizza and move all the people who produce it into producing cola. Point *A* in the figure and possibility *A* in the production table show this case. The quantity of cola produced increases to 15 million cans, and pizza dries up. Alternatively, we might close the cola factories and switch all the resources into producing pizza. In this situation, we produce 5 million pizzas. Point *F* in the figure and possibility *F* in the table show this case.

Production Efficiency

We achieve **production efficiency** if we produce goods and services at the lowest possible cost. This outcome occurs at all the points *on* the *PPF*. At points *inside* the *PPF*, production is inefficient because we are giving up more than necessary of one good to produce a given quantity of the other good.

For example, at point *Z* in Fig. 2.1, we produce 3 million pizzas and 5 million cans of cola. But we have enough resources to produce 3 million pizzas and 9 million cans of cola. Our pizzas cost more cola than necessary. We can get them for a lower cost. Only when we produce *on* the *PPF* do we incur the lowest possible cost of production.

Production is *inefficient* inside the *PPF* because resources are either *unused* or *misallocated* or both.

Resources are *unused* when they are idle but could be working. For example, we might leave some of the factories idle or some workers unemployed.

Resources are *misallocated* when they are assigned to tasks for which they are not the best match. For example, we might assign skilled pizza chefs to work in a cola factory and skilled cola producers to work in a pizza shop. We could get more pizzas *and* more cola from these same workers if we reassigned them to the tasks that more closely match their skills.

Tradeoff Along the *PPF*

Every choice *along* the *PPF* involves a *tradeoff*. On the *PPF* in Fig. 2.1, we trade off cola for pizzas.

Tradeoffs arise in every imaginable real-world situation in which a choice must be made. At any given point in time, we have a fixed amount of labour, land, capital, and entrepreneurship. By using our available technologies, we can employ these resources to produce goods and services, but we are limited in what we can produce. This limit defines a boundary between what we can attain and what we

cannot attain. This boundary is the real-world's production possibilities frontier, and it defines the tradeoffs that we must make. On our real-world *PPF*, we can produce more of any one good or service only if we produce less of some other goods or services.

When doctors want to spend more on AIDS and cancer research, they face a tradeoff: more medical research for less of some other things. When Parliament wants to spend more on education and health care, it faces a tradeoff: more education and health care for less national defence or for higher taxes and less personal spending. When an environmental group argues for less logging, it is suggesting a tradeoff: greater conservation of endangered wildlife for less paper. When you want to study more, you face a tradeoff: more study time for less leisure or sleep.

All tradeoffs involve a cost—an opportunity cost.

Opportunity Cost

The **opportunity cost** of an action is the highest-valued alternative forgone. The *PPF* makes this idea precise and enables us to calculate opportunity cost. Along the *PPF*, there are only two goods, so there is only one alternative forgone: some quantity of the other good. Given our current resources and technology, we can produce more pizzas only if we produce less cola. The opportunity cost of producing an additional pizza is the cola we *must* forgo. Similarly, the opportunity cost of producing an additional can of cola is the quantity of pizzas we must forgo.

In Fig. 2.1, if we move from point *C* to point *D*, we get 1 million more pizzas but 3 million fewer cans of cola. The additional 1 million pizzas *cost* 3 million cans of cola, so one pizza costs 3 cans of cola.

If we move in the opposite direction from point *D* to point *C*, the quantity of cola produced increases by 3 million cans and the quantity of pizzas produced decreases by 1 million. The additional 3 million cans of cola *cost* 1 million pizzas, so one can of cola costs 1/3 of a pizza. The opportunity cost of producing an additional can of cola is equal to the *inverse* of the opportunity cost of producing an additional pizza.

Opportunity Cost Is a Ratio Opportunity cost is a ratio. It is the decrease in the quantity produced of one good divided by the increase in the quantity produced of another good as we move along the production possibilities frontier.

Increasing Opportunity Cost The opportunity cost of a pizza increases as the quantity of pizzas produced increases. The outward-bowed shape of the *PPF* reflects increasing opportunity cost. When we produce a large quantity of cola and a small quantity of pizza—between points *A* and *B* in Fig. 2.1—the frontier has a gentle slope. An increase in the quantity of pizzas costs a small decrease in the quantity of cola—the opportunity cost of a pizza is a small quantity of cola.

When we produce a large quantity of pizzas and a small quantity of cola—between points *E* and *F* in Fig. 2.1—the frontier is steep. A given increase in the quantity of pizzas *costs* a large decrease in the quantity of cola, so the opportunity cost of a pizza is a large quantity of cola.

Economics in Action

Increasing Opportunity Cost at Hydro One

Hydro One, Ontario's electric power producer, faces increasing opportunity cost. At low output rates, it costs 2.3 cents per kilowatt hour (kWh) to produce electricity using hydro-powered generators and 3.2 cents per kWh using nuclear generators. As Hydro One increases its output rate, the opportunity cost increases to 4.1 cents per kWh using coal and 6.6 cents per kWh using gas and oil turbines. The figure shows Hydro One's increasing opportunity cost. (Because nuclear plants can't be turned on and off, they produce some electricity alongside hydro all the time.)

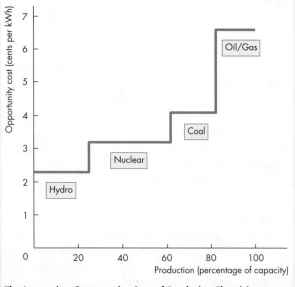

The Increasing Opportunity Cost of Producing Electricity

The *PPF* is bowed outward because resources are not all equally productive in all activities. People with many years of experience working for PepsiCo are good at producing cola but not very good at making pizzas. So if we move some of these people from PepsiCo to Domino's, we get a small increase in the quantity of pizzas but a large decrease in the quantity of cola.

Similarly, people who have spent years working at Domino's are good at producing pizzas, but they have no idea how to produce cola. So if we move some of these people from Domino's to PepsiCo, we get a small increase in the quantity of cola but a large decrease in the quantity of pizzas. As we produce more of one good, we must use resources that are less suited to that activity and more suited to producing the other good, so we face increasing opportunity cost.

Increasing opportunity cost is a universal phenomenon. When the rate of production increases, so does the opportunity cost of production. *Economics in Action* shows the increasing opportunity cost of producing electricity as Ontario's Hydro One power producer steps up its output rate to meet peak demand.

◆ REVIEW QUIZ

1 How does the production possibilities frontier illustrate scarcity?
2 How does the production possibilities frontier illustrate production efficiency?
3 How does the production possibilities frontier show that every choice involves a tradeoff?
4 How does the production possibilities frontier illustrate opportunity cost?
5 Why is opportunity cost a ratio?
6 Why does the *PPF* bow outward and what does that imply about the relationship between opportunity cost and the quantity produced?

You can work these questions in Study Plan 2.1 and get instant feedback.

———————————————————— MyEconLab ◆

We've seen that what we can produce is limited by the production possibilities frontier. We've also seen that production on the *PPF* is efficient. But we can produce many different quantities on the *PPF*. How do we choose among them? How do we know which point on the *PPF* is the best one?

Using Resources Efficiently

We achieve *production efficiency* at every point on the *PPF*, but which point is best? The answer is the point on the *PPF* at which goods and services are produced in the quantities that provide the greatest possible benefit. When goods and services are produced at the lowest possible cost and in the quantities that provide the greatest possible benefit, we have achieved **allocative efficiency**.

The questions that we raised when we reviewed the four big issues in Chapter 1 are questions about allocative efficiency. To answer such questions, we must measure and compare costs and benefits.

The *PPF* and Marginal Cost

The **marginal cost** of a good is the opportunity cost of producing one more unit of it. We calculate marginal cost from the slope of the *PPF*. As the quantity of pizzas produced increases, the *PPF* gets steeper and the marginal cost of a pizza increases. Figure 2.2 illustrates the calculation of the marginal cost of a pizza.

Begin by finding the opportunity cost of producing pizzas in blocks of 1 million pizzas. The cost of the first million pizzas is 1 million cans of cola; the cost of the second million pizzas is 2 million cans of cola; the cost of the third million pizzas is 3 million cans of cola, and so on. The bars in part (a) illustrate these calculations.

The bars in part (b) show the cost of an average pizza in each of the 1 million pizza blocks. Focus on the third million pizzas—the move from *C* to *D* in part (a). Because this block of 1 million pizzas cost 3 million cans of cola, one of these pizzas, on average, costs 3 cans of cola—the height of the bar in part (b).

Next, find the opportunity cost of each additional pizza—the marginal cost of producing a pizza. The marginal cost of producing a pizza increases as the quantity of pizzas produced increases. The marginal cost at point *C* is less than it is at point *D*. On average over the range from *C* to *D*, the marginal cost of a pizza is 3 cans of cola. But it exactly equals 3 cans of cola only in the middle of the range between *C* and *D*.

The red dot in part (b) indicates that the marginal cost of producing a pizza is 3 cans of cola when 2.5 million pizzas are produced. Each black dot in part (b) is interpreted in the same way. The red curve that passes through these dots, labelled *MC*, is the marginal cost curve. It shows the marginal cost of producing a pizza at each quantity of pizzas as we move along the *PPF*.

FIGURE 2.2   The *PPF* and Marginal Cost

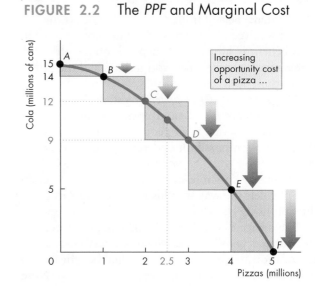

(a) *PPF* and opportunity cost

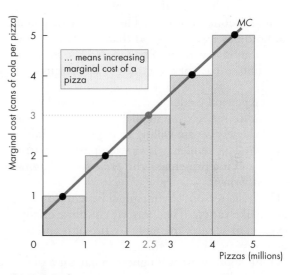

(b) Marginal cost

Marginal cost is calculated from the slope of the *PPF*. As the quantity of pizzas produced increases, the *PPF* gets steeper and the marginal cost of producing a pizza increases. The bars in part (a) show the opportunity cost of pizza in blocks of 1 million pizzas. The bars in part (b) show the cost of an average pizza in each of these 1 million blocks. The red curve, *MC*, shows the marginal cost of producing a pizza at each point along the *PPF*. This curve passes through the centre of each of the bars in part (b).

MyEconLab   animation

Preferences and Marginal Benefit

The **marginal benefit** from a good or service is the benefit received from consuming one more unit of it. This benefit is subjective. It depends on people's **preferences**—people's likes and dislikes and the intensity of those feelings.

Marginal benefit and *preferences* stand in sharp contrast to *marginal cost* and *production possibilities*. Preferences describe what people like and want and the production possibilities describe the limits or constraints on what is feasible.

We need a concrete way of illustrating preferences that parallels the way we illustrate the limits to production using the *PPF*.

The device that we use to illustrate preferences is the **marginal benefit curve**, which is a curve that shows the relationship between the marginal benefit from a good and the quantity consumed of that good. Note that the *marginal benefit curve* is *unrelated* to the *PPF* and cannot be derived from it.

We measure the marginal benefit from a good or service by the most that people are *willing to pay* for an additional unit of it. The idea is that you are willing to pay less for a good than it is worth to you but you are not willing to pay more: The most you are willing to pay for something is its marginal benefit.

It is a general principle that the more we have of any good or service, the smaller is its marginal benefit and the less we are willing to pay for an additional unit of it. This tendency is so widespread and strong that we call it a principle—the *principle of decreasing marginal benefit*.

The basic reason why marginal benefit decreases is that we like variety. The more we consume of any one good or service, the more we tire of it and would prefer to switch to something else.

Think about your willingness to pay for a pizza. If pizza is hard to come by and you can buy only a few slices a year, you might be willing to pay a high price to get an additional slice. But if pizza is all you've eaten for the past few days, you are willing to pay almost nothing for another slice.

You've learned to think about cost as opportunity cost, not as a dollar cost. You can think about marginal benefit and willingness to pay in the same way. The marginal benefit, measured by what you are willing to pay for something, is the quantity of other goods and services that you are willing to forgo. Let's continue with the example of cola and pizza and illustrate preferences this way.

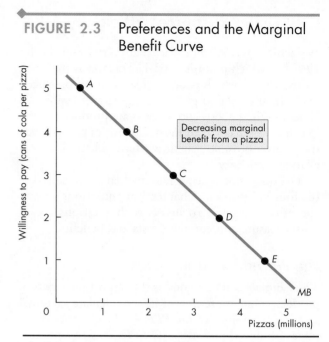

FIGURE 2.3   Preferences and the Marginal Benefit Curve

Possibility	Pizzas (millions)	Willingness to pay (cans of cola per pizza)
A	0.5	5
B	1.5	4
C	2.5	3
D	3.5	2
E	4.5	1

The larger the quantity of pizzas available, the less cola people are willing to give up for an additional pizza. With 0.5 million pizzas available, people are willing to pay 5 cans of cola per pizza, but with 4.5 million pizzas, people are willing to pay only 1 can of cola per pizza. Willingness to pay measures marginal benefit. A universal feature of people's preferences is that as the quantity consumed increases, marginal benefit decreases.

MyEconLab animation

Figure 2.3 illustrates preferences as the willingness to pay for pizza in terms of cola. In row *A*, with 0.5 million pizzas available, people are willing to pay 5 cans of cola per pizza. As the quantity of pizzas increases, the amount that people are willing to pay for a pizza falls. With 4.5 million pizzas available, people are willing to pay only 1 can of cola per pizza.

Let's now use the concepts of marginal cost and marginal benefit to describe allocative efficiency.

FIGURE 2.4   Efficient Use of Resources

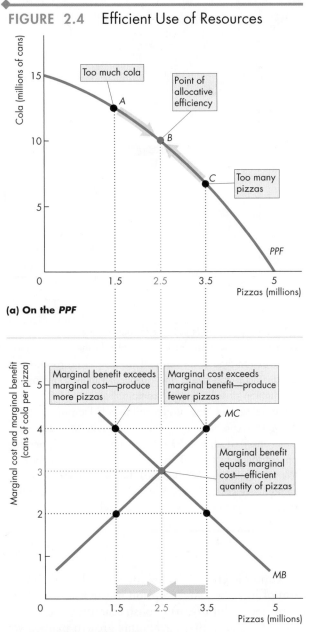

(a) On the PPF

(b) Marginal benefit equals marginal cost

The greater the quantity of pizzas produced, the smaller is the marginal benefit (MB) from a pizza—the less cola people are willing to give up to get an additional pizza. But the greater the quantity of pizzas produced, the greater is the marginal cost (MC) of a pizza—the more cola people must give up to get an additional pizza. When marginal benefit equals marginal cost, resources are being used efficiently.

MyEconLab   animation ◆

Allocative Efficiency

At *any* point on the *PPF*, we cannot produce more of one good without giving up some other good. At the *best* point on the *PPF*, we cannot produce more of one good without giving up some other good that provides greater benefit. We are producing at the point of allocative efficiency—the point on the *PPF* that we prefer above all other points.

Suppose in Fig. 2.4, we produce 1.5 million pizzas. The marginal cost of producing a pizza is 2 cans of cola, and the marginal benefit from a pizza is 4 cans of cola. Because someone values an additional pizza more highly than it costs to produce, we can get more value from our resources by moving some of them out of producing cola and into producing pizza.

Now suppose we produce 3.5 million pizzas. The marginal cost of a pizza is now 4 cans of cola, but the marginal benefit from a pizza is only 2 cans of cola. Because the additional pizza costs more to produce than anyone thinks it is worth, we can get more value from our resources by moving some of them away from producing pizza and into producing cola.

Suppose we produce 2.5 million pizzas. Marginal cost and marginal benefit are now equal at 3 cans of cola. This allocation of resources between pizzas and cola is efficient. If more pizzas are produced, the forgone cola is worth more than the additional pizzas. If fewer pizzas are produced, the forgone pizzas are worth more than the additional cola.

◢ REVIEW QUIZ

1 What is marginal cost? How is it measured?
2 What is marginal benefit? How is it measured?
3 How does the marginal benefit from a good change as the quantity produced of that good increases?
4 What is allocative efficiency and how does it relate to the production possibilities frontier?
5 What conditions must be satisfied if resources are used efficiently?

You can work these questions in Study Plan 2.2 and get instant feedback.

━━━━━━━━━━━━━━━━━━━━━ MyEconLab ◆

You now understand the limits to production and the conditions under which resources are used efficiently. Your next task is to study the expansion of production possibilities.

Economic Growth

During the past 30 years, production per person in Canada has doubled. The expansion of production possibilities is called **economic growth**. Economic growth increases our *standard of living*, but it doesn't overcome scarcity and avoid opportunity cost. To make our economy grow, we face a tradeoff—the faster we make production grow, the greater is the opportunity cost of economic growth.

The Cost of Economic Growth

Economic growth comes from technological change and capital accumulation. **Technological change** is the development of new goods and of better ways of producing goods and services. **Capital accumulation** is the growth of capital resources, including *human capital*.

Technological change and capital accumulation have vastly expanded our production possibilities. We can produce automobiles that provide us with more transportation than was available when we had only horses and carriages. We can produce satellites that provide global communications on a much larger scale than that available with the earlier cable technology. But if we use our resources to develop new technologies and produce capital, we must decrease our production of consumption goods and services. New technologies and new capital have an opportunity cost. Let's look at this opportunity cost.

Instead of studying the *PPF* of pizzas and cola, we'll hold the quantity of cola produced constant and examine the *PPF* for pizzas and pizza ovens. Figure 2.5 shows this *PPF* as the blue curve PPF_0. If we devote no resources to producing pizza ovens, we produce at point *A*. If we produce 3 million pizzas, we can produce 6 pizza ovens at point *B*. If we produce no pizza, we can produce 10 ovens at point *C*.

The amount by which our production possibilities expand depends on the resources we devote to technological change and capital accumulation. If we devote no resources to this activity (point *A*), our *PPF* remains the blue curve PPF_0 in Fig. 2.5. If we cut the current pizza production and produce 6 ovens (point *B*), then in the future, we'll have more capital and our *PPF* will rotate outward to the position shown by the red curve PPF_1. The fewer resources we use for producing pizza and the more resources we use for producing ovens, the greater is the expansion of our future production possibilities.

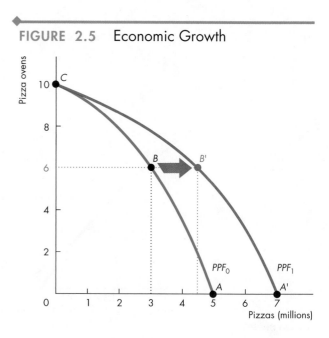

FIGURE 2.5   Economic Growth

PPF_0 shows the limits to the production of pizzas and pizza ovens, with the production of all other goods and services remaining the same. If we devote no resources to producing pizza ovens and produce 5 million pizzas, our production possibilities will remain the same at PPF_0. But if we decrease pizza production to 3 million and produce 6 ovens, at point *B*, our production possibilities expand. After one period, the *PPF* rotates outward to PPF_1 and we can produce at point *B'*, a point outside the original PPF_0. We can rotate the *PPF* outward, but we cannot avoid opportunity cost. The opportunity cost of producing more pizzas in the future is fewer pizzas today.

———————————— MyEconLab animation ◆

Economic growth brings enormous benefits in the form of increased consumption in the future, but it is not free and it doesn't abolish scarcity.

In Fig. 2.5, to make economic growth happen we must use some resources to produce new ovens, which leaves fewer resources to produce pizzas. To move to *B'* in the future, we must move from *A* to *B* today. The opportunity cost of more pizzas in the future is fewer pizzas today. Also, on the new *PPF*, we still face a tradeoff and opportunity cost.

The ideas about economic growth that we have explored in the setting of the pizza industry also apply to nations. Hong Kong and Canada provide a striking case study.

Economics in Action
Hong Kong Overtakes Canada

In 1960, the production possibilities per person in Canada were more than three times those in Hong Kong (see the figure). Canada devotes one-fifth of its resources to accumulating capital and in 1960, Canada was at point *A* on its *PPF*. Hong Kong devotes one-third of its resources to accumulating capital and in 1960, Hong Kong was at point *A* on its *PPF*.

Since 1960, both economies have experienced economic growth, but because Hong Kong devotes a bigger fraction of its resources to accumulating capital, its production possibilities have expanded more quickly.

By 2010, production possibilities per person in Hong Kong were *greater* than those in Canada. Hong Kong has overtaken Canada.

If Hong Kong continues to devote more resources to accumulating capital than Canada does (at point *B* on its 2010 *PPF*), Hong Kong will continue to grow more rapidly. But if it devotes fewer resources to capital accumulation (moving to point *D* on its 2010 *PPF*), then Hong Kong's economic growth rate will slow.

Hong Kong is typical of the fast-growing Asian economies. In China, India, Taiwan, Thailand, and South Korea, production possibilities are expanding at rates of between 5 percent and 10 percent a year.

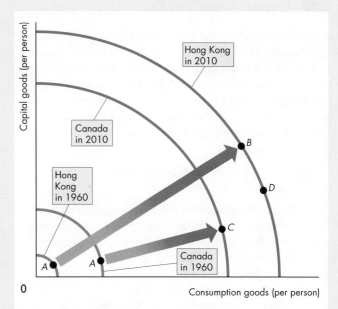

Economic Growth in Canada and Hong Kong

If such high economic growth rates are maintained, these other Asian countries will continue to close the gap between themselves and Canada, and, as Hong Kong has done, eventually overtake Canada. To catch up with Hong Kong, Canada would need to devote a larger part of production to accumulating physical and human capital.

A Nation's Economic Growth

The experiences of Canada and Hong Kong make a striking example of the effects of our choices about consumption and capital goods on the rate of economic growth.

If a nation devotes all its factors of production to producing consumption goods and services and none to advancing technology and accumulating capital, its production possibilities in the future will be the same as they are today.

To expand production possibilities in the future, a nation must devote fewer resources to producing current consumption goods and services and some resources to accumulating capital and developing new technologies. As production possibilities expand, consumption in the future can increase. The decrease in today's consumption is the opportunity cost of tomorrow's increase in consumption.

REVIEW QUIZ

1 What generates economic growth?
2 How does economic growth influence the production possibilities frontier?
3 What is the opportunity cost of economic growth?
4 Why has Hong Kong experienced faster economic growth than Canada?
5 Does economic growth overcome scarcity?

You can work these questions in Study Plan 2.3 and get instant feedback.
———————————————————— MyEconLab ◆

Next, we're going to study another way in which we expand our production possibilities—the amazing fact that *both* buyers and sellers gain from specialization and trade.

◆ Gains from Trade

People can produce for themselves all the goods and services that they consume, or they can produce one good or a few goods and trade with others. Producing only one good or a few goods is called *specialization*. We are going to learn how people gain by specializing in the production of the good in which they have a *comparative advantage* and trading with others.

Comparative Advantage and Absolute Advantage

A person has a **comparative advantage** in an activity if that person can perform the activity at a lower opportunity cost than anyone else. Differences in opportunity costs arise from differences in individual abilities and from differences in the characteristics of other resources.

No one excels at everything. One person is an outstanding pitcher but a poor catcher; another person is a brilliant lawyer but a poor teacher. In almost all human endeavours, what one person does easily, someone else finds difficult. The same applies to land and capital. One plot of land is fertile but has no mineral deposits; another plot of land has outstanding views but is infertile. One machine has great precision but is difficult to operate; another is fast but often breaks down.

Although no one excels at everything, some people excel and can outperform others in a large number of activities—perhaps even in all activities. A person who is more productive than others has an **absolute advantage**.

Absolute advantage involves comparing productivities—production per hour—whereas comparative advantage involves comparing opportunity costs.

A person who has an absolute advantage does not have a *comparative* advantage in every activity. John Grisham is a better lawyer and a better author of fast-paced thrillers than most people. He has an absolute advantage in these two activities. But compared to others, he is a better writer than lawyer, so his *comparative* advantage is in writing.

Because ability and resources vary from one person to another, people have different opportunity costs of producing various goods. These differences in opportunity cost are the source of comparative advantage.

Let's explore the idea of comparative advantage by looking at two smoothie bars: one operated by Liz and the other operated by Joe.

Liz's Smoothie Bar Liz produces smoothies and salads. In Liz's high-tech bar, she can turn out either a smoothie or a salad every 2 minutes—see Table 2.1. If Liz spends all her time making smoothies, she can produce 30 an hour. And if she spends all her time making salads, she can also produce 30 an hour. If she splits her time equally between the two, she can produce 15 smoothies and 15 salads an hour. For each additional smoothie Liz produces, she must decrease her production of salads by one, and for each additional salad she produces, she must decrease her production of smoothies by one. So

> Liz's opportunity cost of producing 1 smoothie is 1 salad,

and

> Liz's opportunity cost of producing 1 salad is 1 smoothie.

Liz's customers buy smoothies and salads in equal quantities, so she splits her time equally between the two items and produces 15 smoothies and 15 salads an hour.

Joe's Smoothie Bar Joe also produces smoothies and salads, but his bar is smaller than Liz's. Also, Joe has only one blender, and it's a slow, old machine. Even if Joe uses all his resources to produce smoothies, he can produce only 6 an hour—see Table 2.2. But Joe is good at making salads. If he uses all his resources to make salads, he can produce 30 an hour.

Joe's ability to make smoothies and salads is the same regardless of how he splits an hour between the two tasks. He can make a salad in 2 minutes or a smoothie in 10 minutes. For each additional smoothie

TABLE 2.1   Liz's Production Possibilities

Item	Minutes to produce 1	Quantity per hour
Smoothies	2	30
Salads	2	30

TABLE 2.2 Joe's Production Possibilities

Item	Minutes to produce 1	Quantity per hour
Smoothies	10	6
Salads	2	30

Joe produces, he must decrease his production of salads by 5. And for each additional salad he produces, he must decrease his production of smoothies by 1/5 of a smoothie. So

>Joe's opportunity cost of producing 1 smoothie is 5 salads,

and

>Joe's opportunity cost of producing 1 salad is 1/5 of a smoothie.

Joe's customers, like Liz's, buy smoothies and salads in equal quantities. So Joe spends 50 minutes of each hour making smoothies and 10 minutes of each hour making salads. With this division of his time, Joe produces 5 smoothies and 5 salads an hour.

Liz's Comparative Advantage In which of the two activities does Liz have a comparative advantage? Recall that comparative advantage is a situation in which one person's opportunity cost of producing a good is lower than another person's opportunity cost of producing that same good. Liz has a comparative advantage in producing smoothies. Her opportunity cost of a smoothie is 1 salad, whereas Joe's opportunity cost of a smoothie is 5 salads.

Joe's Comparative Advantage If Liz has a comparative advantage in producing smoothies, Joe must have a comparative advantage in producing salads. Joe's opportunity cost of a salad is 1/5 of a smoothie, whereas Liz's opportunity cost of a salad is 1 smoothie.

Achieving the Gains from Trade

Liz and Joe run into each other one evening in a singles bar. After a few minutes of getting acquainted, Liz tells Joe about her amazing smoothie business. Her only problem, she tells Joe, is that she would like to produce more because potential customers leave when her lines get too long.

Joe is hesitant to risk spoiling his chances by telling Liz about his own struggling business, but he takes the risk. Joe explains to Liz that he spends 50 minutes of every hour making 5 smoothies and 10 minutes making 5 salads. Liz's eyes pop. "Have I got a deal for you!" she exclaims.

Here's the deal that Liz sketches on a paper napkin. Joe stops making smoothies and allocates all his time to producing salads; Liz stops making salads and allocates all her time to producing smoothies. That is, they both specialize in producing the good in which they have a comparative advantage. Together they produce 30 smoothies and 30 salads in an hour—see Table 2.3(b).

They then trade. Liz sells Joe 10 smoothies and Joe sells Liz 20 salads—the price of a smoothie is 2 salads—see Table 2.3(c).

After the trade, Joe has 10 salads—the 30 he produces minus the 20 he sells to Liz. He also has the 10 smoothies that he buys from Liz. So Joe now has increased the quantities of smoothies and salads that he can sell to his customers—see Table 2.3(d).

TABLE 2.3 Liz and Joe Gain from Trade

(a) Before trade	Liz	Joe
Smoothies	15	5
Salads	15	5

(b) Specialization	Liz	Joe
Smoothies	30	0
Salads	0	30

(c) Trade	Liz	Joe
Smoothies	sell 10	buy 10
Salads	buy 20	sell 20

(d) After trade	Liz	Joe
Smoothies	20	10
Salads	20	10

(e) Gains from trade	Liz	Joe
Smoothies	+5	+5
Salads	+5	+5

Liz has 20 smoothies—the 30 she produces minus the 10 she sells to Joe. She also has the 20 salads that she buys from Joe. Liz has increased the quantities of smoothies and salads that she can sell to her customers—see Table 2.3(d). Liz and Joe both gain 5 smoothies and 5 salads an hour—see Table 2.3(e).

To illustrate her idea, Liz grabs a fresh napkin and draws the graphs in Fig. 2.6. The blue *PPF* in part (a) shows Joe's production possibilities. Before trade, he is producing 5 smoothies and 5 salads an hour at point *A*. The blue *PPF* in part (b) shows Liz's production possibilities. Before trade, she is producing 15 smoothies and 15 salads an hour at point *A*.

Liz's proposal is that they each specialize in producing the good in which they have a comparative advantage. Joe produces 30 salads and no smoothies at point *B* on his *PPF*. Liz produces 30 smoothies and no salads at point *B* on her *PPF*.

Liz and Joe then trade smoothies and salads at a price of 2 salads per smoothie or 1/2 a smoothie per salad. Joe gets smoothies for 2 salads each, which is less than the 5 salads it costs him to produce a smoothie. Liz gets salads for 1/2 a smoothie each, which is less than the 1 smoothie that it costs her to produce a salad.

With trade, Joe has 10 smoothies and 10 salads at point *C*—a gain of 5 smoothies and 5 salads. Joe moves to a point *outside* his *PPF*.

With trade, Liz has 20 smoothies and 20 salads at point *C*—a gain of 5 smoothies and 5 salads. Liz moves to a point *outside* her *PPF*.

Despite Liz being more productive than Joe, both of them gain from specializing—producing the good in which they have a comparative advantage—and trading.

FIGURE 2.6   The Gains from Trade

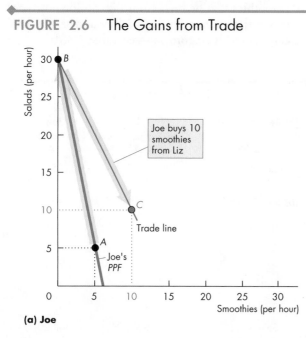

(a) Joe

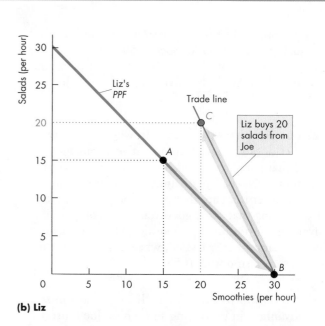

(b) Liz

Initially, Joe produces at point *A* on his *PPF* in part (a), and Liz produces at point *A* on her *PPF* in part (b). Joe's opportunity cost of producing a salad is less than Liz's, so Joe has a comparative advantage in producing salads. Liz's opportunity cost of producing a smoothie is less than Joe's, so Liz has a comparative advantage in producing smoothies.

If Joe specializes in making salads, he produces 30 salads and no smoothies at point *B* on his *PPF*. If Liz specializes

in making smoothies, she produces 30 smoothies and no salads at point *B* on her *PPF*. They exchange salads for smoothies along the red "Trade line." Liz buys salads from Joe for less than her opportunity cost of producing them. Joe buys smoothies from Liz for less than his opportunity cost of producing them. Each goes to point *C*—a point outside his or her *PPF*. With specialization and trade, Joe and Liz gain 5 smoothies and 5 salads each with no extra resources.

Economics in Action
Canada and China Gain from Trade

In Chapter 1 (see p. 5), we asked whether globalization is in the social interest. What you have just learned about the gains from trade provides a big part of the answer. We gain from specialization and trade.

The gains that we achieve from *international* trade are similar to those achieved by Joe and Liz. When Canadians buy clothes that are manufactured in China and when China buys Bombardier regional jets manufactured in Canada, the people of both countries gain.

We could slide along our *PPF* producing fewer regional jets and more jackets. Similarly, China could slide along its *PPF* producing more regional jets and fewer jackets. But everyone would lose. The opportunity cost of our jackets and China's opportunity cost of regional jets would rise.

By specializing in regional jets and trading with China, Canadians get their jackets at a lower cost than that at which Canada can produce them, and China gets its aircraft at a lower cost than that at which it can produce them.

◆ REVIEW QUIZ

1 What gives a person a comparative advantage?
2 Distinguish between comparative advantage and absolute advantage.
3 Why do people specialize and trade?
4 What are the gains from specialization and trade?
5 What is the source of the gains from trade?

You can work these questions in Study Plan 2.4 and get instant feedback.

——————————— MyEconLab ◆

◆ Economic Coordination

People gain by specializing in the production of those goods and services in which they have a comparative advantage and then trading with each other. Liz and Joe, whose production of salads and smoothies we studied earlier in this chapter, can get together and make a deal that enables them to enjoy the gains from specialization and trade. But for billions of individuals to specialize and produce millions of different goods and services, their choices must somehow be coordinated.

Two competing economic coordination systems have been used: central economic planning and decentralized markets.

Central economic planning was tried in Russia and China and is still used in Cuba and North Korea. This system works badly because government economic planners don't know people's production possibilities and preferences. Resources get wasted, production ends up *inside* the *PPF,* and the wrong things get produced.

Decentralized coordination works best but to do so it needs four complementary social institutions. They are

■ Firms
■ Markets
■ Property rights
■ Money

Firms

A **firm** is an economic unit that hires factors of production and organizes those factors to produce and sell goods and services. Examples of firms are Canadian Tire, Tim Hortons, and General Motors.

Firms coordinate a huge amount of economic activity. For example, Canadian Tire buys or rents buildings, equips them with storage shelves and checkout lanes, hires labour, and decides what goods to buy and sell.

Canadian Tire doesn't produce the goods that it sells. It could do so. It could own and coordinate production of all the goods it sells. But John W. and Alfred J. Billes succeeded by specializing in providing good service and retailing supplies from other firms that specialize (just as Liz and Joe did). This trade between firms takes place in markets.

Markets

In ordinary speech, the word *market* means a place where people buy and sell goods such as fish, meat, fruits, and vegetables. In economics, a *market* has a more general meaning. A **market** is any arrangement that enables buyers and sellers to get information and to do business with each other. An example is the market in which oil is bought and sold—the world oil market. The world oil market is not a place. It is the network of oil producers, oil users, wholesalers, and brokers who buy and sell oil. In the world oil market, decision makers do not meet physically. They make deals by telephone, fax, and direct computer link.

Markets have evolved because they facilitate trade. Without organized markets, we would miss out on a substantial part of the potential gains from trade. Enterprising individuals and firms, each pursuing their own self-interest, have profited from making markets—standing ready to buy or sell the items in which they specialize. But markets can work only when property rights exist.

Property Rights

The social arrangements that govern the ownership, use, and disposal of anything that people value are called **property rights**. *Real property* includes land and buildings—the things we call property in ordinary speech—and durable goods such as plant and equipment. *Financial property* includes stocks and bonds and money in the bank. *Intellectual property* is the intangible product of creative effort. This type of property includes books, music, computer programs, and inventions of all kinds and is protected by copyrights and patents.

Where property rights are enforced, people have the incentive to specialize and produce the goods in which they have a comparative advantage. Where people can steal the production of others, resources are devoted not to production but to protecting possessions. Without property rights, we would still be hunting and gathering like our Stone Age ancestors.

Money

Money is any commodity or token that is generally acceptable as a means of payment. Liz and Joe didn't use money in the example above. They exchanged salads and smoothies. In principle, trade in markets can exchange any item for any other item. But you can perhaps imagine how complicated life would be if we exchanged goods for other goods. The "invention" of money makes trading in markets much more efficient.

Circular Flows Through Markets

Figure 2.7 shows the flows that result from the choices that households and firms make. Households specialize and choose the quantities of labour, land, capital, and entrepreneurial services to sell or rent to firms. Firms choose the quantities of factors of production to hire. These (red) flows go through the *factor markets*. Households choose the quantities of goods and services to buy, and firms choose the quantities to produce. These (red) flows go through the *goods markets*. Households receive incomes and make expenditures on goods and services (the green flows).

How do markets coordinate all these decisions?

Coordinating Decisions

Markets coordinate decisions through price adjustments. To see how, think about your local market for hamburgers. Suppose that too few hamburgers are available and some people who want to buy hamburgers are not able to do so. To make buying and selling plans the same, either more hamburgers must be offered for sale or buyers must scale down their appetites (or both). A rise in the price of a hamburger produces this outcome. A higher price encourages producers to offer more hamburgers for sale. It also encourages some people to change their lunch plans. Fewer people buy hamburgers, and more buy hot dogs. More hamburgers (and more hot dogs) are offered for sale.

Alternatively, suppose that more hamburgers are available than people want to buy. In this case, to make the choices of buyers and sellers compatible, more hamburgers must be bought or fewer hamburgers must be offered for sale (or both). A fall in the price of a hamburger achieves this outcome. A lower price encourages people to buy more hamburgers. It also encourages firms to produce a smaller quantity of hamburgers.

FIGURE 2.7   Circular Flows in the Market Economy

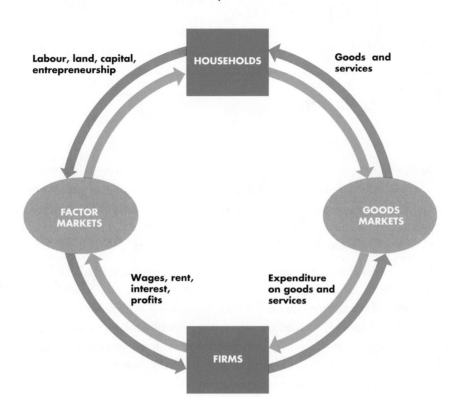

Households and firms make economic choices and markets coordinate these choices.

Households choose the quantities of labour, land, capital, and entrepreneurial services to sell or rent to firms in exchange for wages, rent, interest, and profits. Households also choose how to spend their incomes on the various types of goods and services available.

Firms choose the quantities of factors of production to hire and the quantities of goods and services to produce.

Goods markets and factor markets coordinate these choices of households and firms.

The counterclockwise red flows are real flows—the flow of factors of production from households to firms and the flow of goods and services from firms to households.

The clockwise green flows are the payments for the red flows. They are the flow of income from firms to households and the flow of expenditure on goods and services from households to firms.

MyEconLab   animation ◆

◆ You have now begun to see how economists approach economic questions. Scarcity, choice, and divergent opportunity costs explain why we specialize and trade and why firms, markets, property rights, and money have developed. You can see all around you the lessons you've learned in this chapter. *Reading Between the Lines* on pp. 44–45 provides an opportunity to apply the *PPF* model to deepen your understanding of the reasons for the increase in the cost of food associated with the increase in corn production.

The Rising Opportunity Cost of Food

The Meaning of Agflation

Investors Chronicle
August 11, 2010

The response of the Russian government to a lousy 2010 harvest and soaring wheat prices was as predictable as it was bone-headed. Predictable, because the Russian government has form—by imposing a ban on wheat exports, it was repeating what it did in 2007–08 after a poor harvest. Bone-headed, because in the long run Russia's action will distort markets to the detriment of its consumers—effectively an export ban tells farmers to grow less wheat.

Still, it's not as if Russia's rulers have a monopoly on distorting agricultural markets. In the Land of the Free, they're pretty good at it, too. Take the egregious effect of US politicians' love affair with ethanol production from maize. Thanks to generous state subsidies, this inefficient way of making ethanol now accounts for 85m tonnes of America's annual maize production. While production of maize approaches 300m tonnes most years, that might not matter too much. Except that to fill the tank of a gas-guzzling SUV just once takes as much grain as will feed a person for a year. Small wonder that the U.S. is already giving over more maize to ethanol production than to export. ...

It takes a lot of grain to produce meat. So it is cheaper to eat the stuff as, say, bread, though perhaps it's more appetising to eat it as pork or beef. The trouble is, 3 lbs of grain are needed to raise 1 lb of pork and for beef the ratio is more like eight to one. Yet, thanks to China's economic transformation, the average Chinese is now eating well over 100 lbs of meat a year; maybe three times more than he did 30 years ago. Meat consumption rising at that sort of rate will always mean higher input costs and higher inflation. ...

Excerpted from "The Meaning of Agflation," *Investors Chronicle*, 13 August 2010.
© Financial Times. Reprinted with permission.

ESSENCE OF THE STORY

- Grain production is not keeping up with the amount people want to use as food and fuel.

- Rising global incomes lead to more meat consumption, which increases the amount of grain used to feed animals.

- Ethanol mills use close to one-third of U.S. grain production.

- A drought in Russia in 2010 decreased production.

- All grain prices are likely to keep rising in a process the news article calls "Agflation."

ECONOMIC ANALYSIS

- The United States produces 53 percent of the world's ethanol and Brazil produces 33 percent. Canada produces a bit more than 1 percent (see Fig. 1).

- In Brazil, ethanol is made from sugar but in the United States it is made from corn, so ethanol and food compete to use the same resources.

- To produce more ethanol, U.S. farmers have increased the number of hectares devoted to corn production.

- The amount of land devoted to corn production has also increased in other regions of the world.

- Figure 2 shows the U.S. production possibilities frontier, *PPF*, for corn and other goods and services.

- The increase in the production of corn is illustrated by a movement along the *PPF* in Fig. 1 from point *A* in 2009 to point *B* in 2010.

- In moving from point *A* to point *B*, the United States incurs a higher opportunity cost of producing corn, as the greater slope of the *PPF* at point *B* indicates.

- In other regions of the world, despite the fact that more land was devoted to corn production, the amount of corn produced fell slightly.

- The reason is that droughts in South America and Eastern Europe lowered the crop yield per hectare in those regions.

- Figure 3 shows the rest of the world's *PPF* for corn and other goods and services in 2009 and 2010.

- The increase in the amount of land devoted to producing corn is illustrated by a movement along PPF_{09}.

- With a decrease in the crop yield, production possibilities decrease and the *PPF* rotates inward.

- The rotation from PPF_{10} to PPF_{10} illustrates this decrease in production possibilities.

- The opportunity cost of producing corn in the rest of the world increased for two reasons: the movement along its *PPF* and the inward rotation of the *PPF*.

- With a higher opportunity cost of producing corn, the cost of both ethanol and food increases.

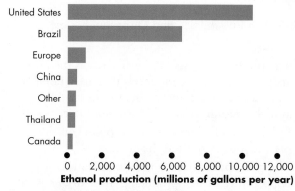

Ethanol production (millions of gallons per year)

Figure 1 Ethanol Production in 2009

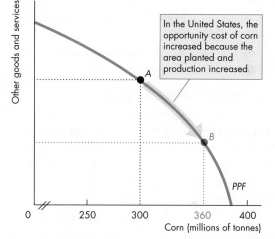

In the United States, the opportunity cost of corn increased because the area planted and production increased

Figure 2 U.S. *PPF*

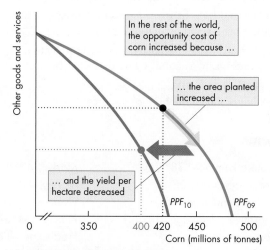

In the rest of the world, the opportunity cost of corn increased because ...

... the area planted increased ...

... and the yield per hectare decreased

Figure 3 Rest of the World *PPF*

45

◆ SUMMARY

Key Points

Production Possibilities and Opportunity Cost

(pp. 30–32)

- The production possibilities frontier is the boundary between production levels that are attainable and those that are not attainable when all the available resources are used to their limit.
- Production efficiency occurs at points on the production possibilities frontier.
- Along the production possibilities frontier, the opportunity cost of producing more of one good is the amount of the other good that must be given up.
- The opportunity cost of all goods increases as the production of the good increases.

Working Problems 1 to 3 will give you a better understanding of production possibilities and opportunity cost.

Using Resources Efficiently (pp. 33–35)

- Allocative efficiency occurs when goods and services are produced at the least possible cost and in the quantities that bring the greatest possible benefit.
- The marginal cost of a good is the opportunity cost of producing one more unit of it.
- The marginal benefit from a good is the benefit received from consuming one more unit of it and is measured by the willingness to pay for it.
- The marginal benefit from a good decreases as the amount of the good available increases.
- Resources are used efficiently when the marginal cost of each good is equal to its marginal benefit.

Working Problems 4 to 10 will give you a better understanding of the efficient use of resources.

Economic Growth (pp. 36–37)

- Economic growth, which is the expansion of production possibilities, results from capital accumulation and technological change.
- The opportunity cost of economic growth is forgone current consumption.
- The benefit of economic growth is increased future consumption.

Working Problem 11 will give you a better understanding of economic growth.

Gains from Trade (pp. 38–41)

- A person has a comparative advantage in producing a good if that person can produce the good at a lower opportunity cost than everyone else.
- People gain by specializing in the activity in which they have a comparative advantage and trading with others.

Working Problems 12 to 17 will give you a better understanding of the gains from trade.

Economic Coordination   (pp. 41–43)

- Firms coordinate a large amount of economic activity, but there is a limit to the efficient size of a firm.
- Markets coordinate the economic choices of people and firms.
- Markets can work efficiently only when property rights exist.
- Money makes trading in markets more efficient.

Working Problem 18 will give you a better understanding of economic coordination.

Key Terms

Absolute advantage, 38
Allocative efficiency, 33
Capital accumulation, 36
Comparative advantage, 38
Economic growth, 36
Firm, 41
Marginal benefit, 34
Marginal benefit curve, 34
Marginal cost, 33

Market, 42
Money, 42
Opportunity cost, 31
Preferences, 34
Production efficiency, 31
Production possibilities frontier, 30
Property rights, 42
Technological change, 36

SCAN THIS

STUDY PLAN PROBLEMS AND APPLICATIONS

MyEconLab ◆ You can work Problems 1 to 21 in Chapter 2 Study Plan and get instant feedback.

Production Possibilities and Opportunity Cost

(Study Plan 2.1)

Use the following data to work Problems 1 to 3. Brazil produces ethanol from sugar, and the land used to grow sugar can be used to grow food crops. Suppose that Brazil's production possibilities for ethanol and food crops are as follows:

Ethanol (barrels per day)		Food crops (tonnes per day)
70	and	0
64	and	1
54	and	2
40	and	3
22	and	4
0	and	5

1. a. Draw a graph of Brazil's *PPF* and explain how your graph illustrates scarcity.
   b. If Brazil produces 40 barrels of ethanol a day, how much food must it produce to achieve production efficiency?
   c. Why does Brazil face a tradeoff on its *PPF*?

2. a. If Brazil increases its production of ethanol from 40 barrels per day to 54 barrels per day, what is the opportunity cost of the additional ethanol?
   b. If Brazil increases its production of food crops from 2 tonnes to 3 tonnes per day, what is the opportunity cost of the additional food?
   c. What is the relationship between your answers to parts (a) and (b)?

3. Does Brazil face an increasing opportunity cost of ethanol? What feature of Brazil's *PPF* illustrates increasing opportunity cost?

Using Resources Efficiently (Study Plan 2.2)

Use the above table to work Problems 4 and 5.

4. Define marginal cost and calculate Brazil's marginal cost of producing a tonne of food when the quantity produced is 2.5 tonnes per day,

5. Define marginal benefit, explain how it is measured, and explain why the data in the table does not enable you to calculate Brazil's marginal benefit from food.

6. Distinguish between *production efficiency* and *allocative efficiency.* Explain why many production possibilities achieve production efficiency but only one achieves allocative efficiency.

Use the following graphs to work Problems 7 to 10. Harry enjoys tennis but wants a high grade in his economics course. The graphs show his *PPF* for these two "goods" and his *MB* curve from tennis.

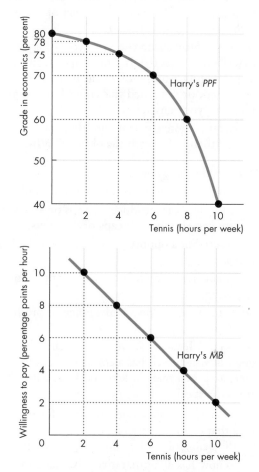

7. What is Harry's marginal cost of tennis if he plays for (i) 3 hours a week; (ii) 5 hours a week; and (iii) 7 hours a week?

8. a. If Harry uses his time to achieve allocative efficiency, what is his economics grade and how many hours of tennis does he play?
   b. Explain why Harry would be worse off getting a grade higher than your answer to part (a).

9. If Harry becomes a tennis superstar with big earnings from tennis, what happens to his *PPF*, his *MB* curve, and his efficient time allocation?

10. If Harry suddenly finds high grades in economics easier to attain, what happens to his *PPF*, his *MB* curve, and his efficient time allocation?

Economic Growth (Study Plan 2.3)

11. A farm grows wheat and produces pork. The marginal cost of producing each of these products increases as more of it is produced.
    a. Make a graph that illustrates the farm's *PPF*.
    b. The farm adopts a new technology that allows it to use fewer resources to fatten pigs. Use your graph to illustrate the impact of the new technology on the farm's *PPF*.
    c. With the farm using the new technology described in part (b), has the opportunity cost of producing a tonne of wheat increased, decreased, or remained the same? Explain and illustrate your answer.
    d. Is the farm more efficient with the new technology than it was with the old one? Why?

Gains from Trade (Study Plan 2.4)

Use the following data to work Problems 12 and 13.
12. In an hour, Sue can produce 40 caps or 4 jackets and Tessa can produce 80 caps or 4 jackets.
    a. Calculate Sue's opportunity cost of producing a cap.
    b. Calculate Tessa's opportunity cost of producing a cap.
    c. Who has a comparative advantage in producing caps?
    d. If Sue and Tessa specialize in producing the good in which each has a comparative advantage, and then trade jackets and caps, who gains from the specialization and trade?

13. Suppose that Tessa buys a new machine for making jackets that enables her to make 20 jackets an hour. (She can still make only 80 caps per hour.)
    a. Who now has a comparative advantage in producing jackets?
    b. Can Sue and Tessa still gain from trade?

Use the following data to work Problems 14 to 17.
Imports accounted for about 70 percent of sales of pork meat in Australia. Pork imports from Denmark, Canada, and the United States rose 48 percent in the past year. Australian producers receive about $2.30 per kilogram, which costs $3 to produce.
14. What does this data suggest about Australia's comparative advantage in pork meat production?
15. Pork imports had grown rapidly in the previous four years. What does this suggest about the change in Australia's comparative advantage in this product and why might that change have occurred?

16. Canada is an important supplier of pork meat to Australia, while Australia exports wine to Canada. Construct both an Australian and a Canadian *PPF* for wine and pork that are consistent with this pattern of trade.
17. The pork industry had sought restrictions on imports but the government decided that there was no case for restricting imports. What would have been the effect of restrictions on imports on production efficiency in Australia?

Economic Coordination (Study Plan 2.5)

18. For 50 years, Cuba has had a centrally planned economy in which the government made the decisions on how resources were allocated.
    a. Why would you expect Cuba's production possibilities (per person) to be smaller than those of Canada?
    b. What are the social institutions that Cuba might lack that help Canada to achieve allocative efficiency?

Economics in the News (Study Plan 2.EN)

Use the following data to work Problems 19 to 21.
Brazil produces ethanol from sugar at a cost of 83 cents per gallon. The United States produces ethanol from corn at a cost of $1.14 per gallon. Sugar grown on one acre of land produces twice the quantity of ethanol as the corn grown on an acre. The United States imports 5 percent of the ethanol it uses and produces the rest itself. Since 2003, U.S. ethanol production has more than doubled and U.S. corn production has increased by 45 percent.

19. a. Does Brazil or the United States have a comparative advantage in producing ethanol?
    b. Sketch the *PPF* for ethanol and other goods and services for the United States.
    c. Sketch the *PPF* for ethanol and other goods and services for Brazil.

20. a. Do you expect the opportunity cost of producing ethanol in the United States to have increased since 2003? Explain why.
    b. Do you think the United States has achieved production efficiency in its manufacture of ethanol? Explain why or why not.
    c. Do you think the United States has achieved allocative efficiency in its manufacture of ethanol? Explain why or why not.

21. Sketch a figure similar to Fig. 2.6 on p. 40 to show how both the United States and Brazil can gain from specialization and trade.

ADDITIONAL PROBLEMS AND APPLICATIONS

MyEconLab ◆ You can work these problems in MyEconLab if assigned by your instructor.

Production Possibilities and Opportunity Cost

Use the following table to work Problems 22 to 23.
The people of Leisure Island have 50 hours of labour a day that can be used to produce entertainment and good food. The table shows the maximum quantity of either entertainment or good food that Leisure Island can produce with different quantities of labour.

Labour (hours)	Entertainment (units per month)		Good food (units per month)
0	0	or	0
10	20	or	30
20	40	or	50
30	60	or	60
40	80	or	65
50	100	or	67

22. Is an output of 50 units of entertainment and 50 units of good food attainable and efficient? With a production of 50 units of entertainment and 50 units of good food, do the people of Leisure Island face a tradeoff?

23. What is the opportunity cost of producing an additional unit of entertainment? Explain how the opportunity cost of a unit of entertainment changes as more entertainment is produced.

Use the following table to work Problems 24 and 25.
Suppose that Sunland's production possibilities are

Food (kilograms per month)		Sunscreen (litres per month)
300	and	0
200	and	50
100	and	100
0	and	150

24. a. Draw a graph of Sunland's *PPF* and explain how your graph illustrates a tradeoff.
   b. If Sunland produces 150 kilograms of food per month, how much sunscreen must it produce if it achieves production efficiency?
   c. What is Sunland's opportunity cost of producing 1 kilogram of food?
   d. What is Sunland's opportunity cost of producing 1 litre of sunscreen?
   e. Explain the relationship between your answers to parts (c) and (d).

25. What feature of a *PPF* illustrates increasing opportunity cost? Explain why the country's opportunity cost does or does not increase.

Using Resources Efficiently

26. In Problem 24, what is the marginal cost of a kilogram of food in Sunland when the quantity produced is 150 kilograms per day? What is special about Sunland's marginal cost of food?

27. The table describes the preferences in Sunland.

Sunscreen (litres per month)	Willingness to pay (kilograms of food per litre)
25	3
75	2
125	1

   a. What is the marginal benefit from sunscreen and how is it measured?
   b. Draw a graph of Sunland's marginal benefit from sunscreen.

Economic Growth

28. Capital accumulation and technological change bring economic growth, which means that the *PPF* keeps shifting outward: Production that was unattainable yesterday becomes attainable today; production that is unattainable today will become attainable tomorrow. Why doesn't this process of economic growth mean that scarcity is being defeated and will one day be gone?

Gains from Trade

Use the following data to work Problems 29 and 30.
Kim can produce 40 pies or 400 cakes an hour. Liam can produce 100 pies or 200 cakes an hour.

29. a. Calculate Kim's opportunity cost of a pie and Liam's opportunity cost of a pie.
   b. If each spends 30 minutes of each hour producing pies and 30 minutes producing cakes, how many pies and cakes does each produce?
   c. Who has a comparative advantage in producing pies? Who has a comparative advantage in producing cakes?

30. a. Draw a graph of Kim's *PPF* and Liam's *PPF*.
   b. On your graph, show the point at which each produces when they spend 30 minutes of each hour producing pies and 30 minutes producing cakes.
   c. On your graph, show what Kim produces and what Liam produces when they specialize.
   d. When they specialize and trade, what are the total gains from trade?

e. If Kim and Liam share the total gains equally, what trade takes place between them?

31. Tony and Patty produce skis and snowboards. The tables show their production possibilities. Tony produces 5 snowboards and 40 skis a week; Patty produces 10 snowboards and 5 skis a week.

Tony's Production Possibilities

Snowboards (per week)		Skis (per week)
25	and	0
20	and	10
15	and	20
10	and	30
5	and	40
0	and	50

Patty's Production Possibilities

Snowboards (per week)		Skis (per week)
20	and	0
10	and	5
0	and	10

a. Who has a comparative advantage in producing snowboards? And who has a comparative advantage in producing skis?

b. If Tony and Patty specialize and trade 1 snowboard for 1 ski, what are the gains from trade?

Economic Coordination

32. Indicate on a graph of the circular flows in the market economy, the real and money flows in which the following items belong:

a. You buy an iPad from the Apple Store.

b. Apple Inc. pays the designers of the iPad.

c. Apple Inc. decides to expand and rents an adjacent building.

d. You buy a new e-book from Amazon.

e. Apple Inc. hires a student as an intern during the summer.

Economics in the News

33. After you have studied *Reading Between the Lines* on pp. 44–45, answer the following questions.

a. How does an increase in the use of corn to produce ethanol affect the opportunity cost of corn?

b. How would you expect an increase in the quantity of corn produced to influence the opportunity cost of producing corn?

c. Why did the cost of producing corn increase in the rest of the world?

d. Is it possible that the increased quantity of corn produced, despite the higher cost of production, represents a move towards allocative efficiency?

34. **Malaria Eradication Back on the Table**
In response to the Gates Malaria Forum in October 2007, countries are debating the pros and cons of eradication. Dr. Arata Kochi of the World Health Organization believes that with enough money malaria cases could be cut by 90 percent, but he believes that it would be very expensive to eliminate the remaining 10 percent of cases. He concluded that countries should not strive to eradicate malaria.
Source: *The New York Times*, March 4, 2008

a. Is Dr. Kochi talking about *production efficiency* or *allocative efficiency* or both?

b. Make a graph with the percentage of malaria cases eliminated on the x-axis and the marginal cost and marginal benefit from driving down malaria cases on the y-axis. On your graph:

(i) Draw a marginal cost curve that is consistent with Dr. Kochi's opinion.

(ii) Draw a marginal benefit curve that is consistent with Dr. Kochi's opinion.

(iii) Identify the quantity of malaria eradicated that achieves allocative efficiency.

35. **Lots of Little Screens**
Inexpensive broadband access has created a generation of television producers for whom the Internet is their native medium. As they redirect the focus from TV to computers, cell phones, and iPods, the video market is developing into an open digital network.
Source: *The New York Times*, December 2, 2007

a. How has inexpensive broadband changed the production possibilities of video entertainment and other goods and services?

b. Sketch a *PPF* for video entertainment and other goods and services before broadband.

c. Show how the arrival of inexpensive broadband has changed the *PPF*.

d. Sketch a marginal benefit curve for video entertainment.

e. Show how the new generation of TV producers for whom the Internet is their native medium might have changed the marginal benefit from video entertainment.

f. Explain how the efficient quantity of video entertainment has changed.

Your Economic Revolution

PART ONE

Three periods in human history stand out as ones of economic revolution. The first, the *Agricultural Revolution,* occurred 10,000 years ago. In what is today Iraq, people learned to domesticate animals and plant crops. People stopped roaming in search of food and settled in villages, towns, and cities where they specialized in the activities in which they had a comparative advantage and developed markets in which to exchange their products. Wealth increased enormously.

You are studying economics at a time that future historians will call the *Information Revolution.* Over the entire world, people are embracing new information technologies and prospering on an unprecedented scale.

Economics was born during the *Industrial Revolution,* which began in England during the 1760s. For the first time, people began to apply science and create new technologies for the manufacture of textiles and iron, to create steam engines, and to boost the output of farms.

During all three economic revolutions, many have prospered but many have been left behind. It is the range of human progress that poses the greatest question for economics and the one that Adam Smith addressed in the first work of economic science: What causes the differences in wealth among nations?

Many people had written about economics before **Adam Smith**, *but he made economics a science. Born in 1723 in Kirkcaldy, a small fishing town near Edinburgh, Scotland, Smith was the only child of the town's customs officer. Lured from his professorship (he was a full professor at 28) by a wealthy Scottish duke who gave him a pension of £300 a year—10 times the average income at that time—Smith devoted 10 years to writing his masterpiece:* An Inquiry into the Nature and Causes of the **Wealth of Nations**, *published in 1776.*

Why, Adam Smith asked, are some nations wealthy while others are poor? He was pondering these questions at the height of the Industrial Revolution, and he answered by emphasizing the role of the division of labour and free markets.

To illustrate his argument, Adam Smith described two pin factories. In the first, one person, using the hand tools available in the 1770s, could make 20 pins a day. In the other, by using those same hand tools but breaking the process into a number of individually small operations in which people specialize—by the division of labour—10 people could make a staggering 48,000 pins a day.

It is not from the benevolence of the butcher, the brewer, or the baker that we expect our dinner, but from their regard to their own interest.

ADAM SMITH
The Wealth of Nations

One draws out the wire, another straightens it, a third cuts it, a fourth points it, a fifth grinds it. Three specialists make the head, and a fourth attaches it. Finally, the pin is polished and packaged.

But a large market is needed to support the division of labour: One factory employing 10 workers would need to sell more than 15 million pins a year to stay in business!

Professor Bhagwati, what attracted you to economics?

When you come from India, where poverty hits the eye, it is easy to be attracted to economics, which can be used to bring prosperity and create jobs to pull up the poor into gainful employment.

I learned later that there are two broad types of economist: those who treat the subject as an arid mathematical toy and those who see it as a serious social science.

If Cambridge, where I went as an undergraduate, had been interested in esoteric mathematical economics, I would have opted for something else. But the Cambridge economists from whom I learned—many among the greatest figures in the discipline—saw economics as a social science. I therefore saw the power of economics as a tool to address India's poverty and was immediately hooked.

Who had the greatest impact on you at Cambridge?

Most of all, it was Harry Johnson, a young Canadian of immense energy and profound analytical gifts. Quite unlike the shy and reserved British dons, Johnson was friendly, effusive, and supportive of students who flocked around him. He would later move to Chicago, where he became one of the most influential members of the market-oriented Chicago school. Another was Joan Robinson, arguably the world's most impressive female economist.

When I left Cambridge for MIT, going from one Cambridge to the other, I was lucky to transition from one phenomenal set of economists to another. At MIT, I learned much from future Nobel laureates Paul Samuelson and Robert Solow. Both would later become great friends and colleagues when I joined the MIT faculty in 1968.

After Cambridge and MIT, you went to Oxford and then back to India. What did you do in India?

I joined the Planning Commission in New Delhi, where my first big job was to find ways of raising the bottom 30 percent of India's population out of poverty to a "minimum income" level.

And what did you prescribe?

My main prescription was to "grow the pie." My research suggested that the share of the bottom 30 percent of the pie did not seem to vary dramatically with differences in economic and political systems. So growth in the pie seemed to be the principal

(but not the only) component of an antipoverty strategy. To supplement growth's good effects on the poor, the Indian planners were also dedicated to education, health, social reforms, and land reforms. Also, the access of the lowest-income and socially disadvantaged groups to the growth process and its benefits

> My main prescription was to "grow the pie" ... Much empirical work shows that where growth has occurred, poverty has lessened.

was to be improved in many ways, such as extension of credit without collateral.

Today, this strategy has no rivals. Much empirical work shows that where growth has occurred, poverty has lessened. It is nice to know that one's basic take on an issue of such central importance to humanity's well-being has been borne out by experience!

You left India in 1968 to come to the United States and an academic job at MIT. Why?

While the decision to emigrate often reflects personal factors—and they were present in my case—the offer of a professorship from MIT certainly helped me

JAGDISH BHAGWATI is University Professor at Columbia University. Born in India in 1934, he studied at Cambridge University in England, MIT, and Oxford University before returning to India. He returned to teach at MIT in 1968 and moved to Columbia in 1980. A prolific scholar, Professor Bhagwati also writes in leading newspapers and magazines throughout the world. He has been much honoured for both his scientific work and his impact on public policy. His greatest contributions are in international trade but extend also to developmental problems and the study of political economy.

Michael Parkin talked with Jagdish Bhagwati about his work and the progress that economists have made in understanding the benefits of economic growth and international trade since the pioneering work of Adam Smith.

make up my mind. At the time, it was easily the world's most celebrated department. Serendipitously, the highest-ranked departments at MIT were not in engineering and the sciences but in linguistics (which had Noam Chomsky) and economics (which had Paul Samuelson). Joining the MIT faculty was a dramatic breakthrough: I felt stimulated each year by several fantastic students and by several of the world's most creative economists.

We hear a lot in the popular press about fair trade and level playing fields. What's the distinction between free trade and fair trade? How can the playing field be unlevel?

Free trade simply means allowing no trade barriers such as tariffs, subsidies, and quotas. Trade barriers make domestic prices different from world prices for traded goods. When this happens, resources are not being used efficiently. Basic economics from the time of Adam Smith tells us why free trade is good for us and why barriers to trade harm us, though our understanding of this doctrine today is far more nuanced and profound than it was at its creation.

Fair trade, on the other hand, is almost always a sneaky way of objecting to free trade. If your rivals are hard to compete with, you are not likely to get protection simply by saying that you cannot hack it. But if you say that your rival is an "unfair" trader, that is an easier sell! As international competition has grown fiercer, cries of "unfair trade" have therefore multiplied. The lesser rogues among the protectionists ask for "free and fair trade," whereas the worst ones ask for "fair, not free, trade."

> Fair trade ... is almost always a sneaky way of objecting to free trade.

At the end of World War II, the General Agreement on Tariffs and Trade (GATT) was established and there followed several rounds of multilateral trade negotiations and reductions in barriers to trade. How do you assess the contribution of GATT and its successor, the World Trade Organization (WTO)?

The GATT has made a huge contribution by overseeing massive trade liberalization in industrial goods among the developed countries. GATT rules, which "bind" tariffs to negotiated ceilings, prevent the raising of tariffs and have prevented tariff wars like those of the 1930s in which mutual and retaliatory tariff barriers were raised, to the detriment of everyone.

The GATT was folded into the WTO at the end of the Uruguay Round of trade negotiations, and the WTO is institutionally stronger. For instance, it has a binding dispute settlement mechanism, whereas the GATT had no such teeth. It is also more ambitious in its scope, extending to new areas such as the environment, intellectual property protection, and investment rules.

Running alongside the pursuit of multilateral free trade has been the emergence of bilateral trade agreements such as NAFTA and the European Union (EU). How do you view the bilateral free trade areas in today's world?

Unfortunately, there has been an explosion of bilateral free trade areas today. By some estimates, the ones in place and others being plotted approach 400! Each bilateral agreement gives preferential treatment to its trading partner over others. Because there are now so many bilateral agreements, such as those between the United States and Israel and between the United States and Jordan, the result is a chaotic pattern of different tariffs depending on where a product comes from. Also, "rules of origin" must be agreed upon to determine whether a product is, say, Jordanian or Taiwanese if Jordan qualifies for a preferential tariff but Taiwan does not and Taiwanese inputs enter the Jordanian manufacture of the product.

I have called the resulting crisscrossing of preferences and rules of origin the "spaghetti bowl" problem. The world trading system is choking under these proliferating bilateral deals. Contrast this complexity with the simplicity of a multilateral system with common tariffs for all WTO members.

We now have a world of uncoordinated and inefficient trade policies. The EU makes bilateral free trade agreements with different non-EU countries, so the United States follows with its own bilateral agreements; and with Europe and the United States doing it, the Asian countries, long wedded to multilateralism, have now succumbed to the mania.

> We now have a world of uncoordinated and inefficient trade policies.

Instead, if the United States had provided leadership by rewriting rules to make the signing of such bilateral agreements extremely difficult, this plague on the trading system today might well have been averted.

Is the "spaghetti bowl" problem getting better or worse?
Unquestionably it is getting worse. Multilateralism is retreating and bilateralism is advancing. The 2010 G-20 meeting in Canada was a disappointment. At the insistence of the United States, a definite date for completing the Doha Round was dropped and instead, unwittingly rubbing salt into the wound, President Barack Obama announced his administration's willingness to see the U.S.–South Korea free trade agreement through.

There are distressing recent reports that the U.S. Commerce Department is exploring ways to strengthen the bite of anti-dumping actions, which are now generally agreed to be a form of discriminatory protectionism aimed selectively at successful exporting nations and firms.

Equally distressing is Obama's decision to sign a bill that raises fees on some temporary work visas in order to pay for higher border-enforcement expenditures. Further, it was asserted that a tax on foreign workers would reduce the numbers coming in and "taking jobs away" from U.S. citizens. Many supporters of the proposal claimed, incoherently, that it would simultaneously discourage foreign workers from entering the United States and increase revenues.

Obama's surrender exemplified the doctrine that one retreat often leads to another, with new lobbyists following in others' footsteps. Perhaps the chief mistake, as with recent "Buy American" provisions in U.S. legislation, was to allow the Employ American Workers Act (EAWA) to be folded into the stimulus bill. This act makes it harder for companies to get governmental support to hire skilled immigrants with H1(b) visas: They must first show that they have not laid off or do not plan to lay off U.S. workers in similar occupations. Whatever the shortcomings of such measures in economic-policy terms, the visa-fee-enhancement provision is de facto discriminatory, and thus violates WTO rules against discrimination between domestic and foreign firms, or between foreign firms from different WTO countries.

While the visa-fee legislation is what lawyers call "facially" non-discriminatory, its design confers an advantage on U.S. firms vis-à-vis foreign firms. Such acts of discrimination in trade policies find succor in the media and in some of America's prominent think tanks. For example, in the wake of the vast misery brought by flooding to the people of Pakistan, the U.S. and other governments have risen to the occasion with emergency aid. But there have also been proposals to grant duty-free access to Pakistan's exports. But this would be discriminatory towards developing countries that do not have duty-free access, helping Pakistan at their expense.

What advice do you have for a student who is just starting to study economics? Is economics a good subject in which to major?
I would say enormously so. In particular, we economists bring three unique insights to good policymaking.

First, economists look for second- and subsequent-round effects of actions.

Second, we correctly emphasize that a policy cannot be judged without using a counterfactual. It is a witticism that an economist, when asked how her husband was, said, "Compared to what?"

Third, we uniquely and systematically bring the principle of social cost and social benefit to our policy analysis.

CHAPTER 3

Demand and Supply

After studying this chapter, you will be able to

◆ Describe a competitive market and think about a price as an opportunity cost

◆ Explain the influences on demand

◆ Explain the influences on supply

◆ Explain how demand and supply determine prices and quantities bought and sold

◆ Use the demand and supply model to make predictions about changes in prices and quantities

What makes the price of coffee double in just two years and then fall by 50 percent? This chapter enables you to answer this and similar questions.

You know that economics is about the choices people make to cope with scarcity and how those choices respond to incentives. Prices act as incentives. You're going to see how people respond to prices and how prices get determined by demand and supply.

The demand and supply model that you study in this chapter is the main tool of economics.

At the end of the chapter, in *Reading Between the Lines*, we'll apply the model to the market for coffee and explain why its price fluctuates so much.

◆ Markets and Prices

When you need a new pair of running shoes, want a bagel and a latte, plan to upgrade your cell phone, or look for a winter break in the sun, you must find a place where people sell those items or offer those services. The place in which you find them is a *market.* You learned in Chapter 2 (p. 42) that a market is any arrangement that enables buyers and sellers to get information and to do business with each other.

A market has two sides: buyers and sellers. There are markets for *goods* such as apples and hiking boots, for *services* such as haircuts and tennis lessons, for *factors of production* such as computer programmers and earthmovers, and for other manufactured *inputs* such as memory chips and auto parts. There are also markets for money such as Japanese yen and for financial securities such as Yahoo! stock. Only our imagination limits what can be traded in markets.

Some markets are physical places where buyers and sellers meet and where an auctioneer or a broker helps to determine the prices. Examples of this type of market are live car auctions and the wholesale fish, meat, and produce markets.

Some markets are groups of people spread around the world who never meet and know little about each other but are connected through the Internet or by telephone and fax. Examples are the e-commerce markets and the currency markets.

But most markets are unorganized collections of buyers and sellers. You do most of your trading in this type of market. An example is the market for basketball shoes. The buyers in this $3-billion-a-year market are the 45 million Canadians and Americans who play basketball (or who want to make a fashion statement). The sellers are the tens of thousands of retail sports equipment and footwear stores. Each buyer can visit several different stores, and each seller knows that the buyer has a choice of stores.

Markets vary in the intensity of competition that buyers and sellers face. In this chapter, we're going to study a **competitive market**—a market that has many buyers and many sellers, so no single buyer or seller can influence the price.

Producers offer items for sale only if the price is high enough to cover their opportunity cost. And consumers respond to changing opportunity cost by seeking cheaper alternatives to expensive items.

We are going to study how people respond to *prices* and the forces that determine prices. But to pursue these tasks, we need to understand the relationship between a price and an opportunity cost.

In everyday life, the *price* of an object is the number of dollars that must be given up in exchange for it. Economists refer to this price as the **money price**.

The *opportunity cost* of an action is the highest-valued alternative forgone. If, when you buy a cup of coffee, the highest-valued thing you forgo is some gum, then the opportunity cost of the coffee is the *quantity* of gum forgone. We can calculate the quantity of gum forgone from the money prices of the coffee and the gum.

If the money price of coffee is $1 a cup and the money price of gum is 50¢ a pack, then the opportunity cost of one cup of coffee is two packs of gum. To calculate this opportunity cost, we divide the price of a cup of coffee by the price of a pack of gum and find the *ratio* of one price to the other. The ratio of one price to another is called a **relative price**, and a *relative price is an opportunity cost.*

We can express the relative price of coffee in terms of gum or any other good. The normal way of expressing a relative price is in terms of a "basket" of all goods and services. To calculate this relative price, we divide the money price of a good by the money price of a "basket" of all goods (called a *price index*). The resulting relative price tells us the opportunity cost of the good in terms of how much of the "basket" we must give up to buy it.

The demand and supply model that we are about to study determines *relative prices,* and the word "price" means *relative* price. When we predict that a price will fall, we do not mean that its *money* price will fall—although it might. We mean that its *relative* price will fall. That is, its price will fall *relative* to the average price of other goods and services.

◢ REVIEW QUIZ

1 What is the distinction between a money price and a relative price?
2 Explain why a relative price is an opportunity cost.
3 Think of examples of goods whose relative price has risen or fallen by a large amount.

You can work these questions in Study Plan 3.1 and get instant feedback.

——————————————————— MyEconLab ◆

Let's begin our study of demand and supply, starting with demand.

◆ Demand

If you demand something, then you

1. Want it,
2. Can afford it, and
3. Plan to buy it.

Wants are the unlimited desires or wishes that people have for goods and services. How many times have you thought that you would like something "if only you could afford it" or "if it weren't so expensive"? Scarcity guarantees that many—perhaps most—of our wants will never be satisfied. Demand reflects a decision about which wants to satisfy.

The **quantity demanded** of a good or service is the amount that consumers plan to buy during a given time period at a particular price. The quantity demanded is not necessarily the same as the quantity actually bought. Sometimes the quantity demanded exceeds the amount of goods available, so the quantity bought is less than the quantity demanded.

The quantity demanded is measured as an amount per unit of time. For example, suppose that you buy one cup of coffee a day. The quantity of coffee that you demand can be expressed as 1 cup per day, 7 cups per week, or 365 cups per year.

Many factors influence buying plans, and one of them is the price. We look first at the relationship between the quantity demanded of a good and its price. To study this relationship, we keep all other influences on buying plans the same and we ask: How, other things remaining the same, does the quantity demanded of a good change as its price changes?

The law of demand provides the answer.

The Law of Demand

The **law of demand** states

> Other things remaining the same, the higher the price of a good, the smaller is the quantity demanded; and the lower the price of a good, the greater is the quantity demanded.

Why does a higher price reduce the quantity demanded? For two reasons:

- Substitution effect
- Income effect

Substitution Effect When the price of a good rises, other things remaining the same, its *relative* price—its opportunity cost—rises. Although each good is unique, it has *substitutes*—other goods that can be used in its place. As the opportunity cost of a good rises, the incentive to economize on its use and switch to a substitute becomes stronger.

Income Effect When a price rises, other things remaining the same, the price rises *relative* to income. Faced with a higher price and an unchanged income, people cannot afford to buy all the things they previously bought. They must decrease the quantities demanded of at least some goods and services. Normally, the good whose price has increased will be one of the goods that people buy less of.

To see the substitution effect and the income effect at work, think about the effects of a change in the price of an energy bar. Several different goods are substitutes for an energy bar. For example, an energy drink could be consumed instead of an energy bar.

Suppose that an energy bar initially sells for $3.00 and then its price falls to $1.50. People now substitute energy bars for energy drinks—the substitution effect. And with a budget that now has some slack from the lower price of an energy bar, people buy even more energy bars—the income effect. The quantity of energy bars demanded increases for these two reasons.

Now suppose that an energy bar initially sells for $3 and then the price doubles to $6. People now buy fewer energy bars and more energy drinks—the substitution effect. And faced with a tighter budget, people buy even fewer energy bars—the income effect. The quantity of energy bars demanded decreases for these two reasons.

Demand Curve and Demand Schedule

You are now about to study one of the two most used curves in economics: the demand curve. You are also going to encounter one of the most critical distinctions: the distinction between *demand* and *quantity demanded*.

The term **demand** refers to the entire relationship between the price of a good and the quantity demanded of that good. Demand is illustrated by the demand curve and the demand schedule. The term *quantity demanded* refers to a point on a demand curve—the quantity demanded at a particular price.

Figure 3.1 shows the demand curve for energy bars. A **demand curve** shows the relationship between the quantity demanded of a good and its price when all other influences on consumers' planned purchases remain the same.

The table in Fig. 3.1 is the demand schedule for energy bars. A *demand schedule* lists the quantities demanded at each price when all the other influences on consumers' planned purchases remain the same. For example, if the price of a bar is 50¢, the quantity demanded is 22 million a week. If the price is $2.50, the quantity demanded is 5 million a week. The other rows of the table show the quantities demanded at prices of $1.00, $1.50, and $2.00.

We graph the demand schedule as a demand curve with the quantity demanded on the *x*-axis and the price on the *y*-axis. The points on the demand curve labelled *A* through *E* correspond to the rows of the demand schedule. For example, point *A* on the graph shows a quantity demanded of 22 million energy bars a week at a price of 50¢ a bar.

Willingness and Ability to Pay Another way of looking at the demand curve is as a willingness-and-ability-to-pay curve. The willingness and ability to pay is a measure of *marginal benefit.*

If a small quantity is available, the highest price that someone is willing and able to pay for one more unit is high. But as the quantity available increases, the marginal benefit of each additional unit falls and the highest price that someone is willing and able to pay also falls along the demand curve.

In Fig. 3.1, if only 5 million energy bars are available each week, the highest price that someone is willing to pay for the 5 millionth bar is $2.50. But if 22 million energy bars are available each week, someone is willing to pay 50¢ for the last bar bought.

A Change in Demand

When any factor that influences buying plans changes, other than the price of the good, there is a **change in demand**. Figure 3.2 illustrates an increase in demand. When demand increases, the demand curve shifts rightward and the quantity demanded at each price is greater. For example, at $2.50 a bar, the quantity demanded on the original (blue) demand curve is 5 million energy bars a week. On the new (red) demand curve, at $2.50 a bar, the quantity demanded is 15 million bars a week. Look closely at the numbers in the table and check that the quantity demanded at each price is greater.

FIGURE 3.1   The Demand Curve

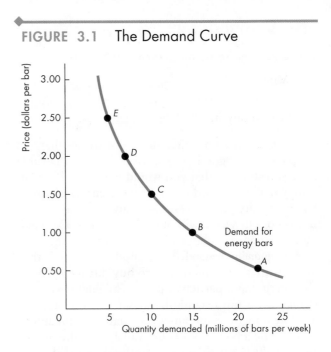

	Price (dollars per bar)	Quantity demanded (millions of bars per week)
A	0.50	22
B	1.00	15
C	1.50	10
D	2.00	7
E	2.50	5

The table shows a demand schedule for energy bars. At a price of 50¢ a bar, 22 million bars a week are demanded; at a price of $1.50 a bar, 10 million bars a week are demanded. The demand curve shows the relationship between quantity demanded and price, other things remaining the same. The demand curve slopes downward: As the price falls, the quantity demanded increases.

The demand curve can be read in two ways. For a given price, the demand curve tells us the quantity that people plan to buy. For example, at a price of $1.50 a bar, people plan to buy 10 million bars a week. For a given quantity, the demand curve tells us the maximum price that consumers are willing and able to pay for the last bar available. For example, the maximum price that consumers will pay for the 15 millionth bar is $1.00.

FIGURE 3.2 An Increase in Demand

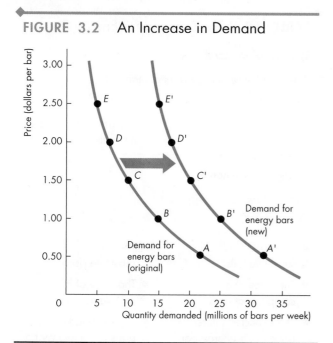

Original demand schedule Original income		New demand schedule New higher income		
	Price (dollars per bar)	Quantity demanded (millions of bars per week)	Price (dollars per bar)	Quantity demanded (millions of bars per week)
A	0.50	22	A'	0.50	32
B	1.00	15	B'	1.00	25
C	1.50	10	C'	1.50	20
D	2.00	7	D'	2.00	17
E	2.50	5	E'	2.50	15

A change in any influence on buying plans other than the price of the good itself results in a new demand schedule and a shift of the demand curve. A change in income changes the demand for energy bars. At a price of $1.50 a bar, 10 million bars a week are demanded at the original income (row C of the table) and 20 million bars a week are demanded at the new higher income (row C'). A rise in income increases the demand for energy bars. The demand curve shifts *rightward*, as shown by the shift arrow and the resulting red curve.

MyEconLab animation

Six main factors bring changes in demand. They are changes in

- The prices of related goods
- Expected future prices
- Income
- Expected future income and credit
- Population
- Preferences

Prices of Related Goods The quantity of energy bars that consumers plan to buy depends in part on the prices of substitutes for energy bars. A **substitute** is a good that can be used in place of another good. For example, a bus ride is a substitute for a train ride; a hamburger is a substitute for a hot dog; and an energy drink is a substitute for an energy bar. If the price of a substitute for an energy bar rises, people buy less of the substitute and more energy bars. For example, if the price of an energy drink rises, people buy fewer energy drinks and more energy bars. The demand for energy bars increases.

The quantity of energy bars that people plan to buy also depends on the prices of complements with energy bars. A **complement** is a good that is used in conjunction with another good. Hamburgers and fries are complements, and so are energy bars and exercise. If the price of an hour at the gym falls, people buy more gym time *and more* energy bars.

Expected Future Prices If the expected future price of a good rises and if the good can be stored, the opportunity cost of obtaining the good for future use is lower today than it will be in the future when people expect the price to be higher. So people retime their purchases—they substitute over time. They buy more of the good now before its price is expected to rise (and less afterward), so the demand for the good today increases.

For example, suppose that a Florida frost damages the season's orange crop. You expect the price of orange juice to rise, so you fill your freezer with enough frozen juice to get you through the next six months. Your current demand for frozen orange juice has increased, and your future demand has decreased.

Similarly, if the expected future price of a good falls, the opportunity cost of buying the good today is high relative to what it is expected to be in the future. So again, people retime their purchases. They buy less of the good now before its price is expected to fall, so the demand for the good decreases today and increases in the future.

Computer prices are constantly falling, and this fact poses a dilemma. Will you buy a new computer now, in time for the start of the school year, or will you wait until the price has fallen some more? Because people expect computer prices to keep falling, the current demand for computers is less (and the future demand is greater) than it otherwise would be.

Income Consumers' income influences demand. When income increases, consumers buy more of most goods; and when income decreases, consumers buy less of most goods. Although an increase in income leads to an increase in the demand for *most* goods, it does not lead to an increase in the demand for *all* goods. A **normal good** is one for which demand increases as income increases. An **inferior good** is one for which demand decreases as income increases. As incomes increase, the demand for air travel (a normal good) increases and the demand for long-distance bus trips (an inferior good) decreases.

Expected Future Income and Credit When expected future income increases or credit becomes easier to get, demand for the good might increase now. For example, a salesperson gets the news that she will receive a big bonus at the end of the year, so she goes into debt and buys a new car now, rather than wait until she receives the bonus.

Population Demand also depends on the size and the age structure of the population. The larger the population, the greater is the demand for all goods and services; the smaller the population, the smaller is the demand for all goods and services. For example, the demand for parking spaces or movies or just about anything that you can imagine is much greater in the Greater Toronto Area (population 5.6 million) than it is in Thunder Bay (population 124,000).

Also, the larger the proportion of the population in a given age group, the greater is the demand for the goods and services used by that age group. For example, in 2010, there were 2.3 million 20- to 24-year-olds in Canada compared with 2.1 million in 2000. As a result, the demand for university places in 2010 was greater than in 2000. Over this same period, the number of Canadians aged 90 years more than doubled to exceed 200,000. As a result, the demand for nursing home services increased.

TABLE 3.1   The Demand for Energy Bars

The Law of Demand

The quantity of energy bars demanded

Decreases if:	Increases if:
■ The price of an energy bar rises	■ The price of an energy bar falls

Changes in Demand

The demand for energy bars

Decreases if:	Increases if:
■ The price of a substitute falls	■ The price of a substitute rises
■ The price of a complement rises	■ The price of a complement falls
■ The expected future price of an energy bar falls	■ The expected future price of an energy bar rises
■ Income falls*	■ Income rises*
■ Expected future income falls or credit becomes harder to get*	■ Expected future income rises or credit becomes easier to get*
■ The population decreases	■ The population increases

*An energy bar is a normal good.

Preferences Demand depends on preferences. *Preferences* determine the value that people place on each good and service. Preferences depend on such things as the weather, information, and fashion. For example, greater health and fitness awareness has shifted preferences in favour of energy bars, so the demand for energy bars has increased.

Table 3.1 summarizes the influences on demand and the direction of those influences.

A Change in the Quantity Demanded Versus a Change in Demand

Changes in the influences on buying plans bring either a change in the quantity demanded or a change in demand. Equivalently, they bring either a movement along the demand curve or a shift of the demand curve. The distinction between a change in the quantity demanded and a change in demand is the same as that between a movement along the demand curve and a shift of the demand curve.

A point on the demand curve shows the quantity demanded at a given price, so a movement along the demand curve shows a **change in the quantity demanded**. The entire demand curve shows demand, so a shift of the demand curve shows a *change in demand*. Figure 3.3 illustrates these distinctions.

Movement Along the Demand Curve If the price of the good changes but no other influence on buying plans changes, we illustrate the effect of the price change as a movement along the demand curve.

A fall in the price of a good increases the quantity demanded of it. In Fig. 3.3, we illustrate the effect of a fall in price as a movement down along the demand curve D_0.

A rise in the price of a good decreases the quantity demanded of it. In Fig. 3.3, we illustrate the effect of a rise in price as a movement up along the demand curve D_0.

A Shift of the Demand Curve If the price of a good remains constant but some other influence on buying plans changes, there is a change in demand for that good. We illustrate a change in demand as a shift of the demand curve. For example, if more people work out at the gym, consumers buy more energy bars regardless of the price of a bar. That is what a rightward shift of the demand curve shows— more energy bars are demanded at each price.

In Fig. 3.3, there is a *change in demand* and the demand curve shifts when any influence on buying plans changes, other than the price of the good. Demand *increases* and the demand curve *shifts rightward* (to the red demand curve D_1) if the price of a substitute rises, the price of a complement falls, the expected future price of the good rises, income increases (for a normal good), expected future income or credit increases, or the population increases. Demand *decreases* and the demand curve *shifts leftward* (to the red demand curve D_2) if the price of a substitute falls, the price of a complement rises, the expected future price of the good falls, income decreases (for a normal good), expected future income or credit decreases, or the population decreases. (For an inferior good, the effects of changes in income are in the opposite direction to those described above.)

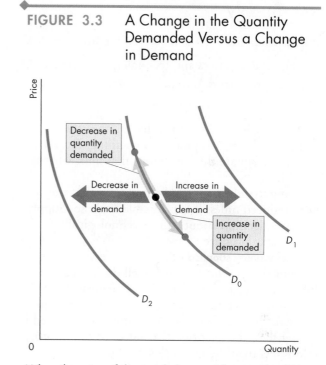

FIGURE 3.3   A Change in the Quantity Demanded Versus a Change in Demand

When the price of the good changes, there is a movement along the demand curve and *a change in the quantity demanded*, shown by the blue arrows on demand curve D_0. When any other influence on buying plans changes, there is a shift of the demand curve and a *change in demand*. An increase in demand shifts the demand curve rightward (from D_0 to D_1). A decrease in demand shifts the demand curve leftward (from D_0 to D_2).

MyEconLab   animation

REVIEW QUIZ

1 Define the quantity demanded of a good or service.
2 What is the law of demand and how do we illustrate it?
3 What does the demand curve tell us about the price that consumers are willing to pay?
4 List all the influences on buying plans that change demand, and for each influence, say whether it increases or decreases demand.
5 Why does demand not change when the price of a good changes with no change in the other influences on buying plans?

You can work these questions in Study Plan 3.2 and get instant feedback.

MyEconLab

◆ Supply

If a firm supplies a good or service, the firm

1. Has the resources and technology to produce it,
2. Can profit from producing it, and
3. Plans to produce it and sell it.

A supply is more than just having the *resources* and the *technology* to produce something. *Resources and technology* are the constraints that limit what is possible.

Many useful things can be produced, but they are not produced unless it is profitable to do so. Supply reflects a decision about which technologically feasible items to produce.

The **quantity supplied** of a good or service is the amount that producers plan to sell during a given time period at a particular price. The quantity supplied is not necessarily the same amount as the quantity actually sold. Sometimes the quantity supplied is greater than the quantity demanded, so the quantity sold is less than the quantity supplied.

Like the quantity demanded, the quantity supplied is measured as an amount per unit of time. For example, suppose that GM produces 1,000 cars a day. The quantity of cars supplied by GM can be expressed as 1,000 a day, 7,000 a week, or 365,000 a year. Without the time dimension, we cannot tell whether a particular quantity is large or small.

Many factors influence selling plans, and again one of them is the price of the good. We look first at the relationship between the quantity supplied of a good and its price. Just as we did when we studied demand, to isolate the relationship between the quantity supplied of a good and its price, we keep all other influences on selling plans the same and ask: How does the quantity supplied of a good change as its price changes when other things remain the same?

The law of supply provides the answer.

The Law of Supply

The **law of supply** states:

> Other things remaining the same, the higher the price of a good, the greater is the quantity supplied; and the lower the price of a good, the smaller is the quantity supplied.

Why does a higher price increase the quantity supplied? It is because *marginal cost increases.* As the quantity produced of any good increases, the marginal cost of producing the good increases. (See Chapter 2, p. 33 to review marginal cost.)

It is never worth producing a good if the price received for the good does not at least cover the marginal cost of producing it. When the price of a good rises, other things remaining the same, producers are willing to incur a higher marginal cost, so they increase production. The higher price brings forth an increase in the quantity supplied.

Let's now illustrate the law of supply with a supply curve and a supply schedule.

Supply Curve and Supply Schedule

You are now going to study the second of the two most used curves in economics: the supply curve. You're also going to learn about the critical distinction between *supply* and *quantity supplied.*

The term **supply** refers to the entire relationship between the price of a good and the quantity supplied of it. Supply is illustrated by the supply curve and the supply schedule. The term *quantity supplied* refers to a point on a supply curve—the quantity supplied at a particular price.

Figure 3.4 shows the supply curve of energy bars. A **supply curve** shows the relationship between the quantity supplied of a good and its price when all other influences on producers' planned sales remain the same. The supply curve is a graph of a supply schedule.

The table in Fig. 3.4 sets out the supply schedule for energy bars. A *supply schedule* lists the quantities supplied at each price when all the other influences on producers' planned sales remain the same. For example, if the price of an energy bar is 50¢, the quantity supplied is zero—in row *A* of the table. If the price of an energy bar is $1.00, the quantity supplied is 6 million energy bars a week—in row *B*. The other rows of the table show the quantities supplied at prices of $1.50, $2.00, and $2.50.

To make a supply curve, we graph the quantity supplied on the *x*-axis and the price on the *y*-axis. The points on the supply curve labelled *A* through *E* correspond to the rows of the supply schedule. For example, point *A* on the graph shows a quantity supplied of zero at a price of 50¢ an energy bar. Point *E* shows a quantity supplied of 15 million bars at $2.50 an energy bar.

FIGURE 3.4   The Supply Curve

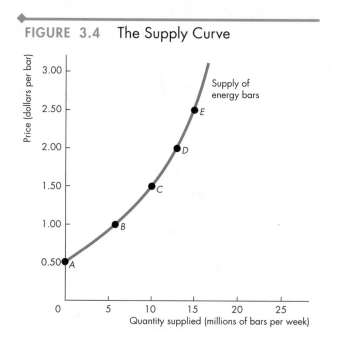

The table shows the supply schedule of energy bars. For example, at a price of $1.00, 6 million bars a week are supplied; at a price of $2.50, 15 million bars a week are supplied. The supply curve shows the relationship between the quantity supplied and the price, other things remaining the same. The supply curve slopes upward: As the price of a good increases, the quantity supplied increases.

A supply curve can be read in two ways. For a given price, the supply curve tells us the quantity that producers plan to sell at that price. For example, at a price of $1.50 a bar, producers are planning to sell 10 million bars a week. For a given quantity, the supply curve tells us the minimum price at which producers are willing to sell one more bar. For example, if 15 million bars are produced each week, the lowest price at which a producer is willing to sell the 15 millionth bar is $2.50.

	Price (dollars per bar)	Quantity supplied (millions of bars per week)
A	0.50	0
B	1.00	6
C	1.50	10
D	2.00	13
E	2.50	15

────── MyEconLab animation ◆

Minimum Supply Price The supply curve can be interpreted as a minimum-supply-price curve—a curve that shows the lowest price at which someone is willing to sell. This lowest price is the *marginal cost*.

If a small quantity is produced, the lowest price at which someone is willing to sell one more unit is low. But as the quantity produced increases, the marginal cost of each additional unit rises, so the lowest price at which someone is willing to sell an additional unit rises along the supply curve.

In Fig. 3.4, if 15 million bars are produced each week, the lowest price at which someone is willing to sell the 15 millionth bar is $2.50. But if 10 million bars are produced each week, someone is willing to accept $1.50 for the last bar produced.

A Change in Supply

When any factor that influences selling plans other than the price of the good changes, there is a **change in supply**. Six main factors bring changes in supply. They are changes in

- The prices of factors of production
- The prices of related goods produced
- Expected future prices
- The number of suppliers
- Technology
- The state of nature

Prices of Factors of Production The prices of the factors of production used to produce a good influence its supply. To see this influence, think about the supply curve as a minimum-supply-price curve. If the price of a factor of production rises, the lowest price that a producer is willing to accept for that good rises, so supply decreases. For example, during 2008, as the price of jet fuel increased, the supply of air travel decreased. Similarly, a rise in the minimum wage decreases the supply of hamburgers.

Prices of Related Goods Produced The prices of related goods that firms produce influence supply. For example, if the price of energy gel rises, firms switch production from bars to gel. The supply of energy bars decreases. Energy bars and energy gel are *substitutes in production*—goods that can be produced by using the same resources. If the price of beef rises, the supply of cowhide increases. Beef and cowhide are *complements in production*—goods that must be produced together.

Expected Future Prices   If the expected future price of a good rises, the return from selling the good in the future increases and is higher than it is today. So supply decreases today and increases in the future.

The Number of Suppliers   The larger the number of firms that produce a good, the greater is the supply of the good. As new firms enter an industry, the supply in that industry increases. As firms leave an industry, the supply in that industry decreases.

Technology   The term "technology" is used broadly to mean the way that factors of production are used to produce a good. A technology change occurs when a new method is discovered that lowers the cost of producing a good. For example, new methods used in the factories that produce computer chips have lowered the cost and increased the supply of chips.

The State of Nature   The state of nature includes all the natural forces that influence production. It includes the state of the weather and, more broadly, the natural environment. Good weather can increase the supply of many agricultural products and bad weather can decrease their supply. Extreme natural events such as earthquakes, tornadoes, and hurricanes can also influence supply.

Figure 3.5 illustrates an increase in supply. When supply increases, the supply curve shifts rightward and the quantity supplied at each price is larger. For example, at $1.00 per bar, on the original (blue) supply curve, the quantity supplied is 6 million bars a week. On the new (red) supply curve, the quantity supplied is 15 million bars a week. Look closely at the numbers in the table in Fig. 3.5 and check that the quantity supplied is larger at each price.

Table 3.2 summarizes the influences on supply and the directions of those influences.

A Change in the Quantity Supplied Versus a Change in Supply

Changes in the influences on selling plans bring either a change in the quantity supplied or a change in supply. Equivalently, they bring either a movement along the supply curve or a shift of the supply curve.

A point on the supply curve shows the quantity supplied at a given price. A movement along the supply curve shows a **change in the quantity supplied**. The entire supply curve shows supply. A shift of the supply curve shows a *change in supply*.

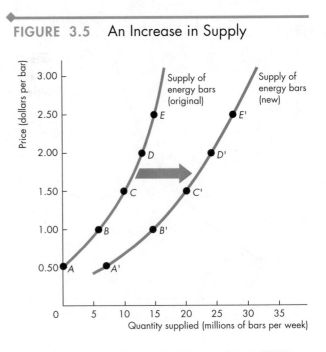

FIGURE 3.5   An Increase in Supply

Original supply schedule Old technology			New supply schedule New technology		
	Price (dollars per bar)	Quantity supplied (millions of bars per week)		Price (dollars per bar)	Quantity supplied (millions of bars per week)
A	0.50	0	A'	0.50	7
B	1.00	6	B'	1.00	15
C	1.50	10	C'	1.50	20
D	2.00	13	D'	2.00	25
E	2.50	15	E'	2.50	27

A change in any influence on selling plans other than the price of the good itself results in a new supply schedule and a shift of the supply curve. For example, a new, cost-saving technology for producing energy bars changes the supply of energy bars. At a price of $1.50 a bar, 10 million bars a week are supplied when producers use the old technology (row C of the table) and 20 million energy bars a week are supplied when producers use the new technology (row C'). An advance in technology *increases* the supply of energy bars. The supply curve shifts *rightward*, as shown by the shift arrow and the resulting red curve.

MyEconLab   animation

Figure 3.6 illustrates and summarizes these distinctions. If the price of the good changes and other things remain the same, there is a *change in the quantity supplied* of that good. If the price of the good falls, the quantity supplied decreases and there is a movement down along the supply curve S_0. If the price of the good rises, the quantity supplied increases and there is a movement up along the supply curve S_0. When any other influence on selling plans changes, the supply curve shifts and there is a *change in supply*. If supply increases, the supply curve shifts rightward to S_1. If supply decreases, the supply curve shifts leftward to S_2.

TABLE 3.2   The Supply of Energy Bars

The Law of Supply

The quantity of energy bars supplied

Decreases if:	*Increases if:*
■ The price of an energy bar falls	■ The price of an energy bar rises

Changes in Supply

The supply of energy bars

Decreases if:	*Increases if:*
■ The price of a factor of production used to produce energy bars rises	■ The price of a factor of production used to produce energy bars falls
■ The price of a substitute in production rises	■ The price of a substitute in production falls
■ The price of a complement in production falls	■ The price of a complement in production rises
■ The expected future price of an energy bar rises	■ The expected future price of an energy bar falls
■ The number of suppliers of bars decreases	■ The number of suppliers of bars increases
■ A technology change decreases energy bar production	■ A technology change increases energy bar production
■ A natural event decreases energy bar production	■ A natural event increases energy bar production

FIGURE 3.6   A Change in the Quantity Supplied Versus a Change in Supply

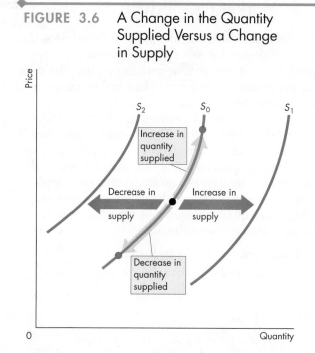

When the price of the good changes, there is a movement along the supply curve and *a change in the quantity supplied,* shown by the blue arrows on supply curve S_0. When any other influence on selling plans changes, there is a shift of the supply curve and a *change in supply.* An increase in supply shifts the supply curve rightward (from S_0 to S_1), and a decrease in supply shifts the supply curve leftward (from S_0 to S_2).

━━━ MyEconLab   animation ◆

REVIEW QUIZ

1 Define the quantity supplied of a good or service.
2 What is the law of supply and how do we illustrate it?
3 What does the supply curve tell us about the producer's minimum supply price?
4 List all the influences on selling plans, and for each influence, say whether it changes supply.
5 What happens to the quantity of cell phones supplied and the supply of cell phones if the price of a cell phone falls?

You can work these questions in Study Plan 3.3 and get instant feedback.

━━━━━━━━━ MyEconLab ◆

Now we're going to combine demand and supply and see how prices and quantities are determined.

Market Equilibrium

We have seen that when the price of a good rises, the quantity demanded *decreases* and the quantity supplied *increases*. We are now going to see how the price adjusts to coordinate buying plans and selling plans and achieve an equilibrium in the market.

An *equilibrium* is a situation in which opposing forces balance each other. Equilibrium in a market occurs when the price balances buying plans and selling plans. The **equilibrium price** is the price at which the quantity demanded equals the quantity supplied. The **equilibrium quantity** is the quantity bought and sold at the equilibrium price. A market moves towards its equilibrium because

- Price regulates buying and selling plans.
- Price adjusts when plans don't match.

Price as a Regulator

The price of a good regulates the quantities demanded and supplied. If the price is too high, the quantity supplied exceeds the quantity demanded. If the price is too low, the quantity demanded exceeds the quantity supplied. There is one price at which the quantity demanded equals the quantity supplied. Let's work out what that price is.

Figure 3.7 shows the market for energy bars. The table shows the demand schedule (from Fig. 3.1) and the supply schedule (from Fig. 3.4). If the price is 50¢ a bar, the quantity demanded is 22 million bars a week but no bars are supplied. There is a shortage of 22 million bars a week. The final column of the table shows this shortage. At a price of $1.00 a bar, there is still a shortage but only of 9 million bars a week.

If the price is $2.50 a bar, the quantity supplied is 15 million bars a week but the quantity demanded is only 5 million. There is a surplus of 10 million bars a week.

The one price at which there is neither a shortage nor a surplus is $1.50 a bar. At that price, the quantity demanded equals the quantity supplied: 10 million bars a week. The equilibrium price is $1.50 a bar, and the equilibrium quantity is 10 million bars a week.

Figure 3.7 shows that the demand curve and the supply curve intersect at the equilibrium price of $1.50 a bar. At each price *above* $1.50 a bar, there is a surplus of bars. For example, at $2.00 a bar, the surplus is 6 million bars a week, as shown by the

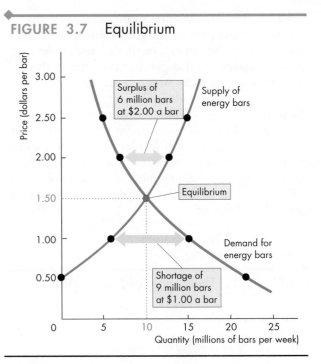

FIGURE 3.7   Equilibrium

Price (dollars per bar)	Quantity demanded	Quantity supplied	Shortage (–) or surplus (+)
	(millions of bars per week)		
0.50	22	0	–22
1.00	15	6	–9
1.50	10	10	0
2.00	7	13	+6
2.50	5	15	+10

The table lists the quantity demanded and the quantity supplied as well as the shortage or surplus of bars at each price. If the price is $1.00 a bar, 15 million bars a week are demanded and 6 million bars are supplied. There is a shortage of 9 million bars a week, and the price rises.

If the price is $2.00 a bar, 7 million bars a week are demanded and 13 million bars are supplied. There is a surplus of 6 million bars a week, and the price falls.

If the price is $1.50 a bar, 10 million bars a week are demanded and 10 million bars are supplied. There is neither a shortage nor a surplus, and the price does not change. The price at which the quantity demanded equals the quantity supplied is the equilibrium price, and 10 million bars a week is the equilibrium quantity.

MyEconLab   animation   ◆

blue arrow. At each price *below* $1.50 a bar, there is a shortage of bars. For example, at $1.00 a bar, the shortage is 9 million bars a week, as shown by the red arrow.

Price Adjustments

You've seen that if the price is below equilibrium, there is a shortage and that if the price is above equilibrium, there is a surplus. But can we count on the price to change and eliminate a shortage or a surplus? We can, because such price changes are beneficial to both buyers and sellers. Let's see why the price changes when there is a shortage or a surplus.

A Shortage Forces the Price Up Suppose the price of an energy bar is $1. Consumers plan to buy 15 million bars a week, and producers plan to sell 6 million bars a week. Consumers can't force producers to sell more than they plan, so the quantity that is actually offered for sale is 6 million bars a week. In this situation, powerful forces operate to increase the price and move it towards the equilibrium price. Some producers, noticing lines of unsatisfied consumers, raise the price. Some producers increase their output. As producers push the price up, the price rises towards its equilibrium. The rising price reduces the shortage because it decreases the quantity demanded and increases the quantity supplied. When the price has increased to the point at which there is no longer a shortage, the forces moving the price stop operating. The price comes to rest at its equilibrium.

A Surplus Forces the Price Down Suppose the price of a bar is $2. Producers plan to sell 13 million bars a week, and consumers plan to buy 7 million bars a week. Producers cannot force consumers to buy more than they plan, so the quantity that is actually bought is 7 million bars a week. In this situation, powerful forces operate to lower the price and move it towards the equilibrium price. Some producers, unable to sell the quantities of energy bars they planned to sell, cut their prices. In addition, some producers scale back production. As producers cut the price, the price falls towards its equilibrium. The falling price decreases the surplus because it increases the quantity demanded and decreases the quantity supplied. When the price has fallen to the point at which there is no longer a surplus, the forces moving the price stop operating. The price comes to rest at its equilibrium.

The Best Deal Available for Buyers and Sellers
When the price is below equilibrium, it is forced upward. Why don't buyers resist the increase and refuse to buy at the higher price? The answer is because they value the good more highly than its current price and they can't satisfy their demand at the current price. In some markets—for example, the markets that operate on eBay—the buyers might even be the ones who force the price up by offering to pay a higher price.

When the price is above equilibrium, it is bid downward. Why don't sellers resist this decrease and refuse to sell at the lower price? The answer is because their minimum supply price is below the current price and they cannot sell all they would like to at the current price. Sellers willingly lower the price to gain market share.

At the price at which the quantity demanded and the quantity supplied are equal, neither buyers nor sellers can do business at a better price. Buyers pay the highest price they are willing to pay for the last unit bought, and sellers receive the lowest price at which they are willing to supply the last unit sold.

When people freely make offers to buy and sell and when demanders try to buy at the lowest possible price and suppliers try to sell at the highest possible price, the price at which trade takes place is the equilibrium price—the price at which the quantity demanded equals the quantity supplied. The price coordinates the plans of buyers and sellers, and no one has an incentive to change it.

◢ REVIEW QUIZ

1 What is the equilibrium price of a good or service?
2 Over what range of prices does a shortage arise? What happens to the price when there is a shortage?
3 Over what range of prices does a surplus arise? What happens to the price when there is a surplus?
4 Why is the price at which the quantity demanded equals the quantity supplied the equilibrium price?
5 Why is the equilibrium price the best deal available for both buyers and sellers?

You can work these questions in Study Plan 3.4 and get instant feedback.

◆ Predicting Changes in Price and Quantity

The demand and supply model that we have just studied provides us with a powerful way of analyzing influences on prices and the quantities bought and sold. According to the model, a change in price stems from a change in demand, a change in supply, or a change in both demand and supply. Let's look first at the effects of a change in demand.

An Increase in Demand

If more people join health clubs, the demand for energy bars increases. The table in Fig. 3.8 shows the original and new demand schedules for energy bars as well as the supply schedule of energy bars.

The increase in demand creates a shortage at the original price and to eliminate the shortage, the price must rise.

Figure 3.8 shows what happens. The figure shows the original demand for and supply of energy bars. The original equilibrium price is $1.50 an energy bar, and the equilibrium quantity is 10 million energy bars a week. When demand increases, the demand curve shifts rightward. The equilibrium price rises to $2.50 an energy bar, and the quantity supplied increases to 15 million energy bars a week, as highlighted in the figure. There is an *increase in the quantity supplied* but *no change in supply*—a movement along, but no shift of, the supply curve.

A Decrease in Demand

We can reverse this change in demand. Start at a price of $2.50 a bar with 15 million energy bars a week being bought and sold, and then work out what happens if demand decreases to its original level. Such a decrease in demand might arise if people switch to energy gel (a substitute for energy bars). The decrease in demand shifts the demand curve leftward. The equilibrium price falls to $1.50 a bar, the quantity supplied decreases, and the equilibrium quantity decreases to 10 million bars a week.

We can now make our first two predictions:

1. When demand increases, the price rises and the quantity increases.
2. When demand decreases, the price falls and the quantity decreases.

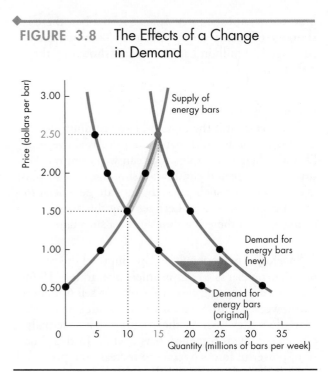

FIGURE 3.8   The Effects of a Change in Demand

Price (dollars per bar)	Quantity demanded (millions of bars per week)		Quantity supplied (millions of bars per week)
	Original	New	
0.50	22	32	0
1.00	15	25	6
1.50	**10**	20	**10**
2.00	7	17	13
2.50	5	15	15

Initially, the demand for energy bars is the blue demand curve. The equilibrium price is $1.50 a bar, and the equilibrium quantity is 10 million bars a week. When more health-conscious people do more exercise, the demand for energy bars increases and the demand curve shifts rightward to become the red curve.

At $1.50 a bar, there is now a shortage of 10 million bars a week. The price of a bar rises to a new equilibrium of $2.50. As the price rises to $2.50, the quantity supplied increases—shown by the blue arrow on the supply curve—to the new equilibrium quantity of 15 million bars a week. Following an increase in demand, the quantity supplied increases but supply does not change—the supply curve does not shift.

MyEconLab   animation ◆

Economics in Action
The Global Market for Crude Oil

The demand and supply model provides insights into all competitive markets. Here, we'll apply what you've learned about the effects of an increase in demand to the global market for crude oil.

Crude oil is like the life-blood of the global economy. It is used to fuel our cars, airplanes, trains, and buses, to generate electricity, and to produce a wide range of plastics. When the price of crude oil rises, the costs of transportation, power, and materials all increase.

In 2001, the price of a barrel of oil was $20 (using the value of money in 2010). In 2008, before the global financial crisis ended a long period of economic expansion, the price peaked at $127 a barrel.

While the price of oil was rising, the quantity of oil produced and consumed also increased. In 2001, the world produced 65 million barrels of oil a day. By 2008, that quantity was 72 million barrels.

Who or what has been raising the price of oil? Is it the action of greedy oil producers? Oil producers might be greedy, and some of them might be big enough to withhold supply and raise the price, but it wouldn't be in their self-interest to do so. The higher price would bring forth a greater quantity supplied from other producers and the profit of the producer limiting supply would fall.

Oil producers could try to cooperate and jointly withhold supply. The Organization of Petroleum Exporting Countries, OPEC, is such a group of producers. But OPEC doesn't control the *world* supply and its members' self-interest is to produce the quantities that give them the maximum attainable profit.

So even though the global oil market has some big players, they don't fix the price. Instead, the actions of thousands of buyers and sellers and the forces of demand and supply determine the price of oil.

So how have demand and supply changed?

Because both the price and the quantity have increased, the demand for oil must have increased. Supply might have changed, too, but here we'll suppose that supply has remained the same.

The global demand for oil has increased for one major reason: World income has increased. The increase has been particularly large in the emerging economies of Brazil, China, and India. Increased world income has increased the demand for oil-using goods such as electricity, gasoline, and plastics, which in turn has increased the demand for oil.

The figure illustrates the effects of the increase in demand on the global oil market. The supply of oil remained constant along supply curve S. The demand for oil in 2001 was D_{2001}, so in 2001 the price was $20 a barrel and the quantity was 65 million barrels per day. The demand for oil increased and by 2008 it had reached D_{2008}. The price of oil increased to $127 a barrel and the quantity increased to 72 million barrels a day. The increase in the quantity is an *increase in the quantity supplied*, not an increase in supply.

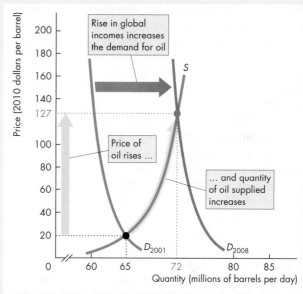

The Global Market for Crude Oil

An Increase in Supply

When Nestlé (the producer of PowerBar) and other energy bar producers switch to a new cost-saving technology, the supply of energy bars increases. Figure 3.9 shows the new supply schedule (the same one that was shown in Fig. 3.5). What are the new equilibrium price and quantity? The price falls to $1.00 a bar, and the quantity increases to 15 million bars a week. You can see why by looking at the quantities demanded and supplied at the old price of $1.50 a bar. The new quantity supplied at that price is 20 million bars a week, and there is a surplus. The price falls. Only when the price is $1.00 a bar does the quantity supplied equal the quantity demanded.

Figure 3.9 illustrates the effect of an increase in supply. It shows the demand curve for energy bars and the original and new supply curves. The initial equilibrium price is $1.50 a bar, and the equilibrium quantity is 10 million bars a week. When supply increases, the supply curve shifts rightward. The equilibrium price falls to $1.00 a bar, and the quantity demanded increases to 15 million bars a week, highlighted in the figure. There is an *increase in the quantity demanded* but *no change in demand*—a movement along, but no shift of, the demand curve.

A Decrease in Supply

Start out at a price of $1.00 a bar with 15 million bars a week being bought and sold. Then suppose that the cost of labour or raw materials rises and the supply of energy bars decreases. The decrease in supply shifts the supply curve leftward. The equilibrium price rises to $1.50 a bar, the quantity demanded decreases, and the equilibrium quantity decreases to 10 million bars a week.

We can now make two more predictions:

1. When supply increases, the price falls and the quantity increases.
2. When supply decreases, the price rises and the quantity decreases.

You've now seen what happens to the price and the quantity when either demand or supply changes while the other one remains unchanged. In real markets, both demand and supply can change together. When this happens, to predict the changes in price and quantity, we must combine the effects that you've just seen. That is your final task in this chapter.

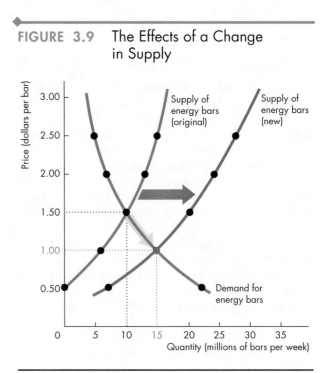

FIGURE 3.9   The Effects of a Change in Supply

Price (dollars per bar)	Quantity demanded (millions of bars per week)	Quantity supplied (millions of bars per week)	
		Original	New
0.50	22	0	7
1.00	15	6	15
1.50	**10**	**10**	20
2.00	7	13	25
2.50	5	15	27

Initially, the supply of energy bars is shown by the blue supply curve. The equilibrium price is $1.50 a bar, and the equilibrium quantity is 10 million bars a week. When the new cost-saving technology is adopted, the supply of energy bars increases and the supply curve shifts rightward to become the red curve.

At $1.50 a bar, there is now a surplus of 10 million bars a week. The price of an energy bar falls to a new equilibrium of $1.00 a bar. As the price falls to $1.00, the quantity demanded increases—shown by the blue arrow on the demand curve—to the new equilibrium quantity of 15 million bars a week. Following an increase in supply, the quantity demanded increases but demand does not change—the demand curve does not shift.

MyEconLab   animation

Economics in Action
The Market for Strawberries

California produces 85 percent of North America's strawberries and its crop, which starts to increase in March, is in top flight by April. During the winter months of January and February, Florida is the main strawberry producer.

In a normal year, the supplies from these two regions don't overlap much. As California's production steps up in March and April, Florida's production falls off. The result is a steady supply of strawberries and not much seasonal fluctuation in the price of strawberries.

But 2010 wasn't a normal year. Florida had exceptionally cold weather, which damaged the strawberry fields, lowered crop yields, and delayed the harvests. The result was unusually high strawberry prices.

With higher-than-normal prices, Florida farmers planted strawberry varieties that mature later than their normal crop and planned to harvest this fruit during the spring. Their plan worked perfectly and good growing conditions delivered a bumper crop by late March.

On the other side of the nation, while Florida was freezing, Southern California was drowning under unusually heavy rains. This wet weather put the strawberries to sleep and delayed their growth. But when the rains stopped and the temperature began to rise, California joined Florida with a super abundance of fruit.

With an abundance of strawberries, the price tumbled. Strawberry farmers in both regions couldn't hire enough labour to pick the super-sized crop, so some fruit was left in the fields to rot.

The figure explains what was happening in the market for strawberries.

Demand, shown by the demand curve, D, didn't change. In January, the failed Florida crop kept supply low and the supply curve was $S_{January}$. The price was high at $7.60 per kilogram and production was 2.50 million kilograms per day.

In April, the bumper crops in both regions increased supply to S_{April}. This increase in supply lowered the price to $2.40 per kilogram and increased the quantity demanded—a movement along the demand curve—to 2.75 million kilograms per day.

You can also see in the figure why farmers left fruit in the field to rot. At the January price of $7.60 a kilogram, farmers would have been paying top wages to hire the workers needed to pick fruit at the rate of 3 million kilograms per day. This is the quantity on supply curve S_{April} at $7.60 a pound.

But with the fall in price to $2.40 a kilogram, growers were not able to make a profit by picking more than 2.75 million kilograms.

For some growers the price wasn't high enough to cover the cost of hiring labour, so they opened their fields to anyone who wanted to pick their own strawberries for free.

The events we've described here in the market for strawberries illustrate the effects of a change in supply with no change in demand.

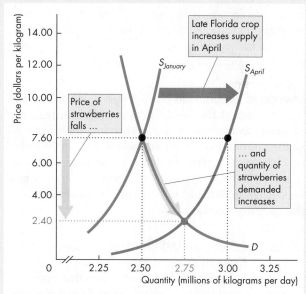

The Market for Strawberries

All the Possible Changes in Demand and Supply

Figure 3.10 brings together and summarizes the effects of all the possible changes in demand and supply. With what you've learned about the effects of a change in *either* demand or supply, you can predict what happens if *both* demand and supply change together. Let's begin by reviewing what you already know.

Change in Demand with No Change in Supply The first row of Fig. 3.10, parts (a), (b), and (c), summarizes the effects of a change in demand with no change in supply. In part (a), with no change in either demand or supply, neither the price nor the quantity changes. With an *increase* in demand and no change in supply in part (b), both the price and quantity increase. And with a *decrease* in demand and no change in supply in part (c), both the price and the quantity decrease.

Change in Supply with No Change in Demand The first column of Fig. 3.10, parts (a), (d), and (g), summarizes the effects of a change in supply with no change in demand. With an *increase* in supply and no change in demand in part (d), the price falls and quantity increases. And with a *decrease* in supply and no change in demand in part (g), the price rises and the quantity decreases.

Increase in Both Demand and Supply You've seen that an increase in demand raises the price and increases the quantity. And you've seen that an increase in supply lowers the price and increases the quantity. Fig. 3.10(e) combines these two changes. Because either an increase in demand or an increase in supply increases the quantity, the quantity also increases when both demand and supply increase. But the effect on the price is uncertain. An increase in demand raises the price and an increase in supply lowers the price, so we can't say whether the price will rise or fall when both demand and supply increase. We need to know the magnitudes of the changes in demand and supply to predict the effects on price. In the example in Fig. 3.10(e), the price does not change. But notice that if demand increases by slightly more than the amount shown in the figure, the price will rise. And if supply increases by slightly more than the amount shown in the figure, the price will fall.

Decrease in Both Demand and Supply Figure 3.10(i) shows the case in which demand and supply *both decrease*. For the same reasons as those we've just reviewed, when both demand and supply decrease, the quantity decreases, and again the direction of the price change is uncertain.

Decrease in Demand and Increase in Supply You've seen that a decrease in demand lowers the price and decreases the quantity. And you've seen that an increase in supply lowers the price and increases the quantity. Fig. 3.10(f) combines these two changes. Both the decrease in demand and the increase in supply lower the price, so the price falls. But a decrease in demand decreases the quantity and an increase in supply increases the quantity, so we can't predict the direction in which the quantity will change unless we know the magnitudes of the changes in demand and supply. In the example in Fig. 3.10(f), the quantity does not change. But notice that if demand decreases by slightly more than the amount shown in the figure, the quantity will decrease; if supply increases by slightly more than the amount shown in the figure, the quantity will increase.

Increase in Demand and Decrease in Supply Figure 3.10(h) shows the case in which demand increases and supply decreases. Now, the price rises, and again the direction of the quantity change is uncertain.

REVIEW QUIZ

What is the effect on the price and quantity of MP3 players (such as the iPod) if

1 The price of a PC falls or the price of an MP3 download rises? (Draw the diagrams!)

2 More firms produce MP3 players or electronics workers' wages rise? (Draw the diagrams!)

3 Any two of the events in questions 1 and 2 occur together? (Draw the diagrams!)

You can work these questions in Study Plan 3.5 and get instant feedback.
——————————————— MyEconLab ◆

◆ To complete your study of demand and supply, take a look at *Reading Between the Lines* on pp. 74–75, which explains why the price of coffee increased in 2010. Try to get into the habit of using the demand and supply model to understand the movements in prices in your everyday life.

FIGURE 3.10   The Effects of All the Possible Changes in Demand and Supply

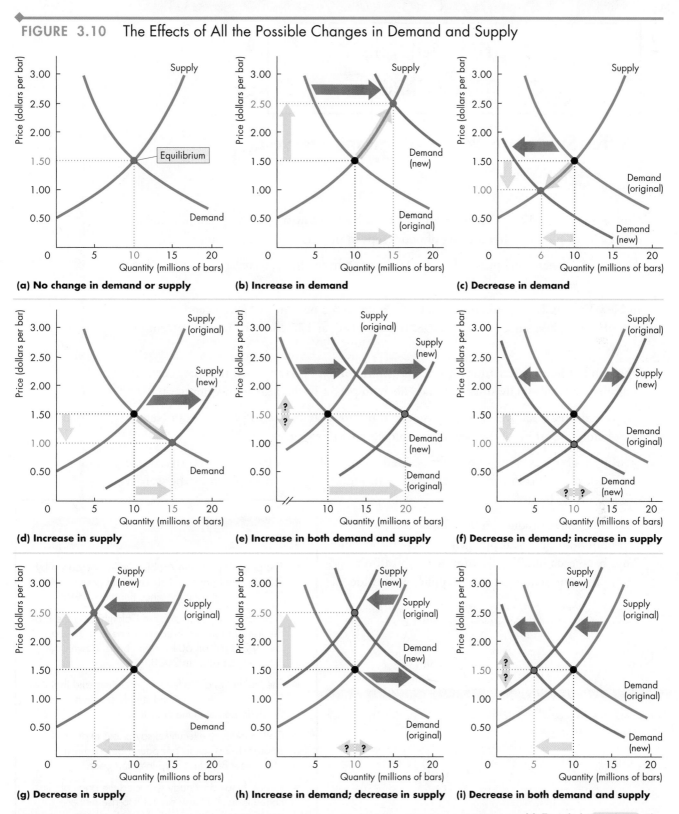

(a) **No change in demand or supply**

(b) **Increase in demand**

(c) **Decrease in demand**

(d) **Increase in supply**

(e) **Increase in both demand and supply**

(f) **Decrease in demand; increase in supply**

(g) **Decrease in supply**

(h) **Increase in demand; decrease in supply**

(i) **Decrease in both demand and supply**

MyEconLab   animation   ◆

Demand and Supply: The Price of Coffee

Coffee Surges on Poor Colombian Harvests

FT.com
July 30, 2010

Coffee prices hit a 12-year high on Friday on the back of low supplies of premium Arabica coffee from Colombia after a string of poor crops in the Latin American country.

The strong fundamental picture has also encouraged hedge funds to reverse their previous bearish views on coffee prices.

In New York, ICE September Arabica coffee jumped 3.2 percent to 178.75 cents per pound, the highest since February 1998. It traded later at 177.25 cents, up 6.8 percent on the week.

The London-based International Coffee Organization on Friday warned that the "current tight demand and supply situation" was "likely to persist in the near to medium term."

Coffee industry executives believe prices could rise towards 200 cents per pound in New York before the arrival of the new Brazilian crop later this year.

"Until October it is going to be tight on high quality coffee," said a senior executive at one of Europe's largest coffee roasters. He said: "The industry has been surprised by the scarcity of high quality beans."

Colombia coffee production, key for supplies of premium beans, last year plunged to a 33-year low of 7.8m bags, each of 60kg, down nearly a third from 11.1m bags in 2008, tightening supplies worldwide. ...

Excerpted from "Coffee Surges on Poor Colombian Harvests" by Javier Blas. *Financial Times*, July 30, 2010. Reprinted with permission.

ESSENCE OF THE STORY

- The price of premium Arabica coffee increased by 3.2 percent to almost 180 cents per pound in July 2010, the highest price since February 1998.

- A sequence of poor crops in Colombia cut the production of premium Arabica coffee to a 33-year low of 7.8 million 60-kilogram bags, down from 11.1 million bags in 2008.

- The International Coffee Organization said that the "current tight demand and supply situation" was "likely to persist in the near to medium term."

- Coffee industry executives say prices might approach 200 cents per pound before the arrival of the new Brazilian crop later this year.

- Hedge funds previously expected the price of coffee to fall but now expect it to rise further.

ECONOMIC ANALYSIS

- This news article reports two sources of changes in supply and demand that changed the price of coffee.

- The first source of change is the sequence of poor harvests in Colombia. These events decreased the world supply of Arabica coffee. (Arabica is the type that Starbucks uses.)

- Before the reported events, the world production of Arabica was 120 million bags per year and its price was 174 cents per pound.

- The decrease in the Colombian harvest decreased world production to about 116 million bags, which is about 3 percent of world production.

- Figure 1 shows the situation before the poor Colombia harvests and the effects of those poor harvests. The demand curve is D and initially, the supply curve was S_0. The market equilibrium is at 120 million bags per year and a price of 174 cents per pound.

- The poor Colombian harvests decreased supply and the supply curve shifted leftward to S_1. The price increased to 180 cents per pound and the quantity decreased to 116 million bags.

- The second source of change influenced both supply and demand. It is a change in the expected future price of coffee.

- The hedge funds referred to in the news article are speculators that try to profit from buying at a low price and selling at a high price.

- With the supply of coffee expected to remain low, the price was expected to rise further—a rise in the expected future price of coffee.

- When the expected future price of coffee rises, some people want to buy more coffee (so they can sell it later)—an increase in the demand today. And some people offer less coffee for sale (so they can sell it later for a higher price)—a decrease in the supply today.

- Figure 2 shows the effects of these changes in the demand and supply today.

- Demand increases and the demand curve shifts from D_0 to D_1. Supply decreases and the supply curve shifts from S_1 to S_2.

- Because demand increases and supply decreases, the price rises. In this example, it rises to 200 cents per pound.

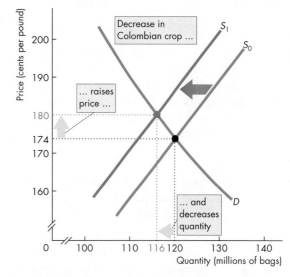

Figure 1 The Effects of the Colombian Crop

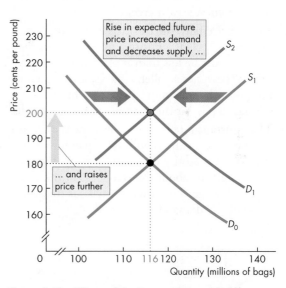

Figure 2 The Effects of the Expected Future Price

- Also, because demand increases and supply decreases, the change in the equilibrium quantity can go in either direction.

- In this example, the increase in demand equals the decrease in supply, so the equilibrium quantity remains constant at 116 million bags per year.

◆ MATHEMATICAL NOTE

Demand, Supply, and Equilibrium

Demand Curve

The law of demand says that as the price of a good or service falls, the quantity demanded of that good or service increases. We can illustrate the law of demand by drawing a graph of the demand curve or writing down an equation. When the demand curve is a straight line, the following equation describes it:

$$P = a - bQ_D,$$

where P is the price and Q_D is the quantity demanded. The a and b are positive constants.

The demand equation tells us three things:

1. The price at which no one is willing to buy the good (Q_D is zero). That is, if the price is a, then the quantity demanded is zero. You can see the price a in Fig. 1. It is the price at which the demand curve hits the y-axis—what we call the demand curve's "y-intercept."

2. As the price falls, the quantity demanded increases. If Q_D is a positive number, then the price P must be less than a. As Q_D gets larger, the price P becomes smaller. That is, as the quantity increases, the maximum price that buyers are willing to pay for the last unit of the good falls.

3. The constant b tells us how fast the maximum price that someone is willing to pay for the good falls as the quantity increases. That is, the constant b tells us about the steepness of the demand curve. The equation tells us that the slope of the demand curve is $-b$.

Supply Curve

The law of supply says that as the price of a good or service rises, the quantity supplied of that good or service increases. We can illustrate the law of supply by drawing a graph of the supply curve or writing down an equation. When the supply curve is a straight line, the following equation describes it:

$$P = c + dQ_S,$$

where P is the price and Q_S is the quantity supplied. The c and d are positive constants.

The supply equation tells us three things:

1. The price at which sellers are not willing to supply the good (Q_S is zero). That is, if the price is c, then no one is willing to sell the good. You can see the price c in Fig. 2. It is the price at which the supply curve hits the y-axis—what we call the supply curve's "y-intercept."

2. As the price rises, the quantity supplied increases. If Q_S is a positive number, then the price P must be greater than c. As Q_S increases, the price P becomes larger. That is, as the quantity increases, the minimum price that sellers are willing to accept for the last unit rises.

3. The constant d tells us how fast the minimum price at which someone is willing to sell the good rises as the quantity increases. That is, the constant d tells us about the steepness of the supply curve. The equation tells us that the slope of the supply curve is d.

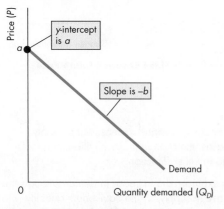

Figure 1 Demand curve

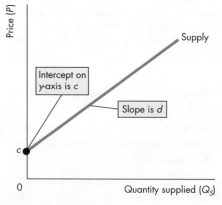

Figure 2 Supply curve

Market Equilibrium

Demand and supply determine market equilibrium. Figure 3 shows the equilibrium price (P^*) and equilibrium quantity (Q^*) at the intersection of the demand curve and the supply curve.

We can use the equations to find the equilibrium price and equilibrium quantity. The price of a good adjusts until the quantity demanded Q_D equals the quantity supplied Q_S. So at the equilibrium price (P^*) and equilibrium quantity (Q^*),

$$Q_D = Q_S = Q^*.$$

To find the equilibrium price and equilibrium quantity, substitute Q^* for Q_D in the demand equation and Q^* for Q_S in the supply equation. Then the price is the equilibrium price (P^*), which gives

$$P^* = a - bQ^*$$
$$P^* = c + dQ^*.$$

Notice that

$$a - bQ^* = c + dQ^*.$$

Now solve for Q^*:

$$a - c = bQ^* + dQ^*$$
$$a - c = (b + d)Q^*$$
$$Q^* = \frac{a - c}{b + d}.$$

To find the equilibrium price, (P^*), substitute for Q^* in either the demand equation or the supply equation.

Using the demand equation, we have

$$P^* = a - b\left(\frac{a - c}{b + d}\right)$$
$$P^* = \frac{a(b + d) - b(a - c)}{b + d}$$
$$P^* = \frac{ad + bc}{b + d}.$$

Alternatively, using the supply equation, we have

$$P^* = c + d\left(\frac{a - c}{b + d}\right)$$
$$P^* = \frac{c(b + d) + d(a - c)}{b + d}$$
$$P^* = \frac{ad + bc}{b + d}.$$

An Example

The demand for ice cream cones is

$$P = 800 - 2Q_D.$$

The supply of ice cream cones is

$$P = 200 + 1Q_S.$$

The price of a cone is expressed in cents, and the quantities are expressed in cones per day.

To find the equilibrium price (P^*) and equilibrium quantity (Q^*), substitute Q^* for Q_D and Q_S and P^* for P. That is,

$$P^* = 800 - 2Q^*$$
$$P^* = 200 + 1Q^*.$$

Now solve for Q^*:

$$800 - 2Q^* = 200 + 1Q^*$$
$$600 = 3Q^*$$
$$Q^* = 200.$$

And

$$P^* = 800 - 2(200)$$
$$= 400.$$

The equilibrium price is $4 a cone, and the equilibrium quantity is 200 cones per day.

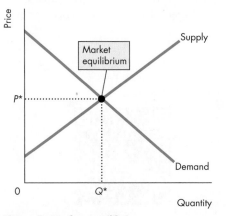

Figure 3 Market equilibrium

SUMMARY

Key Points

Markets and Prices (p. 56)

- A competitive market is one that has so many buyers and sellers that no single buyer or seller can influence the price.
- Opportunity cost is a relative price.
- Demand and supply determine relative prices.

Working Problem 1 will give you a better understanding of markets and prices.

Demand (pp. 57–61)

- Demand is the relationship between the quantity demanded of a good and its price when all other influences on buying plans remain the same.
- The higher the price of a good, other things remaining the same, the smaller is the quantity demanded—the law of demand.
- Demand depends on the prices of related goods (substitutes and complements), expected future prices, income, expected future income and credit, the population, and preferences.

Working Problems 2 to 5 will give you a better understanding of demand.

Supply (pp. 62–65)

- Supply is the relationship between the quantity supplied of a good and its price when all other influences on selling plans remain the same.
- The higher the price of a good, other things remaining the same, the greater is the quantity supplied—the law of supply.

- Supply depends on the prices of factors of production used to produce a good, the prices of related goods produced, expected future prices, the number of suppliers, technology, and the state of nature.

Working Problems 6 to 9 will give you a better understanding of supply.

Market Equilibrium (pp. 66–67)

- At the equilibrium price, the quantity demanded equals the quantity supplied.
- At any price above the equilibrium price, there is a surplus and the price falls.
- At any price below the equilibrium price, there is a shortage and the price rises.

Working Problems 10 and 11 will give you a better understanding of market equilibrium.

Predicting Changes in Price and Quantity (pp. 68–73)

- An increase in demand brings a rise in the price and an increase in the quantity supplied. A decrease in demand brings a fall in the price and a decrease in the quantity supplied.
- An increase in supply brings a fall in the price and an increase in the quantity demanded. A decrease in supply brings a rise in the price and a decrease in the quantity demanded.
- An increase in demand and an increase in supply bring an increased quantity but an uncertain price change. An increase in demand and a decrease in supply bring a higher price but an uncertain change in quantity.

Working Problems 12 to 14 will give you a better understanding of predicting changes in price and quantity.

Key Terms

Change in demand, 58
Change in supply, 63
Change in the quantity demanded, 61
Change in the quantity supplied, 64
Competitive market, 56
Complement, 59
Demand, 57
Demand curve, 58
Equilibrium price, 66
Equilibrium quantity, 66

Inferior good, 60
Law of demand, 57
Law of supply, 62
Money price, 56
Normal good, 60
Quantity demanded, 57
Quantity supplied, 62
Relative price, 56
Substitute, 59
Supply, 62
Supply curve, 62

SCAN THIS

STUDY PLAN PROBLEMS AND APPLICATIONS

MyEconLab ◆ You can work Problems 1 to 17 in Chapter 3 Study Plan and get instant feedback.

Markets and Prices (Study Plan 3.1)

1. William Gregg owned a mill in South Carolina. In December 1862, he placed a notice in the *Edgehill Advertiser* announcing his willingness to exchange cloth for food and other items. Here is an extract:

   1 yard of cloth for 1 pound of bacon

   2 yards of cloth for 1 pound of butter

   4 yards of cloth for 1 pound of wool

   8 yards of cloth for 1 bushel of salt

   a. What is the relative price of butter in terms of wool?

   b. If the money price of bacon was 20¢ a pound, what do you predict was the money price of butter?

   c. If the money price of bacon was 20¢ a pound and the money price of salt was $2.00 a bushel, do you think anyone would accept Mr. Gregg's offer of cloth for salt?

Demand (Study Plan 3.2)

2. The price of food increased during the past year.

   a. Explain why the law of demand applies to food just as it does to all other goods and services.

   b. Explain how the substitution effect influences food purchases and provide some examples of substitutions that people might make when the price of food rises and other things remain the same.

   c. Explain how the income effect influences food purchases and provide some examples of the income effect that might occur when the price of food rises and other things remain the same.

3. Place the following goods and services into pairs of likely substitutes and pairs of likely complements. (You may use an item in more than one pair.) The goods and services are coal, oil, natural gas, wheat, corn, rye, pasta, pizza, sausage, skateboard, roller blades, video game, laptop, iPod, cell phone, text message, e-mail, phone call, voice mail.

4. During 2010, the average income in China increased by 10 percent. Compared to 2009, how do you expect the following would change:

   a. The demand for beef. Explain your answer.

   b. The demand for rice. Explain your answer.

5. In May 2010, the price of gasoline was 99.6 cents per litre. By May 2011, the price had increased to 132 cents per litre. Assume that there were no changes in average income, population, or any other influence on buying plans. Explain how the rise in the price of gasoline would affect

   a. The demand for gasoline.

   b. The quantity of gasoline demanded.

Supply (Study Plan 3.3)

6. From May 2010 to February 2011, the price of corn increased by 100 percent and some barley growers on the Prairies stopped planting barley and started to grow corn.

   a. Does this fact illustrate the law of demand or the law of supply? Explain your answer.

   b. Why would a barley farmer grow corn?

Use the following information to work Problems 7 to 9.

Dairies make low-fat milk from full-cream milk. In making low-fat milk, the dairies produce cream, which is made into ice cream. In the market for low-fat milk, the following events occur one at a time:

   (i)   The wage rate of dairy workers rises.
   (ii) The price of cream rises.
   (iii) The price of low-fat milk rises.
   (iv) With the period of low rainfall extending, dairies raise their expected price of low-fat milk next year.
   (v)   With advice from health-care experts, dairy farmers decide to switch from producing full-cream milk to growing vegetables.
   (vi) A new technology lowers the cost of producing ice cream.

7. Explain the effect of each event on the supply of low-fat milk.

8. Use a graph to illustrate the effect of each event.

9. Does any event (or events) illustrate the law of supply?

Market Equilibrium (Study Plan 3.4)

10. "As more people buy computers, the demand for Internet service increases and the price of Internet service decreases. The fall in the price of Internet service decreases the supply of Internet service." Explain what is wrong with this statement.

11. The demand and supply schedules for gum are

Price (cents per pack)	Quantity demanded (millions of packs a week)	Quantity supplied (millions of packs a week)
20	180	60
40	140	100
60	100	140
80	60	180
100	20	220

   a. Draw a graph of the market for gum and mark in the equilibrium price and quantity.

   b. Suppose that the price of gum is 70¢ a pack. Describe the situation in the gum market and explain how the price adjusts.

   c. Suppose that the price of gum is 30¢ a pack. Describe the situation in the gum market and explain how the price adjusts.

Predicting Changes in Price and Quantity
(Study Plan 3.5)

12. The following events occur one at a time:
    (i)   The price of crude oil rises.
    (ii) The price of a car rises.
    (iii) All speed limits on highways are abolished.
    (iv) Robots cut car production costs.

    Which of these events will increase or decrease (state which occurs)
    a. The demand for gasoline?
    b. The supply of gasoline?
    c. The quantity of gasoline demanded?
    d. The quantity of gasoline supplied?

13. In Problem 11, a fire destroys some factories that produce gum and the quantity of gum supplied decreases by 40 million packs a week at each price.

    a. Explain what happens in the market for gum and draw a graph to illustrate the changes.

    b. If at the time the fire occurs there is an increase in the teenage population, which increases the quantity of gum demanded by 40 million packs a week at each price, what are the new equilibrium price and quantity of gum? Illustrate these changes on your graph.

14. **Tim Hortons' Risk**
    Tim Hortons has exploded to become a dominant player among quick-serve restaurants. In 2001, it took the risk by switching to centralized production of baked goods, which lowered its labour costs and increased its sales volume.
    Source: *Financial Post*, August 12, 2010
    Draw a graph to show the effect of lower labour costs on the price of Tims' baked goods and the quantity sold.

Economics in the News (Study Plan 3.EN)

15. **Don't Look for Cheap Food Anytime Soon**
    Global food prices probably will rise in the first half of this century because of an expanding population and higher incomes and slower crop-yield growth.
    Source: *National Post*, March 9, 2011
    Explain the effect on food prices of
    a. Expanding population and rising incomes.
    b. Slower crop-yield growth.

16. **Frigid Florida Winter Is Bad News for Tomato Lovers**
    An unusually cold January in Florida destroyed entire fields of tomatoes and forced many farmers to delay their harvest. Florida's growers are shipping only a quarter of their usual 2.5 million kilograms a week. The price has risen from $13.00 for a 12.5-kilogram box a year ago to $60 now.
    Source: *USA Today*, March 3, 2010
    a. Make a graph to illustrate the market for tomatoes in January 2009 and January 2010.
    b. On the graph, show how the events in the news clip influence the market for tomatoes.
    c. Why is the news "bad for tomato lovers"?

17. **Gas Prices Jump Across Canada amid Libya Unrest** Oil prices shot up to US$103 a barrel as traders were forced to question how bad the Libyan situation would get and whether the instability could spread to other oil-rich nations. In Toronto, the gas price jumped 3.7 percent to 121.4 cents per litre and after it rose 2 cents a litre earlier in the week.
    Source: CTV News, June 6, 2011
    a. Does demand for or the supply of gasoline or both change when the price of oil soars?
    b. Use a graph to illustrate what happens to the equilibrium price of gasoline and the equilibrium quantity of gasoline bought when the price of oil soars.

ADDITIONAL PROBLEMS AND APPLICATIONS

MyEconLab ◆ You can work these problems in MyEconLab if assigned by your instructor.

Markets and Prices

18. What features of the world market for crude oil make it a competitive market?

19. The money price of a textbook is $90 and the money price of the Wii game *Super Mario Galaxy* is $45.
    a. What is the opportunity cost of a textbook in terms of the Wii game?
    b. What is the relative price of the Wii game in terms of textbooks?

Demand

20. The price of gasoline has increased during the past year.
    a. Explain why the law of demand applies to gasoline just as it does to all other goods and services.
    b. Explain how the substitution effect influences gasoline purchases and provide some examples of substitutions that people might make when the price of gasoline rises and other things remain the same.
    c. Explain how the income effect influences gasoline purchases and provide some examples of the income effects that might occur when the price of gasoline rises and other things remain the same.

21. Think about the demand for the three game consoles: Xbox, PS3, and Wii. Explain the effect of the following events on the demand for Xbox games and the quantity of Xbox games demanded, other things remaining the same.
    a. The price of an Xbox falls.
    b. The prices of a PS3 and a Wii fall.
    c. The number of people writing and producing Xbox games increases.
    d. Consumers' incomes increase.
    e. Programmers who write code for Xbox games become more costly to hire.
    f. The expected future price of an Xbox game falls.
    g. A new game console that is a close substitute for Xbox comes onto the market.

Supply

22. Classify the following pairs of goods and services as substitutes in production, complements in production, or neither.
    a. Bottled water and health club memberships
    b. French fries and baked potatoes
    c. Leather purses and leather shoes
    d. Hybrids and SUVs
    e. Diet coke and regular coke

23. As the global financial crisis hit, the prices of homes fell across the United States and the number of homes offered for sale decreased.
    a. Does this fact illustrate the law of demand or the law of supply? Explain your answer.
    b. Why would home owners decide not to sell?

24. **G.M. Cuts Production for Quarter**
    General Motors cut its fourth-quarter production schedule by 10 percent because Ford Motor, Chrysler, and Toyota sales declined in August.
    Source: *The New York Times*, September 5, 2007
    Explain whether this news clip illustrates a change in the supply of cars or a change in the quantity supplied of cars.

Market Equilibrium

Use the following figure to work Problems 25 and 26.

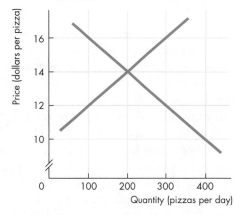

25. a. Label the curves. Which curve shows the willingness to pay for a pizza?
    b. If the price of a pizza is $16, is there a shortage or a surplus and does the price rise or fall?

c. Sellers want to receive the highest possible price, so why would they be willing to accept less than $16 a pizza?

26. a. If the price of a pizza is $12, is there a shortage or a surplus and does the price rise or fall?

b. Buyers want to pay the lowest possible price, so why would they be willing to pay more than $12 for a pizza?

27. The demand and supply schedules for potato chips are

Price (cents per bag)	Quantity demanded	Quantity supplied
	(millions of bags per week)	
50	160	130
60	150	140
70	140	150
80	130	160
90	120	170
100	110	180

a. Draw a graph of the potato chip market and mark in the equilibrium price and quantity.

b. If the price is 60¢ a bag, is there a shortage or a surplus, and how does the price adjust?

Predicting Changes in Price and Quantity

28. In Problem 27, a new dip increases the quantity of potato chips that people want to buy by 30 million bags per week at each price.

a. How does the demand and/or supply of chips change?

b. How does the price and quantity of chips change?

29. In Problem 27, if a virus destroys potato crops and the quantity of potato chips produced decreases by 40 million bags a week at each price, how does the supply of chips change?

30. If the virus in Problem 29 hits just as the new dip in Problem 28 comes onto the market, how does the price and quantity of chips change?

31. The world's largest instant-noodle maker said soaring wheat prices have forced noodle prices up. Despite the rising price, Asia's middle class, with their increasing incomes, are eating more wheat products as they try to diversify their diets from rice and save time with processed foods.

a. Explain the effect of soaring wheat prices on the market for noodles, other things remaining the same.

b. Explain the effect of the middle class switching its diet from rice to noodles on the market for noodles, other things remaining the same.

c. Explain the combined effect of soaring wheat prices and rising incomes on the equilibrium price and quantity of noodles.

d. As the middle class in Asia continues to grow, how might the price of rice change?

Economics in the News

32. After you have studied *Reading Between the Lines* on pp. 74–75, answer the following questions.

a. What happened to the price of coffee in 2010?

b. What substitutions do you expect might have been made to decrease the quantity of coffee demanded?

c. What influenced the demand for coffee in 2010 and what influenced the quantity of coffee demanded?

d. What influenced the supply of coffee during 2010 and how did the supply of coffee change?

e. How did the combination of the factors you have noted in parts (c) and (d) influence the price and quantity of coffee?

f. Was the change in the quantity of coffee a change in the quantity demanded or a change in the quantity supplied?

33. **Strawberry Prices Drop as Late Harvest Hits Market**
Shoppers bought strawberries in March for $1.25 a pound rather than the $3.49 a pound they paid last year. With the price so low, some growers plowed over their strawberry plants to make way for spring melons; others froze their harvests and sold them to juice and jam makers.
Source: *USA Today*, April 5, 2010

a. Explain how the market for strawberries would have changed if growers had not plowed in their plants but offered locals "you pick for free."

b. Describe the changes in demand and supply in the market for strawberry jam.

34. **"Popcorn Movie" Experience Gets Pricier**
Cinemas are raising the price of popcorn. Demand for field corn, which is used for animal feed, corn syrup, and ethanol, has increased and its price has exploded. That's caused some farmers to shift from growing popcorn to easier-to-grow field corn.
Source: *USA Today*, May 24, 2008

Explain and illustrate graphically the events described in the news clip in the market for

a. Popcorn

b. Movie tickets

The Amazing Market

PART TWO

The chapter that you've just studied explains how markets work. The market is an amazing instrument. It enables people who have never met and who know nothing about each other to interact and do business. It also enables us to allocate our scarce resources to the uses that we value most highly. Markets can be very simple or highly organized. Markets are ancient and they are modern.

A simple and ancient market is one that the American historian Daniel J. Boorstin describes in *The Discoverers* (p. 161). In the late fourteenth century,

> *The Muslim caravans that went southward from Morocco across the Atlas Mountains arrived after twenty days at the shores of the Senegal River. There the Moroccan traders laid out separate piles of salt, of beads from Ceutan coral, and cheap manufactured goods. Then they retreated out of sight. The local tribesmen, who lived in the strip mines where they dug their gold, came to the shore and put a heap of gold beside each pile of Moroccan goods. Then they, in turn, went out of view, leaving the Moroccan traders either to take the gold offered for a particular pile or to reduce the pile of their merchandise to suit the offered price in gold. Once again the Moroccan traders withdrew, and the process went on. By this system of commercial etiquette, the Moroccans collected their gold.*

An organized and modern market is an auction at which the U.S. government sells rights to cell phone companies for the use of the airwaves.

Everything and anything that can be exchanged is traded in markets to the benefit of both buyers and sellers.

Alfred Marshall (1842–1924) *grew up in an England that was being transformed by the railroad and by the expansion of manufacturing. Mary Paley was one of Marshall's students at Cambridge, and when Alfred and Mary married in 1877, celibacy rules barred Alfred from continuing to teach at Cambridge. By 1884, with more liberal rules, the Marshalls returned to Cambridge, where Alfred became Professor of Political Economy.*

Many economists had a hand in refining the demand and supply model, but the first thorough and complete statement of the model as we know it today was set out by Alfred Marshall, with the help of Mary Paley Marshall. Published in 1890, this monumental treatise, The Principles of Economics, *became the textbook on economics on both sides of the Atlantic for almost half a century.*

The forces to be dealt with are ... so numerous, that it is best to take a few at a time .... Thus we begin by isolating the primary relations of supply, demand, and price.

ALFRED MARSHALL
The Principles of Economics

What sparked your interest in economics?

I was studying mathematics and computer science, but I felt that the subjects were not as relevant as I would like.

I discovered economics through a research assistantship with a professor who was working on auctions. I had a summer job working for a firm that sold computers to the government through auctions. Eventually my professor, Bob Marshall, wrote two articles on the topic and testified before Congress to help reform the system for government procurement of computers. That really inspired me and showed me the power of economic ideas to change the world and to make things work more efficiently.

This original inspiration has remained and continues to drive much of your research. Can you explain how economists study auctions?

The study of the design of markets and auction-based marketplaces requires you to use all of the different tools that economics offers.

An auction is a well-defined game. You can write down the rules of the game and a formal theoretical model does a great job capturing the real problem that the players face. And theories do an excellent job predicting behaviour.

Buyers have a valuation for an object that is private information. They do not know the valuations of other bidders, and sometimes they don't even know their own valuation. For example, if they're buying oil rights, there may be uncertainty about how much oil there is in the ground. In that case, information about the amount of oil available is dispersed among the bidders, because each bidder has done their own survey. The bidders face a strategic problem of bidding, and they face an informational problem of trying to draw inferences about how valuable the object will be if they win.

Bidders need to recognize that their bid only matters when they win the auction, and they only win when they bid the most. The knowledge that they were the most optimistic of all the competitors should cause them to revise their beliefs.

From the seller's perspective, there are choices about how an auction is designed—auctions can use sealed bidding, where the seller receives bids and then opens them at a pre-determined time, or alternatively bidding may be interactive, where each bidder has an

opportunity to outbid the previous high bidder. There are also different ways to use bids received by the auctioneer to determine the price. The seller may consider revenue, though governments are often most concerned about efficient allocation.

Both revenue and efficiency are affected by auction design. One key question the seller must con-

> **Both revenue and efficiency are affected by auction design.**

sider is how the design will affect the participation of bidders, as this will determine how competitive bidding will be as well as whether the object gets to the potential bidder who values the item the most.

What must the designer of an auction-based marketplace take into account?

An example of an auction-based marketplace is eBay, where the market designer sets the rules for buyers and sellers to interact.

SUSAN ATHEY is Professor of Economics at Harvard University. Born in 1970 in Boston and growing up in Rockville, Maryland, she completed high school in three years, wrapped up three majors—in economics, mathematics, and computer science—at Duke University at 20, completed her Ph.D. at Stanford University at 24, and was voted tenure at MIT and Stanford at 29. After teaching at MIT for six years and Stanford for five years, she moved to Harvard in 2006. Among her many honours and awards, the most prestigious is the John Bates Clark Medal given to the best economist under 40. She is the first woman to receive this award.

Professor Athey's research is broad both in scope and style. A government that wants to auction natural resources will turn to her fundamental discoveries (and possibly consult with her) before deciding how to organize the auction. An economist who wants to test a theory using a large data set will use her work on statistics and econometrics.

Michael Parkin and Robin Bade talked with Susan Athey about her research, the progress that economists have made in understanding and designing markets, and her advice to students.

When you design an auction-based marketplace, you have a whole new set of concerns. The buyers and sellers themselves are independent agents, each acting in their own interest. The design is a two-step process: You need to design an auction that is going to achieve an efficient allocation; and you need to design both the auction and the overall structure of the marketplace to attract participation.

In the case of eBay, the platform itself chooses the possible auction formats: Auctions take place over time and bidders have the opportunity to outbid the standing high bidder during that time. The platform also allows sellers to use the "buy it now" option. The platform also makes certain tools and services available, such as the ability to search for items in various ways, track auctions, provide feedback, and monitor reputation. The sellers can select the level of the reserve price, whether they want to have a secret reserve price, how long the auction will last, whether to use "buy it now," what time of day the auction closes, how much information to provide, how many

pictures they post.

These are all factors that impact participation of bidders and the revenue the seller will receive. The success of the platform hinges on both buyers and sellers choosing to participate.

Does auction theory enable us to predict the differences in the outcomes of an open ascending-bid English auction and a sealed-bid auction?

Sure. In some of my research, I compared open ascending auctions and pay-your-bid, sealed-bid auctions. I showed

> ... sealed-bid auctions can do a better job of deterring collusion ... [and] generate larger revenue.

how the choice of auction format can make a big difference when you have small bidders bidding against larger, stronger bidders who usually (but not always) have higher valuations.

In an open ascending auction, it is hard for a small weaker bidder to ever win, because a stronger bidder can see their bids, respond to them, and outbid them.

But in a pay-your-bid, sealed-bid auction, bidders shade their bids—they bid less than their value, assuring themselves of some profit if they win—and a large bidder doesn't have the opportunity to see and respond to an unusually high bid from a weak bidder. Strong bidders realize that their competition is weak, and they shade their bids a lot—they bid a lot less than their value. That gives a small bidder the opportunity to be aggressive and outbid a larger bidder, even if it has a lower value. So what that does is encourage entry of small bidders. I found empirically that this entry effect was important and it helps sealed-bid auctions generate larger revenue than open ascending-bid auctions.

Does a sealed-bid auction always generate more revenue, other things equal, than an open ascending-bid auction?

Only if you have asymmetric bidders—strong large bidders and weaker small bidders—and even then the effect is ambiguous. It's an empirical question, but it tends to be true. We also showed that sealed-bid auctions can do a better job of deterring collusion. There are theoretical reasons to suggest that sealed bid auctions are more difficult to collude at than open

85

ascending auctions, since at open ascending auctions, bidders can detect an opponent who is bidding higher than an agreement specifies and then respond to that. We found empirically in U.S. Forest Service timber auctions that the gap between sealed-bid auctions and ascending auctions was even greater than what a competitive model would predict, suggesting that some collusion may be at work.

What is the connection between auctions and the supply and demand model?

The basic laws of supply and demand can be seen in evidence in a market like eBay. The more sellers that are selling similar products, the lower the prices they can expect to achieve. Similarly the more buyers there are demanding those objects, the higher the prices the sellers can achieve.

> The basic laws of supply and demand can be seen in evidence in a market like eBay.

An important thing for an auction marketplace is to attract a good balance of buyers and sellers so that both the buyers and the sellers find it more profitable to transact in that marketplace rather than using some other mechanism. From a seller's perspective, the more bidders there are on the platform, the greater the demand and the higher the prices. And from the buyer's perspective, the more sellers there are on the platform, the greater the supply and the lower the prices.

Can we think of this thought experiment you just described as discovering demand and supply curves?

Exactly. When you study supply and demand curves, you wave your hands about how the prices actually get set. In different kinds of market settings, the actual mechanisms for setting prices are different. One way of setting prices is through auctions. But we tend to use auctions in settings where there are unique objects, so there isn't just one market price for the thing you are selling. If you were selling something that had lots of market substitutes, you can think of there being a market price in which this object can transact. An auction is a way to find a market price for something where there might not be a fixed market.

Can we think of an auction as a mechanism for finding the equilibrium price and quantity?

Exactly. We can think of the whole collection of auctions on eBay as being a mechanism to discover a market clearing price, and individual items might sell a little higher or a little lower but overall we believe that the prices on eBay auctions will represent market-clearing (equilibrium) prices.

Is economics a good subject in which to major? What subjects work well as complements with economics?

Of course I think economics is a fabulous major and I am passionate about it. I think it's a discipline that trains you to think rigorously. And if you apply yourself you'll finish an economics major with a more disciplined mind than when you started. Whether you go into the business world or academics, you'll be able to confront and think in a logical and structured way about whether a policy makes sense, a business model makes sense, or an industry structure is likely to be sustainable. You should look for that in an undergraduate major. You should not be looking to just absorb facts, but you should be looking to train your mind and to think in a way that you will be able to apply to the rest of your career. I think that economics combines well with statistics and mathematics or with more policy-oriented disciplines.

Do you have anything special to say to women who might be making a career choice? Why is economics a good field for a woman?

On the academic side, economics is a fairly objective field, where the best ideas win, so it's a level playing field. Academics is not very family friendly before you get tenured and extremely family friendly after. Within academics or outside of it, there are a wide range of fairly high-paying jobs that still allow some autonomy over your schedule and that have a deeper and more compelling meaning. For both men and women, if you choose to have a family, you reevaluate your career choices, and the tradeoff between time and money changes. And you're more likely to stick with and excel in a career if you find some meaning in it. So economics combines some of the advantages of having a strong job market and opportunities to have a large enough salary to pay for child care, and makes it economically worthwhile to stay in the workforce, without sacrificing the sense of the greater good.

CHAPTER
20

Measuring GDP and Economic Growth

**After studying this chapter,
you will be able to**

◆ Define GDP and explain why GDP equals
aggregate expenditure and aggregate
income

◆ Explain how Statistics Canada measures
GDP and real GDP

◆ Describe how real GDP is used and
explain its limitations as a measure of
economic well-being

Will our economy expand more rapidly next year or will it sink into a
"double-dip" recession? Many Canadian businesses want to know the
answer to this question. To assess the state of the economy and to make
big decisions about business expansion, firms such as RIM, the maker of
the BlackBerry, use forecasts of GDP. What exactly is GDP and what does it
tell us about the state of the economy?

In this chapter, you will find out how Statistics Canada measures GDP.
You will also learn about the uses and the limitations of these measures.
In *Reading Between the Lines* at the end of the chapter, we'll look at some
future scenarios for the Canadian economy.

Gross Domestic Product

What exactly is GDP, how is it calculated, what does it mean, and why do we care about it? You are going to discover the answers to these questions in this chapter. First, what *is* GDP?

GDP Defined

GDP, or **gross domestic product**, is the market value of the final goods and services produced within a country in a given time period. This definition has four parts:

- Market value
- Final goods and services
- Produced within a country
- In a given time period

We'll examine each in turn.

Market Value To measure total production, we must add together the production of apples and oranges, computers and popcorn. Just counting the items doesn't get us very far. For example, which is the greater total production: 100 apples and 50 oranges or 50 apples and 100 oranges?

GDP answers this question by valuing items at their *market values*—the prices at which items are traded in markets. If the price of an apple is 10¢, then the market value of 50 apples is $5. If the price of an orange is 20¢, then the market value of 100 oranges is $20. By using market prices to value production, we can add the apples and oranges together. The market value of 50 apples and 100 oranges is $5 plus $20, or $25.

Final Goods and Services To calculate GDP, we value the *final goods and services* produced. A **final good** (or service) is an item that is bought by its final user during a specified time period. It contrasts with an **intermediate good** (or service), which is an item that is produced by one firm, bought by another firm, and used as a component of a final good or service.

For example, a Ford truck is a final good, but a Firestone tire on the truck is an intermediate good. A Dell computer is a final good, but an Intel Pentium chip inside it is an intermediate good.

If we were to add the value of intermediate goods and services produced to the value of final goods and services, we would count the same thing many times—a problem called *double counting*. The value of a truck already includes the value of the tires, and the value of a Dell PC already includes the value of the Pentium chip inside it.

Some goods can be an intermediate good in some situations and a final good in other situations. For example, the ice cream that you buy on a hot summer day is a final good, but the ice cream that a restaurant buys and uses to make sundaes is an intermediate good. The sundae is the final good. So whether a good is an intermediate good or a final good depends on what it is used for, not what it is.

Some items that people buy are neither final goods nor intermediate goods and they are not part of GDP. Examples of such items include financial assets—stocks and bonds—and secondhand goods—used cars or existing homes. A secondhand good was part of GDP in the year in which it was produced, but not in GDP this year.

Produced Within a Country Only goods and services that are produced *within a country* count as part of that country's GDP. Roots, a Canadian firm, produces T-shirts in Taiwan, and the market value of those shirts is part of Taiwan's GDP, not part of Canada's GDP. Toyota, a Japanese firm, produces automobiles in Cambridge, Ontario, and the value of this production is part of Canada's GDP, not part of Japan's GDP.

In a Given Time Period GDP measures the value of production *in a given time period*—normally either a quarter of a year—called the quarterly GDP data—or a year—called the annual GDP data.

GDP measures not only the value of total production but also total income and total expenditure. The equality between the value of total production and total income is important because it shows the direct link between productivity and living standards. Our standard of living rises when our incomes rise and we can afford to buy more goods and services. But we must produce more goods and services if we are to be able to buy more goods and services.

Rising incomes and a rising value of production go together. They are two aspects of the same phenomenon: increasing productivity. To see why, we study the circular flow of expenditure and income.

GDP and the Circular Flow of Expenditure and Income

Figure 20.1 illustrates the circular flow of expenditure and income. The economy consists of households, firms, governments, and the rest of the world (the rectangles), which trade in factor markets and goods (and services) markets. We focus first on households and firms.

Households and Firms   Households sell and firms buy the services of labour, capital, and land in factor markets. For these factor services, firms pay income to households: wages for labour services, interest for the use of capital, and rent for the use of land. A fourth factor of production, entrepreneurship, receives profit.

Firms' retained earnings—profits that are not distributed to households—are part of the household sector's income. You can think of retained earnings as being income that households save and lend back to firms. Figure 20.1 shows the total income—*aggregate income*—received by households, including retained earnings, as the blue flow labelled *Y*.

Firms sell and households buy consumer goods and services—such as inline skates and haircuts—in the goods market. The total payment for these goods and services is **consumption expenditure**, shown by the red flow labelled *C*.

Firms buy and sell new capital equipment—such as computer systems, airplanes, trucks, and assembly line equipment—in the goods market. Some of what firms produce is not sold but is added to inventory. For example, if GM produces 1,000 cars and sells 950 of them, the other 50 cars remain in GM's inventory of unsold cars, which increases by 50 cars. When a firm adds unsold output to inventory, we can think of the firm as buying goods from itself. The

FIGURE 20.1   The Circular Flow of Expenditure and Income

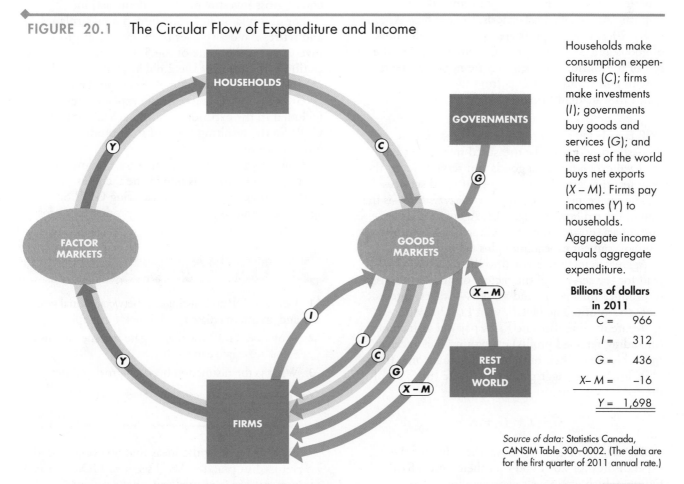

Households make consumption expenditures (*C*); firms make investments (*I*); governments buy goods and services (*G*); and the rest of the world buys net exports (*X − M*). Firms pay incomes (*Y*) to households. Aggregate income equals aggregate expenditure.

Billions of dollars in 2011	
C =	966
I =	312
G =	436
X − M =	−16
Y =	1,698

Source of data: Statistics Canada, CANSIM Table 300–0002. (The data are for the first quarter of 2011 annual rate.)

MyEconLab   animation

purchase of new plant, equipment, and buildings and the additions to inventories are **investment**, shown by the red flow labelled *I*.

Governments   Governments buy goods and services from firms and their expenditure on goods and services is called **government expenditure**. In Fig. 20.1, government expenditure is shown as the red flow *G*.

Governments finance their expenditure with taxes. But taxes are not part of the circular flow of expenditure and income. Governments also make financial transfers to households, such as social security benefits and unemployment benefits, and pay subsidies to firms. These financial transfers, like taxes, are not part of the circular flow of expenditure and income.

Rest of the World   Firms in Canada sell goods and services to the rest of the world—**exports**—and buy goods and services from the rest of the world—**imports**. The value of exports (*X*) minus the value of imports (*M*) is called **net exports**, the red flow *X* − *M* in Fig 20.1. If net exports are positive, the net flow of goods and services is from Canadian firms to the rest of the world. If net exports are negative, the net flow of goods and services is from the rest of the world to Canadian firms.

GDP Equals Expenditure Equals Income   Gross domestic product can be measured in two ways: by the total expenditure on goods and services or by the total income earned producing goods and services.

The total expenditure—*aggregate expenditure*—is the sum of the red flows in Fig. 20.1. Aggregate expenditure equals consumption expenditure plus investment plus government expenditure plus net exports.

Aggregate income is equal to the total amount paid for the services of the factors of production used to produce final goods and services—wages, interest, rent, and profit. The blue flow in Fig. 20.1 shows aggregate income. Because firms pay out as incomes (including retained profits) everything they receive from the sale of their output, aggregate income (the blue flow) equals aggregate expenditure (the sum of the red flows). That is,

$$Y = C + I + G + X - M.$$

The table in Fig. 20.1 shows the values of the expenditures for 2011 and that their sum is $1,698 billion, which also equals aggregate income.

Because aggregate expenditure equals aggregate income, the two methods of measuring GDP give the same answer. So

GDP equals aggregate expenditure and equals aggregate income.

The circular flow model is the foundation on which the national economic accounts are built.

Why Is Domestic Product "Gross"?

"Gross" means before subtracting the depreciation of capital. The opposite of "gross" is "net," which means after subtracting the depreciation of capital.

Depreciation is the decrease in the value of a firm's capital that results from wear and tear and obsolescence. The total amount spent both buying new capital and replacing depreciated capital is called **gross investment**. The amount by which the value of capital increases is called **net investment**. Net investment equals gross investment minus depreciation.

For example, if an airline buys 5 new airplanes and retires 2 old airplanes from service, its gross investment is the value of the 5 new airplanes, depreciation is the value of the 2 old airplanes retired, and net investment is the value of 3 new airplanes.

Gross investment is one of the expenditures included in the expenditure approach to measuring GDP. So the resulting value of total product is a gross measure.

Gross profit, which is a firm's profit before subtracting depreciation, is one of the incomes included in the income approach to measuring GDP. So again, the resulting value of total product is a gross measure.

◆ REVIEW QUIZ

1   Define GDP and distinguish between a final good and an intermediate good. Provide examples.
2   Why does GDP equal aggregate income and also equal aggregate expenditure?
3   What is the distinction between gross and net?

You can work these questions in Study Plan 20.1 and get instant feedback.

——————————————— MyEconLab ◆

Let's now see how the ideas that you've just studied are used in practice. We'll see how GDP and its components are measured in Canada today.

Measuring Canada's GDP

Statistics Canada uses the concepts in the circular flow model to measure GDP and its components in the *National Income and Expenditure Accounts*. Because the value of aggregate production equals aggregate expenditure and aggregate income, there are two approaches available for measuring GDP, and both are used. They are

- The expenditure approach
- The income approach

The Expenditure Approach

The *expenditure approach* measures GDP as the sum of consumption expenditure (C), investment (I), government expenditure on goods and services (G), and net exports of goods and services ($X - M$). These expenditures correspond to the red flows through the goods markets in the circular flow model in Fig. 20.1. Table 20.1 shows these expenditures and the calculation of GDP for 2011.

Consumption expenditure is the expenditure by Canadian households on goods and services produced in Canada and in the rest of the world and is shown by the red flow C in Fig. 20.2. They include goods such as pop and books and services such as banking and legal advice. They also include the

TABLE 20.1   GDP: The Expenditure Approach

Item	Symbol	Amount in 2011 (billions of dollars)	Percentage of GDP
Consumption expenditure	C	966	56.8
Investment	I	312	18.4
Government expenditure on goods and services	G	436	25.7
Net exports of goods and services	$X - M$	−16	−0.9
Gross domestic product	Y	**1,698**	**100.0**

The expenditure approach measures GDP as the sum of personal consumption expenditures (C), investment (I), government expenditure on goods and services (G), and net exports ($X - M$). In 2011, GDP measured by the expenditure approach was $1,698 billion. More than one-half of aggregate expenditure is consumption expenditure.

Source of data: Statistics Canada, CANSIM Table 380–0002.

purchase of consumer durable goods, such as computers and microwave ovens. But they do *not* include the purchase of new homes, which Statistics Canada counts as part of investment.

Investment is the expenditure on capital equipment and buildings by firms and the additions to business inventories. It also includes expenditure on new homes by households. Investment is the red flow I in Fig. 20.2.

Government expenditure on goods and services is the expenditure by all levels of government on goods and services, such as national defence and garbage collection. It does *not* include *transfer payments*, such as unemployment benefits, because they are not expenditures on goods and services. Government expenditure is the red flow G in Fig. 20.2.

Net exports of goods and services are the value of exports minus the value of imports. This item includes telephone equipment that Nortel sells to AT&T (a Canadian export), and Japanese DVD players that Sears buys from Sony (a Canadian import) and is shown by the red flow $X - M$ in Fig. 20.2.

Table 20.1 shows the relative magnitudes of the four items of aggregate expenditure.

FIGURE 20.2   Aggregate Expenditure

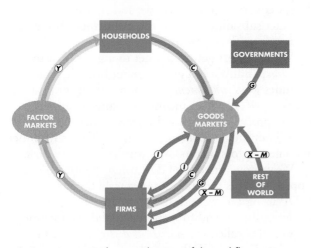

Aggregate expenditure is the sum of the red flows.

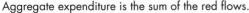

MyEconLab   *animation*

The Income Approach

The income approach measures GDP by summing the incomes that firms pay households for the factors of production they hire—wages for labour, interest for capital, rent for land, and profit for entrepreneurship. These incomes sum to the blue flows through the goods markets in the circular flow model in Fig. 20.1. We divide the incomes in the *National Income and Expenditure Accounts* into two broad categories:

1. Wages, salaries, and supplementary labour income
2. Other factor incomes

Wages, salaries, and supplementary labour income is the payment for labour services. It includes gross wages plus benefits such as pension contributions and is shown by the blue flow *W* in Fig. 20.3.

Other factor incomes include corporate profits, interest, farmers' income, and income from non-farm unincorporated businesses. These incomes are a mixture of interest, rent, and profit and include some labour income from self-employment. They are included in the blue flow *OFI* in Fig. 20.3.

Table 20.2 shows these incomes and their relative magnitudes. They sum to net domestic income at factor cost.

An *indirect tax* is a tax paid by consumers when they buy goods and services. (In contrast, a *direct tax* is a tax on income.) An indirect tax makes the market price exceed factor cost. A *subsidy* is a

TABLE 20.2   GDP: The Income Approach

Item	Amount in 2011 (billions of dollars)	Percentage of GDP
Wages, salaries, and supplementary labour income	880	51.8
Other factor incomes	402	23.7
Net domestic income at factor cost	1,282	75.5
Indirect taxes *less* subsidies	178	10.5
Net domestic income at market prices	1,460	86.0
Depreciation	236	13.9
GDP (income approach)	**1,696**	**99.9**
Statistical discrepancy	2	0.1
GDP (expenditure approach)	**1,698**	**100.0**

The sum of factor incomes equals *net domestic income at factor cost*. GDP equals net domestic income at factor cost plus indirect taxes less subsidies plus depreciation.

In 2011, GDP measured by the income approach was $1,696 billion. This amount is $2 billion less than GDP measured by the expenditure approach—a statistical discrepancy of $2 billion or 0.1 percent of GDP.

Wages, salaries, and supplementary labour income is by far the largest part of aggregate income.

Source of data: Statistics Canada, CANSIM Table 380–0001.

payment by the government to a producer. With a subsidy, factor cost exceeds market price. To get from factor cost to market price, we add indirect taxes and subtract subsidies. Making this adjustment brings us to *net domestic income at market prices.*

We still must get from a *net* to a *gross* measure. Total expenditure is a *gross* number because it includes *gross investment.* Net domestic income at market prices is a net income measure because corporate profits are measured *after deducting depreciation.* They are a net income measure. To get from net income to gross income, we must *add depreciation.*

We've now arrived at GDP using the income approach. This number is not exactly the same as GDP using the expenditure approach. The gap between the expenditure approach and the income approach is called the *statistical discrepancy* and it is calculated as the GDP expenditure total minus the GDP income total. The discrepancy is never large. In 2011, it was 0.1 percent of GDP.

FIGURE 20.3   Aggregate Income

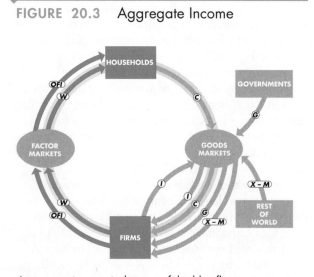

Aggregate income is the sum of the blue flows.

Nominal GDP and Real GDP

Often, we want to *compare* GDP in two periods, say 2001 and 2011. In 2001, GDP was $1,108 billion and in 2011, it was $1,698 billion—53 percent higher than in 2001. This increase in GDP is a combination of an increase in production and a rise in prices. To isolate the increase in production from the rise in prices, we distinguish between *real* GDP and *nominal* GDP.

Real GDP is the value of final goods and services produced in a given year when *valued at the prices of a reference base year.* By comparing the value of production in the two years at the same prices, we reveal the change in production.

Currently, the reference base year is 2002 and we describe real GDP as measured in 2002 dollars—in terms of what the dollar would buy in 2002.

Nominal GDP is the value of final goods and services produced in a given year when valued at the prices of that year. Nominal GDP is just a more precise name for GDP.

Economists at Statistics Canada calculate real GDP using the method described in the Mathematical Note on pp. 484–485. Here, we'll explain the basic idea but not the technical details.

Calculating Real GDP

We'll calculate real GDP for an economy that produces one consumption good, one capital good, and one government service. Net exports are zero.

Table 20.3 shows the quantities produced and the prices in 2002 (the base year) and in 2012. In part (a), we calculate nominal GDP in 2002. For each item, we multiply the quantity produced in 2002 by its price in 2002 to find the total expenditure on the item. We sum the expenditures to find nominal GDP, which in 2002 is $100 million. Because 2002 is the base year, both real GDP and nominal GDP equal $100 million.

In Table 20.3(b), we calculate nominal GDP in 2012, which is $300 million. Nominal GDP in 2012 is three times its value in 2002. But by how much has production increased? Real GDP will tell us.

In Table 20.3(c), we calculate real GDP in 2012. The quantities of the goods and services produced are those of 2012, as in part (b). The prices are those in the reference base year—2002, as in part (a).

For each item, we multiply the quantity produced in 2012 by its price in 2002. We then sum these expenditures to find real GDP in 2012, which is

TABLE 20.3   Calculating Nominal GDP and Real GDP

	Item	Quantity (millions)	Price (dollars)	Expenditure (millions of dollars)
(a) In 2002				
C	T-shirts	10	5	50
I	Computer chips	3	10	30
G	Security services	1	20	20
Y	Real and Nominal GDP in 2002			100
(b) In 2012				
C	T-shirts	4	5	20
I	Computer chips	2	20	40
G	Security services	6	40	240
Y	Nominal GDP in 2012			300
(c) Quantities of 2012 valued at prices of 2002				
C	T-shirts	4	5	20
I	Computer chips	2	10	20
G	Security services	6	20	120
Y	Real GDP in 2012			160

In 2002, the reference base year, real GDP equals nominal GDP and was $100 million. In 2012, nominal GDP increased to $300 million. But real GDP in 2012 in part (c), which is calculated by using the quantities of 2012 in part (b) and the prices of 2002 in part (a), was only $160 million—a 60 percent increase from 2002.

$160 million. This number is what total expenditure would have been in 2012 if prices had remained the same as they were in 2002.

Nominal GDP in 2012 is three times its value in 2002, but real GDP in 2012 is only 1.6 times its 2002 value—a 60 percent increase in production.

◢ REVIEW QUIZ

1 What is the expenditure approach to measuring GDP?
2 What is the income approach to measuring GDP?
3 What adjustments must be made to total income to make it equal GDP?
4 What is the distinction between nominal GDP and real GDP?
5 How is real GDP calculated?

You can work these questions in Study Plan 20.2 and get instant feedback.

MyEconLab ◆

◆ The Uses and Limitations of Real GDP

Economists use estimates of real GDP for two main purposes:

- To compare the standard of living over time
- To compare the standard of living across countries

The Standard of Living Over Time

One method of comparing the standard of living over time is to calculate real GDP per person in different years. **Real GDP per person** is real GDP divided by the population. Real GDP per person tells us the value of goods and services that the average person can enjoy. By using *real* GDP, we remove any influence that rising prices and a rising cost of living might have had on our comparison.

We're interested in both the long-term trends and the shorter-term cycles in the standard of living.

Long-Term Trend   A handy way of comparing real GDP per person over time is to express it as a ratio of some reference year. For example, in 1969, real GDP per person was $19,000 and in 2010, it was $38,000 (both rounded to the nearest thousand). So real GDP per person in 2010 was double its 1969 level. To the extent that real GDP per person measures the standard of living, people were twice as well off in 2010 as their grandparents had been in 1969.

Figure 20.4 shows the path of Canadian real GDP per person from 1961 to 2010 and highlights two features of our expanding living standard:

- The growth of potential GDP per person
- Fluctuations of real GDP per person

The Growth of Potential GDP   **Potential GDP** is the maximum level of real GDP that can be produced while avoiding shortages of labour, capital, land, and entrepreneurial ability that would bring rising inflation. Potential GDP per person, the smoother black line in Fig. 20.4, grows at a steady pace because the quantities of the factors of production and their productivities grow at a steady pace.

But potential GDP per person doesn't grow at a *constant* pace. During the 1960s, it grew at 3.4 percent per year but slowed to only 2.4 percent per year during the 1970s. This slowdown might seem small, but it had big consequences, as you'll soon see.

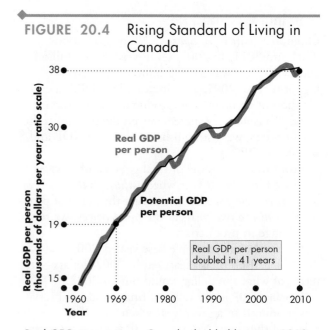

FIGURE 20.4   Rising Standard of Living in Canada

Real GDP per person in Canada doubled between 1969 and 2010. Real GDP per person, the red line, fluctuates around potential GDP per person, the black line. (The *y*-axis is a ratio scale—see the Appendix, pp, 482–483.)

Sources of data: Statistics Canada, CANSIM Tables 380–0017 and 051–0005. Potential GDP is based on the Bank of Canada's output gap measure after 1982 and authors' assumptions before 1982.

━━━━ MyEconLab   animation   ◆

Fluctuations of Real GDP   You can see that real GDP per person shown by the red line in Fig. 20.4 fluctuates around potential GDP per person, and sometimes real GDP per person shrinks.

Let's take a closer look at the two features of our expanding living standard that we've just outlined.

Productivity Growth Slowdown   How costly was the slowdown in productivity growth after 1970? The answer is provided by the *Lucas wedge*, which is the dollar value of the accumulated gap between what real GDP per person would have been if the growth rate of the 1960s had persisted and what real GDP per person turned out to be. (Nobel Laureate Robert E. Lucas Jr. drew attention to this gap.)

Figure 20.5 illustrates the Lucas wedge. The wedge started out small during the 1970s, but by 2010 real GDP per person was $30,700 per year lower than it would have been with no growth slowdown, and the accumulated gap was an astonishing $400,000 per person.

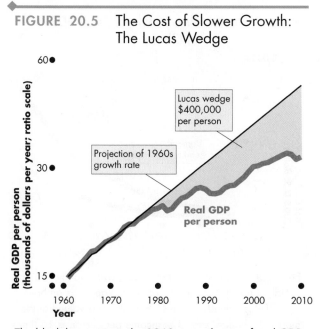

FIGURE 20.5   The Cost of Slower Growth: The Lucas Wedge

The black line projects the 1960s growth rate of real GDP per person to 2010. The Lucas wedge arises from the slow-down of productivity growth that began during the 1970s. The cost of the slowdown is $400,000 per person.

Sources of data: Statistics Canada, CANSIM Tables 380–0017 and 051–0005 and authors' calculations.

MyEconLab   animation ◆

Real GDP Fluctuations—The Business Cycle We call the fluctuations in the pace of expansion of real GDP the **business cycle**. The business cycle is a periodic but irregular up-and-down movement of total production and other measures of economic activity. The business cycle isn't a regular predictable cycle like the phases of the moon, but every cycle has two phases:

1. Expansion
2. Recession

and two turning points:

1. Peak
2. Trough

Figure 20.6 shows these features of the most recent Canadian business cycle.

An **expansion** is a period during which real GDP increases. In the early stage of an expansion real GDP returns to potential GDP and as the expansion progresses, potential GDP grows, and real GDP eventually exceeds potential GDP.

A common definition of **recession** is a period during which real GDP decreases—its growth rate is negative—for at least two successive quarters. A more general definition of recession and one used by the U.S. National Bureau of Economic Research is "a period of significant decline in total output, income, employment, and trade, usually lasting from six months to a year, and marked by contractions in many sectors of the economy."

An expansion ends and recession begins at a business cycle *peak*, which is the highest level that real GDP has attained up to that time. A recession ends at a *trough*, when real GDP reaches a temporary low point and from which the next expansion begins.

In 2008, Canada went into an unusually severe recession. Starting from a long way below potential GDP, a new expansion began in mid-2009. But real GDP was still not back at potential GDP in the first quarter of 2011 (the latest data available when this text was written).

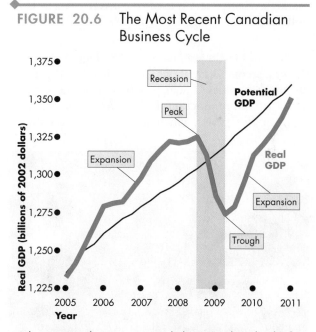

FIGURE 20.6   The Most Recent Canadian Business Cycle

A business cycle expansion ended at a peak in the third quarter of 2008, which was then followed by a recession that ended at a trough in the second quarter of 2009. A new expansion then began.

Sources of data: Statistics Canada, CANSIM Tables 380–0017 and 051–0005. Potential GDP is based on the Bank of Canada's output gap measure.

MyEconLab   animation ◆

The Standard of Living Across Countries

Two problems arise in using real GDP to compare living standards across countries. First, the real GDP of one country must be converted into the same currency units as the real GDP of the other country. Second, the goods and services in both countries must be valued at the same prices. Comparing the United States and China provides a striking example of these two problems.

China and the United States in U.S. Dollars In 2010, real GDP per person in the United States was $42,800 and in China it was 23,400 yuan. The yuan is the currency of China and the price at which the dollar and the yuan exchanged—the *market exchange rate*—was 8.2 yuan per US$1. Using this exchange rate, 23,400 yuan converts to US$2,850. On these numbers, real GDP per person in the United States was 15 times that in China.

The red line in Fig. 20.7 shows real GDP per person in China from 1980 to 2010 when the market exchange rate is used to convert yuan to U.S. dollars.

China and the United States at PPP Figure 20.7 shows a second estimate of China's real GDP per person that values China's production on the same terms as U.S. production. It uses *purchasing power parity* or *PPP* prices, which are the *same prices* for

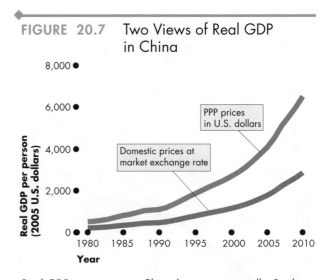

FIGURE 20.7   Two Views of Real GDP in China

Real GDP per person in China has grown rapidly. But how rapidly it has grown and to what level depends on how real GDP is valued. When GDP in 2010 is valued at the market exchange rate, U.S. income per person is 15 times that in China. China looks like a poor developing country. But the comparison is misleading. When GDP is valued at purchasing power parity prices, U.S. income per person is only 6.5 times that in China.

Source of data: International Monetary Fund, *World Economic Outlook database*, April 2010.

———————— MyEconLab   animation ◆

A Big Mac costs $3.75 in Chicago and 13.25 yuan or US$1.62 in Shanghai. To compare real GDP in China and the United States, we must value China's Big Macs at the US$3.75 price—the PPP price.

both countries. The prices of some goods are higher in the United States than in China, so these items get a smaller weight in China's real GDP than they get in U.S. real GDP. An example is a Big Mac that costs $3.75 in Chicago. In Shanghai, a Big Mac costs 13.25 yuan, which is the equivalent of US$1.62. So in China's real GDP, a Big Mac gets less than half the weight that it gets in U.S. real GDP.

Some prices in China are higher than in the United States but more prices are lower, so Chinese prices put a lower value on China's production than do U.S. prices.

According to the PPP comparisons, real GDP per person in the United States in 2010 was 6.5 times that of China, not 15 times.

You've seen how real GDP is used to make standard of living comparisons over time and across countries. But real GDP isn't a perfect measure of the standard of living and we'll now examine its limitations.

Limitations of Real GDP

Real GDP measures the value of goods and services that are bought in markets. Some of the factors that influence the standard of living and that are not part of GDP are

- Household production
- Underground economic activity
- Health and life expectancy
- Leisure time
- Security
- Environmental quality
- Political freedom and social justice

Household Production An enormous amount of production takes place every day in our homes. Preparing meals, cleaning the kitchen, changing a light bulb, cutting grass, washing a car, and caring for a child are all examples of household production. Because these productive activities are not traded in markets, they are not included in GDP.

The omission of household production from GDP means that GDP *underestimates* total production. But it also means that the growth rate of GDP *overestimates* the growth rate of total production. The reason is that some of the growth rate of market production (included in GDP) is a replacement for home production. So part of the increase in GDP arises from a decrease in home production.

Two trends point in this direction. One is the number of women who have jobs, which increased from 38 percent in 1976 to 58 percent in Canada in 2010. The other is the trend in the market purchase of traditionally home-produced goods and services.

For example, more and more families now eat in restaurants—one of the fastest-growing industries in Canada—and use day-care services. This trend means that an increasing proportion of food preparation and child care that were part of household production are now measured as part of GDP. So real GDP grows more rapidly than does real GDP plus home production.

Underground Economic Activity The *underground economy* is the part of the economy that is purposely hidden from the view of the government to avoid taxes and regulations or because the goods and services being produced are illegal. Because underground economic activity is unreported, it is omitted from GDP.

The underground economy is easy to describe, even if it is hard to measure. It includes the production and distribution of illegal drugs, production that uses illegal labour that is paid less than the minimum wage, and jobs done for cash to avoid paying income taxes. This last category might be quite large and includes tips earned by cab drivers, hairdressers, and hotel and restaurant workers.

Estimates of the scale of the underground economy in Canada range between 5 and 15 percent of GDP ($85 billion to $255 billion).

Provided that the underground economy is a stable proportion of the total economy, the growth rate of real GDP still gives a useful estimate of changes in economic well-being and the standard of living. But sometimes production shifts from the underground economy to the rest of the economy, and sometimes it shifts the other way. The underground economy expands relative to the rest of the economy if taxes become especially high or if

Whose production is more valuable: the chef's whose work gets counted in GDP ...

... or the busy mother's whose dinner preparation and child minding don't get counted?

regulations become especially restrictive. And the underground economy shrinks relative to the rest of the economy if the burdens of taxes and regulations are eased. During the 1980s, when tax rates were cut, there was an increase in the reporting of previously hidden income and tax revenues increased. So some part (but probably a very small part) of the expansion of real GDP during the 1980s represented a shift from the underground economy rather than an increase in production.

Health and Life Expectancy   Good health and a long life—the hopes of everyone—do not show up in real GDP, at least not directly. A higher real GDP enables us to spend more on medical research, health care, a good diet, and exercise equipment. And as real GDP has increased, our life expectancy has lengthened—from 70 years at the end of World War II to approaching 80 years today.

But we face new health and life expectancy problems every year. AIDS and drug abuse are taking young lives at a rate that causes serious concern. When we take these negative influences into account, we see that real GDP growth overstates the improvements in the standard of living.

Leisure Time   Leisure time is an economic good that adds to our economic well-being and the standard of living. Other things remaining the same, the more leisure we have, the better off we are. Our working time is valued as part of GDP, but our leisure time is not. Yet that leisure time must be at least as valuable to us as the wage that we earn for the last hour worked. If it were not, we would work instead of taking leisure. Over the years, leisure time has steadily increased. The workweek has become shorter, more people take early retirement, and the number of vacation days has increased. These improvements in economic well-being are not reflected in real GDP.

Security   Security has several dimensions that influence our economic well-being. We value the security that comes from our jobs, the security provided by local police services, and the security that comes from our national defence.

Environmental Quality   Economic activity directly influences the quality of the environment. The burning of hydrocarbon fuels is the most visible activity that damages our environment, but it is not the only

example. The depletion of nonrenewable natural resources, the mass clearing of forests, and the pollution of lakes and rivers are other major environmental consequences of industrial production.

Resources that are used to protect the environment are valued as part of GDP. For example, the value of catalytic converters that help to protect the atmosphere from automobile emissions is part of GDP. But if we did not use such pieces of equipment and instead polluted the atmosphere, we would not count the deteriorating air that we were breathing as a negative part of GDP.

An industrial society possibly produces more atmospheric pollution than an agricultural society does. But pollution does not always increase as we become wealthier. Wealthy people value a clean environment and are willing to pay for one. Compare the pollution in China today with pollution in the Canada. China, a poor country, pollutes its rivers, lakes, and atmosphere in a way that is unimaginable in Canada.

Political Freedom and Social Justice   Most people in the Western world value political freedoms such as those provided by the Canadian Constitution. And they value social justice—equality of opportunity and of access to social security safety nets that protect people from the extremes of misfortune.

A country might have a very large real GDP per person but have limited political freedom and social justice. For example, a small elite might enjoy political liberty and extreme wealth while the vast majority are effectively enslaved and live in abject poverty. Such an economy would generally be regarded as having a lower standard of living than one that had the same amount of real GDP but in which political freedoms were enjoyed by everyone. Today, China has rapid real GDP growth but limited political freedoms, while Poland and Ukraine have moderate real GDP growth but democratic political systems. Economists have no easy way to determine which of these countries is better off.

The Bottom Line   Do we get the wrong message about the level and growth in economic well-being and the standard of living by looking only at the level and growth of real GDP? We do get the wrong message. One of the largest reasons is that developing countries have a larger amount of household production and a larger underground economy than do

Economics in Action

A Broader Indicator of Economic Well-Being

The limitations of real GDP reviewed in this chapter affect the standard of living and general well-being of every country. So to make international comparisons of the general state of economic well-being, we must look at real GDP and other indicators.

The United Nations has constructed a broader measure called the Human Development Index (HDI), which combines real GDP, life expectancy and health, and education. Real GDP per person (measured on the PPP basis) is a major component of the HDI.

The dots in the figure show the relationship between real GDP per person and the HDI. In 2010, Norway had the highest real GDP per person, but the second highest HDI. (Australia was highest.)

Australia and Norway, along with the United States, have higher HDIs than Canada. The HDI of Canada is lower than that of these three other countries for a combination of reasons, one of which is a lower GDP per person.

African nations have the lowest levels of economic

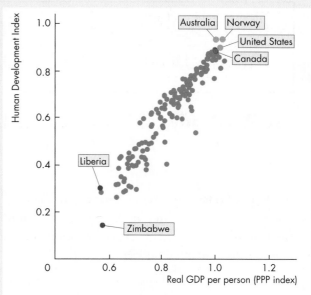

The Human Development Index

Source of data: United Nations hdr.undp.org/en/statistics/data.

well-being. Zimbabwe has both the lowest real GDP per person and the lowest HDI.

developed countries, so the gaps between the standards of living are exaggerated. Also as real GDP grows, part of the measured growth reflects a switch from home production to market production and from underground economic activity to regular production. So the growth rate of real GDP overstates the growth rate in the standard of living.

It is possible to construct broader measures that combine the many influences that contribute to the standard of living. The United Nations' Human Development Index (HDI) described in *Economics in Action* above is one example of a broader measure of economic well-being and the standard of living, but this measure places a good deal of weight on real GDP.

Dozens of other measures have been proposed. One includes resource depletion and emissions in a Green GDP measure. Another emphasizes the enjoyment of life rather than the production of goods in a "genuine progress index" or GPI.

Despite all the alternatives, real GDP per person remains the most widely used indicator of economic well-being and the standard of living.

REVIEW QUIZ

1. Distinguish between real GDP and potential GDP and describe how each grows over time.
2. How does the growth rate of real GDP contribute to an improved standard of living?
3. What is a business cycle and what are its phases and turning points?
4. What is PPP and how does it help us to make valid international comparisons of real GDP?
5. Explain why real GDP might be an unreliable indicator of the standard of living.

You can work these questions in Study Plan 20.3 and get instant feedback.

———————————— MyEconLab ◆

◆ You now know how economists measure GDP and what the GDP data tell us. *Reading Between the Lines* on pp. 480–481 uses GDP to describe some possible future paths as we emerge from recession.

Real GDP Forecasts in the Uncertain Economy of 2011

Are We Ready for That Double Dip?

Financial Post
August 20, 2011

In Ottawa Friday, Minister of Finance Jim Flaherty and Bank of Canada governor Mark Carney gave their updates on the Canadian economy. The big question: How does the darkened global picture affect Canada's economic prospects and the federal government's ability to return to a balanced budget on schedule?

By most accounts, the Canadian economy is doing well. The United States entered recession, defined as a significant decline in economic activity, in December 2007. Canada entered recession later, in fall 2008.

And Canada's recession was shorter: the U.S. economy contracted for 18 months, while the Canadian economy was starting to grow again in June 2009, less than 10 months after its recession's start. ...

The most worrisome prospect for Canada and the world: a double-dip recession in the United States. This outcome, while not yet the most likely one, is becoming more probable: The U.S. manufacturing index just posted its worst reading since July 2009. ...

[S]ales of Canadian goods and services in the United States still account for more than a fifth of our output: a drop of 5 percent in U.S. demand could translate to a 1 percent hit to real growth here. Canada is not an island, and positive market factors cannot undo the arithmetic of globally interlinked economies.

The financial crisis was painful and economic recovery will be slow, punctuated by ups and downs. Pauses or reversals routinely emerge during recoveries, as people and businesses try to make sense of new and volatile economic realities. Yet those are the vagaries of economic life—policymakers' job is to provide the prudent fiscal foundation and supple monetary environment within which the rest of us can do our own best planning. ...

ESSENCE OF THE STORY

- Canada entered recession in the fall of 2008, nine months later than the start of U.S. recession.

- Canada and the United States started to expand again in mid-2009, so Canada's recession was shorter than that of the United States.

- In mid-2011, the Canadian economy was performing well but the risk of a double-dip recession in the United States hung over Canada and the world.

- One-fifth of Canada's production is sold in the United States.

- A drop of 5 percent in U.S. demand could translate to a 1 percent fall in Canada's production.

ECONOMIC ANALYSIS

- Canada's economic performance is strongly influenced by events in the United States and the rest of the world.

- The past few years have seen unusually large swings in production and economic growth.

- In 2008 and 2009, an unusually deep global recession occurred and the United States was hardest hit.

- In the U.S. recession, which started at a peak at the end of 2007 and ended at a trough in mid–2009, real GDP fell by 5.5 percent.

- In the Canadian recession, which started at a peak in the third quarter of 2008 and ended at a trough in mid–2009, real GDP fell by 4.2 percent.

- Figure 1 illustrates these two recessions. To compare the United States and Canada on the same scale, the figure graphs real GDP in the two countries as percentages of their level in the first quarter of 2005.

- You can see that Canadian real GDP expanded more rapidly than U.S. real GDP and you can see that the U.S. recession was deeper and lasted longer than the Canadian recession.

- In the recovery that started at the same time for the two economies, U.S. real GDP grew by 5 percent and Canadian real GDP grew by 6.2 percent.

- In mid-2011, U.S. real GDP had still not returned to its pre-recession peak, while Canada's real GDP was 2.1 percent higher than its pre-recession peak.

- A "double-dip" recession is a second recession that occurs before an expansion has returned real GDP to a level greater than its previous peak.

- A "double-dip" recession in the United States would be bad news for the global economy and for Canada.

- Figure 2 shows what might happen.

- Starting in the third quarter of 2011, U.S. real GDP starts to shrink and a new "double-dip" recession begins. By mid 2012, U.S. real GDP has fallen by 4 percent.

- In Figure 2, Canada takes a big hit with real GDP falling by 3 percent.

- The news article says that a 5 percent drop in U.S. real GDP translates to a 1 percent drop in Canadian real GDP, so why does Fig. 2 show such a big drop for Canada?

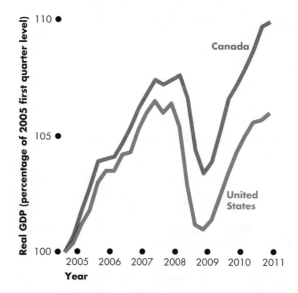

Figure 1 The Recessions Compared

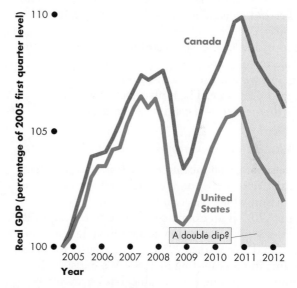

Figure 2 A Double Dip Recession

- The reason is that a fall in U.S. real GDP would lower real GDP in Europe and in Asia so Canadian exports to these regions would fall.

- A "double-dip" U.S. recession, if it happened, would bring a global recession and Canada would see its real GDP fall by much more that one-fifth of the fall in U.S. real GDP.

481

APPENDIX

Graphs in Macroeconomics

After studying this appendix, you will be able to

◆ Make and interpret a time-series graph

◆ Make and interpret a graph that uses a ratio scale

◆ The Time-Series Graph

In macroeconomics we study the fluctuations and trends in the key variables that describe macroeconomic performance and policy. These variables include GDP and its expenditure and income components that you've learned about in this chapter. They also include variables that describe the labour market and consumer prices that you will study in Chapter 21.

Regardless of the variable of interest, we want to be able to compare its value today with that in the past; and we want to describe how the variable has changed over time. The most effective way to do these things is to make a time-series graph.

Making a Time-Series Graph

A **time-series graph** measures time (for example, years, quarters, or months) on the *x*-axis and the variable or variables in which we are interested on the *y*-axis. Figure A20.1 is an example of a time-series graph. It provides some information about unemployment in the United States since 1980. In this figure, we measure time in years starting in 1980. We measure the unemployment rate (the variable that we are interested in) on the *y*-axis.

A time-series graph enables us to visualize how a variable has changed over time and how its value in one period relates to its value in another period. It conveys an enormous amount of information quickly and easily.

Let's see how to "read" a time-series graph.

Reading a Time-Series Graph

To practice reading a time-series graph, take a close look at Fig. A20.1. The graph shows the level, change, and speed of change of the variable.

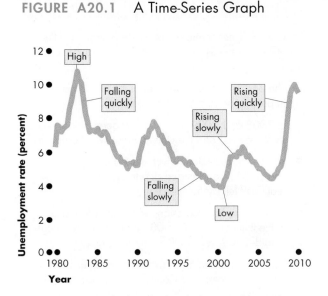

FIGURE A20.1   A Time-Series Graph

A time-series graph plots the level of a variable on the *y*-axis against time (here measured in years) on the *x*-axis. This graph shows the U.S. unemployment rate each year from 1980 to 2010. It shows when unemployment was high, when it was low, when it increased, when it decreased, and when it changed quickly and slowly.

———MyEconLab   animation   ◆

■ The *level* of the variable: It tells us when unemployment is *high* and *low*. When the line is a long distance above the *x*-axis, the unemployment rate is high, as it was, for example, in 1983 and again in 2009. When the line is close to the *x*-axis, the unemployment rate is low, as it was, for example, in 2001.

■ The *change* in the variable: It tells us how unemployment *changes*—whether it *increases* or *decreases*. When the line slopes upward, as it did in 2008 and 2009, the unemployment rate is rising. When the line slopes downward, as it did in 1984 and 1997, the unemployment rate is falling.

■ The *speed of change* in the variable: It tells us whether the unemployment rate is rising or falling *quickly* or *slowly*. If the line is very steep, then the unemployment rate increases or decreases quickly. If the line is not steep, the unemployment rate increases or decreases slowly. For example, the unemployment rate rose quickly in 2008 and slowly in 2003 and it fell quickly in 1984 and slowly in 1997.

Ratio Scale Reveals Trend

A time-series graph also reveals whether a variable has a **cycle**, which is a tendency for a variable to alternate between upward and downward movements, or a **trend**, which is a tendency for a variable to move in one general direction.

The unemployment rate in Fig. A20.1 has a cycle but no trend. When a trend is present, a special kind of time-series graph, one that uses a ratio scale on the *y*-axis, reveals the trend.

A Time-Series with a Trend

Many macroeconomics variables, among them GDP and the average level of prices, have an upward trend. Figure A20.2 shows an example of such a variable: the average prices paid by consumers.

In Fig. A20.2(a), Canadian consumer prices since 1970 are graphed on a normal scale. In 1970 the level is 100. In other years, the average level of prices is measured as a percentage of the 1970 level.

The graph clearly shows the upward trend of prices. But it doesn't tell us when prices were rising fastest or whether there was any change in the trend. Just looking at the upward-sloping line in Fig. A20.2(a) gives the impression that the pace of growth of consumer prices was constant.

Using a Ratio Scale

On a graph axis with a normal scale, the gap between 1 and 2 is the same as that between 3 and 4. On a graph axis with a ratio scale, the gap between 1 and 2 is the same as that between 2 and 4. The ratio 2 to 1 equals the ratio 4 to 2. By using a ratio scale, we can "see" when the growth rate (the percentage change per unit of time) changes.

Figure A20.2(b) shows an example of a ratio scale. Notice that the values on the *y*-axis get closer together but the gap between 400 and 200 equals the gap between 200 and 100: The ratio gaps are equal.

Graphing the data on a ratio scale reveals the trends. In the case of consumer prices, the trend is much steeper during the 1970s and early 1980s than in the later years. The steeper the line in the ratio-scale graph in part (b), the faster are prices rising. Prices rose rapidly during the 1970s and early 1980s and more slowly in the later 1980s and the 1990s. The ratio-scale graph reveals this fact. We use ratio-scale graphs extensively in macroeconomics.

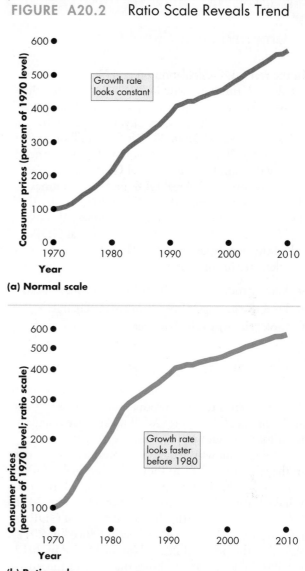

FIGURE A20.2   Ratio Scale Reveals Trend

(a) Normal scale

(b) Ratio scale

The graph shows the average of consumer prices from 1970 to 2010. The level is 100 in 1970 and the value for other years are percentages of the 1970 level. Consumer prices normally rise each year so the line slopes upward. In part (a), where the *y*-axis scale is normal, the rate of increase appears to be constant.

In part (b), where the *y*-axis is a ratio scale (the ratio of 400 to 200 equals the ratio 200 to 100), prices rose faster in the 1970s and early 1980s and slower in the later years. The ratio scale reveals this trend.

——————————— MyEconLab ⟨animation⟩ ◆

◼ MATHEMATICAL NOTE

Chained-Dollar Real GDP

In the real GDP calculation on p. 473, real GDP in 2012 is 1.6 times its value in 2002. But suppose that we use 2012 as the reference base year and value real GDP in 2002 at 2012 prices. If you do the math, you will see that real GDP in 2002 is $150 million at 2012 prices. GDP in 2012 is $300 million (in 2012 prices), so now the numbers say that real GDP has doubled. Which is correct: Did real GDP increase 1.6 times or double? Should we use the prices of 2002 or 2012? The answer is that we need to use *both* sets of prices.

Statistics Canada uses a measure of real GDP called **chained-dollar real GDP**. Three steps are needed to calculate this measure:

- ◼ Value production in the prices of adjacent years
- ◼ Find the average of two percentage changes
- ◼ Link (chain) to the base year

Value Production in Prices of Adjacent Years

The first step is to value production in *adjacent* years at the prices of *both* years. We'll make these calculations for 2012 and its preceding year, 2011.

Table 1 shows the quantities produced and prices in the two years. Part (a) shows the nominal GDP calculation for 2011—the quantities produced in 2011 valued at the prices of 2011. Nominal GDP in 2011 is $145 million. Part (b) shows the nominal GDP calculation for 2012—the quantities produced in 2012 valued at the prices of 2012. Nominal GDP in 2012 is $300 million. Part (c) shows the value of the quantities produced in 2012 at the prices of 2011. This total is $160 million. Finally, part (d) shows the value of the quantities produced in 2011 at the prices of 2012. This total is $275 million.

Find the Average of Two Percentage Changes

The second step is to find the percentage change in the value of production based on the prices in the two adjacent years. Table 2 summarizes these calculations.

Part (a) shows that, valued at the prices of 2011, production increased from $145 million in 2011 to $160 million in 2012, an increase of 10.3 percent.

TABLE 1 Real GDP Calculation Step 1: Value Production in Adjacent Years at Prices of Both Years

Item		Quantity (millions)	Price (dollars)	Expenditure (millions of dollars)
(a) In 2011				
C	T-shirts	3	5	15
I	Computer chips	3	10	30
G	Security services	5	20	100
Y	Nominal GDP in 2011			**145**
(b) In 2012				
C	T-shirts	4	5	20
I	Computer chips	2	20	40
G	Security services	6	40	240
Y	Nominal GDP in 2012			**300**
(c) Quantities of 2012 valued at prices of 2011				
C	T-shirts	4	5	20
I	Computer chips	2	10	20
G	Security services	6	20	120
Y	2012 production at 2011 prices			**160**
(d) Quantities of 2011 valued at prices of 2012				
C	T-shirts	3	5	15
I	Computer chips	3	20	60
G	Security services	5	40	200
Y	2011 production at 2012 prices			**275**

Step 1 is to value the production of adjacent years at the prices of both years. Here, we value the production of 2011 and 2012 at the prices of both 2011 and 2012. The value of 2011 production at 2011 prices, in part (a), is nominal GDP in 2011. The value of 2012 production at 2012 prices, in part (b), is nominal GDP in 2012. Part (c) calculates the value of 2012 production at 2011 prices, and part (d) calculates the value of 2011 production at 2012 prices. We use these numbers in Step 2.

Part (b) shows that, valued at the prices of 2012, production increased from $275 million in 2011 to $300 million in 2012, an increase of 9.1 percent. Part (c) shows that the average of these two percentage changes in the value of production is 9.7. That is, $(10.3 + 9.1) \div 2 = 9.7$.

What we've just calculated is the *growth rate of real GDP* in 2012. But what is the *level* of real GDP? Finding the level of real GDP is what happens in Step 3 that we'll now describe.

TABLE 2   Real GDP Calculation Step 2: Find Average of Two Percentage Changes

Value of Production	Millions of dollars
(a) At 2011 prices	
Nominal GDP in 2011	145
2012 production at 2011 prices	160
Percentage change in production at 2011 prices	10.3
(b) At 2012 prices	
2011 production at 2012 prices	275
Nominal GDP in 2012	300
Percentage change in production at 2012 prices	9.1
(c) Average percentage change in 2012	**9.7**

Using the numbers calculated in Step 1, the percentage change in production from 2011 to 2012 valued at 2011 prices is 10.3 percent, in part (a). The percentage change in production from 2011 to 2012 valued at 2012 prices is 9.1 percent, in part (b). The average of these two percentage changes is 9.7 percent, in part (c).

Link (Chain) to the Base Year

The third step is to measure real GDP in the prices of the *reference base year*. To do this, Statistics Canada selects a base year (currently 2002) in which, *by definition*, real GDP equals nominal GDP. Statistics

Canada performs calculations like the ones that you've just worked through for 2012 to find the percentage change in real GDP in each pair of adjacent years. Finally, it uses the percentage changes calculated in Step 2 to find real GDP in 2002 prices for each year.

Figure 1 illustrates these Step 3 calculations to chain link to the base year. In the reference base year, 2002, real GDP equals nominal GDP, which we'll assume is $100 million (shown in the first link in the chain). Using the same methods that we've just described for 2011 and 2012, we'll assume that the growth rate of real GDP from 2002 to 2003 is 7 percent (also shown in the first link in the chain). If real GDP in 2002 is $100 million and the growth rate in 2003 is 7 percent, then real GDP in 2003 is $107 million—7 percent higher than real GDP in 2002.

By repeating these calculations for each year, we obtain *chained-dollar real GDP* in 2002 dollars for each year. The growth rates shown in the table for 2004 to 2011 take real GDP in 2011 to $179 million. That is, the 2011 *chained-dollar real GDP* in 2002 dollars is $179 million.

We've calculated the growth rate for 2012, which is highlighted in Fig. 1 as 9.7 percent. Applying this growth rate to the $179 million level of real GDP in 2011 gives real GDP in 2012 as $196 million.

Notice that the growth rates depend only on prices and quantities produced in adjacent years and do not depend on what the reference base year is. Changing the reference base year changes the *level* of real GDP in each year, but it does not change the *growth rates*.

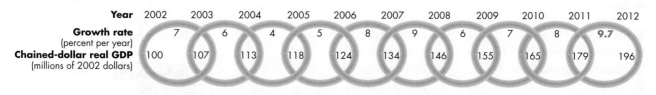

Figure 1 Real GDP Calculation Step 3: Repeat Growth Rate Calculations and Chain Link

Exercise

The table provides data on the economy of Tropical Republic, which produces only bananas and coconuts.

Use this data to calculate Tropical Republic's nominal GDP in 2011 and 2012 and its chained-dollar real GDP in 2012 expressed in 2011 dollars.

	Table	
Quantities	2011	2012
Bananas	1,000 bunches	1,100 bunches
Coconuts	500 bunches	525 bunches
Prices		
Bananas	$2 a bunch	$3 a bunch
Coconuts	$10 a bunch	$8 a bunch

◆ SUMMARY

Key Points

Gross Domestic Product (pp. 468–470)

- GDP, or gross domestic product, is the market value of all the final goods and services produced in a country during a given period.
- A final good is an item that is bought by its final user, and it contrasts with an intermediate good, which is a component of a final good.
- GDP is calculated by using either the expenditure or income totals in the circular flow model.
- Aggregate expenditure on goods and services equals aggregate income and GDP.

Working Problems 1 to 7 will give you a better understanding of gross domestic product.

Measuring Canada's GDP (pp. 471–473)

- Because aggregate expenditure, aggregate income, and the value of aggregate production are equal, we can measure GDP by using the expenditure approach or the income approach.
- The expenditure approach sums consumption expenditure, investment, government expenditure on goods and services, and net exports.
- The income approach sums wages, interest, rent, and profit (plus indirect taxes less subsidies plus depreciation).

- Real GDP is measured using a common set of prices to remove the effects of inflation from GDP.

Working Problems 8 to 15 will give you a better understanding of measuring Canada's GDP.

The Uses and Limitations of Real GDP (pp. 474–479)

- Real GDP is used to compare the standard of living over time and across countries.
- Real GDP per person grows and fluctuates around the more smoothly growing potential GDP.
- Incomes would be much higher today if the growth rate of real GDP per person had not slowed during the 1970s.
- International real GDP comparisons use PPP prices.
- Real GDP is not a perfect measure of the standard of living because it excludes household production, the underground economy, health and life expectancy, leisure time, security, environmental quality, and political freedom and social justice.

Working Problem 16 will give you a better understanding of the uses and limitations of real GDP.

Key Terms

Business cycle, 475
Chained-dollar real GDP, 484
Consumption expenditure, 469
Cycle, 483
Depreciation, 470
Expansion, 475
Exports, 470
Final good, 468
Government expenditure, 470
Gross domestic product (GDP), 468
Gross investment, 470
Imports, 470

Intermediate good, 468
Investment, 470
Net exports, 470
Net investment, 470
Nominal GDP, 473
Potential GDP, 474
Real GDP, 473
Real GDP per person, 474
Recession, 475
Time-series graph, 482
Trend, 483

SCAN THIS

STUDY PLAN PROBLEMS AND APPLICATIONS

MyEconLab ◆ You can work Problems 1 to 17 in Chapter 20 Study Plan and get instant feedback.

Gross Domestic Product (Study Plan 20.1)

1. Classify each of the following items as a final good or service or an intermediate good or service and identify which is a component of consumption expenditure, investment, or government expenditure on goods and services:
   - Banking services bought by a student.
   - New cars bought by Hertz, the car rental firm.
   - Newsprint bought by the *National Post*.
   - The purchase of a new limo for the prime minister.
   - New house bought by Alanis Morissette.

2. The firm that printed this textbook bought the paper from XYZ Paper Mills. Was this purchase of paper part of GDP? If not, how does the value of the paper get counted in GDP?

Use the following figure, which illustrates the circular flow model, to work Problems 3 and 4.

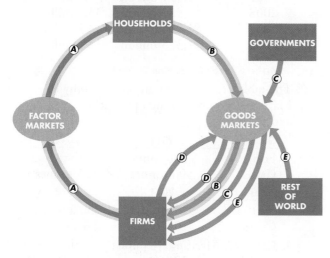

3. During 2008, in an economy:
   - Flow *B* was $900 billion.
   - Flow *C* was $200 billion.
   - Flow *D* was $300 billion.
   - Flow *E* was –$70 billion.
   Name the flows and calculate the value of
   a. Aggregate income.
   b. GDP.

4. During 2009, flow *A* was $1,300 billion, flow *B* was $910 billion, flow *D* was $330 billion, and flow *E* was –$80 billion.

Calculate the 2009 values of
   a. GDP.
   b. Government expenditure.

5. Use the following data to calculate aggregate expenditure and imports of goods and services.
   - Government expenditure: $20 billion
   - Aggregate income: $100 billion
   - Consumption expenditure: $67 billion
   - Investment: $21 billion
   - Exports of goods and services: $30 billion

6. **Canadian Economy Shrinks in May**

   Real GDP grew 1 percent in the first quarter of 2011. Business investment increased 3.2 percent, exports grew 1.6 percent, and imports rose by 2.2 percent.

   Source: Statistics Canada, *The Daily*, July 29, 2011

   Use the letters on the figure in Problem 3 to indicate the flow in which each item in the news clip occurs. How can GDP have grown by only 1.0 percent with business investment and exports up by much more than 1 percent?

7. A U.S. market research firm deconstructed an Apple iPod and studied the manufacturers, costs, and profits of each of the parts and components. The final results are
   - An Apple iPod sells in the United States for $299.
   - A Japanese firm, Toshiba, makes the hard disk and display screen, which cost $93.
   - Other components produced in South Korea cost $25.
   - Other components produced in the United States cost $21.
   - The iPod is assembled in China at a cost of $5.
   - The costs and profits of retailers, advertisers, and transportation firms in the United States are $75.
   a. What is Apple's profit?
   b. Where in the national income and expenditure accounts of the United States, Japan, South Korea, and China are these transactions recorded?
   c. What contribution does one iPod make to world GDP?

Measuring Canada's GDP (Study Plan 20.2)

Use the following data to work Problems 8 and 9.
The table lists some macroeconomic data for Canada in 2008.

Item	Billions of dollars
Wages paid to labour	815
Consumption expenditure	885
Net domestic income at factor cost	1,210
Investment	304
Government expenditure	357
Net exports	32
Depreciation	202

8. Calculate Canada's GDP in 2008.

9. Explain the approach (expenditure or income) that you used to calculate GDP.

Use the following data to work Problems 10 and 11.
The national accounts of Parchment Paradise are kept on (you guessed it) parchment. A fire destroys the statistics office. The accounts are now incomplete but they contain the following data:

- GDP (income approach): $2,900
- Consumption expenditure: $2,000
- Indirect taxes less subsidies: $100
- Net domestic income at factor cost: $2,500
- Investment: $800
- Government expenditure: $400
- Wages: $2,000
- Net exports: –$200

10. Calculate GDP (expenditure approach) and depreciation.

11. Calculate the sum of total income less wages and the statistical discrepancy.

Use the following data to work Problems 12 and 13.
Tropical Republic produces only bananas and coconuts. The base year is 2010, and the table gives the quantities produced and the prices.

Quantities	2010	2011
Bananas	800 bunches	900 bunches
Coconuts	400 bunches	500 bunches

Prices	2010	2011
Bananas	$2 a bunch	$4 a bunch
Coconuts	$10 a bunch	$5 a bunch

12. Calculate nominal GDP in 2010 and 2011.

13. Calculate real GDP in 2011 expressed in base-year prices.

Use the following news clip to work Problems 14 and 15.

Toyota First to Build Electric Vehicles in Canada

Toyota will start assembling electric versions of its RAV4 sport utility vehicle in Woodstock. Governments are contributing $141 million to Toyota for a series of upgrades at plants in Cambridge and Woodstock worth a total of $545 million under the name Project Green Light.

Source: *Toronto Star*, August 4, 2011

14. Explain how this activity by Toyota will influence Canada's GDP and the components of aggregate expenditure.

15. Explain how this activity by Toyota will influence the factor incomes that make up Canada's GDP.

The Uses and Limitations of Real GDP (Study Plan 20.3)

16. Use the following table to work out in which year Canada's standard of living (i) increases and (ii) decreases. Explain your answer.

Year	Real GDP	Population
2007	$1,311 billion	32.9 million
2008	$1,320 billion	33.3 million
2009	$1,284 billion	33.7 million
2010	$1,325 billion	34.1 million

Mathematical Note (Study Plan 20.MN)

17. The table provides data on the economy of Maritime Republic, which produces only fish and crabs.

Quantities	2011	2012
Fish	1,000 tonnes	1,100 tonnes
Crabs	500 tonnes	525 tonnes

Prices	2011	2012
Fish	$20 a tonne	$30 a tonne
Crabs	$10 a tonne	$8 a tonne

a. Calculate Maritime Republic's nominal GDP in 2011 and 2012.

b. Calculate Maritime Republic's chained-dollar real GDP in 2012 expressed in 2011 dollars.

Data Graphing

Use the *Data Grapher* in MyEconLab to work Problems 18 and 19.

18. In which country in 2009 was the growth rate of real GDP per person highest: Canada, Japan, or the United States?

19. In which country in 2009 was the growth rate of real GDP per person lowest: France, China, or the United States?

ADDITIONAL PROBLEMS AND APPLICATIONS

MyEconLab ◆ You can work these problems in MyEconLab if assigned by your instructor.

Gross Domestic Product

20. Classify each of the following items as a final good or service or an intermediate good or service and identify which is a component of consumption expenditure, investment, or government expenditure on goods and services:
    - Banking services bought by Loblaws.
    - Security system bought by the TD Bank.
    - Coffee beans bought by Tim Hortons.
    - New coffee grinders bought by Second Cup.
    - Starbucks grande mocha frappuccino bought by a student at a campus coffee bar.
    - New helicopters bought by Canada's army.

Use the figure in Problem 3 to work Problems 21 and 22.

21. In 2009, flow A was $1,000 billion, flow C was $250 billion, flow B was $650 billion, and flow E was $50 billion. Calculate investment.

22. In 2010, flow D was $2 trillion, flow E was −$1 trillion, flow A was $10 trillion, and flow C was $4 trillion. Calculate consumption expenditure.

Use the following information to work Problems 23 and 24.

The components and robots for Toyota's auto assembly lines in Canada are built in Japan. Toyota assembles cars for the Canadian market in Ontario.

23. Explain where these activities appear in Canada's *National Income and Expenditure Accounts*.

24. Explain where these activities appear in Japan's *National Income and Expenditure Accounts*.

Use the following news clip to work Problems 25 and 26, and use the circular flow model to illustrate your answers.

Boeing Bets the House

Boeing is producing some components of its new 787 Dreamliner in Japan and is assembling it in the United States. Much of the first year's production will be sold to ANA (All Nippon Airways), a Japanese airline.

Source: *The New York Times*, May 7, 2006

25. Explain how Boeing's activities and its transactions affect U.S. and Japanese GDP.

26. Explain how ANA's activities and its transactions affect U.S. and Japanese GDP.

Measuring Canada's GDP

Use the following data to work Problems 27 and 28. The table lists some macroeconomic data for Xanadu in 2012.

Item	Billions of dollars
Wages paid to labour	800
Consumption expenditure	1,000
Profit, interest, and rents	340
Investment	150
Government expenditure	290
Net exports	−34

27. Calculate Xanadu's GDP in 2012.

28. Explain the approach (expenditure or income) that you used to calculate GDP.

Use the following data to work Problems 29 to 31. An economy produces only apples and oranges. The base year is 2011, and the table gives the quantities produced and the prices.

Quantities	2011	2012
Apples	60	160
Oranges	80	220

Prices	2011	2012
Apples	$0.50	$1.00
Oranges	$0.25	$2.00

29. Calculate nominal GDP in 2011 and 2012.

30. Calculate real GDP in 2011 and 2012 expressed in base-year prices.

31. **GDP Expands 11.4 Percent, Fastest in 13 Years**

    China's gross domestic product grew 11.4 percent last year and marked a fifth year of double-digit growth. The increase was especially remarkable given that the United States is experiencing a slowdown due to the sub-prime crisis and housing slump. Citigroup estimates that each 1 percent drop in the U.S. economy will shave 1.3 percent off China's growth, because Americans are heavy users of Chinese products. In spite of the uncertainties, China is expected to post its sixth year of double-digit growth next year.

    Source: *The China Daily*, January 24, 2008

    Use the expenditure approach for calculating China's GDP to explain why "each 1 percent drop in the U.S. economy will shave 1.3 percent off China's growth."

The Uses and Limitations of Real GDP

32. The United Nations' Human Development Index (HDI) is based on real GDP per person, life expectancy at birth, and indicators of the quality and quantity of education.

    a. Explain why the HDI might be better than real GDP as a measure of economic welfare.

    b. Which items in the HDI are part of real GDP and which items are not in real GDP?

    c. Do you think the HDI should be expanded to include items such as pollution, resource depletion, and political freedom? Explain.

    d. What other influences on economic welfare should be included in a comprehensive measure?

33. **U.K. Living Standards Outstrip U.S.**

    Oxford analysts report that living standards in Britain are set to rise above those in America for the first time since the nineteenth century. Real GDP per person in Britain will be £23,500 this year, compared with £23,250 in America, reflecting not only the strength of the pound against the dollar but also the U.K. economy's record run of growth since 2001. But the Oxford analysts also point out that Americans benefit from lower prices than those in Britain.

    Source: *The Sunday Times*, January 6, 2008

    If real GDP per person is greater in the United Kingdom than in the United States but Americans benefit from lower prices, does this comparison of real GDP per person really tell us which country has the higher standard of living?

34. Use the news clip in Problem 31.

    a. Why might China's recent GDP growth rates overstate the actual increase in the level of production taking place in China?

    b. Explain the complications involved with attempting to compare the economic welfare in China and the United States by using the GDP for each country.

35. **Poor India Makes Millionaires at Fastest Pace**

    India, with the world's largest population of poor people, created millionaires at the fastest pace in the world in 2007. India added another 23,000 more millionaires in 2007 to its 2006 tally of 100,000 millionaires measured in dollars. That is 1 millionaire for about 7,000 people living on less than $2 a day.

    Source: *The Times of India*, June 25, 2008

    a. Why might real GDP per person misrepresent the standard of living of the average Indian?

    b. Why might $2 a day underestimate the standard of living of the poorest Indians?

Economics in the News

36. After you have studied *Reading Between the Lines* on pp. 480–481, answer the following questions.

    a. Which economy—Canada or the United States—had the longest and deepest recession in 2008–2009?

    b. What is a "double-dip" recession?

    c. If the United States had a double-dip recession, why would Canada most likely have a recession too?

    d. Why would you expect Canada to experience a recession more severe than one-fifth that of the United States?

37. **Totally Gross**

    GDP has proved useful in tracking both short-term fluctuations and long-run growth. Which isn't to say GDP doesn't miss some things. Amartya Sen, at Harvard, helped create the United Nations' Human Development Index, which combines health and education data with per capita GDP to give a better measure of the wealth of nations. Joseph Stiglitz, at Columbia, advocates a "green net national product" that takes into account the depletion of natural resources. Others want to include happiness in the measure. These alternative benchmarks have merit but can they be measured with anything like the frequency, reliability and impartiality of GDP?

    Source: *Time*, April 21, 2008

    a. Explain the factors that the news clip identifies as limiting the usefulness of GDP as a measure of economic welfare.

    b. What are the challenges involved in trying to incorporate measurements of those factors in an effort to better measure economic welfare?

    c. What does the ranking of Canada in the Human Development Index imply about the levels of health and education relative to other nations?

Mathematical Note

38. Use the information in Problem 29 to calculate the chained-dollar real GDP in 2012 expressed in 2011 dollars.

Monitoring Jobs and Inflation

Each month, we chart the course of unemployment as a measure of Canadian economic health. How do we count the number of people unemployed? Is it a reliable vital sign?

Having a good job that pays a decent wage is only half of the equation that translates into a good standard of living. The other half is the *cost of living* that we measure each month with the Consumer Price Index, or CPI. What is the CPI, how is it calculated, and is it a reliable guide to the cost of living?

Reading Between the Lines, at the end of this chapter, puts the spotlight on employment and unemployment during recession and expansion of the past few years.

After studying this chapter, you will be able to

◆ Explain why unemployment is a problem and define the unemployment rate and other labour market indicators

◆ Explain why unemployment is present even at full employment, and how its rate fluctuates over a business cycle

◆ Explain why inflation is a problem and how we measure it using the CPI

◆ Employment and Unemployment

What kind of job market will you enter when you graduate? Will there be plenty of good jobs to choose among, or will jobs be so hard to find that you end up taking one that doesn't use your education and pays a low wage? The answer depends, to a large degree, on the total number of jobs available and on the number of people competing for them.

The Canadian economy is an incredible job-creating machine. In 2011, 17 million people had jobs, which was 2 million more than in 2001 and 6 million more than in 1981. But not everyone who wants a job can find one. On a typical day, more than 1 million people are unemployed. That's equivalent to the population of Calgary. During a recession, this number rises and during a boom year it falls. At its worst, during the Great Depression, one in every five workers was unemployed.

Why Unemployment Is a Problem

Unemployment is a serious personal and social economic problem for two main reasons. It results in

- Lost incomes and production
- Lost human capital

Lost Incomes and Production The loss of a job brings a loss of income and lost production. These losses are devastating for the people who bear them and they make unemployment a frightening prospect for everyone. Unemployment benefits create a safety net, but they don't fully replace lost earnings.

Lost Human Capital Prolonged unemployment permanently damages a person's job prospects by destroying human capital, which lowers the living standard in both the present and the future.

Think about a manager who loses his job when

Economics in Action

What Keeps Ben Bernanke Awake at Night

The Great Depression began in October 1929, when the U.S. stock market crashed. It reached its deepest point in 1933, when 25 percent of the labour force was unemployed, and lasted until 1941, when the United States entered World War II. The depression quickly spread globally to envelop most nations.

The 1930s were and remain the longest and worst period of high unemployment in history. Failed banks, stores, farms, and factories left millions of Americans and Canadians without jobs, homes, and food. Without the support of government and charities, millions would have starved.

The Great Depression was an enormous political event: It fostered the rise of the German and Japanese militarism that were to bring the most devastating war humans have ever fought. It also led to President Franklin D. Roosevelt's "New Deal," which enhanced the role of government in economic life and made government intervention in markets popular and the market economy unpopular.

The Great Depression also brought a revolution in economics. British economist John Maynard Keynes published his *General Theory of Employment, Interest, and Money* and created what we now call macroeconomics.

Many economists have studied the Great Depression and tried to determine why what started out as an ordinary recession became so devastating. Among them is Ben Bernanke, the chairman of the U.S. Federal Reserve (the U.S. Fed).

One of the reasons the U.S. Fed was so aggressive in cutting interest rates, saving Bear Stearns, and propping up Fannie Mae and Freddie Mac is because Ben Bernanke is so vividly aware of the horrors of total economic collapse and determined to avoid any risk of a repeat of the Great Depression.

his employer downsizes. The only work he can find is driving a taxi. After a year in this work, he discovers that he can't compete with new MBA graduates. Eventually, he gets hired as a manager but in a small firm and at a lower wage than before. He has lost some of his human capital.

Governments make strenuous efforts to measure unemployment accurately and to adopt policies to moderate its level and ease its pain. Let's see how the Canadian government monitors unemployment.

Labour Force Survey

Every month, Statistics Canada conducts a *Labour Force Survey* in which it asks 54,000 households a series of questions about the age and job market status of the members of each household. Figure 21.1 shows the population categories used by Statistics Canada and the relationships among the categories.

The population divides into two broad groups: the working-age population and others who are too young to work or who live in institutions and are unable to work. The **working-age population** is the total number of people aged 15 years and over. The working-age population is also divided into two groups: those in the labour force and those not in the labour force. Members of the labour force are either employed or unemployed. So the **labour force** is the sum of the employed and the unemployed. The employed are either full-time or part-time workers; and part-time workers either want part-time work (voluntary part-time) or want full-time work (involuntary part-time).

To be counted as employed in the Labour Force Survey, a person must have either a full-time job or a part-time job. To be counted as *un*employed, a person must be available for work and must be in one of three categories:

1. Without work but has made specific efforts to find a job within the previous four weeks
2. Laid off from a job and be waiting to be called back to work
3. Waiting to start a new job within four weeks

People who satisfy one of these three criteria are counted as unemployed. People in the working-age population who are neither employed nor unemployed are classified as not in the labour force.

In 2010, the population of Canada was 34.1 million; the working-age population was

FIGURE 21.1   Population Labour Force Categories

The total population consists of the working-age population and others. The working-age population consists of those in the labour force and those not in the labour force. The labour force is either employed or unemployed. The employed are either full-time or part-time employed and the part-time employed are either voluntary or involuntary part-time.

Source of data: Statistics Canada, CANSIM Tables 051–0001, 282–0002, and 282–0014.

———————————— MyEconLab animation ◆

27.7 million. Of this number, 9.2 million were not in the labour force. Most of these people were in school full time or had retired from work. The remaining 18.5 million people made up the Canadian labour force. Of these, 17.0 million were employed and 1.5 million were unemployed. Of the 17.0 million employed, 3.3 million had part-time jobs, and of these, 0.9 million wanted a full-time job but couldn't find one.

Four Labour Market Indicators

Statistics Canada calculates four indicators of the state of the labour market. They are

- The unemployment rate
- The involuntary part-time rate
- The labour force participation rate
- The employment-to-population ratio

The Unemployment Rate The amount of unemployment is an indicator of the extent to which people who want jobs can't find them. The **unemployment rate** is the percentage of the people in the labour force who are unemployed. That is,

$$\text{Unemployment rate} = \frac{\text{Number of people unemployed}}{\text{Labour force}} \times 100$$

and

$$\text{Labour force} = \frac{\text{Number of people}}{\text{employed}} + \frac{\text{Number of people}}{\text{unemployed}}.$$

In 2010, the number of people employed was 17.04 million and the number unemployed was 1.48 million. By using the above equations, you can verify that the labour force was 18.52 million (17.04 million plus 1.48 million) and the unemployment rate was 8 percent (1.48 million divided by 18.52 million, multiplied by 100).

Figure 21.2 shows the unemployment rate from 1960 to 2010. The average unemployment rate during this period was 7.6 percent. The unemployment rate fluctuates over the business cycle: It increases as a recession deepens, reaches a peak after a recession ends, and decreases after a recovery gets going.

The Involuntary Part-Time Rate Part-time workers who want full-time work are underemployed and Statistics Canada counts their number. The *involuntary part-time rate* is the percentage of the people in the labour force who work part time but want full-time jobs.

$$\frac{\text{Involuntary}}{\text{part-time rate}} = \frac{\frac{\text{Number of involuntary}}{\text{part-time workers}}}{\text{Labour force}} \times 100.$$

In 2010, with 920,000 involuntary part-time workers and a labour force of 18.52 million, the involuntary part-time rate was 5 percent.

The Labour Force Participation Rate The number of people in the labour force is an indicator of the willingness of people of working age to take jobs. The **labour force participation rate** is the percentage of the working-age population who are members of the labour force. That is,

$$\frac{\text{Labour force}}{\text{participation rate}} = \frac{\text{Labour force}}{\frac{\text{Working-age}}{\text{population}}} \times 100.$$

In 2010, the labour force was 18.52 million and the working-age population was 27.66 million. By using the above equation, you can verify that the

---

FIGURE 21.2   The Unemployment Rate: 1960–2010

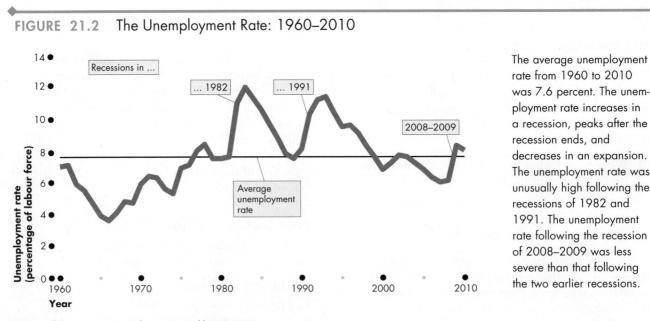

The average unemployment rate from 1960 to 2010 was 7.6 percent. The unemployment rate increases in a recession, peaks after the recession ends, and decreases in an expansion. The unemployment rate was unusually high following the recessions of 1982 and 1991. The unemployment rate following the recession of 2008–2009 was less severe than that following the two earlier recessions.

Source of data: Statistics Canada, CANSIM Table 282–0002.

MyEconLab   animation

FIGURE 21.3   Labour Force Participation and Employment: 1960–2010

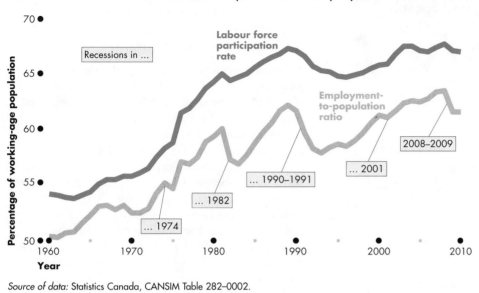

The labour force participation rate and the employment-to-population ratio increased rapidly before 1990 and slowly after 1990. They fluctuate with the business cycle.

The employment-to-population ratio fluctuates more than the labour force participation rate and reflects cyclical fluctuations in the unemployment rate.

Source of data: Statistics Canada, CANSIM Table 282–0002.

MyEconLab   animation ◆

labour force participation rate was 67.0 percent (18.52 million divided by 27.66 million, multiplied by 100).

The Employment-to-Population Ratio The number of people of working age who have jobs is an indicator of both the availability of jobs and the degree of match between people's skills and jobs. The **employment-to-population ratio** is the percentage of people of working age who have jobs. That is,

$$\text{Employment-to-population ratio} = \frac{\text{Number of people employed}}{\text{Working-age population}} \times 100.$$

In 2010, the number of people employed was 17.04 million and the working-age population was 27.66 million. By using the above equation, you can verify that the employment-to-population ratio was 61.6 percent (17.04 million divided by 27.66 million, multiplied by 100).

Figure 21.3 shows the labour force participation rate and the employment-to-population ratio from 1960 to 2010. These indicators follow an upward trend before 1990 and then flatten off. The increase before 1990 means that the Canadian economy created jobs at a faster rate than the working-age population grew.

The employment-to-population ratio fluctuates with the business cycle: It falls in a recession and rises in an expansion. The labour force participation rate has milder business cycle swings that reflect movements into and out of the labour force.

Other Definitions of Unemployment

Do fluctuations in the labour force participation rate over the business cycle mean that people who leave the labour force during a recession should be counted as unemployed? Or are they correctly counted as not in the labour force?

Statistics Canada believes that the official definition of unemployment gives the correct measure of the unemployment rate. But as you've already seen, it doesn't count the underutilized labour of people with part-time jobs who want full-time jobs. The official measure also omits another type of underutilized labour: people known as marginally attached workers. A **marginally attached worker** is a person who currently is neither working nor looking for work but has indicated that he or she wants a job and is available and has looked for work sometime in the recent past. A marginally attached worker who has stopped looking for a job because of repeated failure to find one is called a **discouraged worker**.

The official measure of unemployment excludes marginally attached workers because they haven't

FIGURE 21.4 The Duration of Unemployment Spells

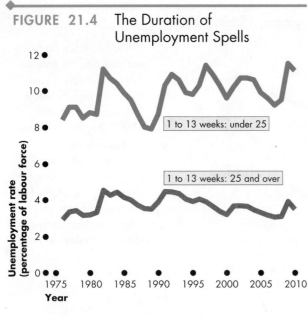

(a) Short-term unemployment

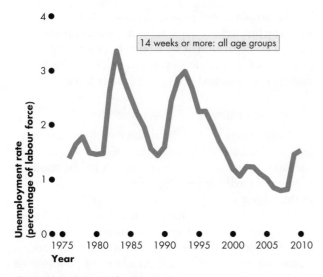

(b) Long-term unemployment

On average, 60 percent of unemployment is short term—1 to 13 weeks. Part (a) shows the incidence of short-term unemployment, which falls much more heavily on under–25-year-olds than on over–25-year-olds. Part (b) shows long-term unemployment—14 weeks or more. This unemployment affects all age groups in a similar way and its rate fluctuates with the business cycle but along a downward trend.

Source of data: Statistics Canada, CANSIM Table 282–0048.

MyEconLab   animation ◆

made specific efforts to find a job within the past four weeks. In all other respects, they are unemployed.

Most Costly Unemployment

All unemployment is costly, but the most costly is long-term unemployment. People who are unemployed for a few weeks and then find another job bear some costs of unemployment. But these costs are low compared to the costs borne by people who remain unemployed for many weeks.

On average, about 60 percent of unemployment is short term—between 1 week and 13 weeks. Figure 21.4(a) shows that for those over 25, short-term unemployment is around 4 percent and fluctuates only slightly over the business cycle. But the figure also shows that the short-term unemployment rate of people under 25 is high and fluctuates more strongly with the business cycle.

Figure 21.4(b) shows the long-term unemployment rate—unemployment spells lasting for 14 weeks or more. The long-term unemployment rate fluctuates with the business cycle but it has trended downward. During the 2008–2009 recession, it was less than half that of the recessions of the early 1980s and early 1990s.

REVIEW QUIZ

1 What determines if a person is in the labour force?
2 What distinguishes an unemployed person from one who is not in the labour force?
3 Describe the trends and fluctuations in the unemployment rate in Canada from 1960 to 2010.
4 Describe the trends and fluctuations in the employment-to-population ratio and labour force participation rate in Canada from 1960 to 2010.
5 Describe the key facts about the duration of unemployment spells.

You can work these questions in Study Plan 21.1 and get instant feedback.

━━━━━━━━━━━━━━━ MyEconLab ◆

You've seen how we measure employment and unemployment. Your next task is to see what we mean by full employment and how unemployment and real GDP fluctuate over the business cycle.

Unemployment and Full Employment

There is always someone without a job who is searching for one, so there is always some unemployment. The key reason is that the economy is a complex mechanism that is always changing—it experiences frictions, structural change, and cycles.

Frictional Unemployment

There is an unending flow of people into and out of the labour force as people move through the stages of life—from being in school to finding a job, to working, perhaps to becoming unhappy with a job and looking for a new one, and, finally, to retiring from full-time work.

There is also an unending process of job creation and job destruction as new firms are born, firms expand or contract, and some firms fail and go out of business.

The flows into and out of the labour force and the processes of job creation and job destruction create the need for people to search for jobs and for businesses to search for workers. Businesses don't usually hire the first person who applies for a job, and unemployed people don't usually take the first job that comes their way. Instead, both firms and workers spend time searching for what they believe will be the best available match. By this process of search, people can match their own skills and interests with the available jobs and find a satisfying job and a good income.

The unemployment that arises from the normal labour turnover we've just described—from people entering and leaving the labour force and from the ongoing creation and destruction of jobs—is called **frictional unemployment**. Frictional unemployment is a permanent and healthy phenomenon in a dynamic, growing economy.

Structural Unemployment

The unemployment that arises when changes in technology or international competition change the skills needed to perform jobs or change the locations of jobs is called **structural unemployment**. Structural unemployment usually lasts longer than frictional unemployment because workers must retrain and possibly relocate to find a job. When a steel plant in Hamilton, Ontario, is automated, some jobs in that

city disappear. Meanwhile, new jobs for security guards, retail clerks, and life-insurance salespeople are created in Toronto and Vancouver. The unemployed former steelworkers remain unemployed for several months until they move, retrain, and get one of these jobs. Structural unemployment is painful, especially for older workers for whom the best available option might be to retire early or take a lower-skilled, lower-paying job.

Cyclical Unemployment

The higher than normal unemployment at a business cycle trough and the lower than normal unemployment at a business cycle peak is called **cyclical unemployment**. A worker who is laid off because the economy is in a recession and who gets rehired some months later when the expansion begins has experienced cyclical unemployment.

"Natural" Unemployment

Natural unemployment is the unemployment that arises from frictions and structural change when there is no cyclical unemployment—when all the unemployment frictional and structural. Natural unemployment expressed as a percentage of the labour force is called the **natural unemployment rate**.

Full employment is defined as a situation in which the unemployment rate equals the natural unemployment rate.

What determines the natural unemployment rate? Is it constant or does it change over time?

The natural unemployment rate is influenced by many factors but the most important ones are

- The age distribution of the population
- The scale of structural change
- The real wage rate
- Unemployment benefits

The Age Distribution of the Population An economy with a young population has a large number of new job seekers every year and has a high level of frictional unemployment. An economy with an aging population has fewer new job seekers and a low level of frictional unemployment.

The Scale of Structural Change The scale of structural change is sometimes small. The same jobs using the same machines remain in place for many years. But sometimes there is a technological upheaval. The old ways are swept aside and millions of jobs are lost and the skill to perform them loses value. The amount of structural unemployment fluctuates with the pace and volume of technological change and the change driven by fierce international competition, especially from fast-changing Asian economies. A high level of structural unemployment is present in many of Canada's provinces today (as you can see in *Economics in Action* opposite).

The Real Wage Rate The natural unemployment rate is influenced by the level of the real wage rate. Real wage rates that bring unemployment are a *minimum wage* and an *efficiency wage*. Chapter 6 (see pp. 131–133) explains how the minimum wage creates unemployment. An *efficiency wage* is a wage set above the going market wage to enable firms to attract the most productive workers, get them to work hard, and discourage them from quitting.

Unemployment Benefits Unemployment benefits increase the natural unemployment rate by lowering the opportunity cost of job search. Canada and the European countries have more generous unemployment benefits and higher natural unemployment rates than the United States. Extending unemployment benefits increases the natural unemployment rate.

There is no controversy about the existence of a natural unemployment rate. Nor is there disagreement that the natural unemployment rate changes. But economists don't know its exact size or the extent to which it fluctuates. There is no official estimate of the natural unemployment rate.

Real GDP and Unemployment Over the Cycle

The quantity of real GDP at full employment is *potential GDP*. Over the business cycle, real GDP fluctuates around potential GDP. The gap between real GDP and potential GDP is called the **output gap**. As the output gap fluctuates over the business cycle, the unemployment rate fluctuates around the natural unemployment rate.

Figure 21.5 illustrates these fluctuations in Canada between 1985 and 2010—the output gap in part (a) and the unemployment rate and natural unemployment rate in part (b).

When the economy is at full employment, the unemployment rate equals the natural employ-

Economics in Action
Structural Unemployment in Canada

In 2010, unemployment rates across Canada's provinces ranged from more than 14 percent in Newfoundland and Labrador to just over 5 percent in Saskachewan. All the provinces west of Ontario had unemployment rates below the national average while Ontario and the Maritimes were above the national average. Quebec unemployment equalled the national average at 8 percent.

This range of unemployment rates across the provinces arises from structural features of the Canadian economy and reflects regional differences in structural unemployment.

The West in general is growing rapidly based largely on the extraction of resources. The Maritimes and to a lesser extent Quebec and Ontario are growing more slowly. People must leave the eastern provinces and move westward to find work. A reluctuance to uproot keeps the unemployment rates widely dispersed.

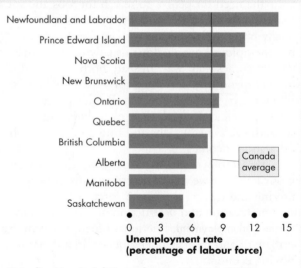

Canadian Provincial Unemployment Rates in 2010

Source of data: Statistics Canada, CANSIM Table 282–0002.

ment rate and real GDP equals potential GDP so the output gap is zero. When the unemployment rate is less than the natural unemployment rate, real GDP is greater than potential GDP and the output gap is positive. And when the unemployment rate is greater

FIGURE 21.5   The Output Gap and the Unemployment Rate

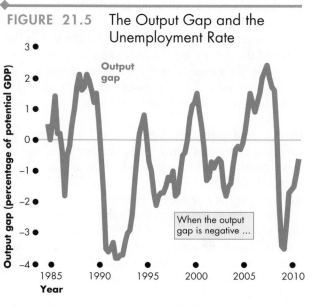

(a) Output gap

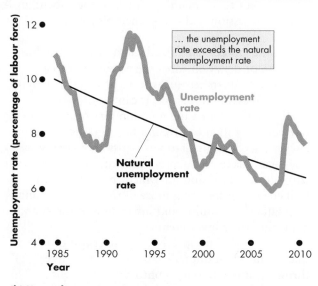

(b) Unemployment rate

As real GDP fluctuates around potential GDP in part (a), the unemployment rate fluctuates around the natural unemployment rate in part (b). In recessions, cyclical unemployment peaks and the output gap becomes negative. In expansions, the unemployment rate falls below the natural unemployment rate and the output gap becomes positive. The natural unemployment rate has trended downward.

Sources of data: Statistics Canada CANSIM Table 282–0002 and Bank of Canada output gap estimates.

MyEconLab   animation ◆

than the natural unemployment rate, real GDP is less than potential GDP and the output gap is negative. The timing of the fluctuations in real GDP and the unemployment rate don't align perfectly and the unemployment rate lags real GDP. But the general tendency for real GDP to rise and the unemployment rate to fall in an expansion and for real GDP to fall and the unemployment rate to rise in a recession is clear in the figure.

The Trend in the Natural Unemployment Rate

Figure 21.5(b) shows our estimate of the natural unemployment rate since 1985. This estimate puts the natural unemployment rate at 10 percent in 1985 and falling steadily through the rest of the 1980s, the 1990s, and the 2000s to a bit more than 6 percent in 2010. This estimate of the natural unemployment rate in Canada is one that many, but not all, economists would agree with.

REVIEW QUIZ

1 Why does unemployment arise and what makes some unemployment unavoidable?
2 Define frictional unemployment, structural unemployment, and cyclical unemployment. Give examples of each type of unemployment.
3 What is the natural unemployment rate?
4 How does the natural unemployment rate change and what factors might make it change?
5 Why is the unemployment rate never zero, even at full employment?
6 What is the output gap? How does it change when the economy goes into recession?
7 How does the unemployment rate fluctuate over the business cycle?

You can work these questions in Study Plan 21.2 and get instant feedback.

━━━━━━━━━ MyEconLab ◆

Your next task is to see how we monitor the price level and the inflation rate. You will learn about the Consumer Price Index (CPI), which is monitored every month. You will also learn about other measures of the price level and the inflation rate.

◆ The Price Level, Inflation, and Deflation

What will it *really* cost you to pay off your student loan? What will your parents' life savings buy when they retire? The answers depend on what happens to the **price level**, the average level of prices, and the value of money. A persistently rising price level is called **inflation**; a persistently falling price level is called **deflation**.

We are interested in the price level and inflation for two main reasons. First, we want to measure the annual percentage change of the price level—the inflation rate or deflation rate. Second, we want to distinguish between the money values and real values of economic variables such as your student loan and your parents' savings.

We begin by explaining why inflation and deflation are problems. Then we'll look at how we measure the price level and the inflation rate. Finally, we'll return to the task of distinguishing real values from money values.

Why Inflation and Deflation are Problems

Low, steady, and anticipated inflation or deflation isn't a problem, but an unexpected burst of inflation or period of deflation brings big problems and costs. An unexpected inflation or deflation

- Redistributes income
- Redistributes wealth
- Lowers real GDP and employment
- Diverts resources from production

Redistributes Income Workers and employers sign wage contracts that last for a year or more. An unexpected burst of inflation raises prices but doesn't immediately raise the wages. Workers are worse off because their wages buy less than they bargained for and employers are better off because their profits rise.

An unexpected period of deflation has the opposite effect. Wage rates don't fall but the prices fall. Workers are better off because their fixed wages buy more than they bargained for and employers are worse off with lower profits.

Redistributes Wealth People enter into loan contracts that are fixed in money terms and that pay an interest rate agreed as a percentage of the money borrowed and lent. With an unexpected burst of inflation, the money that the borrower repays to the lender buys

less than the money originally loaned. The borrower wins and the lender loses. The interest paid on the loan doesn't compensate the lender for the loss in the value of the money loaned. With an unexpected deflation, the money that the borrower repays to the lender buys *more* than the money originally loaned. The borrower loses and the lender wins.

Lowers Real GDP and Employment Unexpected inflation that raises firms' profits brings a rise in investment and a boom in production and employment. Real GDP rises above potential GDP and the unemployment rate falls below the natural rate. But this situation is *temporary*. Profitable investment dries up, spending falls, real GDP falls below potential GDP, and the unemployment rate rises. Avoiding these swings in production and jobs means avoiding unexpected swings in the inflation rate.

An unexpected deflation has even greater consequences for real GDP and jobs. Businesses and households that are in debt (borrowers) are worse off and they cut their spending. A fall in total spending brings a recession and rising unemployment.

Diverts Resources from Production Unpredictable inflation or deflation turns the economy into a casino and diverts resources from productive activities to forecasting inflation. It can become more profitable to forecast the inflation rate or deflation rate correctly than to invent a new product. Doctors, lawyers, accountants, farmers—just about everyone—can make themselves better off, not by specializing in the profession for which they have been trained but by spending more of their time dabbling as amateur economists and inflation forecasters and managing their investments.

From a social perspective, the diversion of talent that results from unpredictable inflation is like throwing scarce resources onto a pile of garbage. This waste of resources is a cost of inflation.

At its worst, inflation becomes **hyperinflation**—an inflation rate of 50 percent a month or higher that grinds the economy to a halt and causes a society to collapse. Hyperinflation is rare, but Zimbabwe in recent years and several European and Latin American countries have experienced it.

We pay close attention to the inflation rate, even when it is low, to avoid its consequences. We monitor the price level every month and devote considerable resources to measuring it accurately. You're now going to see how we do this.

The Consumer Price Index

Every month, Statistics Canada measures the price level by calculating the **Consumer Price Index (CPI)**, which is a measure of the average of the prices paid by urban consumers for a fixed basket of consumer goods and services. What you learn here will help you to make sense of the CPI and relate it to your own economic life. The CPI tells you about the *value* of the money in your pocket.

Reading the CPI Numbers

The CPI is defined to equal 100 for a period called the *reference base period.* Currently, the reference base period is 2002. That is, for the average of the 12 months of 2002, the CPI equals 100.

In July 2011, the CPI was 120. This number tells us that the average of the prices paid by urban consumers for a fixed market basket of consumer goods and services was 20 percent higher in 2011 than it was on the average during 2002.

Constructing the CPI

Constructing the CPI involves three stages:

- Selecting the CPI basket
- Conducting the monthly price survey
- Calculating the CPI

The CPI Basket The first stage in constructing the CPI is to select what is called the *CPI basket.* This basket contains the goods and services represented in the index, each weighted by its relative importance. The idea is to make the relative importance of the items in the CPI basket the same as that in the budget of an average urban household. For example, because people spend more on housing than on bus rides, the CPI places more weight on the price of housing than on the price of a bus ride.

To determine the CPI basket, Statistics Canada conducts a survey of consumer expenditures. Today's CPI basket is based on data gathered in a 2009 survey. Figure 21.6 shows the 2009 CPI basket valued at the prices of April 2011.

As you look at the relative importance of the items in the CPI basket, remember that it applies to the *average* household. *Individual* households' baskets are spread around the average. Think about what you buy and compare *your* basket with the CPI basket of the average household.

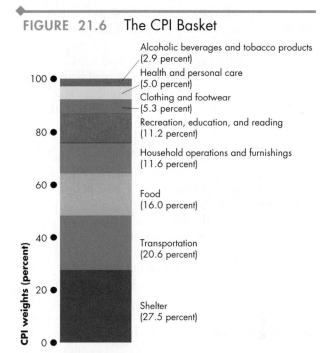

FIGURE 21.6   The CPI Basket

The CPI basket consists of the items that an average urban household buys. The figure shows the percentages.

Sources of data: Statistics Canada, Weighting Diagram of the Consumer Price Index—2009 Basket at April 2011 Prices.

————————————— MyEconLab animation ◆

The Monthly Price Survey Each month, Statistics Canada employees check the prices of the goods and services in the CPI basket in all the major cities. Because the CPI aims to measure price *changes*, it is important that the prices recorded each month refer to exactly the same item. For example, suppose the price of a box of jelly beans has increased but a box now contains more beans. Has the price of jelly beans increased? The Statistics Canada employee must record the details of changes in quality or packaging so that price changes can be calculated.

Once the raw price data are in hand, the next task is to calculate the CPI.

Calculating the CPI To calculate the CPI, we

1. Find the cost of the CPI basket at base-period prices.
2. Find the cost of the CPI basket at current-period prices.
3. Calculate the CPI for the base period and the current period.

We'll work through these three steps for the simple artificial economy in Table 21.1, which shows the quantities in the CPI basket and the prices in the base period (2010) and current period (2012).

Part (a) contains the data for the base period. In that period, consumers bought 10 oranges at $1 each and 5 haircuts at $8 each. To find the cost of the CPI basket in the base-period prices, multiply the quantities in the CPI basket by the base-period prices. The cost of oranges is $10 (10 at $1 each), and the cost of haircuts is $40 (5 at $8 each). So total cost of the CPI basket in the base period of the CPI basket is $50 ($10 + $40).

Part (b) contains the price data for the current period. The price of an orange increased from $1 to $2, which is a 100 percent increase—($1 ÷ $1) × 100 = 100. The price of a haircut increased from $8 to $10, which is a 25 percent increase—($2 ÷ $8) × 100 = 25.

The CPI provides a way of averaging these price increases by comparing the cost of the basket rather than the price of each item. To find the cost of the CPI basket in the current period, 2012, multiply the quantities in the basket by their 2012 prices. The cost of oranges is $20 (10 at $2 each), and the cost of haircuts is $50 (5 at $10 each). So total cost of the fixed CPI basket at current-period prices is $70 ($20 + $50).

You've now taken the first two steps towards calculating the CPI: calculating the cost of the CPI basket in the base period and the current period. The third step uses the numbers you've just calculated to find the CPI for 2010 and 2012.

The formula for the CPI is

$$\text{CPI} = \frac{\text{Cost of CPI basket at current-period prices}}{\text{Cost of CPI basket at base-period prices}} \times 100.$$

In Table 21.1, you established that in 2010 (the base period), the cost of the CPI basket was $50 and in 2012, it was $70. If we use these numbers in the CPI formula, we can find the CPI for 2010 and 2012. For 2010, the CPI is

$$\text{CPI in 2010} = \frac{\$50}{\$50} \times 100 = 100.$$

For 2012, the CPI is

$$\text{CPI in 2012} = \frac{\$70}{\$50} \times 100 = 140.$$

The principles that you've applied in this simplified CPI calculation apply to the more complex calculations performed every month by Statistics Canada.

Measuring the Inflation Rate

A major purpose of the CPI is to measure changes in the cost of living and in the value of money. To measure these changes, we calculate the *inflation rate* as the annual percentage change in the CPI. To calculate the inflation rate, we use the formula:

$$\frac{\text{Inflation}}{\text{rate}} = \frac{\text{CPI this year} - \text{CPI last year}}{\text{CPI last year}} \times 100.$$

We can use this formula to calculate the inflation rate in 2011. The CPI in July 2011 was 120.0, and the CPI in July 2010 was 116.8. So the inflation rate during the 12 months to July 2011 was

$$\frac{\text{Inflation}}{\text{rate}} = \frac{(120.0 - 116.8)}{116.8} \times 100 = 2.7\%.$$

TABLE 21.1   The CPI: A Simplified Calculation

(a) The cost of the CPI basket at base-period prices: 2010

| CPI basket | | | Cost of |
Item	Quantity	Price	CPI Basket
Oranges	10	$1	$10
Haircuts	5	$8	$40
Cost of CPI basket at base-period prices			$50

(b) The cost of the CPI basket at current-period prices: 2012

| CPI basket | | | Cost of |
Item	Quantity	Price	CPI Basket
Oranges	10	$2	$20
Haircuts	5	$10	$50
Cost of CPI basket at current-period prices			$70

Distinguishing High Inflation from a High Price Level

Figure 21.7 shows the CPI and the inflation rate in Canada between 1972 and 2011. The two parts of the figure are related and emphasize the distinction between high inflation and high prices.

When the price level in part (a) *rises rapidly*, (1972 through 1982), the inflation rate in part (b) is *high*. When the price level in part (a) *rises slowly*, (after 1993), the inflation rate in part (b) is *low*.

A high inflation rate means that the price level is rising rapidly. A high price level means that there has been a sustained period of rising prices.

If the price level in part (a) were to *fall*, the inflation rate in part (b) would be negative—deflation.

The CPI is not a perfect measure of the price level and changes in the CPI probably overstate the inflation rate. Let's look at the sources of bias.

The Biased CPI

The main sources of bias in the CPI are

- New goods bias
- Quality change bias
- Commodity substitution bias
- Outlet substitution bias

New Goods Bias If you want to compare the price level in 2012 with that in 1972, you must somehow compare the price of a computer today with that of a typewriter in 1972. Because a PC is more expensive than a typewriter was, the arrival of the PC puts an upward bias into the CPI and its inflation rate.

Quality Change Bias Cars, DVD players, and many other items get better every year. Part of the rise in the prices of these items is a payment for improved quality and is not inflation. But the CPI counts the entire price rise as inflation and so overstates inflation.

Commodity Substitution Bias Changes in relative prices lead consumers to change the items they buy. For example, if the price of beef rises and the price of chicken remains unchanged, people buy more chicken and less beef. This switch from beef to chicken might provide the same amount of protein and the same enjoyment as before and expenditure is the same as before. The price of protein has not changed. But because the CPI ignores the substitution of chicken for beef, it says the price of protein has increased.

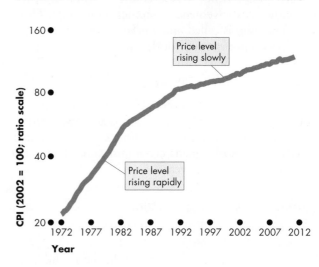

FIGURE 21.7   The CPI and the Inflation Rate

(a) CPI

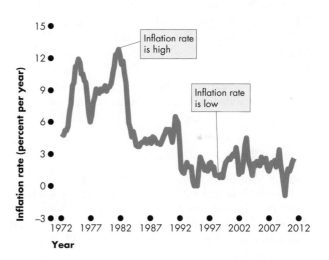

(b) Inflation rate

When the *price level rises rapidly*, the *inflation rate* is *high* and when the *price level rises slowly*, the *inflation rate* is *low*.

From 1972 through 1982, the price level rose rapidly in part (a) and the inflation rate was high in part (b). Between 1982 and 1993, the price level rose more slowly in part (a) and the inflation rate fell in part (b). After 1993, the price level rose slowly in part (a) and the inflation rate was low in part (b).

Source of data: Statistics Canada, CANSIM Table 326–0020.

— MyEconLab animation ◆

Outlet Substitution Bias When confronted with higher prices, people use discount stores more frequently and convenience stores less frequently. This phenomenon is called *outlet substitution*. The CPI surveys do not monitor outlet substitutions.

The Magnitude of the Bias

You've reviewed the sources of bias in the CPI. But how big is the bias? This question is addressed periodically and the most recent estimate is provided in a study by Bank of Canada economist James Rossiter at about 0.6 percent per year.

Some Consequences of the Bias

The bias in the CPI distorts private contracts and increases government outlays. Many private agreements, such as wage contracts, are linked to the CPI. For example, a firm and its workers might agree to a three-year wage deal that increases the wage rate by 2 percent a year plus the percentage increase in the CPI. Such a deal ends up giving the workers more real income than the firm intended.

Close to a third of federal government outlays are linked directly to the CPI. And while a bias of 0.6 percent a year seems small, accumulated over a decade it adds up to several billion dollars of additional expenditures.

Alternative Price Indexes

The CPI is just one of many alternative price level index numbers and because of the bias in the CPI, other measures are used for some purposes. We'll describe two alternatives to the CPI and explain when and why they might be preferred to the CPI. The alternatives are

- GDP deflator
- Chained price index for consumption

GDP Deflator The **GDP deflator** is an index of the prices of all the items included in GDP and is the ratio of nominal GDP to real GDP. That is,

$$\text{GDP deflator} = \frac{\text{Nominal GDP}}{\text{Real GDP}} \times 100.$$

Because real GDP includes consumption expenditure, investment, government expenditure, and net exports, the GDP deflator is an index of the prices of all these items.

Real GDP is calculated using the chained-dollar method (see Chapter 20, pp. 484–485), which means that the weights attached to each item in the GDP deflator are the components of GDP in both the current year and the preceding year.

Because it uses current period and previous period quantities rather than fixed quantities from an earlier period, a chained-dollar price index incorporates substitution effects and new goods and overcomes the sources of bias in the CPI.

Since 2000, the GDP deflator has increased at an average rate of 2.6 percent per year, which is 0.3 percentage points above the CPI inflation rate.

The GDP deflator is appropriate for macroeconomics because, like GDP, it is a comprehensive measure of the cost of the real GDP basket of goods and services. But as a measure of the cost of living, it is too broad—it includes items that consumers don't buy.

Chained Price Index for Consumption The **chained price index for consumption (CPIC)** is an index of the prices of all the items included in consumption expenditure in GDP and is the ratio of nominal consumption expenditure to real consumption expenditure. That is,

$$\text{CPIC} = \frac{\text{Nominal consumption expenditure}}{\text{Real consumption expenditure}} \times 100.$$

Like the GDP deflator, because the CPIC uses current period and previous period quantities rather than fixed quantities from an earlier period, it incorporates substitution effects and new goods and overcomes the sources of bias in the CPI.

Since 2000, the CPIC has increased at an average rate of 1.6 percent per year, which is 0.7 percentage points below the CPI inflation rate.

Core Inflation

No matter whether we calculate the inflation rate using the CPI, the GDP deflator, or the CPIC, the number bounces around a good deal from month to month or quarter to quarter. To determine whether the inflation rate is trending upward or downward, we need to strip the raw numbers of their volatility. The **core inflation rate**, which is the inflation rate excluding volatile elements, attempts to do just that and reveal the underlying inflation trend.

The most commonly used measure of core inflation is the core CPI inflation rate and as a practical matter, the core CPI inflation rate is calculated as the percentage change in the CPI excluding food and fuel. The prices of these two items are among the most volatile.

While the core CPI inflation rate removes the volatile elements in inflation, it can give a misleading view of the true underlying inflation rate. If the relative prices of the excluded items are changing, the core inflation rate will give a biased measure of the true underlying inflation rate.

Such a misleading account was given during the years between 2000 and 2011 when the relative prices of food and fuel were rising. The result was a core CPI inflation rate that was systematically below the CPI rate by an average of 0.3 percentage points.

Figure 21.7 shows the two series since 1993. More refined measures of core inflation that eliminate the bias have been suggested but are not in common use.

The Real Variables in Macroeconomics

You saw in Chapter 3 the distinction between a money price and a relative price (see p. 56). Another name for a money price is a nominal price. In macroeconomics, we often want to distinguish between a real variable and its corresponding nominal variable. We want to distinguish a real price from its corresponding nominal price because a real price is an opportunity cost that influences choices. And we want to distinguish a real quantity (like real GDP) from a nominal quantity (like nominal GDP) because we want to see what is "really" happening to variables that influence the standard of living.

You've seen in this chapter how we view real GDP as nominal GDP deflated by the GDP deflator. Viewing real GDP in this way opens up the idea of using the same method to calculate other real variables. By using the GDP deflator, we can deflate any nominal variable and find its corresponding real values. An important example is the wage rate, which is the price of labour. We measure the economy's real wage rate as the nominal wage rate divided by the GDP deflator.

There is one variable that is a bit different—an interest rate. A real interest rate is not a nominal interest rate divided by the price level. You'll learn how to adjust interest rates for inflation to find a real interest rate in Chapter 23. But all the other real variables of macroeconomics are calculated by dividing a nominal variable by the price level.

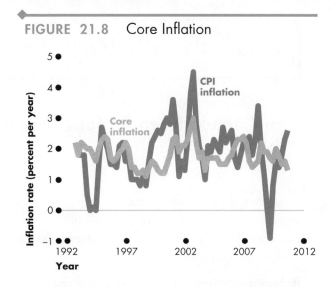

FIGURE 21.8   Core Inflation

The core CPI inflation rate excludes volatile price changes of food and fuel. Since 2000, the core CPI inflation rate on average has been below the CPI inflation rate on average because the relative prices of food and fuel have been rising.

Sources of data: Statistics Canada CANSIM Table 380–0020 and Bank of Canada Core inflation rate.

MyEconLab animation

REVIEW QUIZ

1 What is the price level?
2 What is the CPI and how is it calculated?
3 How do we calculate the inflation rate and what is its relationship with the CPI?
4 What are the four main ways in which the CPI is an upward-biased measure of the price level?
5 What problems arise from the CPI bias?
6 What are the alternative measures of the price level and how do they address the problem of bias in the CPI?

You can work these questions in Study Plan 21.3 and get instant feedback.

MyEconLab

You've now completed your study of the measurement of macroeconomic performance. Your next task is to learn what determines that performance. But first, take a look at how the U.S. economy influences the Canadian labour market in *Reading Between the Lines* on pp. 506–507.

Jobs Growth Lags Recovery

Can Canada Keep Its Jobs Pace as U.S. Stumbles? ...

Toronto Star
July 9, 2011

Two years after the official end of the recession, the heap of troubles facing the world's biggest economy seems to be growing—the anemic labour market, the still-struggling real estate sector, sagging consumer confidence, the political stalemate between Republicans and Democrats, and the looming Aug. 2 deadline to raise the statutory annual debt ceiling.

Robust in recovery, Canada has charged ahead. But the question now is, can Canada keep its stride as the U.S. economy stumbles?

There's no doubt our economies are still intertwined. ... And yet, labour market reports released in Canada and the U.S. on Friday highlight stark differences.

The U.S. economy gained a measly 18,000 jobs last month, the weakest showing since fall. The jobless rate edged up to 9.2 percent in June.

Even worse, the U.S. Labor Department estimated only 25,000 jobs were added in May, less than half of the 54,000 reported earlier.

Canada, one-tenth the size of our southern neighbour, added a respectable 28,000 positions in June.

The increase was largely due to part-time positions, but it was enough to keep the unemployment rate steady at 7.4 percent. That's on top of 22,000 jobs gained the month before. ...

"The concern is that without the U.S. recovery moving onto stronger footing, Canada's economy can really only take it so far," said Doug Porter, deputy chief economist at BMO Capital Markets. ...

Canada has benefited from the global boom in demand for timber, oil, precious metals, and other commodities, adding diversity to the economy and providing a welcome cushion against the dip in U.S. trade that came with the recession. ...

Reprinted with permission—Torstar Syndication Services.

ESSENCE OF THE STORY

- Employment in the United States increased by only 25,000 in May (2011) and 18,000 in June and the unemployment rate increased to 9.2 percent.

- Employment in Canada (one-tenth the size of the United States) increased by 22,000 in May and 28,000 in June and the unemployment rate held steady at 7.4 percent.

- Canadian job gains were mostly part time.

- Canada has benefited from the global boom in timber, oil, precious metals, and other commodities.

- Economists were concerned that Canada's continued success will be limited by a weak U.S. economy.

ECONOMIC ANALYSIS

- This news article reports some Canadian and U.S. labour market data for May and June 2011 and says that the two economies are closely linked but that Canada has benefited from a global resources boom.

- The global recession of 2008–2009 had a bigger effect on the U.S. economy than on the Canadian economy and the recovery during 2010 and 2011 was weaker in the United States than in Canada.

- The three figures compare the labour markets of Canada and the United States during 2008–2011.

- Figure 1 shows that the employment-to-population ratio in the United States is lower than in Canada and that it fell more steeply in the United States in the recession.

- Figure 1 also shows that through 2010 and 2011, when the employment-to-population ratio in Canada was rising slightly, the U.S. kept falling.

- Figure 2 shows the unemployment rates. Before the recession, Canada had a higher unemployment rate than the United States.

- Figure 2 also shows that during 2008, the U.S. unemployment rate climbed steeply and by the end of 2008, the U.S. unemployment rate was above the Canadian rate.

- Figure 3 shows that during the 2008–2009 recession, part-time employment expanded as a percentage of total employment.

- Figure 3 also shows that Canada started the recession with more employment in part-time jobs (as a percentage of total jobs) than the United States, but during the expansion of 2010 and 2011, the part-time employment was a similar percentage in the two economies.

- Canada's relatively stronger performance during 2010 and 2011 is driven by the strength of the Asian economies—China and India in particular—and the resource exports to these economies.

- If the United States goes into a new, "double-dip" recession, it is unlikely that Canada will continue to perform as well as it did during 2010 and 2011.

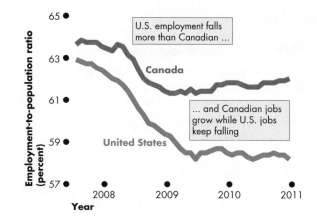

Figure 1 Employment

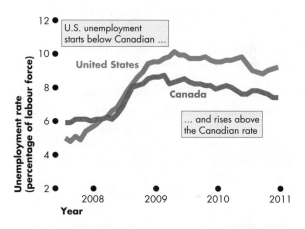

Figure 2 Unemployment

Figure 3 Part-time employment

SUMMARY

Key Points

Employment and Unemployment (pp. 492–496)

- Unemployment is a serious personal, social, and economic problem because it results in lost output and income and a loss of human capital.
- The unemployment rate averaged 7.6 percent between 1960 and 2010. It increases in recessions and decreases in expansions.
- The labour force participation rate and the employment-to-population ratio have an upward trend and fluctuate with the business cycle.
- About 60 percent of unemployment lasts for 1 to 13 weeks.
- Long-term unemployment spells—14 weeks or longer—have trended downward.

Working Problems 1 to 4 will give you a better understanding of employment and unemployment.

Unemployment and Full Employment (pp. 497–499)

- Some unemployment is unavoidable because people are constantly entering and leaving the labour force and losing or quitting jobs; also firms that create jobs are constantly being born, expanding, contracting, and dying.
- Unemployment can be frictional, structural, or cyclical.
- When all unemployment is frictional and structural, the unemployment rate equals the natural unemployment rate, the economy is at full employment, and real GDP equals potential GDP.

- Over the business cycle, real GDP fluctuates around potential GDP and the unemployment rate fluctuates around the natural unemployment rate.

Working Problems 5 to 11 will give you a better understanding of unemployment and full employment.

The Price Level and Inflation (pp. 500–505)

- Inflation (or deflation) that is unexpected redistributes income and wealth and diverts resources from production.
- The Consumer Price Index (CPI) is a measure of the average of the prices paid by urban consumers for a fixed basket of consumer goods and services.
- The CPI is defined to equal 100 for a reference base period—currently 2002.
- The inflation rate is the percentage change in the CPI from one period to the next.
- Changes in the CPI probably overstate the inflation rate because of the bias that arises from new goods, quality changes, commodity substitution, and outlet substitution.
- The bias in the CPI distorts private contracts and increases government outlays.
- Alternative price level measures avoid the bias of the CPI but do not make a large difference to the measured inflation rate.
- Real economic variables are calculated by dividing nominal variables by the price level.

Working Problems 12 to 20 will give you a better understanding of the price level and inflation.

Key Terms

Chained price index for
   consumption (CPIC), 504
Consumer Price Index (CPI), 501
Core inflation rate, 504
Cyclical unemployment, 497
Deflation, 500
Discouraged worker, 495
Employment-to-population ratio, 495
Frictional unemployment, 497
Full employment, 497
GDP deflator, 504

Hyperinflation, 500
Inflation, 500
Labour force, 493
Labour force participation rate, 494
Marginally attached worker, 495
Natural unemployment rate, 497
Output gap, 498
Price level, 500
Structural unemployment, 497
Unemployment rate, 494
Working-age population, 493

SCAN THIS

STUDY PLAN PROBLEMS AND APPLICATIONS

MyEconLab ◆ You can work Problems 1 to 20 in Chapter 21 Study Plan and get instant feedback.

Employment and Unemployment (Study Plan 21.1)

1. Statistics Canada reported the following data for June 2011:

   Labour force: 19,021,600

   Employment: 17,693,300

   Working-age population: 27,975,700

   Calculate the
   a. Unemployment rate.
   b. Labour force participation rate.
   c. Employment-to-population ratio.

2. In July 2012, in the economy of Sandy Island, 10,000 people were employed, 1,000 were unemployed, and 5,000 were not in the labour force. During August 2012, 80 people lost their jobs and didn't look for new ones, 20 people quit their jobs and retired, 150 unemployed people were hired, 50 people quit the labour force, and 40 people entered the labour force to look for work. Calculate for July 2012
   a. The unemployment rate.
   b. The employment-to-population ratio.

   And calculate for the end of August 2012
   c. The number of people unemployed.
   d. The number of people employed.
   e. The unemployment rate.

Use the following information to work Problems 3 and 4.

In January 2008, the Canadian unemployment rate was 5.9 percent. In August 2009, the unemployment rate was 8.7 percent. Predict what happened to

3. Unemployment between January 2008 and August 2009, assuming that the labour force was constant.

4. The labour force between January 2008 and August 2009, assuming that unemployment was constant.

Unemployment and Full Employment (Study Plan 21.2)

5. **Regional Jet Orders Dry Up, Jobs at Risk**

   The world's third largest plane maker, Bombardier, didn't book one order for its new Q400 regional jet during the second quarter of 2011. Regional jet orders simply disappeared.

Bombardier said it would make a decision about production at its Mirabel, Quebec, plant that employs 1,200 skilled workers.

   Source: *Financial Post*, September 1, 2011

   If Bombardier were to close its Mirabel plant and lay off the 1,200 workers employed there, what would happen to frictional, structural, and cyclical unemployment, and what would happen to the natural unemployment rate?

Use the following news clip to work Problems 6 to 8.

Economic Conditions at the Cycle Bottom

Employment rebounded by 0.1 percent in August 2008, its first gain in four months. All of the increase was in full-time jobs. The unemployment rate in August 2008 was 8.7 percent, up from 8.6 percent a month earlier.

   Source: *Canadian Economic Observer*, September 2008

6. How did the unemployment rate in August 2008 compare to the unemployment rate during the recessions of the early 1980s and early 1990s?

7. How can the unemployment rate rise when employment rises?

8. How does the unemployment rate in August 2008 compare to the estimated natural unemployment rate? What does this imply about the relationship between real GDP and potential GDP at this time?

Use the following news clip to work Problems 9 and 10.

Some Firms Struggle to Hire Despite High Unemployment

Matching people with available jobs is always difficult after a recession as the economy remakes itself. But U.S. data suggest the disconnect is particularly acute this time. Since the recovery began, the number of job openings has risen more than twice as fast as actual hires. If the job market were working normally, openings would be getting filled as they appear. Some five million more would be employed and the unemployment rate would be 6.8%, instead of 9.5%.

   Source: *The Wall Street Journal*, August 9, 2010

9. If the labour market is working properly, why would there be any unemployment at all?

10. Are the 5 million workers who cannot find jobs because of mismatching in the labour market counted as part of the economy's structural unemployment or part of its cyclical unemployment?

11. Which of the following people are unemployed because of labour market mismatching?
    - Michael has unemployment benefits of $450 a week and he turned down a full-time job paying $7.75 an hour.
    - Tory used to earn $60,000 a year and he turned down a low-paying job to search for one that pays at least $50,000 a year.
    - David turned down a temporary full-time job paying $15 an hour because it was an hour's drive away and the gas cost would be high.

The Price Level and Inflation (Study Plan 21.3)

Use the following information to work Problems 12 and 13.

The people on Coral Island buy only juice and cloth. The CPI basket contains the quantities bought in 2009. The average household spent $60 on juice and $30 on cloth in 2009 when the price of juice was $2 a bottle and the price of cloth was $5 a metre. In 2010, juice was $4 a bottle and cloth was $6 a metre.

12. Calculate the CPI basket and the percentage of the household's budget spent on juice in 2009.

13. Calculate the CPI and the inflation rate in 2010.

Use the following data to work Problems 14 to 16.

The Lucky Country reported the following CPI data:

June 2010	201.9
June 2011	207.2
June 2012	217.4

14. Calculate the inflation rates for the years ended June 2011 and June 2012. How did the inflation rate change in 2012?

15. Why might these CPI numbers be biased?

16. How do alternative price indexes help to avoid the bias in the CPI numbers?

17. **Inflation Can Act as a Safety Valve**

    Workers will more readily accept a real wage cut that arises from an increase in the price level than a cut in their nominal wage rate.

    Source: FT.com, May 28, 2009

    Explain why inflation influences a worker's real wage rate. Why might this observation be true?

18. The IMF *World Economic Outlook* reported the following price level data (2000 = 100):

Region	2006	2007	2008
United States	117.1	120.4	124.0
Euro area	113.6	117.1	119.6
Japan	98.1	98.1	98.8

a. In which region was the inflation rate highest in 2007 and in 2008?

b. Describe the path of the price level in Japan.

19. **CPI Report**

Consumer prices rose 2.7 percent in the 12 months to July 2011, primarily the result of higher prices for gasoline and food. This follows a 3.1 percent increase in June and a 3.7 percent advance in May. Energy prices advanced 12.9 percent during the 12 months to July, following a 15.7 percent increase in June. On a year-over-year basis, gasoline prices rose 23.5 percent, compared with the 28.5 percent gain in June. In contrast, natural gas prices fell. Food prices rose 4.3 percent in the 12 months to July, matching the increase in June. Excluding food and energy, the Consumer Price Index (CPI) increased 1.2 percent in the 12 months to July, after advancing 1.4 percent in June.

Source: Statistics Canada, *The Daily*, August 19, 2011

Did the inflation rate increase, decrease, or remain the same in July 2011? In your answer, distinguish between the CPI and the core CPI. Why might the core CPI be a useful measurement and why might it be misleading?

20. **Dress for Less**

Since 1998, the price of the Louis Vuitton "Speedy" handbag has more than doubled, to $685, while the price of Joe Boxer's "licky face" underwear has dropped by nearly half, to $8.99. As luxury fashion has become more expensive, mainstream apparel has become markedly less so. Clothing is one of the few categories in the CPI in which overall prices have declined—about 10 percent—since 1998.

Source: *The New York Times*, May 29, 2008

If luxury clothing prices have increased dramatically since the late 1990s, why has the clothing category of the CPI actually declined by about 10 percent?

ADDITIONAL PROBLEMS AND APPLICATIONS

MyEconLab ◆ You can work these problems in MyEconLab if assigned by your instructor.

Employment and Unemployment

21. What is the unemployment rate supposed to measure and why is it an imperfect measure?

22. Statistics Canada reported the following data for June 2011:

    Labour force participation rate: 68 percent
    Working-age population: 27,975,700
    Employment-to-population ratio: 63.2

    Calculate the
    a. Labour force.
    b. Employment.
    c. Unemployment rate.

23. In Nova Scotia in May 2011, the labour force was 501,700 and 458,100 people were unemployed. In June 2011, the labour force increased by 4,600 and the number employed increased by 9,300. Calculate the unemployment rate in May 2011 and in June 2011.

24. Statistics Canada reported the following data for Ontario in May and June in 2011: The unemployment rate fell from 8.3 percent to 7.6 percent. The employment-to-population ratio increased from 62.2 percent to 63 percent and the labour force participation rate increased from 67.9 percent to 68.2 percent.

    a. Did the number employed increase by more than the number unemployed fell? How can you tell?
    b. If the number employed did increase by more than the number unemployed fell, what happened to the number of marginally attached workers?

25. A high unemployment rate tells us a large percentage of the labour force is unemployed, but it doesn't tell us why the unemployment rate is high. What extra information tells us if (i) people are taking longer than usual to find a job, and (ii) more people are involuntary part-time workers?

26. **Some Firms Struggle to Hire Despite High Unemployment**

    With about 1.5 million Canadians looking for work, some employers are swamped with job applicants, but many employers can't hire enough workers. What has changed in the jobs market? During the recession, millions of middle-skill, middle-wage jobs disappeared. Now with the recovery, these people can't find the skilled jobs that they seek and have a hard time adjusting to lower-skilled work with less pay.

    Source: *The Wall Street Journal*, August 9, 2010

    How would an increase in unemployment benefits influence the cost of unemployment? Would firms that seek to hire more labour find it easier to hire workers?

27. Why might the unemployment rate underestimate the underutilization of labour resources?

Unemployment and Full Employment

Use the following data to work Problems 28 to 30. The IMF *World Economic Outlook* reports the following unemployment rates:

Region	2010	2011
United States	9.6	8.5
United Kingdom	7.8	7.7
Japan	5.1	4.9

28. What do these numbers tell us about the phase of the business cycle in the United States, the United Kingdom, and Japan in 2011?

29. What do these numbers tell us about the relative size of the natural unemployment rates in the United States, the United Kingdom, and Japan?

30. Do these numbers tell us anything about the relative size of the labour force participation rates and employment-to-population ratios in the three regions?

31. **A Half-Year of Job Losses**

    Employers trimmed jobs in June for the sixth straight month, with the total for the first six months at 438,000 jobs lost by the U.S. economy. The job losses in June were concentrated in manufacturing and construction, two sectors that have been badly battered in the recession.

    Source: CNN, July 3, 2008

    a. Based on the news clip, what might be the main source of increased unemployment?
    b. Based on the news clip, what might be the main type of increased unemployment?

32. **Tax Imports When Companies Close Canadian Plants**

The government should charge higher import taxes on companies that deliberately close operations in Canada, causing job losses in factories and farming, only to move operations to the U.S. with the sole purpose of producing goods for sale in the Canadian market.

Source: Letter to *The Hamilton Spectator,* August 31, 2011

a. What type of unemployment does the author of this letter want to avoid? Explain.

b. How might the recommended policy impact Ontario's natural unemployment rate? Explain.

The Price Level and Inflation

33. A typical family on Sandy Island consumes only juice and cloth. Last year, which was the base year, the family spent $40 on juice and $25 on cloth. In the base year, juice was $4 a bottle and cloth was $5 a length. This year, juice is $4 a bottle and cloth is $6 a length. Calculate

a. The CPI basket.

b. The CPI in the current year.

c. The inflation rate in the current year.

34. Amazon.ca agreed to pay its workers $20 an hour in 1999 and $22 an hour in 2001. The price level for these years was 166 in 1999 and 180 in 2001. Calculate the real wage rate in each year. Did these workers really get a pay raise between 1999 and 2001?

35. **News Release**

Real personal expenditure on consumption goods and services in 2002 chained dollars was $814.2 billion in 2009 and $841.5 billion in 2010. Personal expenditure on consumption goods and services in current dollars was $898.2 billion in 2009 and $940.6 billion in 2011.

Source: Statistics Canada

a. Calculate the chained price index for consumption (CPIC) for 2009 and 2010.

b. Calculate the CPIC inflation rate for 2010.

c. Why might the CPIC inflation rate be preferred to the CPI inflation rate?

d. Did real personal expenditure on consumption goods and services increase by more or by less than the increase measured in current dollars? Why?

Economics in the News

36. After you have studied *Reading Between the Lines* on pp. 506–507, answer the following questions:

a. What are the key differences in performance of the U.S. and Canadian job markets during 2008–2011?

b. How do the part-time employment rates of the two countries compare?

c. Why might the U.S. job market have been so much weaker than the Canadian job market during 2008–2010?

d. Do you think the differences between the U.S. and Canadian job markets in 2008–2010 are frictional, structural, or cyclical?

37. **Out of a Job and Out of Luck at 54**

Too young to retire, too old to get a new job. That's how many older workers feel after getting the pink slip and spending time on the unemployment line. Many lack the skills to craft resumes and search online, experts say. Older workers took an average of about 5 weeks longer than younger people to land a job. "Older workers will be more adversely affected because of the time it takes to transition into another job," said Deborah Russell, AARP's director of workforce issues.

Source: CNN, May 21, 2008

a. What type of unemployment might older workers be more prone to experience?

b. Explain how the unemployment rate of older workers is influenced by the business cycle.

c. Why might older unemployed workers become marginally attached or discouraged workers during a recession?

Data Graphing

Use the *Data Grapher* in MyEconLab to work Problems 38 to 40.

38. In which country in 2010 was the unemployment rate highest and in which was it lowest: Canada, Japan, France, or the United States?

39. In which country in 2010 was the inflation rate highest and in which was it lowest: Canada, Japan, France, or the United States?

40. Make a scatter diagram of Canadian inflation and unemployment. Describe the relationship.

The Big Picture

PART SEVEN

Macroeconomics is a large and controversial subject that is interlaced with political ideological disputes. And it is a field in which charlatans as well as serious thinkers have much to say.

You have just learned in Chapters 20 and 21 how we monitor and measure the main macroeconomic variables. We use real GDP to calculate the rate of economic growth and business cycle fluctuations. And we use the CPI and other measures of the price level to calculate the inflation rate and to "deflate" nominal values to find *real* values.

In the chapters that lie ahead, you will learn the theories that economists have developed to explain economic growth, fluctuations, and inflation.

First, in Chapters 22 through 25, you will study the long-term trends. This material is central to the oldest question in macroeconomics that Adam Smith tried to answer: What are the causes of the wealth of nations? You will also study three other old questions that Adam Smith's contemporary and friend David Hume first addressed: What causes inflation? What causes international deficits and surpluses? And why do exchange rates fluctuate?

In Chapters 26 through 28, you will study macroeconomic fluctuations.

Finally, in Chapters 29 and 30, you will study the policies that the federal government and Bank of Canada might adopt to make the economy perform well.

David Hume, *a Scot who lived from 1711 to 1776, did not call himself an economist. "Philosophy and general learning" is how he described the subject of his life's work. Hume was an extraordinary thinker and writer. Published in 1742, his* Essays, Moral and Political *range across economics, political science, moral philosophy, history, literature, ethics, and religion and explore such topics as love, marriage, divorce, suicide, death, and the immortality of the soul!*

His economic essays provide astonishing insights into the forces that cause inflation, business cycle fluctuations, balance of payments deficits, and interest rate fluctuations; and they explain the effects of taxes and government deficits and debts.

Data were scarce in Hume's day, so he was not able to draw on detailed evidence to support his analysis. But he was empirical. He repeatedly appealed to experience and evidence as the ultimate judge of the validity of an argument. Hume's fundamentally empirical approach dominates macroeconomics today.

> ... in every kingdom into which money begins to flow in greater abundance than formerly, everything takes a new face: labour and industry gain life; the merchant becomes more enterprising, the manufacturer more diligent and skillful, and even the farmer follows his plow with greater alacrity and attention.
>
> **DAVID HUME**
> *Essays, Moral and Political*

Peter, what attracted you to economics?

When I was in high school I had a part-time job as office boy with a small company that imported wool from around the world and sold it to textile mills in Ontario and Quebec. I was fascinated by the way wool prices went up and down all the time and this curiosity led me to enroll in an honours economics course. My interests soon switched to macroeconomics, but I was always driven by curiosity to find out more about the workings of the human anthill.

You have made outstanding contributions to our understanding of all the major problems of macroeconomics, notably unemployment, economic growth, and inflation. Which of these issues do you believe is the most serious one for Canada today? Can they be separated?

Canada has suffered much less from the global financial crisis than the United States and most other countries. There are a number of reasons for this. Canadian banks have been more prudent in their lending and investment strategies, we did not have the explosion of household debt, especially mortgage debt, or the bubble in housing prices that occurred in the United States, and both the Bank of Canada's inflation-targeting policy and our relatively small government deficits gave our policymakers more room to stimulate the economy without stoking fears of inflation.

My biggest concern is that Canada seems to be losing many of these advantages, and we may be headed for our own crisis. In particular, household debt is still rising at a rapid rate in Canada, to the point where it is now a larger proportion of household income than in the United States. The longer this credit boom continues, the more exposed our financial system becomes in the event of a downturn in housing prices or a rise in unemployment.

Either of these events would lead to a rise in loan defaults, as it has already in the United States where people are walking away from mortgages on houses whose prices have fallen below the amount owed (i.e., mortgages that are "underwater") and where many unemployed people find themselves no longer able to pay back their debts.

If that starts happening in Canada, then banks and other lenders in Canada will find themselves with a lot of bad loans on their books, and as a result will

be less willing to extend further credit. This will result in less investment in fixed capital, research and development, and education and training, all of which are highly dependent on credit from the financial system.

Less investment would result not just in higher unemployment but also in slower economic growth. Indeed, this scenario of increased household financial distress spilling over to banking problems, less investment, and slower economic growth may well take place even if housing prices don't turn down and even if unemployment continues to fall. The reason is that interest rates are bound to rise from their currently very low values, and when they do there will be increasing financial distress among Canadian households who will find it difficult to meet the increased interest payments on the large debts that they have run up over the past few years.

So in summary, my biggest concern at the moment is that we may yet be headed for a credit crisis that would result in high unemployment and low economic growth.

> My biggest concern ... is that we may be headed for a credit crisis that would result in high unemployment and low economic growth.

PETER HOWITT is Lyn Crost Professor of Social Sciences in the Department of Economics at Brown University. Born in 1946 in Toronto, he was an undergraduate at McGill University and a graduate student at Northwestern University.

Professor Howitt began his research and teaching career at the University of Western Ontario in 1972, where he spent many productive years before moving to the United States in 1996.

Professor Howitt is a past president of the Canadian Economics Association and is one of the world's leading macroeconomists. He has done research on all aspect of macroeconomics, with a focus in recent years on economic growth.

Michael Parkin and Robin Bade talked with Peter Howitt about his work and the major macroeconomic problems facing Canada today.

Even though I think a rise in unemployment is a bigger danger now than a rise in inflation, nevertheless I believe that the Bank of Canada should err on the side of higher interest rates than would normally be justified by its inflation target, because higher interest rates will help to slow the credit boom.

Although higher interest rates may depress aggregate demand and result in some short-term increase in unemployment, and although higher interest rates will immediately put households under even more financial stress, both of these problems will be less severe if the interest rate increases come sooner rather than later.

If we wait until households have reached their borrowing limits before raising interest rates I think we may be in for a deep and prolonged recession. Canada could end up in the situation of the United States right now, where banks are reluctant to lend, and probably will be for a long time given that almost a quarter of all mortgages are underwater and hence in danger of default.

In retrospect (hindsight always being 20/20) the Federal Reserve System probably should have followed such a pre-emptive policy in the early 2000s to choke off the booms in housing prices and in household indebtedness that ultimately brought down some of the most trusted American financial institutions and jammed global credit markets.

More generally, I think one of the most important lessons of the financial crisis has been that monetary policy needs to be aimed at preventing not only inflation but also financial crises.

Exactly how to kill these two birds with one stone is a difficult question that we cannot answer with any certainty right now, but a lot of research is being undertaken aimed at finding an answer. Some of that research suggests that increases in house prices and increases in household debt are important leading indicators of banking crises. My hope is that we can profit from that research even at this early stage by taking pre-emptive action to avert banking crises, especially since we have seen how costly it is to wait until the crisis hits and then have to clean up afterward.

> ... the most important lesson is ... monetary policy needs to be aimed at preventing not only inflation but also financial crises.

What does your research tell us about the main sources of Canada's persistently high unemployment rate during the 1980s and 1990s?

A lot of what has taken place in Canada is an example of the effects of creative destruction that I talked about. A lot of technological change destroys low-skill jobs, and also destroys the value of old skills. In particular, a lot of clerical and middle management jobs have been made redundant by computers. Computers open up new jobs for people able to master the technology, but a lot of people don't have the skills or the knowledge to profit from these opportunities.

This is a global phenomenon, not just limited to Canada. Computers are having a revolutionary effect on economic life all over the world. In the United States it hasn't appeared to produce much unemployment. Instead what you see is a growing gap between the wages of skilled and unskilled workers. In Canada that gap isn't as visible, largely because we have more generous minimum wages and unemployment insurance benefits, which means that a fall in the demand for low-skill workers shows up more in a rise in unemployment and less in a fall in their wages than in the United States.

515

Why did our economic growth rate slow during the 1980s?

The short answer is that no one knows. But I think the answer probably lies in the computer revolution. Ultimately, I think this revolution is going to give us a higher growth rate. But we have to accumulate a lot of knowledge in order to profit from it. We have been going through a collective learning experience that has been enormously costly, and this has been a continual drag on productivity, even though in the end I expect it will greatly enhance productivity.

Also, I think we are underestimating growth rates nowadays. This is because we are investing a lot in knowledge—knowledge of how to harness the power of the computer and to exploit the opportunities that it presents. Investment in knowledge is like investment in machinery in that it entails the sacrifice of resources now in return for the promise of more income in the future. But while the national income accountant measures investment in machines as part of the economy's output, investment in knowledge is just treated as wasted resources.

> ... income accountant measures investment in machines as part of the economy's output, investment in knowledge as ... wasted resources.

Was the pursuit of low inflation worthwhile? Have we now got too low an inflation rate?

I think the pursuit of low inflation was definitely worthwhile, although in retrospect maybe we should have been more patient. Inflation impairs one of the most useful devices in the economic system—the conventional measure of value. Now that we have almost eliminated inflation we have a much healthier economic system. I don't think we should go much further, however, because you may have to raise unemployment even higher in order to get inflation all the way down to zero. Once you have it down to 2 percent you have little more to gain by reducing it further.

Also, further reductions in inflation may impair the working of the labour market. That is, people whose real wages are falling for whatever reason may be more inclined to continue working if they can at least avoid having to submit to a nominal wage cut, but can instead take the real-wage cut through the back door of inflation. With 2 percent inflation there is still lots of room for this sort of real-wage flexibility, but with no inflation there is none at all.

Some economists say that the Bank of Canada can speed up the economic growth rate by forgetting about low inflation and keeping interest rates low. Others say the best hope for increasing the growth rate is low inflation. Who is right?

The first group is certainly now right, except perhaps in a very short-run sense. You can't sustain a high growth rate for long by printing more money. Before long you'll end up with a higher rate of inflation and even higher interest rates as lenders seek compensation for the fall in the value of money. A lot of recent econometric evidence has been produced by various writers studying the experience of different countries that shows over long periods of time that inflation and growth are negatively correlated. More inflation from one decade to the next is likely to produce a fall in the growth rate rather than a rise. The effect doesn't appear to be numerically very large, but even a small drop in the growth rate can have a significant depressing effect on the level of real income if sustained for a decade or two.

What advice would you give to a student who wants to become a professional economist today?

My first advice for anyone interested in doing economics is to give full reign to your curiosity. The greatest satisfaction that I have received as an economist has been from discovering things about how the world works, from seeing a little more clearly some of the complex interactions between the different parts of the economy. I can still remember the excitement I felt when I started to see how demand and supply work, and when I learned about the circular flow of economic activity and how it can be affected by saving and investment decisions. I am happy to say that this sense of excitement has never left me. Furthermore, one of the great things about economics is that you can be paid well for spending your time satisfying your curiosity. Satisfying your curiosity is enjoyable, but if you want to accomplish something you can't let yourself be satisfied easily. You have to keep asking questions, and trying to answer them. It's easy to think you have solved a problem when you haven't explored things deeply enough. The best way for a student to do this is to do lots of exercises, and to discuss what you are doing with others. The same applies throughout one's career.

CHAPTER
22

Economic Growth

After studying this chapter, you will be able to

◆ Define the economic growth rate and explain the implications of sustained growth

◆ Describe the economic growth trends in Canada and other countries and regions

◆ Explain how labour productivity growth makes potential GDP grow

◆ Explain the sources of labour productivity growth

◆ Explain the theories of economic growth and policies to increase the growth rate

Real GDP *per person* in Canada tripled between 1961 and 2011. If you live in a dorm that was built during the 1960s, it is likely to have just two power outlets: one for a desk lamp and one for a bedside lamp. Today your room bulges with a personal computer, TV and DVD player, microwave, refrigerator, coffeemaker, smart phone, and iPod. Economic growth has brought about this improvement in living standards.

In this chapter, we study the forces that make real GDP grow and living standards improve. In *Reading Between the Lines* at the end of the chapter, we look at China, the fastest-growing economy, and see how its GDP growth compares with that of Japan and the United States.

The Basics of Economic Growth

Economic growth is a sustained expansion of production possibilities measured as the increase in real GDP over a given period. Rapid economic growth maintained over a number of years can transform a poor nation into a rich one. Such have been the stories of Hong Kong, South Korea, and some other Asian economies. Slow economic growth or the absence of growth can condemn a nation to devastating poverty. Such has been the fate of Sierra Leone, Somalia, Zambia, and much of the rest of Africa.

The goal of this chapter is to help you to understand why some economies expand rapidly and others stagnate. We'll begin by learning how to calculate the economic growth rate and by discovering the magic of sustained growth.

Calculating Growth Rates

We express the **economic growth rate** as the annual percentage change of real GDP. To calculate this growth rate, we use the formula:

$$\text{Real GDP growth rate} = \frac{\text{Real GDP in current year} - \text{Real GDP in previous year}}{\text{Real GDP in previous year}} \times 100.$$

For example, if real GDP in the current year is $1,650 billion and if real GDP in the previous year was $1,500 billion, then the economic growth rate is 10 percent—($150 ÷ $1500) × 100 = 10.

The growth rate of real GDP tells us how rapidly the *total* economy is expanding. This measure is useful for telling us about potential changes in the balance of power among nations. But it does not tell us about changes in the standard of living.

The standard of living depends on **real GDP per person** (also called *per capita* real GDP), which is real GDP divided by the population. So the contribution of real GDP growth to the change in the standard of living depends on the growth rate of real GDP per person. We use the above formula to calculate this growth rate, replacing real GDP with real GDP per person.

Suppose, for example, that in the current year, when real GDP is $1,650 billion, the population is 30.3 million. Then real GDP per person is $1,650 billion divided by 30.3 million, which equals $54,455. And suppose that in the previous year, when real GDP was $1,500 billion, the population

was 30 million. Then real GDP per person in that year was $1,500 billion divided by 30 million, which equals $50,000.

Use these two values of real GDP per person with the growth formula above to calculate the growth rate of real GDP per person. That is,

$$\text{Real GDP per person growth rate} = \frac{\$54,455 - \$50,000}{\$50,000} \times 100 = 8.9 \text{ percent.}$$

The growth rate of real GDP per person can also be calculated *approximately* by subtracting the population growth rate from the real GDP growth rate. In the example you've just worked through, the growth rate of real GDP is 10 percent. The population changes from 30 million to 30.3 million, so the population growth rate is 1 percent. The growth rate of real GDP per person is approximately equal to 10 percent minus 1 percent, which equals 9 percent.

Real GDP per person grows only if real GDP grows faster than the population grows. If the growth rate of the population exceeds the growth of real GDP, then real GDP per person falls.

The Magic of Sustained Growth

Sustained growth of real GDP per person can transform a poor society into a wealthy one. The reason is that economic growth is like compound interest.

Compound Interest Suppose that you put $100 in the bank and earn 5 percent a year interest on it. After 1 year, you have $105. If you leave that $105 in the bank for another year, you earn 5 percent interest on the original $100 *and on the $5 interest that you earned last year*. You are now earning interest on interest! The next year, things get even better. Then you earn 5 percent on the original $100 and on the interest earned in the first year and the second year. You are even earning interest on the interest that you earned on the interest of the first year.

Your money in the bank is growing at a rate of 5 percent a year. Before too many years have passed, your initial deposit of $100 will have grown to $200. But after how many years?

The answer is provided by a formula called the **Rule of 70**, which states that the number of years it takes for the level of any variable to double is approximately 70 divided by the annual percentage

FIGURE 22.1   The Rule of 70

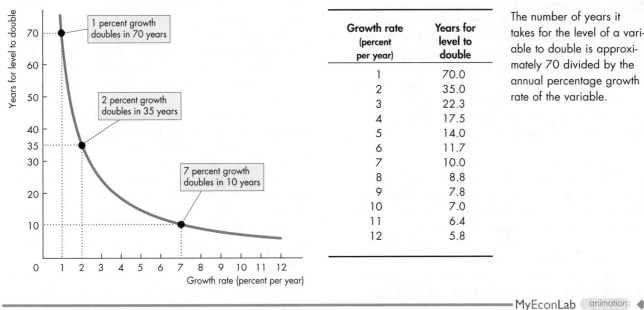

Growth rate (percent per year)	Years for level to double
1	70.0
2	35.0
3	22.3
4	17.5
5	14.0
6	11.7
7	10.0
8	8.8
9	7.8
10	7.0
11	6.4
12	5.8

The number of years it takes for the level of a variable to double is approximately 70 divided by the annual percentage growth rate of the variable.

growth rate of the variable. Using the Rule of 70, you can now calculate how many years it takes your $100 to become $200. It is 70 divided by 5, which is 14 years.

Applying the Rule of 70

The Rule of 70 applies to any variable, so it applies to real GDP per person. Figure 22.1 shows the doubling time for growth rates of 1 percent per year to 12 percent per year.

You can see that real GDP per person doubles in 70 years (70 divided by 1)—an average human life span—if the growth rate is 1 percent a year. It doubles in 35 years if the growth rate is 2 percent a year and in just 10 years if the growth rate is 7 percent a year.

We can use the Rule of 70 to answer other questions about economic growth. For example, in 2011, Canadian real GDP per person was approximately 4 times that of China. China's recent growth rate of real GDP per person was 10 percent a year. If this growth rate were maintained, how long would it take China's real GDP per person to reach that of Canada in 2011? The answer, provided by the Rule of 70, is 14 years. China's real GDP per person doubles in

7 years (70 divided by 10). It doubles again to 4 times its current level in another 7 years. So after 14 years of growth at 10 percent a year, China's real GDP per person is 4 times its current level and equals that of Canada in 2011. Of course, after 14 years, Canadian real GDP per person would have increased, so China would still not have caught up to Canada. At the current growth rates, China's real GDP per person will equal that of Canada by 2030.

REVIEW QUIZ

1 What is economic growth and how do we calculate its rate?
2 What is the relationship between the growth rate of real GDP and the growth rate of real GDP per person?
3 Use the Rule of 70 to calculate the growth rate that leads to a doubling of real GDP per person in 20 years.

You can work these questions in Study Plan 22.1 and get instant feedback.

◆ Economic Growth Trends

You have just seen the power of economic growth to increase incomes. At a 1 percent growth rate, it takes a human life span to double the standard of living. But at a 7 percent growth rate, the standard of living doubles every decade. How fast is our economy growing? How fast are other economies growing? Are poor countries catching up to rich ones, or do the gaps between the rich and poor persist or even widen? Let's answer these questions.

Growth in the Canadian Economy

Figure 22.2 shows *real GDP per person* in Canada for the 84 years from 1926 to 2010. The average growth rate over this period is 2 percent per year.

The earliest years in the graph are dominated by two extraordinary events: the Great Depression of the 1930s and World War II in the 1940s. The fall in real GDP during the depression and the bulge during the war obscure the changes in the long-term

growth trend that occurred within these years. Averaging out the depression and the war, the long-term growth rate was close to its 84-year average of 2 percent a year.

The 1950s had slow growth but then, during the 1960s, the growth rate speeded up and averaged 3.3 percent a year. The 1970s growth slowed to 2.1 percent a year and in the 1980s the growth rate slowed to a crawl of 0.7 percent a year. After 1996, the growth rate increased again but didn't return to its long-term average. Over the 15 years between 1996 and 2010, the growth rate averaged 1.6 percent.

A major goal of this chapter is to explain why our economy grows and why the long-term growth rate varies. Why did growth speed up during the 1960s, slow through the 1970s and 1980s, and then speed up again during the late 1990s? Another goal is to explain variations in the growth rate across countries.

Let's look at some facts about the growth rates of other nations and compare them with Canada's growth rate.

◆ **FIGURE 22.2** Economic Growth in Canada: 1926–2010

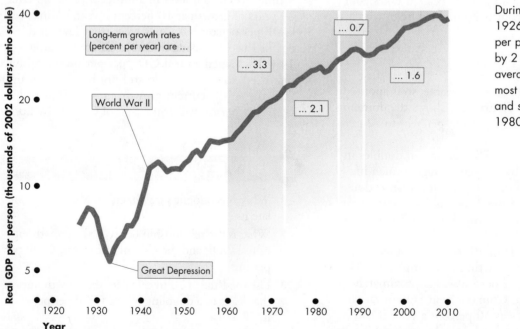

During the 84 years from 1926 to 2010, real GDP per person in Canada grew by 2 percent a year, on average. Growth was the most rapid during the 1960s and slowest during the 1980s.

Sources of data: F.H. Leacy (ed.), *Historical Statistics of Canada*, 2nd ed., catalogue 11-516, series A1, F32, F55, Statistics Canada, Ottawa, 1983; Statistics Canada, Tables 380-0002 and 051-0005.

MyEconLab animation ◆

Real GDP Growth in the World Economy

Figure 22.3 shows real GDP per person in Canada and in other countries between 1960 and 2010. Part (a) looks at the seven richest countries—known as the G7 nations. Among these nations, the United States has the highest real GDP per person. In 2010, Canada had the second-highest real GDP per person, ahead of Japan and France, Germany, Italy, and the United Kingdom (collectively the Europe Big 4).

During the 50 years shown here, the gaps between Canada, the United States, and the Europe Big 4 have been almost constant. But starting from a long way below, Japan grew fastest. It caught up to Europe in 1970 and to Canada in 1990. But during the 1990s, Japan's economy stagnated.

Many other countries have lower incomes per person than Canada and some are growing more slowly than Canada and falling further behind. Figure 22.3(b) looks at some of these countries.

Real GDP per person in Central and South America was 35 percent of the Canadian level in 1960. The region grew more slowly than Canada and dropped to 25 percent of the Canadian level by 2000, but then growth speeded and by 2010, real GDP per person in these countries was 27 percent of the Canadian level.

Growth has also been slow in Eastern Europe. There, real GDP per person fell from 34 percent of the Canadian level in 1980 to 20 percent in 1993. Eastern European growth speeded up during the 2000s and income per person climbed to 32 percent of the Canadian level by 2010.

Real GDP per person in Africa, the world's poorest continent, fell from 12 percent of the Canadian level in 1960 to 7 percent in 2010.

FIGURE 22.3   Economic Growth Around the World

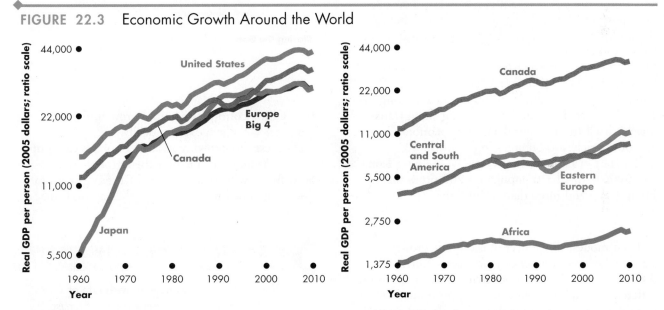

(a) Growth in the rich G7

(b) Persistent gaps between rich and poor

Real GDP per person has grown throughout the world. Among the rich industrial countries in part (a), real GDP per person has grown slightly faster in the United States than in Canada and the four big countries of Europe (France, Germany, Italy, and the United Kingdom). Japan had the fastest growth rate before 1973 but then growth slowed and Japan's economy stagnated during the 1990s.

Among a wider range of countries shown in part (b), growth rates have been lower than that of Canada. The gaps between the real GDP per person in Canada and in these countries have widened. The gap between the real GDP per person in Canada and Africa has widened by a large amount.

Sources of data: (1960–2007) Alan Heston, Robert Summers, and Bettina Aten, Penn World Table Version 6.3, Center for International Comparisons of the University of Pennsylvania (CICUP), August 2009; and (2008–2010) International Monetary Fund, *World Economic Outlook*, April 2010.

Economics in Action
Fast Trains on the Same Track

Four Asian economies, Hong Kong, Korea, Singapore, and China, have experienced spectacular growth, which you can see in the figure. During the 1960s, real GDP per person in these economies ranged from 2.5 to 25 percent of that Canada. But by 1990, real GDP per person in Hong Kong had surpassed that in Canada and by 1993, real GDP per person in Singapore had overtaken that in Canada. By 2005, Korea was only a short distance behind.

The figure also shows that China is catching up but from a long way behind. China's real GDP per person increased from 2.5 percent of the Canadian level in 1960 to 15 percent in 2010.

The Asian economies shown here are like fast trains running on the same track at similar speeds and with a roughly constant gap between them. Singapore and Hong Kong are hooked together as the lead train, which runs about 12 years in front of Korea and about 40 years in front of China.

Real GDP per person in Korea in 2010 was similar to that in Hong Kong in 1988, and real GDP in China in 2010 was similar to that of Hong Kong in 1976. Between 1976 and 2010, Hong Kong transformed itself from a poor developing economy into one of the richest economies in the world.

The rest of China is now doing what Hong Kong has done. China has a population 200 times that of Hong Kong and more than 4 times that of Canada.

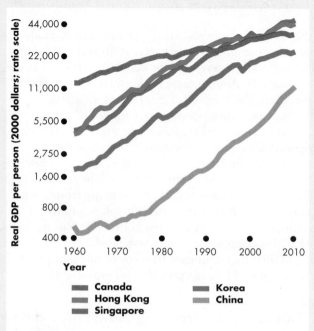

Closing the Gap

Sources of data: See Fig. 22.3 on p. 521.

So if China continues its rapid growth, the world economy will change dramatically.

As these fast-growing Asian economies catch up with Canada, we can expect their growth rates to slow. But it will be surprising if China's growth rate slows much before it has closed the gap on Canada.

Even modest differences in economic growth rates sustained over a number of years bring enormous differences in the standard of living. And some of the differences that you've just seen are enormous. So the facts about economic growth in Canada and around the world raise some big questions.

What are the preconditions for economic growth? What sustains economic growth once it gets going? How can we identify the sources of economic growth and measure the contribution that each source makes? What can we do to increase the sustainable rate of economic growth?

We're now going to address these questions and discover the causes of economic growth. We start by seeing how potential GDP is determined and what makes it grow. You will see that labour productivity growth is the key to rising living standards and go on to explore the sources of this growth.

► REVIEW QUIZ

1 What has been the average growth rate of Canadian real GDP per person over the past 84 years? In which periods was growth most rapid and in which periods was it slowest?

2 Describe the gaps between real GDP per person in Canada and in other countries. For which countries is the gap narrowing? For which is it widening? For which is it the same?

3 Compare real GDP per person and its growth rate in Hong Kong, Korea, Singapore, China, and Canada. In terms of real GDP per person, how far is China behind these others?

You can work these questions in Study Plan 22.2 and get instant feedback.

────────── MyEconLab ◆

How Potential GDP Grows

Economic growth occurs when real GDP increases. But a one-shot rise in real GDP or a recovery from recession isn't economic growth. Economic growth is a sustained, year-after-year increase in *potential GDP*.

So what determines potential GDP and what are the forces that make it grow?

What Determines Potential GDP?

Labour, capital, land, and entrepreneurship produce real GDP, and the productivity of the factors of production determines the quantity of real GDP that can be produced.

The quantity of land is fixed and on any given day, the quantities of entrepreneurial ability and capital are also fixed and their productivities are given. The quantity of labour employed is the only *variable* factor of production. Potential GDP is the level of real GDP when the quantity of labour employed is the full-employment quantity.

To determine potential GDP, we use a model with two components:

- An aggregate production function
- An aggregate labour market

Aggregate Production Function When you studied the limits to production in Chapter 2 (see p. 30), you learned that the *production possibilities frontier* is the boundary between the combinations of goods and services that can be produced and those that cannot. We're now going to think about the production possibilities frontier for two special "goods": real GDP and the quantity of leisure time.

Think of real GDP as a number of big shopping carts. Each cart contains some of each kind of different goods and services produced, and one cartload of items costs $1 billion. To say that real GDP is $1,400 billion means that it is 1,400 very big shopping carts of goods and services.

The quantity of leisure time is the number of hours spent not working. Each leisure hour could be spent working. If we spent all our time taking leisure, we would do no work and produce nothing. Real GDP would be zero. The more leisure we forgo, the greater is the quantity of labour we supply and the greater is the quantity of real GDP produced.

But labour hours are not all equally productive. We use our most productive hours first and as more hours are worked, less and less productive hours are used. So for each additional hour of leisure forgone (each additional hour of labour), real GDP increases but by successively smaller amounts.

The **aggregate production function** is the relationship that tells us how real GDP changes as the quantity of labour changes when all other influences on production remain the same. Figure 22.4 shows this relationship—the curve labelled *PF*. An increase in the quantity of labour (and a corresponding decrease in leisure hours) brings a movement along the production function and an increase in real GDP.

Aggregate Labour Market In macroeconomics, we pretend that there is one large labour market that determines the quantity of labour employed and the quantity of real GDP produced. To see how this aggregate labour market works, we study the demand for labour, the supply of labour, and labour market equilibrium.

The Demand for Labour The *demand for labour* is the relationship between the quantity of labour demanded and the real wage rate. The quantity of labour demanded is the hours of labour demanded by all the firms in the economy in a given period.

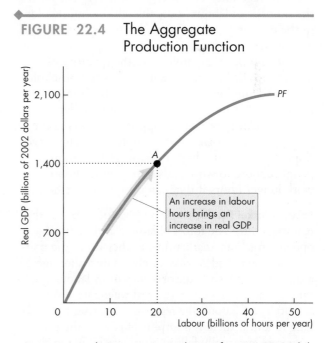

FIGURE 22.4   The Aggregate Production Function

At point *A* on the aggregate production function *PF*, 20 billion hours of labour produce $1,400 billion of real GDP.

MyEconLab animation ◆

This quantity depends on the price of labour, which is the real wage rate.

The **real wage rate** is the money wage rate divided by the price level. The real wage rate is the quantity of goods and services that an hour of labour earns. It contrasts with the money wage rate, which is the number of dollars that an hour of labour earns.

The *real* wage rate influences the quantity of labour demanded because what matters to firms is not the number of dollars they pay (money wage rate) but how much output they must sell to earn those dollars.

The quantity of labour demanded *increases* as the real wage rate *decreases*—the demand for labour curve slopes downward. Why? The answer lies in the shape of the production function.

You've seen that along the production function, each additional hour of labour increases real GDP by successively smaller amounts. This tendency has a name: the *law of diminishing returns*. Because of diminishing returns, firms will hire more labour only if the real wage rate falls to match the fall in the extra output produced by that labour.

The Supply of Labour   The *supply of labour* is the relationship between the quantity of labour supplied and the real wage rate. The quantity of labour supplied is the number of labour hours that all the households in the economy plan to work during a given period. This quantity depends on the real wage rate.

The *real* wage rate influences the quantity of labour supplied because what matters to households is not the number of dollars they earn (money wage rate) but what they can buy with those dollars.

The quantity of labour supplied *increases* as the real wage rate *increases*—the supply of labour curve slopes upward. At a higher real wage rate, more people choose to work and more people choose to work longer hours if they can earn more per hour.

Labour Market Equilibrium   The price of labour is the real wage rate. The forces of supply and demand operate in labour markets just as they do in the markets for goods and services to eliminate a shortage or a surplus. But a shortage or a surplus of labour brings only a gradual change in the real wage rate. If there is a shortage of labour, the real wage rate rises to eliminate it; and if there is a surplus of labour, the real wage rate eventually falls to eliminate it. When there is neither a shortage nor a surplus, the labour market is in equilibrium—a full-employment equilibrium.

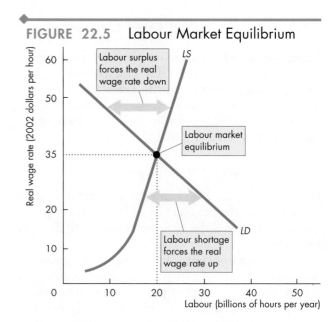

FIGURE 22.5   Labour Market Equilibrium

Labour market equilibrium occurs when the quantity of labour demanded equals the quantity of labour supplied. The equilibrium real wage rate is $35 an hour, and equilibrium employment is 20 billion hours per year.

At a wage rate above $35 an hour, there is a surplus of labour and the real wage rate falls to eliminate the surplus. At a wage rate below $35 an hour, there is a shortage of labour and the real wage rate rises to eliminate the shortage.

MyEconLab   animation

Figure 22.5 illustrates labour market equilibrium. The demand for labour curve is *LD* and the supply of labour curve is *LS*. This labour market is in equilibrium at a real wage rate of $35 an hour and 20 billion hours a year are employed.

If the real wage rate exceeds $35 an hour, the quantity of labour supplied exceeds the quantity demanded and there is a surplus of labour. When there is a surplus of labour, the real wage rate falls towards the equilibrium real wage rate where the surplus is eliminated.

If the real wage rate is less than $35 an hour, the quantity of labour demanded exceeds the quantity supplied and there is a shortage of labour. When there is a shortage of labour, the real wage rate rises towards the equilibrium real wage rate where the shortage is eliminated.

If the real wage rate is $35 an hour, the quantity of labour demanded equals the quantity supplied and there is neither a shortage nor a surplus of labour. In this situation, there is no pressure in either direction on the real wage rate. So the real wage rate remains constant and the market is in equilibrium. At this equilibrium real wage rate and level of employment, the economy is at *full employment*.

Potential GDP You've seen that the production function tells us the quantity of real GDP that a given amount of labour can produce—see Fig. 22.4. The quantity of real GDP produced increases as the quantity of labour increases. At the equilibrium quantity of labour, the economy is at full employment, and the quantity of real GDP at full employment is potential GDP. So the full-employment quantity of labour produces potential GDP.

Figure 22.6 illustrates the determination of potential GDP. Part (a) shows labour market equilibrium. At the equilibrium real wage rate, equilibrium employment is 20 billion hours. Part (b) shows the production function. With 20 billion hours of labour, the economy can produce a real GDP of $1,400 billion. This amount is potential GDP.

What Makes Potential GDP Grow?

We can divide all the forces that make potential GDP grow into two categories:

- Growth of the supply of labour
- Growth of labour productivity

Growth of the Supply of Labour When the supply of labour grows, the supply of labour curve shifts rightward. The quantity of labour at a given real wage rate increases.

The quantity of labour is the number of workers employed multiplied by average hours per worker; and the number employed equals the employment-to-population ratio multiplied by the working-age population (see Chapter 22, p. 495). So the quantity of labour changes as a result of changes in

1. Average hours per worker
2. The employment-to-population ratio
3. The working-age population

Average hours per worker have decreased as the workweek has become shorter, and the employment-to-population ratio has increased as more women have entered the labour force. The combined effect

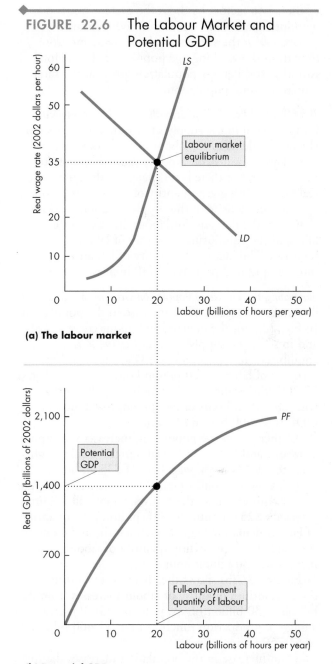

FIGURE 22.6 The Labour Market and Potential GDP

(a) The labour market

(b) Potential GDP

The economy is at full employment when the quantity of labour demanded equals the quantity of labour supplied, in part (a). The real wage rate is $35 an hour, and employment is 20 billion hours a year. Part (b) shows potential GDP. It is the quantity of real GDP determined by the production function at the full-employment quantity of labour.

━━━━━━━━━━━━━ MyEconLab animation ◆

of these two factors has kept the average hours per working-age person (approximately) constant.

Growth in the supply of labour has come from growth in the working-age population. In the long run, the working-age population grows at the same rate as the total population.

The Effects of Population Growth Population growth brings growth in the supply of labour, but it does not change the demand for labour or the production function. The economy can produce more output by using more labour, but there is no change in the quantity of real GDP that a given quantity of labour can produce.

With an increase in the supply of labour and no change in the demand for labour, the real wage rate falls and the equilibrium quantity of labour increases. The increased quantity of labour produces more output and potential GDP increases.

Illustrating the Effects of Population Growth Figure 22.7 illustrates the effects of an increase in the population. In Fig. 22.7(a), the demand for labour curve is LD and initially the supply of labour curve is LS_0. The equilibrium real wage rate is $35 an hour and the quantity of labour is 20 billion hours a year. In Fig. 22.7(b), the production function (PF) shows that with 20 billion hours of labour employed, potential GDP is $1,400 billion at point A.

An increase in the population increases the supply of labour and the supply of labour curve shifts rightward to LS_1. At a real wage rate of $35 an hour, there is now a surplus of labour. So the real wage rate falls. In this example, the real wage rate will fall until it reaches $25 an hour. At $25 an hour, the quantity of labour demanded equals the quantity of labour supplied. The equilibrium quantity of labour increases to 30 billion hours a year.

Figure 22.7(b) shows the effect on real GDP. As the equilibrium quantity of labour increases from 20 billion to 30 billion hours, potential GDP increases along the production function from $1,400 billion to $1,750 billion at point B.

So an increase in the population increases the full-employment quantity of labour, increases potential GDP, and lowers the real wage rate. But the population increase *decreases* potential GDP per hour of labour. Initially, it was $70 ($1,400 billion divided by 20 billion). With the population increase, potential GDP per hour of labour is $58.33 ($1,750 billion divided by 30 billion). Diminishing returns are the source of the decrease in potential GDP per hour of labour.

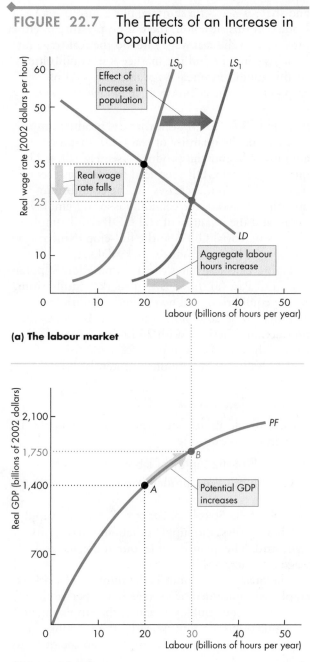

FIGURE 22.7   The Effects of an Increase in Population

(a) The labour market

(b) Potential GDP

An increase in the population increases the supply of labour. In part (a), the supply of labour curve shifts rightward. The real wage rate falls and aggregate labour hours increase. In part (b), the increase in aggregate labour hours brings an increase in potential GDP. But diminishing returns bring a decrease in potential GDP per hour of labour.

 MyEconLab   animation

Growth of Labour Productivity **Labour productivity** is the quantity of real GDP produced by an hour of labour. It is calculated by dividing real GDP by aggregate labour hours. For example, if real GDP is $1,400 billion and aggregate hours are 20 billion, labour productivity is $70 per hour.

When labour productivity grows, real GDP per person grows and brings a rising standard of living. Let's see how an increase in labour productivity changes potential GDP.

Effects of an Increase in Labour Productivity If labour productivity increases, production possibilities expand. The quantity of real GDP that any given quantity of labour can produce increases. If labour is more productive, firms are willing to pay more for a given number of hours of labour so the demand for labour also increases.

With an increase in the demand for labour and *no change in the supply of labour*, the real wage rate rises and the quantity of labour supplied increases. The equilibrium quantity of labour also increases.

So an increase in labour productivity increases potential GDP for two reasons: Labour is more productive and more labour is employed.

Illustrating the Effects of an Increase in Labour Productivity Figure 22.8 illustrates the effects of an increase in labour productivity.

In part (a), the production function initially is PF_0. With 20 billion hours of labour employed, potential GDP is $1,400 billion at point *A*.

In part (b), the demand for labour curve is LD_0 and the supply of labour curve is *LS*. The real wage rate is $35 an hour, and the equilibrium quantity of labour is 20 billion hours a year.

Now labour productivity increases. In Fig. 22.8(a), the increase in labour productivity shifts the production function upward to PF_1. At each quantity of labour, more real GDP can be produced. For example, at 20 billion hours, the economy can now produce $2,000 billion of real GDP at point *B*.

In Fig. 22.8(b), the increase in labour productivity increases the demand for labour and the demand for labour curve shifts rightward to LD_1. At the initial real wage rate of $35 an hour, there is now a shortage of labour. The real wage rate rises. In this example, the real wage rate will rise until it reaches $45 an hour. At $45 an hour, the quantity of labour demanded equals the quantity of labour supplied and the equilibrium quantity of labour is 22.5 billion hours a year.

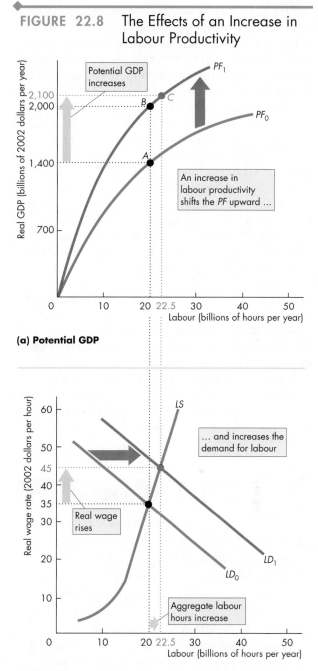

FIGURE 22.8 The Effects of an Increase in Labour Productivity

(a) Potential GDP

(b) The labour market

An increase in labour productivity shifts the production function upward from PF_0 to PF_1 in part (a) and shifts the demand for labour curve rightward from LD_0 to LD_1 in part (b). The real wage rate rises to $45 an hour, and aggregate labour hours increase from 20 billion to 22.5 billion. Potential GDP increases from $1,400 billion to $2,100 billion.

MyEconLab   animation

Figure 22.8(a) shows how the increase in labour productivity changes potential GDP. First, at the initial quantity of labour, real GDP increases to point *B* on the new production function. Second, as the equilibrium quantity of labour increases from 20 billion to 22.5 billion hours, potential GDP increases to $2,100 billion at point *C*.

Potential GDP per hour of labour also increases. Initially, it was $70 ($1,400 billion divided by 20 billion). With the increase in labour productivity, potential GDP per hour of labour is $93.33 ($2,100 billion divided by 22.5 billion).

The increase in aggregate labour hours that you have just seen is a consequence of an increase in labour productivity. This increase in aggregate labour hours and labour productivity is an example of the interaction effects that economists seek to identify in their search for the ultimate *causes* of economic growth. In the case that we've just studied, aggregate labour hours increase but that increase is a *consequence*, not a cause, of the growth of potential GDP. The source of the increase in potential GDP is an increase in labour productivity.

Labour productivity is the key to increasing output per hour of labour and rising living standards, but what brings an increase in labour productivity? The next section answers this question.

◆ REVIEW QUIZ

1 What is the aggregate production function?
2 What determines the demand for labour, the supply of labour, and labour market equilibrium?
3 What determines potential GDP?
4 What are the two broad sources of potential GDP growth?
5 What are the effects of an increase in the population on potential GDP, the quantity of labour, the real wage rate, and potential GDP per hour of labour?
6 What are the effects of an increase in labour productivity on potential GDP, the quantity of labour, the real wage rate, and potential GDP per hour of labour?

You can work these questions in Study Plan 22.3 and get instant feedback.

———————— MyEconLab ◆

◆ Why Labour Productivity Grows

You've seen that labour productivity growth makes potential GDP grow; and you've seen that labour productivity growth is essential if real GDP per person and the standard of living are to grow. But *why* does labour productivity grow? What are the preconditions that make labour productivity growth possible and what are the forces that make it grow? Why does labour productivity grow faster at some times and in some places than others?

Preconditions for Labour Productivity Growth

The fundamental precondition for labour productivity growth is the *incentive* system created by firms, markets, property rights, and money. These four social institutions are the same as those described in Chapter 2 (see pp. 41–42) that enable people to gain by specializing and trading.

Economics in Action
Intellectual Property Rights Propel Growth

In 1760, when North America was developing an agricultural economy, England was on the cusp of an economic revolution, the *Industrial Revolution*.

For 70 dazzling years, technological advances in the use of steam power; the manufacture of cotton, wool, iron, and steel; and in transportation, accompanied by massive capital investment associated with these technologies, transformed the economy of England. Incomes rose and brought an explosion in an increasingly urbanized population.

By 1825, advances in steam technology had reached a level of sophistication that enabled Robert Stevenson to build the world's first steam-powered rail engine (the Rocket pictured here) and the birth of the world's first railroad.

Why did the Industrial Revolution happen? Why did it start in 1760? And why in England?

Economic historians say that intellectual property rights—England's patent system—provide the answer. England's patent system began with the Statute of Monopolies of 1624, which gave inventors a monopoly to use their idea for a term of 14 years. For about 100 years, the system was used to reward friends of the royal court rather than true inventors.

It was the presence of secure property rights in Britain in the middle 1700s that got the Industrial Revolution going (see *Economics in Action* below). And it is their absence in some parts of Africa today that is keeping labour productivity stagnant.

With the preconditions for labour productivity growth in place, three things influence its pace:

- Physical capital growth
- Human capital growth
- Technological advances

Physical Capital Growth

As the amount of capital per worker increases, labour productivity also increases. Production processes that use hand tools can create beautiful objects, but production methods that use large amounts of capital per worker are much more productive. The accumulation of capital on farms, in textile factories, in iron

But from around 1720 onward, the system started to work well. To be granted a 14-year monopoly, an inventor only had to pay the required £100 fee (about $22,000 in today's money) and register his or her invention. The inventor was not required to describe the invention in too much detail, so registering and getting a patent didn't mean sharing the invention with competitors.

This patent system, which is in all essentials the same as today's, aligned the self-interest of entrepreneurial inventors with the social interest and unleashed a flood of inventions, the most transformative of which was steam power and, by 1825, the steam locomotive.

foundries and steel mills, in coal mines, on building sites, in chemical plants, in auto plants, in banks and insurance companies, and in shopping malls has added incredibly to the labour productivity of our economy. The next time you see a movie that is set in the Old West or colonial times, look carefully at the small amount of capital around. Try to imagine how productive you would be in such circumstances compared with your productivity today.

Human Capital Growth

Human capital—the accumulated skill and knowledge of human beings—is the fundamental source of labour productivity growth. Human capital grows when a new discovery is made and it grows as more and more people learn how to use past discoveries.

The development of one of the most basic human skills—writing—was the source of some of the earliest major gains in productivity. The ability to keep written records made it possible to reap ever-larger gains from specialization and trade. Imagine how hard it would be to do any kind of business if all the accounts, invoices, and agreements existed only in people's memories.

Later, the development of mathematics laid the foundation for the eventual extension of knowledge about physical forces and chemical and biological processes. This base of scientific knowledge was the foundation for the technological advances of the Industrial Revolution and of today's information revolution.

But a lot of human capital that is extremely productive is much more humble. It takes the form of millions of individuals learning and becoming remarkably more productive by repetitively doing simple production tasks. One much-studied example of this type of human capital growth occurred in World War II. With no change in physical capital, thousands of workers and managers in U.S. shipyards learned from experience and accumulated human capital that more than doubled their productivity in less than two years.

Technological Advances

The accumulation of physical capital and human capital have made a large contribution to labour productivity growth. But technological change—the discovery and the application of new technologies—has made an even greater contribution.

FIGURE 22.9   The Sources of Economic Growth

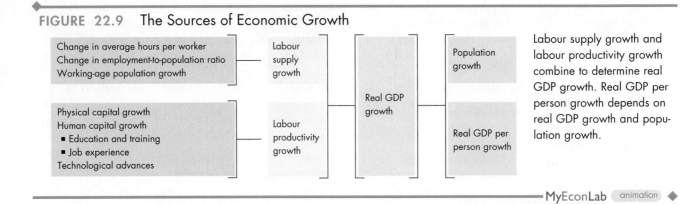

| Change in average hours per worker / Change in employment-to-population ratio / Working-age population growth | → Labour supply growth |
| Physical capital growth / Human capital growth / ■ Education and training / ■ Job experience / Technological advances | → Labour productivity growth |

Real GDP growth → Population growth / Real GDP per person growth

Labour supply growth and labour productivity growth combine to determine real GDP growth. Real GDP per person growth depends on real GDP growth and population growth.

MyEconLab   animation ◆

Economics in Action
Women Are the Better Borrowers

Economic growth is driven by the decisions made by billions of individuals to save and invest, and to borrow and lend. But most people are poor, have no credit history, and can't borrow from a bank.

These people—many of whom are women—can, however, start a business, employ a few people, and earn an income with the help of a *microloan*.

Microloans originated in Bangladesh but have spread throughout the developing world. Kiva.org and MicroPlace.com (owned by eBay) are Web sites that enable people to lend money that is used to make microloans in developing economies.

Throughout the developing world, microloans are helping women to feed and clothe their families and to grow their small businesses, often in agriculture. As the incomes of microloan borrowers rise, they pay off their loans and accumulate capital. A billion microloans pack a macro punch.

Labour is many times more productive today than it was a hundred years ago but not because we have more steam engines and more horse-drawn carriages per person. Rather, it is because we have transportation equipment that uses technologies that were unknown a hundred years ago and that are more productive than the old technologies were.

Technological advance arises from formal research and development programs and from informal trial and error, and it involves discovering new ways of getting more out of our resources.

To reap the benefits of technological change, capital must increase. Some of the most powerful and far-reaching fundamental technologies are embodied in human capital—for example, language, writing, and mathematics. But most technologies are embodied in physical capital. For example, to reap the benefits of the internal combustion engine, millions of horse-drawn carriages had to be replaced with automobiles; and to reap the benefits of digital music, millions of Discmans had to be replaced with iPods.

Figure 22.9 summarizes the sources of labour productivity growth and more broadly of real GDP growth. The figure also emphasizes that for real GDP per person to grow, real GDP must grow faster than the population.

◆ REVIEW QUIZ

1   What are the preconditions for labour productivity growth?
2   Explain the influences on the pace of labour productivity growth.

You can work these questions in Study Plan 22.4 and get instant feedback.

MyEconLab ◆

Growth Theories, Evidence, and Policies

You've seen how population growth and labour productivity growth make potential GDP grow. You've also seen that the growth of physical capital and human capital and technological advances make labour productivity grow. How do all these factors interact? What is cause and what is effect? Growth theories address these questions.

Alternative theories of economic growth provide insights into the process of economic growth, but none provides a complete and definite answer to the basic questions: What causes economic growth and why do growth rates vary? Economics has some way to go before it can provide definite answers to these questions. We look at the current state of the empirical evidence. Finally, we'll look at the policies that might achieve faster growth.

Let's start by studying the three main theories of economic growth:

- Classical growth theory
- Neoclassical growth theory
- New growth theory

Classical Growth Theory

Classical growth theory is the view that the growth of real GDP per person is temporary and that when it rises above the subsistence level, a population explosion eventually brings it back to the subsistence level. Adam Smith, Thomas Robert Malthus, and David Ricardo—the leading economists of the late eighteenth century and early nineteenth century—proposed this theory, but the view is most closely associated with the name of Malthus and is sometimes called the *Malthusian theory*. Charles Darwin's ideas about evolution by natural selection were inspired by the insights of Malthus.

Modern-Day Malthusians Many people today are Malthusians. They say that if today's global population of 6.9 billion explodes to 11 billion by 2050 and perhaps 35 billion by 2300, we will run out of resources, real GDP per person will decline, and we will return to a primitive standard of living. We must, say Malthusians, contain population growth.

Modern-day Malthusians also point to global warming and climate change as reasons to believe that eventually, real GDP per person will decrease.

Neoclassical Growth Theory

Neoclassical growth theory is the proposition that real GDP per person grows because technological change induces saving and investment that make capital per hour of labour grow. Growth ends if technological change stops because of diminishing marginal returns to both labour and capital. Robert Solow of MIT suggested the most popular version of this growth theory in the 1950s.

Neoclassical growth theory's big break with its classical predecessor is its view about population growth.

The Neoclassical Theory of Population Growth The population explosion of eighteenth century Europe that created the classical theory of population eventually ended. The birth rate fell, and while the population continued to increase, its rate of increase moderated.

The key economic influence that slowed the population growth rate is the opportunity cost of a woman's time. As women's wage rates increase and their job opportunities expand, the opportunity cost of having children increases. Faced with a higher opportunity cost, families choose to have fewer children and the birth rate falls.

Technological advances that bring higher incomes also bring advances in health care that extend lives. So as incomes increase, both the birth rate and the death rate decrease. These opposing forces offset each other and result in a slowly rising population.

This modern view of population growth and the historical trends that support it contradict the views of the classical economists. They also call into question the modern doomsday view that the planet will be swamped with more people than it can support.

Technological Change and Diminishing Returns In neoclassical growth theory, the pace of technological change influences the economic growth rate but economic growth does not influence the pace of technological change. It is assumed that technological change results from chance. When we're lucky, we have rapid technological change, and when bad luck strikes, the pace of technological advance slows.

To understand neoclassical growth theory, imagine the world of the mid-1950s, when Robert Solow is explaining his idea. Income per person is around $12,000 a year in today's money. The population is growing at about 1 percent a year. Saving and investment are about 20 percent of GDP, enough to keep the quantity of capital per hour of labour constant. Income per person is growing but not very quickly.

Then technology begins to advance at a more rapid pace across a range of activities. The transistor revolutionizes an emerging electronics industry. New plastics revolutionize the manufacture of household appliances. The interstate highway system revolutionizes road transportation. Jet airliners start to replace piston-engine airplanes and speed air transportation.

These technological advances bring new profit opportunities. Businesses expand, and new businesses are created to exploit the newly available profitable technologies. Investment and saving increase. The economy enjoys new levels of prosperity and growth. But will the prosperity last? And will the growth last? Neoclassical growth theory says that the *prosperity* will last but the *growth* will not last unless technology keeps advancing.

According to neoclassical growth theory, the prosperity will persist because there is no classical population growth to induce the wage rate to fall. So the gains in income per person are permanent.

But growth will eventually stop if technology stops advancing because of diminishing marginal returns to capital. The high profit rates that result from technological change bring increased saving and capital accumulation. But as more capital is accumulated, more and more projects are undertaken that have lower rates of return—diminishing marginal returns. As the return on capital falls, the incentive to keep investing weakens. With weaker incentives to save and invest, saving decreases and the rate of capital accumulation slows. Eventually, the pace of capital accumulation slows so that it is only keeping up with population growth. Capital per worker remains constant.

A Problem with Neoclassical Growth Theory All economies have access to the same technologies, and capital is free to roam the globe, seeking the highest available real interest rate. Capital will flow between countries until real interest rates are equal, and they will be equal when capital per hour of labour is identical. Real GDP growth rates and income levels per person around the world will converge. Figure 22.3 on p. 521 shows that while there is some sign of convergence among the rich countries in part (a), convergence is slow, and part (b) shows that it does not appear to be imminent for all countries. New growth theory overcomes this shortcoming of neoclassical growth theory. It also explains what determines the pace of technological change.

New Growth Theory

New growth theory holds that real GDP per person grows because of the choices people make in the pursuit of profit and that growth will persist indefinitely. Paul Romer of Stanford University developed this theory during the 1980s, based on ideas of Joseph Schumpeter during the 1930s and 1940s.

According to the new growth theory, the pace at which new discoveries are made—and at which technology advances—is not determined by chance. It depends on how many people are looking for a new technology and how intensively they are looking. The search for new technologies is driven by incentives.

Profit is the spur to technological change. The forces of competition squeeze profits, so to increase profit, people constantly seek either lower-cost methods of production or new and better products for which people are willing to pay a higher price. Inventors can maintain a profit for several years by taking out a patent or a copyright, but eventually, a new discovery is copied, and profits disappear. So more research and development is undertaken in the hope of creating a new burst of profitable investment and growth.

Two facts about discoveries and technological knowledge play a key role in the new growth theory: Discoveries are (at least eventually) a public capital good; and knowledge is capital that is not subject to diminishing marginal returns.

Economists call a good a *public good* when no one can be excluded from using it and when one person's use does not prevent others from using it. National defence is the classic example of a public good. The programming language used to write apps for the iPhone is another.

Because knowledge is a public good, as the benefits of a new discovery spread, free resources become available. Nothing is given up when they are used: They have a zero opportunity cost. When a student in Waterloo writes a new iPhone app, his use of the programming language doesn't prevent another student in Vancouver from using it.

Knowledge is even more special because it is *not* subject to diminishing returns. But increasing the stock of knowledge makes both labour and machines more productive. Knowledge capital does not bring diminishing returns. Biotech knowledge illustrates this idea well. Biologists have spent a lot of time developing DNA sequencing technology. As more has been discovered, the productivity of this knowledge capital has relentlessly increased. In 1990, it cost about $50 to sequence one DNA base pair. That cost had fallen to $1 by 2000 and to 1/10,000th of a penny by 2010.

The implication of this simple and appealing observation is astonishing. Unlike the other two theories, new growth theory has no growth-stopping mechanism. As physical capital accumulates, the return to capital—the real interest rate—falls. But the incentive to innovate and earn a higher profit becomes stronger. So innovation occurs, capital becomes more productive, the demand for capital increases, and the real interest rate rises again.

Labour productivity grows indefinitely as people discover new technologies that yield a higher real interest rate. The growth rate depends only on people's incentives and ability to innovate.

A Perpetual Motion Economy New growth theory sees the economy as a perpetual motion machine, which Fig. 22.10 illustrates.

No matter how rich we become, our wants exceed our ability to satisfy them. We always want a higher standard of living. In the pursuit of a higher standard of living, human societies have developed incentive systems—markets, property rights, and money—that enable people to profit from innovation. Innovation leads to the development of new and better techniques of production and new and better products. To take advantage of new techniques and to produce new products, new firms start up and old firms go out of business—firms are born and die. As old firms die and new firms are born, some jobs are destroyed and others are created. The new jobs created are better than the old ones and they pay higher real wage rates. Also, with higher wage rates and more productive techniques, leisure increases. New and better jobs and new and better products lead to more consumption goods and services and, combined with increased leisure, bring a higher standard of living.

But our insatiable wants are still there, so the process continues: Wants and incentives create innovation, new and better products, and a yet higher standard of living.

FIGURE 22.10   A Perpetual Motion Machine

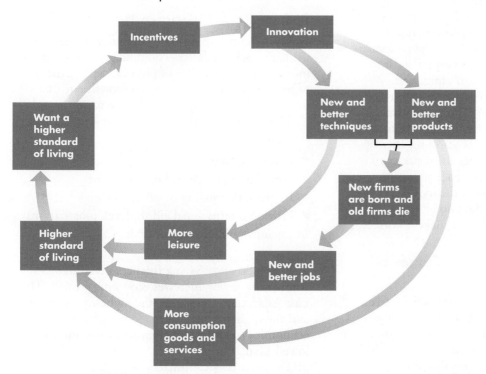

People want a higher standard of living and are spurred by profit incentives to make the innovations that lead to new and better techniques and new and better products.

These new and better techniques and products, in turn, lead to the birth of new firms and the death of some old firms, new and better jobs, and more leisure and more consumption goods and services.

The result is a higher standard of living, but people want a still higher standard of living, and the growth process continues.

Source: Based on a similar figure in *These Are the Good Old Days: A Report on U.S. Living Standards*, Federal Reserve Bank of Dallas 1993 Annual Report.

MyEconLab   animation

New Growth Theory Versus Malthusian Theory

The contrast between the Malthusian theory and new growth theory couldn't be more sharp. Malthusians see the end of prosperity as we know it today and new growth theorists see unending plenty. The contrast becomes clearest by thinking about the differing views about population growth.

To a Malthusian, population growth is part of the problem. To a new growth theorist, population growth is part of the solution. People are the ultimate economic resource. A larger population brings forth more wants, but it also brings a greater amount of scientific discovery and technological advance. So rather than being the source of falling real GDP per person, population growth generates faster labour productivity growth and rising real GDP per person. Resources are limited, but the human imagination and ability to increase productivity are unlimited.

Sorting Out the Theories

Which theory is correct? None of them tells us the whole story, but each teaches us something of value.

Classical growth theory reminds us that our physical resources are limited and that without advances in technology, we must eventually hit diminishing returns.

Neoclassical growth theory reaches the same conclusion but not because of a population explosion. Instead, it emphasizes diminishing returns to capital and reminds us that we cannot keep growth going just by accumulating physical capital. We must also advance technology and accumulate human capital. We must become more creative in our use of scarce resources.

New growth theory emphasizes the capacity of human resources to innovate at a pace that offsets diminishing returns. New growth theory fits the facts of today's world more closely than do either of the other two theories. But that doesn't make it correct.

The Empirical Evidence on the Causes of Economic Growth

Economics makes progress by the interplay between theory and empirical evidence. A theory makes predictions about what we will observe if the theory is correct. Empirical evidence—the data generated by history and the natural experiments that it performs—provides the data for testing the theory.

Economists have done an enormous amount of research confronting theories of growth with the empirical evidence. The way in which this research has been conducted has changed over the years.

In 1776, when Adam Smith wrote about "the nature and causes of the Wealth of Nations" in his celebrated book, empirical evidence took the form of carefully selected facts described in words and stories. Today, large databases, sophisticated statistical methods, and fast computers provide numerical measurements of the causes of economic growth.

Economists have looked at the growth rate data for more than 100 countries for the period since 1960 and explored the correlations between the growth rate and more than 60 possible influences on it. The conclusion of this data crunching is that most of these possible influences have variable and unpredictable effects, but a few of them have strong and clear effects. Table 22.1 summarizes these more robust influences. They are arranged in order of difficulty (or in the case of region, impossiblity) of changing. Political and economic systems are hard to change, but market distortions, investment, and openness to international trade are features of a nation's economy that can be influenced by policy.

Let's now look at growth policies.

Policies for Achieving Faster Growth

Growth theory supported by empirical evidence tells us that to achieve faster economic growth, we must increase the growth rate of physical capital, the pace of technological advance, or the growth rate of human capital and openness to international trade.

The main suggestions for achieving these objectives are

- Stimulate saving
- Stimulate research and development
- Improve the quality of education
- Provide international aid to developing nations
- Encourage international trade

Stimulate Saving Saving finances investment so stimulating saving increases economic growth. The East Asian economies have the highest growth rates and the highest saving rates. Some African economies have the lowest growth rates and the lowest saving rates.

Tax incentives can increase saving. Registered Retirement Saving Plans (RRSPs) are a tax incentive to save. Economists claim that a tax on consumption rather than income provides the best saving incentive.

TABLE 22.1   The Influences on Economic Growth

Influence	Good for Economic Growth	Bad for Economic Growth
Region	■ Far from equator	■ Sub-Sahara Africa
Politics	■ Rule of law	■ Revolutions
	■ Civil liberties	■ Military coups
		■ Wars
Economic system	■ Capitalist	
Market distortions		■ Exchange rate distortions
		■ Price controls and black markets
Investment	■ Human capital	
	■ Physical capital	
International trade	■ Open to trade	

Source of data: Xavier Sala-i-Martin, "I Just Ran Two Million Regressions," *The American Economic Review*, Vol. 87, No 2, (May 1997), pp. 178–183.

Stimulate Research and Development   Everyone can use the fruits of *basic* research and development efforts. For example, all biotechnology firms can use advances in gene-splicing technology. Because basic inventions can be copied, the inventor's profit is limited and the market allocates too few resources to this activity. Governments can direct public funds towards financing basic research, but this solution is not foolproof. It requires a mechanism for allocating the public funds to their highest-valued use.

Improve the Quality of Education   The free market produces too little education because it brings benefits beyond those valued by the people who receive the education. By funding basic education and by ensuring high standards in basic skills such as language, mathematics, and science, governments can contribute to a nation's growth potential. Education can also be stimulated and improved by using tax incentives to encourage improved private provision.

Provide International Aid to Developing Nations   It seems obvious that if rich countries give financial aid to developing countries, investment and growth will increase in the recipient countries. Unfortunately, the obvious does not routinely happen. A large amount of data-driven research on the effects of aid on growth has turned up a zero and even negative effect. Aid often gets diverted and spent on consumption.

Encourage International Trade   Trade, not aid, stimulates economic growth. It works by extracting the available gains from specialization and trade. The fastest-growing nations are those most open to trade. If the rich nations truly want to aid economic development, they will lower their trade barriers against developing nations, especially in farm products. The World Trade Organization's efforts to achieve more open trade are being resisted by the richer nations.

REVIEW QUIZ

1   What is the key idea of classical growth theory that leads to the dismal outcome?
2   What, according to neoclassical growth theory, is the fundamental cause of economic growth?
3   What is the key proposition of new growth theory that makes economic growth persist?

You can work these questions in Study Plan 22.5 and get instant feedback.

───────────── MyEconLab ◆

◆ To complete your study of economic growth, take a look at *Reading Between the Lines* on pp. 536–537 and see how economic growth is changing the GDP ranking of nations.

Economic Growth in China

China Pips Japan but "Still a Developing Nation"

www.afp.com

August 17, 2010

China insisted Tuesday it was still a developing nation despite overtaking Japan as the world's second largest economy, in the face of pressure to take on a greater role in global affairs. ...

Thirty years after opening its doors to the outside world, China has enjoyed spectacular economic growth and already claimed the titles of world's top exporter, auto market, and steelmaker.

After outpacing its neighbour in the second quarter, China is on course this year to officially confirm its position as world number two—a title Japan held for 40 years—underscoring its emergence as a global economic and political force.

While some analysts are predicting that China could take on the top spot from the United States within a few decades, commentators insisted it remained a developing nation with tens of millions living in poverty.

Commerce ministry spokesman Yao Jian said China still lagged far behind its rivals in per capita terms and has a long way to go to becoming a world-class power.

"The quality of China's economic growth still needs to be improved, no matter whether it is in terms of people's quality of life or in terms of science, technology, and environmental protection," the spokesman said.

"We still have an enormous gap to make up."

He said China's per capita GDP was 3,800 dollars—putting it around 105th in the world—and that 150 million of its 1.3 billion people live below the poverty line, according to UN standards.

"China's economy will continue to develop because China has a large population and its economy lagged behind," he said. ...

ESSENCE OF THE STORY

- China is a large developing nation that ranks at 105 in the world on per capita income, with 150 million of its 1.3 billion people living below the UN poverty line.

- After opening to global trade and investment 30 years ago, China has experienced rapid economic growth.

- In mid-2010, China displaced Japan as the world's number two economy. Japan held this spot for 40 years.

- Some analysts predict that China will take the top spot from the United States within a few decades.

- A commerce ministry spokesman says people's quality of life, and science, technology, and environmental protection need to be improved.

ECONOMIC ANALYSIS

- The news that China overtook Japan in mid-2010 to become the world's second largest economy is based on GDP data.

- When the GDP of China measured in yuan and the GDP of Japan measured in yen are converted to U.S. dollars at the current exchange rate, China's GDP became slightly larger than Japan's in the second quarter of 2010.

- Figure 1 shows the data on GDP in China, Japan, and the United States. You can see that Japan has stagnated since 1995 while China has streaked upward.

- You learned in Chapter 20 that PPP prices provide a more useful international comparison of GDP. You also learned that real GDP measures economic growth and nominal GDP (in Fig. 1) measures a combination of economic growth and inflation (or deflation).

- Comparing China and Japan using real GDP in PPP prices (in Fig. 2), China became the number two economy in 2000, and on the International Monetary Fund (IMF) projections, China will catch up to the United States to become joint number one economy in 2015.

- In 2010, China had more than four times as many people as the United States and they earned, on average, 16 percent of U.S. income. So total income in China was about 70 percent of U.S. income.

- China remains a poor country in three respects: Income per person is low; income inequality is large, so many people live in poverty; and most of the country's advanced technology is imported from the United States and Europe.

- How poor China appears depends on the numbers used. At the current exchange rate and in China's prices, income per person was $3,800 in 2010, but in 2005 PPP prices, it was $6,800. Figure 3 shows how far China's income per person is behind that in Japan and the United States when valued in PPP prices.

- The growth of physical capital and human capital and technological change are proceeding at a rapid pace in China and bringing rapid growth in real GDP per person.

- But China lags a long way behind the United States in science, technology, and environmental protection.

- As China's economy continues to expand, it will devote more resources to narrowing the gap in these areas as well as narrowing the income gap.

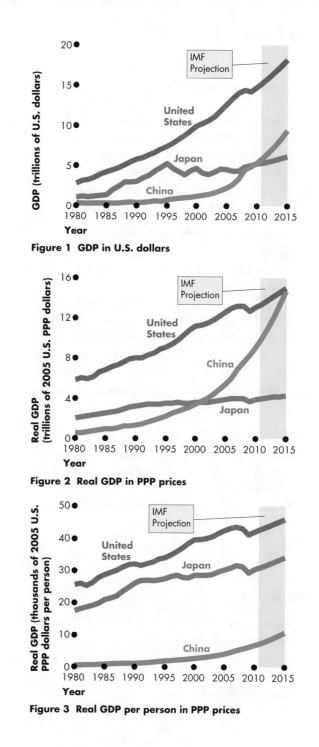

Figure 1 GDP in U.S. dollars

Figure 2 Real GDP in PPP prices

Figure 3 Real GDP per person in PPP prices

SUMMARY

Key Points

The Basics of Economic Growth (pp. 518–519)

- Economic growth is the sustained expansion of production possibilities and is measured as the annual percentage rate of change of real GDP.
- The Rule of 70 tells us the number of years in which real GDP doubles—70 divided by the annual percentage growth rate.

Working Problems 1 to 5 will give you a better understanding of the basics of economic growth.

Economic Growth Trends (pp. 520–522)

- Real GDP per person in Canada grows at an average rate of 2 percent a year. Growth was most rapid during the 1960s.
- The gaps in real GDP per person among the rich G7 countries and between Canada and Africa and Central and Eastern Europe have persisted.
- The gaps between Canada and Singapore, Hong Kong, Korea, and China have narrowed.

Working Problem 6 will give you a better understanding of economic growth trends.

How Potential GDP Grows (pp. 523–528)

- The aggregate production function and equilibrium in the aggregate labour market determine potential GDP.
- Potential GDP grows if the labour supply grows or if labour productivity grows.

- Only labour productivity growth makes real GDP per person and the standard of living grow.

Working Problems 7 to 14 will give you a better understanding of how potential GDP grows.

Why Labour Productivity Grows (pp. 528–530)

- Labour productivity growth requires an incentive system created by firms, markets, property rights, and money.
- The sources of labour productivity growth are growth of physical capital and human capital and advances in technology.

Working Problems 15 and 16 will give you a better understanding of why labour productivity grows.

Growth Theories, Evidence, and Policies (pp. 531–535)

- In classical theory, real GDP per person keeps returning to the subsistence level.
- In neoclassical growth theory, diminishing returns to capital limit economic growth.
- In new growth theory, economic growth persists indefinitely at a rate determined by decisions that lead to innovation and technological change.
- Policies for achieving faster growth include stimulating saving and research and development, encouraging international trade, and improving the quality of education.

Working Problems 17 and 18 will give you a better understanding of growth theories, evidence, and policies.

Key Terms

Aggregate production function, 523
Classical growth theory, 531
Economic growth rate, 518
Labour productivity, 527
Neoclassical growth theory, 531

New growth theory, 532
Real GDP per person, 518
Real wage rate, 524
Rule of 70, 518

SCAN THIS

STUDY PLAN PROBLEMS AND APPLICATIONS

MyEconLab ◆ You can work Problems 1 to 18 in Chapter 22 Study Plan and get instant feedback.

The Basics of Economic Growth (Study Plan 22.1)

1. Brazil's real GDP was 1,360 trillion reais in 2009 and 1,434 trillion reais in 2010. Brazil's population was 191.5 million in 2009 and 193.3 million in 2010. Calculate
   a. The economic growth rate.
   b. The growth rate of real GDP per person.
   c. The approximate number of years it takes for real GDP per person in Brazil to double if the 2010 economic growth rate and population growth rate are maintained.

2. Japan's real GDP was 525 trillion yen in 2009 and 535 trillion yen in 2010. Japan's population was 127.6 million in 2009 and 127.5 million in 2010. Calculate
   a. The economic growth rate.
   b. The growth rate of real GDP per person.
   c. The approximate number of years it takes for real GDP per person in Japan to double if the real GDP economic growth rate returns to 3 percent a year and the population growth rate is maintained.

Use the following data to work Problems 3 and 4. China's real GDP per person was 9,280 yuan in 2009 and 10,110 yuan in 2010. India's real GDP per person was 30,880 rupees in 2009 and 32,160 rupees in 2010.

3. By maintaining their current growth rates, which country will double its 2010 standard of living first?

4. The population of China is growing at 1 percent a year and the population of India is growing at 1.4 percent a year. Calculate the growth rate of real GDP in each country.

5. **China's Economy Picks Up Speed**
   China's trend growth rate of real GDP per person was 2.2 percent a year before 1980 and 8.7 percent a year after 1980. In the year to August 2009, China's output increased by 11.3 percent.
   Source: *World Economic Outlook* and FT.com, September 14, 2009
   Distinguish between a rise in China's economic growth rate and a temporary cyclical expansion.

How long, at the current growth rate, will it take for China to double its real GDP per person?

Economic Growth Trends (Study Plan 22.2)

6. China was the largest economy for centuries because everyone had the same type of economy—subsistence—and so the country with the most people would be economically biggest. Then the Industrial Revolution sent the West on a more prosperous path. Now the world is returning to a common economy, this time technology- and information-based, so once again population triumphs.
   a. Why was China the world's largest economy until 1890?
   b. Why did the United States surpass China in 1890 to become the world's largest economy?

How Potential GDP Grows (Study Plan 22.3)

Use the following information to work Problems 7 and 8.

Suppose that the United States cracks down on illegal immigrants and returns millions of workers to their home countries.

7. Explain what will happen to U.S. potential GDP, employment, and the real wage rate.

8. Explain what will happen in the countries to which the immigrants return to potential GDP, employment, and the real wage rate.

Use the following news clip to work Problems 9 to 11.

U.S. Workers World's Most Productive

Americans work longer hours than those in other rich nations. Americans also produce more per person but only part of the U.S. productivity growth can be explained by the longer hours they work. Americans also create more wealth per hour of work. U.S. employees worked an average of 1,804 hours in 2006, compared to 1,564.4 for the French, but far less than the 2,200 hours that Asians worked. But in Asian countries the average labour productivity is lower.
Source: CBS News, September 3, 2007

9. What is the difference between productivity in this news clip and real GDP per person?

10. Identify and correct a confusion between levels and growth rates of productivity in the news clip.

11. If workers in developing Asian economies work more hours than Americans, why are they not the world's most productive?

Use the following tables to work Problems 12 to 14. The tables describe an economy's labour market and its production function in 2010.

Real wage rate (dollars per hour)	Labour hours supplied	Labour hours demanded
80	45	5
70	40	10
60	35	15
50	30	20
40	25	25
30	20	30
20	15	35

Labour (hours)	Real GDP (2005 dollars)
5	425
10	800
15	1,125
20	1,400
25	1,625
30	1,800
35	1,925
40	2,000

12. What are the equilibrium real wage rate, the quantity of labour employed in 2010, labour productivity, and potential GDP in 2010?

13. In 2011, the population increases and labour hours supplied increase by 10 at each real wage rate. What are the equilibrium real wage rate, labour productivity, and potential GDP in 2011?

14. In 2011, the population increases and labour hours supplied increase by 10 at each real wage rate. Does the standard of living in this economy increase in 2011? Explain why or why not.

Why Labour Productivity Grows (Study Plan 22.4)

15. **Productivity Trends in the Canadian Economy**

From 1987 to 1997, labour productivity fell at an annual average rate of 0.3 percent in small firms and rose by 1.3 percent in large corporations. Between 1997 and 2005, labour productivity increased 3.2 percent per year in small firms and by 1.5 percent per year in large corporations.

Source: Statistics Canada, *The Daily*, October 18, 2010

Explain how the productivity trends described in the news clip would change real GDP and employment. Draw a diagram similar to Fig. 22.8 to illustrate your answer.

16. For three years, there was no technological change in Longland but capital per hour of labour increased from $10 to $20 to $30 and real GDP per hour of labour increased from $3.80 to $5.70 to $7.13. Then, in the fourth year, capital per hour of labour remained constant but real GDP per hour of labour increased to $10. Does Longland experience diminishing returns? Explain.

Growth Theories, Evidence, and Policies
(Study Plan 22.5)

17. Explain the processes that will bring the growth of real GDP per person to a stop according to
   a. Classical growth theory.
   b. Neoclassical growth theory.
   c. New growth theory.

18. In the economy of Cape Despair, the subsistence real wage rate is $15 an hour. Whenever real GDP per hour rises above $15, the population grows, and whenever real GDP per hour of labour falls below this level, the population falls. The table shows Cape Despair's production function:

Labour (billions of hours per year)	Real GDP (billions of 2000 dollars)
0.5	8
1.0	15
1.5	21
2.0	26
2.5	30
3.0	33
3.5	35

Initially, the population of Cape Despair is constant and real GDP per hour of labour is at the subsistence level of $15. Then a technological advance shifts the production function upward by 50 percent at each level of labour.

   a. What are the initial levels of real GDP and labour productivity?
   b. What happens to labour productivity immediately following the technological advance?
   c. What happens to the population growth rate following the technological advance?
   d. What are the eventual levels of real GDP and real GDP per hour of labour?

ADDITIONAL PROBLEMS AND APPLICATIONS

MyEconLab ◆ You can work these problems in MyEconLab if assigned by your instructor.

The Basics of Economic Growth

19. If in 2010 China's real GDP is growing at 9 percent a year, its population is growing at 1 percent a year, and these growth rates continue, in what year will China's real GDP per person be twice what it is in 2010?

20. Mexico's real GDP was 8,600 trillion pesos in 2009 and 8,688 trillion pesos in 2010. Mexico's population was 107 million in 2009 and 108 million in 2010. Calculate

   a. The economic growth rate.

   b. The growth rate of real GDP per person.

   c. The approximate number of years it takes for real GDP per person in Mexico to double if the 2010 economic growth rate and population growth rate are maintained.

21. Venezuela's real GDP was 57,049 trillion bolivares in 2009 and 56,764 trillion bolivares in 2010. Venezuela's population was 28.6 million in 2009 and 29.2 million in 2010. Calculate

   a. The economic growth rate.

   b. The growth rate of real GDP per person.

   c. The approximate number of years it takes for real GDP per person in Venezuela to double if economic growth returns to its average since 2009 of 3.6 percent a year and is maintained.

Economic Growth Trends

22. **The New World Order**

   While gross domestic product growth is cooling a bit in emerging market economies, the results are still tremendous compared with the United States and much of Western Europe. The emerging market economies posted a 6.7 percent jump in real GDP in 2008, down from 7.5 percent in 2007. The advanced economies grew an estimated 1.6 percent in 2008. The difference in growth rates represents the largest spread between emerging market economies and advanced economies in the 37-year history of the survey.

   Source: *Fortune*, July 14, 2008

   Do growth rates over the past few decades indicate that gaps in real GDP per person around the world are shrinking, growing, or staying the same? Explain.

How Potential GDP Grows

23. If a large increase in investment increases labour productivity, explain what happens to

   a. Potential GDP.

   b. Employment.

   c. The real wage rate.

24. If a severe drought decreases labour productivity, explain what happens to

   a. Potential GDP.

   b. Employment.

   c. The real wage rate.

Use the following tables to work Problems 25 to 27. The first table describes an economy's labour market in 2010 and the second table describes its production function in 2010.

Real wage rate (dollars per hour)	Labour hours supplied	Labour hours demanded
80	55	15
70	50	20
60	45	25
50	40	30
40	35	35
30	30	40
20	25	45

Labour (hours)	Real GDP (2005 dollars)
15	1,425
20	1,800
25	2,125
30	2,400
35	2,625
40	2,800
45	2,925
50	3,000

25. What are the equilibrium real wage rate and the quantity of labour employed in 2010?

26. What are labour productivity and potential GDP in 2010?

27. Suppose that labour productivity increases in 2010. What effect does the increased labour productivity have on the demand for labour, the supply of labour, potential GDP, and real GDP per person?

Why Labour Productivity Grows

28. Canada's Productivity Performance

Between 1961 and 2008, productivity in Canada rose 2.0 percent a year on average, compared with 2.3 percent in the United States and in recent years, the gap in productivity growth between the two countries has steadily widened. From 2000 to 2008, labour productivity in Canada increased at less than one-third of the pace in the United States.

Source: Statistics Canada, *The Daily*, August 4, 2009

Explain the sources of labour productivity growth that might account for the trends described in the news clip.

Growth Theories, Evidence, and Policies

29. The Productivity Watch

According to former Federal Reserve chairman Alan Greenspan, IT investments in the 1990s boosted productivity, which boosted corporate profits, which led to more IT investments, and so on, leading to a nirvana of high growth.

Source: *Fortune*, September 4, 2006

Which of the growth theories that you've studied in this chapter best corresponds to the explanation given by Mr. Greenspan?

30. Is faster economic growth always a good thing? Argue the case for faster growth and the case for slower growth. Then reach a conclusion on whether growth should be increased or slowed.

31. Makani Power: A Mighty Wind

Makani Power aims to generate energy from what are known as high-altitude wind-extraction technologies. And that's about all its 34-year-old Aussie founder, Saul Griffith, wants to say about it. But Makani can't hide entirely, not when its marquee investor is Google.org, the tech company's philanthropic arm. Makani's plan is to capture that high-altitude wind with a very old tool: kites. Harnessing higher-altitude wind, at least in theory, has greater potential than the existing wind industry because at a thousand feet above the ground, the wind is stronger and more consistent.

Source: *Fortune*, April 28, 2008

Explain which growth theory best describes the news clip.

Economics in the News

32. After you have studied *Reading Between the Lines* on pp. 536–537, answer the following questions.

   a. On what criterion is China the second largest economy in the world?

   b. What is the distinction between the size of an economy and the standard of living of its people?

   c. Where does China rank on a standard of living comparison? How is that rank changing and why?

   d. What is the distinction between market prices and PPP prices?

   e. Using PPP prices, where does China's economy rank in size and standard of living?

   f. For what might the size of an economy matter?

33. Make Way for India—The Next China

China grows at around 9 percent a year, but its one-child policy will start to reduce the size of China's working-age population within the next 10 years. India, by contrast, will have an increasing working-age population for another generation at least.

Source: *The Independent*, March 1, 2006

   a. Given the expected population changes, do you think China or India will have the greater economic growth rate? Why?

   b. Would China's growth rate remain at 9 percent a year without the restriction on its population growth rate?

   c. India's population growth rate is 1.6 percent a year, and in 2005 its economic growth rate was 8 percent a year. China's population growth rate is 0.6 percent a year, and in 2005 its economic growth rate was 9 percent a year. In what year will real GDP per person double in each country?

Data Graphing

Use the *Data Grapher* to create a graph of the growth rate of real GDP per person in Canada, the United States, Germany, and the United Kingdom.

34. Which of these four countries had the fastest growth of real GDP per person since 1980 and which had the slowest?

35. In which of these four countries has real GDP per person fluctuated most? In which country has real GDP per person fluctuated least?

Finance, Saving, and Investment

After studying this chapter, you will be able to

◆ Describe the flows of funds through financial markets and the financial institutions

◆ Explain how borrowing and lending decisions interact in financial markets

◆ Explain the effects of government borrowing and lending in financial markets

◆ Explain the effects of international borrowing and lending in financial markets

During normal times, financial markets play their quiet, unseen role channelling funds from savers and lenders to investors and borrowers. But since 2008, times have not been normal. Financial markets have been volatile and in turmoil. Banks have failed and governments have bailed out some of them and put their own financial position at risk. This chapter explains how financial markets work—in normal times and in times like today.

In *Reading Between the Lines* at the end of the chapter, we'll look at the effects of government budget deficits in the global economy and in the deeply troubled and closely watched market for the debt of the Government of Greece.

◆ Financial Institutions and Financial Markets

The financial institutions and markets that we study in this chapter play a crucial role in the economy. They provide the channels through which saving flows to finance the investment in new capital that makes the economy grow.

In studying the economics of financial institutions and markets, we distinguish between

- Finance and money
- Physical capital and financial capital

Finance and Money

In economics, we use the term *finance* to describe the activity of providing the funds that finance expenditures on capital. The study of finance looks at how households and firms obtain and use financial resources and how they cope with the risks that arise in this activity.

Money is what we use to pay for goods and services and factors of production and to make financial transactions. The study of money looks at how households and firms use it, how much of it they hold, how banks create and manage it, and how its quantity influences the economy.

In the economic lives of individuals and businesses, finance and money are closely interrelated. And some of the main financial institutions, such as banks, provide both financial services and monetary services. Nevertheless, by distinguishing between *finance* and *money* and studying them separately, we will better understand our financial and monetary markets and institutions.

For the rest of this chapter, we study finance. Money is the topic of the next chapter.

Physical Capital and Financial Capital

Economists distinguish between physical capital and financial capital. *Physical capital* is the tools, instruments, machines, buildings, and other items that have been produced in the past and that are used today to produce goods and services. Inventories of raw materials, semifinished goods, and components are part of physical capital. When economists use the term capital, they mean *physical* capital. The funds that firms use to buy physical capital are called **financial capital**.

Along the *aggregate production function* in Chapter 22 (see p. 523), the quantity of capital is fixed. An increase in the quantity of capital increases production possibilities and shifts the aggregate production function upward. You're going to see, in this chapter, how investment, saving, borrowing, and lending decisions influence the quantity of capital and make it grow and, as a consequence, make real GDP grow.

We begin by describing the links between capital and investment and between wealth and saving.

Capital and Investment

The quantity of capital changes because of investment and depreciation. *Investment* increases the quantity of capital and *depreciation* decreases it (see Chapter 20, p. 470). The total amount spent on new capital is called **gross investment**. The change in the value of capital is called **net investment**. Net investment equals gross investment minus depreciation.

Figure 23.1 illustrates these terms. On January 1, 2011, Ace Bottling Inc. had machines worth $30,000—Ace's initial capital. During 2011, the market value of Ace's machines fell by 67 percent—$20,000. After this depreciation, Ace's machines were valued at $10,000. During 2011, Ace spent $30,000 on new machines. This amount is Ace's gross investment. By December 31, 2011, Ace Bottling had capital valued at $40,000, so its capital had increased by $10,000. This amount is Ace's net investment. Ace's net investment equals its gross investment of $30,000 minus depreciation of its initial capital of $20,000.

Wealth and Saving

Wealth is the value of all the things that people own. What people own is related to what they earn, but it is not the same thing. People earn an *income*, which is the amount they receive during a given time period from supplying the services of the resources they own. **Saving** is the amount of income that is not paid in taxes or spent on consumption goods and services. Saving increases wealth. Wealth also increases when the market value of assets rises—called *capital gains*—and decreases when the market value of assets falls—called *capital losses*.

For example, at the end of the school year you have $250 in the bank and a coin collection worth $300, so your wealth is $550. During the summer, you earn $5,000 (net of taxes) and spend $1,000 on

FIGURE 23.1   Capital and Investment

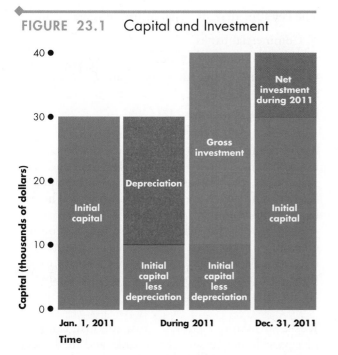

On January 1, 2011, Ace Bottling had capital worth $30,000. During the year, the value of Ace's capital fell by $20,000—depreciation—and it spent $30,000 on new capital—gross investment. Ace's net investment was $10,000 ($30,000 gross investment minus $20,000 depreciation) so that at the end of 2011, Ace had capital worth $40,000.

——————— MyEconLab animation ◆

consumption goods and services, so your saving is $4,000. Your bank account increases to $4,250 and your wealth becomes $4,550. The $4,000 increase in wealth equals saving. If coins rise in value and your coin collection is now worth $500, you have a capital gain of $200, which is also added to your wealth.

National wealth and national saving work like this personal example. The wealth of a nation at the end of a year equals its wealth at the start of the year plus its saving during the year, which equals (after-tax) income minus consumption expenditure.

To make real GDP grow, saving and wealth must be transformed into investment and capital. This transformation takes place in the markets for financial capital and through the activities of financial institutions. We're now going to describe these markets and institutions.

Financial Capital Markets

Saving is the source of the funds that are used to finance investment, and these funds are supplied and demanded in three types of financial markets:

- Loan markets
- Bond markets
- Stock markets

Loan Markets Businesses often want short-term finance to buy inventories or to extend credit to their customers. Sometimes they get this finance in the form of a loan from a bank. Households often want finance to purchase big ticket items, such as automobiles or household furnishings and appliances. They get this finance as bank loans, often in the form of outstanding credit card balances.

Households also get finance to buy new homes. (Expenditure on new homes is counted as part of investment.) These funds are usually obtained as a loan that is secured by a **mortgage**—a legal contract that gives ownership of a home to the lender in the event that the borrower fails to meet the agreed loan payments (repayments and interest). Mortgage loans in the United States were at the centre of what became a global financial crisis in 2007 and 2008.

All of these types of financing take place in loan markets.

Bond Markets When McDonald's spends $1 billion rebranding its restaurants, it gets the finance it needs by selling bonds. Governments—federal, provincial, and municipal—also raise finance by issuing bonds.

A **bond** is a promise to make specified payments on specified dates. For example, you can buy a McDonald's Corporation bond that promises to pay $3.50 every year until 2020 and then to make a final payment of $100 on July 15, 2020.

The buyer of a bond from McDonald's makes a loan to the company and is entitled to the payments promised by the bond. When a person buys a newly issued bond, he or she may hold the bond until the borrower has repaid the amount borrowed or sell it to someone else. Bonds issued by firms and governments are traded in the **bond market**.

The term of a bond might be long (decades) or short (just a month or two). Firms often issue very short-term bonds as a way of getting paid for their sales before the buyer is able to pay. For example, Bombardier sells $100 million of railway locomotives to VIA Rail and wants to be paid when the items are shipped. But VIA Rail doesn't want to pay until the locomotives are earning an income. In this situation, VIA Rail might promise to pay Bombardier $101 million three months in the future. A bank would be willing to buy this promise for (say) $100 million. Bombardier gets $100 million immediately and the bank gets $101 million in three months when VIA Rail honours its promise. The Government of Canada issues promises of this type, called Treasury bills.

Another type of bond is a **mortgage-backed security**, which entitles its holder to the income from a package of mortgages. Mortgage lenders create mortgage-backed securities. They make mortgage loans to homebuyers and then create securities that they sell to obtain more funds to make more mortgage loans. The holder of a mortgage-backed security is entitled to receive payments that derive from the payments received by the mortgage lender from the homebuyer–borrower.

Mortgage-backed securities were at the centre of the financial market storm of 2007–2008.

Stock Markets   When Petro-Canada wants finance to expand an Alberta oilsands project, it issues stock. A **stock** is a certificate of ownership and claim to the firm's profits. Petro-Canada has issued 484 million shares of its stock. So if you owned 484 Petro-Canada shares, you would own one millionth of the firm and be entitled to receive one millionth of its profits.

Unlike a stockholder, a bondholder does not own part of the firm that issued the bond.

A **stock market** is a financial market in which shares of stocks of corporations are traded. The Toronto Stock Exchange, the New York Stock Exchange (in the United States), the London Stock Exchange (in England), and the Tokyo Stock Exchange (in Japan) are all examples of stock markets.

Financial Institutions

Financial markets are highly competitive because of the role played by financial institutions in those markets. A **financial institution** is a firm that operates on both sides of the markets for financial capital. The financial institution is a borrower in one market and a lender in another.

Financial institutions also stand ready to trade so that households with funds to lend and firms or households seeking funds can always find someone on the other side of the market with whom to trade.

The key Canadian financial institutions are

- Commercial banks
- Trust and loan companies
- Credit unions and caisses populaires
- Pension funds
- Insurance companies

Banks   Banks accept deposits and use the funds to buy government bonds and other securities and to make loans. Canada has 14 domestic banks, and a further 33 foreign banks operate in Canada. These banks hold more than 70 percent of the total assets of the Canadian financial services sector. Economists distinguish banks from other financial institutions because bank deposits are money. We'll return to these institutions in Chapter 24, where we study the role of money in our economy.

Trust and Loan Companies   Trust and loan companies provide similar services to banks and the largest of them are owned by banks. They accept deposits and make personal loans and mortgage loans. They also administer estates, trusts, and pension plans.

Credit Unions and Caisses Populaires   Credit unions and caisses populaires are banks that are owned and controlled by their depositors and borrowers, are regulated by provincial rules, and operate only inside their own provincial boundaries. These institutions are large in number but small in size.

Pension Funds   Pension funds are financial institutions that receive the pension contributions of firms and workers. They use these funds to buy a diversified portfolio of bonds and stocks that they expect to generate an income that balances risk and return. The income is used to pay pension benefits.

Some pension funds invest in mortgage-backed securities of the type that collapsed in value during the 2008 financial crisis.

Pension funds can be very large and play an active role in the firms whose stock they hold.

Insurance Companies   Insurance companies provide risk-sharing services. They enter into agreements with households and firms to provide compensation in the event of accident, theft, fire, ill health, and a host of other misfortunes. They receive premiums from their customers and make payments against claims.

Insurance companies use the funds they have received but not paid out as claims to buy bonds and stocks on which they earn an interest income.

Some insurance companies also insure corporate bonds and other risky financial assets. They provide insurance that pays out if a firm fails and cannot meet its bond obligations. Some insurance companies insure other insurers in a complex network of reinsurance.

In normal times, insurance companies have a steady flow of funds coming in from premiums and interest on the financial assets they hold and a steady, but smaller, flow of funds paying claims. Their profit is the gap between the two flows. But in unusual times, when large and widespread losses are being incurred, insurance companies can run into difficulty in meeting their obligations. Such a situation arose in 2008 for one of the world's biggest insurers, AIG, and the firm was taken into public ownership.

Canadian insurance companies have very large international operations and earn 70 percent of their income outside Canada.

All financial institutions face risk and this risk poses two problems: a solvency problem and a liquidity problem.

Insolvency and Illiquidity

A financial institution's **net worth** is the market value of what it has lent minus the market value of what it has borrowed. If net worth is positive, the institution is *solvent*. But if net worth is negative, the institution is *insolvent* and must go out of business. The owners of an insolvent financial institution—usually its stockholders—bear the loss.

A financial institution both borrows and lends, so it is exposed to the risk that its net worth might become negative. To limit that risk, financial institutions are regulated and a minimum amount of their lending must be backed by their net worth.

Sometimes, a financial institution is solvent but illiquid. A firm is *illiquid* if it has made long-term loans with borrowed funds and is faced with a sudden demand to repay more of what it has borrowed than its available cash. In normal times, a financial institution that is illiquid can borrow from another institution. But if all the financial institutions are short of cash, the market for loans among financial institutions dries up.

Insolvency and illiquidity were at the core of a global financial meltdown in 2007–2008.

Economics in Action
At the Centre of a Financial Storm

Bear Stearns: absorbed by JPMorgan Chase with help from the Federal Reserve. Lehman Brothers: gone. Fannie Mae and Freddie Mac: taken into government oversight with U.S. taxpayer guarantees. Merrill Lynch: absorbed by Bank of America. AIG: given an $85 billion lifeline by the Federal Reserve and sold off in parcels to financial institutions around the world. Wachovia: taken over by Citigroup. Washington Mutual: taken over by JPMorgan. Morgan Stanley: 20 percent bought by Mitsubishi, a large Japanese bank. These are some of the events in the financial crisis of 2008. What is going on?

Between 2002 and 2005, mortgage lending exploded and home prices rose. Mortgage lenders bundled their loans into *mortgage-backed securities* and sold them to eager buyers around the world.

In 2006, interest rates began to rise and the values of financial assets fell. With lower asset values, financial institutions took big losses. Some losses of some institutions were too big to bear and these institutions became insolvent.

Interest Rates and Asset Prices

Stocks, bonds, short-term securities, and loans are collectively called *financial assets*. The interest rate on a financial asset is the interest received expressed as a percentage of the price of the asset.

Because the interest rate is a percentage of the price of an asset, if the asset price rises, other things remaining the same, the interest rate falls. Conversely, if the asset price falls, other things remaining the same, the interest rate rises.

To see this inverse relationship between an asset price and the interest rate, let's look at an example. We'll consider a bond that promises to pay its holder $5 a year forever. What is the rate of return—the interest rate—on this bond? The answer depends on the price of the bond. If you could buy this bond for $50, the interest rate would be 10 percent per year:

Interest rate = ($5 ÷ $50) × 100 = 10 percent.

But if the price of this bond increased to $200, its rate of return or interest rate would be only 2.5 percent per year. That is,

Interest rate = ($5 ÷ $200) × 100 = 2.5 percent.

This relationship means that the price of an asset and the interest rate on that asset are determined simultaneously—one implies the other.

This relationship also means that if the interest rate on the asset rises, the price of the asset falls, debts become harder to pay, and the net worth of the financial institution falls. Insolvency can arise from a previously unexpected large rise in the interest rate.

In the next part of this chapter, we learn how interest rates and asset prices are determined in the financial markets.

◆ REVIEW QUIZ

1 Distinguish between physical capital and financial capital and give two examples of each.
2 What is the distinction between gross investment and net investment?
3 What are the three main types of markets for financial capital?
4 Explain the connection between the price of a financial asset and its interest rate.

You can work these questions in Study Plan 23.1 and get instant feedback.

——————————— MyEconLab ◆

◆ The Loanable Funds Market

In macroeconomics, we group all the financial markets that we described in the previous section into a single loanable funds market. The **loanable funds market** is the aggregate of all the individual financial markets.

The circular flow model of Chapter 20 (see p. 469) can be extended to include flows in the loanable funds market that finance investment.

Funds that Finance Investment

Figure 23.2 shows the flows of funds that finance investment. They come from three sources:

1. Household saving
2. Government budget surplus
3. Borrowing from the rest of the world

Households' income, Y, is spent on consumption goods and services, C, saved, S, or paid in net taxes, T. **Net taxes** are the taxes paid to governments minus the cash transfers received from governments (such as Social Security and unemployment benefits). So income is equal to the sum of consumption expenditure, saving, and net taxes:

$$Y = C + S + T.$$

You saw in Chapter 21 (p. 492) that Y also equals the sum of the items of aggregate expenditure: consumption expenditure, C, investment, I, government expenditure, G, and exports, X, minus imports, M. That is:

$$Y = C + I + G + X - M.$$

By using these two equations, you can see that

$$I + G + X = M + S + T.$$

Subtract G and X from both sides of the last equation to obtain

$$I = S + (T - G) + (M - X).$$

This equation tells us that investment, I, is financed by household saving, S, the government budget surplus, $(T - G)$, and borrowing from the rest of the world, $(M - X)$.

A government budget surplus $(T > G)$ contributes funds to finance investment, but a government budget deficit $(T < G)$ competes with investment for funds.

FIGURE 23.2   Financial Flows and the Circular Flow of Expenditure and Income

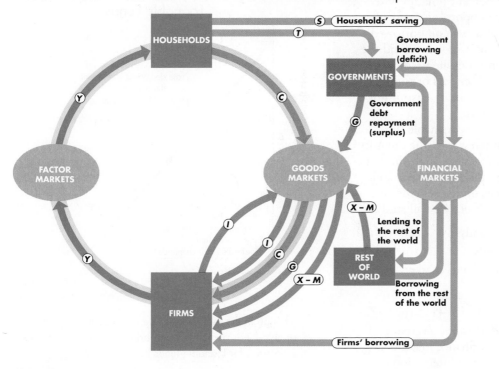

Households use their income for consumption expenditure (C), saving (S), and net taxes (T). Firms borrow to finance their investment expenditure. Governments borrow to finance a budget deficit or repay debt if they have a budget surplus. The rest of the world borrows to finance its deficit or lends its surplus.

MyEconLab animation

If we export less than we import, we borrow (M – X) from the rest of the world to finance some of our investment. If we export more than we import, we lend (X – M) to the rest of the world and part of our saving finances investment in other countries.

The sum of private saving, S, and government saving, (T – G), is called **national saving**. National saving and foreign borrowing finance investment.

In 2011, Canadian investment was $310 billion and governments (federal, provincial, and local combined) had a deficit of $51 billion. The total of these items of $361 billion was financed by private saving of $345 billion and borrowing from the rest of the world (negative net exports) of $16 billion.

You're going to see how investment and saving and the flows of loanable funds—all measured in constant 2002 dollars—are determined. The price in the loanable funds market that achieves equilibrium is an interest rate, which we also measure in real terms as the *real* interest rate. In the loanable funds market, there is just one interest rate, which is an average of the interest rates on all the different types of financial securities that we described earlier. Let's see what we mean by the real interest rate.

The Real Interest Rate

The **nominal interest rate** is the number of dollars that a borrower pays and a lender receives in interest in a year expressed as a percentage of the number of dollars borrowed and lent. For example, if the annual interest paid on a $500 loan is $25, the nominal interest rate is 5 percent per year: $25 ÷ $500 × 100 or 5 percent.

The **real interest rate** is the nominal interest rate adjusted to remove the effects of inflation on the buying power of money. The real interest rate is approximately equal to the nominal interest rate minus the inflation rate.

You can see why if you suppose that you have put $500 in a savings account that earns 5 percent a year. At the end of a year, you have $525 in your savings account. Suppose that the inflation rate is 2 percent per year—during the year, all prices increased by 2 percent. Now, at the end of the year, it costs $510 to buy what $500 would have bought 1 year ago. Your money in the bank has really only increased by $15, from $510 to $525. That $15 is equivalent to a real interest rate of 3 percent a year on your original

$500. So the real interest rate is the 5 percent nominal interest rate minus the 2 percent inflation rate.[1]

The real interest rate is the opportunity cost of loanable funds. The real interest *paid* on borrowed funds is the opportunity cost of borrowing. And the real interest rate *forgone* when funds are used either to buy consumption goods and services or to invest in new capital goods is the opportunity cost of not saving or not lending those funds.

We're now going to see how the loanable funds market determines the real interest rate, the quantity of funds loaned, saving, and investment. In the rest of this section, we will ignore the government and the rest of the world and focus on households and firms in the loanable funds market. We will study

- The demand for loanable funds
- The supply of loanable funds
- Equilibrium in the loanable funds market

The Demand for Loanable Funds

The *quantity of loanable funds demanded* is the total quantity of funds demanded to finance investment, the government budget deficit, and international investment or lending during a given period. Our focus here is on investment. We'll bring the other two items into the picture in later sections of this chapter.

What determines investment and the demand for loanable funds to finance it? Many details influence this decision, but we can summarize them in two factors:

1. The real interest rate
2. Expected profit

Firms invest in capital only if they expect to earn a profit and fewer projects are profitable at a high real interest rate than at a low real interest rate, so

Other things remaining the same, the higher the real interest rate, the smaller is the quantity of loanable funds demanded; and the lower the real interest rate, the greater the quantity of loanable funds demanded.

---

[1]The *exact* real interest rate formula, which allows for the change in the purchasing power of both the interest and the loan is: Real interest rate = (Nominal interest rate − Inflation rate) ÷ (1 + Inflation rate/100). If the nominal interest rate is 5 percent a year and the inflation rate is 2 percent a year, the real interest rate is (5 − 2) ÷ (1 + 0.02) = 2.94 percent a year.

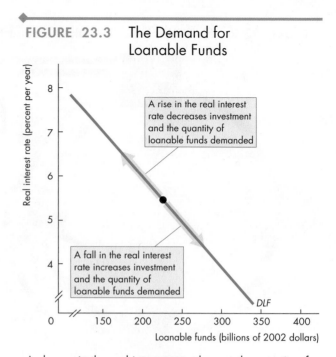

FIGURE 23.3   The Demand for Loanable Funds

A change in the real interest rate changes the quantity of loanable funds demanded and brings a movement along the demand for loanable funds curve.

MyEconLab   animation

Demand for Loanable Funds Curve   The **demand for loanable funds** is the relationship between the quantity of loanable funds demanded and the real interest rate, when all other influences on borrowing plans remain the same. The demand curve *DLF* in Fig. 23.3 is a demand for loanable funds curve.

To understand the demand for loanable funds, think about Bell Canada's decision to borrow $100 million to buy some new phone mail servers. If Bell expects to get a return of $5 million a year from this investment before paying interest costs and the interest rate is less than 5 percent a year, Bell would make a profit, so it buys some new phone mail servers. But if the interest rate is more than 5 percent a year, Bell would incur a loss, so it doesn't buy new phone mail servers. The quantity of loanable funds demanded is greater the lower is the real interest rate.

Changes in the Demand for Loanable Funds   When the expected profit changes, the demand for loanable funds changes. Other things remaining the same, the greater the expected profit from new capital, the greater is the amount of investment and the greater the demand for loanable funds.

Expected profit rises during a business cycle expansion and falls during a recession; rises when technological change creates profitable new products; rises as a growing population brings increased demand for goods and services; and fluctuates with contagious swings of optimism and pessimism, called "animal spirits" by John Maynard Keynes and "irrational exuberance" by Alan Greenspan.

When expected profit changes, the demand for loanable funds curve shifts.

The Supply of Loanable Funds

The *quantity of loanable funds supplied* is the total funds available from private saving, the government budget surplus, and international borrowing during a given period. Our focus here is on saving. We'll bring the other two items into the picture later.

How do you decide how much of your income to save and supply in the loanable funds market? Your decision is influenced by many factors, but chief among them are

1. The real interest rate
2. Disposable income
3. Expected future income
4. Wealth
5. Default risk

We begin by focusing on the real interest rate.

Other things remaining the same, the higher the real interest rate, the greater is the quantity of loanable funds supplied; and the lower the real interest rate, the smaller is the quantity of loanable funds supplied.

The Supply of Loanable Funds Curve The **supply of loanable funds** is the relationship between the quantity of loanable funds supplied and the real interest rate when all other influences on lending plans remain the same. The curve *SLF* in Fig. 23.4 is a supply of loanable funds curve.

Think about a student's decision to save some of what she earns from her summer job. With a real interest rate of 2 percent a year, she decides that it is not worth saving much—better to spend the income and take a student loan if funds run out during the semester. But if the real interest rate jumped to 10 percent a year, the payoff from saving would be high enough to encourage her to cut back on spending and increase the amount she saves.

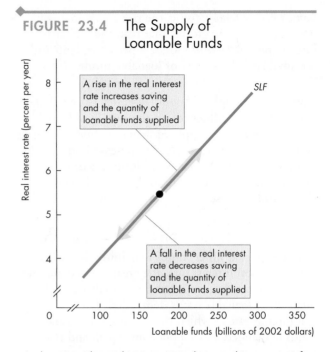

FIGURE 23.4   The Supply of Loanable Funds

A rise in the real interest rate increases saving and the quantity of loanable funds supplied

A fall in the real interest rate decreases saving and the quantity of loanable funds supplied

A change in the real interest rate changes the quantity of loanable funds supplied and brings a movement along the supply of loanable funds curve.

MyEconLab animation

Changes in the Supply of Loanable Funds A change in disposable income, expected future income, wealth, or default risk changes the supply of loanable funds.

Disposable Income A household's *disposable income* is the income earned minus net taxes. When disposable income increases, other things remaining the same, consumption expenditure increases but by less than the increase in income. Some of the increase in income is saved. So the greater a household's disposable income, other things remaining the same, the greater is its saving.

Expected Future Income The higher a household's expected future income, other things remaining the same, the smaller is its saving today.

Wealth The higher a household's wealth, other things remaining the same, the smaller is its saving. If a person's wealth increases because of a capital gain, the person sees less need to save. For example, from 2002 through 2006, when house prices were rising rapidly, wealth increased despite the fact that personal saving decreased.

Default Risk Default risk is the risk that a loan will not be repaid. The greater that risk, the higher is the interest rate needed to induce a person to lend and the smaller is the supply of loanable funds.

Shifts of the Supply of Loanable Funds Curve When any of the four influences on the supply of loanable funds changes, the supply of loanable funds changes and the supply curve shifts. An increase in disposable income, a decrease in expected future income, a decrease in wealth, or a fall in default risk increases saving and increases the supply of loanable funds.

Equilibrium in the Loanable Funds Market

You've seen that other things remaining the same, the higher the real interest rate, the greater is the quantity of loanable funds supplied and the smaller is the quantity of loanable funds demanded. There is one real interest rate at which the quantities of loanable funds demanded and supplied are equal, and that interest rate is the equilibrium real interest rate.

Figure 23.5 shows how the demand for and supply of loanable funds determine the real interest rate. The *DLF* curve is the demand curve and the *SLF* curve is the supply curve. If the real interest rate exceeds 6 percent a year, the quantity of loanable funds supplied exceeds the quantity demanded—a surplus of funds. Borrowers find it easy to get funds, but lenders are unable to lend all the funds they have available. The real interest rate falls and continues to fall until the quantity of funds supplied equals the quantity of funds demanded.

If the real interest rate is less than 6 percent a year, the quantity of loanable funds supplied is less than the quantity demanded—a shortage of funds. Borrowers can't get the funds they want, but lenders are able to lend all the funds they have. So the real interest rate rises and continues to rise until the quantity of funds supplied equals the quantity demanded.

Regardless of whether there is a surplus or a shortage of loanable funds, the real interest rate changes and is pulled towards an equilibrium level. In Fig. 23.5, the equilibrium real interest rate is 6 percent a year. At this interest rate, there is neither a surplus nor a shortage of loanable funds. Borrowers can get the funds they want, and lenders can lend all the funds they have available. The investment plans of borrowers and the saving plans of lenders are consistent with each other.

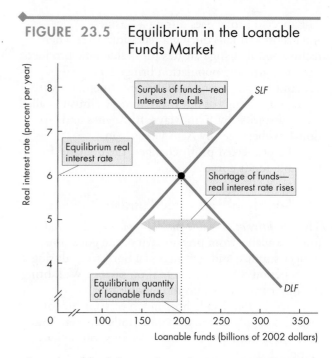

FIGURE 23.5 Equilibrium in the Loanable Funds Market

A surplus of funds lowers the real interest rate and a shortage of funds raises it. At an interest rate of 6 percent a year, the quantity of funds demanded equals the quantity supplied and the market is in equilibrium.

—————— MyEconLab animation ◆

Changes in Demand and Supply

Financial markets are highly volatile in the short run but remarkably stable in the long run. Volatility in the market comes from fluctuations in either the demand for loanable funds or the supply of loanable funds. These fluctuations bring fluctuations in the real interest rate and in the equilibrium quantity of funds lent and borrowed. They also bring fluctuations in asset prices.

Here we'll illustrate the effects of *increases* in demand and supply in the loanable funds market.

An Increase in Demand If the profits that firms expect to earn increase, they increase their planned investment and increase their demand for loanable funds to finance that investment. With an increase in the demand for loanable funds, but no change in the supply of loanable funds, there is a shortage of funds. As borrowers compete for funds, the interest rate rises and lenders increase the quantity of funds supplied.

Figure 23.6(a) illustrates these changes. An increase in the demand for loanable funds shifts the demand curve rightward from DLF_0 to DLF_1. With

FIGURE 24.6   Changes in Demand and Supply

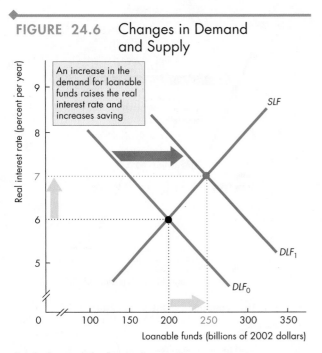

An increase in the demand for loanable funds raises the real interest rate and increases saving

(a) An increase in demand

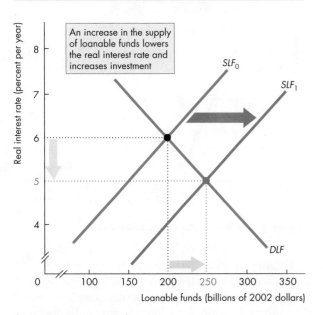

An increase in the supply of loanable funds lowers the real interest rate and increases investment

(b) An increase in supply

In part (a), the demand for loanable funds increases and supply doesn't change. The real interest rate rises (financial asset prices fall) and the quantity of funds increases.

In part (b), the supply of loanable funds increases and demand doesn't change. The real interest rate falls (financial asset prices rise) and the quantity of funds increases.

MyEconLab   animation ◆

no change in the supply of loanable funds, there is a shortage of funds at a real interest rate of 6 percent a year. The real interest rate rises until it is 7 percent a year. Equilibrium is restored and the equilibrium quantity of funds has increased.

An Increase in Supply If one of the influences on saving plans changes and increases saving, the supply of loanable funds increases. With no change in the demand for loanable funds, the market is flush with loanable funds. Borrowers find bargains and lenders find themselves accepting a lower interest rate. At the lower interest rate, borrowers find additional investment projects profitable and increase the quantity of loanable funds that they borrow.

Figure 23.6(b) illustrates these changes. An increase in supply shifts the supply curve rightward from SLF_0 to SLF_1. With no change in demand, there is a surplus of funds at a real interest rate of 6 percent a year. The real interest rate falls until it is 5 percent a year. Equilibrium is restored and the equilibrium quantity of funds has increased.

Long-Run Growth of Demand and Supply Over time, both demand and supply in the loanable funds market fluctuate and the real interest rate rises and falls. Both the supply of loanable funds and the demand for loanable funds tend to increase over time. On the average, they increase at a similar pace, so although demand and supply trend upward, the real interest rate has no trend. It fluctuates around a constant average level.

◢ REVIEW QUIZ

1 What is the loanable funds market?
2 Why is the real interest rate the opportunity cost of loanable funds?
3 How do firms make investment decisions?
4 What determines the demand for loanable funds and what makes it change?
5 How do households make saving decisions?
6 What determines the supply of loanable funds and what makes it change?
7 How do changes in the demand for and supply of loanable funds change the real interest rate and quantity of loanable funds?

You can work these questions in Study Plan 23.2 and get instant feedback.

MyEconLab ◆

Economics in Action

Loanable Funds Fuel Home Price Bubble

The financial crisis that gripped the U.S. and global economies in 2007 and cascaded through the financial markets in 2008 had its origins much earlier in events taking place in the loanable funds market.

Between 2001 and 2005, a massive injection of loanable funds occurred. Some funds came from the rest of the world, but that source of supply has been stable. The Federal Reserve, the U.S. central bank known as "the Fed," provided funds to keep interest rates low and that was a major source of the increase in the supply of funds. (The next chapter explains how a central bank does this.)

Figure 1 illustrates the loanable funds market starting in 2001. In that year, the demand for loanable funds was DLF_{01} and the supply of loanable funds was SLF_{01}. The equilibrium real interest rate was 4 percent a year and the equilibrium quantity of loanable funds was $29 trillion (in 2005 U.S. dollars).

During the ensuing four years, a massive increase in the supply of loanable funds shifted the supply curve rightward to SLF_{05}. A smaller increase in demand shifted the demand for loanable funds curve to DLF_{05}. The real interest rate fell to 1 percent a year and the quantity of loanable funds increased to $36 trillion—a 24 percent increase in just four years.

With this large increase in available funds, much of it in the form of mortgage loans to home buyers, the demand for homes increased by more than the increase in the supply of homes. Home prices rose and the expectation of further increases fuelled the demand for loanable funds.

By 2006, the expectation of continued rapidly rising home prices brought a very large increase in the demand for loanable funds. At the same time, the Fed began to tighten credit. (Again, you'll learn how this is done in the next chapter). The result of the Fed's tighter credit policy was a slowdown in the pace of increase in the supply of loanable funds.

Figure 2 illustrates these events. In 2006, the demand for loanable funds increased from DLF_{05} to DLF_{06} and the supply of loanable funds increased by a smaller amount from SLF_{05} to SLF_{06}. The real interest rate increased to 3 percent a year.

The rise in the real interest rate (and a much higher rise in the nominal interest rate) put many homeowners in financial difficulty. Mortgage payments increased and some borrowers stopped repaying their loans.

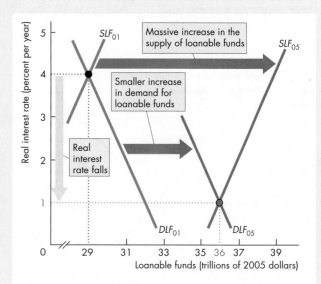

Figure 1 The Foundation of the Crisis: 2001–2005

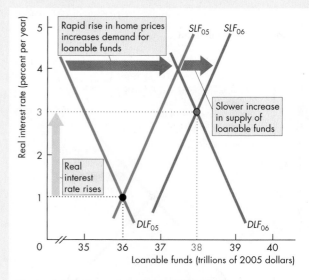

Figure 2 The Start of the Crisis: 2005–2006

By August 2007, the damage from mortgage default and foreclosure was so large that the credit market began to dry up. A large decrease in both demand and supply kept interest rates roughly constant but decreased the quantity of loans.

The quantity of outstanding loans didn't decrease, but the rate of increase slowed to a snail's pace and financial institutions most exposed to the bad mortgage debts and the securities that they backed (described on p. 547) began to fail.

These events illustrate the crucial role played by the loanable funds market.

Government in the Loanable Funds Market

Government enters the loanable funds market when it has a budget surplus or budget deficit. A government budget surplus increases the supply of loanable funds and contributes to financing investment; a government budget deficit increases the demand for loanable funds and competes with businesses for funds. Let's study the effects of government on the loanable funds market.

A Government Budget Surplus

A government budget surplus increases the supply of loanable funds. The real interest rate falls, which decreases household saving and decreases the quantity of private funds supplied. The lower real interest rate increases the quantity of loanable funds demanded and increases investment.

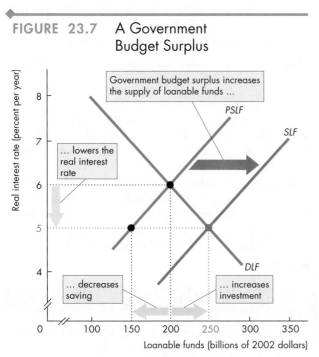

FIGURE 23.7   A Government Budget Surplus

A government budget surplus of $100 billion is added to private saving and the private supply of loanable funds (*PSLF*) to determine the supply of loanable funds, *SLF*. The real interest rate falls to 5 percent a year, private saving decreases, but investment increases to $250 billion.

MyEconLab   animation ◆

Figure 23.7 shows these effects of a government budget surplus. The private supply of loanable funds curve is *PSLF*. The supply of loanable funds curve, *SLF*, shows the sum of private supply and the government budget surplus. Here, the government budget surplus is $100 billion, so at each real interest rate the *SLF* curve lies $100 billion to the right of the *PSLF* curve. That is, the horizontal distance between the *PSLF* curve and the *SLF* curve equals the government budget surplus.

With no government surplus, the real interest rate is 6 percent a year, the quantity of loanable funds is $200 billion a year, and investment is $200 billion a year. But with the government surplus of $100 billion a year, the equilibrium real interest rate falls to 5 percent a year and the equilibrium quantity of loanable funds increases to $250 billion a year.

The fall in the interest rate decreases private saving to $150 billion, but investment increases to $250 billion, which is financed by private saving plus the government budget surplus (government saving).

A Government Budget Deficit

A government budget deficit increases the demand for loanable funds. The real interest rate rises, which increases household saving and increases the quantity of private funds supplied. But the higher real interest rate decreases investment and the quantity of loanable funds demanded by firms to finance investment.

Figure 23.8 shows these effects of a government budget deficit. The private demand for loanable funds curve is *PDLF*. The demand for loanable funds curve, *DLF*, shows the sum of private demand and the government budget deficit. Here, the government budget deficit is $100 billion, so at each real interest rate the *DLF* curve lies $100 billion to the right of the *PDLF* curve. That is, the horizontal distance between the *PDLF* curve and the *DLF* curve equals the government budget deficit.

With no government deficit, the real interest rate is 6 percent a year, the quantity of loanable funds is $200 billion a year, and investment is $200 billion a year. But with the government budget deficit of $100 billion a year, the equilibrium real interest rate rises to 7 percent a year and the equilibrium quantity of loanable funds increases to $250 billion a year.

The rise in the real interest rate increases private saving to $250 billion, but investment decreases to $150 billion because $100 billion of private saving must finance the government budget deficit.

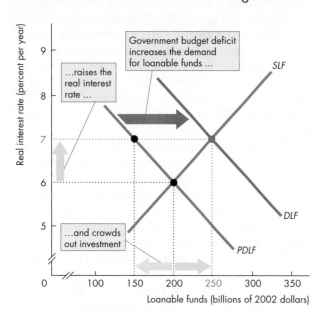

FIGURE 23.8   A Government Budget Deficit

A government budget deficit adds to the private demand for loanable funds curve (*PDLF*) to determine the demand for loanable funds curve, *DLF*. The real interest rate rises, saving increases, but investment decreases—a crowding-out effect.

MyEconLab   animation ◆

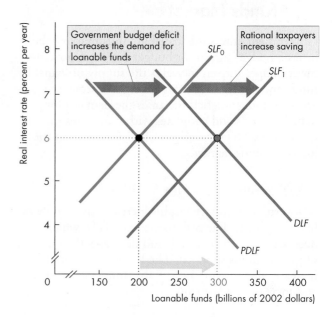

FIGURE 23.9   The Ricardo-Barro Effect

A budget deficit increases the demand for loanable funds. Rational taxpayers increase saving, which shifts the supply of loanable funds curve from SLF_0 to SLF_1. Crowding out is avoided: Increased saving finances the budget deficit.

MyEconLab   animation ◆

The Crowding-Out Effect The tendency for a government budget deficit to raise the real interest rate and decrease investment is called the **crowding-out effect**. The budget deficit crowds out investment by competing with businesses for scarce financial capital.

The crowding-out effect does not decrease investment by the full amount of the government budget deficit because the higher real interest rate induces an increase in private saving that partly contributes towards financing the deficit.

The Ricardo–Barro Effect First suggested by the English economist David Ricardo in the nineteenth century and refined by Robert J. Barro of Harvard University, the **Ricardo–Barro effect** holds that both of the effects we've just shown are wrong and the government budget, whether in surplus or deficit, has no effect on either the real interest rate or investment.

Barro says that taxpayers are rational. They can see that a budget deficit today means that future taxes will be higher and future disposable incomes will be smaller. With smaller expected future dispos-

able incomes, saving increases today. Private saving and the private supply of loanable funds increase to match the quantity of loanable funds demanded by the government. So the budget deficit has no effect on either the real interest rate or investment. Figure 23.9 shows this outcome.

Most economists regard the Ricardo–Barro view as extreme. But there might be some change in private saving that goes in the direction suggested by the Ricardo–Barro effect that lessens the crowding-out effect.

REVIEW QUIZ

1 How does a government budget surplus or deficit influence the loanable funds market?
2 What is the crowding-out effect and how does it work?
3 What is the Ricardo–Barro effect and how does it modify the crowding-out effect?

You can work these questions in Study Plan 23.3 and get instant feedback.

MyEconLab ◆

The Global Loanable Funds Market

The loanable funds market is global, not national. Lenders on the supply side of the market want to earn the highest possible real interest rate and they will seek it by looking everywhere in the world. Borrowers on the demand side of the market want to pay the lowest possible real interest rate and they will seek it by looking everywhere in the world. Financial capital is mobile: It moves to the best advantage of lenders and borrowers.

International Capital Mobility

If a Canadian supplier of loanable funds can earn a higher interest rate in Tokyo than in Toronto, funds supplied in Japan will increase and funds supplied in Canada will decrease—funds will flow from Canada to Japan.

If a Canadian demander of loanable funds can pay a lower interest rate in Paris than in Toronto, the demand for funds in France will increase and the demand for funds in Canada will decrease—funds will flow from France to Canada.

Because lenders are free to seek the highest real interest rate and borrowers are free to seek the lowest real interest rate, the loanable funds market is a single, integrated, global market. Funds flow into the country in which the interest rate is highest and out of the country in which the interest rate is lowest.

When funds leave the country with the lowest interest rate, a shortage of funds raises the real interest rate. When funds move into the country with the highest interest rate, a surplus of funds lowers the real interest rate. The free international mobility of financial capital pulls real interest rates around the world towards equality.

Only when the real interest rates in Toronto, Tokyo, and Paris are equal does the incentive to move funds from one country to another stop.

Equality of real interest rates does not mean that if you calculate the average real interest rate in Toronto, Tokyo, and Paris, you'll get the same number. To compare real interest rates, we must compare financial assets of *equal risk*.

Lending is risky. A loan might not be repaid. Or the price of a stock or bond might fall. Interest rates include a risk premium—the riskier the loan, other things remaining the same, the higher is the interest rate. The interest rate on a risky loan minus that on a safe loan is called the *risk premium*.

International capital mobility brings *real* interest rates in all parts of the world to equality, except for differences that reflect differences in risk—differences in the risk premium.

International Borrowing and Lending

A country's loanable funds market connects with the global market through net exports. If a country's net exports are negative ($X < M$), the rest of the world supplies funds to that country and the quantity of loanable funds in that country is greater than national saving. If a country's net exports are positive ($X > M$), the country is a net supplier of funds to the rest of the world and the quantity of loanable funds in that country is less than national saving.

Demand and Supply in the Global and National Markets

The demand for and supply of funds in the global loanable funds market determines the world equilibrium real interest rate. This interest rate makes the quantity of loanable funds demanded equal the quantity supplied in the world economy. But it does not make the quantity of funds demanded and supplied equal in each national economy. The demand for and supply of funds in a national economy determine whether the country is a lender to or a borrower from the rest of the world.

The Global Loanable Funds Market Figure 23.10(a) illustrates the global market. The demand for loanable funds, DLF_W, is the sum of the demands in all countries. Similarly, the supply of loanable funds, SLF_W, is the sum of the supplies in all countries. The world equilibrium real interest rate makes the quantity of funds supplied in the world as a whole equal to the quantity demanded. In this example, the equilibrium real interest rate is 5 percent a year and the quantity of funds is $10 trillion.

An International Borrower Figure 23.10(b) shows the loanable funds market in a country that borrows from the rest of the world. The country's demand for loanable funds, DLF, is part of the world demand in Fig. 23.10(a). The country's supply of loanable funds, SLF_D, is part of the world supply.

FIGURE 23.10   Borrowing and Lending in the Global Loanable Funds Market

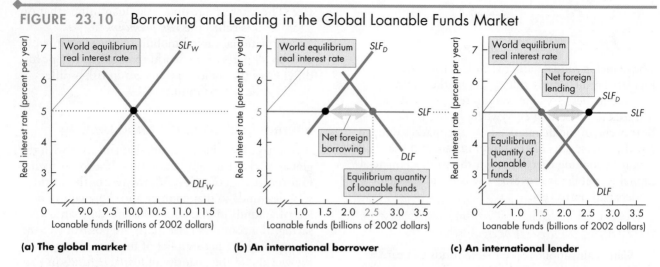

(a) The global market   **(b) An international borrower**   **(c) An international lender**

In the global loanable funds market in part (a), the demand for loanable funds, DLF_W, and the supply of funds, SLF_W, determine the world real interest rate. Each country can get funds at the world real interest rate and faces the (horizontal) supply curve SLF in parts (b) and (c).

At the world real interest rate, borrowers in part (b)

want more funds than the quantity supplied by domestic lenders (SLF_D). The shortage is made up by international borrowing.

Domestic suppliers of funds in part (c) want to lend more than domestic borrowers demand. The excess quantity supplied goes to foreign borrowers.

MyEconLab   animation

If this country were isolated from the global market, the real interest rate would be 6 percent a year (where the DLF and SLF_D curves intersect). But if the country is integrated into the global economy, with an interest rate of 6 percent a year, funds would *flood into* it. With a real interest rate of 5 percent a year in the rest of the world, suppliers of loanable funds would seek the higher return in this country. In effect, the country faces the supply of loanable funds curve SLF, which is horizontal at the world equilibrium real interest rate.

The country's demand for loanable funds and the world interest rate determine the equilibrium quantity of loanable funds—$2.5 billion in Fig. 23.10(b).

An International Lender   Figure 23.10(c) shows the situation in a country that lends to the rest of the world. As before, the country's demand for loanable funds, DLF, is part of the world demand and the country's supply of loanable funds, SLF_D, is part of the world supply in Fig. 23.10(a).

If this country were isolated from the global economy, the real interest rate would be 4 percent a year (where the DLF and SLF_D curves intersect). But if this country is integrated into the global economy, with an interest rate of 4 percent a year, funds would

quickly *flow out* of it. With a real interest rate of 5 percent a year in the rest of the world, domestic suppliers of loanable funds would seek the higher return in other countries. Again, the country faces the supply of loanable funds curve SLF, which is horizontal at the world equilibrium real interest rate.

The country's demand for loanable funds and the world interest rate determine the equilibrium quantity of loanable funds—$1.5 billion in Fig. 23.10(c).

Changes in Demand and Supply   A change in the demand or supply in the global loanable funds market changes the real interest rate in the way shown in Fig. 23.6 (see p. 553). The effect of a change in demand or supply in a national market depends on the size of the country. A change in demand or supply in a small country has no significant effect on global demand or supply, so it leaves the world real interest rate unchanged and changes only the country's net exports and international borrowing or lending. A change in demand or supply in a large country has a significant effect on global demand or supply, so it changes the world real interest rate as well as the country's net exports and international borrowing or lending. Every country feels some of the effect of a large country's change in demand or supply.

Economics in Action
Greenspan's Interest Rate Puzzle

The real interest rate paid by big corporations in the United States fell from 5.5 percent a year in 2001 to 2.5 percent a year in 2005. Alan Greenspan, then Chairman of the Federal Reserve, said he was puzzled that the real interest rate was falling at a time when the U.S. government budget deficit was increasing.

Why did the real interest rate fall?

The answer lies in the global loanable funds market. Rapid economic growth in Asia and Europe brought a large increase in global saving, which in turn increased the global supply of loanable funds. The supply of loanable funds increased because Asian and European saving increased strongly.

The U.S. government budget deficit increased the U.S. and global demand for loanable funds. But this increase was very small compared to the increase in the global supply of loanable funds.

The result of a large increase in supply and a small increase in demand was a fall in the world equilibrium real interest rate and an increase in the equilibrium quantity of loanable funds.

The figure illustrates these events. The supply of loanable funds increased from SLF_{01} in 2001 to SLF_{05} in 2005. (In the figure, we ignore the change in the global demand for loanable funds because it was small relative to the increase in supply.)

With the increase in supply, the real interest rate

fell from 5.5 percent to 2.5 percent a year and the quantity of loanable funds increased.

In the United States, borrowing from the rest of the world increased to finance the increased government budget deficit.

The interest rate puzzle illustrates the important fact that the loanable funds market is a global market, not a national market.

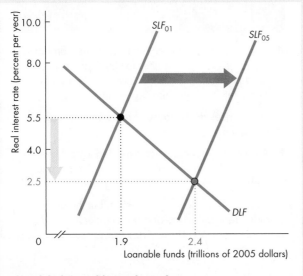

The Global Loanable Funds Market

REVIEW QUIZ

1 Why do loanable funds flow among countries?
2 What determines the demand for and supply of loanable funds in an individual economy?
3 What happens if a country has a shortage of loanable funds at the world real interest rate?
4 What happens if a country has a surplus of loanable funds at the world real interest rate?
5 How is a government budget deficit financed in an open economy?

You can work these questions in Study Plan 23.4 and get instant feedback.

———————————————— MyEconLab ◆

◆ To complete your study of financial markets, take a look at *Reading Between the Lines* on pp. 560–561 and see how you can use the model of the loanable funds market to understand the events in global financial markets in 2010 and 2011.

Euro Crisis and the Global Market

Markets Plunge Following Resignation of German ECB Official

www.guardian.co.uk

September 9, 2011

The dramatic resignation of a senior European central banker sent stock markets plunging, amid fears that Greece is on the brink of default and the fragile consensus in Berlin over support for the ailing Italian and Spanish economies was close to disintegration.

Bank stocks, down more than 5% in some cases, were the worst affected as the Dow Jones dropped almost 3% to below 11,000. European exchanges joined the panic with the FTSE falling more than 100 points to 5,230. Speculation that several French and German banks would soon embark on massive capital raising schemes to offset write-offs on holdings of Greek debt, added to the febrile atmosphere.

Greece issued a statement to say it remained solvent and would not need to seek funds beyond the sums already agreed with the EU and International Monetary Fund. Deputy prime minister Evangelos Venizelos said: "It is not the first time we see an organized wave of 'rumours' about an upcoming Greek default. This is a game of a very bad taste."

But the statement from Athens failed to rally markets, which have remained wary of assurances by EU leaders that they will do everything necessary to keep peripheral eurozone countries afloat.

Nick Bennenbroek, head of currency strategy at Wells Fargo Bank, said investors globally were concerned at the potential collapse of a European sovereign. "The European troubles are permeating across global financial markets." …

ESSENCE OF THE STORY

- A top European central banker resigned and on the same day, stock prices fell by 2 percent in London and 3 percent in New York. Some bank stocks fell by more than 5 percent.

- Stock prices fell because of fears that Greece might default.

- A default by Greece was expected to spill over to Italy and Spain and inflict losses on French and German banks that hold Greek government debt.

- Greece said it would not default, but the promise didn't reassure stock- and bondholders.

ECONOMIC ANALYSIS

- The Government of Greece has a large budget deficit and a debt that exceeds Greek GDP.

- Greece is a member of the European Union and uses the euro as its currency.

- To help prevent Greece from defaulting on its debt, other EU governments, notably those of Germany and France, have extended loans to Greece.

- Events such as those reported in the news article make Greek government bondholders nervous and cause some to sell their Greek bonds.

- A greater expectation of default by Greece lowers the expected value of the stocks of banks and other institutions that hold Greek bonds. So investors sell bank stocks.

- Bond and stock markets are interlinked in the global loanable funds market, so selling ripples through the market, prices fall, and the real interest rate rises.

- Despite daily volatility in the global loanable funds market, averaged over a year, the market has been remarkably stable. It has even displayed a Ricardo–Barro rationality.

- Figure 1 shows the global loanable funds market in 2010 and 2011.

- In 2010, the demand for loanable funds (government and private) was DLF_0 and the supply of loanable funds (government and private) was SLF_0. The real interest rate was 3 percent a year.

- In 2011, government budget deficits around the world increased the demand for loanable funds to DLF_1. The supply of loanable funds increased to SLF_1 and the real interest rate remained at 3 percent a year.

- The situation in the market for Greek government debt was very different from that in the global market and Figure 2 shows how different.

- In 2010, the demand for loanable funds (government and private) was DLF_0 and the supply of loanable funds (government and private) was SLF_0. The real interest rate was 10 percent a year, reflecting a high risk of default.

- In 2011, the Greek government's budget deficit increased the demand for loanable funds to DLF_1 and at the same time increased the risk of a default. With a more likely default, the supply of loanable funds in Greece *decreased* to SLF_1.

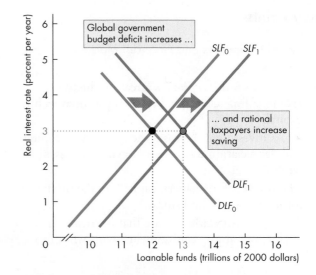

Figure 1 The Global Loanable Funds Market

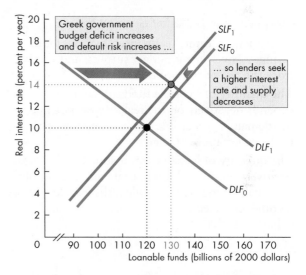

Figure 2 The Market for Greece's Government Debt

- The increase in the demand for loanable funds exceeded the decrease in supply, so the quantity of loanable funds increased.

- Because demand increased and supply decreased, the interest rate increased to 14 percent a year.

- The performance of the global loanable funds market demonstrates the ability of the large global market to withstand large fluctuations in risk and interest rates in one small part of the global economy.

SUMMARY

Key Points

Financial Institutions and Financial Markets (pp. 544–548)

- Capital (*physical capital*) is a real productive resource; financial capital is the funds used to buy capital.
- Gross investment increases the quantity of capital and depreciation decreases it. Saving increases wealth.
- The markets for financial capital are the markets for loans, bonds, and stocks.
- Financial institutions ensure that borrowers and lenders can always find someone with whom to trade.

Working Study Plan Problems 1 to 5 will give you a better understanding of financial institutions and markets.

The Loanable Funds Market (pp. 548–554)

- Investment in capital is financed by household saving, a government budget surplus, and funds from the rest of the world.
- The quantity of loanable funds demanded depends negatively on the real interest rate and the demand for loanable funds changes when profit expectations change.
- The quantity of loanable funds supplied depends positively on the real interest rate and the supply of loanable funds changes when disposable income, expected future income, wealth, and default risk change.

- Equilibrium in the loanable funds market determines the real interest rate and quantity of funds.

Working Study Plan Problems 6 to 9 will give you a better understanding of the loanable funds market.

Government in the Loanable Funds Market (pp. 555–556)

- A government budget surplus increases the supply of loanable funds, lowers the real interest rate, and increases investment and the equilibrium quantity of loanable funds.
- A government budget deficit increases the demand for loanable funds, raises the real interest rate, and increases the equilibrium quantity of loanable funds, but decreases investment in a crowding-out effect.
- The Ricardo–Barro effect is the response of rational taxpayers to a budget deficit: Private saving increases to finance the budget deficit. The real interest rate remains constant and the crowding-out effect is avoided.

Working Study Plan Problems 10 to 15 will give you a better understanding of government in the loanable funds market.

The Global Loanable Funds Market (pp. 557–559)

- The loanable funds market is a global market.
- The equilibrium real interest rate is determined in the global loanable funds market and national demand and supply determine the quantity of international borrowing or lending.

Working Study Plan Problems 16 to 18 will give you a better understanding of the global loanable funds market.

Key Terms

Bond, 545
Bond market, 545
Crowding-out effect, 556
Demand for loanable funds, 550
Financial capital, 544
Financial institution, 546
Gross investment, 544
Loanable funds market, 548
Mortgage, 545
Mortgage-backed security, 546
National saving, 549

Net investment, 544
Net taxes, 548
Net worth, 547
Nominal interest rate, 549
Real interest rate, 549
Ricardo–Barro effect, 556
Saving, 544
Stock, 546
Stock market, 546
Supply of loanable funds, 551
Wealth, 544

SCAN THIS

STUDY PLAN PROBLEMS AND APPLICATIONS

MyEconLab ◆ You can work Problems 1 to 18 in Chapter 23 Study Plan and get instant feedback.

Financial Institutions and Financial Markets
(Study Plan 23.1)

Use the following information to work Problems 1 and 2.

Michael is an Internet service provider. On December 31, 2011, he bought an existing business with servers and a building worth $400,000. During his first year of operation, his business grew and he bought new servers for $500,000. The market value of some of his older servers fell by $100,000.

1. Calculate Michael's gross investment, depreciation, and net investment during 2012.

2. What is the value of Michael's capital at the end of 2012?

3. Lori is a student who teaches golf on the weekend and in a year earns $20,000 after paying her taxes. At the beginning of 2012, Lori owned $1,000 worth of books, CDs, and golf clubs and she had $5,000 in a savings account at the bank. During 2012, the interest on her savings account was $300 and she spent a total of $15,300 on consumption goods and services. There was no change in the market values of her books, CDs, and golf clubs.
   a. How much did Lori save in 2012?
   b. What was her wealth at the end of 2012?

4. In a speech to financial analysts, William Poole, a former Chairman of the St. Louis Federal Reserve Bank, said:

   Over most of the post–World War II period, the personal saving rate averaged about 6 percent, with some higher years from the mid-1970s to mid-1980s. The negative trend in the saving rate started in the mid-1990s, about the same time the stock market boom started. Thus it is hard to dismiss the hypothesis that the decline in the measured saving rate in the late 1990s reflected the response of consumption to large capital gains from corporate equity [stock]. Evidence from panel data of households also supports the conclusion that the decline in the personal saving rate since 1984 is largely a consequence of capital gains on corporate equities.

   a. Is the purchase of corporate equities part of household consumption or saving? Explain your answer.
   b. Equities reap a capital gain in the same way that houses reap a capital gain. Does this mean that the purchase of equities is investment? If not, explain why it is not.

5. **G-20 Leaders Look to Shake off Lingering Economic Troubles**

   The G-20 aims to take stock of the economic recovery. One achievement of the G-20 in Pittsburgh could be a deal to require that financial institutions hold more capital.
   Source: *ABC News*, September 24, 2009

   What are the financial institutions that the G-20 might require to hold more capital? What exactly is the "capital" referred to in the news clip? How might the requirement to hold more capital make financial institutions safer?

The Loanable Funds Market (Study Plan 23.2)

Use the following information to work Problems 6 and 7.

First Call, Inc., is a cell phone company. It plans to build an assembly plant that costs $10 million if the real interest rate is 6 percent a year. If the real interest rate is 5 percent a year, First Call will build a larger plant that costs $12 million. And if the real interest rate is 7 percent a year, First Call will build a smaller plant that costs $8 million.

6. Draw a graph of First Call's demand for loanable funds curve.

7. First Call expects its profit from the sale of cell phones to double next year. If other things remain the same, explain how this increase in expected profit influences First Call's demand for loanable funds.

8. Draw a graph to illustrate how an increase in the supply of loanable funds and a decrease in the demand for loanable funds can lower the real interest rate and leave the equilibrium quantity of loanable funds unchanged.

9. Use the information in Problem 4.

   a. U.S. household income has grown considerably since 1984. Has U.S. saving been on a downward trend because Americans feel wealthier?

   b. Explain why households preferred to buy corporate equities rather than bonds.

Government in the Loanable Funds Market
(Study Plan 23.3)

Use the following table to work Problems 10 to 12. The table shows an economy's demand for loanable funds and the supply of loanable funds schedules when the government's budget is balanced.

Real interest rate (percent per year)	Loanable funds demanded	Loanable funds supplied
	(trillions of 2005 dollars)	
4	8.5	5.5
5	8.0	6.0
6	7.5	6.5
7	7.0	7.0
8	6.5	7.5
9	6.0	8.0
10	5.5	8.5

10. Suppose that the government has a budget surplus of $1 trillion. What are the real interest rate, the quantity of investment, and the quantity of private saving? Is there any crowding out in this situation?

11. Suppose that the government has a budget deficit of $1 trillion. What are the real interest rate, the quantity of investment, and the quantity of private saving? Is there any crowding out in this situation?

12. Suppose that the government has a budget deficit of $1 trillion and the Ricardo–Barro effect occurs. What are the real interest rate and the quantity of investment?

Use the table in Problem 10 and the following information to work Problems 13 to 15.

Suppose that the quantity of loanable funds demanded increases by $1 trillion at each real interest rate and the quantity of loanable funds supplied increases by $2 trillion at each interest rate.

13. If the government budget is balanced, what are the real interest rate, the quantity of loanable funds, investment, and private saving? Does any crowding out occur?

14. If the government budget becomes a deficit of $1 trillion, what are the real interest rate, the quantity of loanable funds, investment, and private saving? Does any crowding out occur?

15. If the government wants to stimulate investment and increase it to $9 trillion, what must it do?

The Global Loanable Funds Market (Study Plan 23.4)

Use the following information to work Problems 16 and 17.

Global Saving Glut and U.S. Current Account, remarks by Ben Bernanke (when a governor of the Federal Reserve) on March 10, 2005:

The U.S. economy appears to be performing well: Output growth has returned to healthy levels, the labour market is firming, and inflation appears to be under control. But, one aspect of U.S. economic performance still evokes concern: the nation's large and growing current account deficit (negative net exports). Most forecasters expect the nation's current account imbalance to decline slowly at best, implying a continued need for foreign credit and a concomitant decline in the U.S. net foreign asset position.

16. Why is the United States, with the world's largest economy, borrowing heavily on international capital markets—rather than lending, as would seem more natural?

17. a. What implications do the U.S. current account deficit (negative net exports) and the United States' reliance on foreign credit have for the performance of the U.S. economy?

   b. What policies, if any, should be used to address this situation?

18. **IMF Says It Battled Crisis Well**

   The International Monetary Fund (IMF) reported that it acted effectively in combating the global recession. Since September 2008, the IMF made $163 billion available to developing countries. While the IMF urged developed countries and China to run deficits to stimulate their economies, the IMF required developing countries with large deficits to cut spending and not increase spending.

   Source: *The Wall Street Journal*, September 29, 2009

   a. Explain how increased government budget deficits change the loanable funds market.

   b. Would the global recession have been less severe had the IMF made larger loans to developing countries?

ADDITIONAL PROBLEMS AND APPLICATIONS

MyEconLab ◆ You can work these problems in MyEconLab if assigned by your instructor.

Financial Institutions and Financial Markets

19. On January 1, 2011, Terry's Towing Service owned 4 tow trucks valued at $300,000. During 2011, Terry's bought 2 new trucks for a total of $180,000. At the end of 2011, the market value of all of the firm's trucks was $400,000. What was Terry's gross investment? Calculate Terry's depreciation and net investment.

Use the following information to work Problems 20 and 21.

Statistics Canada reported that the capital stock was $6,113 billion at the end of 2008, $6,266 billion at the end of 2009, and $6,510 billion at the end of 2010. Depreciation in 2009 was $166 billion, and gross investment during 2010 was $361 billion.

20. Calculate Canadian net investment and gross investment during 2009.

21. Calculate Canadian depreciation and net investment during 2010.

22. Annie runs a fitness centre. On December 31, 2011, she bought an existing business with exercise equipment and a building worth $300,000. During 2012, business improved and she bought some new equipment for $50,000. At the end of 2012, her equipment and buildings were worth $325,000. Calculate Annie's gross investment, depreciation, and net investment during 2012.

23. Karrie is a golf pro, and after she paid taxes, her income from golf and interest from financial assets was $1,500,000 in 2012. At the beginning of 2012, she owned $900,000 worth of financial assets. At the end of 2012, Karrie's financial assets were worth $1,900,000.
    a. How much did Karrie save during 2012?
    b. How much did she spend on consumption goods and services?

The Loanable Funds Market

Use the following information to work Problems 24 and 25.

In 2012, the Lee family had disposable income of $80,000, wealth of $140,000, and an expected future income of $80,000 a year. At a real interest

rate of 4 percent a year, the Lee family saves $15,000 a year; at a real interest rate of 6 percent a year, they save $20,000 a year; and at a real interest rate of 8 percent, they save $25,000 a year.

24. Draw a graph of the Lee family's supply of loanable funds curve.

25. In 2013, suppose that the stock market crashes and the default risk increases. Explain how this increase in default risk influences the Lee family's supply of loanable funds curve.

26. Draw a graph to illustrate the effect of an increase in the demand for loanable funds and an even larger increase in the supply of loanable funds on the real interest rate and the equilibrium quantity of loanable funds.

27. **Greenspan's Conundrum Spells Confusion for Us All**

    In January 2005, the interest rate on bonds was 4% a year and it was expected to rise to 5% a year by the end of 2005. As the rate rose to 4.3% during February, most commentators focused, not on why the interest rate rose, but on why it was so low before. Explanations of this "conundrum" included that unusual buying and expectations for an economic slowdown were keeping the interest rate low.

    Source: *Financial Times*, February 26, 2005

    a. Explain how "unusual buying" might lead to a low real interest rate.
    b. Explain how investors' "expectations for an economic slowdown" might lead to a lower real interest rate.

Government in the Loanable Funds Market

Use the following information to work Problems 28 and 29.

India's Economy Hits the Wall

At the start of 2008, India had an annual growth of 9%, huge consumer demand, and increasing foreign investment. But by July 2008, India had 11.4% inflation, large government deficits, and rising interest rates. Economic growth is expected to fall to 7% by the end of 2008. A Goldman Sachs report suggests that India needs to lower the government's deficit, raise educational achievement, control inflation, and liberalize its financial markets.

Source: *Business Week*, July 1, 2008

28. If the Indian government reduces its deficit and returns to a balanced budget, how will the demand for or supply of loanable funds in India change?

29. With economic growth forecasted to slow, future incomes are expected to fall. If other things remain the same, how will the demand or supply of loanable funds in India change?

30. **Canadian Debt and Deficit**

    Statistics Canada reported that at the end of the first quarter of 2011, the federal government's debt was $550 billion. During that quarter, the government received $59 billion in revenue and spent $76 billion.

    Source: Statistics Canada, CANSIM Table 385-0032

    Explain the effect of the federal deficit and the mounting debt on Canadian economic growth.

The Global Loanable Funds Market

31. **The Global Savings Glut and Its Consequences**

    Several developing countries are running large current account surpluses (representing an excess of savings over investment) and rapid growth has led to high saving rates as people save a large fraction of additional income. In India, the saving rate has risen from 23% a decade ago to 33% today. China's saving rate is 55%. The glut of saving in Asia is being put into U.S. bonds. When a poor country buys U.S. bonds, it is in effect lending to the United States.

    Source: *The Cato Institute*, June 8, 2007

    a. Graphically illustrate and explain the impact of the "glut of savings" on the real interest rate and the quantity of loanable funds.

    b. How do the high saving rates in Asia impact investment in the United States?

Use the following information to work Problems 32 to 35.

Most economists agree that the problems we are witnessing today developed over a long period of time. For more than a decade, a massive amount of money flowed into the United States from investors abroad, because our country is an attractive and secure place to do business. This large influx of money to U.S. financial institutions—along with low interest rates—made it easier for Americans to get credit. These developments allowed more families to borrow money for cars and homes and college tuition—some for the first time. They allowed more entrepreneurs to get loans to start new businesses and create jobs.

President George W. Bush, *Address to the Nation*, September 24, 2008

32. Explain why, for more than a decade, a massive amount of money flowed into the United States. Compare and contrast your explanation with that of the president.

33. Provide a graphical analysis of the reasons why the interest rate was low.

34. Funds have been flowing into the United States since the early 1980s. Why might they have created problems in 2008 but not earlier?

35. Could the United States stop funds from flowing in from other countries? How?

Economics in the News

36. After you have studied *Reading Between the Lines* on pp. 560–561, answer the following questions.
    a. What event sent the world's stock prices down on September 8, 2011?
    b. What feature of the financial markets translated the event into a stock price fall?
    c. How did the global loanable funds market respond to daily shocks over the whole of 2010–2011?
    d. How would you explain the stark difference in the performance of the global loanable funds market and the market for Greek government debt?
    e. Why would Germany and France want to prevent a Greek government default?
    f. If Greece did default, what do you think would happen in the global loanable funds market?
    g. Illustrate your answer to part (f) with an appropriate graphical analysis of the global loanable funds market.

CHAPTER
24

Money, the Price Level, and Inflation

After studying this chapter, you will be able to

◆ Define money and describe its functions

◆ Explain the economic functions of banks and the Bank of Canada

◆ Explain how the banking system creates money

◆ Explain how the demand for money and the supply of money influence interest rates

◆ Explain how money growth influences inflation

Money has been around for a long time, and it has taken many forms. It was wampum (beads made from shells) for North American Indians, whale's teeth for Fijians, and tobacco for early American colonists. Today, when we want to buy something, we use coins or dollar bills, write a cheque, or swipe a debit card or a credit card. Soon, we'll be using a "smart card" or a cell phone to make payments. Are all these things money?

The Bank of Canada regulates the quantity of money in our economy. How? And what happens if too much money or too little money is created?

These are the questions we study in this chapter. In *Reading Between the Lines* at the end of the chapter, we look at the extraordinary monetary situation in our big neighbour and the dangers that U.S. monetary policy poses for Canada.

What Is Money?

What do wampum, tobacco, and nickels and dimes have in common? They are all examples of **money**, which is defined as any commodity or token that is generally acceptable as a means of payment. A **means of payment** is a method of settling a debt. When a payment has been made, there is no remaining obligation between the parties to a transaction. So what wampum, tobacco, and nickels and dimes have in common is that they have served (or still do serve) as the means of payment. Money serves three other functions:

- Medium of exchange
- Unit of account
- Store of value

Medium of Exchange

A *medium of exchange* is any object that is generally accepted in exchange for goods and services. Without a medium of exchange, goods and services must be exchanged directly for other goods and services—an exchange called *barter*. Barter requires a *double coincidence of wants*, a situation that rarely occurs. For example, if you want a hamburger, you might offer a DVD in exchange for it. But you must find someone who is selling hamburgers and wants your DVD.

A medium of exchange overcomes the need for a double coincidence of wants. Money acts as a medium of exchange because people with something to sell will always accept money in exchange for it. But money isn't the only medium of exchange. You can buy with a credit card, but a credit card isn't money. It doesn't make a final payment, and the debt it creates must eventually be settled by using money.

Unit of Account

A *unit of account* is an agreed measure for stating the prices of goods and services. To get the most out of your budget, you have to figure out whether seeing one more movie is worth its opportunity cost. But that cost is not dollars and cents. It is the number of ice cream cones, movies, or cups of coffee that you must give up. It's easy to do such calculations when all these goods have prices in terms of dollars and cents (see Table 24.1). If the price of a movie is $8 and the price of a cappuccino is $4, you know right away that seeing 1 movie costs you 2 cappuccinos.

TABLE 24.1 The Unit of Account Function of Money Simplifies Price Comparisons

Good	Price in money units	Price in units of another good
Movie	$8 each	2 cappuccinos
Cappuccino	$4 each	2 ice cream cones
Ice cream	$2 per cone	2 packs of jelly beans
Jelly beans	$1 per pack	2 sticks of gum
Gum	$0.50 per stick	

Money as a unit of account: The price of a movie is $8 and the price of a stick of gum is 50¢, so the opportunity cost of a movie is 16 sticks of gum ($8 ÷ 50¢ = 16).

No unit of account: You go to a movie theatre and learn that the cost of seeing a movie is 2 cappuccinos. You go to a grocery store and learn that a pack of jelly beans costs 2 sticks of gum. But how many sticks of gum does seeing a movie cost you? To answer that question, you go to the coffee shop and find that a cappuccino costs 2 ice cream cones. Now you head for the ice cream shop, where an ice cream cone costs 2 packs of jelly beans. Now you get out your pocket calculator: 1 movie costs 2 cappuccinos, or 4 ice cream cones, or 8 packs of jelly beans, or 16 sticks of gum!

If jelly beans are $1 a pack, 1 movie costs 8 packs of jelly beans. You need only one calculation to figure out the opportunity cost of any pair of goods and services.

Imagine how troublesome it would be if your local movie theatre posted its price as 2 cappuccinos, the coffee shop posted the price of a cappuccino as 2 ice cream cones, the ice cream shop posted the price of an ice cream cone as 2 packs of jelly beans, and the grocery store priced a pack of jelly beans as 2 sticks of gum! Now how much running around and calculating will you have to do to find out how much that movie is going to cost you in terms of the cappuccinos, ice cream cones, jelly beans, or gum that you must give up to see it? You get the answer for cappuccinos right away from the sign posted on the movie theatre. But for all the other goods, you're going to have to visit many different stores to establish the price of each good in terms of another and then calculate the prices in units that are relevant for your own decision. The hassle of doing all this research might be enough to make a person swear off movies! You can see how much simpler it is if all the prices are expressed in dollars and cents.

Store of Value

Money is a *store of value* in the sense that it can be held and exchanged later for goods and services. If money were not a store of value, it could not serve as a means of payment.

Money is not alone in acting as a store of value. A house, a car, and a work of art are other examples.

The more stable the value of a commodity or token, the better it can act as a store of value and the more useful it is as money. No store of value has a completely stable value. The value of a house, a car, or a work of art fluctuates over time. The value of the commodities and tokens that are used as money also fluctuate over time.

Inflation lowers the value of money and the values of other commodities and tokens that are used as money. To make money as useful as possible as a store of value, a low inflation rate is needed.

Money in Canada Today

In Canada today, money consists of

- Currency
- Deposits at banks and other depository institutions

Currency The notes and coins held by individuals and businesses are known as **currency**. Notes are money because the government declares them so with the words "Ce billet a cours légal–this note is legal tender." Notes and coins *inside* banks are not counted as currency because they are not held by individuals and businesses. Currency is convenient for settling small debts and buying low-priced items.

Deposits Deposits of individuals and businesses at banks and other depository institutions, such as trust and mortgage companies, credit unions, and caisses populaires, are also counted as money. Deposits are money because the owners of the deposits can use them to make payments.

Official Measures of Money Two official measures of money in Canada today are known as M1 and M2.

M1 consists of currency held by individuals and businesses plus chequable deposits owned by individuals and businesses. M1 does *not* include notes and coins held by banks, and it does not include chequable deposits owned by the Government of Canada. **M2** consists of M1 plus all other deposits—non-chequable deposits and fixed term deposits.

Economics in Action
Official Measures of Money in Canada

The figure shows the relative magnitudes of the items in M1 and M2. Notice how small currency is.

	$ billions in July 2011
M2	1,040
Comprises all in M1, plus...	
Fixed term deposits	303
Non-chequable deposits, non-personal	29
Non-chequable deposits, personal	163
M1	545
Chequable deposits, non-personal	277
Chequable deposits, personal	211
Currency held by individuals and businesses	57

Two Official Measures of Money

M1
- Currency held by individuals and businesses
- Personal chequable deposits
- Non-personal chequable deposits

M2
- M1
- Personal non-chequable deposits
- Non-personal non-chequable deposits
- Fixed term deposits

Source of data: Statistics Canada, CANSIM Table 176–0020. In the Bank of Canada's official statistics, M1 is called M1+ (gross) and M2 is called M2 (gross).

Are M1 and M2 Really Money? Money is the means of payment. So the test of whether an asset is money is whether it serves as a means of payment. Currency passes the test. But what about deposits? Chequable deposits are money because they can be transferred from one person to another by writing a cheque or using a debit card. Such a transfer of ownership is equivalent to handing over currency. Because M1 consists of currency plus chequable deposits and each of these is a means of payment, *M1 is money.*

But what about M2? Some of the savings deposits in M2 are just as much a means of payment as the chequable deposits in M1. You can use an ATM to get funds from your savings account to pay for your purchase at the grocery store or the gas station. But some savings deposits are not a means of payment. These deposits are known as liquid assets. *Liquidity* is the property of being easily convertible into a means of payment without loss in value. Because the deposits in M2 that are not means of payment are quickly and easily converted into a means of payment—into currency or chequable deposits—they are counted as money.

Deposits Are Money but Cheques Are Not In defining money, we include, along with currency, deposits at banks and other depository institutions. But we do not count the cheques that people write as money. Why are deposits money and cheques not?

To see why deposits are money but cheques are not, think about what happens when Colleen buys some roller-blades for $100 from Rocky's Rollers. When Colleen goes to Rocky's shop, she has $500 in her deposit account at the Laser Bank. Rocky has $1,000 in his deposit account—at the same bank, as it happens. The total deposits of these two people are $1,500. Colleen writes a cheque for $100. Rocky takes the cheque to the bank right away and deposits it. Rocky's bank balance rises from $1,000 to $1,100, and Colleen's balance falls from $500 to $400. The total deposits of Colleen and Rocky are still the same as before: $1,500. Rocky now has $100 more than before, and Colleen has $100 less.

This transaction has transferred money from Colleen to Rocky, but the cheque itself was never money. There wasn't an extra $100 of money while the cheque was in circulation. The cheque instructs the bank to transfer money from Colleen to Rocky.

If Colleen and Rocky use different banks, there is an extra step. Rocky's bank credits $100 to Rocky's account and then takes the cheque to a cheque-clearing centre. The cheque is then sent to Colleen's bank, which pays Rocky's bank $100 and then debits Colleen's account $100. This process can take a few days, but the principles are the same as when two people use the same bank.

Credit Cards Are Not Money You've just seen that cheques are not money. What about credit cards? Isn't having a credit card in your wallet and presenting the card to pay for your roller-blades the same thing as using money? Why aren't credit cards somehow valued and counted as part of the quantity of money?

When you pay by cheque, you are frequently asked to prove your identity by showing your driver's licence. It would never occur to you to think of your driver's licence as money. It's just an ID card. A credit card is also an ID card, but one that lets you take out a loan at the instant you buy something. When you sign a credit card sales slip, you are saying, "I agree to pay for these goods when the credit card company bills me." Once you get your statement from the credit card company, you must make at least the minimum payment due. To make that payment, you need money—you need to have currency or a chequable deposit to pay the credit card company. So although you use a credit card when you buy something, the credit card is not the *means of payment* and it is not money.

⬛ **REVIEW QUIZ**

1 What makes something money? What functions does money perform? Why do you think packs of chewing gum don't serve as money?
2 What are the problems that arise when a commodity is used as money?
3 What are the main components of money in Canada today?
4 What are the official measures of money? Are all the measures really money?
5 Why are cheques and credit cards not money?

You can work these questions in Study Plan 24.1 and get instant feedback.

——————————— MyEconLab ◆

We've seen that the main component of money in Canada is deposits at banks and other depository institutions. Let's take a closer look at these institutions.

◆ The Banking System

The banking system consists of private and public institutions that create money and manage the nation's monetary and payments systems. These institutions play a crucial role in financial markets and have profound effects on overall economic performance. To describe these institutions and explain their functions, we'll divide them into two parts:

- Depository institutions
- The Bank of Canada

Depository Institutions

A **depository institution** is a private firm that takes deposits from households and firms and makes loans to other households and firms. The deposits of three types of depository institution make up the nation's money. They are

- Chartered banks
- Credit unions and caisses populaires
- Trust and mortgage loan companies

Chartered Banks A **chartered bank** is a private firm, chartered under the Bank Act of 1992 to receive deposits and make loans. The chartered banks are by far the largest institutions in the banking system and conduct all types of banking and financial business. In 2008, 14 Canadian-owned banks (including the Royal Bank of Canada, CIBC, Bank of Montreal, Bank of Nova Scotia, National Bank of Canada, and TD Canada Trust) and 33 foreign-owned banks had the bulk of the deposits in M1 and M2.

Credit Unions and Caisses Populaires A *credit union* is a cooperative organization that operates under the Co-operative Credit Association Act of 1992 and that receives deposits from and makes loans to its members. A caisse populaire is a similar type of institution that operates in Quebec.

Trust and Mortgage Loan Companies A *trust and mortgage loan company* is a privately owned depository institution that operates under the Trust and Loan Companies Act of 1992. These institutions receive deposits, make loans, and act as trustee for pension funds and for estates.

All Banks Now Historically, Canada made a sharp legal distinction between banks and other depository institutions. But the economic functions of all depository institutions have grown increasingly similar. This fact is recognized in laws governing these institutions that became effective in 1992. Because they all perform the same essential economic functions, we'll call all these institutions banks unless we need to distinguish among them.

What Depository Institutions Do Depository institutions provide services such as cheque clearing, account management, credit cards, and Internet banking, all of which provide an income from service fees.

But depository institutions earn most of their income by using the funds they receive from depositors to make loans and buy securities that earn a higher interest rate than that paid to depositors. In this activity, a depository institution must perform a balancing act weighing return against risk. To see this balancing act, we'll focus on the chartered banks.

A chartered bank puts the funds it receives from depositors and other funds that it borrows into four types of assets:

1. Reserves A depository institution's **reserves** are notes and coins in its vault or its deposit account at the Bank of Canada. (We study the Bank of Canada later in this chapter.) These funds are used to meet depositors' currency withdrawals and to make payments to other banks. In normal times, a bank keeps about a half of 1 percent of deposits as reserves.

2. Liquid Assets Liquid assets are Government of Canada Treasury bills and commercial bills. These assets are the banks' first line of defence if they need reserves. Liquid assets can be sold and instantly converted into reserves with virtually no risk of loss. Because they have a low risk, they also earn a low interest rate.

3. Securities Securities are Government of Canada bonds and other bonds such as mortgage-backed securities. These assets can be converted into reserves but at prices that fluctuate. Because their prices fluctuate, these assets are riskier than liquid assets, but they also have a higher interest rate.

4. Loans Loans are commitments of funds for an agreed-upon period of time. Banks make loans to corporations to finance the purchase of capital. They also make mortgage loans to finance the purchase of homes, and personal loans to finance consumer durable goods, such as cars or boats. The outstanding balances on credit card accounts are also bank loans. Loans are the riskiest assets of a bank. They cannot be converted into reserves until they are due to be repaid. And some borrowers default and never repay. These assets earn the highest interest rate.

Table 24.2 provides a snapshot of the sources and uses of funds of all the chartered banks in 2011.

Economic Benefits Provided by Depository Institutions

You've seen that a depository institution earns part of its profit because it pays a lower interest rate on deposits than what it earns on loans. What benefits do these institutions provide that make depositors willing to put up with a low interest rate and borrowers willing to pay a higher one?

Depository institutions provide four benefits:

■ Create liquidity
■ Pool risk
■ Lower the cost of borrowing
■ Lower the cost of monitoring borrowers

Create Liquidity Depository institutions create liquidity by *borrowing short and lending long*—taking deposits and standing ready to repay them on short notice or on demand and making loan commitments that run for terms of many years.

Pool Risk A loan might not be repaid—a default. If you lend to one person who defaults, you lose the entire amount loaned. If you lend to 1,000 people (through a bank) and one person defaults, you lose almost nothing. Depository institutions pool risk.

Lower the Cost of Borrowing Imagine there are no depository institutions and a firm is looking for $1 million to buy a new factory. It hunts around for several dozen people from whom to borrow the funds. Depository institutions lower the cost of this search. The firm gets its $1 million from a single institution that gets deposits from a large number of people but spreads the cost of this activity over many borrowers.

Lower the Cost of Monitoring Borrowers By monitoring borrowers, a lender can encourage good decisions that prevent defaults. But this activity is costly. Imagine how costly it would be if each household that lent money to a firm incurred the costs of monitoring that firm directly. Depository institutions can perform this task at a much lower cost.

You now know what money is and that the bulk of the nation's money is deposits in banks and other institutions. Your next task is to learn about the Bank of Canada and the ways in which it can influence the quantity of money.

The Bank of Canada

The Bank of Canada is Canada's **central bank**, a public authority that supervises other banks and financial institutions, financial markets, and the payments system, and conducts monetary policy.

The Bank of Canada is a bank. And like all banks, it accepts deposits, make loans, and holds investment securities. But the Bank of Canada is special in three important ways. It is the

■ Banker to banks and government
■ Lender of last resort
■ Sole issuer of bank notes

Banker to Banks and Government The Bank of Canada has a restricted list of customers. They are the chartered banks, credit unions and caisses populaires, and trust and mortgage loan companies that make up the banking system; the Government of Canada; and the central banks of other countries. The Bank of Canada accepts deposits from these customers. And these deposits are part of the reserves of the banks.

Lender of Last Resort The Bank of Canada makes loans to banks. And it is the **lender of last resort**,

---

TABLE 24.2   Chartered Banks: Sources and Uses of Funds

	$ billions June 2011	Percentage of deposits
Total funds	2,052.5	162.3
Sources		
Deposits	1,264.8	100.0
Borrowing and own capital	787.7	62.3
Uses		
Reserves	4.4	0.3
Liquid assets	306.0	24.2
Securities and other assets	391.0	30.9
Loans	1,351.1	106.8

Chartered banks get three-fifths of their funds from depositors and use most of them to make loans. Banks hold about 0.3 percent of deposits as reserves and almost a quarter of their deposits as liquid assets.

Source of data: Statistics Canada CANSIM Table 176–0011

which means that it stands ready to make loans when the banking system as a whole is short of reserves. If some banks are short of reserves while others have surplus reserves, the overnight loan market moves the funds from one bank to another.

Sole Issuer of Bank Notes The Bank of Canada is the only bank that is permitted to issue bank notes. You might think that such a monopoly is natural, but it isn't. In some banking systems—those of Ireland and Scotland are examples—private banks also issue bank notes. But in Canada and most other countries, the central bank has a monopoly on this activity.

The Bank of Canada's Balance Sheet The Bank of Canada influences the economy by changing interest rates. You'll learn the details of the Bank's monetary policy strategy in Chapter 30 when you've studied all the tools needed to understand monetary policy. But to influence interest rates, the Bank must change the quantity of money in the economy. This quantity depends on the size and composition of its balance sheet—its assets and liabilities. Lets look at the Bank of Canada's balance sheet, starting with its assets.

The Bank of Canada's Assets The Bank of Canada has two main assets:

1. Government securities
2. Loans to depository institutions

The Bank of Canada holds Government of Canada securities—Treasury bills—that it buys in the bills market. The Bank of Canada makes loans to depository institutions. When these institutions in aggregate are short of reserves, they can borrow from the Bank of Canada. In normal times this item is small, or zero as it was in 2011 (see Table 24.3).

The Bank of Canada's Liabilities The Bank of Canada has two liabilities:

1. Bank of Canada notes
2. Depository institution deposits

Bank of Canada notes are the dollar bills that we use in our daily transactions. Some of these notes are held by individuals and businesses; others are in the tills and vaults of banks and other depository institutions. Depository institution deposits at the Bank of Canada are part of the reserves of these institutions (see p. 571).

The Monetary Base The Bank of Canada's liabilities together with coins issued by the Royal Canadian Mint (coins are not liabilities of the Bank of Canada)

make up the monetary base. That is, the **monetary base** is the sum of Bank of Canada notes, coins, and depository institution deposits at the Bank of Canada. The monetary base is so named because it acts like a base that supports the nation's money. Table 24.3 provides a snapshot of the sources and uses of the monetary base in August 2011.

Open Market Operation To change the monetary base, the Bank of Canada conducts an **open market operation**, which is the purchase or sale of government securities by the Bank of Canada in the open market. Let's see how an open market operation works and what it does.

An Open Market Purchase An open market operation changes bank reserves. To see how, suppose the Bank of Canada buys $100 million of government securities from CIBC. When the Bank of Canada makes this transaction, two things happen:

1. CIBC has $100 million less securities, and the Bank of Canada has $100 million more securities.
2. The Bank of Canada pays for the securities by placing $100 million in CIBC's deposit account at the Bank of Canada.

Figure 24.1 shows the effects of these actions on the balance sheets of the Bank of Canada and CIBC. Ownership of the securities passes from CIBC to the Bank of Canada, so CIBC's assets decrease by $100 million and the Bank of Canada's assets increase by $100 million, as shown by the blue arrow running from CIBC to the Bank of Canada.

The Bank of Canada pays for the securities by placing $100 million in CIBC's reserve account, as shown by the green arrow running from the Bank of Canada to CIBC.

TABLE 24.3   The Sources and Uses of the Monetary Base

Sources (billions of dollars)		Uses (billions of dollars)	
Government of Canada securities	57.3	Notes	56.9
Loans to depository institutions	0	Reserves of depository institutions	0.4
Monetary base	57.3	Monetary base	57.3

Source of data: Statistics Canada CANSIM Table 176–0011. The data are for August 2011.

Economics in Action

A Tale of Two Central Banks

Figure 1 shows the balance sheet of the Bank of Canada. Almost all its assets (sources of monetary base) in part (a) are government securities. Almost all of its liabilities (uses of monetary base) in part (b) are notes and coins. The monetary base grew between 2007, the last year before a global financial crisis, and 2011 at an average annual rate of 4.5 percent.

Figure 2 shows the balance sheet of the U.S. Federal Reserve (the Fed). In 2007, before the financial crisis, this balance sheet looked like Canada's. Almost all its assets in part (a) were government securities and almost all of its liabilities in part (b) were notes and coins.

But through the financial crisis and still in place in mid-2011 and expected to be in place well into 2012, the Fed loaned billions of dollars to banks and other troubled institutions and created $1.8 trillion of monetary base—an increase of 125 percent or 22 percent per year on average. Most of this new monetary base is held by the banks as reserves.

When, and how quickly, the Fed unwinds this large increase in the monetary base and bank reserves will have a major influence on the U.S. and Canadian economies.

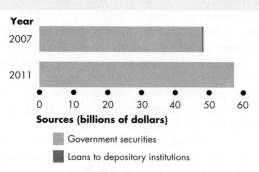

(a) Sources of monetary base

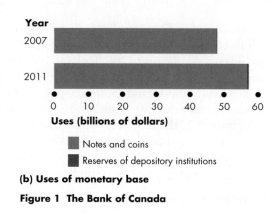

(b) Uses of monetary base

Figure 1 The Bank of Canada

Source of data: Statistics Canada, CANSIM Table 176–0011.

FIGURE 24.1   The Bank of Canada Buys Securities in the Open Market

The Bank of Canada

Assets		Liabilities	
Securities	+$100	Reserves of CIBC	+$100

The Bank of Canada buys securities from a bank ... | ... and pays for the securities by increasing the reserves of the bank

CIBC

Assets		Liabilities
Securities	–$100	
Reserves	+$100	

When the Bank of Canada buys securities in the open market, its assets and liabilities increase. The Bank creates bank reserves and CIBC exchanges securities for reserves.

—————— MyEconLab animation ◆

The Bank of Canada's assets and liabilities increase by $100 million. The CIBC's *total* assets are unchanged: It sold securities to increase its reserves.

An Open Market Sale If the Bank of Canada *sells* $100 million of government securities to CIBC:

1. CIBC has $100 million more securities and the Bank of Canada has $100 million less securities.
2. CIBC pays for the securities by using $100 million of its reserve deposit.

You can follow the effects of these actions by reversing the arrows and the plus and minus signs in Fig. 24.1. Ownership of the securities passes from the Bank of Canada to CIBC, so the Bank of Canada's assets decrease by $100 million and CIBC's assets increase by $100 million.

CIBC uses $100 million of its reserves to pay for the securities.

The Bank of Canada's assets and liabilities decrease by $100 million. CIBC's total assets are unchanged: It has used reserves to buy securities.

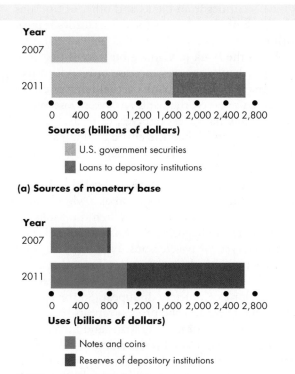

Year

2007

2011

0   400   800   1,200   1,600   2,000   2,400   2,800

Sources (billions of dollars)

◼ U.S. government securities

◼ Loans to depository institutions

(a) Sources of monetary base

Year

2007

2011

0   400   800   1,200   1,600   2,000   2,400   2,800

Uses (billions of dollars)

◼ Notes and coins

◼ Reserves of depository institutions

(b) Uses of monetary base

Figure 2   The U.S. Federal Reserve

Source of data: The Federal Reserve Board.

REVIEW QUIZ

1   What are Canada's depository institutions?
2   What are the functions of depository institutions?
3   How do depository institutions balance risk and return?
4   How do depository institutions create liquidity, pool risks, and lower the cost of borrowing?
5   How does the Bank of Canada differ from other banks?
6   What is the monetary base and how does it relate to the Bank of Canada's balance sheet?
7   What is an open market operation and how does it work?

You can work these questions in Study Plan 24.2 and get instant feedback.

───────────────────────── MyEconLab ◆

Next, we're going to see how the banking system—the banks and the Bank of Canada—creates money.

How Banks Create Money

Banks create money. But this doesn't mean that they have smoke-filled back rooms in which counterfeiters are busily working. Remember, money is both currency and bank deposits. What banks create is deposits, and they do so by making loans.

Let's see how this process works.

Creating Deposits by Making Loans

The easiest way to see that banks create deposits is to think about what happens when Andy, who has a Visa card issued by CIBC, uses his card to buy a tank of gas from Shell. When Andy signs the card sales slip, he takes a loan from CIBC and obligates himself to repay the loan at a later date. At the end of the business day, a Shell clerk takes a pile of signed credit card sales slips, including Andy's, to Shell's bank. For now, let's assume that Shell also banks at CIBC. The bank immediately credits Shell's account with the value of the slips (minus the bank's commission).

You can see that these transactions have created a bank deposit and a loan. Andy has increased the size of his loan (his credit card balance), and Shell has increased the size of its bank deposit. Because bank deposits are money, CIBC has created money.

If, as we've just assumed, Andy and Shell use the same bank, no further transactions take place. But the outcome is essentially the same when two banks are involved. If Shell's bank is the Royal Bank of Canada, then CIBC uses its reserves to pay the Royal Bank. CIBC has an increase in loans and a decrease in reserves; the Royal Bank has an increase in reserves and an increase in deposits. The banking system as a whole has an increase in loans and deposits but no change in reserves.

If Andy had swiped his card at an automatic payment pump, all these transactions would have occurred at the time he filled his tank, and the quantity of money would have increased by the amount of his purchase (minus the bank's commission for conducting the transactions).

Three factors limit the quantity of loans and deposits that the banking system can create through transactions like Andy's. They are

■ The monetary base
■ Desired reserves
■ Desired currency holding

The Monetary Base You've seen that the *monetary base* is the sum of Bank of Canada notes, coins, and banks' deposits at the Bank of Canada. The size of the monetary base limits the total quantity of money that the banking system can create. The reason is that banks have a desired level of reserves, households and firms have a desired holding of currency, and both of these desired holdings of the monetary base depend on the quantity of deposits.

Desired Reserves A bank's *desired reserves* are the reserves that it *plans* to hold. They contrast with a bank's *required reserves*, which is the minimum quantity of reserves that a bank *must* hold.

The quantity of desired reserves depends on the level of deposits and is determined by the **desired reserve ratio**—the ratio of reserves to deposits that the banks *plan* to hold. The *desired* reserve ratio exceeds the *required* reserve ratio by an amount that the banks determine to be prudent on the basis of their daily business requirements and in the light of the current outlook in financial markets.

Desired Currency Holding The proportions of money held as currency and bank deposits—the ratio of currency to deposits—depend on how households and firms choose to make payments: whether they plan to use currency or debit cards and cheques.

Choices about how to make payments change slowly so the ratio of desired currency to deposits also changes slowly, and at any given time this ratio is fixed. If bank deposits increase, desired currency holding also increases. For this reason, when banks make loans that increase deposits, some currency leaves the banks—the banking system leaks reserves. We call the leakage of bank reserves into currency the *currency drain*, and we call the ratio of currency to deposits the **currency drain ratio**.

We've sketched the way that a loan creates a deposit and described the three factors that limit the amount of loans and deposits that can be created. We're now going to examine the money creation process more closely and discover a money multiplier.

The Money Creation Process

The money creation process begins with an increase in the monetary base, which occurs if the Bank of Canada conducts an open market operation in which it buys securities from banks and other institutions. The Bank of Canada pays for the securities it buys with newly created bank reserves.

When the Bank of Canada buys securities from a bank, the bank's reserves increase but its deposits don't change. When a bank's actual reserves exceed its desired reserves, the bank has **excess reserves**. And when a bank has excess reserves, it makes loans and creates deposits. When the entire banking system has excess reserves, total loans and deposits increase and the quantity of money increases.

One bank can make a loan and get rid of excess reserves. But the banking system as a whole can't get rid of excess reserves so easily. When the banks make loans and create deposits, the extra deposits lower excess reserves for two reasons. First, the increase in deposits increases desired reserves. Second, a currency drain decreases total reserves. But excess reserves don't completely disappear. So the banks lend some more and the process repeats.

As the process of making loans and increasing deposits repeats, desired reserves increase, total reserves decrease through the currency drain, and eventually enough new deposits have been created to use all the new monetary base.

Figure 24.2 summarizes one round in the process we've just described. The sequence has the following eight steps:

1. Banks have excess reserves.
2. Banks lend excess reserves.
3. The quantity of money increases.
4. New money is used to make payments.
5. Some of the new money remains on deposit.
6. Some of the new money is a *currency drain*.
7. Desired reserves increase because deposits have increased.
8. Excess reserves decrease.

If the Bank of Canada *sells* securities in an open market operation, then banks have negative excess reserves—they are short of reserves. When the banks are short of reserves, loans and deposits decrease and the process we've described above works in a downward direction until desired reserves plus desired currency holding has decreased by an amount equal to the decrease in monetary base.

A money multiplier determines the change in the quantity of money that results from a change in the monetary base.

FIGURE 24.2   How the Banking System Creates Money by Making Loans

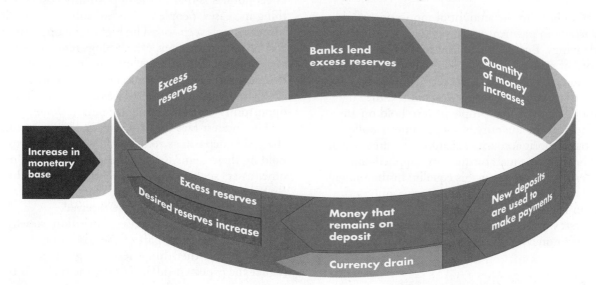

The Bank of Canada increases the monetary base, which increases bank reserves and creates excess reserves. Banks lend the excess reserves, which creates new deposits. The quantity of money increases. New deposits are used to make payments. Some of the new money remains on deposit at banks and some leaves the banks in a currency drain. The increase in bank deposits increases banks' desired reserves. But the banks still have excess reserves, though less than before. The process repeats until excess reserves have been eliminated.

MyEconLab   animation ◆

The Money Multiplier

The **money multiplier** is the ratio of the change in the quantity of money to the change in monetary base. For example, if a $1 million increase in the monetary base increases the quantity of money by $2.5 million, then the money multiplier is 2.5.

The smaller the banks' desired reserve ratio and the smaller the currency drain ratio, the larger is the money multiplier. (See the Mathematical Note on pp. 586–587 for details on the money multiplier.)

◆ REVIEW QUIZ

1   How do banks create money?
2   What limits the quantity of money that the banking system can create?
3   A bank manager tells you that she doesn't create money. She just lends the money that people deposit. Explain why she's wrong.

You can work these questions in Study Plan 24.3 and get instant feedback.
MyEconLab ◆

Economics in Action
The Variable Money Multipliers

We can measure the money multiplier, other things remaining the same, as the ratio of the quantity of money to the monetary base. Because there are two definitions of money, M1 and M2, there are two money multipliers. These money multipliers, it turns out, are not constant.

In 1990, the M1 multiplier—the ratio of M1 to the monetary base—was about 5.5; and the M2 multiplier—the ratio of M2 to the monetary base—was about 16. Through the 1990s and 2000s, the currency drain ratio gradually decreased and so did the reserve ratio of the banks. Because these two uses of monetary base decreased relative to deposits, the money multipliers increased.

By 2010 the M1 multiplier was 10, almost double its 1990 value, and the M2 multiplier was 18.

Because the money multipliers have increased over time, the quantity of monetary base has grown more slowly than the quantities of M1 and M2.

◆ The Money Market

There is no limit to the amount of money we would like to *receive* in payment for our labour or as interest on our savings. But there *is* a limit to how big an inventory of money we would like to *hold* and neither spend nor use to buy assets that generate an income. The *quantity of money demanded* is the inventory of money that people plan to hold on any given day. It is the quantity of money in our wallets and in our deposit accounts at banks. The quantity of money held must equal the quantity supplied, and the forces that bring about this equality in the money market have powerful effects on the economy, as you will see in the rest of this chapter.

But first, we need to explain what determines the amount of money that people plan to hold.

The Influences on Money Holding

The quantity of money that people plan to hold depends on four main factors:

- The price level
- The *nominal* interest rate
- Real GDP
- Financial innovation

The Price Level The quantity of money measured in dollars is *nominal money*. The quantity of nominal money demanded is proportional to the price level, other things remaining the same. If the price level rises by 10 percent, people hold 10 percent more nominal money than before, other things remaining the same. If you hold $20 to buy your weekly movies and pop, you will increase your money holding to $22 if the prices of movies and pop—and your wage rate—increase by 10 percent.

The quantity of money measured in constant dollars (for example, in 2002 dollars) is real money. *Real money* is equal to nominal money divided by the price level and is the quantity of money measured in terms of what it will buy. In the above example, when the price level rises by 10 percent and you increase your money holding by 10 percent, your *real* money holding is constant. Your $22 at the new price level buys the same quantity of goods and is the same quantity of *real money* as your $20 at the original price level. The quantity of real money demanded is independent of the price level.

The *Nominal* Interest Rate A fundamental principle of economics is that as the opportunity cost of something increases, people try to find substitutes for it. Money is no exception. The higher the opportunity cost of holding money, other things remaining the same, the smaller is the quantity of real money demanded. The nominal interest rate on other assets minus the nominal interest rate on money is the opportunity cost of holding money.

The interest rate that you earn on currency and chequable deposits is zero. So the opportunity cost of holding these items is the nominal interest rate on other assets such as a savings bond or Treasury bill. By holding money instead, you forgo the interest that you otherwise would have received.

Money loses value because of inflation, so why isn't the inflation rate part of the cost of holding money? It is. Other things remaining the same, the higher the expected inflation rate, the higher is the nominal interest rate.

Real GDP The quantity of money that households and firms plan to hold depends on the amount they are spending. The quantity of money demanded in the economy as a whole depends on aggregate expenditure—real GDP.

Again, suppose that you hold an average of $20 to finance your weekly purchases of movies and pop. Now imagine that the prices of these goods and of all other goods remain constant but that your income increases. As a consequence, you now buy more goods and services and you also keep a larger amount of money on hand to finance your higher volume of expenditure.

Financial Innovation Technological change and the arrival of new financial products influence the quantity of money held. Financial innovations include

1. Daily interest chequable deposits
2. Automatic transfers between chequable and saving deposits
3. Automatic teller machines
4. Credit cards and debit cards
5. Internet banking and bill paying

These innovations have occurred because of the development of computing power that has lowered the cost of calculations and record keeping.

We summarize the effects of the influences on money holding by using a demand for money curve.

The Demand for Money

The **demand for money** is the relationship between the quantity of real money demanded and the nominal interest rate when all other influences on the amount of money that people wish to hold remain the same.

Figure 24.3 shows a demand for money curve, *MD*. When the interest rate rises, other things remaining the same, the opportunity cost of holding money rises and the quantity of real money demanded decreases—there is a movement up along the demand for money curve. Similarly, when the interest rate falls, the opportunity cost of holding money falls, and the quantity of real money demanded increases—there is a movement down along the demand for money curve.

When any influence on money holding other than the interest rate changes, there is a change in the demand for money and the demand for money curve shifts. Let's study these shifts.

Shifts in the Demand for Money Curve

A change in real GDP or financial innovation changes the demand for money and shifts the demand for money curve.

Figure 24.4 illustrates the change in the demand for money. A decrease in real GDP decreases the demand for money and shifts the demand for money curve leftward from MD_0 to MD_1. An increase in real GDP has the opposite effect: It increases the demand for money and shifts the demand for money curve rightward from MD_0 to MD_2.

The influence of financial innovation on the demand for money curve is more complicated. It decreases the demand for currency and might increase the demand for some types of deposits and decrease the demand for others. But generally, financial innovation decreases the demand for money.

Changes in real GDP and financial innovation have brought large shifts in the demand for money in Canada.

FIGURE 24.3   The Demand for Money

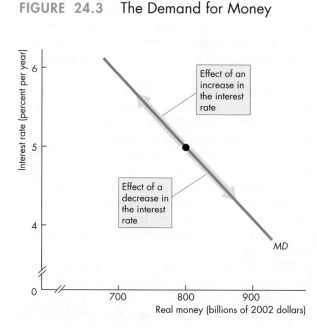

The demand for money curve, *MD*, shows the relationship between the quantity of real money that people plan to hold and the nominal interest rate, other things remaining the same. The interest rate is the opportunity cost of holding money. A change in the interest rate brings a movement along the demand for money curve.

FIGURE 24.4   Changes in the Demand for Money

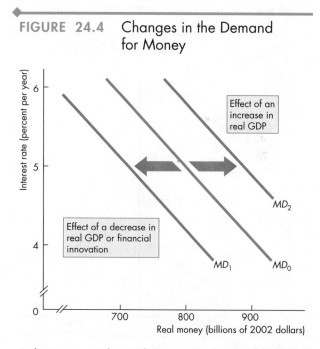

A decrease in real GDP decreases the demand for money. The demand for money curve shifts leftward from MD_0 to MD_1. An increase in real GDP increases the demand for money. The demand for money curve shifts rightward from MD_0 to MD_2. Financial innovation generally decreases the demand for money.

Money Market Equilibrium

You now know what determines the demand for money, and you've seen how the banking system creates money. Let's now see how the money market reaches an equilibrium.

Money market equilibrium occurs when the quantity of money demanded equals the quantity of money supplied. The adjustments that occur to bring money market equilibrium are fundamentally different in the short run and the long run.

Short-Run Equilibrium The quantity of money supplied is determined by the actions of the banks and the Bank of Canada. As the Bank of Canada adjusts the quantity of money, the interest rate changes.

In Fig. 24.5, the Bank of Canada uses open market operations to make the quantity of real money supplied $800 billion and the supply of money curve *MS*. With demand for money curve *MD*, the equilibrium interest rate is 5 percent a year.

If the interest rate were 4 percent a year, people would want to hold more money than is available.

FIGURE 24.5   Money Market Equilibrium

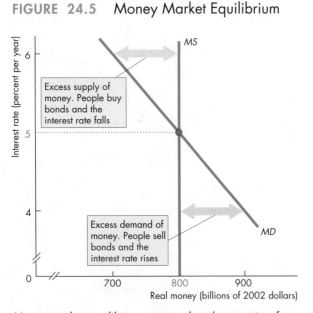

Money market equilibrium occurs when the quantity of money demanded equals the quantity supplied. In the short run, real GDP determines the demand for money curve, *MD*, and the Bank of Canada determines the supply of money curve, *MS*. The interest rate adjusts to achieve equilibrium, here 5 percent a year.

——MyEconLab animation ◆

They would sell bonds, bid down their price, and the interest rate would rise. If the interest rate were 6 percent a year, people would want to hold less money than is available. They would buy bonds, bid up their price, and the interest rate would fall.

The Short-Run Effect of a Change in the Supply of Money Starting from a short-run equilibrium, if the Bank of Canada increases the quantity of money, people find themselves holding more money than the quantity demanded. With a surplus of money holding, people enter the loanable funds market and buy bonds. The increase in demand for bonds raises the price of a bond and lowers the interest rate (refresh your memory by looking at Chapter 23, p. 548).

If the Bank of Canada decreases the quantity of money, people find themselves holding less money than the quantity demanded. They now enter the loanable funds market to sell bonds. The decrease in the demand for bonds lowers their price and raises the interest rate.

Figure 24.6 illustrates the effects of the changes in the quantity of money that we've just described. When the supply of money curve shifts rightward from MS_0 to MS_1, the interest rate falls to 4 percent a year; when the supply of money curve shifts leftward to MS_2, the interest rate rises to 6 percent a year.

Long-Run Equilibrium You've just seen how the nominal interest rate is determined in the money market at the level that makes the quantity of money demanded equal the quantity supplied by the Bank of Canada. You learned in Chapter 23 (on p. 552) that the real interest rate is determined in the loanable funds market at the level that makes the quantity of loanable funds demanded equal the quantity of loanable funds supplied. You also learned in Chapter 23 (on p. 549) that the real interest rate equals the nominal interest rate minus the inflation rate.

When the inflation rate equals the expected (or forecasted) inflation rate and when real GDP equals potential GDP, the money market, the loanable funds market, the goods market, and the labour market are in long-run equilibrium—the economy is in long-run equilibrium.

If in long-run equilibrium, the Bank of Canada increases the quantity of money, eventually a new long-run equilibrium is reached in which nothing real has changed. Real GDP, employment, the real quantity of money, and the real interest rate all return to their original levels. But something does

FIGURE 24.6 A Change in the Supply of Money

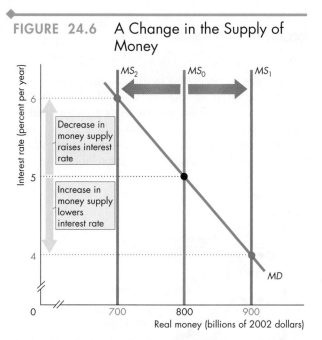

An increase in the supply of money shifts the supply of money curve from MS_0 to MS_1 and the interest rate falls. A decrease in the supply of money shifts the supply of money curve from MS_0 to MS_2 and the interest rate rises.

— MyEconLab animation ◆

change: the price level. The price level rises by the same percentage as the rise in the quantity of money. Why does this outcome occur in the long run?

The reason is that real GDP and employment are determined by the demand for labour, the supply of labour, and the production function—the real forces described in Chapter 22 (pp. 523–525); and the real interest rate is determined by the demand for and supply of (real) loanable funds—the real forces described in Chapter 23 (pp. 550–552). The only variable that is free to respond to a change in the supply of money in the long run is the price level. The price level adjusts to make the quantity of real money supplied equal to the quantity demanded.

So when the nominal quantity of money changes, in the long run the price level changes by the same percentage as the change in the quantity of nominal money. That is, the change in the price level is proportional to the change in the quantity of money.

The Transition from the Short Run to the Long Run

How does the economy move from the first short-run response to an increase in the quantity of money to the long-run response?

The adjustment process is lengthy and complex. Here, we'll only provide a sketch of the process. A more thorough account must wait until you've studied Chapter 26.

We start out in long-run equilibrium and the Bank of Canada increases the quantity of money by 10 percent. Here are the steps in what happens next.

First, the nominal interest rate falls (just like you saw on p. 580 and in Fig. 24.5). The real interest rate falls too, as people try to get rid of their excess money holdings and buy bonds.

With a lower real interest rate, people want to borrow and spend more. Firms want to borrow to invest and households want to borrow to invest in bigger homes or to buy more consumer goods.

The increase in the demand for goods cannot be met by an increase in supply because the economy is already at full employment. So there is a general shortage of all kinds of goods and services.

The shortage of goods and services forces the price level to rise.

As the price level rises, the real quantity of money decreases. The decrease in the quantity of real money raises the nominal interest rate and the real interest rate. As the interest rate rises, spending plans are cut back, and eventually the original full-employment equilibrium is restored. At the new long-run equilibrium, the price level has risen by 10 percent and nothing real has changed.

◢◣ REVIEW QUIZ

1 What are the main influences on the quantity of real money that people and businesses plan to hold?

2 Show the effects of a change in the nominal interest rate and a change in real GDP using the demand for money curve.

3 How is money market equilibrium determined in the short run?

4 How does a change in the supply of money change the interest rate in the short run?

5 How does a change in the supply of money change the interest rate in the long run?

You can work these questions in Study Plan 24.4 and get instant feedback.

————————— MyEconLab ◆

Let's explore the long-run link between money and the price level a bit further.

◆ The Quantity Theory of Money

In the long run, the price level adjusts to make the quantity of real money demanded equal the quantity supplied. A special theory of the price level and inflation—the quantity theory of money—explains this long-run adjustment of the price level.

The **quantity theory of money** is the proposition that in the long run, an increase in the quantity of money brings an equal percentage increase in the price level. To explain the quantity theory of money, we first need to define *the velocity of circulation*.

The **velocity of circulation** is the average number of times a dollar of money is used annually to buy the goods and services that make up GDP. But GDP equals the price level (P) multiplied by *real* GDP (Y). That is,

$$GDP = PY.$$

Call the quantity of money M. The velocity of circulation, V, is determined by the equation

$$V = PY/M.$$

For example, if GDP is $1,000 billion ($PY = $1,000 billion) and the quantity of money is $250 billion, then the velocity of circulation is 4.

From the definition of the velocity of circulation, the *equation of exchange* tells us how M, V, P, and Y are connected. This equation is

$$MV = PY.$$

Given the definition of the velocity of circulation, the equation of exchange is always true—it is true by definition. It becomes the quantity theory of money if the quantity of money does not influence the velocity of circulation or real GDP. In this case, the equation of exchange tells us that in the long run, the price level is determined by the quantity of money. That is,

$$P = M(V/Y),$$

where (V/Y) is independent of M. So a change in M brings a proportional change in P.

We can also express the equation of exchange in growth rates,[1] in which form it states that

$$\frac{\text{Money}}{\text{growth rate}} + \frac{\text{Rate of}}{\substack{\text{velocity} \\ \text{change}}} = \frac{\text{Inflation}}{\text{rate}} + \frac{\text{Real GDP}}{\text{growth rate}}$$

Economics in Action
Does the Quantity Theory Work?

On average, as predicted by the quantity theory of money, the inflation rate fluctuates in line with fluctuations in the money growth rate minus the real GDP growth rate. Figure 1 shows the relationship between money growth (M2 definition) and inflation in Canada. You can see a clear relationship between the two variables.

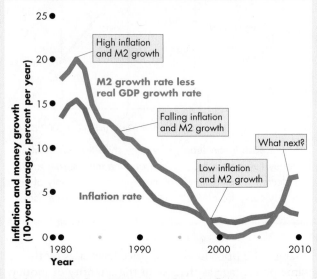

Figure 1 Canadian Money Growth and Inflation

Sources of data: Statistics Canada, CANSIM Tables 176–0020 and 380–0002.

Solving this equation for the inflation rate gives

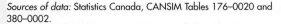

$$\frac{\text{Inflation}}{\text{rate}} = \frac{\text{Money}}{\text{growth rate}} + \frac{\text{Rate of}}{\substack{\text{velocity} \\ \text{change}}} - \frac{\text{Real GDP}}{\text{growth rate}}$$

In the long run, the rate of velocity change is not influenced by the money growth rate. More strongly, in the long run, the rate of velocity change

---

[1] To obtain this equation, begin with
$$MV = PY.$$
Then changes in these variables are related by the equation
$$V\Delta M + M\Delta V = Y\Delta P + P\Delta Y.$$
Divide this equation by the equation of exchange to obtain
$$\Delta M/M + \Delta V/V = \Delta P/P + \Delta Y/Y.$$
The term $\Delta M/M$ is the money growth rate, $\Delta V/V$ is the rate of velocity change, $\Delta P/P$ is the inflation rate, and $\Delta Y/Y$ is the real GDP growth rate.

International data also support the quantity theory. Figure 2 shows a scatter diagram of the inflation rate and the money growth rate in 134 countries and Fig. 3 shows the inflation rate and money growth rate in countries with inflation rates below 20 percent a year. You can see a general tendency for money growth and inflation to be correlated, but the quantity theory (the red line) does not predict inflation precisely.

The correlation between money growth and inflation isn't perfect, and the correlation does not tell us that money growth *causes* inflation. Money growth might cause inflation; inflation might cause money growth; or some third variable might cause both inflation and money growth. Other evidence does confirm, though, that causation runs from money growth to inflation.

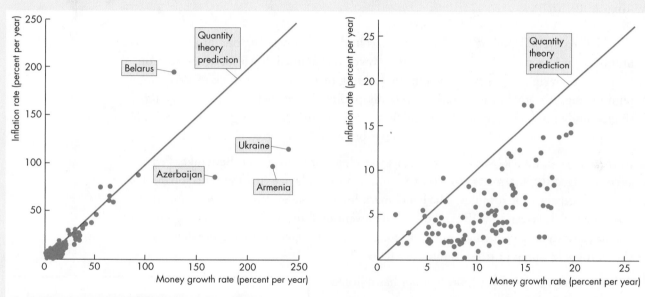

Figure 2 134 Countries: 1990–2005

Figure 3 Lower-Inflation Countries: 1990–2005

Sources of data: International Financial Statistics Yearbook, 2008 and International Monetary Fund, *World Economic Outlook*, October, 2008.

is approximately zero. With this assumption, the inflation rate in the long run is determined as

$$\text{Inflation rate} = \text{Money growth rate} - \text{Real GDP growth rate}.$$

In the long run, fluctuations in the money growth rate minus the real GDP growth rate bring equal fluctuations in the inflation rate.

Also, in the long run, with the economy at full employment, real GDP equals potential GDP, so the real GDP growth rate equals the potential GDP growth rate. This growth rate might be influenced by inflation, but the influence is most likely small and the quantity theory assumes that it is zero. So the real GDP growth rate is given and doesn't change when the money growth rate changes—inflation is correlated with money growth.

REVIEW QUIZ

1 What is the quantity theory of money?
2 How is the velocity of circulation calculated?
3 What is the equation of exchange?
4 Does the quantity theory correctly predict the effects of money growth on inflation?

You can work these questions in Study Plan 24.5 and get instant feedback.

———————————————— MyEconLab ◆

◆ You now know what money is, how the banks create it, and how the quantity of money influences the nominal interest rate in the short run and the price level in the long run. *Reading Between the Lines* on pp. 584–585 looks at the Fed's incredible actions in the recent financial crisis.

Can More Money Keep a Recovery Going?

It Falls to the Fed to Fuel Recovery

The Financial Times
August 30, 2010

The U.S. recovery is stalling. ... The recovery is in danger of petering out altogether. Recent numbers have been dismal. Second-quarter growth was marked down to 1.6 percent on Friday. Earlier, signs of a new crunch in the housing market gave the stock market another pummelling. Already low expectations were disappointed nonetheless: Sales of existing single-family homes in July fell by nearly 30 percent, to their lowest for 15 years. Sales of new homes were at their lowest since the series began to be reported in 1963. ...

At the end of last week, speaking at the Jackson Hole conference, Ben Bernanke, Fed chief, acknowledged the faltering recovery, and reminded his audience that the central bank has untapped capacity for stimulus. The benchmark interest rate is effectively zero, but that leaves quantitative easing (QE) and other unconventional measures. So far as QE goes, the Fed has already pumped trillions of U.S. dollars into the economy by buying debt. If it chose, it could pump in trillions more. ...

As the monetary economist Scott Sumner has pointed out, Milton Friedman—name me a less reconstructed monetarist—talked of "the fallacy of identifying tight money with high interest rates and easy money with low interest rates." When long-term nominal interest rates are very low, and inflation expectations are therefore also very low, money is tight in the sense that matters. When money is loose, inflation expectations rise, and so do long-term interest rates. ... Under current circumstances, better to print money and be damned. ...

ESSENCE OF THE STORY

- The 2010 second-quarter U.S. real GDP growth rate was a low 1.6 percent a year and home sales were at their lowest since measurement started in 1963.

- U.S. Federal Reserve Chairman Ben Bernanke agreed the recovery is weak but said the Fed has weapons to fight recession.

- Interest rates are close to zero but the Fed has pumped trillions of U.S. dollars into the economy by buying debt (quantitative easing) and the Fed can pump in trillions more.

- Economist Scott Sumner, citing Milton Friedman, says the interest rate that influences spending decisions is the real interest rate and that isn't low when inflation is expected to be low.

- With the U.S. recovery stalling and possibly ending, the Fed should pump in more money.

ECONOMIC ANALYSIS

- Between October 2007 and October 2008, to counter a global financial crisis, the U.S. Federal Reserve cut the interest rates to almost zero.

- Between October 2008 and October 2009, the Fed increased the monetary base by an unprecedented $900 billion.

- Between October 2009 and March 2010, the Fed added a further $300 billion to the monetary base—a total increase of $1.2 trillion over 18 months.

- Figure 1 shows these extraordinary increases in the U.S. monetary base.

- As you've seen in this chapter (on p. 575), most of the increase in monetary base was held by the banks. They increased their reserves.

- These monetary actions by the Fed lowered the interest rates that firms and households pay on very short-term loans, as you can see in Fig. 2.

- But the interest rate on long-term loans that finance business investment barely changed.

- You can see in Fig. 2 that the long-term corporate bond rate (the rate paid by the safest big firms) hovered around 5.5 percent.

- For the Fed's injection of monetary base to lower the long-term corporate bond rate, the banks would have to get into the loanable funds market and start to lend their large volume of reserves.

- As the news article notes, it is the real interest rate, not the nominal interest rate, that influences expenditure. And because for a few months, deflation (a falling price level) was expected, the real interest rate spiked upward.

- Figure 3 shows the real interest rate on long-term corporate borrowing.

- Despite massive injections of monetary base (quantitative easing) and powerful effects on the short-term interest rate, it is hard to see the effects of the Fed's actions on the long-term real interest rate.

- Increasing the monetary base further, as advocated in the news article, might lower the long-term real interest rate, but it might alternatively merely add to bank reserves and leave the long-term interest rate unchanged.

- The Bank of Canada cut Canadian interest rates in line with the U.S. interest rates but, as you saw on p. 574, this action didn't require a massive increase in Canada's monetary base.

- The prolonged period of low interest rates in the United States almost certainly means that Canada's interest rates will remain low for an extended period.

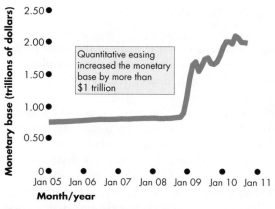

Figure 1 U.S. Monetary Base

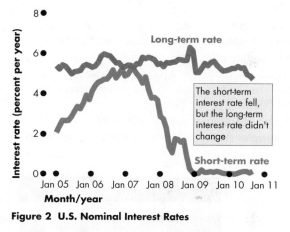

Figure 2 U.S. Nominal Interest Rates

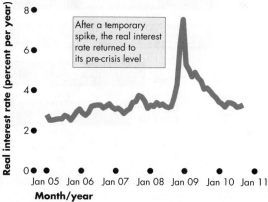

Figure 3 U.S. Long-term Real Interest Rate

- Low interest rates and a large increase in the quantity of money might increase the price level.

- A rapid increase in the growth rate of money might increase the inflation rate.

MATHEMATICAL NOTE

The Money Multiplier

This note explains the basic math of the money multiplier and shows how the value of the multiplier depends on the banks' desired reserve ratio and the currency drain ratio.

To make the process of money creation concrete, we work through an example for a banking system in which each bank has a desired reserve ratio of 10 percent *of deposits* and the currency drain ratio is 50 percent *of deposits*. (Although these ratios are larger than the ones in the Canadian economy, they make the process end more quickly and enable you to see more clearly the principles at work.)

The figure keeps track of the numbers. Before the process begins, all the banks have no excess reserves. Then the monetary base increases by $100,000 and one bank has excess reserves of this amount.

The bank lends the $100,000 of excess reserves. When this loan is made, new money increases by $100,000.

Some of the new money will be held as currency and some as deposits. With a currency drain ratio of 50 percent of deposits, one third of the new money will be held as currency and two thirds will be held as deposits. That is, $33,333 drains out of the banks as currency and $66,667 remains in the banks as deposits. The increase in the quantity of money of $100,000 equals the increase in deposits plus the increase in currency holdings.

The increased bank deposits of $66,667 generate an increase in desired reserves of 10 percent of that amount, which is $6,667. Actual reserves have increased by the same amount as the increase in deposits: $66,667. So the banks now have excess reserves of $60,000.

The process we've just described repeats but begins with excess reserves of $60,000. The figure shows the next round. At the end of the process, the quantity of money has increased by a multiple of the increase in the monetary base. In this case, the increase is $250,000, which is 2.5 times the increase in the monetary base.

The sequence in the figure shows the first stages of the process that finally reaches the total shown in the final row of the "money" column.

To calculate what happens at the later stages in the process and the final increase in the quantity of money, look closely at the numbers in the figure.

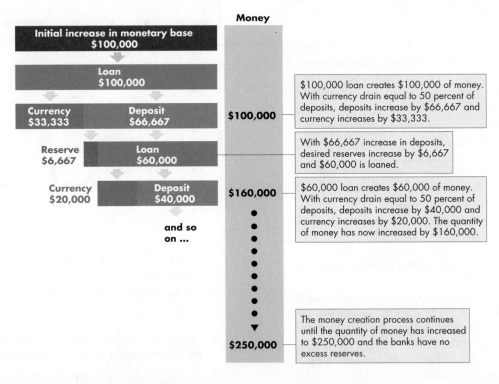

Figure 1 The money creation process

The initial increase in reserves is $100,000 (call it A). At each stage, the loan is 60 percent (0.6) of the previous loan and the quantity of money increases by 0.6 of the previous increase. Call that proportion L ($L = 0.6$). We can write down the complete sequence for the increase in the quantity of money as

$$A + AL + AL^2 + AL^3 + AL^4 + AL^5 + \dots \ .$$

Remember, L is a fraction, so at each stage in this sequence, the amount of new loans and new money gets smaller. The total value of loans made and money created at the end of the process is the sum of the sequence, which is[1]

$$A/(1 - L).$$

If we use the numbers from the example, the total increase in the quantity of money is

$100,000 + 60,000 + 36,000 + \dots$

$= \$100,000 \ (1 + 0.6 + 0.36 + \dots)$

$= \$100,000 \ (1 + 0.6 + 0.6^2 + \dots)$

$= \$100,000 \times 1/(1 - 0.6)$

$= \$100,000 \times 1/(0.4)$

$= \$100,000 \times 2.5$

$= \$250,000.$

The magnitude of the money multiplier depends on the desired reserve ratio and the currency drain ratio. Let's explore this relationship.

The money multiplier is the ratio of money to the monetary base. Call the money multiplier mm, the quantity of money M, and the monetary base MB.

Then

$$mm = M/MB.$$

Next recall that money, M, is the sum of deposits and currency. Call deposits D and currency C. Then

$$M = D + C.$$

Finally, recall that the monetary base, MB, is the sum of banks' reserves and currency. Call banks' reserves R. Then

$$MB = R + C.$$

Use the equations for M and MB in the mm equation to give:

$$mm = M/MB = (D + C)/(R + C).$$

Now divide all the variables on the right side of the equation by D to give:

$$mm = M/MB = (1 + C/D))/(R/D + C/D).$$

In this equation, C/D is the currency ratio and R/D is the banks' reserve ratio. If we use the values in the example on the previous page, C/D is 0.5 and R/D is 0.1, and

$$mm = (1 + 0.5)/(0.1 + 0.5)$$
$$= 1.5/0.6 = 2.5.$$

The Canadian Money Multiplier

The money multiplier in Canada can be found by using the formula above along with the values of C/D and R/D in Canada. With two definitions of money, M1 and M2, we have two money multipliers. Call the M1 deposits $D1$ and call the M2 deposits $D2$.

The numbers for M1 in 2010 are $C/D1 = 0.1059$ and $R/D1 = 0.0026$. So

M1 multiplier $= (1 + 0.1059)/(0.0026 + 0.1059)$

$= 10.2.$

For M2 in 2010, $C/D2 = 0.0577$ and $R/D2 = 0.0014$, so

M2 multiplier $= (1 + 0.0577)/(0.0014 + 0.0577)$

$= 17.9.$

---

[1] The sequence of values is called a convergent geometric series. To find the sum of a series such as this, begin by calling the sum S. Then write the sum as

$$S = A + AL + AL^2 + AL^3 + AL^4 + AL^5 + \dots \ .$$

Multiply by L to get

$$LS = AL + AL^2 + AL^3 + AL^4 + AL^5 + \dots$$

and then subtract the second equation from the first to get

$$S(1 - L) = A$$

or

$$S = A/(1 - L).$$

SUMMARY

Key Points

What Is Money? (pp. 568–570)

- Money is the means of payment. It functions as a medium of exchange, a unit of account, and a store of value.
- Today, money consists of currency and bank deposits.

Working Problems 1 to 4 will give you a better understanding of what money is.

The Banking System (pp. 571–575)

- The banking system consists of depository institutions (chartered banks, credit unions and caisses populaires, and trust and mortgage loan companies) whose deposits are money, and the Bank of Canada.
- Depository institutions provide four main economic services: They create liquidity, minimize the cost of obtaining funds, minimize the cost of monitoring borrowers, and pool risks.
- The Bank of Canada is Canada's central bank.

Working Problems 5 to 9 will give you a better understanding of the banking system.

How Banks Create Money (pp. 575–577)

- Banks create money by making loans.
- The total quantity of money that can be created depends on the monetary base, the desired reserve ratio, and the currency drain ratio.

Working Problems 10 to 14 will give you a better understanding of how banks create money.

The Money Market (pp. 578–581)

- The quantity of money demanded is the amount of money that people plan to hold.
- The quantity of real money equals the quantity of nominal money divided by the price level.
- The quantity of real money demanded depends on the nominal interest rate, real GDP, and financial innovation.
- The nominal interest rate makes the quantity of money demanded equal the quantity supplied.
- When the Bank of Canada increases the supply of money, the nominal interest rate falls (the short-run effect).
- In the long run, when the Bank of Canada increases the supply of money, the price level rises and the nominal interest rate returns to its initial level.

Working Problems 15 and 16 will give you a better understanding of the money market.

The Quantity Theory of Money (pp. 582–583)

- The quantity theory of money is the proposition that money growth and inflation move up and down together in the long run.
- Canadian and international evidence is consistent with the quantity theory of money, on average.

Working Problem 17 will give you a better understanding of the quantity theory of money.

Key Terms

Central bank, 572
Chartered bank, 571
Currency, 569
Currency drain ratio, 576
Demand for money, 579
Depository institution, 571
Desired reserve ratio, 576
Excess reserves, 576
Lender of last resort, 572
M1, 569

M2, 569
Means of payment, 568
Monetary base, 573
Money, 568
Money multiplier, 577
Open market operation, 573
Quantity theory of money, 582
Reserves, 571
Velocity of circulation, 582

SCAN THIS

STUDY PLAN PROBLEMS AND APPLICATIONS

MyEconLab ◆ You can work Problems 1 to 19 in Chapter 24 Study Plan and get instant feedback.

What Is Money? (Study Plan 24.1)

1. In Canada today, money includes which of the following items?
   a. Bank of Canada bank notes in CIBC's ATM machines
   b. Your Visa card
   c. Coins inside a vending machine
   d. A Bank of Canada $20 note in your wallet
   e. The cheque you have just written to pay for your rent
   f. The student loan you took out last August

2. In January 2011, currency was $57 billion and banks held $4 billion of notes and coins; personal chequable deposits were $204 billion; non-personal chequable deposits were $264 billion; personal non-chequable deposits were $159 billion; non-personal non-chequable deposits were $29 billion; and fixed term deposits were $306 billion. Calculate M1 and M2 in January 2011.

3. In May 2011, M1 was $537 billion; M2 was $1,034 billion; personal chequable deposits were $206 billion; non-personal chequable deposits were $273 billion; personal non-chequable deposits were $162 billion; and non-personal non-chequable deposits were $30 billion. Calculate currency held by individuals and businesses and calculate fixed term deposits.

4. **Money Transfers By Text Message**
   Bermuda residents will be able to transfer their money to almost anyone in the world via text messaging, thanks to a new service being offered by Bermuda Financial Network Ltd.
   Source: royalgazette.com, September 6, 2011
   If Canadian residents got the service that is coming to Bermuda residents, will currency disappear? How will the components of M1 change?

The Banking System (Study Plan 24.2)

Use the following news clip to work Problems 5 and 6.

BNP Paribas avoids Downgrade
Moody's credit rating agency says two of France's biggest banks are holding too much risky Greek government debt. Another French bank escaped a downgrade by selling €70bn of investments in risky yacht and jets-leasing businesses.
Source: cityam.com, September 15, 2011

5. Explain how this news clip illustrates a bank's "balancing act" and how the over-pursuit of profit or underestimation of risk can lead to a bank failure.

6. During a time of uncertainty, why might a bank sell some of its risky assets? What might it do with the funds it gets from the sell off?

7. Suppose that at the end of December 2010, the monetary base in Canada was $55 billion, and depository institutions were holding reserves at the Bank of Canada of $1 billion and notes and coins of $3 billion. What quantity of notes and coins was held outside the depository institutions?

8. **Risky Assets: Counting to a Trillion**
   Prior to the financial crisis, the U.S. Federal Reserve held less than $1 trillion in assets and most were in safe U.S. government securities. By mid-December 2008, the Fed's balance sheet had increased to over $2.3 trillion. The massive expansion began when the Fed rolled out its lending program: sending banks cash in exchange for risky assets.
   Source: CNN Money, September 29, 2009
   What did the U.S. Federal Reserve do to increase its assets to $2.3 trillion in 2008? Trace the types of transactions it must have undertaken.

9. The Bank of Canada sells $2 million of securities to the Bank of Nova Scotia. Enter the transactions that take place to show the changes in the following balance sheets.

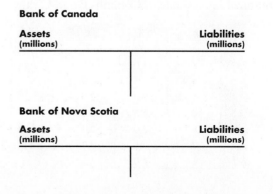

Bank of Canada

Assets (millions)	Liabilities (millions)

Bank of Nova Scotia

Assets (millions)	Liabilities (millions)

How Banks Create Money (Study Plan 24.3)

10. The commercial banks in Zap have

Reserves	$250 million
Loans	$1,000 million
Deposits	$2,000 million
Total assets	$2,500 million

If the banks hold no excess reserves, calculate their desired reserve ratio.

Use the following information to work Problems 11 and 12.

In the economy of Nocoin, banks have deposits of $300 billion. Their reserves are $15 billion, two thirds of which is in deposits with the central bank. Households and firms hold $30 billion in bank notes. There are no coins!

11. Calculate the monetary base and the quantity of money.

12. Calculate the banks' desired reserve ratio and the currency drain ratio (as percentages).

Use the following news clip to work Problems 13 and 14.

Banks Drop on Higher Reserve Requirement

China's central bank will raise its reserve ratio requirement by a percentage point to a record 17.5 percent, stepping up a battle to contain lending growth. Banks' ratio of excess reserves to deposits was 2 percent. Every half-point increase in the required reserve ratio cuts banks' profits by 1.5 percent.

Source: *People's Daily Online*, June 11, 2008

13. Explain how increasing the required reserve ratio impacts banks' money creation process.

14. Why might a higher required reserve ratio decrease bank profits?

The Money Market (Study Plan 24.4)

15. The spreadsheet provides information about the demand for money in Minland. Column A is the nominal interest rate, r. Columns B and C show

	A	B	C
1	r	Y_0	Y_1
2	7	1.0	1.5
3	6	1.5	2.0
4	5	2.0	2.5
5	4	2.5	3.0
6	3	3.0	3.5
7	2	3.5	4.0
8	1	4.0	4.5

the quantity of money demanded at two values of real GDP: Y_0 is $10 billion and Y_1 is $20 billion. The quantity of money supplied is $3 billion. Initially, real GDP is $20 billion. What happens in Minland if the interest rate (i) exceeds 4 percent a year and (ii) is less than 4 percent a year?

16. The figure shows the demand for money curve.

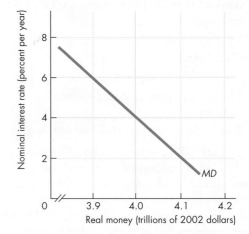

If the central bank decreases the quantity of real money supplied from $4 trillion to $3.9 trillion, explain how the price of a bond will change.

The Quantity Theory of Money (Study Plan 24.5)

17. Quantecon is a country in which the quantity theory of money operates. In year 1, the economy is at full employment and real GDP is $400 million, the price level is 200, and the velocity of circulation is 20. In year 2, the quantity of money increases by 20 percent. Calculate the quantity of money, the price level, real GDP, and the velocity of circulation in year 2.

Mathematical Note (Study Plan 24.MN)

18. In Problem 11, the banks have no excess reserves. Suppose that the Bank of Nocoin, the central bank, increases bank reserves by $0.5 billion.
    a. What happens to the quantity of money?
    b. Explain why the change in the quantity of money is not equal to the change in the monetary base.
    c. Calculate the money multiplier.

19. In Problem 11, the banks have no excess reserves. Suppose that the Bank of Nocoin, the central bank, decreases bank reserves by $0.5 billion.
    a. Calculate the money multiplier.
    b. What happens to the quantity of money, deposits, and currency?

ADDITIONAL PROBLEMS AND APPLICATIONS

MyEconLab ◆ You can work these problems in MyEconLab if assigned by your instructor.

What Is Money?

20. Sara withdraws $1,000 from her savings account at the TD Bank, keeps $50 in cash, and deposits the balance in her chequable account at the TD Bank. What is the immediate change in M1 and M2?

21. Rapid inflation in Brazil in the early 1990s caused the cruzeiro to lose its ability to function as money. Which of the following commodities would most likely have taken the place of the cruzeiro in the Brazilian economy? Explain why.
    a. Tractor parts
    b. Packs of cigarettes
    c. Loaves of bread
    d. Impressionist paintings
    e. Baseball trading cards

22. **From Paper-Clip to House, in 14 Trades**
    A 26-year-old Montreal man appears to have succeeded in his quest to barter a single, red paper-clip all the way up to a house. It took almost a year and 14 trades.
    Source: *CBC News*, July 7, 2006
    Is barter a means of payment? Is it just as efficient as money when trading on e-Bay? Explain.

The Banking System

Use the following news clip to work Problems 23 and 24.

Investment in the Future

The RBC says lines of credit for education are popular and the size of loans to students has been going up as tuition costs have increased. Compared to "good debt" like a mortgage, student loan rates are higher, because the debt is riskier. Financial institutions know that students need help and have created financial-management websites and other educational material to help students
Source: *Winnipeg Free Press*, September 17, 2011

23. Explain how this news clip illustrates the attempts by banks to maximize profits. Why are interest rates on student loans higher than those on mortgages?

24. Why would banks create websites to educate students about financial management?

25. How does a central bank differ from a chartered bank?

26. If the Bank of Canada makes an open market sale of $1 million of securities to a chartered bank, what initial changes occur in the economy?

27. Set out the transactions that the Bank of Canada must undertake to increase the quantity of money.

28. Describe the Bank of Canada's assets and liabilities. What is the monetary base and how does it relate to the Bank of Canada's balance sheet?

29. **World Central Banks Act as EU Growth Stalls**
    The European Central Bank (ECB), along with its U.S., Japanese, Swiss, and British counterparts, announced they would inject extra U.S. dollar liquidity into banks facing a shortage of the U.S. dollars.
    European bank shares have plunged over the past weeks as their usual sources of U.S. dollars have dried up on concerns they might be hit by a Greek debt default, and the announcement sparked a strong bank and general stocks rally.
    Source: AFP, September 15, 2011
    How can a group of central banks "inject extra U.S. dollar liquidity"? What will such an action do to the quantity of U.S. dollars in Europe?

How Banks Create Money

30. Banks in New Transylvania have a desired reserve ratio of 10 percent and no excess reserves. The currency drain ratio is 50 percent. Then the central bank increases the monetary base by $1,200 billion.
    a. How much do the banks lend in the first round of the money creation process?
    b. How much of the initial amount lent flows back to the banking system as new deposits?
    c. How much of the initial amount lent does not return to the banks but is held as currency?
    d. Why does a second round of lending occur?
    e. If the currency drain ratio increased to 60 percent, what would happen to the money multiplier?

f. If the desired reserve ratio decreased to 5 percent, what would happen to the money multiplier?

The Money Market

31. Explain the change in the nominal interest rate in the short run if
    a. Real GDP increases.
    b. The money supply increases.
    c. The price level rises.

32. In Minland in Problem 15, the interest rate is 4 percent a year. Suppose that real GDP decreases to $10 billion and the quantity of money supplied remains unchanged. Do people buy bonds or sell bonds? Explain how the interest rate changes.

The Quantity Theory of Money

33. The table provides some data for the United States in the first decade following the Civil War.

	1869	1879
Quantity of money	$1.3 billion	$1.7 billion
Real GDP (1929 dollars)	$7.4 billion	Z
Price level (1929 = 100)	X	54
Velocity of circulation	4.50	4.61

Source of data: Milton Friedman and Anna J. Schwartz, A Monetary History of the United States 1867–1960.

    a. Calculate the value of X in 1869.
    b. Calculate the value of Z in 1879.
    c. Are the data consistent with the quantity theory of money? Explain your answer.

Mathematical Note

34. In the United Kingdom, the currency drain ratio is 0.38 of deposits and the reserve ratio is 0.002. In Australia, the quantity of money is $150 billion, the currency drain ratio is 33 percent of deposits, and the reserve ratio is 8 percent.
    a. Calculate the U.K. money multiplier.
    b. Calculate the monetary base in Australia.

Economics in the News

35. After you have studied Reading Between the Lines on pp. 584–585, answer the following questions.
    a. What changes in the U.S. monetary base have occurred since October 2008?
    b. How did the Fed bring about an increase in the monetary base?
    c. How did the increase in the monetary base change the quantities of M1 and M2? Why?
    d. How did the change in monetary base influence short-term nominal interest rates? Why?
    e. How did the change in monetary base influence long-term nominal interest rates? Why?
    f. How did the change in monetary base influence long-term real interest rates? Why?

36. **Fed at Odds with ECB over Value of Policy Tool**

Financial innovation and the spread of U.S. currency throughout the world has broken down relationships between money, inflation, and growth, making monetary gauges a less useful tool for policy makers, the U.S. Federal Reserve chairman, Ben Bernanke, said. Many other central banks use monetary aggregates as a guide to policy decision, but Bernanke believes reliance on monetary aggregates would be unwise because the empirical relationship between U.S. money growth, inflation, and output growth is unstable. Bernanke said that the Fed had "philosophical" and economic differences with the European Central Bank and the Bank of England regarding the role of money and that debate between institutions was healthy. "Unfortunately, forecast errors for money growth are often significant," reducing their effectiveness as a tool for policy, Bernanke said. "There are differences between the U.S. and Europe in terms of the stability of money demand," Bernanke said. Ultimately, the risk of bad policy arising from a devoted following of money growth led the Fed to downgrade the importance of money measures.

Source: International Herald Tribune, November 10, 2006

    a. Explain how the debate surrounding the quantity theory of money could make "monetary gauges a less useful tool for policy makers."
    b. What do Bernanke's statements reveal about his stance on the accuracy of the quantity theory of money?

CHAPTER
25

The Exchange Rate and the Balance of Payments

After studying this chapter, you will be able to

◆ Explain how the exchange rate is determined

◆ Explain the trends and fluctuations in the exchange rate

◆ Explain the effects of alternative exchange rate policies

◆ Explain what causes international deficits and surpluses

The Canadian dollar—the loonie—is one of more than a hundred different monies. But most international payments are made using the U.S dollar ($), the euro (€), or the Japanese yen (¥). The value of the Canadian dollar rises and falls against these other monies. Why? Can or should Canada do anything to stabilize the value of its dollar? Sometimes we borrow from foreigners and at other times we repay our international debts. Why? What causes international deficits and surpluses?

In this chapter, you're going to discover the answers to these questions. And in *Reading Between the Lines* at the end of the chapter, we'll look at China's foreign exchange rate policy and see why it troubles many people.

◆ The Foreign Exchange Market

When Canadian Tire imports snow blowers from China, it pays for them using Chinese yuan. And when China Airlines buys an airplane from Bombardier, it pays using Canadian dollars. Whenever people buy things from another country, they use the currency of that country to make the transaction. It doesn't make any difference what the item is that is being traded internationally. It might be a snow blower, an airplane, insurance or banking services, real estate, the stocks and bonds of a government or corporation, or even an entire business.

Foreign money is just like Canadian money. It consists of notes and coins issued by a central bank and mint and deposits in banks and other depository institutions. When we described Canadian money in Chapter 24, we distinguished between notes and coins and bank deposits. But when we talk about foreign money, we refer to it as foreign currency. **Foreign currency** is the money of other countries regardless of whether that money is in the form of notes, coins, or bank deposits.

We buy these foreign currencies and foreigners buy Canadian dollars in the foreign exchange market.

Trading Currencies

The currency of one country is exchanged for the currency of another in the **foreign exchange market.** The foreign exchange market is not a place like a downtown flea market or a fruit and vegetable market. The foreign exchange market is made up of thousands of people—importers and exporters, banks, international investors and speculators, international travellers, and specialist traders called *foreign exchange brokers.*

The foreign exchange market opens on Monday morning in Sydney, Australia, and Hong Kong, which is still Sunday evening in Toronto. As the day advances, markets open in Singapore, Tokyo, Bahrain, Frankfurt, London, New York, Chicago, and San Francisco. As the West Coast markets close, Sydney is only an hour away from opening for the next day of business. The sun barely sets in the foreign exchange market. Dealers around the world are in continual contact by telephone and computer, and on a typical day in 2011, around $3 trillion (of all currencies) were traded in the foreign exchange market—or more than $600 trillion in a year.

Exchange Rates

An **exchange rate** is the price at which one currency exchanges for another currency in the foreign exchange market. For example, on September 1, 2011, one Canadian dollar would buy 79 Japanese yen. So the exchange rate was 79 yen per Canadian dollar.

The exchange rate fluctuates. Sometimes it rises and sometimes it falls. A rise in the exchange rate is called an *appreciation* of the dollar, and a fall in the exchange rate is called a *depreciation* of the dollar. For example, when the exchange rate rises from 79 yen to 100 yen per dollar, the dollar appreciates, and when the exchange rate falls from 100 yen to 79 yen per dollar, the dollar depreciates.

Economics in Action on the next page shows the fluctuations in the Canadian dollar against three currencies since 2000.

Questions About the Canadian Dollar Exchange Rate

The performance of the Canadian dollar in the foreign exchange market raises a number of questions that we address in this chapter.

First, how is the exchange rate determined? Why did the Canadian dollar appreciate against the U.S. dollar from 2003 to 2008, depreciate in 2009, and then appreciate?

Second, how do the Bank of Canada and other central banks operate in the foreign exchange market? In particular, how is the exchange rate between the Chinese yuan and other currencies determined and why did it remain constant against the U.S. dollar for many years?

Third, how do exchange rate fluctuations influence our international trade and international payments? Could we influence our international deficit by changing the exchange rate? Would an appreciation of the Chinese yuan change the balance of payments between China and the rest of the world?

We begin by learning how trading in the foreign exchange market determines the exchange rate.

An Exchange Rate Is a Price

An exchange rate is a price—the price of one currency in terms of another. And like all prices, an exchange rate is determined in a market—the *foreign exchange market.*

The Canadian dollar trades in the foreign exchange market and is supplied and demanded by

Economics in Action
The Canadian Dollar: More Up than Down

The figure shows the Canadian dollar exchange rate against the three currencies that feature prominently in Canadian imports—the U.S. dollar, the European euro, and the Japanese yen—between 2000 and 2011.

Against the U.S.dollar and the yen, the Canadian dollar has tended to appreciate. It depreciated only in 2008 and 2009. The Canadian dollar has fluctuated both up and down against the euro but has had no trend. It depreciated slightly against the euro up to 2005 and appreciated slightly after 2005.

Notice the high-frequency fluctuations (rapid brief up and down movements) of the value of the Canadian dollar against the other three currencies.

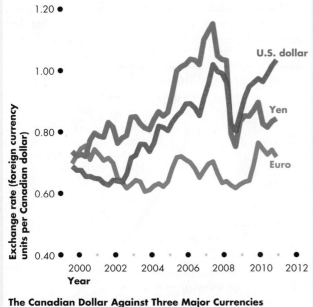

The Canadian Dollar Against Three Major Currencies

Source of data: Pacific Exchange Rate Service.

tens of thousands of traders every hour of every business day. Because it has many traders and no restrictions on who may trade, the foreign exchange market is a *competitive market*.

In a competitive market, demand and supply determine the price. So to understand the forces that determine the exchange rate, we need to study the factors that influence demand and supply in the foreign exchange market. But there is a feature of the foreign exchange market that makes it special.

The Demand for One Money Is the Supply of Another Money

When people who are holding the money of some other country want to exchange it for Canadian dollars, they demand Canadian dollars and supply that other country's money. And when people who are holding Canadian dollars want to exchange them for the money of some other country, they supply Canadian dollars and demand that other country's money.

So the factors that influence the demand for Canadian dollars also influence the supply of U.S. dollars, euros, or yen. And the factors that influence the demand for that other country's money also influence the supply of Canadian dollars.

We'll first look at the influences on the demand for Canadian dollars in the foreign exchange market.

Demand in the Foreign Exchange Market

People buy Canadian dollars in the foreign exchange market so that they can buy Canadian-produced goods and services—Canadian exports. They also buy Canadian dollars so that they can buy Canadian assets such as bonds, stocks, businesses, and real estate or so that they can keep part of their money holding in a Canadian dollar bank account.

The quantity of Canadian dollars demanded in the foreign exchange market is the amount that traders plan to buy during a given time period at a given exchange rate. This quantity depends on many factors, but the main ones are

1. The exchange rate
2. World demand for Canadian exports
3. Interest rates in Canada and other countries
4. The expected future exchange rate

We look first at the relationship between the quantity of Canadian dollars demanded in the foreign exchange market and the exchange rate when the other three influences remain the same.

The Law of Demand for Foreign Exchange The law of demand applies to Canadian dollars just as it does to anything else that people value. Other things remaining the same, the higher the exchange rate, the smaller is the quantity of Canadian dollars demanded in the foreign exchange market. For example, if the price of the Canadian dollar rises from 80 U.S. cents to 90 U.S. cents but nothing else changes, the quantity of Canadian dollars that people plan to buy in the foreign exchange market decreases.

The exchange rate influences the quantity of Canadian dollars demanded for two reasons:

- Exports effect
- Expected profit effect

Exports Effect The larger the value of Canadian exports, the larger is the quantity of Canadian dollars demanded in the foreign exchange market. But the value of Canadian exports depends on the prices of Canadian-produced goods and services *expressed in the currency of the foreign buyer*. And these prices depend on the exchange rate. The lower the exchange rate, other things remaining the same, the lower are the prices of Canadian-produced goods and services to foreigners and the greater is the volume of Canadian exports. So if the exchange rate falls (and other influences remain the same), the quantity of Canadian dollars demanded in the foreign exchange market increases.

To see the exports effect at work, think about orders for Bombardier's regional jet. If the price of a plane is $8 million and the exchange rate is 75 euro cents per Canadian dollar, the price of this airplane to KLM, a European airline, is €6 million. KLM decides that this price is too high, so it doesn't buy a new airplane. If the exchange rate falls to 60 euro cents per Canadian dollar and other things remain the same, the price of a regional jet falls to €4.8 million. KLM now decides to buy a plane from Bombardier and buys Canadian dollars in the foreign exchange market.

Expected Profit Effect The larger the expected profit from holding Canadian dollars, the greater is the quantity of Canadian dollars demanded in the foreign exchange market. But expected profit depends on the exchange rate. For a given expected future exchange rate, the lower the exchange rate today, the larger is the expected profit from buying Canadian dollars today and holding them, so the greater is the quantity of Canadian dollars demanded in the foreign exchange market today. Let's look at an example.

Suppose that Mizuho Bank, a Japanese bank, expects the exchange rate to be 120 yen per Canadian dollar at the end of the year. If today's exchange rate is also 120 yen per Canadian dollar, Mizuho Bank expects no profit from buying Canadian dollars and holding them until the end of

the year. But if today's exchange rate is 100 yen per Canadian dollar and Mizuho Bank buys Canadian dollars, it expects to sell those dollars at the end of the year for 120 yen per dollar and make a profit of 20 yen per Canadian dollar.

The lower the exchange rate today, other things remaining the same, the greater is the expected profit from holding Canadian dollars and the greater is the quantity of Canadian dollars demanded in the foreign exchange market today.

Demand Curve for Canadian Dollars

Figure 25.1 shows the demand curve for Canadian dollars in the foreign exchange market. A change in the exchange rate, other things remaining the same, brings a change in the quantity of Canadian dollars demanded and a movement along the demand curve. The arrows show such movements.

We will look at the factors that *change* demand in the next section of this chapter. Before doing that, let's see what determines the supply of Canadian dollars.

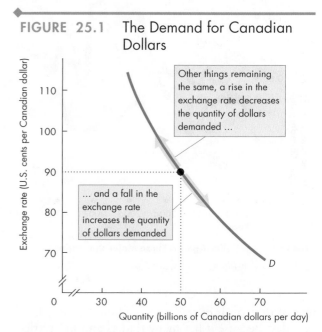

FIGURE 25.1 The Demand for Canadian Dollars

Other things remaining the same, a rise in the exchange rate decreases the quantity of dollars demanded ...

... and a fall in the exchange rate increases the quantity of dollars demanded

The quantity of Canadian dollars demanded depends on the exchange rate. Other things remaining the same, if the exchange rate rises, the quantity of Canadian dollars demanded decreases and there is a movement up along the demand curve of Canadian dollars. If the exchange rate falls, the quantity of Canadian dollars demanded increases and there is a movement down along the demand curve of Canadian dollars.

MyEconLab animation

Supply in the Foreign Exchange Market

People sell Canadian dollars and buy other currencies so that they can buy foreign-produced goods and services—Canadian imports. People also sell Canadian dollars and buy foreign currencies so that they can buy foreign assets such as bonds, stocks, businesses, and real estate or so that they can hold part of their money in bank deposits denominated in a foreign currency.

The quantity of Canadian dollars supplied in the foreign exchange market is the amount that traders plan to sell during a given time period at a given exchange rate. This quantity depends on many factors, but the main ones are

1. The exchange rate
2. Canadian demand for imports
3. Interest rates in Canada and other countries
4. The expected future exchange rate

Let's look at the law of supply in the foreign exchange market—the relationship between the quantity of Canadian dollars supplied in the foreign exchange market and the exchange rate when the other three influences remain the same.

The Law of Supply of Foreign Exchange   Other things remaining the same, the higher the exchange rate, the greater is the quantity of Canadian dollars supplied in the foreign exchange market. For example, if the exchange rate rises from 100 yen to 120 yen per Canadian dollar and other things remain the same, the quantity of Canadian dollars that people plan to sell in the foreign exchange market increases.

The exchange rate influences the quantity of dollars supplied for two reasons:

- Imports effect
- Expected profit effect

Imports Effect   The larger the value of Canadian imports, the larger is the quantity of Canadian dollars supplied in the foreign exchange market. But the value of Canadian imports depends on the prices of foreign-produced goods and services *expressed in Canadian dollars.* These prices depend on the exchange rate. The higher the exchange rate, other things remaining the same, the lower are the prices of foreign-produced goods and services to Canadians and the greater is the volume of Canadian imports. So if the exchange rate rises (and other influences remain the same), the quantity of Canadian dollars supplied in the foreign exchange market increases.

Expected Profit Effect   This effect works just like that on the demand for the Canadian dollar but in the opposite direction. The higher the exchange rate today, other things remaining the same, the larger is the expected profit from selling Canadian dollars today and holding foreign currencies, so the greater is the quantity of Canadian dollars supplied.

Supply Curve for Canadian Dollars

Figure 25.2 shows the supply curve of Canadian dollars in the foreign exchange market. A change in the exchange rate, other things remaining the same, brings a change in the quantity of Canadian dollars supplied and a movement along the supply curve. The arrows show such movements.

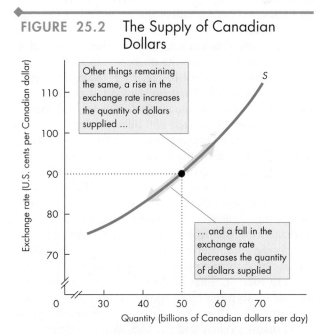

FIGURE 25.2   The Supply of Canadian Dollars

Other things remaining the same, a rise in the exchange rate increases the quantity of dollars supplied ...

... and a fall in the exchange rate decreases the quantity of dollars supplied

The quantity of Canadian dollars supplied depends on the exchange rate. Other things remaining the same, if the exchange rate rises, the quantity of Canadian dollars supplied increases and there is a movement up along the supply curve of Canadian dollars. If the exchange rate falls, the quantity of Canadian dollars supplied decreases and there is a movement down along the supply curve of Canadian dollars.

MyEconLab   animation   ◆

Market Equilibrium

Equilibrium in the foreign exchange market depends on how the Bank of Canada and other central banks operate. Here, we will study equilibrium when central banks keep out of this market. In a later section (on pp. 604–606), we examine the effects of alternative actions that the Bank of Canada or another central bank might take in the foreign exchange market.

Figure 25.3 shows the demand curve for Canadian dollars, *D*, from Fig. 25.1 and the supply curve of Canadian dollars, *S*, from Fig. 25.2, and the equilibrium exchange rate.

The exchange rate acts as a regulator of the quantities demanded and supplied. If the exchange rate is too high, there is a surplus—the quantity supplied exceeds the quantity demanded. For example, in Fig. 25.3, if the exchange rate is 100 U.S. cents per Canadian dollar, there is a surplus of Canadian dollars. If the exchange rate is too low, there is a shortage—the quantity supplied is less than the quantity demanded. For example, if the exchange rate is 80 U.S. cents per Canadian dollar, there is a shortage of Canadian dollars.

At the equilibrium exchange rate, there is neither a shortage nor a surplus—the quantity supplied equals the quantity demanded. In Fig. 25.3, the equilibrium exchange rate is 90 U.S. cents per Canadian dollar. At this exchange rate, the quantity demanded and the quantity supplied are each $50 billion a day.

The foreign exchange market is constantly pulled to its equilibrium by the forces of supply and demand. Foreign exchange traders are constantly looking for the best price they can get. If they are selling, they want the highest price available. If they are buying, they want the lowest price available. Information flows from trader to trader through the worldwide computer network, and the price adjusts minute by minute to keep buying plans and selling plans in balance. That is, the price adjusts minute by minute to keep the exchange rate at its equilibrium.

Figure 25.3 shows how the exchange rate between the Canadian dollar and the U.S. dollar is determined. The exchange rates between the Canadian dollar and all other currencies are determined in a similar way. So are the exchange rates among the other currencies. But the exchange rates are tied together so that no profit can be made by buying one currency, selling it for a second one, and then buying back the first one. If such a profit were available, traders would spot it, demand and supply would change, and the exchange rates would snap into alignment.

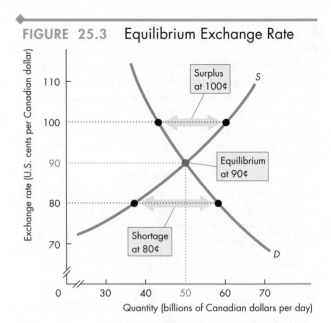

FIGURE 25.3   Equilibrium Exchange Rate

The demand curve for Canadian dollars is *D*, and the supply curve of Canadian dollars is *S*. If the exchange rate is 100 U.S. cents per Canadian dollar, there is a surplus of Canadian dollars and the exchange rate falls. If the exchange rate is 80 U.S. cents per Canadian dollar, there is a shortage of Canadian dollars and the exchange rate rises. If the exchange rate is 90 U.S. cents per Canadian dollar, there is neither a shortage nor a surplus of Canadian dollars and the exchange rate remains constant. The foreign exchange market is in equilibrium.

MyEconLab   animation

REVIEW QUIZ

1 What are the influences on the demand for Canadian dollars in the foreign exchange market?
2 Provide an example of the exports effect on the demand for Canadian dollars.
3 What are the influences on the supply of Canadian dollars in the foreign exchange market?
4 Provide an example of the imports effect on the supply of Canadian dollars.
5 How is the equilibrium exchange rate determined?
6 What happens if there is a shortage or a surplus of Canadian dollars in the foreign exchange market?

You can work these questions in Study Plan 25.1 and get instant feedback.

MyEconLab

Exchange Rate Fluctuations

You've seen (in the box on p. 595) that the Canadian dollar fluctuates against the U.S. dollar, the yen, and the euro. Changes in the demand for Canadian dollars or the supply of Canadian dollars bring these exchange rate fluctuations. We'll now look at the factors that make demand and supply change, starting with the demand side of the market.

A Change in Demand for Canadian Dollars

The demand for Canadian dollars in the foreign exchange market changes when there is a change in

- World demand for Canadian exports
- Canadian interest rate relative to the foreign interest rate
- The expected future exchange rate

World Demand for Canadian Exports An increase in world demand for Canadian exports increases the demand for Canadian dollars. To see this effect, think about Bombardier's airplane sales. An increase in demand for air travel in Australia sends that country's airlines on a global shopping spree. They decide that the Bombardier regional jet is the ideal product, so they order 50 airplanes from Bombardier. The demand for Canadian dollars now increases.

Canadian Interest Rate Relative to the Foreign Interest Rate People buy financial assets to make a return. The higher the interest rate that people can make on Canadian assets compared with foreign assets, the more Canadian assets they buy.

What matters is not the *level* of the Canadian interest rate, but the Canadian interest rate minus the foreign interest rate—a gap that is called the **Canadian interest rate differential**. If the Canadian interest rate rises and the foreign interest rate remains constant, the Canadian interest rate differential increases. The larger the Canadian interest rate differential, the greater is the demand for Canadian assets and the greater is the demand for Canadian dollars in the foreign exchange market.

The Expected Future Exchange Rate For a given current exchange rate, other things remaining the same, a rise in the expected future exchange rate increases the profit that people expect to make by

holding Canadian dollars and the demand for Canadian dollars increases today.

Figure 25.4 summarizes the influences on the demand for Canadian dollars. An increase in the demand for Canadian exports, a rise in the Canadian interest rate differential, or a rise in the expected future exchange rate increases the demand for Canadian dollars today and shifts the demand curve rightward from D_0 to D_1. A decrease in the demand for Canadian exports, a fall in the Canadian interest rate differential, or a fall in the expected future exchange rate decreases the demand for Canadian dollars today and shifts the demand curve leftward from D_0 to D_2.

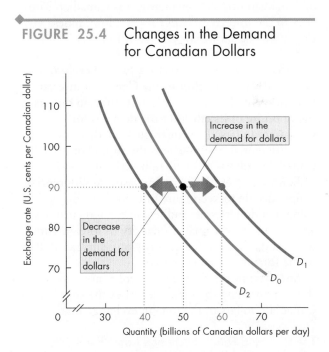

FIGURE 25.4 Changes in the Demand for Canadian Dollars

A change in any influence on the quantity of Canadian dollars that people plan to buy, other than the exchange rate, brings a change in the demand for Canadian dollars.

The demand for Canadian dollars

Increases if:

- World demand for Canadian exports increases
- The Canadian interest rate differential rises
- The expected future exchange rate rises

Decreases if:

- World demand for Canadian exports decreases
- The Canadian interest rate differential falls
- The expected future exchange rate falls

MyEconLab   animation

A Change in Supply of Canadian Dollars

The supply of Canadian dollars in the foreign exchange market changes when there is a change in

- Canadian demand for imports
- Canadian interest rate relative to the foreign interest rate
- The expected future exchange rate

Canadian Demand for Imports   An increase in the Canadian demand for imports increases the supply of Canadian dollars in the foreign exchange market. For example, an increase in demand for snow blowers sends Canadian Tire shopping in China. The supply of Canadian dollars now increases as Canadian Tire goes to the foreign exchange market for Chinese yuan to pay for the snow blowers that it imports.

Canadian Interest Rate Relative to the Foreign Interest Rate   The effect of the Canadian interest rate differential on the supply of Canadian dollars is the opposite of its effect on the demand for Canadian dollars. The larger the Canadian interest rate differential, the *smaller* is the supply of Canadian dollars in the foreign exchange market.

With a higher Canadian interest rate differential, people decide to keep more of their funds in Canadian dollar assets and less in foreign currency assets. They buy a smaller quantity of foreign currency and sell a smaller quantity of Canadian dollars in the foreign exchange market.

So, a rise in the Canadian interest rate, other things remaining the same, decreases the supply of Canadian dollars in the foreign exchange market.

The Expected Future Exchange Rate   For a given current exchange rate, other things remaining the same, a fall in the expected future exchange rate decreases the profit that can be made by holding Canadian dollars and decreases the quantity of Canadian dollars that people want to hold. To reduce their holdings of Canadian dollar assets, people must sell Canadian dollars. When they do so, the supply of Canadian dollars in the foreign exchange market increases.

Figure 25.5 summarizes the influences on the supply of Canadian dollars. If the supply of Canadian dollars decreases, the supply curve shifts leftward from S_0 to S_1. And if the supply of Canadian dollars increases, the supply curve shifts rightward from S_0 to S_2.

FIGURE 25.5   Changes in the Supply of Canadian Dollars

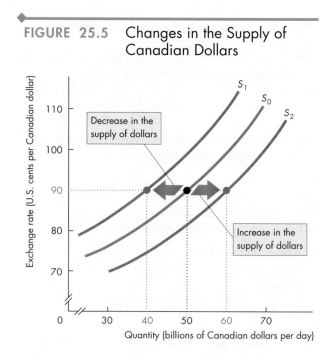

A change in any influence on the quantity of Canadian dollars that people plan to sell, other than the exchange rate, brings a change in the supply of dollars.

The supply for Canadian dollars

Increases if:

- Canadian demand for imports increases
- The Canadian interest rate differential falls
- The expected future exchange rate falls

Decreases if:

- Canadian demand for imports decreases
- The Canadian interest rate differential rises
- The expected future exchange rate rises

——————— MyEconLab   animation ◆

Changes in the Exchange Rate

If the demand for Canadian dollars increases and the supply does not change, the exchange rate rises. If the demand for Canadian dollars decreases and the supply does not change, the exchange rate falls. Similarly, if the supply of Canadian dollars decreases and the demand does not change, the exchange rate rises. If the supply of Canadian dollars increases and the demand does not change, the exchange rate falls.

These predictions are exactly the same as those for any other market. Two episodes in the life of the Canadian dollar (next page) illustrate these predictions.

Economics in Action
The Dollar on a Roller Coaster

The foreign exchange market is a striking example of a competitive market. The expectations of thousands of traders around the world influence this market minute-by-minute throughout the 24-hour global trading day.

Demand and supply rarely stand still and their fluctuations bring a fluctuating exchange rate. Two episodes in the life of the dollar illustrate these fluctuations: 2007–2009, when the dollar depreciated, and 2009–2011, when the dollar appreciated.

A Depreciating Canadian Dollar: 2007–2009

Between October 2007 and February 2009, the Canadian dollar depreciated against the U.S dollar. It fell from 100 U.S. cents to 80 U.S. cents per Canadian dollar. Part (a) of the figure illustrates this depreciation. In 2007, the demand and supply curves were those labelled D_{07} and S_{07}. The exchange rate was 100 U.S. cents per Canadian dollar.

During the last quarter of 2007 and the whole of 2008, the global economy was in recession. The demand by China and other Asian economies for Canadian energy and raw material exports decreased, which decreased the demand the Canadian dollars. The effect of the global recession on the Canadian dollar was anticipated by foreign exchange traders, who reacted by selling more Canadian dollars—an increase in the supply of Canadian dollars.

The combination of a decrease in demand for and an increase in supply of Canadian dollars sent the exchange rate down.

In part (a) of the figure, the demand curve shifted leftward from D_{07} to D_{09}, the supply curve shifted rightward from S_{07} to S_{09}, and the exchange rate fell to 80 U.S. cents per Canadian dollar.

An Appreciating Canadian Dollar: 2009–2011

Between February 2009 and May 2011, the Canadian dollar appreciated against the U.S. dollar. It rose from 80 U.S. cents to 103 U.S. cents per Canadian dollar. Part (b) of the figure illustrates this appreciation.

The demand and supply curves labelled D_{09} and S_{09} are the same as in part (a). During 2009 and 2010, the Asian economy began to expand rapidly and lead the world from recession. China's demand for Canadian energy and raw materials increased and so did the demand for the Canadian dollar.

Again, this increase in demand was anticipated and traders, expecting a higher Canadian dollar, held on to their dollars so the supply of Canadian dollars decreased. In the figure, the demand curve shifted rightward from D_{09} to D_{11} and the supply curve shifted leftward from S_{09} to S_{11}. The exchange rate rose to 103 U.S. cents per Canadian dollar.

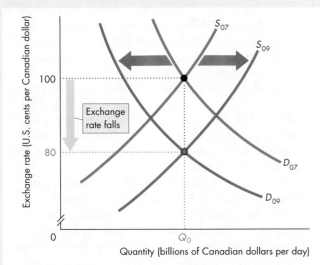

(a) 2007–2009

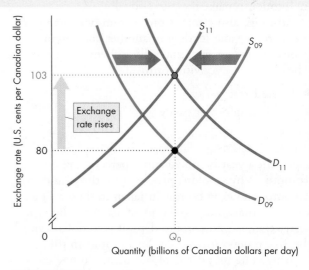

(b) 2009–2011

The Falling and Rising Canadian Dollar

Fundamentals, Expectations, and Arbitrage

Changes in the *expected* exchange rate change the *actual* exchange rate. But what makes the expected exchange rate change? The answer is new information about the *fundamental influences* on the exchange rate—the world demand for Canadian exports, Canadian demand for imports, and the Canadian interest rate relative to the foreign interest rate. Expectations about these variables change the exchange rate through their influence on the expected exchange rate, and the effect is instant.

To see why, suppose news breaks that the Bank of Canada will raise the interest rate next week. Traders now expect the demand for dollars to increase and the dollar to appreciate: They expect to profit by buying dollars today and selling them next week for a higher price than they paid. The rise in the expected future value of the dollar increases the demand for dollars today, decreases the supply of dollars today, and raises the exchange rate. The exchange rate changes as soon as the news about a fundamental influence is received.

Profiting by trading in the foreign exchange market often involves *arbitrage*—the practice of buying in one market and selling for a higher price in another related market. Arbitrage ensures that the exchange rate is the same in Toronto, New York, and all other trading centres. It isn't possible to buy at a low price in London and sell for a higher price in Toronto. If it were possible, demand would increase in London and decrease in Toronto to make the prices equal.

Arbitrage also removes profit from borrowing in one currency and lending in another and buying goods in one currency and selling them in another. These arbitrage activities bring about

- Interest rate parity
- Purchasing power parity

Interest Rate Parity   Suppose a bank deposit earns 1 percent a year in Tokyo and 3 percent a year in Toronto. Why wouldn't people move their funds to Toronto, and even borrow in Japan to do so? The answer is that some would, in an activity called the "carry trade." The Toronto deposit is in dollars and the Tokyo deposit is in yen. So a change in the exchange rate brings risk to borrowing in one currency and lending in another. If investors *expect* the yen to appreciate by 2 percent a year and they buy and hold yen for a year they will earn 1 percent interest and *expect* a 2 percent return from the higher

yen. The total *expected* return is 3 percent, the same as on Canadian dollars in Toronto.

This situation is called **interest rate parity**, which means *equal rates of return*. Adjusted for risk, interest rate parity always prevails. Funds move to get the highest *expected* return available. If for a few seconds a higher return is available in Toronto than in Tokyo, the demand for Canadian dollars increases and the exchange rate rises until the expected rates of return are equal.

Purchasing Power Parity   Suppose a memory stick costs 5,000 yen in Tokyo and $50 in Toronto. If the exchange rate is 100 yen per dollar, the two monies have the same value. You can buy a memory stick in either Tokyo or Toronto for the same price. You can express that price as either 5,000 yen or $50, but the price is the same in the two currencies.

The situation we've just described is called **purchasing power parity**, which means *equal value of money*. If purchasing power parity does not prevail, powerful arbitrage forces go to work. To see these forces, suppose that the price of a memory stick in Toronto rises to $60, but in Tokyo it remains at 5,000 yen. Further, suppose the exchange rate remains at 100 yen per dollar. In this case, a memory stick in Tokyo still costs 5,000 yen or $50, but in Toronto, it costs $60 or 6,000 yen. Money buys more in Japan than in Canada. Money is not of equal value in the two countries.

If all (or most) prices have increased in Canada and not increased in Japan, then people will generally expect that the value of the Canadian dollar in the foreign exchange market must fall. In this situation, the exchange rate is expected to fall. The demand for Canadian dollars decreases, and the supply of Canadian dollars increases. The exchange rate falls, as expected. If the exchange rate falls to 83.33 yen per dollar and there are no further price changes, purchasing power parity is restored. A memory stick that costs $60 in Toronto also costs the equivalent of $60 ($60 \times 83.33 = 5,000$) in Tokyo.

If prices rise in Japan and other countries but remain constant in Canada, then people will expect the Canadian dollar to appreciate. The demand for Canadian dollars increases, and the supply of Canadian dollars decreases. The exchange rate rises, as expected.

So far we've been looking at the forces that determine the *nominal* exchange rate—the amount of one money that another money buys. We're now going to study the *real* exchange rate.

The Real Exchange Rate

The **real exchange rate** is the relative price of Canadian-produced goods and services to foreign-produced goods and services. It is a measure of the quantity of the real GDP of other countries that a unit of Canadian real GDP buys. The real Canadian dollar–yen exchange rate, RER, is

$$RER = (E \times P)/P^*,$$

where E is the exchange rate (yen per Canadian dollar), P is the Canadian price level, and P^* is the Japanese price level.

To understand the real exchange rate, suppose that each country produces only one good and that the exchange rate E is 100 yen per dollar. Canada produces only computer chips priced at $150 each, so P equals $150 and $E \times P$ equals 15,000 yen. Japan produces only iPods priced at 5,000 yen each, so P^* equals 5,000 yen. Then the real Canadian dollar–Japanese yen exchange rate is

$$RER = (100 \times 150)/5,000 = 3 \text{ iPods per chip.}$$

The Short Run In the short run, if the nominal exchange rate changes, the real exchange rate also changes. The reason is that prices and the price levels in Canada and Japan don't change every time the exchange rate changes. Sticking with the chips and iPods example, if the dollar appreciates to 200 yen per dollar and prices don't change, the real exchange rate rises to 6 iPods per chip. The price of an iPod in Canada falls to $25 (5,000 yen ÷ 200 yen per dollar = $25).

Changes in the real exchange rate bring short-run changes in the quantity of imports demanded and the quantity of exports supplied.

The Long Run But in the long run, the situation is radically different: In the long run, the nominal exchange rate and the price level are determined together and the real exchange rate does *not* change when the nominal exchange rate changes.

In the long run, demand and supply in the markets for goods and services determine prices. In the chips and iPod example, the world markets for chips and iPods determine their *relative* price. In our example the relative price is 3 iPods per chip. The same forces determine all relative prices and so determine nations' relative price levels.

In the long run, if the dollar appreciates prices *do* change. To see why, recall the quantity theory of money that you met in Chapter 24 (pp. 582–583).

In the long run, the quantity of money determines the price level. But the quantity theory of money applies to all countries, so the quantity of money in Japan determines the price level in Japan, and the quantity of money in Canada determines the price level in Canada.

For a given real exchange rate, a change in the quantity of money brings a change in the price level *and* a change in the exchange rate.

Suppose that the quantity of money doubles in Japan. The dollar appreciates (the yen depreciates) from 100 yen per dollar to 200 yen per dollar and all prices double, so the price of an iPod rises from 5,000 yen to 10,000 yen.

At the new price in Japan and the new exchange rate, an iPod still costs $50 (10,000 yen ÷ 200 yen per dollar = $50). The real exchange rate remains at 3 iPods per chip.

If Japan and Canada produced identical goods (if GDP in both countries consisted only of computer chips), the real exchange rate in the long run would equal 1.

In reality, although there is overlap in what each country produces, Canadian real GDP is a different bundle of goods and services from Japanese real GDP. So the relative price of Japanese and Canadian real GDP—the real exchange rate—is not 1, and it changes over time. The forces of demand and supply in the markets for the millions of goods and services that make up real GDP determine the relative price of Japanese and Canadian real GDP, and changes in these forces change the real exchange rate.

REVIEW QUIZ

1 Why do the demand for and supply of Canadian dollars change?
2 What makes the Canadian dollar exchange rate fluctuate?
3 What is interest rate parity and what happens when this condition doesn't hold?
4 What is purchasing power parity and what happens when this condition doesn't hold?
5 What determines the real exchange rate and the nominal exchange rate in the short run?
6 What determines the real exchange rate and the nominal exchange rate in the long run?

You can work these questions in Study Plan 25.2 and get instant feedback.

MyEconLab ◆

Exchange Rate Policy

Because the exchange rate is the price of a country's money in terms of another country's money, governments and central banks must have a policy towards the exchange rate. Three possible exchange rate policies are

- Flexible exchange rate
- Fixed exchange rate
- Crawling peg

Flexible Exchange Rate

A **flexible exchange rate** is an exchange rate that is determined by demand and supply in the foreign exchange market with no direct intervention by the central bank.

Most countries, including Canada, operate a flexible exchange rate, and the foreign exchange market that we have studied so far in this chapter is an example of a flexible exchange rate regime.

But even a flexible exchange rate is influenced by central bank actions. If the Bank of Canada raises the Canadian interest rate and other countries keep their interest rates unchanged, the demand for Canadian dollars increases, the supply of Canadian dollars decreases, and the exchange rate rises. (Similarly, if the Bank of Canada lowers the Canadian interest rate, the demand for Canadian dollars decreases, the supply increases, and the exchange rate falls.)

In a flexible exchange rate regime, when the central bank changes the interest rate, its purpose is not usually to influence the exchange rate, but to achieve some other monetary policy objective. (We return to this topic at length in Chapter 30.)

Fixed Exchange Rate

A **fixed exchange rate** is an exchange rate that is determined by a decision of the government or the central bank and is achieved by central bank intervention in the foreign exchange market to block the unregulated forces of demand and supply.

The world economy operated a fixed exchange rate regime from the end of World War II to the early 1970s. China had a fixed exchange rate until recently. Hong Kong has had a fixed exchange rate for many years and continues with that policy today.

Active intervention in the foreign exchange market is required to achieve a fixed exchange rate.

If the Bank of Canada wanted to fix the Canadian dollar exchange rate against the U.S. dollar, the Bank of Canada would have to sell Canadian dollars to prevent the exchange rate from rising above the target value and buy Canadian dollars to prevent the exchange rate from falling below the target value.

There is no limit to the quantity of Canadian dollars that the Bank of Canada can *sell*. The Bank of Canada creates Canadian dollars and can create any quantity it chooses. But there is a limit to the quantity of Canadian dollars the Bank of Canada can *buy*. That limit is set by Canadian official foreign currency reserves because to buy Canadian dollars the Bank of Canada must sell foreign currency. Intervention to buy Canadian dollars stops when Canadian official foreign currency reserves run out.

Let's look at the foreign exchange interventions that the Bank of Canada can make.

Suppose the Bank of Canada wants to keep the exchange rate at 90 U.S. cents per Canadian dollar. If the exchange rate rises above 90 cents, the Bank sells Canadian dollars. If the exchange rate falls below 90 cents, the Bank buys Canadian dollars. By these actions, the Bank keeps the exchange rate close to its target rate of 90 U.S. cents per Canadian dollar.

Figure 25.6 shows the Bank of Canada's intervention in the foreign exchange market. The supply of Canadian dollars is S and initially the demand for dollars is D_0. The equilibrium exchange rate is 90 U.S. cents per Canadian dollar. This exchange rate is also the Bank of Canada's target exchange rate, shown by the horizontal red line.

When the demand for Canadian dollars increases and the demand curve shifts rightward to D_1, the Bank of Canada sells 10 billion Canadian dollars. This action prevents the exchange rate from rising. When the demand for Canadian dollars decreases and the demand curve shifts leftward to D_2, the Bank of Canada buys 10 billion Canadian dollars. This action prevents the exchange rate from falling.

If the demand for Canadian dollars fluctuates between D_1 and D_2 and on average is D_0, the Bank can repeatedly intervene in the way we've just seen. Sometimes the Bank of Canada buys and sometimes it sells but, on average, it neither buys nor sells.

But suppose the demand for Canadian dollars *increases permanently* from D_0 to D_1. To maintain the exchange rate at 90 U.S. cents per Canadian dollar, the Bank of Canada must sell Canadian dollars and buy foreign currency, so Canadian official foreign currency reserves would be increasing. At some point, the Bank of Canada would abandon the exchange rate of 90 U.S. cents per Canadian dollar and stop piling up foreign currency reserves.

FIGURE 25.6   Foreign Exchange Market Intervention

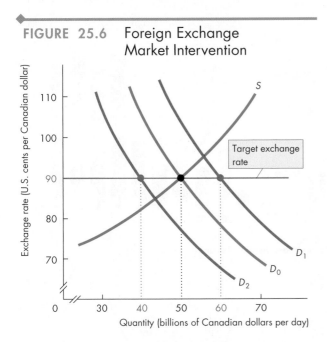

Initially, the demand for Canadian dollars is D_0, the supply of Canadian dollars is S, and the exchange rate is 90 U.S. cents per Canadian dollar. The Bank of Canada can intervene in the foreign exchange market to keep the exchange rate close to its target rate (90 U.S. cents in this example). If the demand for Canadian dollars increases and the demand curve shifts from D_0 to D_1, the Bank of Canada sells Canadian dollars. If the demand for Canadian dollars decreases and the demand curve shifts from D_0 to D_2, the Bank of Canada buys Canadian dollars. Persistent intervention on one side of the market cannot be sustained.

—— MyEconLab   ⟨animation⟩   ◆

Now suppose the demand for Canadian dollars *decreases permanently* from D_0 to D_2. In this situation, the Bank of Canada *cannot* maintain the exchange rate at 90 U.S. cents per Canadian dollar indefinitely. To hold the exchange rate at 90 U.S. cents, the Bank of Canada must *buy* Canadian dollars. When the Bank of Canada buys Canadian dollars in the foreign exchange market, it uses Canadian official foreign currency reserves. So the Bank of Canada's action decreases its foreign currency reserves. Eventually, the Bank of Canada would run out of foreign currency and would then have to abandon the target exchange rate of 90 U.S. cents per Canadian dollar.

Crawling Peg

A **crawling peg** is an exchange rate that follows a path determined by a decision of the government or the central bank and is achieved in a similar way to a fixed exchange rate by central bank intervention in the foreign exchange market. A crawling peg works like a fixed exchange rate except that the target value changes. The target might change at fixed intervals (daily, weekly, monthly) or at random intervals.

The Bank of Canada has never operated a crawling peg, but some prominent countries do use this system. When China abandoned its fixed exchange rate, it replaced it with a crawling peg. Developing countries might use a crawling peg as a method of trying to control inflation—of keeping the inflation rate close to target.

The ideal crawling peg sets a target for the exchange rate equal to the equilibrium exchange rate

Economics in Action
The People's Bank of China in the Foreign Exchange Market

The exchange rate between the Chinese yuan and the U.S. dollar was constant for several years before 2005. The reason for this constant exchange rate is that China's central bank, the People's Bank of China, intervened to operate a *fixed exchange rate policy*. From 1997 until 2005, the yuan was pegged at 8.28 yuan per U.S. dollar. Since 2005, the yuan has appreciated but it has not been permitted to fluctuate freely. Since 2005, the yuan has been on a crawling peg.

Why Does China Manage Its Exchange Rate? The popular story is that China manages its exchange rate to keep its export prices low and to make it easier to compete in world markets. You've seen that this story is correct *only in the short run*. With prices in China unchanged, a lower yuan–U.S. dollar exchange rate brings lower U.S. dollar prices for China's exports. But the yuan–U.S. dollar exchange rate was fixed for almost 10 years and has been managed for 5 more years. This long period of a fixed exchange rate has long-run, not short-run, effects. In the long run, the exchange rate has no effect on competitiveness. The reason is that prices adjust to reflect the exchange rate and the real exchange rate is unaffected by the nominal exchange rate.

So why does China fix its exchange rate? The most convincing answer is that China sees a fixed exchange rate as a way of controlling its inflation rate. By making the yuan crawl against the U.S. dollar, China's inflation rate is anchored to the U.S. inflation rate and will depart from U.S. inflation by an amount determined by the speed of the crawl.

The bottom line is that in the long run, exchange rate policy is monetary policy, not foreign trade policy. To change its exports and imports, a country must change its comparative advantage (Chapter 2).

How Does China Manage Its Exchange Rate? The People's Bank pegs the yuan by intervening in the foreign exchange market and buying U.S. dollars. But to do so, it must pile up U.S. dollars.

Part (a) of the figure shows the scale of China's increase in official foreign currency reserves, some of which are euros and yen but most of which are U.S. dollars. You can see that China's reserves increased by more than $400 billion in 2007, 2008, 2009, and 2010.

The demand and supply curves in part (b) of the figure illustrate what is happening in the market for U.S. dollars priced in terms of the yuan and explains why China's reserves have increased. The demand curve *D* and supply curve *S* intersect at 5 yuan per U.S. dollar. If the People's Bank of China takes no actions in the market, this exchange rate is the equilibrium rate (an assumed value).

The consequence of the fixed (and crawling peg) yuan exchange rate is that China has piled up U.S. dollar reserves on a huge scale. At the end of 2005, China's official foreign currency reserves were $820 billion and by the end of 2011, they had reached $2.8 trillion!

If the People's Bank stopped buying U.S. dollars, the U.S. dollar would depreciate and the yuan would appreciate—the yuan–U.S. dollar exchange rate would fall—and China would stop piling up U.S. dollar reserves.

In the example in the figure, the dollar would depreciate to 5 yuan per dollar.

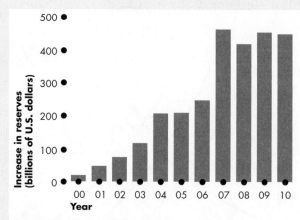

(a) Increase in U.S. dollar reserves

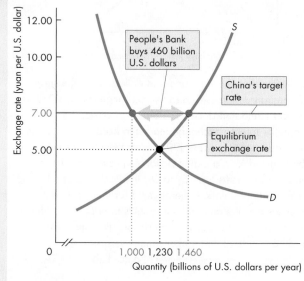

(b) Pegging the yuan

China's Foreign Exchange Market Intervention

on average. The peg seeks only to prevent large swings in the expected future exchange rate that change demand and supply and make the exchange rate fluctuate too wildly.

A crawling peg departs from the ideal if, as often happens with a fixed exchange rate, the target rate departs from the equilibrium exchange rate for too long. When this happens, the country either runs out of reserves or piles up reserves.

Reading Between the Lines on pp. 612–613 looks further at China's crawling peg exchange rate policy.

In the final part of this chapter, we explain how the balance of international payments is determined.

REVIEW QUIZ

1 What is a flexible exchange rate and how does it work?
2 What is a fixed exchange rate and how is its value fixed?
3 What is a crawling peg and how does it work?
4 How has China operated in the foreign exchange market, why, and with what effect?

You can work these questions in Study Plan 25.3 and get instant feedback.

◆ Financing International Trade

You now know how the exchange rate is determined, but what is the effect of the exchange rate? How does currency depreciation or currency appreciation influence our international trade and payments? We're going to lay the foundation for addressing these questions by looking at the scale of international trading, borrowing, and lending and at the way in which we keep our records of international transactions. These records are called the *balance of payments accounts.*

Balance of Payments Accounts

A country's **balance of payments accounts** records its international trading, borrowing, and lending in three accounts:

1. Current account
2. Capital and financial account
3. Official settlements account

The **current account** records receipts from exports of goods and services sold abroad, payments for imports of goods and services from abroad, net interest income paid abroad, and net transfers abroad (such as foreign aid payments). The *current account balance* equals the sum of exports minus imports, net interest income, and net transfers.

The **capital and financial account** records foreign investment in Canada minus Canadian investment abroad. (This account also has a statistical discrepancy that arises from errors and omissions in measuring international capital transactions.)

The **official settlements account** records the change in **Canadian official reserves**, which are the government's holdings of foreign currency. If Canadian official reserves *increase*, the official settlements account balance is *negative*. The reason is that holding foreign money is like investing abroad. Canadian investment abroad is a minus item in the capital and financial account and in the official settlements account.

The sum of the balances on the three accounts *always* equals zero. That is, to pay for our current account deficit, we must either borrow more from abroad than we lend abroad or use our official reserves to cover the shortfall.

Table 25.1 shows the Canadian balance of payments accounts in 2010. Items in the current account and the capital and financial account that provide foreign currency to Canada have a plus sign; items that cost Canada foreign currency have a minus sign. The table shows that in 2010, Canadian imports exceeded Canadian exports and the current account had a deficit of $51 billion. How do we pay for imports that exceed the value of our exports? That is, how do we pay for our current account deficit?

We pay by borrowing from the rest of the world. The capital account tells us by how much. We borrowed from the rest of the world (foreign investment in Canada) and we lent to the rest of the world (Canadian investment abroad). Our *net* foreign borrowing was $54 billion. There is almost always a statistical discrepancy between our capital account and current account transactions, and in 2010, the discrepancy was $1 billion. Combining the discrepancy with the measured net foreign borrowing gives a capital and financial account balance of $55 billion.

TABLE 25.1   Canadian Balance of Payments Accounts in 2010

Current account	Billions of dollars
Exports of goods and services	+476
Imports of goods and services	−508
Net interest income	+16
Net transfers	−3
Current account balance	−51

Capital and financial account	
Net foreign investment in Canada	+54
Statistical discrepancy	1
Capital and financial account balance	+55

Official settlements account	
Official settlements account balance	−4

Source of data: Statistics Canada CANSIM Tables 376–0001 and 376–0002.

The capital and financial account balance plus the current account balance equals the change in Canadian official reserves. In 2010, the capital and financial account balance of $55 billion plus the current account balance of –$51 billion equalled $4 billion. Official reserves *increased* in 2010 by $4 billion. Holding more foreign reserves is like lending to the rest of the world, so this amount appears in the official settlements account in Table 25.1 as –$4 billion. The sum of the balances on the three balance of payments accounts equals zero.

To see more clearly what the nation's balance of payments accounts mean, think about your own balance of payments accounts. They are similar to the nation's accounts.

An Individual's Balance of Payments Accounts An individual's current account records the income from supplying the services of factors of production and the expenditure on goods and services. Consider Jackie, for example. She worked in 2010 and earned an income of $25,000. Jackie has $10,000 worth of investments that earned her an interest income of $1,000. Jackie's current account shows an income of $26,000. Jackie spent $18,000 buying consumption goods and services. She also bought a new house, which cost her $60,000. So Jackie's total expenditure was $78,000. Jackie's expenditure minus her income is $52,000 ($78,000 minus $26,000). This amount is Jackie's current account deficit.

Economics in Action
Three Decades of Deficits

The numbers that you reviewed in Table 25.1 give a snapshot of the balance of payments accounts in 2010. The figure below puts that snapshot into perspective by showing the balance of payments between 1985 and 2010.

Because the economy grows and the price level rises, changes in the dollar value of the balance of payments do not convey much information. To remove the influences of economic growth and infla-

tion, the figure shows the balance of payments expressed as a percentage of nominal GDP.

As you can see, a large current account deficit emerged during the 1980s but declined during the 1990s and moved into surplus in the 2000s before returning to deficit in 2009 and 2010.

The capital and financial account balance is almost a mirror image of the current account balance. The reason is that the official settlements balance is very small in comparison with the balances on the other two accounts and the three balances sum to zero.

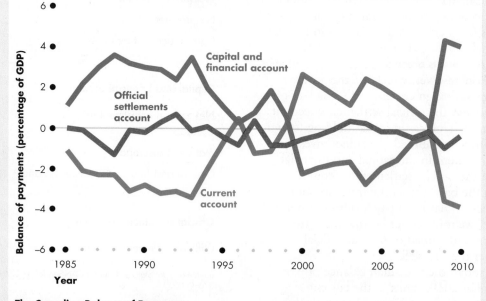

The Canadian Balance of Payments

Source of data: Statistics Canada CANSIM Tables 376–0001 and 376–0002.

To pay for expenditure of $52,000 in excess of her income, Jackie must either use the money that she has in the bank or take out a loan. Suppose that Jackie took out a loan of $50,000 to help buy her house and that this loan was the only borrowing that she did. Borrowing is an *inflow* in the capital account, so Jackie's capital account *surplus* was $50,000. With a current account deficit of $52,000 and a capital account surplus of $50,000, Jackie was still $2,000 short. She got that $2,000 from her own bank account. Her cash holdings decreased by $2,000.

Jackie's income from her work is like a country's income from its exports. Her income from her investments is like a country's interest income from foreigners. Her purchases of goods and services, including her purchase of a house, are like a country's imports. Jackie's loan—borrowing from someone else—is like a country's borrowing from the rest of the world. The change in Jackie's bank account is like the change in the country's official reserves.

Borrowers and Lenders

A country that is borrowing more from the rest of the world than it is lending to the rest of the world is called a **net borrower**. Similarly, a **net lender** is a country that is lending more to the rest of the world than it is borrowing from the rest of the world.

Canada was a net borrower in 2009 and 2010 and a net lender between 1999 and 2008. Through most of the 1980s and 1990s, Canada was a net borrower.

The United States is the world's largest net borrower. Since the early 1980s, with the exception of only a single year, 1991, the United States has been a net borrower from the rest of the world. And during the years since 1992, the scale of U.S. borrowing has mushroomed.

Most countries are net borrowers like the United States. But a few countries, including China, Japan, and oil-rich Saudi Arabia, are net lenders. In 2010, when the United States borrowed $470 billion from the rest of the world, China alone lent $300 billion.

Debtors and Creditors

A net borrower might be decreasing its net assets held in the rest of the world, or it might be going deeper into debt. A nation's total stock of foreign investment determines whether it is a debtor or a creditor. A **debtor nation** is a country that during its entire history has borrowed more from the rest of the world than it has lent to it. It has a stock of outstanding debt to the rest of the world that exceeds the stock of its own claims on the rest of the world. A **creditor nation** is a country that during its entire history has invested more in the rest of the world than other countries have invested in it.

Canada is a debtor nation. Throughout the nineteenth century we borrowed from Europe to finance our westward expansion, railroads, and industrialization. The capital-hungry developing countries (like Canada during the nineteenth century) are among the largest debtor nations. The international debt of these countries grew from less than a third to more than a half of their gross domestic product during the 1980s and created what was called the "Third World debt crisis."

But the United States is the world's largest debtor nation. Since 1986, the total stock of U.S. borrowing from the rest of the world has exceeded U.S. lending to the rest of the world by $7.4 trillion (almost as much as Canada's gross domestic product).

Is U.S. International Borrowing a Problem?

Should the world be concerned that the United States is a massive net borrower and a very large debtor nation? Does the global economy need to be rebalanced and the U.S. deficit eliminated?

The answer to this question depends mainly on what the United States is doing with the borrowed money. If borrowing is financing investment that in turn is generating economic growth and higher income, borrowing is not a problem. It earns a return that more than pays the interest. But if borrowed money is used to finance consumption, to pay the interest and repay the loan, consumption will eventually have to be reduced. In this case, the greater the borrowing and the longer it goes on, the greater is the reduction in consumption that will eventually be necessary.

In 2010, U.S. borrowing from abroad was $439 billion. In that year, private investment in buildings, plant, and equipment was $1,840 billion and government investment in defence equipment and social projects was $500 billion. All this investment added to U.S. capital and increased productivity.

Government also spends on education and health care services, which increase *human capital*. U.S. international borrowing is financing private and public investment, not consumption.

Current Account Balance

What determines a country's current account balance and net foreign borrowing? You've seen that net exports (NX) is the main item in the current account. We can define the current account balance (CAB) as

$$CAB = NX + \text{Net interest income} + \text{Net transfers}.$$

We can study the current account balance by looking at what determines net exports because the other two items are small and do not fluctuate much.

Net Exports

Net exports are determined by the government budget and private saving and investment. To see how net exports are determined, we need to recall some of the things that we learned in Chapter 23 about the flows of funds that finance investment. Table 25.2 refreshes your memory and summarizes some calculations.

Part (a) lists the national income variables that are needed, with their symbols. Part (b) defines three balances: net exports, the government sector balance, and the private sector balance.

Net exports is exports of goods and services minus imports of goods and services.

The **government sector balance** is equal to net taxes minus government expenditure on goods and services. If that number is positive, a government sector surplus is lent to other sectors; if that number is negative, a government deficit must be financed by borrowing from other sectors. The government sector deficit is the sum of the deficits of the federal, provincial, and local governments.

The **private sector balance** is saving minus investment. If saving exceeds investment, a private sector surplus is lent to other sectors. If investment exceeds saving, a private sector deficit is financed by borrowing from other sectors.

Part (b) also shows the values of these balances for Canada in 2010. As you can see, net exports were –$31 billion, a deficit of $31 billion. The government sector's revenue from *net* taxes was $365 billion and its expenditure was $421 billion, so the government sector balance was –$56 billion—a deficit of $56 billion. The private sector saved $318 billion and invested $293 billion, so its balance was $25 billion—a surplus of $25 billion.

Part (c) shows the relationship among the three balances. From the national income accounts, we know that real GDP, Y, is the sum of consumption

TABLE 25.2   Net Exports, the Government Budget, Saving, and Investment

	Symbols and equations	Canada in 2010 (billions of dollars)
(a) Variables		
Exports*	X	478
Imports*	M	509
Government expenditure	G	421
Net taxes	T	365
Investment	I	293
Saving	S	318
(b) Balances		
Net exports	$X - M$	$478 - 509 = -31$
Government sector	$T - G$	$365 - 421 = -56$
Private sector	$S - I$	$318 - 293 = 25$
(c) Relationship among balances		
National accounts	$Y = C + I + G + X - M$	
	$= C + S + T$	
Rearranging:	$X - M = S - I + T - G$	
Net exports equals:	$X - M$	-31
Government sector plus	$T - G$	-56
Private sector	$S - I$	25

Source of data: Statistics Canada, CANSIM Tables 380–0002 and 380–0017.

* The national income accounts measures of exports and imports are different from the balance of payments accounts measures in Table 25.1 on p. 607.

expenditure (C), investment, government expenditure, and net exports. Real GDP also equals the sum of consumption expenditure, saving, and net taxes. Rearranging these equations tells us that net exports is the sum of the government sector balance and the private sector balance. In Canada in 2010, the government sector balance was –$56 billion and the private sector balance was $25 billion. The government

Economics in Action

The Three Sector Balances

You've seen that net exports equal the sum of the government sector balance and the private sector balance. How do these three sector balances fluctuate over time?

The figure answers this question. It shows the government sector balance (red line), net exports (blue line), and the private sector balance (green line).

The private sector balance and the government sector balance move in opposite directions. When the government sector deficit increased during the early 1980s and early 1990s, the private sector surplus increased. And when the government sector deficit decreased during the late 1990s and became a surplus during the early 2000s, the private sector's surplus decreased and became a deficit. In the late 2000s, when the government surplus shrank and became a deficit, the private sector deficit shrank and became a surplus.

Sometimes the government sector deficit and the net export surplus are correlated, but the net export balance does not follow the government sector balance closely. Rather, net exports respond to the *sum* of the government sector and private sector balances.

When the private sector surplus exceeds the government sector deficit, net exports are positive. When the government sector deficit exceeds the private sector surplus, net exports are negative.

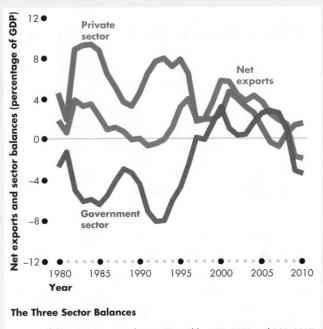

The Three Sector Balances

Source of data: Statistics Canada, CANSIM Tables 380–0002 and 380–0017.

sector balance plus the private sector balance equalled net exports of –$31 billion.

Where Is the Exchange Rate?

We haven't mentioned the exchange rate while discussing the balance of payments. Doesn't it play a role? The answer is that in the short run it does but in the long run it doesn't.

In the short run, a fall in the dollar lowers the real exchange rate, which makes Canadian imports more costly and Canadian exports more competitive. A higher price of imported consumption goods and services might induce a decrease in consumption expenditure and an increase in saving. A higher price of imported capital goods might induce a decrease in investment. Other things remaining the same, an increase in saving or a decrease in investment decreases the private sector deficit and decreases the current account deficit.

But in the long run, a change in the nominal exchange rate leaves the real exchange rate unchanged and plays no role in influencing the current account balance.

REVIEW QUIZ

1 What are the transactions that the balance of payments accounts record?
2 Is Canada a net borrower or a net lender? Is it a debtor or a creditor nation?
3 How are net exports and the government sector balance linked?

You can work these questions in Study Plan 25.4 and get instant feedback.

——————————————— MyEconLab ◆

Reading Between the Lines on pp. 612–613 looks at China's crawling exchange rate policy.

China's Exchange Rate Policy

China Central Bank Sets Yuan Post at Record

www.wsj.com

September 27, 2011

China's central bank set the yuan's official guidepost at a new high Monday even as global investors continued to push the currency lower, suggesting that Beijing will continue to let the Chinese currency strengthen despite global economic jitters.

The People's Bank of China, which guides the yuan's daily trading range, didn't respond to requests for comment Monday.

But observers said the move suggests Chinese officials won't let unease over the world economic outlook get in the way of efforts to gradually guide the yuan higher, as they have since Beijing essentially removed the currency's peg to the U.S. dollar in June 2010. A stronger yuan makes China's manufacturers less competitive abroad. But it also puts downward pressure on domestic inflation, strengthens consumption and burnishes the yuan's case for becoming a more global currency—something Chinese officials see as key to reducing Beijing's dependence on the U.S. dollar. China also faces international pressure, particularly from the U.S., to let the yuan rise and reduce what some U.S. lawmakers say is an unfair boost for China's exporters.

Monday's move by the People's Bank of China is "a signal to the market that China will keep letting the yuan appreciate despite the risk aversion in the rest of the world," said Dariusz Kowalczyk, Hong Kong-based economist …

ESSENCE OF THE STORY

- The People's Bank of China, China's central bank, moved the yuan to a new high on September 26.

- Market forces (global investors) were pushing the currency down.

- The People's Bank of China guides the yuan's daily trading range.

- Observers say unease over the world economic outlook will not stop a gradual move to a higher yuan.

- A stronger yuan makes Chinese exports less competitive, but it puts downward pressure on inflation, lessens China's dependence on the U.S. dollar, and reduces criticism of China's exchange rate policy.

ECONOMIC ANALYSIS

- China's exchange rate was pegged at 8.28 yuan per U.S. dollar until July 2005.

- In July 2005, the yuan appreciated against the U.S. dollar (the U.S. dollar depreciated against the yuan) by 2.1 percent.

- Since July 2005, the yuan has slowly but persistently appreciated against the dollar (the dollar has persistently depreciated against the yuan).

- Figure 1 shows the path of the depreciating U.S. dollar against the yuan.

- To peg the yuan before July 2005 and since then to keep the exchange rate from rising more than it wants, the People's Bank of China buys U.S. dollars in the foreign exchange market.

- The result of these foreign exchange market transactions has been a strong growth in China's foreign reserves.

- Figure 2 shows the buildup of China's reserves, which by 2010 were $2.8 trillion.

- Americans are concerned about the yuan–U.S. dollar exchange rate because China has a large trade surplus with the United States.

- But China's overall current account surplus is not large and is a fraction of the large U.S. current account deficit.

- Figure 3 shows the U.S. current account deficit and China's current account surplus.

- The analysis in this chapter explains that a current account deficit results from too little private and government saving relative to investment.

- China saves more than it invests, and the United States invests more than it saves.

- A change in the nominal exchange rate between the U.S. dollar and the Chinese yuan cannot make a large contribution to changing these imbalances.

- The main effect of the appreciation of the yuan against the U.S. dollar will be to slow China's inflation rate relative to the U.S. inflation rate.

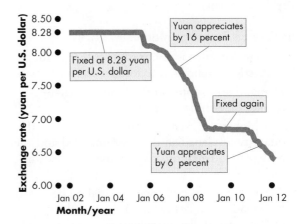

Figure 1 The Yuan–U.S. Dollar Exchange Rate

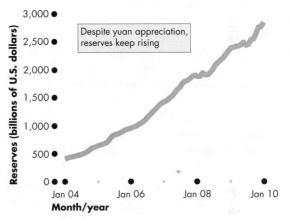

Figure 2 China's Reserves Pile Up

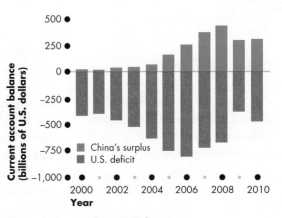

Figure 3 Current Account Balances

SUMMARY

Key Points

The Foreign Exchange Market (pp. 594–598)

- Foreign currency is obtained in exchange for domestic currency in the foreign exchange market.
- Demand and supply in the foreign exchange market determine the exchange rate.
- The higher the exchange rate, the smaller is the quantity of Canadian dollars demanded and the greater is the quantity of Canadian dollars supplied.
- The equilibrium exchange rate makes the quantity of Canadian dollars demanded equal the quantity of Canadian dollars supplied.

Working Problems 1 to 6 will give you a better understanding of the foreign exchange market.

Exchange Rate Fluctuations (pp. 599–603)

- Changes in the world demand for Canadian exports, the Canadian interest rate differential, or the expected future exchange rate change the demand for Canadian dollars.
- Changes in Canadian demand for imports, the Canadian interest rate differential, or the expected future exchange rate change the supply of Canadian dollars.
- Exchange rate expectations are influenced by purchasing power parity and interest rate parity.

- In the long run, the nominal exchange rate is a monetary phenomenon and the real exchange rate is independent of the nominal exchange rate.

Working Problems 7 to 15 will give you a better understanding of exchange rate fluctuations.

Exchange Rate Policy (pp. 604–606)

- An exchange rate can be flexible, fixed, or a crawling peg.
- To achieve a fixed or a crawling exchange rate, a central bank must intervene in the foreign exchange market and either buy or sell foreign currency.

Working Problems 16 and 17 will give you a better understanding of exchange rate policy.

Financing International Trade (pp. 607–611)

- International trade, borrowing, and lending are financed by using foreign currency.
- A country's international transactions are recorded in its current account, capital account, and official settlements account.
- The current account balance is similar to net exports and is determined by the government sector balance plus the private sector balance.

Working Problems 18 and 19 will give you a better understanding of financing international trade.

Key Terms

Balance of payments accounts, 607
Canadian interest rate differential, 599
Canadian official reserves, 607
Capital and financial account, 607
Crawling peg, 605
Creditor nation, 609
Current account, 607
Debtor nation, 609
Exchange rate, 594
Fixed exchange rate, 604

Flexible exchange rate, 604
Foreign currency, 594
Foreign exchange market, 594
Government sector balance, 610
Interest rate parity, 602
Net borrower, 609
Net exports, 610
Net lender, 609
Official settlements account, 607
Private sector balance, 610
Purchasing power parity, 602
Real exchange rate, 603

SCAN THIS

STUDY PLAN PROBLEMS AND APPLICATIONS

MyEconLab ◆ You can work Problems 1 to 19 in Chapter 25 Study Plan and get instant feedback.

The Foreign Exchange Market (Study Plan 25.1)

Use the following data to work Problems 1 to 3.

The Canadian dollar exchange rate increased from $0.94 U.S. in June 2010 to $1.04 U.S. in June 2011, and it decreased from 77 euro cents in June 2010 to 71 euro cents in June 2011.

1. Did the Canadian dollar appreciate or depreciate against the U.S. dollar? Did the Canadian dollar appreciate or depreciate against the euro?

2. What was the value of the U.S. dollar in terms of Canadian dollars in June 2010 and June 2011? Did the U.S. dollar appreciate or depreciate against the Canadian dollar over the year June 2010 to June 2011?

3. What was the value of one euro (100 euro cents) in terms of Canadian dollars in June 2010 and June 2011? Did the euro appreciate or depreciate against the Canadian dollar over the year June 2010 to June 2011?

Use the following data to work Problems 4 to 6.

In June 2010, the exchange rate was 90 yen per Canadian dollar. By October 2010, the exchange rate had fallen to 79 yen per Canadian dollar.

4. Explain the exports effect of this change in the exchange rate.

5. Explain the imports effect of this change in the exchange rate.

6. Explain the expected profit effect of this change in the exchange rate.

Exchange Rate Fluctuations (Study Plan 25.2)

7. On August 3, 2010, the U.S. dollar was trading at 86 yen per U.S. dollar on the foreign exchange market. On September 13, 2010, the U.S. dollar was trading at 83 yen per U.S. dollar.

   a. What events in the foreign exchange market might have brought this fall in the value of the U.S. dollar?

   b. Did the events change the demand for U.S. dollars, the supply of U.S. dollars, or both demand and supply in the foreign exchange market?

8. Colombia is the world's biggest producer of roses. The global demand for roses increases and, at the same time, the central bank in Colombia increases the interest rate. In the foreign exchange market for Colombian pesos, what happens to

   a. The demand for pesos?

   b. The supply of pesos?

   c. The quantity of pesos demanded?

   d. The quantity of pesos supplied?

   e. The exchange rate of the peso against the Canadian dollar?

9. If a euro deposit in a bank in Paris, France, earns interest of 4 percent a year and a yen deposit in Tokyo, Japan, earns 0.5 percent a year, everything else remaining the same and adjusted for risk, what is the exchange rate expectation of the Japanese yen?

10. The U.K. pound is trading at 1.54 Canadian dollars per U.K. pound. There is purchasing power parity at this exchange rate. The interest rate in Canada is 2 percent a year and the interest rate in the United Kingdom is 4 percent a year.

    a. Calculate the Canadian interest rate differential.

    b. What is the U.K. pound expected to be worth in terms of Canadian dollars one year from now?

    c. Which country more likely has the lower inflation rate? How can you tell?

11. You can purchase a laptop in Detroit, Michigan, for $1,296 U.S. If the exchange rate is $1.08 U.S per Canadian dollar and if purchasing power parity prevails, at what price can you buy an identical computer in Windsor, Ontario?

12. **When the Chips Are Down**

    The *Economist* magazine uses the price of a Big Mac to determine whether a currency is undervalued or overvalued. In July 2010, the price of a Big Mac was $3.73 in New York, 13.2 yuan in Beijing, and 6.50 Swiss francs in Geneva. The exchanges rates were 6.78 yuan per U.S. dollar and 1.05 Swiss francs per U.S. dollar.

    Source: *The Economist*, July 22, 2010

    a. Was the yuan undervalued or overvalued relative to purchasing power parity?

    b. Was the Swiss franc undervalued or overvalued relative to purchasing power parity?

c. Do you think the price of a Big Mac in different countries provides a valid test of purchasing power parity?

13. The price level in the Eurozone is 112.4, the price level in the United States is 109.1, and the nominal exchange rate was 80 euro cents per U.S. dollar. What is the real exchange rate expressed as Eurozone real GDP per unit of U.S. real GDP?

14. The Canadian price level is 106.3, the Japanese price level is 95.4, and the real exchange rate is 103.6 Japanese real GDP per unit of Canadian real GDP. What is the nominal exchange rate?

15. **Canadian Currency Climbs Against Yen as Central Banks Intervene**

The Canadian dollar gained the most against the yen in 10 months as the Group of Seven nations, including Canada, intervened in the foreign exchange markets to stabilize the Japanese currency. Canada's dollar had its biggest weekly loss in four months versus the U.S. dollar after a nuclear power-plant crisis caused by Japan's worst earthquake damped investor appetite for higher-yielding currencies.

Source: *Bloomberg News*, March 18, 2011

Explain the changes in demand and supply that brought a rise in the Canadian dollar against the yen and a fall against the U.S. dollar.

Illustrate your answer with graphs of the foreign exchange market.

Exchange Rate Policy (Study Plan 25.3)

16. With the strengthening of the yen against other currencies in 2010, Japan's central bank did not take any action. A leading Japanese politician has called on the central bank to take actions to weaken the yen, saying it will help exporters in the short run and have no long-run effects.

a. What is Japan's current exchange rate policy?

b. What does the politician want the exchange rate policy to be in the short run? Why would such a policy have no effect on the exchange rate in the long run?

17. **Canada's Experience with Flexible Exchange Rate in the 1950s: Valuable Lessons Learned**

Canada had a flexible exchange rate from 1933 to 1939, 1950 to 1962, and has maintained one since 1970. A flexible exchange rate regime insulates the domestic economy from external shocks and permits the operation of an independent

national monetary policy. Canada's experience led to a better understanding of the impact of monetary and fiscal policies in an open economy with a high degree of capital mobility and provided evidence to support the case for a flexible rate as a viable alternative to a fixed exchange rate.

Source: *Bank of Canada Review*, Spring 2008

a. Explain the difference between the flexible exchange rate policy that Canada pioneered and a fixed exchange rate policy.

b. Explain the advantages of a flexible exchange rate policy over a fixed exchange rate policy.

c. If a fixed exchange rate does not influence competitiveness in the long run, why might a country adopt this policy?

Financing International Trade (Study Plan 25.4)

18. The table gives some information about U.S. international transactions in a year.

Item	Billions of U.S. dollars
Imports of goods and services	2,561
Foreign investment in the United States	955
Exports of goods and services	1,853
U.S. investment abroad	300
Net interest income	121
Net transfers	−123
Statistical discrepancy	66

a. Calculate the current account balance.

b. Calculate the capital and financial account balance.

c. Did U.S. official reserves increase or decrease?

d. Was the United States a net borrower or a net lender in this year? Explain your answer.

19. **The Biggest Debtor Nation**

The United States is the biggest debtor nation. For the past 30 years it has been piling up large trade deficits. The current account peaked at 7 percent of GDP in 2007, and is financed by capital inflows. Foreigners purchase large amounts of U.S. assets, or the current account deficit cannot be financed.

Source: *Economic Times*, September 28, 2011

a. Explain why a current account deficit is financed by capital inflows.

b. Under what circumstances would the debtor nation status of the United States become a concern?

ADDITIONAL PROBLEMS AND APPLICATIONS

MyEconLab ◆ You can work these problems in MyEconLab if assigned by your instructor.

The Foreign Exchange Market

20. Suppose that yesterday, the Canadian dollar was trading on the foreign exchange market at 0.75 euros per Canadian dollar and today the Canadian dollar is trading at 0.78 euros per Canadian dollar. Which of the two currencies (the Canadian dollar or the euro) has appreciated and which has depreciated today?

21. Suppose that the exchange rate fell from 84 yen per Canadian dollar to 71 yen per Canadian dollar. What is the effect of this change on the quantity of Canadian dollars that people plan to buy in the foreign exchange market?

22. Suppose that the exchange rate rose from 71 yen per Canadian dollar to 100 yen per Canadian dollar. What is the effect of this change on the quantity of Canadian dollars that people plan to sell in the foreign exchange market?

23. Today's exchange rate between the yuan and the U.S. dollar is 6.78 yuan per dollar and the central bank of China is buying U.S. dollars in the foreign exchange market. If the central bank of China did not purchase U.S. dollars, would there be excess demand or excess supply of U.S. dollars in the foreign exchange market? Would the exchange rate remain at 6.78 yuan per U.S. dollar? If not, which currency would appreciate?

Exchange Rate Fluctuations

24. Yesterday, the current exchange rate was $1.05 U.S. per Canadian dollar and traders expected the exchange rate to remain unchanged for the next month. Today, with new information, traders now expect the exchange rate next month to fall to $1 U.S. per Canadian dollar. Explain how the revised expected future exchange rate influences the demand for Canadian dollars, the supply of Canadian dollars, or both in the foreign exchange market.

25. On January 1, 2010, the exchange rate was 91 yen per U.S. dollar. Over the year, the supply of U.S. dollars increased and by January, 2011, the exchange rate fell to 84 yen per U.S. dollar. What happened to the quantity of U.S. dollars that people planned to buy in the foreign exchange market?

26. On August 1, 2010, the exchange rate was 84 yen per U.S. dollar. Over the year, the demand for U.S. dollars increased and by August 1, 2011, the exchange rate was 100 yen per U.S. dollar. What happened to the quantity of U.S. dollars that people planned to sell in the foreign exchange market?

Use the following news clip to work Problems 27 and 28.

Top U.S. Real Estate Markets for Investment

Rahul Reddy has been investing in Australian real estate for the last two years. Now, with the Australian dollar growing in strength and the American housing market strained, he's got his eye on real estate in Florida and California. Encouraged by a weak dollar and a belief in the resiliency of the U.S. economy, investors are seeking investment properties and development opportunities in the United States. "The United States is good for speculative higher-risk investments from our perspective because the strong Australian dollar will enable us to gain hold of real estate at prices we will probably not see for a long time," says Reddy. "The United States is an economic powerhouse that I think will recover, and if the exchange rate goes back to what it was a few years ago, we will benefit."

Source: *Forbes*, July 10, 2008

27. Explain why foreigners are "seeking investment properties and development opportunities in the United States."

28. Explain what would happen if the speculation made by Reddy became widespread. Would expectations become self-fulfilling?

Use the following information to work Problems 29 and 30.

Brazil's Overvalued Real

The Brazilian real has appreciated 33 percent against the U.S. dollar and has pushed up the price of a Big Mac in Sao Paulo to $4.60, higher than the New York price of $3.99. Despite Brazil's interest rate being at 8.75 percent a year compared to the U.S. interest rate at near zero, foreign funds flowing into Brazil surged in October.

Source: Bloomberg News, October 27, 2009

29. Does purchasing power parity hold? If not, does purchasing power parity predict that the Brazilian real will appreciate or depreciate against the U.S. dollar? Explain.

30. Does interest rate parity hold? If not, why not? Will the Brazilian real appreciate further or depreciate against the U.S. dollar if the U.S. central bank (Federal Reserve) raises the U.S. interest rate while the Brazilian interest rate remains at 8.75 percent a year?

Exchange Rate Policy

Use the following news clip to work Problems 31 to 34.

U.S. Declines to Cite China as Currency Manipulator

The Bush administration has declined to cite China for manipulating its currency to gain unfair trade advantages against the United States. America's growing trade deficit with China, which last year hit an all-time high of $256.3 billion, is the largest deficit ever recorded with a single country. Chinese currency, the yuan, has risen in value by 18.4 percent against the U.S. dollar since the Chinese government loosened its currency system in July 2005. However, American manufacturers contend the yuan is still undervalued by as much as 40 percent, making Chinese products more competitive in this country and U.S. goods more expensive in China. China buys U.S. dollar-denominated securities to maintain the value of the yuan in terms of the U.S. dollar.

Source: MSN, May 15, 2008

31. What was the exchange rate policy adopted by China until July 2005? Explain how it worked. Draw a graph to illustrate your answer.

32. What was the exchange rate policy adopted by China after July 2005? Explain how it works.

33. Explain how fixed and crawling peg exchange rates can be used to manipulate trade balances in the short run, but not the long run.

34. Explain the long-run effect of China's current exchange rate policy.

35. **Aussie Dollar Hit by Interest Rate Talk**

The Australian dollar fell against the U.S. dollar to its lowest value in the past two weeks. The CPI inflation rate was reported to be generally as expected but not high enough to justify previous expectations for an aggressive interest rate rise by Australia's central bank next week.

Source: Reuters, October 28, 2009

a. What is Australia's exchange rate policy? Explain why expectations about the Australian interest rate lowered the value of the Australian dollar against the U.S. dollar.

b. To avoid the fall in the value of the Australian dollar against the U.S. dollar, what action could the central bank of Australia have taken? Would such an action signal a change in Australia's exchange rate policy?

Financing International Trade

Use the following table to work Problems 36 to 38. The table gives some data about the U.K. economy:

Item	Billions of U.K. pounds
Consumption expenditure	721
Exports of goods and services	277
Government expenditure	230
Net taxes	217
Investment	181
Saving	162

36. Calculate the private sector balance.

37. Calculate the government sector balance.

38. Calculate net exports and show the relationship between the government sector balance and net exports.

Economics in the News

39. After you have studied *Reading Between the Lines* on pp. 612–613, answer the following questions.

a. Do you think the yuan–U.S. dollar exchange rate is a problem for Americans or the source of the U.S. current account deficit?

b. Do you think that appreciation of the yuan against the U.S. dollar can help the United States to eliminate its current account deficit?

c. What do you predict would be the main effects of an increase in the yuan–U.S. dollar exchange rate?

d. What, if anything, could U.S. policy do to reduce the U.S. current account deficit?

e. Why do you think China was reluctant to see the yuan appreciate before 2005 but now is increasingly wanting it to appreciate?

f. Why do you think China was intervening to make the yuan appreciate during 2011?

Expanding the Frontier

Economics is about how we cope with scarcity. We cope as individuals by making choices that balance marginal benefits and marginal costs so that we use our scarce resources efficiently. We cope as societies by creating incentive systems and social institutions that encourage specialization and exchange.

These choices and the incentive systems that guide them determine what we specialize in; how much work we do; how hard we work at school to learn the mental skills that form our human capital and that determine the kinds of jobs we get and the incomes we earn; how much we save for future big-ticket expenditures; how much businesses and governments spend on new capital—on auto assembly lines, computers and fibre cables for improved Internet services, shopping malls, highways, bridges, and tunnels; how intensively existing capital and natural resources are used and how quickly they wear out or are used up; and the problems that scientists, engineers, and other inventors work on to develop new technologies.

All the choices we've just described combine to determine the standard of living and the rate at which it improves—the economic growth rate.

Money that makes specialization and exchange in markets possible is a huge contributor to economic growth. But too much money brings a rising cost of living with no improvement in the standard of living.

Joseph Schumpeter, *the son of a textile factory owner, was born in Austria in 1883. He moved from Austria to Germany during the tumultuous 1920s when those two countries experienced hyperinflation. In 1932, in the depths of the Great Depression, he came to the United States and became a professor of economics at Harvard University.*

This creative economic thinker wrote about economic growth and development, business cycles, political systems, and economic biography. He was a person of strong opinions who expressed them forcefully and delighted in verbal battles.

Schumpeter saw the development and diffusion of new technologies by profit-seeking entrepreneurs as the source of economic progress. But he saw economic progress as a process of creative destruction—the creation of new profit opportunities and the destruction of currently profitable businesses. For Schumpeter, economic growth and the business cycle were a single phenomenon.

Economic progress, in capitalist society, means turmoil.

JOSEPH SCHUMPETER
Capitalism, Socialism, and Democracy

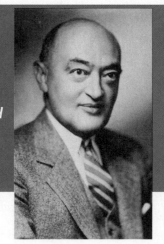

What attracted you to economics?

It was a random event. I wanted to be rich, so I asked my mom, "In my family, who is the richest guy?" She said, "Your uncle John." And I asked, "What did he study?" And she said, "Economics." So I went into economics!

In Spain, there are no liberal arts colleges where you can study lots of things. At age 18, you must decide what career you will follow. If you choose economics, you go to economics school and take economics five years in a row. So you have to make a decision in a crazy way, like I did.

How did economic growth become your major field of research?

I studied economics. I liked it. I studied mathematical economics. I liked it too, and I went to graduate school. In my second year at Harvard, Jeffrey Sachs hired me to go to Bolivia. I saw poor people for the first time in my life. I was shocked. I decided I should try to answer the question "Why are these people so poor and why are we so rich, and what can we do to turn their state into our state?" We live in a bubble world in the United States and Europe, and we don't realize how poor people really are. When you see poverty at first hand, it is very hard to think about something else. So I decided to study economic growth. Coincidentally, when I returned from Bolivia, I was assigned to be Robert Barro's teaching assistant. He was teaching economic growth, so I studied with him and eventually wrote books and articles with him.

In your first research on economic growth, you tested the neoclassical growth model using data for a number of countries and for the states of the United States. What did you discover?

Neoclassical theory was criticized on two grounds. First, its source of growth, technological change, is exogenous—not explained. Second, its assumption of diminishing marginal returns to capital seems to imply that income per person should converge to the same level in every country. If you are poor, your marginal product should be high. Every cookie that you save should generate huge growth. If you are rich, your marginal product should be low. Every

cookie you save should generate very little growth. Therefore poor countries should grow faster than rich countries, and convergence of income levels should occur. Convergence doesn't occur, so, said its critics, neoclassical theory must be wrong.

It turned out that it was this criticism that was wrong. Growth depends on the productivity of your cookies and on how many cookies you save. If you don't save any cookies, you don't grow, even if your marginal product is large.

Conditional convergence is the idea that income per person will converge only if countries have similar savings rates, similar technologies, and similar everything. That's what I tested. To hold every relevant factor equal, I tested the hypothesis using regions: states within the United States or countries that are similar. And once you're careful to hold other things

> **Growth through capital accumulation is very, very hard. Growth has to come from other things, such as technological change.**

Xavier Sala-i-Martin is Professor of Economics at Columbia University. He is also a Research Associate at the National Bureau of Economic Research, Senior Economic Advisor to the World Economic Forum, Associate Editor of the *Journal of Economic Growth*, founder and CEO of Umbele Foundation: A Future for Africa, and President of the Economic Commission of the Barcelona Football Club.

Professor Sala-i-Martin was an undergraduate at Universitat Autonoma de Barcelona and a graduate student at Harvard University, where he obtained his Ph.D. in 1990.

In 2004, he was awarded the Premio Juan Carlos I de Economía, a biannual prize given by the Bank of Spain to the best economist in Spain and Latin America. With Robert Barro, he is the author of *Economic Growth* Second Edition (MIT Press, 2003), the definitive graduate level text on this topic.

Michael Parkin and Robin Bade talked with Xavier Sala-i-Martin about his work and the progress that economists have made in understanding economic growth.

equal, you see a perfect negative relationship between growth rates and income levels.

As predicted by neoclassical theory, poor countries grow faster than rich countries if they are similar. So my research shows that it is not so easy to reject neoclassical theory. The law of diminishing returns that comes from Adam Smith and Malthus and Ricardo is very powerful. Growth through capital accumulation is very, very hard. Growth has to come from other things, such as technological change.

What do we know today about the nature and causes of the wealth of nations that Adam Smith didn't know?

Actually, even though over the last 200 years some of the best minds have looked at the question, we know surprisingly little. We have some general principles that are not very easy to apply in practice. We know, for example, that markets are good. We know that for the economy to work, we need property rights to be guaranteed. If there are thieves—government or private thieves—that can steal the proceeds of the investment, there's no investment and there's no growth. We know that the incentives are very important.

These are general principles. Because we know these principles we should ask: How come Africa is still poor? The answer is, it is very hard to translate "Markets are good" and "Property rights work" into practical actions. We know that Zimbabwe has to guarantee property rights. With the government it has, that's not going to work. The Canadian constitution works in the United States. If you try to copy the constitution and impose the system in Zimbabwe, it's not going to work.

You've done a lot of work on distribution of income, and you say we've made a lot of progress. What is the evidence to support this conclusion?

There are two issues: poverty and inequality. When in 2001 I said poverty is going down, everyone said I was crazy. The United Nations Development Report, which uses World Bank data, was saying the exact opposite. I said the World Bank methodology was flawed. After a big public argument that you can see in *The Economist*, the World Bank revised their poverty numbers and they now agree with me that poverty rates are falling.

Poverty rates are falling.

Now why is poverty falling? In 1970, 80 percent of the world's poor were in Asia—in China, India, Bangladesh, and Indonesia. China's "Great Leap Forward" was a great leap backward. People were starving to death. Now, the growth of these countries has been spectacular and the global poverty rate has fallen. Yes, if you look at Africa, Africa is going backwards. But Africa has 700 million people. China has 1.3 billion. India has 1.1 billion. Indonesia has 300 million. Asia has 4 billion of the world's 6 billion people. These big guys are growing. It's impossible that global poverty is not going down.

But what we care about is poverty in different regions of the world. Asia has been doing very well, but Africa has not. Unfortunately, Africa is still going in the wrong direction.

You've made a big personal commitment to Africa. What is the Africa problem? Why does this continent lag behind Asia? Why, as you've just put it, is Africa going in the wrong direction?

Number one, Africa is a very violent continent. There are 22 wars in Africa as we speak. Two, nobody will invest in Africa. Three, we in the rich world—the United States, Europe, and Japan—won't let them trade. Because we have agricultural subsidies, trade barriers, and tariffs for their products, they can't sell to us.

Africans should globalize themselves. They should open, and we should let them open. They should introduce markets. But to get markets, you need legal systems, police, transparency, less red tape. You need a lot of the things we have now. They have corrupt economies, very bureaucratic, with no property rights, the judiciary is corrupt. All of that has to change.

They need female education. One of the biggest rates of return that we have is educating girls. To educate girls, they'll need to build schools, they need to pay teachers, they need to buy uniforms, they need to provide the incentives for girls to go to school, which usually is like a string. You pull it, you don't push it. Pushing education doesn't work. What you need is: Let the girls know that the rate of return on education is very high by providing jobs after they leave school. So you need to change the incentives of the girls to go to school and educate themselves. That's going to increase the national product, but it will also increase health, and it will also reduce fertility.

Returning to the problems of poverty and inequality, how can inequality be increasing within countries but decreasing globally—across countries?

Because most inequality comes from the fact that some people live in rich countries and some people live in poor countries. The big difference across people is not that there are rich Americans and poor Americans. Americans are very close to each other relative to the difference between Americans and people from Senegal. What is closing today is the gap *across* countries—and for the first time in history. Before the Industrial Revolution, everybody was equal.

Equal and poor. Equally poor. People were living at subsistence levels, which means you eat, you're clothed, you have a house, you die. No movies, no travel, no music, no toothbrush. Just subsist. And if the weather is not good, one third of the population dies. That was the history of the world between 10,000 B.C. and today.

Yes, there was a king, there was Caesar, but the majority of the population were peasants.

All of a sudden, the Industrial Revolution means that one small country, England, takes off and there is 2 percent growth every year. The living standard of the workers of England goes up and up and up. Then the United States, then France, then the rest of Europe, then Canada all begin to grow.

In terms of today's population, 1 billion people become rich and 5 billion remain poor. Now for the first time in history, the majority of these 5 billion people are growing more rapidly than the rich guys. They're catching up quickly. The incomes of the majority of poor citizens of the world are growing faster than those of Americans.

What advice do you have for someone who is just beginning to study economics?

Question! Question everything! Take some courses in history and math. And read my latest favourite book, Bill Easterly's *White Man's Burden.** It shows why we have not been doing the right thing in the aid business. I'm a little bit less dramatic than he is. He says that nothing has worked. I think some things have worked, and we have to take advantage of what has worked to build on it. But I agree with the general principle that being nice, being good, doesn't necessarily mean doing good. Lots of people with good intentions do harm. Economic science teaches us that incentives are the key.

> **Question!
> Question everything!**

---

*William Easterly, *The White Man's Burden: Why the West's Efforts to Aid the Rest Have Done So Much Ill and So Little Good.* New York, Penguin Books, 2006.

CHAPTER

26

Aggregate Supply and Aggregate Demand

After studying this chapter, you will be able to

◆ Explain what determines aggregate supply

◆ Explain what determines aggregate demand

◆ Explain what determines real GDP and the price level and how economic growth, inflation, and the business cycle arise

◆ Describe the main schools of thought in macroeconomics today

The uneven pace at which production grows and prices rise—the busi-ness cycle—and the uneven pace of economic growth and inflation are the subject of this chapter and the two that follow it.

This chapter explains the *aggregate supply–aggregate demand model* or *AS-AD model*. The model provides a framework for understanding the forces that make our economy expand, that bring inflation, and that cause business cycle fluctuations. The *AS-AD* model also provides a framework within which we can see the range of views of macroeconomists in different schools of thought.

In *Reading Between the Lines* at the end of the chapter, we use the *AS-AD* model to interpret the course of Canadian real GDP and the price level in 2011.

Aggregate Supply

The purpose of the aggregate supply–aggregate demand model that you study in this chapter is to explain how real GDP and the price level are determined and how they interact. The model uses similar ideas to those that you encountered in Chapter 3 when you learned how the quantity and price in a competitive market are determined. But the *aggregate supply–aggregate demand* model (*AS-AD* model) isn't just an application of the competitive market model. Some differences arise because the *AS-AD* model is a model of an imaginary market for the total of all the final goods and services that make up real GDP. The quantity in this "market" is real GDP and the price is the price level measured by the GDP deflator.

One thing that the *AS-AD* model shares with the competitive market model is that both distinguish between *supply* and the *quantity supplied*. We begin by explaining what we mean by the quantity of real GDP supplied.

Quantity Supplied and Supply

The *quantity of real GDP supplied* is the total quantity of goods and services, valued in constant base-year (2002) dollars, that firms plan to produce during a given period. This quantity depends on the quantity of labour employed, the quantity of physical and human capital, and the state of technology.

At any given time, the quantity of capital and the state of technology are fixed. They depend on decisions that were made in the past. The population is also fixed. But the quantity of labour is not fixed. It depends on decisions made by households and firms about the supply of and demand for labour.

The labour market can be in any one of three states: at full employment, above full employment, or below full employment. At full employment, the quantity of real GDP supplied is *potential GDP*, which depends on the full-employment quantity of labour (see Chapter 22, pp. 521–523). Over the business cycle, employment fluctuates around full employment and the quantity of real GDP supplied fluctuates around potential GDP.

Aggregate supply is the relationship between the quantity of real GDP supplied and the price level. This relationship is different in the long run than in the short run and to study aggregate supply, we distinguish between two time frames:

- Long-run aggregate supply
- Short-run aggregate supply

Long-Run Aggregate Supply

Long-run aggregate supply is the relationship between the quantity of real GDP supplied and the price level when the money wage rate changes in step with the price level to maintain full employment. The quantity of real GDP supplied at full employment equals potential GDP and this quantity is the same regardless of the price level.

The long-run aggregate supply curve in Fig. 26.1 illustrates long-run aggregate supply as the vertical line at potential GDP labelled *LAS*. Along the long-run aggregate supply curve, as the price level changes, the money wage rate also changes so the real wage rate remains at the full-employment equilibrium level and real GDP remains at potential GDP. The long-run aggregate supply curve is always vertical and is always located at potential GDP.

The long-run aggregate supply curve is vertical because potential GDP is independent of the price level. The reason for this independence is that a movement along the *LAS* curve is accompanied by a change in *two* sets of prices: the prices of goods and services (the price level) and the prices of the factors of production, most notably, the money wage rate. A 10 percent increase in the prices of goods and services is matched by a 10 percent increase in the money wage rate. Because the price level and the money wage rate change by the same percentage, the *real wage rate* remains unchanged at its full-employment equilibrium level. So when the price level changes and the real wage rate remains constant, employment remains constant and real GDP remains constant at potential GDP.

Production at a Pepsi Plant   You can see more clearly why real GDP is unchanged when all prices change by the same percentage by thinking about production decisions at a Pepsi bottling plant. How does the quantity of Pepsi supplied change if the price of Pepsi changes and the wage rate of the workers and prices of all the other resources used vary by the same percentage? The answer is that the quantity supplied doesn't change. The firm produces the quantity that maximizes profit. That quantity depends on the price of Pepsi relative to the cost of producing it. With no change in price *relative to cost*, production doesn't change.

Short-Run Aggregate Supply

Short-run aggregate supply is the relationship between the quantity of real GDP supplied and the price level *when the money wage rate, the prices of other resources, and potential GDP remain constant.* Figure 26.1 illustrates this relationship as the short-run aggregate supply curve *SAS* and the short-run aggregate supply schedule. Each point on the *SAS* curve corresponds to a row of the short-run aggregate supply schedule. For example, point *A* on the *SAS* curve and row *A* of the schedule tell us that if the price level is 100, the quantity of real GDP supplied is $1,100 billion. In the short run, a rise in the price level brings an increase in the quantity of real GDP supplied. The short-run aggregate supply curve slopes upward.

With a given money wage rate, there is one price level at which the real wage rate is at its full-employment equilibrium level. At this price level, the quantity of real GDP supplied equals potential GDP and the *SAS* curve intersects the *LAS* curve. In this example, that price level is 110. If the price level rises above 110, the quantity of real GDP supplied increases along the *SAS* curve and exceeds potential GDP; if the price level falls below 110, the quantity of real GDP supplied decreases along the *SAS* curve and is less than potential GDP.

Back at the Pepsi Plant You can see why the short-run aggregate supply curve slopes upward by returning to the Pepsi bottling plant. If production increases, marginal cost rises and if production decreases, marginal cost falls (see Chapter 2, p. 33).

If the price of Pepsi rises with no change in the money wage rate and other costs, Pepsi can increase profit by increasing production. Pepsi is in business to maximize its profit, so it increases production.

Similarly, if the price of Pepsi falls while the money wage rate and other costs remain constant, Pepsi can avoid a loss by decreasing production. The lower price weakens the incentive to produce, so Pepsi decreases production.

What's true for Pepsi bottlers is true for the producers of all goods and services. When all prices rise, the *price level rises.* If the price level rises and the money wage rate and other factor prices remain constant, all firms increase production and the quantity of real GDP supplied increases. A fall in the price level has the opposite effect and decreases the quantity of real GDP supplied.

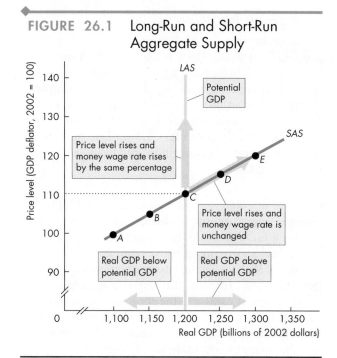

FIGURE 26.1   Long-Run and Short-Run Aggregate Supply

	Price level (GDP deflator)	Real GDP supplied (billions of 2002 dollars)
A	100	1,100
B	105	1,150
C	**110**	**1,200**
D	115	1,250
E	120	1,300

In the long run, the quantity of real GDP supplied is potential GDP and the *LAS* curve is vertical at potential GDP.

In the short run, the quantity of real GDP supplied increases if the price level rises, while all other influences on supply plans remain the same.

The short-run aggregate supply curve, *SAS*, slopes upward. The short-run aggregate supply curve is based on the aggregate supply schedule in the table. Each point *A* through *E* on the curve corresponds to the row in the table identified by the same letter.

When the price level is 110, the quantity of real GDP supplied is $1,200 billion, which is potential GDP. If the price level rises above 110, the quantity of real GDP supplied increases and exceeds potential GDP; if the price level falls below 110, the quantity of real GDP supplied decreases below potential GDP.

MyEconLab   animation   ◆

Changes in Aggregate Supply

A change in the price level changes the quantity of real GDP supplied, which is illustrated by a movement along the short-run aggregate supply curve. It does not change aggregate supply. Aggregate supply changes when an influence on production plans other than the price level changes. These other influences include changes in potential GDP and changes in the money wage rate. Let's begin by looking at a change in potential GDP.

Changes in Potential GDP When potential GDP changes, aggregate supply changes. An increase in potential GDP increases both long-run aggregate supply and short-run aggregate supply.

Figure 26.2 shows the effects of an increase in potential GDP. Initially, the long-run aggregate supply curve is LAS_0 and the short-run aggregate supply curve is SAS_0. If potential GDP increases to $1,300 billion, long-run aggregate supply increases and the long-run aggregate supply curve shifts rightward to LAS_1. Short-run aggregate supply also increases, and the short-run aggregate supply curve shifts rightward to SAS_1. The two supply curves shift by the same amount only if the full-employment price level remains constant, which we will assume to be the case.

Potential GDP can increase for any of three reasons:

- An increase in the full-employment quantity of labour
- An increase in the quantity of capital
- An advance in technology

Let's look at these influences on potential GDP and the aggregate supply curves.

An Increase in the Full-Employment Quantity of Labour
A Pepsi bottling plant that employs 100 workers bottles more Pepsi than does an otherwise identical plant that employs 10 workers. The same is true for the economy as a whole. The larger the quantity of labour employed, the greater is real GDP.

With constant capital and technology, *potential* GDP increases if the *full-employment* quantity of labour increases. An increase in employment that results from a fall in cyclical unemployment increases real GDP but it doesn't increase potential GDP. It brings a movement along the *SAS* curve, but it does

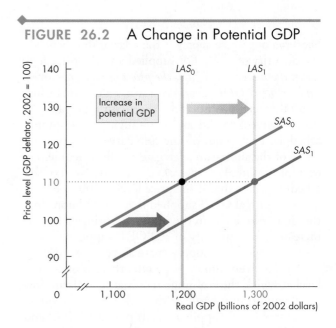

An increase in potential GDP increases both long-run aggregate supply and short-run aggregate supply. The long-run aggregate supply curve shifts rightward from LAS_0 to LAS_1 and the short-run aggregate supply curve shifts from SAS_0 to SAS_1.

———————————— MyEconLab   animation ◆

not change potential GDP and the long-run aggregate supply curve.

An Increase in the Quantity of Capital A Pepsi bottling plant with two production lines bottles more Pepsi than does an otherwise identical plant that has only one production line. For the economy, the larger the quantity of capital, the more productive is the labour force and the greater is its potential GDP. Potential GDP per person in the capital-rich United States is vastly greater than that in capital-poor China or Russia.

Capital includes *human capital*. One Pepsi plant is managed by an economics major with an MBA and has a labour force with an average of 10 years of experience. This plant produces a larger output than does an otherwise identical plant that is managed by someone with no business training or experience and that has a young labour force that is new to bottling. The first plant has a greater amount of human capital than the second. For the economy as a whole, the larger the quantity of *human capital*—the skills that people have acquired in school and through on-the-job training—the greater is potential GDP.

An Advance in Technology A Pepsi plant that has pre-computer age machines produces less than one that uses the latest robot technology. Technological change enables firms to produce more from any given amount of factors of production. So even with fixed quantities of labour and capital, improvements in technology increase potential GDP.

Technological advances are by far the most important source of increased production over the past two centuries. As a result of technological advances, one farmer in Canada today can feed 100 people and in a year one autoworker can produce almost 14 cars and trucks.

Let's now look at the effects of changes in the money wage rate.

Changes in the Money Wage Rate
When the money wage rate (or the money price of any other factor of production such as oil) changes, short-run aggregate supply changes but long-run aggregate supply does not change.

Figure 26.3 shows the effect of an increase in the money wage rate. Initially, the short-run aggregate supply curve is SAS_0. A rise in the money wage rate *decreases* short-run aggregate supply and shifts the short-run aggregate supply curve leftward to SAS_2.

A rise in the money wage rate decreases short-run aggregate supply because it increases firms' costs. With increased costs, the quantity that firms are willing to supply at each price level decreases, which is shown by a leftward shift of the SAS curve.

A change in the money wage rate does not change long-run aggregate supply because on the LAS curve, the change in the money wage rate is accompanied by an equal percentage change in the price level. With no change in *relative* prices, firms have no incentive to change production and real GDP remains constant at potential GDP. With no change in potential GDP, the long-run aggregate supply curve LAS does not shift.

What Makes the Money Wage Rate Change?
The money wage rate can change for two reasons: departures from full employment and expectations about inflation. Unemployment above the natural rate puts downward pressure on the money wage rate, and unemployment below the natural rate puts upward pressure on it. An expected rise in the inflation rate makes the money wage rate rise faster, and an expected fall in the inflation rate slows the rate at which the money wage rate rises.

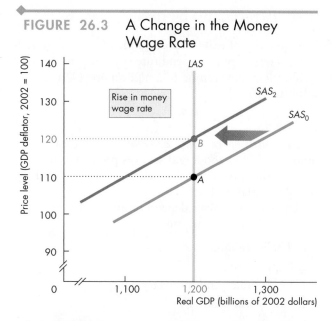

FIGURE 26.3   A Change in the Money Wage Rate

A rise in the money wage rate decreases short-run aggregate supply and shifts the short-run aggregate supply curve leftward from SAS_0 to SAS_2. A rise in the money wage rate does not change potential GDP, so the long-run aggregate supply curve does not shift.

—— MyEconLab   animation ◆

REVIEW QUIZ

1 If the price level and the money wage rate rise by the same percentage, what happens to the quantity of real GDP supplied? Along which aggregate supply curve does the economy move?

2 If the price level rises and the money wage rate remains constant, what happens to the quantity of real GDP supplied? Along which aggregate supply curve does the economy move?

3 If potential GDP increases, what happens to aggregate supply? Does the LAS curve shift or is there a movement along the LAS curve? Does the SAS curve shift or is there a movement along the SAS curve?

4 If the money wage rate rises and potential GDP remains the same, does the LAS curve or the SAS curve shift or is there a movement along the LAS curve or the SAS curve?

You can work these questions in Study Plan 26.1 and get instant feedback.

—— MyEconLab ◆

◆ Aggregate Demand

The quantity of real GDP demanded (Y) is the sum of real consumption expenditure (C), investment (I), government expenditure (G), and exports (X) minus imports (M). That is,

$$Y = C + I + G + X - M.$$

The *quantity of real GDP demanded* is the total amount of final goods and services produced in Canada that people, businesses, governments, and foreigners plan to buy.

These buying plans depend on many factors. Some of the main ones are

1. The price level
2. Expectations
3. Fiscal policy and monetary policy
4. The world economy

We first focus on the relationship between the quantity of real GDP demanded and the price level. To study this relationship, we keep all other influences on buying plans the same and ask: How does the quantity of real GDP demanded vary as the price level varies?

The Aggregate Demand Curve

Other things remaining the same, the higher the price level, the smaller is the quantity of real GDP demanded. This relationship between the quantity of real GDP demanded and the price level is called **aggregate demand**. An *aggregate demand schedule* and an *aggregate demand curve* describe aggregate demand.

Figure 26.4 shows an aggregate demand curve (*AD*) and an aggregate demand schedule. Each point on the *AD* curve corresponds to a row of the schedule. For example, point C' on the *AD* curve and row C' of the schedule tell us that if the price level is 110, the quantity of real GDP demanded is $1,200 billion.

The aggregate demand curve slopes downward for two reasons:

- Wealth effect
- Substitution effects

Wealth Effect　When the price level rises but other things remain the same, *real* wealth decreases. Real

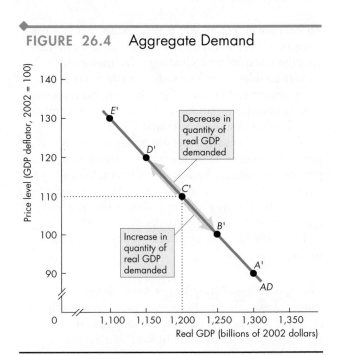

FIGURE 26.4　Aggregate Demand

	Price level (GDP deflator)	Real GDP demanded (billions of 2002 dollars)
A'	90	1,300
B'	100	1,250
C'	**110**	**1,200**
D'	120	1,150
E'	130	1,100

The aggregate demand curve (*AD*) shows the relationship between the quantity of real GDP demanded and the price level. The aggregate demand curve is based on the aggregate demand schedule in the table. Each point A' through E' on the curve corresponds to the row in the table identified by the same letter. When the price level is 110, the quantity of real GDP demanded is $1,200 billion, as shown by point C' in the figure. A change in the price level, when all other influences on aggregate buying plans remain the same, brings a change in the quantity of real GDP demanded and a movement along the AD curve.

━━━━━━━ MyEconLab　animation　◆

wealth is the amount of money in the bank, bonds, stocks, and other assets that people own, measured not in dollars but in terms of the goods and services that the money, bonds, and stocks will buy.

People save and hold money, bonds, and stocks for many reasons. One reason is to build up funds for education expenses. Another reason is to build up enough funds to meet home renovation expenses or other big bills. But the biggest reason is to build up enough funds to provide a retirement income.

If the price level rises, real wealth decreases. People then try to restore their wealth. To do so, they must increase saving and, equivalently, decrease current consumption. Such a decrease in consumption is a decrease in aggregate demand.

Maria's Wealth Effect You can see how the wealth effect works by thinking about Maria's buying plans. Maria lives in Moscow, Russia. She has worked hard all summer and saved 20,000 rubles (the ruble is the currency of Russia), which she plans to spend attending graduate school when she has finished her economics degree. So Maria's wealth is 20,000 rubles. Maria has a part-time job, and her income from this job pays her current expenses. The price level in Russia rises by 100 percent, and now Maria needs 40,000 rubles to buy what 20,000 once bought. To try to make up some of the fall in value of her savings, Maria saves even more and cuts her current spending to the bare minimum.

Substitution Effects When the price level rises and other things remain the same, interest rates rise. The reason is related to the wealth effect that you've just studied. A rise in the price level decreases the real value of the money in people's pockets and bank accounts. With a smaller amount of real money around, banks and other lenders can get a higher interest rate on loans. But faced with a higher interest rate, people and businesses delay plans to buy new capital and consumer durable goods and cut back on spending.

This substitution effect involves changing the timing of purchases of capital and consumer durable goods and is called an *intertemporal* substitution effect—a substitution across time. Saving increases to increase future consumption.

To see this intertemporal substitution effect more clearly, think about your own plan to buy a new computer. At an interest rate of 5 percent a year, you might borrow $1,000 and buy the new computer. But at an interest rate of 10 percent a year, you might decide that the payments would be too high. You don't abandon your plan to buy the computer, but you decide to delay your purchase.

A second substitution effect works through international prices. When the Canadian price level rises and other things remain the same, Canadian-made goods and services become more expensive relative to foreign-made goods and services. This change in *relative prices* encourages people to spend less on Canadian-made items and more on foreign-made items. For example, if the Canadian price level rises relative to the Japanese price level, Japanese consumers buy fewer Canadian-made cars (Canadian exports decrease) and Canadians buy more Japanese-made cars (Canadian imports increase). Canadian GDP decreases.

Maria's Substitution Effects In Moscow, Russia, Maria makes some substitutions. She was planning to trade in her old motor scooter and get a new one. But with a higher price level and a higher interest rate, she decides to make her old scooter last one more year. Also, with the prices of Russian goods sharply increasing, Maria substitutes a low-cost dress made in Malaysia for the Russian-made dress she had originally planned to buy.

Changes in the Quantity of Real GDP Demanded
When the price level rises and other things remain the same, the quantity of real GDP demanded decreases—a movement up along the *AD* curve as shown by the arrow in Fig. 26.4. When the price level falls and other things remain the same, the quantity of real GDP demanded increases—a movement down along the *AD* curve.

We've now seen how the quantity of real GDP demanded changes when the price level changes. How do other influences on buying plans affect aggregate demand?

Changes in Aggregate Demand

A change in any factor that influences buying plans other than the price level brings a change in aggregate demand. The main factors are

- Expectations
- Fiscal policy and monetary policy
- The world economy

Expectations An increase in expected future income increases the amount of consumption goods (especially big-ticket items such as cars) that people plan to buy today and increases aggregate demand.

An increase in the expected future inflation rate increases aggregate demand today because people decide to buy more goods and services at today's relatively lower prices.

An increase in expected future profits increases the investment that firms plan to undertake today and increases aggregate demand.

Fiscal Policy and Monetary Policy The government's attempt to influence the economy by setting and changing taxes, making transfer payments, and purchasing goods and services is called **fiscal policy**. A tax cut or an increase in transfer payments—for example, unemployment benefits or welfare payments—increases aggregate demand. Both of these influences operate by increasing households' *disposable* income. **Disposable income** is aggregate income minus taxes plus transfer payments. The greater the disposable income, the greater is the quantity of consumption goods and services that households plan to buy and the greater is aggregate demand.

Government expenditure on goods and services is one component of aggregate demand. So if the government spends more on spy satellites, schools, and highways, aggregate demand increases.

The Bank of Canada's attempt to influence the economy by changing interest rates and the quantity of money is called **monetary policy**. The Bank influences the quantity of money and interest rates by using the tools and methods described in Chapter 24.

An increase in the quantity of money increases aggregate demand through two main channels: It lowers interest rates and makes it easier to get a loan.

With lower interest rates, businesses plan a greater level of investment in new capital and households plan greater expenditure on new homes, home improvements, automobiles, and a host of other consumer durable goods. Banks and others eager to lend lower their standards for making loans and more people are able to get home loans and other consumer loans.

A decrease in the quantity of money has the opposite effects and lowers aggregate demand.

The World Economy Two main influences that the world economy has on aggregate demand are the exchange rate and foreign income. The *exchange rate* is the amount of a foreign currency that you can buy with a Canadian dollar. Other things remaining the same, a rise in the exchange rate decreases aggregate

Economics in Action
Fiscal Policy to Fight Recession

In the slowing economy of 2008, the U.S. government used fiscal policy in an attempt to stimulate expenditure and increase aggregate demand.

In Canada, the government relied on the automatic tendency for tax revenues to fall and spending on unemployment benefits to rise as the economy slows.

The past few years have seen lively debate between government and opposition about how much fiscal stimulus is needed.

Monetary Policy to Fight Recession

Starting in the fall of 2008, the Bank of Canada, in concert with the U.S. Federal Reserve, the European Central Bank, and the Bank of England, cut the interest rate and took other measures to ease credit and encourage banks and other financial institutions to increase their lending. The U.S. interest rate was pushed to the lowest level (see below).

Like fiscal stimulus, the idea of these interest rate cuts and easier credit was to stimulate business investment and consumption expenditure and increase aggregate demand.

Jim Flaherty versus John McCallum on fiscal stimulus

Ben Bernanke
Federal Reserve — 0.05%

Jean-Claude Trichet
ECB — 1.00%

Mervyn King
Bank of England — 0.50%

Mark Carney
Bank of Canada — 0.25%

FIGURE 26.5   Changes in Aggregate Demand

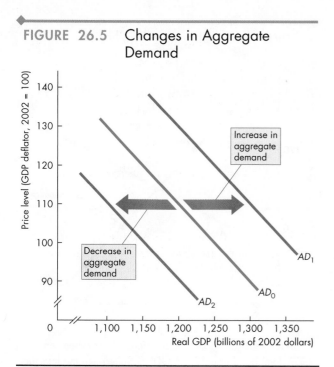

Aggregate demand

Decreases if:

- Expected future income, inflation, or profit decreases

- Fiscal policy decreases government expenditure, increases taxes, or decreases transfer payments

- Monetary policy decreases the quantity of money and increases interest rates

- The exchange rate increases or foreign income decreases

Increases if:

- Expected future income, inflation, or profit increases

- Fiscal policy increases government expenditure, decreases taxes, or increases transfer payments

- Monetary policy increases the quantity of money and decreases interest rates

- The exchange rate decreases or foreign income increases

MyEconLab   animation ◆

demand. To see how the exchange rate influences aggregate demand, suppose that the exchange rate is 1.20 euros per Canadian dollar. A Nokia smart phone made in Finland costs 120 euros, and a BlackBerry costs $110. In Canadian dollars, the Nokia phone costs $100, so people around the world buy the cheaper phone from Finland. Now suppose

the exchange rate falls to 1 euro per Canadian dollar. The Nokia phone now costs $120 and is more expensive than the BlackBerry. People will switch from the Nokia phone to the BlackBerry. Canadian exports will increase and Canadian imports will decrease, so Canadian aggregate demand will increase.

An increase in foreign income increases Canadian exports and increases Canadian aggregate demand. For example, an increase in income in Japan and Germany increases Japanese and German consumers' and producers' planned expenditures on Canadian-produced goods and services.

Shifts of the Aggregate Demand Curve   When aggregate demand changes, the aggregate demand curve shifts. Figure 26.5 shows two changes in aggregate demand and summarizes the factors that bring about such changes.

Aggregate demand increases and the *AD* curve shifts rightward from AD_0 to AD_1 when expected future income, inflation, or profit increases; government expenditure on goods and services increases; taxes are cut; transfer payments increase; the quantity of money increases and the interest rate falls; the exchange rate falls; or foreign income increases.

Aggregate demand decreases and the *AD* curve shifts leftward from AD_0 to AD_2 when expected future income, inflation, or profit decreases; government expenditure on goods and services decreases; taxes increase; transfer payments decrease; the quantity of money decreases and the interest rate rises; the exchange rate rises; or foreign income decreases.

◤ REVIEW QUIZ

1 What does the aggregate demand curve show? What factors change and what factors remain the same when there is a movement along the aggregate demand curve?

2 Why does the aggregate demand curve slope downward?

3 How do changes in expectations, fiscal policy and monetary policy, and the world economy change aggregate demand and the aggregate demand curve?

You can work these questions in Study Plan 26.2 and get instant feedback.

MyEconLab ◆

Explaining Macroeconomic Trends and Fluctuations

The purpose of the *AS-AD* model is to explain changes in real GDP and the price level. The model's main purpose is to explain business cycle fluctuations in these variables. But the model also aids our understanding of economic growth and inflation trends. We begin by combining aggregate supply and aggregate demand to determine real GDP and the price level in equilibrium. Just as there are two time frames for aggregate supply, there are two time frames for macroeconomic equilibrium: a long-run equilibrium and a short-run equilibrium. We'll first look at short-run equilibrium.

Short-Run Macroeconomic Equilibrium

The aggregate demand curve tells us the quantity of real GDP demanded at each price level, and the short-run aggregate supply curve tells us the quantity of real GDP supplied at each price level. **Short-run macroeconomic equilibrium** occurs when the quantity of real GDP demanded equals the quantity of real GDP supplied. That is, short-run macroeconomic equilibrium occurs at the point of intersection of the *AD* curve and the *SAS* curve.

Figure 26.6 shows such an equilibrium at a price level of 110 and real GDP of $1,200 billion (points *C* and *C'*).

To see why this position is the equilibrium, think about what happens if the price level is something other than 110. Suppose, for example, that the price level is 120 and that real GDP is $1,300 billion (at point *E* on the *SAS* curve). The quantity of real GDP demanded is less than $1,300 billion, so firms are unable to sell all their output.

Unwanted inventories pile up, and firms cut both production and prices. Production and prices are cut until firms can sell all their output. This situation occurs only when real GDP is $1,200 billion and the price level is 110.

Now suppose the price level is 100 and real GDP is $1,100 billion (at point *A* on the *SAS* curve). The quantity of real GDP demanded exceeds $1,100 billion, so firms are unable to meet the demand for their output. Inventories decrease, and customers clamour for goods and services, so firms increase production and raise prices. Production and prices increase until firms can meet the demand for their

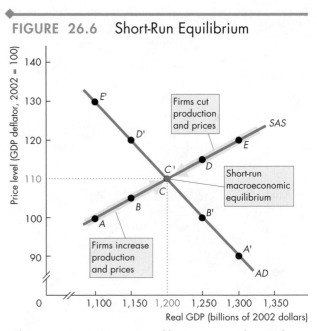

FIGURE 26.6   Short-Run Equilibrium

Short-run macroeconomic equilibrium occurs when real GDP demanded equals real GDP supplied—at the intersection of the aggregate demand curve (*AD*) and the short-run aggregate supply curve (*SAS*).

output. This situation occurs only when real GDP is $1,200 billion and the price level is 110.

In the short run, the money wage rate is fixed. It does not adjust to move the economy to full employment. So in the short run, real GDP can be greater than or less than potential GDP. But in the long run, the money wage rate does adjust and real GDP moves towards potential GDP. Let's look at long-run equilibrium and see how we get there.

Long-Run Macroeconomic Equilibrium

Long-run macroeconomic equilibrium occurs when real GDP equals potential GDP—equivalently, when the economy is on its *LAS* curve.

When the economy is away from long-run equilibrium, the money wage rate adjusts. If the money wage rate is too high, short-run equilibrium is below potential GDP and the unemployment rate is above the natural rate. With an excess supply of labour, the money wage rate falls. If the money wage rate is too low, short-run equilibrium is above potential GDP and the unemployment rate is below the natural rate.

With an excess demand for labour, the money wage rate rises.

Figure 26.7 shows the long-run equilibrium and how it comes about. If the short-run aggregate supply curve is SAS_1, the money wage rate is too high to achieve full employment. A fall in the money wage rate shifts the SAS curve to SAS^* and brings full employment. If the short-run aggregate supply curve is SAS_2, the money wage rate is too low to achieve full employment. Now, a rise in the money wage rate shifts the SAS curve to SAS^* and brings full employment.

In long-run equilibrium, potential GDP determines real GDP, and potential GDP and aggregate demand together determine the price level. The money wage rate adjusts until the SAS curve passes through the long-run equilibrium point.

Let's now see how the $AS\text{-}AD$ model helps us to understand economic growth and inflation.

Economic Growth and Inflation in the AS-AD Model

Economic growth results from a growing labour force and increasing labour productivity, which together make potential GDP grow (Chapter 22, pp. 524–526). Inflation results from a growing quantity of money that outpaces the growth of potential GDP (Chapter 24, pp. 582–583).

The $AS\text{-}AD$ model explains and illustrates economic growth and inflation. It explains economic growth as increasing long-run aggregate supply and it explains inflation as a persistent increase in aggregate demand at a faster pace than that of the increase in potential GDP.

FIGURE 26.7   Long-Run Equilibrium

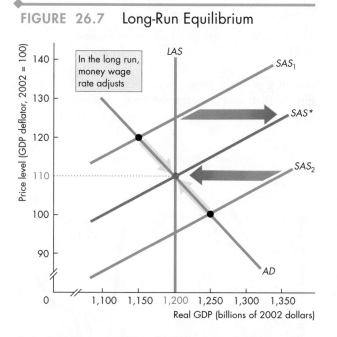

In long-run macroeconomic equilibrium, real GDP equals potential GDP. So long-run equilibrium occurs where the aggregate demand curve, AD, intersects the long-run aggregate supply curve, LAS. In the long run, aggregate demand determines the price level and has no effect on real GDP. The money wage rate adjusts in the long run, so that the SAS curve intersects the LAS curve at the long-run equilibrium price level.

MyEconLab   animation   ◆

Economics in Action

Canadian Economic Growth and Inflation

The figure is a *scatter diagram* of Canadian real GDP and the price level. The graph has the same axes as those of the $AS\text{-}AD$ model. Each dot represents a year between 1961 and 2010. The red dots are recession years. The pattern formed by the dots shows the combination of economic growth and inflation. Economic growth was fastest during the 1960s; inflation was fastest during the 1970s.

The $AS\text{-}AD$ model interprets each dot as being at the intersection of the SAS and AD curves.

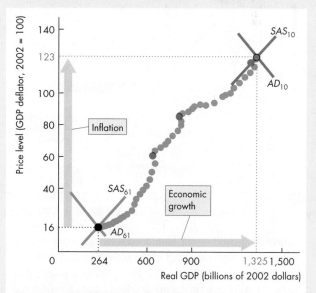

The Path of Real GDP and the Price Level

Source of data: Statistics Canada.

Figure 26.8 illustrates this explanation in terms of the shifting *LAS* and *AD* curves.

When the *LAS* curve shifts rightward from LAS_0 to LAS_1, potential GDP grows from \$1,200 billion to \$1,300 billion and in long-run equilibrium, real GDP also grows to \$1,300 billion.

When the *AD* curve shifts rightward from AD_0 to AD_1, which is a growth of aggregate demand that outpaces the growth of potential GDP, the price level rises from 110 to 120.

If aggregate demand were to increase at the same pace as long-run aggregate supply, real GDP would grow with no inflation.

Our economy experiences periods of growth and inflation, like those shown in Fig. 26.8, but it does not experience *steady* growth and *steady* inflation. Real GDP fluctuates around potential GDP in a business cycle. When we study the business cycle, we ignore economic growth and focus on the fluctuations around the trend. By doing so, we see the business cycle more clearly. Let's now see how the *AS-AD* model explains the business cycle.

FIGURE 26.8   Economic Growth and Inflation

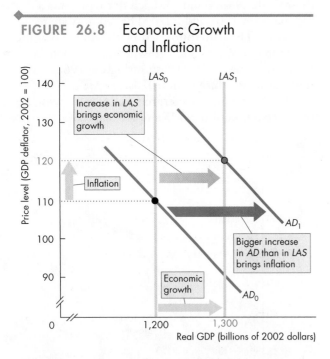

Economic growth results from a persistent increase in potential GDP—a rightward shift of the *LAS* curve. Inflation results from persistent growth in the quantity of money that shifts the *AD* curve rightward at a faster pace than the real GDP growth rate.

───── MyEconLab (animation) ◆

The Business Cycle in the *AS-AD* Model

The business cycle occurs because aggregate demand and short-run aggregate supply fluctuate but the money wage rate does not adjust quickly enough to keep real GDP at potential GDP. Figure 26.9 shows three types of short-run equilibrium.

Figure 26.9(a) shows an above full-employment equilibrium. An **above full-employment equilibrium** is an equilibrium in which real GDP exceeds potential GDP. The gap between real GDP and potential GDP is the **output gap**. When real GDP exceeds potential GDP, the output gap is called an **inflationary gap**.

The above full-employment equilibrium shown in Fig. 26.9(a) occurs where the aggregate demand curve AD_0 intersects the short-run aggregate supply curve SAS_0 at a real GDP of \$1,220 billion. There is an inflationary gap of \$20 billion.

Economics in Action
The Canadian Business Cycle

The Canadian economy had an inflationary gap in 2007 (point *A*), full employment in 2008 (at *B*), and a recessionary gap in 2009 (at *C*). The fluctuating output gap in the figure is the real-world version of Fig. 26.9(d) and is generated by fluctuations in aggregate demand and short-run aggregate supply.

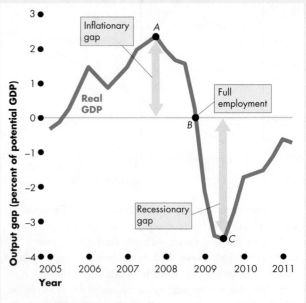

The Canadian Output Gap

Source of data: Bank of Canada output gap, www.bankofcanada.ca/en/rates/indinf/product_data_en.html.

Figure 26.9(b) is an example of **full-employment equilibrium**, in which real GDP equals potential GDP. In this example, the equilibrium occurs where the aggregate demand curve AD_1 intersects the short-run aggregate supply curve SAS_1 at an actual and potential GDP of $1,200 billion.

In part (c), there is a below full-employment equilibrium. A **below full-employment equilibrium** is an equilibrium in which potential GDP exceeds real GDP. When potential GDP exceeds real GDP, the output gap is called a **recessionary gap**.

The below full-employment equilibrium shown in Fig. 26.9(c) occurs where the aggregate demand curve AD_2 intersects the short-run aggregate supply curve SAS_2 at a real GDP of $1,180 billion. Potential GDP is $1,200 billion, so the recessionary gap is $20 billion.

The economy moves from one type of macroeconomic equilibrium to another as a result of fluctuations in aggregate demand and in short-run aggregate supply. These fluctuations produce fluctuations in real GDP. Figure 26.9(d) shows how real GDP fluctuates around potential GDP.

Let's now look at some of the sources of these fluctuations around potential GDP.

FIGURE 26.9   The Business Cycle

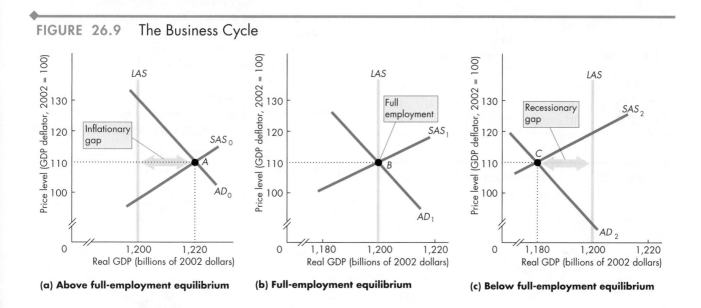

(a) Above full-employment equilibrium   **(b) Full-employment equilibrium**   **(c) Below full-employment equilibrium**

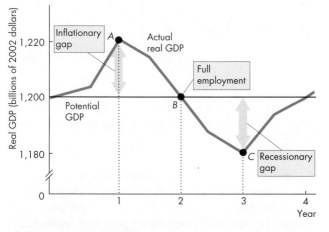

(d) Fluctuations in real GDP

Part (a) shows an above full-employment equilibrium in year 1; part (b) shows a full-employment equilibrium in year 2; and part (c) shows a below full-employment equilibrium in year 3. Part (d) shows how real GDP fluctuates around potential GDP in a business cycle.

In year 1, an inflationary gap exists and the economy is at point A in parts (a) and (d). In year 2, the economy is at full employment and the economy is at point B in parts (b) and (d). In year 3, a recessionary gap exists and the economy is at point C in parts (c) and (d).

Fluctuations in Aggregate Demand

One reason real GDP fluctuates around potential GDP is that aggregate demand fluctuates. Let's see what happens when aggregate demand increases.

Figure 26.10(a) shows an economy at full employment. The aggregate demand curve is AD_0, the short-run aggregate supply curve is SAS_0, and the long-run aggregate supply curve is LAS. Real GDP equals potential GDP at $1,200 billion, and the price level is 110.

Now suppose that the world economy expands and that the demand for Canadian-produced goods increases in Asia and Europe. The increase in Canadian exports increases aggregate demand in Canada, and the aggregate demand curve shifts rightward from AD_0 to AD_1 in Fig. 26.10(a).

Faced with an increase in demand, firms increase production and raise prices. Real GDP increases to $1,250 billion, and the price level rises to 115. The economy is now in an above full-employment equilibrium. Real GDP exceeds potential GDP, and there is an inflationary gap.

The increase in aggregate demand has increased the prices of all goods and services. Faced with higher prices, firms increased their output rates. At this stage, prices of goods and services have increased but the money wage rate has not changed. (Recall that as we move along the SAS curve, the money wage rate is constant.)

The economy cannot produce in excess of potential GDP forever. Why not? What are the forces at work that bring real GDP back to potential GDP?

Because the price level has increased and the money wage rate is unchanged, workers have experienced a fall in the buying power of their wages and firms' profits have increased. Under these circumstances, workers demand higher wages, and firms, anxious to maintain their employment and output levels, meet those demands. If firms do not raise the money wage rate, they will either lose workers or have to hire less productive ones.

As the money wage rate rises, the short-run aggregate supply begins to decrease. In Fig. 26.10(b), the short-run aggregate supply curve begins to shift from

FIGURE 26.10   An Increase in Aggregate Demand

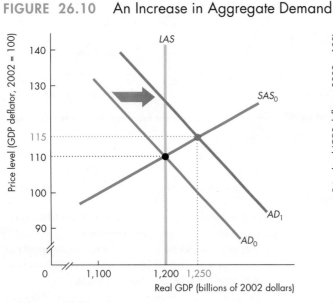

(a) Short-run effect

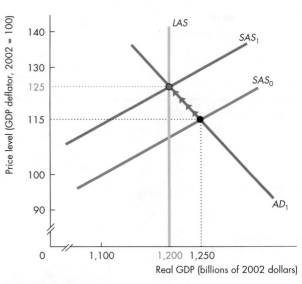

(b) Long-run effect

An increase in aggregate demand shifts the aggregate demand curve from AD_0 to AD_1. In the short run, equilibrium real GDP increases to $1,250 billion and the price level rises to 115. In this situation, an inflationary gap exists. In the long run in part (b), the money wage rate rises and the short-run aggregate

supply curve shifts leftward. As short-run aggregate supply decreases, the SAS curve shifts from SAS_0 to SAS_1 and intersects the aggregate demand curve AD_1 at higher price levels. Real GDP decreases. Eventually, the price level rises to 125 and real GDP decreases to $1,200 billion—potential GDP.

SAS_0 towards SAS_1. The rise in the money wage rate and the shift in the SAS curve produce a sequence of new equilibrium positions. Along the adjustment path, real GDP decreases and the price level rises. The economy moves up along its aggregate demand curve as shown by the arrows in the figure.

Eventually, the money wage rate rises by the same percentage as the price level. At this time, the aggregate demand curve AD_1 intersects SAS_1 at a new full-employment equilibrium. The price level has risen to 125, and real GDP is back where it started, at potential GDP.

A decrease in aggregate demand has effects similar but opposite to those of an increase in aggregate demand. That is, a decrease in aggregate demand shifts the aggregate demand curve leftward. Real GDP decreases to less than potential GDP, and a recessionary gap emerges. Firms cut prices. The lower price level increases the purchasing power of wages and increases firms' costs relative to their output prices because the money wage rate is unchanged. Eventually, the money wage rate falls and the short-run aggregate supply increases.

Let's now work out how real GDP and the price level change when aggregate supply changes.

Fluctuations in Aggregate Supply

Fluctuations in short-run aggregate supply can bring fluctuations in real GDP around potential GDP. Suppose that initially real GDP equals potential GDP. Then there is a large but temporary rise in the price of oil. What happens to real GDP and the price level?

Figure 26.11 answers this question. The aggregate demand curve is AD_0, the short-run aggregate supply curve is SAS_0, and the long-run aggregate supply curve is LAS. Real GDP is $1,200 billion, which equals potential GDP, and the price level is 110. Then the price of oil rises. Faced with higher energy and transportation costs, firms decrease production. Short-run aggregate supply decreases, and the short-run aggregate supply curve shifts leftward to SAS_1. The price level rises to 120, and real GDP decreases to $1,150 billion. Because real GDP decreases, the economy experiences recession. Because the price level increases, the economy experiences inflation. A combination of recession and inflation, called **stagflation**, actually occurred in Canada in the mid-1970s and early 1980s, but events like this are not common.

When the price of oil returns to its original level, the economy returns to full employment.

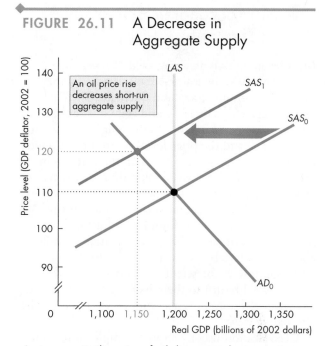

FIGURE 26.11   A Decrease in Aggregate Supply

An oil price rise decreases short-run aggregate supply

An increase in the price of oil decreases short-run aggregate supply and shifts the short-run aggregate supply curve from SAS_0 to SAS_1. Real GDP falls from $1,200 billion to $1,150 billion, and the price level rises from 110 to 120. The economy experiences stagflation.

MyEconLab   animation

REVIEW QUIZ

1 Does economic growth result from increases in aggregate demand, short-run aggregate supply, or long-run aggregate supply?
2 Does inflation result from increases in aggregate demand, short-run aggregate supply, or long-run aggregate supply?
3 Describe three types of short-run macroeconomic equilibrium.
4 How do fluctuations in aggregate demand and short-run aggregate supply bring fluctuations in real GDP around potential GDP?

You can work these questions in Study Plan 26.3 and get instant feedback.

MyEconLab

We can use the *AS-AD* model to explain and illustrate the views of the alternative schools of thought in macroeconomics. That is your next task.

◆ Macroeconomic Schools of Thought

Macroeconomics is an active field of research, and much remains to be learned about the forces that make our economy grow and fluctuate. There is a greater degree of consensus and certainty about economic growth and inflation—the longer-term trends in real GDP and the price level—than there is about the business cycle—the short-term fluctuations in these variables. Here, we'll look only at differences of view about short-term fluctuations.

The *AS-AD* model that you've studied in this chapter provides a good foundation for understanding the range of views that macroeconomists hold about this topic. But what you will learn here is just a first glimpse at the scientific controversy and debate. We'll return to these issues at various points later in the text and deepen your appreciation of the alternative views.

Classification usually requires simplification, and classifying macroeconomists is no exception to this general rule. The classification that we'll use here is simple, but it is not misleading. We're going to divide macroeconomists into three broad schools of thought and examine the views of each group in turn. The groups are

- Classical
- Keynesian
- Monetarist

The Classical View

A **classical** macroeconomist believes that the economy is self-regulating and always at full employment. The term "classical" derives from the name of the founding school of economics that includes Adam Smith, David Ricardo, and John Stuart Mill.

A **new classical** view is that business cycle fluctuations are the efficient responses of a well-functioning market economy that is bombarded by shocks that arise from the uneven pace of technological change.

The classical view can be understood in terms of beliefs about aggregate demand and aggregate supply.

Aggregate Demand Fluctuations In the classical view, technological change is the most significant influence on both aggregate demand and aggregate supply. For this reason, classical macroeconomists

don't use the *AS-AD* framework. But their views can be interpreted in this framework. A technological change that increases the productivity of capital brings an increase in aggregate demand because firms increase their expenditure on new plant and equipment. A technological change that lengthens the useful life of existing capital decreases the demand for new capital, which decreases aggregate demand.

Aggregate Supply Response In the classical view, the money wage rate that lies behind the short-run aggregate supply curve is instantly and completely flexible. The money wage rate adjusts so quickly to maintain equilibrium in the labour market that real GDP always adjusts to equal potential GDP.

Potential GDP itself fluctuates for the same reasons that aggregate demand fluctuates: technological change. When the pace of technological change is rapid, potential GDP increases quickly and so does real GDP. And when the pace of technological change slows, so does the growth rate of potential GDP.

Classical Policy The classical view of policy emphasizes the potential for taxes to stunt incentives and create inefficiency. By minimizing the disincentive effects of taxes, employment, investment, and technological advance are at their efficient levels and the economy expands at an appropriate and rapid pace.

The Keynesian View

A **Keynesian** macroeconomist believes that left alone, the economy would rarely operate at full employment and that to achieve and maintain full employment, active help from fiscal policy and monetary policy is required.

The term "Keynesian" derives from the name of one of the twentieth century's most famous economists, John Maynard Keynes (see p. 723).

The Keynesian view is based on beliefs about the forces that determine aggregate demand and short-run aggregate supply.

Aggregate Demand Fluctuations In the Keynesian view, *expectations* are the most significant influence on aggregate demand. Those expectations are based on herd instinct, or what Keynes himself called "animal spirits." A wave of pessimism about future profit prospects can lead to a fall in aggregate demand and plunge the economy into recession.

Aggregate Supply Response In the Keynesian view, the money wage rate that lies behind the short-run aggregate supply curve is extremely sticky in the downward direction. Basically, the money wage rate doesn't fall. So if there is a recessionary gap, there is no automatic mechanism for getting rid of it. If it were to happen, a fall in the money wage rate would increase short-run aggregate supply and restore full employment. But the money wage rate doesn't fall, so the economy remains stuck in recession.

A modern version of the Keynesian view, known as the **new Keynesian** view, holds not only that the money wage rate is sticky but also that prices of goods and services are sticky. With a sticky price level, the short-run aggregate supply curve is horizontal at a fixed price level.

Policy Response Needed The Keynesian view calls for fiscal policy and monetary policy to actively offset changes in aggregate demand that bring recession.

By stimulating aggregate demand in a recession, full employment can be restored.

The Monetarist View

A **monetarist** is a macroeconomist who believes that the economy is self-regulating and that it will normally operate at full employment, provided that monetary policy is not erratic and that the pace of money growth is kept steady.

The term "monetarist" was coined by an outstanding twentieth-century economist, Karl Brunner, to describe his own views and those of Milton Friedman (see p. 781).

The monetarist view can be interpreted in terms of beliefs about the forces that determine aggregate demand and short-run aggregate supply.

Aggregate Demand Fluctuations In the monetarist view, *the quantity of money* is the most significant influence on aggregate demand. The quantity of money is determined by the Bank of Canada. If the Bank of Canada keeps money growing at a steady pace, aggregate demand fluctuations will be minimized and the economy will operate close to full employment. But if the Bank of Canada decreases the quantity of money or even just slows its growth rate too abruptly, the economy will go into recession. In the monetarist view, all recessions result from inappropriate monetary policy.

Aggregate Supply Response The monetarist view of short-run aggregate supply is the same as the Keynesian view: The money wage rate is sticky. If the economy is in recession, it will take an unnecessarily long time for it to return unaided to full employment.

Monetarist Policy The monetarist view of policy is the same as the classical view on fiscal policy. Taxes should be kept low to avoid disincentive effects that decrease potential GDP. Provided that the quantity of money is kept on a steady growth path, no active stabilization is needed to offset changes in aggregate demand.

The Way Ahead

In the chapters that follow, you're going to encounter Keynesian, classical, and monetarist views again. In the next chapter, we study the original Keynesian model of aggregate demand. This model remains useful today because it explains how expenditure fluctuations are magnified and bring changes in aggregate demand that are larger than the changes in expenditure. We then go on to apply the *AS-AD* model to a deeper look at Canadian inflation and business cycles.

Our attention then turns to short-run macroeconomic policy—the fiscal policy of the government and the monetary policy of the Bank of Canada.

◆▮ REVIEW QUIZ

1   What are the defining features of classical macroeconomics and what policies do classical macroeconomists recommend?
2   What are the defining features of Keynesian macroeconomics and what policies do Keynesian macroeconomists recommend?
3   What are the defining features of monetarist macroeconomics and what policies do monetarist macroeconomists recommend?

You can work these questions in Study Plan 26.4 and get instant feedback.

——————————————— MyEconLab ◆

◆ To complete your study of the *AS-AD* model, *Reading Between the Lines* on pp. 640–641 looks at the Canadian economy in 2011 through the eyes of this model.

Aggregate Supply and Aggregate Demand in Action

Canadian Economy Contracts

Financial Post
September 1, 2011

The Canadian economy shrank in this year's second quarter for the first time since the end of the recession in mid-2009.

Statistics Canada said gross domestic product contracted 0.4 percent between the second and first quarters of this year, when expressed in annualized terms. That's the weakest performance since the 3.7 percent decline seen in the second quarter of 2009. ...

Two straight quarters or more of economic contraction meet the commonly accepted criteria for a recession in Canada. However, TD Economics economist Diana Petramala said that's unlikely to happen this time around.

"Economic growth is likely to pick up over the second half of 2011 as temporary factors fall out of the equation," she said in a research note, referring to things such as shutdowns at energy-sector facilities in Alberta and disruptions caused by the March earthquake in Japan. ...

Statistics Canada said the lower GDP levels seen in the three months ended in June were mostly due to the 2.1 percent decline in exports, noting that domestic demand was up 0.7 percent.

The export decline, which followed two quarters of gains, was led by a 6.7 percent drop in energy shipments out of Canada. Oil-and-gas extraction was down 3.6 percent. ...

Statistics Canada said consumer spending was up 0.4 percent in the second quarter, while goods-production expanded 0.8 percent. ...

ESSENCE OF THE STORY

- Canadian real GDP fell at a rate of 0.4 percent per year in the second quarter of 2011.

- In the second quarter of 2009, real GDP fell at a 3.7 percent annual rate.

- A recession—two successive quarters of contraction—was not expected.

- The source of the negative growth was a 2.1 percent fall in exports that resulted from shutdowns at energy facilities in Alberta and disruptions from Japan's March earthquake, both temporary factors.

- Domestic demand increased by 0.7 percent and consumer spending by 0.4 percent, both at annual rates.

ECONOMIC ANALYSIS

- Canadian real GDP has been below potential GDP since the first quarter of 2009.

- The recessionary gap narrowed through 2009 and 2010 and the first quarter of 2011.

- In the second quarter of 2011, real GDP shrank and the output gap widened.

- Figure 1 shows real GDP, potential GDP, and the output gap (recessionary gap) since the first quarter of 2009 (09/Q1).

- The economy had a recessionary gap because equilibrium real GDP was below potential GDP.

- Figure 2 illustrates the situation in the first quarter of 2011. Potential GDP was $1,360 billion, so the *LAS* curve was *LAS*$_{Q1}$. Aggregate demand was *AD*$_{Q1}$, and short-run aggregate supply was *SAS*$_{Q1}$. The *AD* and *SAS* curves intersect at an equilibrium real GDP of $1,351 and a price level of 126.

- The recessionary gap in the first quarter of 2011 was $9 billion or 0.7 percent of potential GDP.

- During the second quarter of 2011, oil production in Alberta was disrupted and oil exports decreased. Also, the Japanese earthquake and tsunami of March 2011 slowed exports to Japan during the second quarter.

- The decrease in exports decreased aggregate demand and the *AD* curve shifted leftward to *AD*$_{Q2}$ in Fig. 3. An increase in the money wage rate decreased short-run aggregate supply and the *SAS* curve shifted leftward to *SAS*$_{Q2}$. Real GDP decreased to $1,349 billion.

- While real GDP was shrinking, labour force growth and an increase in capital increased potential GDP. The *LAS* curve shifted rightward to *LAS*$_{Q2}$.

- The recessionary gap widened to $17 billion or 1.2 percent of potential GDP.

- With real GDP forecast to grow in the third quarter of 2011, the recessionary gap was expected to narrow and the economy was expected to return to full employment over the coming few quarters.

- Negative shocks from Europe and the United States were risk factors that could keep real GDP below potential GDP for an extended period.

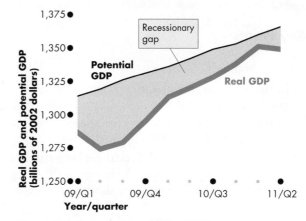

Figure 1 Actual and Potential Real GDP

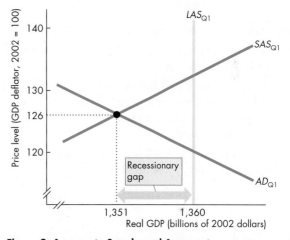

Figure 2 Aggregate Supply and Aggregate Demand in 2011 Q1

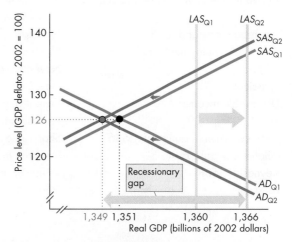

Figure 3 Aggregate Supply and Aggregate Demand in 2011 Q2

◆ SUMMARY

Key Points

Aggregate Supply (pp. 624–627)

- In the long run, the quantity of real GDP supplied is potential GDP.
- In the short run, a rise in the price level increases the quantity of real GDP supplied.
- A change in potential GDP changes long-run and short-run aggregate supply. A change in the money wage rate changes only short-run aggregate supply.

Working Problems 1 to 4 will give you a better understanding of aggregate supply.

Aggregate Demand (pp. 628–631)

- A rise in the price level decreases the quantity of real GDP demanded.
- Changes in expected future income, inflation, and profit; in fiscal policy and monetary policy; and in foreign income and the exchange rate change aggregate demand.

Working Problems 5 to 8 will give you a better understanding of aggregate demand.

Explaining Macroeconomic Trends and Fluctuations (pp. 632–637)

- Aggregate demand and short-run aggregate supply determine real GDP and the price level.
- In the long run, real GDP equals potential GDP and aggregate demand determines the price level.
- The business cycle occurs because aggregate demand and aggregate supply fluctuate.

Working Problems 9 to 18 will give you a better understanding of macroeconomic trends and fluctuations.

Macroeconomic Schools of Thought (pp. 638–639)

- Classical economists believe that the economy is self-regulating and always at full employment.
- Keynesian economists believe that full employment can be achieved only with active policy.
- Monetarist economists believe that recessions result from inappropriate monetary policy.

Working Problems 19 to 21 will give you a better understanding of the macroeconomic schools of thought.

Key Terms

Above full-employment equilibrium, 634
Aggregate demand, 628
Below full-employment equilibrium, 635
Classical, 638
Disposable income, 630
Fiscal policy, 630
Full-employment equilibrium, 635
Inflationary gap, 634
Keynesian, 638
Long-run aggregate supply, 624

Long-run macroeconomic equilibrium, 632
Monetarist, 639
Monetary policy, 630
New classical, 638
New Keynesian, 639
Output gap, 634
Recessionary gap, 635
Short-run aggregate supply, 625
Short-run macroeconomic equilibrium, 632
Stagflation, 637

SCAN THIS

STUDY PLAN PROBLEMS AND APPLICATIONS

MyEconLab ◆ You can work Problems 1 to 21 in Chapter 26 Study Plan and get instant feedback.

Aggregate Supply (Study Plan 26.1)

1. Explain the influence of each of the following events on the quantity of real GDP supplied and aggregate supply in India and use a graph to illustrate.
   - Canadian firms move their call handling, IT, and data functions to India.
   - Fuel prices rise.
   - Wal-Mart and Starbucks open in India.
   - Universities in India increase the number of engineering graduates.
   - The money wage rate rises.
   - The price level in India increases.

Use the following news clip for Problems 2 and 3.

Earnings Growth Slows

In July 2011, average weekly wage rates increased 0.1 percent from the previous month to $872.70. On a year-over-year basis, average weekly wage rates grew by 2.2 percent. This was the slowest wages growth since January 2010.

Source: *The Daily*, Statistics Canada, September 29, 2011

2. Explain how the slow rate of growth in the average weekly wage rate influences aggregate supply.
3. Explain why the wage rate influences only short-run aggregate supply and not potential GDP.
4. Chinese Premier Wen Jiabao has warned Japan that its companies operating in China should raise pay for their workers. Explain how a rise in wages in China will influence the quantity of real GDP supplied and aggregate supply in China.

Aggregate Demand (Study Plan 26.2)

5. Canada trades with the United States. Explain the effect of each of the following events on Canada's aggregate demand.
   - The Government of Canada cuts income taxes.
   - The United States experiences strong economic growth.
   - Canada sets new environmental standards that require power utilities to upgrade their production facilities.
6. The Bank of Canada cuts the quantity of money and all other things remain the same. Explain the effect of the cut in the quantity of money on aggregate demand in the short run.

7. Mexico trades with Canada. Explain the effect of each of the following events on the quantity of real GDP demanded and aggregate demand in Mexico.
   - Canada goes into a recession.
   - The price level in Mexico rises.
   - Mexico increases the quantity of money.

8. **Canadian Economic Accounts**

   Business investment in plant and equipment increased 3.7 percent, housing investment edged up 0.2 percent, consumer spending on goods and services increased 0.4 percent, and expenditures on durable goods rose 0.4 percent.

   Source: *The Daily*, Statistics Canada, August 31, 2011

   Explain how the items in the news clip influence Canadian aggregate demand.

Explaining Macroeconomic Trends and Fluctuations
(Study Plan 26.3)

Use the following graph to work Problems 9 to 11.

Initially, the short-run aggregate supply curve is SAS_0 and the aggregate demand curve is AD_0.

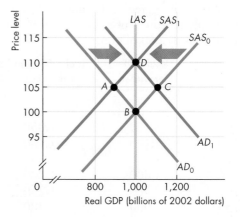

9. Some events change aggregate demand from AD_0 to AD_1. Describe two events that could have created this change in aggregate demand. What is the equilibrium after aggregate demand changed? If potential GDP is $1,000 billion, the economy is at what type of macroeconomic equilibrium?

10. Some events change aggregate supply from SAS_0 to SAS_1. Describe two events that could have created this change in aggregate supply. What is the equilibrium after aggregate supply changed?

If potential GDP is $1,000 billion, does the economy have an inflationary gap, a recessionary gap, or no output gap?

11. Some events change aggregate demand from AD_0 to AD_1 and aggregate supply from SAS_0 to SAS_1. What is the new macroeconomic equilibrium?

Use the following data to work Problems 12 to 14.

The following events have occurred in the history of Canada:

- A deep recession hits the world economy.
- The world oil price rises sharply.
- Canadian businesses expect future profits to fall.

12. Explain for each event whether it changes short-run aggregate supply, long-run aggregate supply, aggregate demand, or some combination of them.

13. Explain the separate effects of each event on Canadian real GDP and the price level, starting from a position of long-run equilibrium.

14. Explain the combined effects of these events on Canadian real GDP and the price level, starting from a position of long-run equilibrium.

Use the following data to work Problems 15 and 16.

The table shows the aggregate demand and short-run aggregate supply schedules of a country in which potential GDP is $1,050 billion.

Price level	Real GDP demanded	Real GDP supplied in the short run
	(billions of 2005 dollars)	
100	1,150	1,050
110	1,100	1,100
120	1,050	1,150
130	1,000	1,200
140	950	1,250
150	900	1,300
160	850	1,350

15. What is the short-run equilibrium real GDP and price level?

16. Does the country have an inflationary gap or a recessionary gap and what is its magnitude?

Use the following news clip to work Problems 17 and 18.

Harper: Economic Outlook 'Not So Positive'

Prime Minister Stephen Harper emerged from a meeting with Finance Minister Jim Flaherty and Bank of Canada governor Mark Carney in Ottawa saying the world economic picture is "not so positive." The fear is that a failure to contain the European debt crisis will push a weak global economy into a recession.

Harper and British Prime Minister David Cameron ended their meeting in Ottawa with a call for European leaders to take decisive action to avoid a second downturn and warned that governments must commit to cutting their debts and deficits and to resisting protectionism.

Source: CBC, September 27, 2011

17. a. What does Stephen Harper mean by "not so positive" and how would Canada be affected by a global recession?
    b. Illustrate the effects on Canada's short-run macroeconomic equilibrium.

18. How would "resisting protectionism" help avoid recession? How would it affect Canada's aggregate demand and aggregate supply?

Macroeconomic Schools of Thought (Study Plan 26.4)

19. Describe what a classical macroeconomist, a Keynesian, and a monetarist would want to do in response to each of the events listed in Problem 11.

Use the following news clip for Problems 20 and 21.

Comparing the Platforms

Liberal Leader Dalton McGuinty said the NDP planned to "increase taxes by $9 billion on job creators." Progressive Conservative Leader Tim Hudak agreed and said that his party if elected would cut the income tax on corporations. NDP leader Andrea Horwath defended her plan to raise corporate taxes, noting the party is planning to give a tax break to companies that create jobs.

Source: CBC, September 26, 2011

20. Do the three Ontario political leaders most likely follow the same macroeconomic school of thought? If not, which school does each follow?

21. Which of the Ontario policies mentioned in the news clip would be most likely to create jobs and which school of macroeconomic thought is closest to that policy?

ADDITIONAL PROBLEMS AND APPLICATIONS

MyEconLab ◆ You can work these problems in MyEconLab if assigned by your instructor.

Aggregate Supply

22. Explain for each event whether it changes the quantity of real GDP supplied, short-run aggregate supply, long-run aggregate supply, or a combination of them.
    - Automotive firms in Canada switch to a new technology that raises productivity.
    - Toyota and Honda build additional plants in Canada.
    - The prices of auto parts imported from China rise.
    - Autoworkers agree to a cut in the nominal wage rate.
    - The Canadian price level rises.

Aggregate Demand

23. Explain for each event whether it changes the quantity of real GDP demanded or aggregate demand.
    - Automotive firms in Canada switch to a new technology that raises productivity.
    - Toyota and Honda build new plants in Canada.
    - Autoworkers agree to a lower money wage rate.
    - The Canadian price level rises.

24. **Business Inventories Build Up** Business inventories increased $19 billion in the second quarter of 2011, more than double the accumulation in the first quarter.

    Source: *The Daily*, Statistics Canada, August 31, 2011

    Explain how a buildup in inventories influences current aggregate demand.

25. **U.S. Consumers Spend More, Bring Home Less**

    U.S. consumers spent slightly more last month but earned less for the first time in nearly two years. The new data on spending and incomes suggest Americans tapped their savings to cope with steep gas prices and a weaker economy. Americans saved less money. The savings rate fell to its lowest level since late 2009. A decline in income growth could slow the economy, if it causes households to cut back.

    Source: CBC, September 30, 2011

Explain how a fall in consumer expenditure influences the quantity of real GDP demanded and aggregate demand.

Explaining Macroeconomic Trends and Fluctuations

Use the following information to work Problems 26 to 28.

The following events have occurred at times in the history of Canada:
- The world economy goes into an expansion.
- Canadian businesses expect future profits to rise.
- The government increases its expenditure on goods and services in a time of war or increased international tension.

26. Explain for each event whether it changes short-run aggregate supply, long-run aggregate supply, aggregate demand, or some combination of them.

27. Explain the separate effects of each event on Canadian real GDP and the price level, starting from a position of long-run equilibrium.

28. Explain the combined effects of these events on Canadian real GDP and the price level, starting from a position of long-run equilibrium.

Use the following information to work Problems 29 and 30.

In Japan, potential GDP is 600 trillion yen and the table shows the aggregate demand and short-run aggregate supply schedules.

Price level	Real GDP demanded	Real GDP supplied in the short run
	(trillions of 2005 yen)	
75	600	400
85	550	450
95	500	500
105	450	550
115	400	600
125	350	650
135	300	700

29. a. Draw a graph of the aggregate demand curve and the short-run aggregate supply curve.
    b. What is the short-run equilibrium real GDP and price level?

30. Does Japan have an inflationary gap or a recessionary gap and what is its magnitude?

Use the following information to work Problems 31 and 32.

Spending by Women Jumps

The magazine *Women of China* reported that Chinese women in big cities spent 63% of their income on consumer goods last year, up from a meager 26% in 2007. Clothing accounted for the biggest chunk of that spending, at nearly 30%, followed by digital products such as cell phones and cameras (11%) and travel (10%). Chinese consumption as a whole grew faster than the overall economy in the first half of the year and is expected to reach 42% of GDP by 2020, up from the current 36%.

Source: *The Wall Street Journal*,
August 27, 2010

31. Explain the effect of a rise in consumption expenditure on real GDP and the price level in the short run.

32. If the economy had been operating at a full-employment equilibrium,
    a. Describe the macroeconomic equilibrium after the rise in consumer spending.
    b. Explain and draw a graph to illustrate how the economy can adjust in the long run to restore a full-employment equilibrium.

33. Why do changes in consumer spending play a large role in the business cycle?

34. **It's Pinching Everyone**

The current inflationary process is a global phenomenon, but emerging and developing countries have been growing significantly faster than the rest of the world. Because there is no reason to believe that world production will rise miraculously at least in the immediate future, many people expect that prices will keep on rising. These expectations in turn exacerbate the inflationary process. Households buy more of non-perishable goods than they need for their immediate consumption because they expect prices to go up even further. What is worse is that traders withhold stocks from the market in the hope of being able to sell these at higher prices later on. In other words, expectations of higher prices become self-fulfilling.

Source: *The Times of India*,
June 24, 2008

Explain and draw a graph to illustrate how inflation and inflation expectations "become self-fulfilling."

Macroeconomic Schools of Thought

35. **Should Congress Pass a New Stimulus Bill? No, Cut Taxes and Curb Spending Instead**

The first stimulus was not too meager, but it was the wrong policy prescription. Anybody who studies economic history would know that government spending doesn't produce long-term, sustainable growth, and jobs. The only sure way to perk up the job market is to cut taxes permanently and rein in public spending and excessive regulation.

Source: sgvtribune.com, September 11, 2010

Economists from which macroeconomic school of thought would recommend a second spending stimulus and which a permanent tax cut?

Economics in the News

36. After you have studied *Reading Between the Lines* on pp. 640–641, answer the following questions.
    a. What are the main features of the Canadian economy in the second quarter of 2011?
    b. Did Canada have a recessionary gap or an inflationary gap in 2011? How do you know?
    c. Looking at Fig. 1 on p. 641, use the *AS-AD* model to show the changes in aggregate demand and aggregate supply that occurred in 2009 and 2010 that brought the economy to its situation at the end of 2010.
    d. Use the *AS-AD* model to show the changes in aggregate demand and aggregate supply that would occur if monetary policy cut the interest rate and increased the quantity of money by enough to restore full employment.
    e. Use the *AS-AD* model to show the changes in aggregate demand and aggregate supply that would occur if the federal government increased its expenditure on goods and services or cut taxes by enough to restore full employment.
    f. Use the *AS-AD* model to show the changes in aggregate demand and aggregate supply that would occur if monetary and fiscal policy stimulus turned out to be too much and took the economy into an inflationary gap. Show the short-run and the long-run effects.

Expenditure Multipliers: The Keynesian Model

After studying this chapter, you will be able to

◆ Explain how expenditure plans are determined

◆ Explain how real GDP is determined at a fixed price level

◆ Explain the expenditure multiplier

◆ Explain the relationship between aggregate expenditure and aggregate demand

Investment and exports fluctuate like the volume of Céline Dion's voice in a concert and the surface of a potholed road. But how does the economy react to those fluctuations? Does it behave like an amplifier, blowing up the fluctuations and spreading them out to affect the many millions of participants in an economic concert? Or does it react like a limousine, absorbing the shocks and providing a smooth ride for the economy's passengers?

You will explore these questions in this chapter and in *Reading Between the Lines* at the end of the chapter you will see the role played by inventory investment during 2011 in a sluggish recovery.

◆ Fixed Prices and Expenditure Plans

In the Keynesian model that we study in this chapter, all the firms are like the grocery store where you shop: They set their prices and sell the quantities their customers are willing to buy. If they persistently sell a greater quantity than they plan to and are constantly running out of inventory, they eventually raise their prices. And if they persistently sell a smaller quantity than they plan to and have inventories piling up, they eventually cut their prices. But on any given day, their prices are fixed and the quantities they sell depend on demand, not supply.

Because each firm's prices are fixed, for the economy as a whole,

1. The *price level* is fixed.
2. *Aggregate demand* determines real GDP.

The Keynesian model explains fluctuations in aggregate demand at a fixed price level by identifying the forces that determine expenditure plans.

Expenditure Plans

Aggregate expenditure has four components: consumption expenditure, investment, government expenditure on goods and services, and net exports (exports *minus* imports). These four components of aggregate expenditure sum to real GDP (see Chapter 20, pp. 469–470).

Aggregate planned expenditure is equal to the sum of the *planned* levels of consumption expenditure, investment, government expenditure on goods and services, and exports minus imports. Two of these components of planned expenditure, consumption expenditure and imports, change when income changes and so they depend on real GDP.

A Two-Way Link Between Aggregate Expenditure and Real GDP

There is a two-way link between aggregate expenditure and real GDP. Other things remaining the same,

- An increase in real GDP increases aggregate expenditure, and
- An increase in aggregate expenditure increases real GDP.

You are now going to study this two-way link.

Consumption and Saving Plans

Several factors influence consumption expenditure and saving plans. The more important ones are

1. Disposable income
2. Real interest rate
3. Wealth
4. Expected future income

Disposable income is aggregate income minus taxes plus transfer payments. Aggregate income equals real GDP, so disposable income depends on real GDP. To explore the two-way link between real GDP and planned consumption expenditure, we focus on the relationship between consumption expenditure and disposable income when the other three factors listed above are constant.

Consumption Expenditure and Saving The table in Fig. 27.1 lists the consumption expenditure and the saving that people plan at each level of disposable income. Households can only spend their disposable income on consumption or save it, so planned consumption expenditure plus planned saving *always* equals disposable income.

The relationship between consumption expenditure and disposable income, other things remaining the same, is called the **consumption function**. The relationship between saving and disposable income, other things remaining the same, is called the **saving function**.

Consumption Function Figure 27.1(a) shows a consumption function. The *y*-axis measures consumption expenditure, and the *x*-axis measures disposable income. Along the consumption function, the points labelled *A* through *F* correspond to the rows of the table. For example, point *E* shows that when disposable income is $800 billion, consumption expenditure is $750 billion. As disposable income increases, consumption expenditure also increases.

At point *A* on the consumption function, consumption expenditure is $150 billion even though disposable income is zero. This consumption expenditure is called *autonomous consumption*, and it is the amount of consumption expenditure that would take place in the short run even if people had no current income. Consumption expenditure in excess of this amount is called *induced consumption*, which is the consumption expenditure that is induced by an increase in disposable income.

45° Line Figure 27.1(a) also contains a 45° line, the height of which measures disposable income. At each point on this line, consumption expenditure equals disposable income. Between *A* and *D*, consumption expenditure exceeds disposable income; between *D* and *F*, consumption expenditure is less than disposable income; and at point *D*, consumption expenditure equals disposable income.

Saving Function Figure 27.1(b) shows a saving function. Again, the points *A* through *F* correspond to the rows of the table. For example, point *E* shows that when disposable income is $800 billion, saving is $50 billion. As disposable income increases, saving increases. Notice that when consumption expenditure exceeds disposable income in part (a), saving is negative—called *dissaving*, in part (b).

FIGURE 27.1   Consumption Function and Saving Function

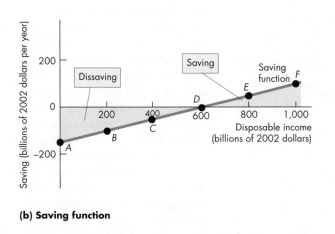

(a) Consumption function

(b) Saving function

	Disposable income	Planned consumption expenditure	Planned saving
		(billions of 2002 dollars)	
A	0	150	−150
B	200	300	−100
C	400	450	−50
D	600	600	0
E	800	750	50
F	1,000	900	100

The table shows consumption expenditure and saving plans at various levels of disposable income. Part (a) of the figure shows the relationship between consumption expenditure and disposable income (the consumption function). The height of the consumption function measures consumption expenditure at each level of disposable income. Part (b) shows the relationship between saving and disposable income (the saving function). The height of the saving function measures saving at each level of disposable income. Points *A* through *F* on the consumption and saving functions correspond to the rows in the table.

The height of the 45° line in part (a) measures disposable income. So along the 45° line, consumption expenditure equals disposable income. Consumption expenditure plus saving equals disposable income. When the consumption function is above the 45° line, saving is negative (dissaving occurs). When the consumption function is below the 45° line, saving is positive. At the point where the consumption function intersects the 45° line, all disposable income is spent on consumption and saving is zero.

Marginal Propensities to Consume and Save

The **marginal propensity to consume** (*MPC*) is the fraction of a *change* in disposable income that is spent on consumption. It is calculated as the *change* in consumption expenditure (ΔC) divided by the *change* in disposable income (ΔYD). The formula is

$$MPC = \frac{\Delta C}{\Delta YD}.$$

In the table in Fig. 27.1, when disposable income increases by $200 billion, consumption expenditure increases by $150 billion. The *MPC* is $150 billion divided by $200 billion, which equals 0.75.

The **marginal propensity to save** (*MPS*) is the fraction of a *change* in disposable income that is saved. It is calculated as the *change* in saving (ΔS) divided by the *change* in disposable income (ΔYD). The formula is

$$MPS = \frac{\Delta S}{\Delta YD}.$$

In the table in Fig. 27.1, when disposable income increases by $200 billion, saving increases by $50 billion. The *MPS* is $50 billion divided by $200 billion, which equals 0.25.

Because an increase in disposable income is either spent on consumption or saved, the marginal propensity to consume plus the marginal propensity to save equals 1. You can see why by using the equation:

$$\Delta C + \Delta S = \Delta YD.$$

Divide both sides of the equation by the change in disposable income to obtain

$$\frac{\Delta C}{\Delta YD} + \frac{\Delta S}{\Delta YD} = 1.$$

$\Delta C / \Delta YD$ is the marginal propensity to consume (*MPC*), and $\Delta S / \Delta YD$ is the marginal propensity to save (*MPS*), so

$$MPC + MPS = 1.$$

Slopes and Marginal Propensities

The slope of the consumption function is the marginal propensity to consume, and the slope of the saving function is the marginal propensity to save.

Figure 27.2(a) shows the *MPC* as the slope of the consumption function. An increase in disposable income of $200 billion is the base of the red triangle. The increase in consumption expenditure that results from this increase in disposable income is $150 billion and is the height of the triangle. The slope of the consumption function is given by the formula "slope equals rise over run" and is $150 billion divided by $200 billion, which equals 0.75—the *MPC*.

Figure 27.2(b) shows the *MPS* as the slope of the saving function. An increase in disposable income of $200 billion (the base of the red triangle) increases saving by $50 billion (the height of the triangle). The slope of the saving function is $50 billion divided by $200 billion, which equals 0.25—the *MPS*.

FIGURE 27.2 The Marginal Propensities to Consume and Save

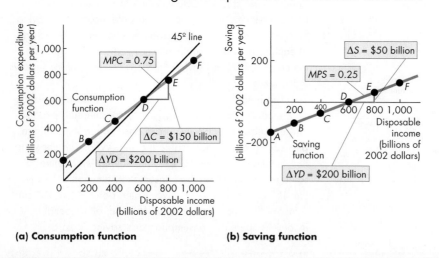

(a) Consumption function

(b) Saving function

The marginal propensity to consume, *MPC*, is equal to the change in consumption expenditure divided by the change in disposable income, other things remaining the same. It is measured by the slope of the consumption function. In part (a), the *MPC* is 0.75.

The marginal propensity to save, *MPS*, is equal to the change in saving divided by the change in disposable income, other things remaining the same. It is measured by the slope of the saving function. In part (b), the *MPS* is 0.25.

MyEconLab animation

Economics in Action
The Canadian Consumption Function

The figure shows the Canadian consumption function. Each point identified by a blue dot represents consumption expenditure and disposable income for a particular year. (The dots are for the years 1970 to 2010, and the dots for five of those years are identified in the figure.)

The Canadian consumption function is CF_{70} in 1970 and CF_{10} in 2010.

The slope of the consumption function in the figure is 0.85, which means that a $1 increase in disposable income increases consumption expenditure by 85¢. This slope, which is an estimate of the marginal propensity to consume, is an assumption that is at the upper end of the range of values that economists have estimated for the marginal propensity to consume.

The consumption function shifts upward over time as other influences on consumption expenditure change. Of these other influences, the real interest rate and wealth fluctuate and so bring upward and downward shifts in the consumption function.

But rising wealth and rising expected future income bring a steady upward shift in the consumption function. As the consumption function shifts upward, autonomous consumption increases.

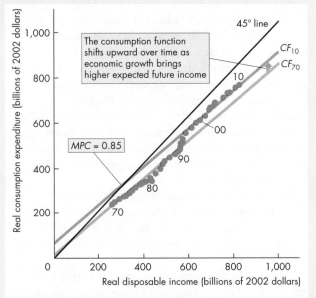

The Canadian Consumption Function

Source of data: Statistics Canada, CANSIM Tables 380-0002 and 380-0004.

Consumption as a Function of Real GDP

Consumption expenditure changes when disposable income changes and disposable income changes when real GDP changes. So consumption expenditure depends not only on disposable income but also on real GDP. We use this link between consumption expenditure and real GDP to determine equilibrium expenditure. But before we do so, we need to look at one further component of aggregate expenditure: imports. Like consumption expenditure, imports are influenced by real GDP.

Import Function

Of the many influences on Canadian imports in the short run, Canadian real GDP is the main influence. Other things remaining the same, an increase in Canadian real GDP increases the quantity of Canadian imports.

The relationship between imports and real GDP is determined by the **marginal propensity to import**, which is the fraction of an increase in real GDP that is spent on imports. It is calculated as the change in imports divided by the change in real GDP, other things remaining the same. For example, if a $100 billion increase in real GDP brings a $25 billion increase in imports, the marginal propensity to import is 0.25.

REVIEW QUIZ

1 Which components of aggregate expenditure are influenced by real GDP?
2 Define and explain how we calculate the marginal propensity to consume and the marginal propensity to save.
3 How do we calculate the effects of real GDP on consumption expenditure and imports by using the marginal propensity to consume and the marginal propensity to import?

You can work these questions in Study Plan 27.1 and get instant feedback.

━━━━━━━━━━━━━ MyEconLab ◆

Real GDP influences consumption expenditure and imports, which in turn influence real GDP. Your next task is to study this second piece of the two-way link between aggregate expenditure and real GDP and see how all the components of aggregate planned expenditure interact to determine real GDP.

◆ Real GDP with a Fixed Price Level

You are now going to see how, at a given price level, aggregate expenditure plans determine real GDP. We start by looking at the relationship between aggregate planned expenditure and real GDP. This relationship can be described by an aggregate expenditure schedule or an aggregate expenditure curve. The *aggregate expenditure schedule* lists aggregate planned expenditure generated at each level of real GDP. The *aggregate expenditure curve* is a graph of the aggregate expenditure schedule.

Aggregate Planned Expenditure

The table in Fig. 27.3 sets out an aggregate expenditure schedule. To calculate aggregate planned expenditure at a given real GDP, we add the expenditure components together. The first column of the table shows real GDP, and the second column shows the planned consumption at each level of real GDP. A $100 billion increase in real GDP increases consumption expenditure by $70 billion—the *MPC* is 0.7.

The next two columns show investment and government expenditure on goods and services, both of which are independent of the level of real GDP. Investment depends on the real interest rate and the expected profit (see Chapter 23, p. 550). At a given point in time, these factors generate a given level of investment. Suppose this level of investment is $200 billion. Also, suppose that government expenditure is $220 billion.

The next two columns show exports and imports. Exports are influenced by events in the rest of the world, prices of foreign-produced goods and services relative to the prices of similar Canadian-produced goods and services, and exchange rates. But they are not directly affected by Canadian real GDP. Exports are a constant $180 billion. Imports increase as Canadian real GDP increases. A $100 billion increase in Canadian real GDP generates a $20 billion increase in imports—the marginal propensity to import is 0.2.

The final column shows aggregate planned expenditure—the sum of planned consumption expenditure, investment, government expenditure on goods and services, and exports minus imports.

Figure 27.3 plots an aggregate expenditure curve. Real GDP is shown on the *x*-axis, and aggregate planned expenditure is shown on the *y*-axis. The aggregate expenditure curve is the red line *AE*. Points

A through *F* on that curve correspond to the rows of the table. The *AE* curve is a graph of aggregate planned expenditure (the last column) plotted against real GDP (the first column).

Figure 27.3 also shows the components of aggregate expenditure. The constant components—investment (I), government expenditure on goods and services (G), and exports (X)—are shown by the horizontal lines in the figure. Consumption expenditure (C) is the vertical gap between the lines labelled $I + G + X$ and $I + G + X + C$.

To construct the *AE* curve, subtract imports (M) from the $I + G + X + C$ line. Aggregate expenditure is expenditure on Canadian-produced goods and services. But the components of aggregate expenditure—C, I, and G—include expenditure on imported goods and services. For example, if you buy a new cell phone, your expenditure is part of consumption expenditure. But if the cell phone is a Nokia made in Finland, your expenditure on it must be subtracted from consumption expenditure to find out how much is spent on goods and services produced in Canada—on Canadian real GDP. Money paid to Nokia for cell phone imports from Finland does not add to aggregate expenditure in Canada.

Because imports are only a part of aggregate expenditure, when we subtract imports from the other components of aggregate expenditure, aggregate planned expenditure still increases as real GDP increases, as you can see in Fig. 27.3.

Consumption expenditure minus imports, which varies with real GDP, is called **induced expenditure**. The sum of investment, government expenditure, and exports, which does not vary with real GDP, is called **autonomous expenditure**. Consumption expenditure and imports can also have an autonomous component—a component that does not vary with real GDP. Another way of thinking about autonomous expenditure is that it would be the level of aggregate planned expenditure if real GDP were zero.

In Fig. 27.3, autonomous expenditure is $600 billion—aggregate planned expenditure when real GDP is zero (point *A*). For each $100 billion increase in real GDP, induced expenditure increases by $50 billion.

The aggregate expenditure curve summarizes the relationship between aggregate *planned* expenditure and real GDP. But what determines the point on the aggregate expenditure curve at which the economy operates? What determines *actual* aggregate expenditure?

FIGURE 27.3   Aggregate Planned Expenditure: The AE Curve

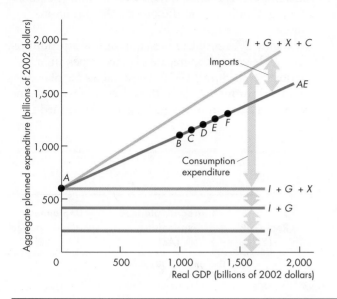

Aggregate planned expenditure is the sum of planned consumption expenditure, investment, government expenditure on goods and services, and exports minus imports. For example, in row B of the table, when real GDP is $1,000 billion, planned consumption expenditure is $700 billion, planned investment is $200 billion, planned government expenditure is $220 billion, planned exports are $180 billion, and planned imports are $200 billion. So when real GDP is $1,000 billion, aggregate planned expenditure is $1,100 billion ($700 + $200 + $220 + $180 − $200). The schedule shows that aggregate planned expenditure increases as real GDP increases. This relationship is graphed as the aggregate expenditure curve AE. The components of aggregate expenditure that increase with real GDP are consumption expenditure and imports. The other components—investment, government expenditure, and exports—do not vary with real GDP.

	Real GDP (Y)	Planned expenditure					Aggregate planned expenditure (AE = C + I + G + X − M)
		Consumption expenditure (C)	Investment (I)	Government expenditure (G)	Exports (X)	Imports (M)	
		(billions of 2002 dollars)					
A	0	0	200	220	180	0	600
B	1,000	700	200	220	180	200	1,100
C	1,100	770	200	220	180	220	1,150
D	1,200	840	200	220	180	240	1,200
E	1,300	910	200	220	180	260	1,250
F	1,400	980	200	220	180	280	1,300

MyEconLab   animation ◆

Actual Expenditure, Planned Expenditure, and Real GDP

Actual aggregate expenditure is always equal to real GDP, as we saw in Chapter 20 (p. 470). But aggregate *planned* expenditure is not always equal to actual aggregate expenditure and therefore is not always equal to real GDP. How can actual expenditure and planned expenditure differ? The answer is that firms can end up with inventories that are greater or smaller than planned. People carry out their

consumption expenditure plans, the government implements its planned expenditure on goods and services, and net exports are as planned. Firms carry out their plans to purchase new buildings, plant, and equipment. But one component of investment is the change in firms' inventories. If aggregate planned expenditure is less than real GDP, firms sell less than they planned to sell and end up with unplanned inventories. If aggregate planned expenditure exceeds real GDP, firms sell more than they planned to sell and end up with inventories being too low.

Equilibrium Expenditure

Equilibrium expenditure is the level of aggregate expenditure that occurs when aggregate *planned* expenditure equals real GDP. Equilibrium expenditure is a level of aggregate expenditure and real GDP at which spending plans are fulfilled. At a given price level, equilibrium expenditure determines real GDP. When aggregate planned expenditure and actual aggregate expenditure are unequal, a process of convergence towards equilibrium expenditure occurs. Throughout this process, real GDP adjusts. Let's examine equilibrium expenditure and the process that brings it about.

Figure 27.4(a) illustrates equilibrium expenditure. The table sets out aggregate planned expenditure at various levels of real GDP. These values are plotted as points *A* through *F* along the *AE* curve. The 45° line shows all the points at which aggregate planned

FIGURE 27.4   Equilibrium Expenditure

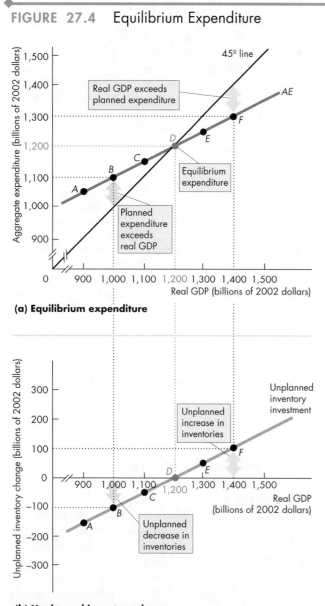

(a) Equilibrium expenditure

(b) Unplanned inventory changes

	Real GDP (Y)	Aggregate planned expenditure (AE)	Unplanned inventory change (Y – AE)
	(billions of 2002 dollars)		
A	900	1,050	−150
B	1,000	1,100	−100
C	1,100	1,150	−50
D	1,200	1,200	0
E	1,300	1,250	50
F	1,400	1,300	100

The table shows expenditure plans at different levels of real GDP. When real GDP is $1,200 billion, aggregate planned expenditure equals real GDP.

Part (a) of the figure illustrates equilibrium expenditure, which occurs when aggregate planned expenditure equals real GDP at the intersection of the 45° line and the *AE* curve. Part (b) of the figure shows the forces that bring about equilibrium expenditure. When aggregate planned expenditure exceeds real GDP, inventories decrease—for example, at point *B* in both parts of the figure. Firms increase production, and real GDP increases.

When aggregate planned expenditure is less than real GDP, inventories increase—for example, at point *F* in both parts of the figure. Firms decrease production, and real GDP decreases. When aggregate planned expenditure equals real GDP, there are no unplanned inventory changes and real GDP remains constant at equilibrium expenditure.

MyEconLab   animation

expenditure equals real GDP. So where the *AE* curve lies above the 45° line, aggregate planned expenditure exceeds real GDP; where the *AE* curve lies below the 45° line, aggregate planned expenditure is less than real GDP; and where the *AE* curve intersects the 45° line, aggregate planned expenditure equals real GDP. Point *D* illustrates equilibrium expenditure. At this point, real GDP is $1,200 billion.

Convergence to Equilibrium

What are the forces that move aggregate expenditure towards its equilibrium level? To answer this question, we must look at a situation in which aggregate expenditure is away from its equilibrium level.

From Below Equilibrium Suppose that in Fig. 27.4, real GDP is $1,000 billion. With real GDP at $1,000 billion, actual aggregate expenditure is also $1,000 billion. But aggregate *planned* expenditure is $1,100 billion, point *B* in Fig. 27.4(a). Aggregate planned expenditure exceeds *actual* expenditure. When people spend $1,100 billion and firms produce goods and services worth $1,000 billion, firms' inventories fall by $100 billion—point *B* in Fig. 27.4(b). Because the change in inventories is part of investment, *actual* investment is $100 billion less than *planned* investment.

Real GDP doesn't remain at $1,000 billion for very long. Firms have inventory targets based on their sales. When inventories fall below target, firms increase production to restore inventories to the target level. To increase inventories, firms hire additional labour and increase production. Suppose that they increase production in the next period by $100 billion. Real GDP increases by $100 billion to $1,100 billion. But again, aggregate planned expenditure exceeds real GDP. When real GDP is $1,100 billion, aggregate planned expenditure is $1,150 billion—point *C* in Fig. 27.4(a). Again, inventories decrease, but this time by less than before. With real GDP of $1,100 billion and aggregate planned expenditure of $1,150 billion, inventories decrease by $50 billion—point *C* in Fig. 27.4(b). Again, firms hire additional labour and production increases; real GDP increases yet further.

The process that we've just described—planned expenditure exceeds real GDP, inventories decrease, and production increases to restore inventories—ends when real GDP has reached $1,200 billion. At

this real GDP, there is equilibrium. Unplanned inventory changes are zero. Firms do not change their production.

From Above Equilibrium If in Fig. 27.4, real GDP is $1,400 billion, the process that we've just described works in reverse. With real GDP at $1,400 billion, actual aggregate expenditure is also $1,400 billion. But aggregate planned expenditure is $1,300 billion—point *F* in Fig. 27.4(a). Actual expenditure *exceeds* planned expenditure. When firms produce goods and services worth $1,400 billion and people spend only $1,300 billion, firms' inventories rise by $100 billion—point *F* in Fig. 27.4(b). Now, real GDP begins to fall.

As long as actual expenditure exceeds planned expenditure, inventories rise and firms cut production. Again, the process ends when real GDP has reached $1,200 billion, the equilibrium at which unplanned inventory changes are zero and firms do not change their production.

REVIEW QUIZ

1 What is the relationship between aggregate planned expenditure and real GDP at equilibrium expenditure?

2 How does equilibrium expenditure come about? What adjusts to achieve equilibrium?

3 If real GDP and aggregate expenditure are less than equilibrium expenditure, what happens to firms' inventories? How do firms change their production? And what happens to real GDP?

4 If real GDP and aggregate expenditure are greater than equilibrium expenditure, what happens to firms' inventories? How do firms change their production? And what happens to real GDP?

You can work these questions in Study Plan 27.2 and get instant feedback.

──────────────── MyEconLab ◆

We've learned that when the price level is fixed, real GDP is determined by equilibrium expenditure. And we have seen how unplanned changes in inventories and the production response they generate bring a convergence towards equilibrium expenditure. We're now going to study *changes* in equilibrium expenditure and discover an economic amplifier called the *multiplier*.

The Multiplier

Investment and exports can change for many reasons. A fall in the real interest rate might induce firms to increase their planned investment. A wave of innovation, such as occurred with the spread of multimedia computers in the 1990s, might increase expected future profits and lead firms to increase their planned investment. An economic boom in Western Europe and Japan might lead to a large increase in their expenditure on Canadian-produced goods and services—on Canadian exports. These are all examples of increases in autonomous expenditure.

When autonomous expenditure increases, aggregate expenditure increases and so does equilibrium expenditure and real GDP. But the increase in real GDP is *larger* than the change in autonomous expenditure. The **multiplier** is the amount by which a change in autonomous expenditure is magnified or multiplied to determine the change in equilibrium expenditure and real GDP.

To get the basic idea of the multiplier, we'll work with an example economy in which there are no income taxes and no imports. So we'll first assume that these factors are absent. Then, when you understand the basic idea, we'll bring these factors back into play and see what difference they make to the multiplier.

The Basic Idea of the Multiplier

Suppose that investment increases. The additional expenditure by businesses means that aggregate expenditure and real GDP increase. The increase in real GDP increases disposable income, and with no income taxes, real GDP and disposable income increase by the same amount. The increase in disposable income brings an increase in consumption expenditure. And the increased consumption expenditure adds even more to aggregate expenditure. Real GDP and disposable income increase further, and so does consumption expenditure. The initial increase in investment brings an even bigger increase in aggregate expenditure because it induces an increase in consumption expenditure. The magnitude of the increase in aggregate expenditure that results from an increase in autonomous expenditure is determined by the *multiplier*.

The table in Fig. 27.5 sets out an aggregate planned expenditure schedule. Initially, when real GDP is $1,100 billion, aggregate planned expenditure is $1,125 billion. For each $100 billion increase in real GDP, aggregate planned expenditure increases by $75 billion. This aggregate expenditure schedule is shown in the figure as the aggregate expenditure curve AE_0. Initially, equilibrium expenditure is $1,200 billion. You can see this equilibrium in row B of the table and in the figure where the curve AE_0 intersects the 45° line at the point marked B.

Now suppose that autonomous expenditure increases by $50 billion. What happens to equilibrium expenditure? You can see the answer in Fig. 27.5. When this increase in autonomous expenditure is added to the original aggregate planned expenditure, aggregate planned expenditure increases by $50 billion at each level of real GDP. The new aggregate expenditure curve is AE_1. The new equilibrium expenditure, highlighted in the table (row D'), occurs where AE_1 intersects the 45° line and is $1,400 billion (point D'). At this real GDP, aggregate planned expenditure equals real GDP.

The Multiplier Effect

In Fig. 27.5, the increase in autonomous expenditure of $50 billion increases equilibrium expenditure by $200 billion. That is, the change in autonomous expenditure leads, like Céline Dion's electronic equipment, to an amplified change in equilibrium expenditure. This amplified change is the *multiplier effect*—equilibrium expenditure increases by *more than* the increase in autonomous expenditure. The multiplier is greater than 1.

Initially, when autonomous expenditure increases, aggregate planned expenditure exceeds real GDP. As a result, inventories decrease. Firms respond by increasing production so as to restore their inventories to the target level. As production increases, so does real GDP. With a higher level of real GDP, *induced expenditure* increases. Equilibrium expenditure increases by the sum of the initial increase in autonomous expenditure and the increase in induced expenditure. In this example, equilibrium expenditure increases by $200 billion following the increase in autonomous expenditure of $50 billion, so induced expenditure increases by $150 billion.

Although we have just analyzed the effects of an *increase* in autonomous expenditure, this analysis also applies to a decrease in autonomous expenditure. If initially the aggregate expenditure curve is AE_1, equilibrium expenditure and real GDP are $1,400 billion. A decrease in autonomous expenditure of $50 billion shifts the aggregate expenditure curve

FIGURE 27.5   The Multiplier

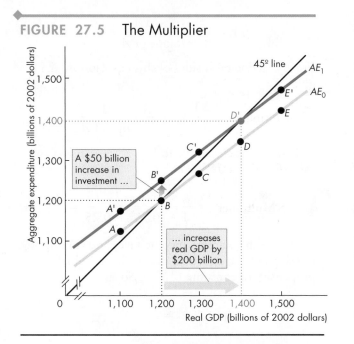

A $50 billion increase in investment ...

... increases real GDP by $200 billion

Real GDP (Y)	Aggregate planned expenditure			
	Original (AE₀)		New (AE₁)	
	(billions of 2002 dollars)			
1,100	A	1,125	A'	1,175
1,200	**B**	**1,200**	**B'**	**1,250**
1,300	C	1,275	C'	1,325
1,400	D	1,350	D'	1,400
1,500	E	1,425	E'	1,475

A $50 billion increase in autonomous expenditure shifts the AE curve upward by $50 billion from AE_0 to AE_1. Equilibrium expenditure increases by $200 billion from $1,200 billion to $1,400 billion. The increase in equilibrium expenditure is 4 times the increase in autonomous expenditure, so the multiplier is 4.

———— MyEconLab animation ◆

downward by $50 billion to AE_0. Equilibrium expenditure decreases from $1,400 billion to $1,200 billion. The decrease in equilibrium expenditure ($200 billion) is larger than the decrease in autonomous expenditure that brought it about ($50 billion).

Why Is the Multiplier Greater Than 1?

We've seen that equilibrium expenditure increases by more than the increase in autonomous expenditure. This makes the multiplier greater than 1. How come? Why does equilibrium expenditure increase by more than the increase in autonomous expenditure?

The multiplier is greater than 1 because induced expenditure increases—an increase in autonomous expenditure *induces* further increases in expenditure. If Rogers Communications Inc. spends $10 million on a new pay-per-view system, real GDP increases by $10 million. But that isn't the end of the story. Video systems designers now have more income, and they spend part of the extra income on goods and services. Real GDP now rises by the initial $10 million plus the extra consumption expenditure induced by the $10 million increase in income. The producers of cars, flat-screen TVs, vacations, and other goods and services now have increased incomes, and they, in turn, spend part of the increase in their incomes on consumption goods and services. Additional income induces additional expenditure, which creates additional income.

How big is the multiplier effect?

The Size of the Multiplier

Suppose that the economy is in a recession. Profit prospects start to look better, and firms are planning a large increase in investment. The world economy is also heading towards expansion. The question on everyone's lips is: How strong will the expansion be? This is a hard question to answer, but an important ingredient in the answer is the size of the multiplier.

The *multiplier* is the amount by which a change in autonomous expenditure is multiplied to determine the change in equilibrium expenditure that it generates. To calculate the multiplier, we divide the change in equilibrium expenditure by the change in autonomous expenditure.

Let's calculate the multiplier for the example in Fig. 27.5. Initially, equilibrium expenditure is $1,200 billion. When autonomous expenditure increases by $50 billion, equilibrium expenditure increases by $200 billion, to $1,400 billion. Then

$$\text{Multiplier} = \frac{\text{Change in equilibrium expenditure}}{\text{Change in autonomous expenditure}}$$

$$\text{Multiplier} = \frac{\$200 \text{ billion}}{\$50 \text{ billion}} = 4.$$

The Multiplier and the Slope of the *AE* Curve

The magnitude of the multiplier depends on the slope of the *AE* curve. In Fig. 27.6, the *AE* curve in part (a) is steeper than the *AE* curve in part (b), and the multiplier is larger in part (a) than in part (b). To see why, let's do a calculation.

Aggregate expenditure and real GDP change because induced expenditure and autonomous expenditure change. The change in real GDP (ΔY) equals the change in induced expenditure (ΔN) plus the change in autonomous expenditure (ΔA). That is,

$$\Delta Y = \Delta N + \Delta A.$$

But the change in induced expenditure is determined by the change in real GDP and the slope of the *AE* curve. To see why, begin with the fact that the slope of the *AE* curve equals the "rise," ΔN, divided by the "run," ΔY. That is,

$$\text{Slope of } AE \text{ curve } = \Delta N \div \Delta Y.$$

So

$$\Delta N = \text{Slope of } AE \text{ curve} \times \Delta Y.$$

Now, use this equation to replace ΔN in the first equation above to give

$$\Delta Y = \text{Slope of } AE \text{ curve} \times \Delta Y + \Delta A.$$

Now, solve for ΔY as

$$(1 - \text{Slope of } AE \text{ curve}) \times \Delta Y = \Delta A$$

and rearrange to give

$$\Delta Y = \frac{\Delta A}{1 - \text{Slope of } AE \text{ curve}}.$$

Finally, divide both sides of this equation by ΔA to give

$$\text{Multiplier} = \frac{\Delta Y}{\Delta A} = \frac{1}{1 - \text{Slope of } AE \text{ curve}}.$$

If we use the example in Fig. 27.5, the slope of the *AE* curve is 0.75, so

$$\text{Multiplier} = \frac{1}{1 - 0.75} = \frac{1}{0.25} = 4.$$

Where there are no income taxes and no imports, the slope of the *AE* curve equals the marginal propensity to consume (*MPC*). So

$$\text{Multiplier} = \frac{1}{1 - MPC}.$$

But $(1 - MPC)$ equals *MPS*. So another formula is

$$\text{Multiplier} = \frac{1}{MPS}.$$

Again using the numbers in Fig. 27.5, we have

$$\text{Multiplier} = \frac{1}{0.25} = 4.$$

Because the marginal propensity to save (*MPS*) is a fraction—a number between 0 and 1—the multiplier is greater than 1.

FIGURE 27.6   The Multiplier and the Slope of the *AE* Curve

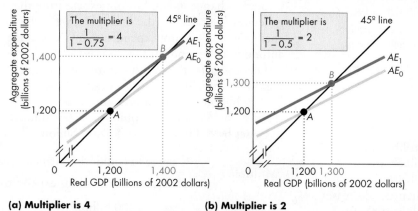

(a) Multiplier is 4

(b) Multiplier is 2

Imports and income taxes make the *AE* curve less steep and reduce the value of the multiplier. In part (a), with no imports and no income taxes, the slope of the *AE* curve is 0.75 (the marginal propensity to consume) and the multiplier is 4. But with imports and income taxes, the slope of the *AE* curve is less than the marginal propensity to consume. In part (b), the slope of the *AE* curve is 0.5. In this case, the multiplier is 2.

Imports and Income Taxes

Imports and income taxes influence the size of the multiplier and make it smaller than it otherwise would be.

To see why imports make the multiplier smaller, think about what happens following an increase in investment. The increase in investment increases real GDP, which in turn increases consumption expenditure. But part of the increase in expenditure is on imported goods and services. Only expenditure on Canadian-produced goods and services increases Canadian real GDP. The larger the marginal propensity to import, the smaller is the change in Canadian real GDP. The Mathematical Note on pp. 668–671 shows the effects of imports and income taxes on the multiplier.

Income taxes also make the multiplier smaller than it otherwise would be. Again, think about what happens following an increase in investment. The increase in investment increases real GDP. Income tax payments increase so disposable income increases by less than the increase in real GDP and consumption expenditure increases by less than it would if taxes had not changed. The larger the income tax rate, the smaller is the change in real GDP.

The marginal propensity to import and the income tax rate together with the marginal propensity to consume determine the multiplier. And their combined influence determines the slope of the *AE* curve.

Over time, the value of the multiplier changes as tax rates change and as the marginal propensity to consume and the marginal propensity to import change. These ongoing changes make the multiplier hard to predict. But they do not change the fundamental fact that an initial change in autonomous expenditure leads to a magnified change in aggregate expenditure and real GDP.

The Multiplier Process

The multiplier effect isn't a one-shot event. It is a process that plays out over a few months. Figure 27.7 illustrates the multiplier process. Autonomous expenditure increases by $50 billion and real GDP increases by $50 billion (the green bar in round 1). This increase in real GDP increases induced expenditure in round 2. With the slope of the *AE* curve equal to 0.75, induced expenditure increases by 0.75 times the increase in real GDP, so the increase in real GDP of $50 billion induces a further increase in expendi-

ture of $37.5 billion. This change in induced expenditure (the green bar in round 2), when added to the previous increase in expenditure (the blue bar in round 2), increases real GDP by $87.5 billion. The round 2 increase in real GDP induces a round 3 increase in induced expenditure. The process repeats through successive rounds. Each increase in real GDP is 0.75 times the previous increase and eventually real GDP increases by $200 billion.

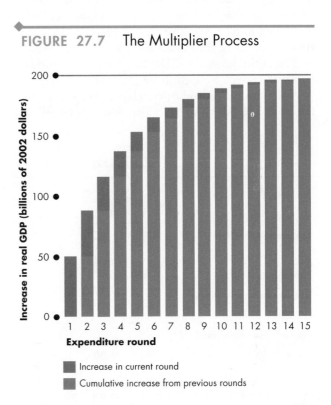

FIGURE 27.7   The Multiplier Process

Autonomous expenditure increases by $50 billion. In round 1, real GDP increases by the same amount. With the slope of the *AE* curve equal to 0.75, each additional dollar of real GDP induces an additional 0.75 of a dollar of induced expenditure. The round 1 increase in real GDP brings an increase in induced expenditure of $37.5 billion in round 2. At the end of round 2, real GDP has increased by $87.5 billion. The extra $37.5 billion of real GDP in round 2 brings a further increase in induced expenditure of $28.1 billion in round 3. At the end of round 3, real GDP has increased by $115.6 billion. This process continues with real GDP increasing by ever-smaller amounts. When the process comes to an end, real GDP has increased by a total of $200 billion.

MyEconLab   animation

Economics in Action
The Multiplier in the Great Depression

The aggregate expenditure model and its multiplier were developed during the 1930s by John Maynard Keynes to understand the most traumatic event in economic history, the *Great Depression*.

In 1929, the Canadian and global economies were booming. Canadian real GDP and real GDP per person had never been higher. By 1933, real GDP had fallen to 67 percent of its 1929 level and more than a quarter of the labour force was unemployed.

The table shows the GDP numbers and components of aggregate expenditure in 1929 and 1933.

Autonomous expenditure collapsed as investment fell from $16 billion to $1 billion and exports fell by a large amount. Government expenditure held steady.

The figure uses the *AE* model to illustrate the Great Depression. In 1929, with autonomous expenditure of $40 billion, the *AE* curve was AE_{29}. Equilibrium expenditure and real GDP were $80 billion.

By 1933, autonomous expenditure had fallen by $13 billion to $27 billion and the *AE* curve had shifted downward to AE_{33}. Equilibrium expenditure and real GDP had fallen to $54 billion.

The decrease in autonomous expenditure of $13 billion brought a decrease in real GDP of $26 billion. The multiplier was $26/$13 = 2. The slope of the *AE* curve is 0.5—the fall in induced expenditure, $13 billion, divided by the fall in real GDP, $26 billion. The multiplier formula, $1/(1 - \text{Slope of } AE \text{ curve})$, delivers a multiplier equal to 2.

	1929	1933
	(billions of 2002 dollars)	
Induced consumption	53	36
Induced imports	−13	−8
Induced expenditure	40	27
Autonomous consumption	−3	4
Investment	16	1
Government expenditure	13	12
Exports	14	10
Autonomous expenditure	40	27
GDP	**80**	**54**

Source of data: Statistics Canada, *Historical Statistics of Canada*, Second Edition, F. H. Leacy (ed.) Ottawa, 1939. Data is recalculated in 2002 dollars.

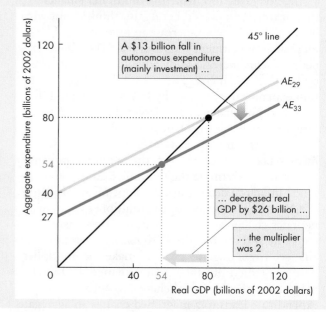

Business Cycle Turning Points

At business cycle turning points, the economy moves from expansion to recession or from recession to expansion. Economists understand these turning points as seismologists understand earthquakes. They know quite a lot about the forces and mechanisms that produce them, but they can't predict them. The forces that bring business cycle turning points are the swings in autonomous expenditure, such as investment and exports. The multiplier that you've just studied is the mechanism that gives momentum to the economy's new direction.

REVIEW QUIZ

1 What is the multiplier? What does it determine? Why does it matter?

2 How do the marginal propensity to consume, the marginal propensity to import, and the income tax rate influence the multiplier?

3 How do fluctuations in autonomous expenditure influence real GDP?

You can work these questions in Study Plan 27.3 and get instant feedback.

──────────── MyEconLab ◆

◆ The Multiplier and the Price Level

We have just considered adjustments in spending that occur in the very short run when the price level is fixed. In this time frame, the economy's cobblestones, which are changes in investment and exports, are not smoothed by shock absorbers like those on a car. Instead, they are amplified like a singer's voice. But these outcomes occur only when the price level is fixed. We now investigate what happens after a long enough time lapse for the price level to change.

Adjusting Quantities and Prices

When firms can't keep up with sales and their inventories fall below target, they increase production, but at some point, they raise their prices. Similarly, when firms find unwanted inventories piling up, they decrease production, but eventually they cut their prices. So far, we've studied the macroeconomic consequences of firms changing their production levels when their sales change, but we haven't looked at the effects of price changes. When individual firms change their prices, the economy's price level changes.

To study the simultaneous determination of real GDP and the price level, we use the *AS-AD model,* which is explained in Chapter 26. But to understand how aggregate demand adjusts, we need to work out the connection between the *AS-AD* model and the aggregate expenditure model that we've used in this chapter. The key to understanding the relationship between these two models is the distinction between the aggregate *expenditure* and aggregate *demand* and the related distinction between the aggregate *expenditure curve* and the aggregate *demand curve.*

Aggregate Expenditure and Aggregate Demand

The aggregate expenditure curve is the relationship between the aggregate planned expenditure and real GDP, all other influences on aggregate planned expenditure remaining the same. The aggregate demand curve is the relationship between the aggregate quantity of goods and services demanded and the price level, all other influences on aggregate demand remaining the same. Let's explore the links between these two relationships.

Deriving the Aggregate Demand Curve

When the price level changes, aggregate planned expenditure changes and the quantity of real GDP demanded changes. The aggregate demand curve slopes downward. Why? There are two main reasons:

- Wealth effect
- Substitution effects

Wealth Effect   Other things remaining the same, the higher the price level, the smaller is the purchasing power of wealth. For example, suppose you have $100 in the bank and the price level is 105. If the price level rises to 125, your $100 buys fewer goods and services. You are less wealthy. With less wealth, you will probably want to try to spend a bit less and save a bit more. The higher the price level, other things remaining the same, the lower is aggregate planned expenditure.

Substitution Effects   For a given expected future price level, a rise in the price level today makes current goods and services more expensive relative to future goods and services and results in a delay in purchases—an *intertemporal substitution.* A rise in the Canadian price level, other things remaining the same, makes Canadian-produced goods and services more expensive relative to foreign-produced goods and services. As a result, Canadian imports increase and Canadian exports decrease—an *international substitution.*

When the price level rises, each of these effects reduces aggregate planned expenditure at each level of real GDP. As a result, when the price level *rises,* the aggregate expenditure curve shifts *downward.* A fall in the price level has the opposite effect. When the price level *falls,* the aggregate expenditure curve shifts *upward.*

Figure 27.8(a) shows the shifts of the *AE* curve. When the price level is 110, the aggregate expenditure curve is AE_0, which intersects the 45° line at point *B.* Equilibrium expenditure is $1,200 billion. If the price level increases to 130, the aggregate expenditure curve shifts downward to AE_1, which intersects the 45° line at point *A.* Equilibrium expenditure decreases to $1,100 billion. If the price level decreases to 90, the aggregate expenditure curve shifts upward to AE_2, which intersects the 45° line at point *C*. Equilibrium expenditure increases to $1,300 billion.

We've just seen that when the price level changes, other things remaining the same, the aggregate expenditure curve shifts and the equilibrium expenditure changes. But when the price level changes, other things remaining the same, there is a movement along the aggregate demand curve.

Figure 27.8(b) shows the movements along the *AD* curve. At a price level of 110, the aggregate quantity of goods and services demanded is $1,200 billion—point *B* on the *AD* curve. If the price level rises to 130, the aggregate quantity of goods and services demanded decreases to $1,100 billion. There is a movement up along the aggregate demand curve to point *A*. If the price level falls to 90, the aggregate quantity of goods and services demanded increases to $1,300 billion. There is a movement down along the aggregate demand curve to point *C*.

Each point on the aggregate demand curve corresponds to a point of equilibrium expenditure. The equilibrium expenditure points *A*, *B*, and *C* in Fig. 27.8(a) correspond to the points *A*, *B*, and *C* on the aggregate demand curve in Fig. 27.8(b).

Changes in Aggregate Expenditure and Aggregate Demand

When any influence on aggregate planned expenditure other than the price level changes, both the aggregate expenditure curve and the aggregate demand curve shift. For example, an increase in investment or exports increases both aggregate planned expenditure and aggregate demand and shifts both the *AE* curve and the *AD* curve.

Figure 27.9 illustrates the effect of such an increase.

Initially, the aggregate expenditure curve is *AE*$_0$ in part (a) and the aggregate demand curve is *AD*$_0$ in part (b). The price level is 110, real GDP is $1,200 billion, and the economy is at point *A* in both parts of Fig. 27.9. Now suppose that investment increases by $100 billion. At a constant price level of 110, the aggregate expenditure curve shifts upward to *AE*$_1$. This curve intersects the 45° line at an equilibrium expenditure of $1,400 billion (point *B*). This equilibrium expenditure of $1,400 billion is the aggregate quantity of goods and services demanded at a price level of 110, as shown by point *B* in part (b). Point *B* lies on a new aggregate demand curve. The

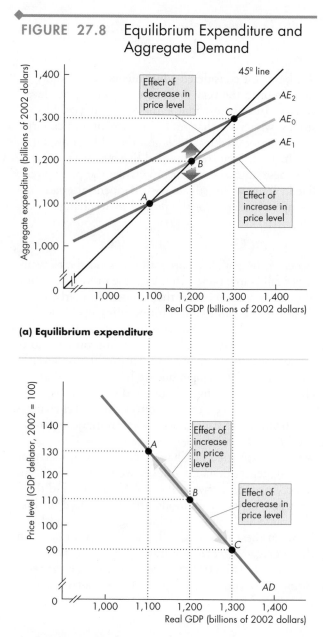

FIGURE 27.8   Equilibrium Expenditure and Aggregate Demand

(a) Equilibrium expenditure

(b) Aggregate demand

A change in the price level *shifts* the *AE* curve and results in a *movement along* the *AD* curve. When the price level is 110, the *AE* curve is *AE*$_0$ and equilibrium expenditure is $1,200 billion at point *B*. When the price level rises to 130, the *AE* curve is *AE*$_1$ and equilibrium expenditure is $1,100 billion at point *A*. When the price level falls to 90, the *AE* curve is *AE*$_2$ and equilibrium expenditure is $1,300 billion at point *C*. Points *A*, *B*, and *C* on the *AD* curve in part (b) correspond to the equilibrium expenditure points *A*, *B*, and *C* in part (a).

MyEconLab   animation

FIGURE 27.9   A Change in Aggregate Demand

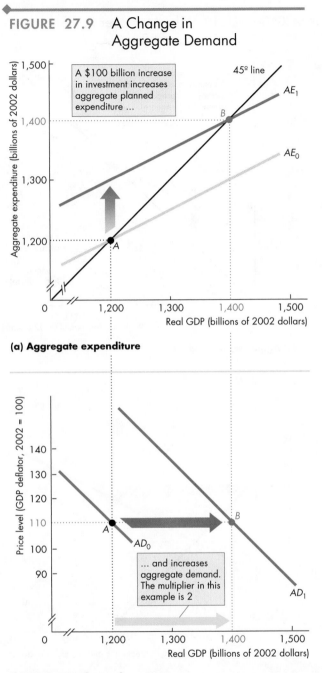

A \$100 billion increase in investment increases aggregate planned expenditure ...

(a) Aggregate expenditure

... and increases aggregate demand. The multiplier in this example is 2

(b) Aggregate demand

The price level is 110. When the aggregate expenditure curve is AE_0 in part (a), the aggregate demand curve is AD_0 in part (b). An increase in autonomous expenditure shifts the AE curve upward to AE_1. In the new equilibrium, real GDP is \$1,400 billion (at point B). Because the quantity of real GDP demanded at a price level of 110 increases to \$1,400 billion, the AD curve shifts rightward to AD_1.

— MyEconLab   animation   ◆

aggregate demand curve has shifted rightward to AD_1.

But how do we know by how much the AD curve shifts? The multiplier determines the answer. The larger the multiplier, the larger is the shift in the aggregate demand curve that results from a given change in autonomous expenditure. In this example, the multiplier is 2. A \$100 billion increase in investment produces a \$200 billion increase in the aggregate quantity of goods and services demanded at each price level. That is, a \$100 billion increase in autonomous expenditure shifts the aggregate demand curve rightward by \$200 billion.

A decrease in autonomous expenditure shifts the aggregate expenditure curve downward and shifts the aggregate demand curve leftward. You can see these effects by reversing the change that we've just described. If the economy is initially at point B on the aggregate expenditure curve AE_1 and on the aggregate demand curve AD_1, a decrease in autonomous expenditure shifts the aggregate expenditure curve downward to AE_0. The aggregate quantity of goods and services demanded decreases from \$1,400 billion to \$1,200 billion, and the aggregate demand curve shifts leftward to AD_0.

Let's summarize what we have just discovered:

If some factor other than a change in the price level increases autonomous expenditure, the AE curve shifts upward and the AD curve shifts rightward. The size of the AD curve shift equals the change in autonomous expenditure multiplied by the multiplier.

Equilibrium Real GDP and the Price Level

In Chapter 26, we learned that aggregate demand and short-run aggregate supply determine equilibrium real GDP and the price level. We've now put aggregate demand under a more powerful microscope and have discovered that a change in investment (or in any component of autonomous expenditure) changes aggregate demand and shifts the aggregate demand curve. The magnitude of the shift depends on the multiplier. But whether a change in autonomous expenditure results ultimately in a change in real GDP, a change in the price level, or a combination of the two depends on aggregate supply. There are two time frames to consider: the short run and the long run. First we'll see what happens in the short run.

An Increase in Aggregate Demand in the Short Run
Figure 27.10 describes the economy. Initially, in part (a), the aggregate expenditure curve is AE_0 and equilibrium expenditure is $1,200 billion—point A. In part (b), aggregate demand is AD_0 and the short-run aggregate supply curve is SAS. (Chapter 26, pp. 625–627, explains the SAS curve.) Equilibrium is at point A in part (b), where the aggregate demand and short-run aggregate supply curves intersect. The price level is 110, and real GDP is $1,200 billion.

Now suppose that investment increases by $100 billion. With the price level fixed at 110, the aggregate expenditure curve shifts upward to AE_1. Equilibrium expenditure increases to $1,400 billion—point B in part (a). In part (b), the aggregate demand curve shifts rightward by $200 billion, from AD_0 to AD_1. How far the aggregate demand curve shifts is determined by the multiplier when the price level is fixed.

But with this new aggregate demand curve, the price level does not remain fixed. The price level rises, and as it does, the aggregate expenditure curve shifts downward. The short-run equilibrium occurs when the aggregate expenditure curve has shifted downward to AE_2 and the new aggregate demand curve, AD_1, intersects the short-run aggregate supply curve at point C in both part (a) and part (b). Real GDP is $1,330 billion, and the price level is 123.

When price level effects are taken into account, the increase in investment still has a multiplier effect on real GDP, but the multiplier is smaller than it would be if the price level were fixed. The steeper the slope of the short-run aggregate supply curve, the larger is the increase in the price level and the smaller is the multiplier effect on real GDP.

An Increase in Aggregate Demand in the Long Run
Figure 27.11 illustrates the long-run effect of an increase in aggregate demand. In the long run, real GDP equals potential GDP and there is full employment. Potential GDP is $1,200 billion, and the long-run aggregate supply curve is LAS. Initially, the economy is at point A in parts (a) and (b).

Investment increases by $100 billion. In Fig. 27.11, the aggregate expenditure curve shifts to AE_1 and the aggregate demand curve shifts to AD_1. With no change in the price level, the economy would move to point B and real GDP would increase to $1,400 billion. But in the short run, the price level rises to 123 and real GDP increases to only

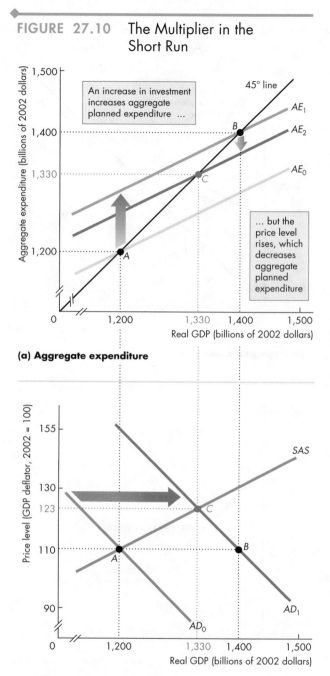

FIGURE 27.10   The Multiplier in the Short Run

(a) Aggregate expenditure

(b) Aggregate demand

An increase in investment shifts the AE curve from AE_0 to AE_1 and the AD curve from AD_0 to AD_1. The price level rises, and the higher price level shifts the AE curve downward from AE_1 to AE_2. The economy moves to point C in both parts. In the short run, when prices are flexible, the multiplier effect is smaller than when the price level is fixed.

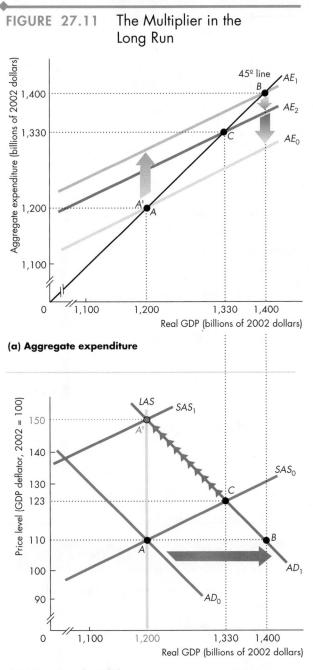

FIGURE 27.11   The Multiplier in the Long Run

(a) Aggregate expenditure

(b) Aggregate demand

Starting from point A, an increase in investment shifts the AE curve to AE_1 and the AD curve to AD_1. In the short run, the economy moves to point C. In the long run, the money wage rate rises and the SAS curve shifts to SAS_1. As the price level rises, the AE curve shifts back to AE_0 and the economy moves to point A'. In the long run, the multiplier is zero.

— MyEconLab animation ◆

$1,330 billion. With the higher price level, the AE curve shifts from AE_1 to AE_2. The economy is now in a short-run equilibrium at point C in both part (a) and part (b).

Real GDP now exceeds potential GDP. The labour force is more than fully employed, and in the long run, shortages of labour increase the money wage rate. The higher money wage rate increases firms' costs, which decreases short-run aggregate supply and shifts the SAS curve leftward to SAS_1. The price level rises further, and real GDP decreases. There is a movement along AD_1, and the AE curve shifts downward from AE_2 towards AE_0. When the money wage rate and the price level have increased by the same percentage, real GDP is again equal to potential GDP and the economy is at point A'. In the long run, the multiplier is zero.

REVIEW QUIZ

1 How does a change in the price level influence the AE curve and the AD curve?

2 If autonomous expenditure increases with no change in the price level, what happens to the AE curve and the AD curve? Which shift is determined by the multiplier and why?

3 How does an increase in autonomous expenditure change real GDP in the short run? Does real GDP change by the same amount as the change in aggregate demand? Why or why not?

4 How does real GDP change in the long run when autonomous expenditure increases? Does real GDP change by the same amount as the change in aggregate demand? Why or why not?

You can work these questions in Study Plan 27.4 and get instant feedback.

━━━━━━━━━━━━━━ MyEconLab ◆

◆ You are now ready to build on what you've learned about aggregate expenditure fluctuations. We'll study the business cycle and the roles of fiscal policy and monetary policy in smoothing the cycle while achieving price stability and sustained economic growth. In Chapter 28 we study the Canadian business cycle and inflation, and in Chapters 29 and 30 we study fiscal policy and monetary policy, respectively. But before you leave the current topic, look at *Reading Between the Lines* on pp. 666–667 and see the aggregate expenditure model in action in the Canadian economy in 2011.

Inventory Investment in a 2011 Contraction

Income and Expenditure Accounts 2011 Q2

www.statcan.gc.ca

August 31, 2011

Real gross domestic product (GDP) declined 0.1 percent in the second quarter, following a 0.9 percent increase the previous quarter. The decline in the second quarter was largely a result of a 2.1 percent drop in exports. Final domestic demand rose 0.7 percent. On a monthly basis, real GDP by industry increased 0.2 percent in June.

Export volume declined 2.1 percent after two quarters of gains. Energy exports contributed the most to this second quarter decline, down 6.7 percent.

Business investment in plant and equipment increased 3.7 percent, the sixth consecutive quarterly advance. Housing investment edged up 0.2 percent.

Consumer spending on goods and services increased 0.4 percent, after remaining unchanged in the first quarter. Expenditures on durable goods rose 0.4 percent.

Business inventories increased $19 billion in the second quarter, more than double the accumulation in the first quarter.

Durable goods held by manufacturers accounted for almost half of the inventory buildup in the second quarter. Retail and wholesale trade inventories accounted for most of the remainder. However, these trade inventories grew less than they did in the first quarter.

Farm inventories increased for a second consecutive quarter.

…

Statistics Canada, Canadian economic accounts, *The Daily*, 11-001-XWE, August 31, 2011; www.statcan.gc.ca/daily-quotidien/110831/dq110831a-eng.htm.

ESSENCE OF THE STORY

- Real GDP decreased in the second quarter of 2011.
- Exports decreased.
- Business investment increased.
- Consumer expenditure increased.
- Business inventories increased.
- Farm inventories increased.

- The news article reports that when real GDP decreased in the second quarter of 2011, inventories *increased*.

- We can interpret the change in inventories using the aggregate expenditure model.

- The table shows the real GDP and aggregate expenditure numbers for the first and second quarters of 2011. Real GDP was $1,349 billion in the second quarter and inventories increased by $19 billion.

- Figure 1 provides an interpretation of what was happening.

- In Fig. 1(a), the *AE* curve tells us the level of aggregate planned expenditure. (The slope of the *AE* curve is 0.2 and is an assumption. This slope depends on the marginal propensity to consume, the marginal propensity to import, and the marginal tax rate, as explained in the Mathematical Note on p. 668.)

- At real GDP of $1,349 billion, aggregate planned expenditure is $1,330 billion—$19 billion below actual expenditure.

- The gap between actual and planned expenditure is an unplanned increase in inventories of $19 billion, which is shown in Fig. 1(b).

- With no change in autonomous expenditure (investment, exports, government expenditure, and autonomous consumption expenditure), real GDP will continue to fall and converge on an equilibrium expenditure of $1,325 billion.

- The news article says that the reason real GDP fell was a fall in exports. The table shows that exports fell by $10 billion.

- The news article also says that the fall in exports was most likely temporary.

- If the fall in exports turns out to be temporary, the *AE* curve will shift upward in the third and fourth quarters of 2011 and the equilibrium expenditure towards which real GDP converges will increase.

Table 1 The Components of Aggregate Expenditure

Item	2011 Q2	2011 Q2	Change
	(billions of 2002 dollars)		
Consumption expenditure	852	855	+3
Investment	323	329	+6
Government expenditure	283	284	+1
Exports	464	454	−10
Imports	596	610	+14
Residual*	16	18	+2
Real GDP	**1,351**	**1,349**	**−2**
Change in inventories	9	19	+10

*The residual arises because chain-dollar real variables are calculated for each expenditure component independently of chain-dollar real GDP and the components don't exactly sum to real GDP.

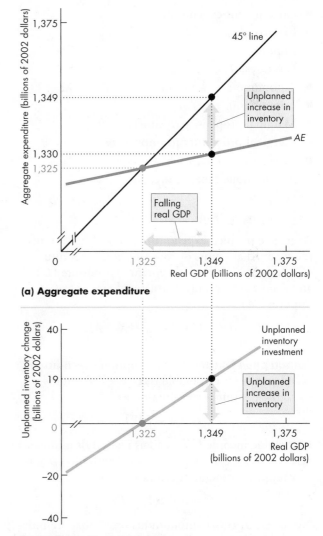

(a) Aggregate expenditure

(b) Unplanned inventory changes

Figure 1 Convergence to Equilibrium Expenditure

◢ MATHEMATICAL NOTE

The Algebra of the Keynesian Model

This mathematical note derives formulas for equilibrium expenditure and the multipliers when the price level is fixed. The variables are

- Aggregate planned expenditure, AE
- Real GDP, Y
- Consumption expenditure, C
- Disposable income, YD
- Investment, I
- Government expenditure, G
- Exports, X
- Imports, M
- Net taxes, T
- Autonomous consumption expenditure, a
- Autonomous taxes, T_a
- Marginal propensity to consume, b
- Marginal propensity to import, m
- Marginal tax rate, t
- Autonomous expenditure, A

Aggregate Expenditure

Aggregate planned expenditure (AE) is the sum of the planned amounts of consumption expenditure (C), investment (I), government expenditure (G), and exports (X) minus the planned amount of imports (M).

$$AE = C + I + G + X - M.$$

Consumption Function Consumption expenditure (C) depends on disposable income (YD), and we write the consumption function as

$$C = a + bYD.$$

Disposable income (YD) equals real GDP minus net taxes ($Y - T$). So if we replace YD with ($Y - T$), the consumption function becomes

$$C = a + b(Y - T).$$

Net taxes, T, equal autonomous taxes (that are independent of income), T_a, plus induced taxes (that vary with income), tY.

So we can write net taxes as

$$T = T_a + tY.$$

Use this last equation to replace T in the consumption function. The consumption function becomes

$$C = a - bT_a + b(1 - t)Y.$$

This equation describes consumption expenditure as a function of real GDP.

Import Function Imports depend on real GDP, and the import function is

$$M = mY.$$

Aggregate Expenditure Curve Use the consumption function and the import function to replace C and M in the AE equation. That is,

$$AE = a - bT_a + b(1 - t)Y + I + G + X - mY.$$

Collect the terms that involve Y on the right side of the equation to obtain

$$AE = (a - bT_a + I + G + X) + [b(1 - t) - m]Y.$$

Autonomous expenditure (A) is $(a - bT_a + I + G + X)$, and the slope of the AE curve is $[b(1 - t) - m]$. So the equation for the AE curve, which is shown in Fig. 1, is

$$AE = A + [b(1 - t) - m]Y.$$

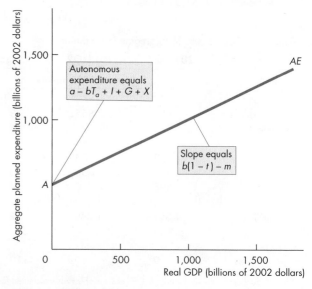

Figure 1 The AE curve

Equilibrium Expenditure

Equilibrium expenditure occurs when aggregate planned expenditure (AE) equals real GDP (Y). That is,

$$AE = Y.$$

In Fig. 2, the scales of the x-axis (real GDP) and the y-axis (aggregate planned expenditure) are identical, so the 45° line shows the points at which aggregate planned expenditure equals real GDP.

Figure 2 shows the point of equilibrium expenditure at the intersection of the AE curve and the 45° line.

To calculate equilibrium expenditure, solve the equations for the AE curve and the 45° line for the two unknown quantities AE and Y. So starting with

$$AE = A + [b(1 - t) - m]Y$$

$$AE = Y,$$

replace AE with Y in the AE equation to obtain

$$Y = A + [b(1 - t) - m]Y.$$

The solution for Y is

$$Y = \frac{1}{1 - [b(1 - t) - m]}A.$$

The Multiplier

The *multiplier* equals the change in equilibrium expenditure and real GDP (Y) that results from a change in autonomous expenditure (A) divided by the change in autonomous expenditure.

A change in autonomous expenditure (ΔA) changes equilibrium expenditure and real GDP by

$$\Delta Y = \frac{1}{1 - [b(1 - t) - m]}\Delta A.$$

$$\text{Multiplier} = \frac{1}{1 - [b(1 - t) - m]}.$$

The size of the multiplier depends on the slope of the AE curve, $b(1 - t) - m$. The larger the slope, the larger is the multiplier. So the multiplier is larger,

- The greater the marginal propensity to consume (b)
- The smaller the marginal tax rate (t)
- The smaller the marginal propensity to import (m)

An economy with no imports and no income taxes has $m = 0$ and $t = 0$. In this special case, the multiplier equals $1/(1 - b)$. If b is 0.75, then the multiplier is 4, as shown in Fig. 3.

In an economy with imports and income taxes, if $b = 0.75$, $t = 0.2$, and $m = 0.1$, the multiplier equals 1 divided by $[1 - 0.75(1 - 0.2) - 0.1]$, which equals 2. Make up some more examples to show the effects of b, t, and m on the multiplier.

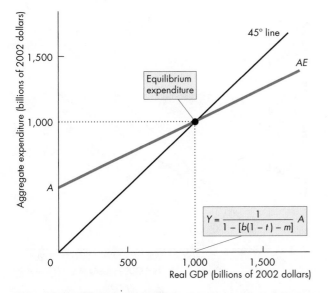

Figure 2 Equilibrium expenditure

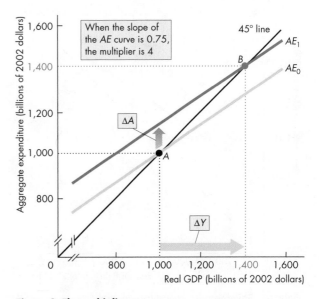

Figure 3 The multiplier

Government Expenditure Multiplier

The **government expenditure multiplier** equals the change in equilibrium expenditure and real GDP (Y) that results from a change in government expenditure (G) divided by the change in government expenditure. Because autonomous expenditure is equal to

$$A = a - bT_a + I + G + X,$$

the change in autonomous expenditure equals the change in government expenditure. That is,

$$\Delta A = \Delta G.$$

You can see from the solution for equilibrium expenditure Y that

$$\Delta Y = \frac{1}{1 - [b(1 - t) - m]} \Delta G.$$

The government expenditure multiplier equals

$$\frac{1}{1 - [b(1 - t) - m]}.$$

In an economy in which $t = 0$ and $m = 0$, the government expenditure multiplier is $1/(1 - b)$. With $b = 0.75$, the government expenditure multiplier is 4, as Fig. 4 shows. Make up some examples and use the above formula to show how b, m, and t influence the government expenditure multiplier.

Autonomous Tax Multiplier

The **autonomous tax multiplier** equals the change in equilibrium expenditure and real GDP (Y) that results from a change in autonomous taxes (T_a) divided by the change in autonomous taxes. Because autonomous expenditure is equal to

$$A = a - bT_a + I + G + X,$$

the change in autonomous expenditure equals *minus* b multiplied by the change in autonomous taxes. That is,

$$\Delta A = -b\Delta T_a.$$

You can see from the solution for equilibrium expenditure Y that

$$\Delta Y = \frac{-b}{1 - [b(1 - t) - m]} \Delta T_a.$$

The autonomous tax multiplier equals

$$\frac{-b}{1 - [b(1 - t) - m]}.$$

In an economy in which $t = 0$ and $m = 0$, the autonomous tax multiplier is $-b/(1 - b)$. In this special case, with $b = 0.75$, the autonomous tax multiplier equals -3, as Fig. 5 shows. Make up some examples and use the above formula to show how b, m, and t influence the autonomous tax multiplier.

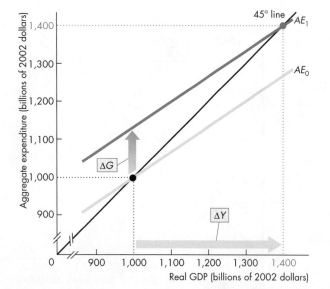

Figure 4 Government expenditure multiplier

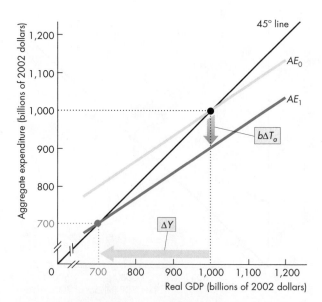

Figure 5 Autonomous tax multiplier

Balanced Budget Multiplier

The **balanced budget multiplier** equals the change in equilibrium expenditure and real GDP (Y) that results from equal changes in government expenditure and taxes divided by the change in government expenditure. Because government expenditure and taxes change by the same amount, the budget balance does not change.

The change in equilibrium expenditure that results from the change in government expenditure is

$$\Delta Y = \frac{1}{1 - [b(1 - t) - m]} \Delta G.$$

And the change in equilibrium expenditure that results from the change in autonomous taxes is

$$\Delta Y = \frac{-b}{1 - [b(1 - t) - m]} \Delta T_a.$$

So the change in equilibrium expenditure resulting from the changes in government expenditure and autonomous taxes is

$$\Delta Y = \frac{1}{1 - [b(1 - t) - m]} \Delta G +$$

$$\frac{-b}{1 - [b(1 - t) - m]} \Delta T_a.$$

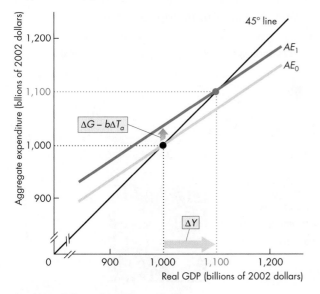

Figure 6 Balanced budget multiplier

Notice that

$$\frac{1}{1 - [b(1 - t) - m]}$$

is common to both terms on the right side. So we can rewrite the equation as

$$\Delta Y = \frac{1}{1 - [b(1 - t) - m]} (\Delta G - b\Delta T_a)$$

The AE curve shifts upward by $\Delta G - b\Delta T_a$ as shown in Fig. 6.

But to keep the budget balanced, the change in autonomous taxes equals the change in government expenditure minus the change in induced taxes. That is,

$$\Delta T_a = \Delta G - t\Delta Y.$$

So we can write the equation for the change in real GDP as

$$\Delta Y = \frac{1}{1 - [b(1 - t) - m]} (\Delta G - b\Delta G - bt\Delta Y).$$

We can simplify this equation. To do so, multiply both sides by $1 - [b(1 - t) - m]$ to give

$$(1 - [b(1 - t) - m])\Delta Y = (1 - b)\Delta G + bt\Delta Y.$$

Now notice that we can subtract $bt\Delta Y$ from both sides of the equation to get

$$(1 - b + m)\Delta Y = (1 - b)\Delta G.$$

So,

$$\Delta Y = \frac{1 - b}{1 - b + m} \Delta G.$$

and the balanced budget multiplier is

$$\frac{1 - b}{1 - b + m}.$$

In an economy in which $m = 0$, the balanced budget multiplier is $(1 - b)/(1 - b)$, which equals 1.

SUMMARY

Key Points

Fixed Prices and Expenditure Plans (pp. 648–651)

- When the price level is fixed, expenditure plans determine real GDP.
- Consumption expenditure is determined by disposable income, and the marginal propensity to consume (*MPC*) determines the change in consumption expenditure brought about by a change in disposable income. Real GDP determines disposable income.
- Imports are determined by real GDP, and the marginal propensity to import determines the change in imports brought about by a change in real GDP.

Working Problems 1 to 3 will give you a better understanding of fixed prices and expenditure plans.

Real GDP with a Fixed Price Level (pp. 652–655)

- Aggregate *planned* expenditure depends on real GDP.
- Equilibrium expenditure occurs when aggregate planned expenditure equals actual expenditure and real GDP.

Working Problems 4 to 7 will give you a better understanding of real GDP with a fixed price level.

The Multiplier (pp. 656–660)

- The multiplier is the magnified effect of a change in autonomous expenditure on equilibrium expenditure and real GDP.

- The multiplier is determined by the slope of the *AE* curve.
- The slope of the *AE* curve is influenced by the marginal propensity to consume, the marginal propensity to import, and the income tax rate.

Working Problems 8 to 11 will give you a better understanding of the multiplier.

The Multiplier and the Price Level (pp. 661–665)

- The *AD* curve is the relationship between the quantity of real GDP demanded and the price level, other things remaining the same.
- The *AE* curve is the relationship between aggregate planned expenditure and real GDP, other things remaining the same.
- At a given price level, there is a given *AE* curve. A change in the price level changes aggregate planned expenditure and shifts the *AE* curve. A change in the price level also creates a movement along the *AD* curve.
- A change in autonomous expenditure that is not caused by a change in the price level shifts the *AE* curve and shifts the *AD* curve. The magnitude of the shift of the *AD* curve depends on the multiplier and on the change in autonomous expenditure.
- The multiplier decreases as the price level changes, and the long-run multiplier is zero.

Working Problems 12 to 21 will give you a better understanding of the multiplier and the price level.

Key Terms

Aggregate planned expenditure, 648
Autonomous expenditure, 652
Autonomous tax multiplier, 670
Balanced budget multiplier, 671
Consumption function, 648
Disposable income, 648
Equilibrium expenditure, 654

Government expenditure multiplier, 670
Induced expenditure, 652
Marginal propensity to consume, 650
Marginal propensity to import, 651
Marginal propensity to save, 650
Multiplier, 656
Saving function, 648

SCAN THIS

STUDY PLAN PROBLEMS AND APPLICATIONS

MyEconLab ◆ You can work Problems 1 to 22 in Chapter 27 Study Plan and get instant feedback.

Fixed Prices and Expenditure Plans (Study Plan 27.1)

Use the following data to work Problems 1 and 2.
You are given the following information about the economy of the United Kingdom.

Disposable income	Consumption expenditure
(billions of pounds per year)	
300	340
400	420
500	500
600	580
700	660

1. Calculate the marginal propensity to consume.
2. Calculate saving at each level of disposable income and calculate the marginal propensity to save.
3. **The U.S. and China's Savings Problems**
   Last year China saved about half of its gross domestic product while the United States saved only 13 percent of its national income. The contrast is even starker at the household level—a personal saving rate in China of about 30 percent of household income, compared with a U.S. rate that dipped into negative territory last year (–0.4 percent of after-tax household income). Similar extremes show up in the consumption shares of the two economies.

   Source: *Fortune*, March 8, 2006

   Compare the *MPC* and *MPS* in the United States and China. Why might they differ?

Real GDP with a Fixed Price Level (Study Plan 27.2)

Use the following figure to work Problems 4 and 5.
The figure illustrates the components of aggregate planned expenditure on Turtle Island. Turtle Island has no imports or exports, no incomes taxes, and the price level is fixed.

4. Calculate autonomous expenditure and the marginal propensity to consume.
5. a. What is aggregate planned expenditure when real GDP is $6 billion?
   b. If real GDP is $4 billion, what is happening to inventories?

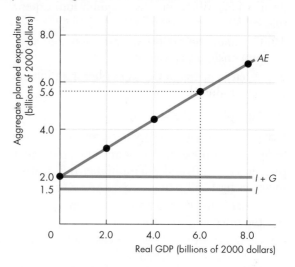

c. If real GDP is $6 billion, what is happening to inventories?

6. Explain the difference between induced consumption expenditure and autonomous consumption expenditure. Why isn't all consumption expenditure induced expenditure?

7. **Recovery?**

   In the second quarter, businesses increased spending on equipment and software by 21.9 percent, while a category that includes home building grew amid a rush by consumers to take advantage of tax credits for homes.

   Source: *The Wall Street Journal*, July 31, 2010

   Explain how an increase in business investment at a constant price level changes equilibrium expenditure.

The Multiplier (Study Plan 27.3)

Use the following data to work Problems 8 and 9.

An economy has a fixed price level, no imports, and no income taxes. *MPC* is 0.80, and real GDP is $150 billion. Businesses increase investment by $5 billion.

8. Calculate the multiplier and the change in real GDP.
9. Calculate the new real GDP and explain why real GDP increases by more than $5 billion.

Use the following data to work Problems 10 and 11.

An economy has a fixed price level, no imports, and no income taxes. An increase in autonomous expenditure of $2 trillion increases equilibrium expenditure by $8 trillion.

10. Calculate the multiplier and the marginal propensity to consume.

11. What happens to the multiplier if an income tax is introduced?

The Multiplier and the Price Level (Study Plan 27.4)

Use the following data to work Problems 12 to 16.

Suppose that the economy is at full employment, the price level is 100, and the multiplier is 2. Investment increases by $100 billion.

12. What is the change in equilibrium expenditure if the price level remains at 100?

13. a. What is the immediate change in the quantity of real GDP demanded?
    b. In the short run, does real GDP increase by more than, less than, or the same amount as the immediate change in the quantity of real GDP demanded?

14. In the short run, does the price level remain at 100? Explain why or why not.

15. a. In the long run, does real GDP increase by more than, less than, or the same amount as the immediate increase in the quantity of real GDP demanded?
    b. Explain how the price level changes in the long run.

16. Are the values of the multipliers in the short run and the long run larger or smaller than 2?

Use the following news clip to work Problems 17 and 18.

Stimulus Calls Rising in Ottawa

Amid building fear of a global financial crisis and return to recession, the federal Conservatives' commitment to deficit reduction is facing heightened scrutiny. "It's important we have up our sleeves, as a nation, ways to control the headwinds we're applying on the economy domestically, because we can't control the external ones," said Michael Gregory, senior economist at BMO Capital Markets. The government has pledged to return to balanced budgets by 2014–15.

Source: *Financial Post*, September 28, 2011

17. If a return to balanced budgets means spending cuts, will aggregate expenditure fall by more

than, less than, or exactly the same as the spending cuts? Explain.

18. Explain and draw a graph to illustrate the effects of "ways to control the headwinds" on aggregate expenditure and aggregate demand in both the short run and the long run.

Use the following news clip to work Problems 19 to 21.

Corporate Tax Cuts Fail to Help Economy: Study

Stephen Harper's plan to reduce corporate taxes further was a flashpoint in the 2011 federal election campaign. The Conservatives' plan is to reduce federal corporate taxes to 15 percent in 2012 from 16.5 percent in 2011 and 18 percent in 2010, while the Liberals and NDP both want to halt those planned cuts.

A new report from the labour-oriented Canadian Centre for Policy Alternatives says business fixed capital spending has declined as a share of GDP since the early 1980s, despite a series of federal and provincial corporate tax cuts from over 50 percent in the early 1980s to 29.5 percent in 2010.

Source: CBC, April 13, 2011

19. Explain and draw a graph to illustrate the effects that Stephen Harper believes result from a cut in corporate taxes.

20. Explain and draw a graph to illustrate the effects that the Canadian Centre for Policy Alternatives believes result from a cut in corporate taxes.

21. What other influences on business investment might explain the trend in business investment's share of GDP?

Mathematical Note (Study Plan 27.MN)

22. In the Canadian economy, autonomous consumption expenditure is $50 billion, investment is $200 billion, and government expenditure is $250 billion. The marginal propensity to consume is 0.7 and net taxes are $250 billion. Exports are $500 billion and imports are $450 billion. Assume that net taxes and imports are autonomous and the price level is fixed.
    a. What is the consumption function?
    b. What is the equation of the *AE* curve?
    c. Calculate equilibrium expenditure.
    d. Calculate the multiplier.
    e. If investment decreases to $150 billion, what is the change in equilibrium expenditure?
    f. Describe the process in part (e) that moves the economy to its new equilibrium expenditure.

ADDITIONAL PROBLEMS AND APPLICATIONS

MyEconLab ◆ You can work these problems in MyEconLab if assigned by your instructor.

Fixed Prices and Expenditure Plans

Use the following data to work Problems 23 and 24. You are given the following information about the economy of Australia.

Disposable income	Saving
(billions of dollars per year)	
0	−5
100	20
200	45
300	70
400	95

23. Calculate the marginal propensity to save.

24. Calculate consumption at each level of disposable income. Calculate the marginal propensity to consume.

Use the following news clip to work Problems 25 to 27.

Americans $1.7 trillion Poorer

Americans saw their net worth decline by $1.7 trillion in the first quarter of 2008. Until then, net worth had been rising steadily since 2003. "The recent declines, however, may not affect consumer spending," said Michael Englund, senior economist with Action Economics. Americans have actually spent more in recent months—spending everything in their wallet and borrowing more. Household debt grew by 3.5 percent with consumer credit rising at an annual rate of 5.75 percent.

Source: CNN, June 5, 2008

25. Explain and draw a graph to illustrate how a decrease in household wealth theoretically impacts the consumption function and the saving function.

26. According to the news clip, how did consumption expenditure respond in the first quarter of 2008? What factors might explain why consumers' actual response differs from what the consumption function model predicts?

27. Draw a graph of a consumption function and show at what point consumers were actually operating in the first quarter. Explain your answer.

Real GDP with a Fixed Price Level

Use the following spreadsheet, which lists real GDP (Y) and the components of aggregate planned expenditure in billions of dollars, to work Problems 28 and 29.

	A	B	C	D	E	F	G
1		Y	C	I	G	X	M
2	A	100	110	50	60	60	15
3	B	200	170	50	60	60	30
4	C	300	230	50	60	60	45
5	D	400	290	50	60	60	60
6	E	500	350	50	60	60	75
7	F	600	410	50	60	60	90

28. Calculate autonomous expenditure. Calculate the marginal propensity to consume.

29. a. What is aggregate planned expenditure when real GDP is $200 billion?
    b. If real GDP is $200 billion, explain the process that moves the economy towards equilibrium expenditure.
    c. If real GDP is $500 billion, explain the process that moves the economy towards equilibrium expenditure.

30. **Business Inventories Decline, GDP Rises**

    Real gross domestic product (GDP) rose in the fourth quarter, led by exports. Consumer spending also increased. Business investment in plant and equipment expanded for the fourth consecutive quarter. Businesses reduced inventories by $5 billion after strong build-ups in the two previous quarters.

    Source: The Daily, Statistics Canada, February 28, 2011

    Explain why business inventories fall when real GDP rises. Of the expenditure items referred to in the news clip, which were a cause of the rise in real GDP and which were effects? Explain your answer with a diagram.

The Multiplier

31. **For a Rainy Day, and for Today**

    In the past fiscal year, B.C. juiced its spending with $2.8 billion from non-renewable resources; Newfoundland, $2.4 billion; Alberta, a whopping $8 billion.

    Source: *Canadian Business*, September 22, 2011

    If the slope of the *AE* curve is 0.7, calculate the immediate change in aggregate planned expenditure that results from the expenditures in the news clip and find the change in real GDP in the short run if the price level remains unchanged.

32. **Recession Threat Demands 'Immediate Action'**

    Investing in infrastructure and green energy programs would give the economy the kickstart it needs more than corporate tax cuts, the NDP said.

    Source: CBC, September 29, 2011

    If taxes fall by $10 billion and the spending on infrastructure and green energy programs increase by $10 billion, which of the two actions would have the larger effect on equilibrium expenditure, other things remaining the same?

The Multiplier and the Price Level

33. **Inflation Rate Rises to 3.1% in August**

    Canada's annual inflation rate was stronger than expected in August, checking in at 3.1 percent. The August rise followed increases of 2.7 percent in July and 3.1 percent in June. Economists had been forecasting a 2.9 percent year-over-year rate of inflation for August.

    Source: CBC News, September 21, 2011

    Explain and draw a graph to illustrate the effect on equilibrium expenditure of the rise in the price level described in the news clip.

Use the following news clip to work Problems 34 to 36.

Where Americans Will (and Won't) Cut Back

Consumer confidence has tumbled but even as consumers cut back on spending, there are some things they refuse to give up. Market research reports that Americans are demonstrating a strong reluctance to give up everyday pleasures, but many are forced to prioritize and scale back some of their spending.

Spending on dining out, out-of-the-home entertainment, clothes, vacations, and buying lunch tend to be the first to be cut and many Americans are driving less and staying at home more. A whopping 50 percent of Americans plan to buy an HD or flat-panel TV in the next year. Cable and satellite TV subscriptions are also way down the list on cutbacks. Despite the expense, another thing consumers refuse to go without completely is travel. Even in these tough times, 59 percent of Americans plan to take a trip in the next six months.

Source: CNN, July 16, 2008

34. Which of the expenditures listed in the news clip are part of induced consumption expenditure and which are part of autonomous consumption expenditure? Explain why all consumption expenditure is not induced expenditure.

35. Explain and draw a graph to illustrate how declining consumer confidence influences aggregate expenditure and aggregate demand in the short run.

36. Explain and draw a graph to illustrate the long-run effect on aggregate expenditure and aggregate demand of the decline in consumer confidence.

Economics in the News

37. After you have studied *Reading Between the Lines* on pp. 666–667, answer the following questions.

    a. If the changes in inventories in the second quarter of 2011 were mainly *planned* changes, what role did they play in shifting the *AE* curve and changing equilibrium expenditure? Use a two-part figure (similar to that on p. 654) to answer this question.

    b. What do you predict will happen to unplanned inventory changes if exports and investment increase and real GDP returns to potential GDP?

Mathematical Note

38. In an economy, autonomous spending is $20 trillion and the slope of the *AE* curve is 0.6.

    a. What is the equation of the *AE* curve?

    b. Calculate equilibrium expenditure.

    c. Calculate the multiplier if the price level is fixed.

Canadian Inflation, Unemployment, and Business Cycle

After studying this chapter, you will be able to

◆ Explain how demand-pull and cost-push forces bring cycles in inflation and output

◆ Explain the short-run and long-run trade-off between inflation and unemployment

◆ Explain how the mainstream business cycle theory and real business cycle theory account for fluctuations in output and employment

We care about inflation because it raises our cost of living. We care about unemployment because either it hits us directly and takes our jobs or it scares us into thinking that we might lose our jobs. And we care about real GDP growth because it directly affects our standard of living. We want low inflation, low unemployment, and rapid income growth. But can we have all these things at the same time? Or do we face a tradeoff among them? As this chapter explains, we face a tradeoff in the short run but not in the long run.

At the end of the chapter, in *Reading Between the Lines*, we examine the labour market during the slow recovery.

◆ Inflation Cycles

In the long run, inflation is a monetary phenomenon. It occurs if the quantity of money grows faster than potential GDP. But in the short run, many factors can start an inflation, and real GDP and the price level interact. To study these interactions, we distinguish between two sources of inflation:

- Demand-pull inflation
- Cost-push inflation

Demand-Pull Inflation

An inflation that starts because aggregate demand increases is called **demand-pull inflation**. Demand-pull inflation can be kicked off by *any* of the factors that change aggregate demand. Examples are a cut in the interest rate, an increase in the quantity of money, an increase in government expenditure, a tax cut, an increase in exports, or an increase in investment stimulated by an increase in expected future profits.

Initial Effect of an Increase in Aggregate Demand

Suppose that last year the price level was 110 and real GDP was $1,200 billion. Potential GDP was also $1,200 billion. Figure 28.1(a) illustrates this situation. The aggregate demand curve is AD_0, the short-run aggregate supply curve is SAS_0, and the long-run aggregate supply curve is LAS.

Now suppose that the Bank of Canada cuts the interest rate. The quantity of money increases and the aggregate demand curve shifts from AD_0 to AD_1. With no change in potential GDP and no change in the money wage rate, the long-run aggregate supply curve and the short-run aggregate supply curve remain at LAS and SAS_0, respectively.

The price level and real GDP are determined at the point where the aggregate demand curve AD_1 intersects the short-run aggregate supply curve. The price level rises to 113, and real GDP increases above potential GDP to $1,250 billion. Unemployment falls below its natural rate. The economy is at an above full-employment equilibrium and there is an inflationary gap. The next step in the unfolding story is a rise in the money wage rate.

FIGURE 28.1 A Demand-Pull Rise in the Price Level

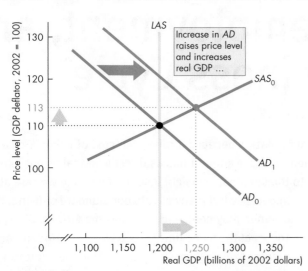

(a) Initial effect

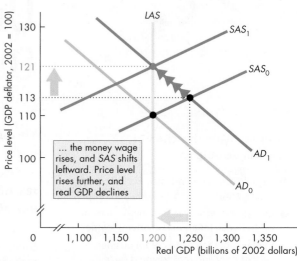

(b) The money wage adjusts

In part (a), the aggregate demand curve is AD_0, the short-run aggregate supply curve is SAS_0, and the long-run aggregate supply curve is LAS. The price level is 110, and real GDP is $1,200 billion, which equals potential GDP. Aggregate demand increases to AD_1. The price level rises to 113, and real GDP increases to $1,250 billion.

In part (b), starting from the above full-employment equilibrium, the money wage rate begins to rise and the short-run aggregate supply curve shifts leftward towards SAS_1. The price level rises further, and real GDP returns to potential GDP.

Money Wage Rate Response Real GDP cannot remain above potential GDP forever. With unemployment below its natural rate, there is a shortage of labour. In this situation, the money wage rate begins to rise. As it does so, short-run aggregate supply decreases and the *SAS* curve starts to shift leftward. The price level rises further, and real GDP begins to decrease.

With no further change in aggregate demand—that is, the aggregate demand curve remains at AD_1—this process ends when the short-run aggregate supply curve has shifted to SAS_1 in Fig. 28.1(b). At this time, the price level has increased to 121 and real GDP has returned to potential GDP of $1,200 billion, the level at which it started.

A Demand-Pull Inflation Process The events that we've just described bring a *one-time rise in the price level*, not an inflation. For inflation to proceed, aggregate demand must *persistently* increase.

The only way in which aggregate demand can persistently increase is if the quantity of money persistently increases. Suppose that every day, the Bank of Canada buys bonds in an open market operation (see Chapter 24, pp. 573–574). When the Bank of Canada buys bonds, it creates monetary base and an expanding monetary base increases the quantity of money. If the quantity of money keeps growing, aggregate demand keeps increasing. This persistent increase in aggregate demand puts continual upward pressure on the price level. The economy now experiences demand-pull inflation.

Figure 28.2 illustrates the process of demand-pull inflation. The starting point is the same as that shown in Fig. 28.1. The aggregate demand curve is AD_0, the short-run aggregate supply curve is SAS_0, and the long-run aggregate supply curve is *LAS*. Real GDP is $1,200 billion, and the price level is 110. Aggregate demand increases, shifting the aggregate demand curve to AD_1. Real GDP increases to $1,250 billion, and the price level rises to 113. The economy is at an above full-employment equilibrium. There is a shortage of labour, and the money wage rate rises. The short-run aggregate supply curve shifts to SAS_1. The price level rises to 121, and real GDP returns to potential GDP.

But the Bank of Canada increases the quantity of money again, and aggregate demand continues to increase. The aggregate demand curve shifts rightward to AD_2. The price level rises further to 125,

FIGURE 28.2   A Demand-Pull Inflation Spiral

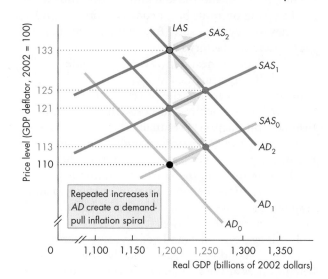

Each time the quantity of money increases, aggregate demand increases and the aggregate demand curve shifts rightward from AD_0 to AD_1 to AD_2, and so on. Each time real GDP increases above potential GDP, the money wage rate rises and the short-run aggregate supply curve shifts leftward from SAS_0 to SAS_1 to SAS_2, and so on. The price level rises from 110 to 113, 121, 125, 133, and so on. There is a demand-pull inflation spiral. Real GDP fluctuates between $1,200 billion and $1,250 billion.

MyEconLab   animation ◆

and real GDP again exceeds potential GDP at $1,250 billion. Yet again, the money wage rate rises and decreases short-run aggregate supply. The *SAS* curve shifts to SAS_2, and the price level rises further, to 133. As the quantity of money continues to grow, aggregate demand increases and the price level rises in an ongoing demand-pull inflation process.

The process you have just studied generates inflation—an ongoing process of a rising price level.

Demand-Pull Inflation in Chatham You may better understand the inflation process that we've just described by considering what is going on in an individual part of the economy, such as a Chatham ketchup-bottling plant. Initially, when aggregate demand increases, the demand for ketchup increases and the price of ketchup rises. Faced with a higher price, the ketchup plant works overtime and increases production. Conditions are good for workers in Chatham, and the ketchup factory finds it hard to hang on to its best people. To do so, it offers a higher money wage rate. As the wage rate rises, so do the ketchup factory's costs.

What happens next depends on aggregate demand. If aggregate demand remains constant, the firm's costs increase but the price of ketchup does not increase as quickly as its costs. In this case, the firm cuts production. Eventually the money wage rate and costs increase by the same percentage as the rise in the price of ketchup. In real terms, the ketchup factory is in the same situation as it was initially. It produces the same amount of ketchup and employs the same amount of labour as before demand increased.

But if aggregate demand continues to increase, so does the demand for ketchup and the price of ketchup rises at the same rate as wages. The ketchup factory continues to operate at above full employment and there is a persistent shortage of labour. Prices and wages chase each other upward in a demand-pull inflation spiral.

Demand-Pull Inflation in Canada A demand-pull inflation like the one you've just studied occurred in Canada during the late 1960s and early 1970s. In 1960, inflation was a moderate 2 percent a year, but its rate increased slowly through the mid-1960s. Then, between 1966 and 1969, the inflation rate surged upward. Inflation then decreased slightly during 1970 and 1971, but it took off again in 1972. By 1973, the inflation rate was almost 10 percent a year.

These increases in inflation resulted from increases in aggregate demand that had two main sources. The first was a large increase in U.S. government expenditure and the quantity of money in the United States, which increased aggregate demand in the entire world economy. The second source was an increase in Canadian government expenditure and the quantity of money.

With unemployment below its natural rate, the money wage rate started to rise more quickly and the SAS curve shifted leftward. The Bank of Canada responded with a further increase in the money growth rate, and a demand-pull inflation spiral unfolded. By 1974, the inflation rate had reached double digits.

Next, let's see how shocks to aggregate supply can create cost-push inflation.

Cost-Push Inflation

An inflation that is kicked off by an increase in costs is called **cost-push inflation**. The two main sources of cost increases are

1. An increase in the money wage rate
2. An increase in the money prices of raw materials

At a given price level, the higher the cost of production, the smaller is the amount that firms are willing to produce. So if the money wage rate rises or if the prices of raw materials (for example, oil) rise, firms decrease their supply of goods and services. Aggregate supply decreases, and the short-run aggregate supply curve shifts leftward.[1] Let's trace the effects of such a decrease in short-run aggregate supply on the price level and real GDP.

Initial Effect of a Decrease in Aggregate Supply
Suppose that last year the price level was 110 and real GDP was $1,200 billion. Potential real GDP was also $1,200 billion. Figure 28.3(a) illustrates this situation. The aggregate demand curve was AD_0, the short-run aggregate supply curve was SAS_0, and the long-run aggregate supply curve was LAS. In the current year, the world's oil producers form a price-fixing organization that strengthens their market power and increases the relative price of oil. They raise the price of oil, and this action decreases short-run aggregate supply. The short-run aggregate supply curve shifts leftward to SAS_1. The price level rises to 117, and real GDP decreases to $1,150 billion. The economy is at a below full-employment equilibrium and there is a recessionary gap.

This event is a *one-time rise in the price level.* It is not inflation. In fact, a supply shock on its own cannot cause inflation. Something more must happen to enable a one-time supply shock, which causes a one-time rise in the price level, to be converted into a process of ongoing inflation. The quantity of money must persistently increase. Sometimes it does increase, as you will now see.

---

[1] Some cost-push forces, such as an increase in the price of oil accompanied by a decrease in the availability of oil, can also decrease long-run aggregate supply. We'll ignore such effects here and examine cost-push factors that change only short-run aggregate supply. Later in the chapter, we study the effects of shocks to long-run aggregate supply.

FIGURE 28.3   A Cost-Push Rise in the Price Level

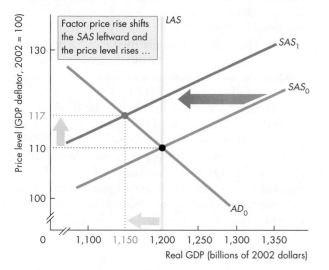

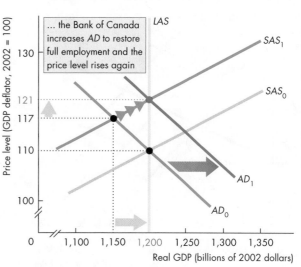

(a) Initial cost push

Initially, the aggregate demand curve is AD_0, the short-run aggregate supply curve is SAS_0, and the long-run aggregate supply curve is LAS. A decrease in aggregate supply (for example, resulting from a rise in the world price of oil) shifts the short-run aggregate supply curve to SAS_1. The economy moves to the point where the short-run aggregate supply curve SAS_1 intersects the aggregate demand curve

(b) The Bank of Canada responds

AD_0. The price level rises to 117, and real GDP decreases to $1,150 billion.

In part (b), if the Bank of Canada responds by increasing aggregate demand to restore full employment, the aggregate demand curve shifts rightward to AD_1. The economy returns to full employment, but the price level rises further to 121.

MyEconLab   animation

Aggregate Demand Response When real GDP decreases, unemployment rises above its natural rate. In such a situation, there is often an outcry of concern and a call for action to restore full employment. Suppose that the Bank of Canada cuts the interest rate and increases the quantity of money. Aggregate demand increases. In Fig. 28.3(b), the aggregate demand curve shifts rightward to AD_1 and full employment is restored. But the price level rises further to 121.

A Cost-Push Inflation Process The oil producers now see the prices of everything they buy increasing, so oil producers increase the price of oil again to restore its new high relative price. Figure 28.4 continues the story. The short-run aggregate supply curve now shifts to SAS_2. The price level rises and real GDP decreases.

The price level rises further, to 129, and real GDP decreases to $1,150 billion. Unemployment increases

above its natural rate. If the Bank of Canada responds yet again with an increase in the quantity of money, aggregate demand increases and the aggregate demand curve shifts to AD_2. The price level rises even higher—to 133—and full employment is again restored. A cost-push inflation spiral results. The combination of a rising price level and decreasing real GDP is called **stagflation**.

You can see that the Bank of Canada has a dilemma. If it does not respond when producers raise the oil price, the economy remains below full employment. If the Bank of Canada increases the quantity of money to restore full employment, it invites another oil price hike that will call forth yet a further increase in the quantity of money.

If the Bank of Canada responds to each oil price hike by increasing the quantity of money, inflation will rage along at a rate decided by oil producers. But if the Bank of Canada doesn't increase the quantity of money, the economy remains below full employment.

FIGURE 28.4   A Cost-Push Inflation Spiral

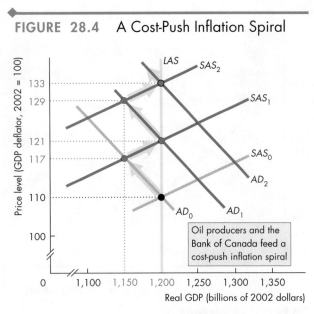

Each time a cost increase occurs, the short-run aggregate supply curve shifts leftward from SAS_0 to SAS_1 to SAS_2, and so on. Each time real GDP decreases below potential GDP, the Bank of Canada increases the quantity of money and the aggregate demand curve shifts rightward from AD_0 to AD_1 to AD_2, and so on. The price level rises from 110 to 117, 121, 129, 133, and so on. There is a cost-push inflation spiral. Real GDP fluctuates between $1,200 billion and $1,150 billion.

————— MyEconLab   animation ◆

Cost-Push Inflation in Chatham

What is going on in the Chatham ketchup-bottling plant when the economy is experiencing cost-push inflation?

When the oil price increases, so do the costs of bottling ketchup. These higher costs decrease the supply of ketchup, increasing its price and decreasing the quantity produced. The ketchup plant lays off some workers.

This situation persists until either the Bank of Canada increases aggregate demand or the price of oil falls. If the Bank of Canada increases aggregate demand, the demand for ketchup increases and so does its price. The higher price of ketchup brings higher profits, and the bottling plant increases its production. The ketchup factory rehires the laid-off workers.

Cost-Push Inflation in Canada

A cost-push inflation like the one you've just studied occurred in Canada during the 1970s. It began in 1974 when the

Organization of the Petroleum Exporting Countries (OPEC) raised the price of oil fourfold. The higher oil price decreased aggregate supply, which caused the price level to rise more quickly and real GDP to shrink. The Bank of Canada then faced a dilemma: Would it increase the quantity of money and accommodate the cost-push forces, or would it keep aggregate demand growth in check by limiting money growth? In 1975, 1976, and 1977, the Bank of Canada repeatedly allowed the quantity of money to grow quickly and inflation proceeded at a rapid rate. In 1979 and 1980, OPEC was again able to push oil prices higher. On that occasion, the Bank of Canada decided not to respond to the oil price hike with an increase in the quantity of money. The result was a recession but also, eventually, a fall in inflation.

Expected Inflation

If inflation is expected, the fluctuations in real GDP that accompany demand-pull and cost-push inflation that you've just studied don't occur. Instead, inflation proceeds as it does in the long run, with real GDP equal to potential GDP and unemployment at its natural rate. Figure 28.5 explains why.

Suppose that last year the aggregate demand curve was AD_0, the aggregate supply curve was SAS_0, and the long-run aggregate supply curve was LAS. The price level was 110, and real GDP was $1,200 billion, which is also potential GDP.

To keep things as simple as possible, suppose that potential GDP does not change, so the LAS curve doesn't shift. Also suppose that aggregate demand is *expected to increase* to AD_1.

In anticipation of this increase in aggregate demand, the money wage rate rises and the short-run aggregate supply curve shifts leftward. If the money wage rate rises by the same percentage as the price level is expected to rise, the short-run aggregate supply curve for next year is SAS_1.

If aggregate demand turns out to be the same as expected, the aggregate demand curve is AD_1. The short-run aggregate supply curve, SAS_1, and AD_1 determine the actual price level at 121. Between last year and this year, the price level increased from 110 to 121 and the economy experienced an inflation rate equal to that expected. If this inflation is ongoing, aggregate demand increases (as expected) in the following year and the aggregate demand curve shifts to AD_2. The money wage rate rises to reflect the expected inflation, and the short-run aggregate

FIGURE 28.5   Expected Inflation

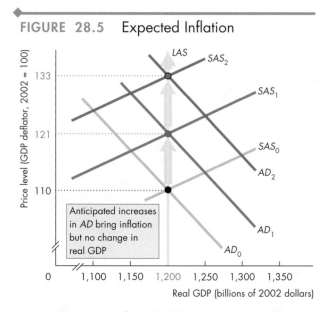

Potential real GDP is $1,200 billion. Last year, aggregate demand was AD_0 and the short-run aggregate supply curve was SAS_0. The actual price level was the same as the expected price level: 110. This year, aggregate demand is expected to increase to AD_1 and the price level is expected to rise from 110 to 121. As a result, the money wage rate rises and the short-run aggregate supply curve shifts to SAS_1.

If aggregate demand actually increases as expected, the actual aggregate demand curve AD_1 is the same as the expected aggregate demand curve. Real GDP is $1,200 billion, and the actual price level rises to 121. The inflation is expected.

Next year, the process continues with aggregate demand increasing as expected to AD_2 and the money wage rate rising to shift the short-run aggregate supply curve to SAS_2. Again, real GDP remains at $1,200 billion, and the price level rises, as expected, to 133.

———— MyEconLab   animation ◆

supply curve shifts to SAS_2. The price level rises, as expected, to 133.

What caused this inflation? The immediate answer is that because people expected inflation, the money wage rate increased and the price level increased. But the expectation was correct. Aggregate demand was expected to increase, and it did increase. It is the actual and expected increase in aggregate demand that caused the inflation.

An expected inflation at full employment is exactly the process that the quantity theory of money

predicts. To review the quantity theory of money, see Chapter 24, pp. 582–583.

This broader account of the inflation process and its short-run effects show why the quantity theory of money doesn't explain the *fluctuations* in inflation. The economy follows the course described in Fig. 28.5, but as predicted by the quantity theory, only if aggregate demand growth is forecasted correctly.

Forecasting Inflation

To anticipate inflation, people must forecast it. Some economists who work for macroeconomic forecasting agencies, banks, insurance companies, labour unions, and large corporations specialize in inflation forecasting. The best forecast available is one that is based on all the relevant information and is called a **rational expectation**. A rational expectation is not necessarily a correct forecast. It is simply the best forecast with the information available. It will often turn out to be wrong, but no other forecast that could have been made with the information available could do better.

Inflation and the Business Cycle

When the inflation forecast is correct, the economy operates at full employment. If aggregate demand grows faster than expected, real GDP rises above potential GDP, the inflation rate exceeds its expected rate, and the economy behaves like it does in a demand-pull inflation. If aggregate demand grows more slowly than expected, real GDP falls below potential GDP and the inflation rate slows.

◆ **REVIEW QUIZ**

1 How does demand-pull inflation begin?
2 What must happen to create a demand-pull inflation spiral?
3 How does cost-push inflation begin?
4 What must happen to create a cost-push inflation spiral?
5 What is stagflation and why does cost-push inflation cause stagflation?
6 How does expected inflation occur?
7 How do real GDP and the price level change if the forecast of inflation is incorrect?

You can work these questions in Study Plan 28.1 and get instant feedback.

———————————————— MyEconLab ◆

Inflation and Unemployment: The Phillips Curve

Another way of studying inflation cycles focuses on the relationship and the short-run tradeoff between inflation and unemployment, a relationship called the **Phillips curve**—so named because it was first suggested by New Zealand economist A.W. Phillips.

Why do we need another way of studying inflation? What is wrong with the *AS-AD* explanation of the fluctuations in inflation and real GDP? The first answer to both questions is that we often want to study changes in both the expected and actual inflation rates and for this purpose, the Phillips curve provides a simpler tool and clearer insights than the *AS-AD* model provides. The second answer to both questions is that we often want to study changes in the short-run tradeoff between inflation and real economic activity (real GDP and unemployment) and again, the Phillips curve serves this purpose well.

To begin our explanation of the Phillips curve, we distinguish between two time frames (similar to the two aggregate supply time frames). We study

- The short-run Phillips curve
- The long-run Phillips curve

The Short-Run Phillips Curve

The **short-run Phillips curve** shows the relationship between inflation and unemployment, holding constant,

1. The expected inflation rate
2. The natural unemployment rate

You've just seen what determines the expected inflation rate. The natural unemployment rate and the factors that influence it are explained in Chapter 21, pp. 497–498.

Figure 28.6 shows a short-run Phillips curve, *SRPC*. Suppose that the expected inflation rate is 10 percent a year and the natural unemployment rate is 6 percent, point *A* in the figure. A short-run Phillips curve passes through this point. If inflation rises above its expected rate, unemployment falls below its natural rate. This joint movement in the inflation rate and the unemployment rate is illustrated as a movement up along the short-run Phillips curve from point *A* to point *B*. Similarly, if inflation falls below its expected rate, unemployment rises above

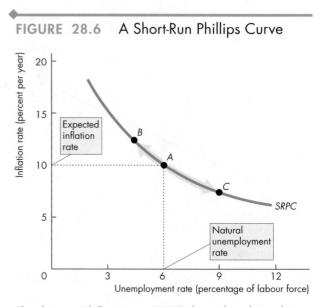

FIGURE 28.6   A Short-Run Phillips Curve

The short-run Phillips curve (*SRPC*) shows the relationship between inflation and unemployment at a given expected inflation rate and a given natural unemployment rate. With an expected inflation rate of 10 percent a year and a natural unemployment rate of 6 percent, the short-run Phillips curve passes through point *A*.

An unexpected increase in aggregate demand lowers unemployment and increases the inflation rate—a movement up along the short-run Phillips curve to point *B*. An unexpected decrease in aggregate demand increases unemployment and lowers the inflation rate—a movement down along the short-run Phillips curve to point *C*.

——————— MyEconLab   animation ◆

its natural rate. In this case, there is movement down along the short-run Phillips curve from point *A* to point *C*.

The short-run Phillips curve is like the short-run aggregate supply curve. A movement along the *SAS* curve that brings a higher price level and an increase in real GDP is equivalent to a movement along the short-run Phillips curve from *A* to *B* that brings an increase in the inflation rate and a decrease in the unemployment rate.

Similarly, a movement along the *SAS* curve that brings a lower price level and a decrease in real GDP is equivalent to a movement along the short-run Phillips curve from *A* to *C* that brings a decrease in the inflation rate and an increase in the unemployment rate.

The Long-Run Phillips Curve

The **long-run Phillips curve** shows the relationship between inflation and unemployment when the actual inflation rate equals the expected inflation rate. The long-run Phillips curve is vertical at the natural unemployment rate. In Fig. 28.7, it is the vertical line *LRPC*.

The long-run Phillips curve tells us that any expected inflation rate is possible at the natural unemployment rate. This proposition is consistent with the *AS-AD* model, which predicts (and which Fig. 28.5 illustrates) that when inflation is expected, real GDP equals potential GDP and unemployment is at its natural rate.

The short-run Phillips curve intersects the long-run Phillips curve at the expected inflation rate. A change in the expected inflation rate shifts the short-run Phillips curve but it does not shift the long-run Phillips curve.

In Fig. 28.7, if the expected inflation rate is 10 percent a year, the short-run Phillips curve is

$SRPC_0$. If the expected inflation rate falls to 6 percent a year, the short-run Phillips curve shifts downward to $SRPC_1$. The vertical distance by which the short-run Phillips curve shifts from point *A* to point *D* is equal to the change in the expected inflation rate. If the actual inflation rate also falls from 10 percent to 6 percent, there is a movement down the long-run Phillips curve from *A* to *D*. An increase in the expected inflation rate has the opposite effect to that shown in Fig. 28.7.

The other source of a shift in the Phillips curve is a change in the natural unemployment rate.

Changes in the Natural Unemployment Rate

The natural unemployment rate changes for many reasons (see Chapter 21, pp. 497–498). A change in the natural unemployment rate shifts both the short-run and long-run Phillips curves. Figure 28.8 illustrates such shifts.

FIGURE 28.7 Short-Run and Long-Run Phillips Curves

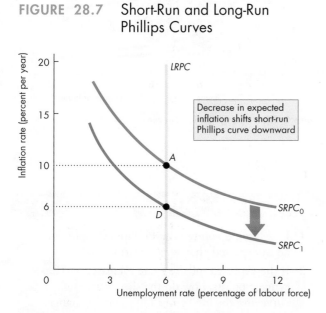

The long-run Phillips curve is *LRPC*. A fall in expected inflation from 10 percent a year to 6 percent a year shifts the short-run Phillips curve downward from $SRPC_0$ to $SRPC_1$. The long-run Phillips curve does not shift. The new short-run Phillips curve intersects the long-run Phillips curve at the new expected inflation rate—point *D*.

FIGURE 28.8 A Change in the Natural Unemployment Rate

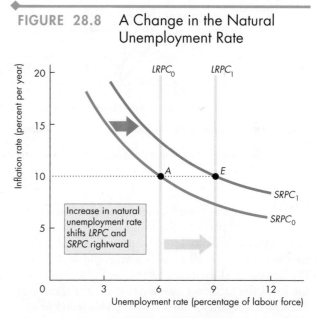

A change in the natural unemployment rate shifts both the short-run and long-run Phillips curves. An increase in the natural unemployment rate from 6 percent to 9 percent shifts the Phillips curves rightward to $SRPC_1$ and $LRPC_1$. The new long-run Phillips curve intersects the new short-run Phillips curve at the expected inflation rate—point *E*.

Economics in Action

The Shifting Short-Run Tradeoff

Figure 1 is a scatter diagram of the Canadian inflation rate (measured by the GDP deflator) and the unemployment rate since 1962. In Fig. 2 we interpret the data in terms of the shifting short-run Phillips curve.

During the 1960s, the short-run Phillips curve was $SRPC_0$, with a natural unemployment rate of 5 percent and an expected inflation rate of 2 percent a year (point A).

During the early 1970s, the short-run Phillips curve was $SRPC_1$, with a natural unemployment rate of 6 percent and an expected inflation rate of 10 percent a year (point B).

During the 1980s, the natural unemployment rate increased to 10 percent and the expected inflation rate fell to 8 percent a year (point C). The short-run Phillips curve shifted rightward to $SRPC_2$.

During the 1990s and 2000s, the expected inflation rate fell to 2 percent a year and the natural unemployment rate decreased to 6 percent (point D). The short-run Phillips curve shifted leftward to $SRPC_3$ and was almost back to $SRPC_0$, where it had been during the 1960s.

Figure 1 Phillips Curve Data in Canada: The Time Sequence

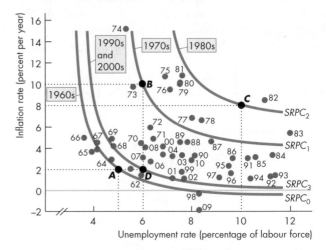

Figure 2 The Shifting Phillips Curves

Source of data: Statistics Canada, CANSIM Tables 380–0002 and 380–0056.

If the natural unemployment rate increases from 6 percent to 9 percent, the long-run Phillips curve shifts from $LRPC_0$ to $LRPC_1$, and if expected inflation is constant at 10 percent a year, the short-run Phillips curve shifts from $SRPC_0$ to $SRPC_1$. Because the expected inflation rate is constant, the short-run Phillips curve $SRPC_1$ intersects the long-run curve $LRPC_1$ (point E) at the same inflation rate at which the short-run Phillips curve $SRPC_0$ intersects the long-run curve $LRPC_0$ (point A).

Changes in both the expected inflation rate and the natural unemployment rate have shifted the Canadian Phillips curve but the expected inflation rate has had the greater effect.

REVIEW QUIZ

1 How would you use the Phillips curve to illustrate an unexpected change in inflation?

2 If the expected inflation rate increases by 10 percentage points, how do the short-run Phillips curve and the long-run Phillips curve change?

3 If the natural unemployment rate increases, what happens to the short-run Phillips curve and the long-run Phillips curve?

4 Does Canada have a stable short-run Phillips curve? Explain why or why not.

You can work these questions in Study Plan 28.2 and get instant feedback.

MyEconLab ◆

The Business Cycle

The business cycle is easy to describe but hard to explain and business cycle theory remains unsettled and a source of controversy. We'll look at two approaches to understanding the business cycle:

■ Mainstream business cycle theory
■ Real business cycle theory

Mainstream Business Cycle Theory

The mainstream business cycle theory is that potential GDP grows at a steady rate while aggregate demand grows at a fluctuating rate. Because the money wage rate is sticky, if aggregate demand grows faster than potential GDP, real GDP moves above potential GDP and an inflationary gap emerges. And if aggregate demand grows slower than potential GDP, real GDP moves below potential GDP and a recessionary gap emerges. If aggregate demand decreases, real GDP also decreases in a recession.

Figure 28.9 illustrates this business cycle theory. Initially, actual and potential GDP are $900 billion. The long-run aggregate supply curve is LAS_0, the aggregate demand curve is AD_0, and the price level is 110. The economy is at full employment at point A.

An expansion occurs when potential GDP increases and the LAS curve shifts rightward to LAS_1. During an expansion, aggregate demand also increases, and usually by more than potential GDP, so the price level rises. Assume that in the current expansion, the price level is expected to rise to 120 and the money wage rate has been set based on that expectation. The short-run aggregate supply curve is SAS_1.

If aggregate demand increases to AD_1, real GDP increases to $1,200 billion, the new level of potential GDP, and the price level rises, as expected, to 120. The economy remains at full employment but now at point B.

If aggregate demand increases more slowly to AD_2, real GDP grows by less than potential GDP and the economy moves to point C, with real GDP at $1,150 billion and the price level at 117. Real GDP growth is slower and inflation is lower than expected.

If aggregate demand increases more quickly to AD_3, real GDP grows by more than potential GDP and the economy moves to point D, with real GDP at $1,250 billion and the price level at 123. Real GDP growth is faster and inflation is higher than expected.

Growth, inflation, and the business cycle arise from the relentless increases in potential GDP, faster (on average) increases in aggregate demand, and fluctuations in the pace of aggregate demand growth.

FIGURE 28.9   The Mainstream Business Cycle Theory

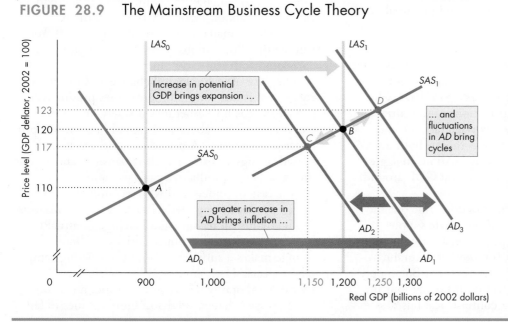

In a business cycle expansion, potential GDP increases and the LAS curve shifts rightward from LAS_0 to LAS_1. A greater than expected increase in aggregate demand brings inflation.

If the aggregate demand curve shifts to AD_1, the economy remains at full employment. If the aggregate demand curve shifts to AD_2, a recessionary gap arises. If the aggregate demand curve shifts to AD_3, an inflationary gap arises.

This mainstream theory comes in a number of special forms that differ regarding the source of fluctuations in aggregate demand growth and the source of money wage stickiness.

Keynesian Cycle Theory   In **Keynesian cycle theory**, fluctuations in investment driven by fluctuations in business confidence—summarized by the phrase "animal spirits"—are the main source of fluctuations in aggregate demand.

Monetarist Cycle Theory   In **monetarist cycle theory**, fluctuations in both investment and consumption expenditure, driven by fluctuations in the growth rate of the quantity of money, are the main source of fluctuations in aggregate demand.

Both the Keynesian and monetarist cycle theories simply assume that the money wage rate is rigid and don't explain that rigidity.

Two newer theories seek to explain money wage rate rigidity and to be more careful about working out its consequences.

New Classical Cycle Theory   In **new classical cycle theory**, the rational expectation of the price level, which is determined by potential GDP and *expected* aggregate demand, determines the money wage rate and the position of the *SAS* curve. In this theory, only *unexpected* fluctuations in aggregate demand bring fluctuations in real GDP around potential GDP.

New Keynesian Cycle Theory   The **new Keynesian cycle theory** emphasizes the fact that today's money wage rates were negotiated at many past dates, which means that *past* rational expectations of the current price level influence the money wage rate and the position of the *SAS* curve. In this theory, both unexpected and currently expected fluctuations in aggregate demand bring fluctuations in real GDP around potential GDP.

The mainstream cycle theories don't rule out the possibility that occasionally an aggregate supply shock might occur. An oil price rise, a widespread drought, a major hurricane, or another natural disaster, could, for example, bring a recession. But supply shocks are not the normal source of fluctuations in the mainstream theories. In contrast, real business cycle theory puts supply shocks at centre stage.

Real Business Cycle Theory

The newest theory of the business cycle, known as **real business cycle theory** (or RBC theory), regards random fluctuations in productivity as the main source of economic fluctuations. These productivity fluctuations are assumed to result mainly from fluctuations in the pace of technological change, but they might also have other sources, such as international disturbances, climate fluctuations, or natural disasters. The origins of RBC theory can be traced to the rational expectations revolution set off by Robert E. Lucas Jr., but the first demonstrations of the power of this theory were given by Edward Prescott and Finn Kydland and by John Long and Charles Plosser. Today, RBC theory is part of a broad research agenda called dynamic general equilibrium analysis, and hundreds of young macroeconomists do research on this topic.

We'll explore RBC theory by looking first at its impulse and then at the mechanism that converts that impulse into a cycle in real GDP.

The RBC Impulse   The impulse in RBC theory is the growth rate of productivity that results from technological change. RBC theorists believe this impulse to be generated mainly by the process of research and development that leads to the creation and use of new technologies.

To isolate the RBC theory impulse, economists measure the change in the combined productivity of capital and labour. Figure 28.10 shows the RBC impulse for Canada from 1962 through 2010. You can see that fluctuations in productivity growth are correlated with real GDP fluctuations.

The pace of technological change and productivity growth is not constant. Sometimes productivity growth speeds up, sometimes it slows, and occasionally it even *falls*—labour and capital become less productive, on average. A period of rapid productivity growth brings a business cycle expansion, and a slowdown or fall in productivity triggers a recession.

It is easy to understand why technological change brings productivity growth. But how does it *decrease* productivity? All technological change eventually increases productivity. But if initially, technological change makes a sufficient amount of existing capital—especially human capital—obsolete, productivity can temporarily fall. At such a time, more jobs are destroyed than created and more businesses fail than start up.

FIGURE 28.10   The Real Business Cycle Impulse

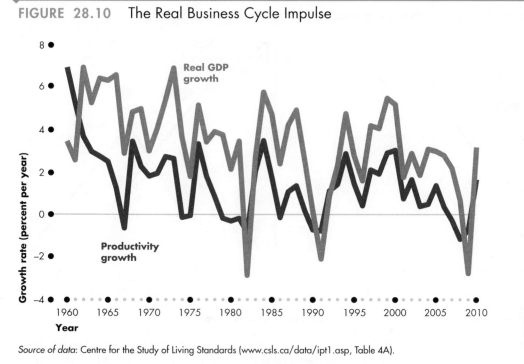

The real business cycle is caused by changes in technology that bring fluctuations in the productivity. growth* rate. Productivity fluctuations are correlated with real GDP fluctuations and most recessions are associated with a slowdown in productivity growth. Economists are not sure what the productivity variable actually measures or what causes it to fluctuate.

*Productivity growth calculations are based on authors' assumptions about the aggregate production function.

Source of data: Centre for the Study of Living Standards (www.csls.ca/data/ipt1.asp, Table 4A).

MyEconLab   animation ◆

The RBC Mechanism Two effects follow from a change in productivity that sparks an expansion or a contraction:

1. Investment demand changes.
2. The demand for labour changes.

We'll study these effects and their consequences during a recession. In an expansion, they work in the direction opposite to what is described here.

Technological change makes some existing capital obsolete and temporarily decreases productivity. Firms expect the future profits to fall and see their labour productivity falling. With lower profit expectations, they cut back their purchases of new capital, and with lower labour productivity, they plan to lay off some workers. So the initial effect of a temporary fall in productivity is a decrease in investment demand and a decrease in the demand for labour.

Figure 28.11 illustrates these two initial effects of a decrease in productivity. Part (a) shows the effects of a decrease in investment demand in the loanable funds market. The demand for loanable funds curve is *DLF* and the supply of loanable funds curve is *SLF* (both of which are explained in Chapter 23,

pp. 548–554). Initially, the demand for loanable funds curve is DLF_0 and the equilibrium quantity of funds is $200 billion at a real interest rate of 6 percent a year. A decrease in productivity decreases investment demand, and the demand for loanable funds curve shifts leftward from DLF_0 to DLF_1. The real interest rate falls to 4 percent a year, and the equilibrium quantity of loanable funds decreases to $170 billion.

Figure 28.11(b) shows the demand for labour and supply of labour (which are explained in Chapter 22, pp. 523–524). Initially, the demand for labour curve is LD_0, the supply of labour curve LS_0, and equilibrium employment is 20 billion hours a year at a real wage rate of $35 an hour. The decrease in productivity decreases the demand for labour, and the demand for labour curve shifts leftward from LD_0 to LD_1.

Before we can determine the new level of employment and real wage rate, we need to take a ripple effect into account—the key effect in RBC theory.

The Key Decision: When to Work? According to RBC theory, people decide *when* to work by doing a cost-benefit calculation. They compare the return

FIGURE 28.11   Loanable Funds and Labour Markets in a Real Business Cycle

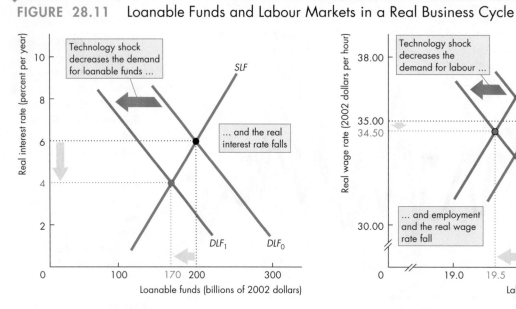

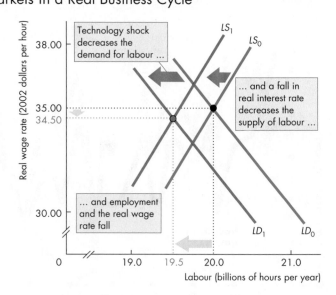

(a) Loanable funds and interest rate

(b) Labour and wage rate

In part (a), the supply of loanable funds *SLF* and initial demand for loanable funds DLF_0 determine the real interest rate at 6 percent a year. In part (b), the initial demand for labour, LD_0, and supply of labour, LS_0, determine the real wage rate at $35 an hour and employment at 20 billion hours. A technological change temporarily decreases productivity, and both the demand for loanable funds and the

demand for labour decrease. The two demand curves shift leftward to DLF_1 and LD_1. In part (a), the real interest rate falls to 4 percent a year. In part (b), the fall in the real interest rate decreases the supply of labour (the when-to-work decision) and the supply of labour curve shifts leftward to LS_1. Employment decreases to 19.5 billion hours, and the real wage rate falls to $34.50 an hour. A recession is underway.

MyEconLab   animation

from working in the current period with the *expected* return from working in a later period. You make such a comparison every day in school. Suppose your goal in this course is to get an A. To achieve this goal, you work hard most of the time. But during the few days before the midterm and final exams, you work especially hard. Why? Because you believe that the return from studying close to the exam is greater than the return from studying when the exam is a long time away. So during the term, you take time off for the movies and other leisure pursuits, but at exam time, you study every evening and weekend.

RBC theory says that workers behave like you. They work fewer hours, sometimes zero hours, when the real wage rate is temporarily low, and they work more hours when the real wage rate is temporarily high. But to properly compare the current wage rate with the expected future wage rate, workers must use

the real interest rate. If the real interest rate is 6 percent a year, a real wage of $1 an hour earned this week will become $1.06 a year from now. If the real wage rate is expected to be $1.05 an hour next year, today's real wage of $1 looks good. By working longer hours now and shorter hours a year from now, a person can get a 1 percent higher real wage. But suppose the real interest rate is 4 percent a year. In this case, $1 earned now is worth $1.04 next year. Working fewer hours now and more next year is the way to get a 1 percent higher real wage.

So the when-to-work decision depends on the real interest rate. The lower the real interest rate, other things remaining the same, the smaller is the supply of labour today. Many economists believe this *intertemporal substitution* effect to be of negligible size. RBC theorists believe that the effect is large, and it is the key feature of the RBC mechanism.

You saw in Fig. 28.11(a) that the decrease in the demand for loanable funds lowers the real interest rate. This fall in the real interest rate lowers the return to current work and decreases the supply of labour.

In Fig. 28.11(b), the labour supply curve shifts leftward to LS_1. The effect of the decrease in productivity on the demand for labour is larger than the effect of the fall in the real interest rate on the supply of labour. That is, the demand curve shifts farther leftward than does the supply curve. As a result, the real wage rate falls to $34.50 an hour and employment decreases to 19.5 billion hours. A recession has begun and is intensifying.

What Happened to Money?   The name *real* business cycle theory is no accident. It reflects the central prediction of the theory. Real things, not nominal or monetary things, cause the business cycle. If the quantity of money changes, aggregate demand changes. But if there is no real change—with no change in the use of resources and no change in potential GDP—the change in the quantity of money changes only the price level. In RBC theory, this outcome occurs because the aggregate supply curve is the *LAS* curve, which pins real GDP down at potential GDP, so when aggregate demand changes, only the price level changes.

Cycles and Growth   The shock that drives the business cycle of RBC theory is the same as the force that generates economic growth: technological change. On average, as technology advances, productivity grows; but as you saw in Fig. 28.10, it grows at an uneven pace. Economic growth arises from the upward trend in productivity growth and, according to RBC theory, the mostly positive but occasionally negative higher frequency shocks to productivity bring the business cycle.

Criticisms and Defenses of RBC Theory   The three main criticisms of RBC theory are that (1) the money wage rate *is* sticky, and to assume otherwise is at odds with a clear fact; (2) intertemporal substitution is too weak a force to account for large fluctuations in labour supply and employment with small real wage rate changes; and (3) productivity shocks are as likely to be caused by *changes in aggregate demand* as by technological change.

If aggregate demand fluctuations cause the fluctuations in productivity, then the traditional aggregate demand theories are needed to explain them. Fluctuations in productivity do not cause the business cycle but are caused by it!

Building on this theme, the critics point out that the so-called productivity fluctuations are correlated with changes in the growth rate of money and other indicators of changes in aggregate demand.

The defenders of RBC theory claim that the theory explains the macroeconomic facts about the business cycle and is consistent with the facts about economic growth. In effect, a single theory explains *both growth and the business cycle.* Productivity increases explain both slowly changing trends and the more frequent business cycle swings. Its defenders also claim that RBC theory is consistent with a wide range of *micro*-economic evidence about labour supply decisions, labour demand and investment demand decisions, and information on the distribution of income between labour and capital.

◆ REVIEW QUIZ

1 Explain the mainstream theory of the business cycle.
2 What are the four special forms of the mainstream theory of the business cycle and how do they differ?
3 According to RBC theory, what is the source of the business cycle? What is the role of fluctuations in the rate of technological change?
4 According to RBC theory, how does a fall in productivity growth influence investment demand, the market for loanable funds, the real interest rate, the demand for labour, the supply of labour, employment, and the real wage rate?
5 What are the main criticisms of RBC theory and how do its supporters defend it?

You can work these questions in Study Plan 28.3 and get instant feedback.

—————————— MyEconLab ◆

◆ You can complete your study of economic fluctuations in *Reading Between the Lines* on pp. 692–693, which looks at the Canadian and U.S. labour markets during the recent recession and slow recovery.

Labour Markets in Slow Recovery

Canada Outshines U.S. with Remarkable Growth in Job Rate

The Calgary Herald
October 7, 2011

Canada churned out a stunning 60,900 jobs in September, once again outshining the United States with an economy that is humming along even as other rich nations struggle with debt and slumping confidence.

The jobless rate fell unexpectedly to 7.1 percent from 7.3 percent in August, Statistics Canada reported on Friday, compared with a U.S. rate that has stayed stubbornly above 9 percent. The U.S. unemployment rate was 9.1 percent in September.

Adjusted to take account of the relative sizes of the two economies and slightly different statistical methods, Canada's gain in new jobs would be comparable to half a million new U.S. positions. U.S. employment rose 103,000 in September. ...

One caveat is that 38,400 of the new jobs were in education, as teachers and assistants returned to work after summer layoffs. ...

Adding to the positive news, September saw 63,800 full-time additions, while part-time employment declined by 2,900. ...

However, Royal Bank of Canada chief economist Craig Wright [said] ... "The challenge lies outside our borders and we're still waiting for more proactive policy from the euro zone, near term, and longer term out of the U.S."...

Scotiabank economists Derek Holt and Karen Cordes Woods, who have often taken a more bearish view, said they could not be "over the moon" over what they said was a misleadingly positive report.

Besides the education distortions, they pointed to a rise of 38,900 in self-employment, which they described as soft, and among actual employees, private sector jobs fell 14,900.

ESSENCE OF THE STORY

- The Canadian economy added 60,900 new jobs in September 2011.

- The unemployment rate fell to 7.1 percent, its lowest level since 2008.

- In contrast, U.S. unemployment remained at 9.1 percent in September.

- Almost all the new jobs are full-time ones but some are part-time and some are in the public sector.

- Europe's government-debt crisis and a weak U.S. economy continued to pose problems for the Canadian economy.

ECONOMIC ANALYSIS

- The most recent phase of the Canadian business cycle is very different from that in the United States.

- The news article provides one indicator of the business cycle: employment numbers during September 2011.

- The data graphed in the figures put the 2011 employment numbers in a longer perspective.

- In 2001, the United States had a mild recession and Canada had a growth rate slowdown.

- Figure 1 shows that following the 2001 recession, the labour force participation rate in Canada surged from 66 percent to 68 percent. At the same time, the U.S. labour force participation rate sagged from 67 percent to 66 percent.

- Figure 2 shows that following the 2001 recession, the employment rate (the employment-to-population ratio) in the United States kept falling. It did not turn upward until late 2003 and it stopped rising at the end of 2006. Through 2007 and 2008, the U.S. employment rate plunged from 63 percent to 61 percent.

- Figure 2 also shows that Canadian employment surged from around 61 percent to 64 percent and kept on rising through 2007 while U.S. employment was falling. Canadian employment fell only slightly during 2008.

- Figure 3 shows that the Canadian unemployment rate has been higher than the U.S. rate. But the Canadian unemployment rate kept falling through 2007 while the U.S. rate was rising. The rapid rise in the U.S. unemployment rate during 2008 is not matched by the Canadian rate.

- Why did Canada escape the severe fall in employment and rise in unemployment that the United States experienced?

- The trigger that sent the U.S. economy crashing was a collapse in house prices and its effects on the credit markets. This problem was much less severe in Canada.

- Canada produces more resources (oil, natural gas, and minerals) than the United States and the prices of all of these resources continued to boom through the last recession.

- The Canadian dollar depreciated, which helped to keep Canadian exports high and imports low and prevent aggregate demand from falling.

Figure 1 Labour Force Participation Rates

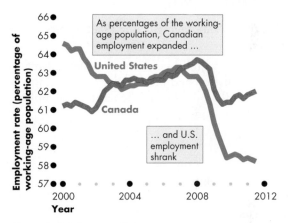

Figure 2 Employment Rates

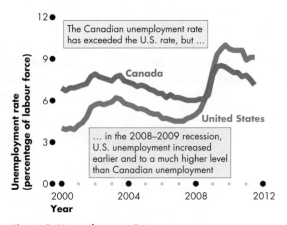

Figure 3 Unemployment Rates

◆ SUMMARY

Key Points

Inflation Cycles (pp. 678–683)

- Demand-pull inflation is triggered by an increase in aggregate demand and fuelled by ongoing money growth. Real GDP cycles above full employment.
- Cost-push inflation is triggered by an increase in the money wage rate or raw material prices and is fuelled by ongoing money growth. Real GDP cycles below full employment in a stagflation.
- When the forecast of inflation is correct, real GDP remains at potential GDP.

Working Problems 1 to 11 will give you a better understanding of inflation cycles.

Inflation and Unemployment: The Phillips Curve (pp. 684–686)

- The short-run Phillips curve shows the tradeoff between inflation and unemployment when the expected inflation rate and the natural unemployment rate are constant.

- The long-run Phillips curve, which is vertical, shows that when the actual inflation rate equals the expected inflation rate, the unemployment rate equals the natural unemployment rate.

Working Problems 12 to 14 will give you a better understanding of inflation and unemployment: the Phillips curve.

The Business Cycle (pp. 687–691)

- The mainstream business cycle theory explains the business cycle as fluctuations of real GDP around potential GDP and as arising from a steady expansion of potential GDP combined with an expansion of aggregate demand at a fluctuating rate.
- Real business cycle theory explains the business cycle as fluctuations of potential GDP, which arise from fluctuations in the influence of technological change on productivity growth.

Working Problem 15 will give you a better understanding of the business cycle.

Key Terms

Cost-push inflation, 680
Demand-pull inflation, 678
Keynesian cycle theory, 688
Long-run Phillips curve, 685
Monetarist cycle theory, 688
New classical cycle theory, 688

New Keynesian cycle theory, 688
Phillips curve, 684
Rational expectation, 683
Real business cycle theory, 688
Short-run Phillips curve, 684
Stagflation, 681

SCAN THIS

STUDY PLAN PROBLEMS AND APPLICATIONS

MyEconLab ◆ You can work Problems 1 to 15 in Chapter 28 Study Plan and get instant feedback.

Inflation Cycles (Study Plan 28.1)

1. **Pakistan: Is It Cost-Push Inflation?**

   With CPI already spiking 11.8 percent for the first ten months of the fiscal year, the average CPI inflation for the same period last year stood at 22.35 percent. Some economists insist the current bout of inflationary pressures is spawned by increasing prices of fuel, food, raw materials, transportation, construction materials, elimination of energy subsidies, etc. as indicated by the spike in the wholesale price index (WPI), which rose 21.99 percent in April from a year earlier.

   Source: *Daily the Pak Banker*, May 22, 2010

   Explain what type of inflation Pakistan is experiencing.

Use the following figure to answer Problems 2, 3, 4, and 5. In each question, the economy starts out on the curves labelled AD_0 and SAS_0.

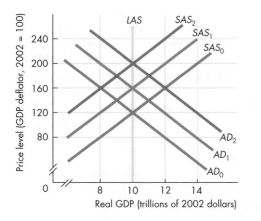

2. Some events occur and the economy experiences a demand-pull inflation.
   a. List the events that might cause a demand-pull inflation.
   b. Describe the initial effects of a demand-pull inflation.
   c. Describe what happens as a demand-pull inflation spiral proceeds.

3. Some events occur and the economy experiences a cost-push inflation.
   a. List the events that might cause a cost-push inflation.
   b. Describe the initial effects of a cost-push inflation.
   c. Describe what happens as a cost-push inflation spiral proceeds.

4. Some events occur and the economy is expected to experience inflation.
   a. List the events that might cause an expected inflation.
   b. Describe the initial effects of an expected inflation.
   c. Describe what happens as an expected inflation proceeds.

5. Suppose that people expect deflation (a falling price level), but aggregate demand remains at AD_0.
   a. What happens to the short-run and long-run aggregate supply curves? (Draw some new curves if you need to.)
   b. Describe the initial effects of an expected deflation.
   c. Describe what happens as it becomes obvious to everyone that the expected deflation is not going to occur.

Use the following news clip to work Problems 6 to 8.

China's Inflation Up at 5.4 percent

China's inflation accelerated in May to 5.4 percent, adding to the case for the central bank to tighten monetary policy.

Inflation has been fueled by a rise in food prices, made worse by severe drought in farming areas. Some economists say inflation is also the result of China's massive stimulus during the global financial crisis.

Like elsewhere, China is coping with a rise in global commodity prices, which are adding to inflationary concerns for policymakers.

China's economy expanded in 2010 by 10.3 percent, a pace that slowed in the first quarter to 9.7 percent.

Source: Reuters, June 13, 2011

6. Is China experiencing demand-pull or cost-push inflation? Explain.

7. Draw a graph to illustrate the initial effects of a one-time rise in commodity prices.

8. Draw a graph to illustrate and explain how China might experience an inflation spiral.

Use the following news clip to work Problems 9 to 11.

Tight Money Won't Slay Food, Energy Inflation

It's important to differentiate between a general increase in prices—a situation in which aggregate demand exceeds their aggregate supply—and a relative price shock. For example, a specific shock to energy prices can become generalized if producers are able to pass on the higher costs. So far, global competition has made that difficult for companies, while higher input costs have largely been neutralized by rising labour productivity. Since 2003, core inflation has averaged less than 2 percent a year in the 30 major economies. History also suggests gambling that slowing growth will shackle core inflation is a winning wager. The risk is that if U.S. consumers don't believe price increases will slow, growing inflation expectations may become self-fulfilling.

Source: *Bloomberg*, May 9, 2008

9. a. Explain the two types of inflation described in this news clip.
   b. Explain why "rising labour productivity" can neutralize the effect on inflation of "higher input costs."

10. Explain how "slowing growth" can reduce inflationary pressure.

11. Draw a graph to illustrate and explain how "growing inflation expectations may become self-fulfilling."

Inflation and Unemployment: The Phillips Curve
(Study Plan 28.2)

12. **Iran Postpones Cutting Gasoline Subsidies**

Inflation is about 10 percent and the unemployment rate is about 14 percent. Earlier this month Iran's main audit body slammed the government's plan to scrap gasoline subsidies, warning that implementing such a reform might result in unrest. The government also intends to scrap subsidies on natural gas, which most Iranians use for cooking and heating, as well as electricity, but the new prices are still not known. However, in recent weeks some households have received electricity bills with nearly sevenfold price increases.

Source: AFP, September 15, 2010

a. If Iran removes the subsidies and consumers don't know what the higher prices will be, draw a graph to show the most likely path of inflation and unemployment.

b. If Iran removes the subsidies and announces the new prices so that consumers know what they are, draw a graph to show the most likely path of inflation and unemployment.

13. **Recession? Maybe. Depression? Get Real.**

The unemployment rate during the Great Depression peaked at nearly 25 percent in 1933, after an initial spike from 3 percent in 1929 to nearly 8.7 percent in 1930. The unemployment rate is just 5 percent, only up from 4.5 percent a year ago. Also during the Great Depression there was deflation, which is not happening today.

Source: CNN, May 28, 2008

a. Can the inflation and unemployment trends during the Great Depression be explained by a movement along a short-run Phillips curve?

b. Can the inflation and unemployment trends during 2008 be explained by a movement along a short-run Phillips curve?

14. **Growth Concern**

Despite higher-than-forecast inflation, Bank of Canada Governor Mark Carney said he may keep interest rates low beyond when full output is restored as the domestic recovery is hobbled by a weak economy in the U.S., the nation's biggest trade partner. "Given current material headwinds, the policy rate can return to its long-run level after inflation is projected to reach the 2 percent target and output is projected to reach its potential," Carney said.

Source: *Bloomberg*, September 21, 2011

Is Mark Carney predicting that the Canadian economy is being pushed along a short-run Phillips curve or that the short-run Phillips curve is shifting? In which direction is the economy being pushed and how will Carney's plan counter it?

The Business Cycle (Study Plan 28.3)

15. **Debate on Causes of Joblessness Grows**

One side says unemployment is a cyclical problem. The other side says it is structural.

Source: *The Wall Street Journal*, September 4, 2010

Which business cycle theory would say that the rise in U.S. unemployment is cyclical? Which would say it is an increase in the natural rate? Why?

ADDITIONAL PROBLEMS AND APPLICATIONS

MyEconLab ◆ You can work these problems in MyEconLab if assigned by your instructor.

Inflation Cycles

Use the following news clip to work Problems 16 and 17.

Bernanke Sees No Repeat of 1970s-Style Inflation

There is little indication today of the beginnings of a 1970s-style wage-price spiral. Then, as now, a serious oil price shock occurred, but today's economy is more flexible in responding to difficulties and the country is more energy efficient than a generation ago, Bernanke said. Also, today the Federal Reserve (the Fed) monitors "inflation expectations." If people believe inflation will keep going up, they will change their behavior in ways that aggravate inflation—thus, a self-fulfilling prophecy. In the 1970s, people were demanding—and getting —higher wages in anticipation of rapidly rising prices; hence, the "wage-price" spiral Bernanke cited. The inflation rate has averaged about 3.5 percent over the past four quarters. That is "significantly higher" than the Fed would like but much less than the double-digit inflation rates of the mid-1970s and 1980, Bernanke said.

Source: *USA Today*, June 4, 2008

16. Draw a graph to illustrate and explain the inflation spiral that the U.S. experienced in the 1970s.

17. a. Explain the role that inflation expectations play in creating a self-fulfilling prophecy.
    b. Explain Bernanke's predictions about the impact of the 2008 oil price shock as compared to the 1970s shock.

Inflation and Unemployment: The Phillips Curve

Use the following information to work Problems 18 and 19.

The Reserve Bank of New Zealand signed an agreement with the New Zealand government in which the Bank agreed to maintain inflation inside a low target range. Failure to achieve the target would result in the governor of the Bank (the equivalent of the governor of the Bank of Canada) losing his job.

18. Explain how this arrangement might have influenced New Zealand's short-run Phillips curve.

19. Explain how this arrangement might have influenced New Zealand's long-run Phillips curve.

Use the following information to work Problems 20 and 21.

An economy has an unemployment rate of 4 percent and an inflation rate of 5 percent a year at point *A* in the figure.

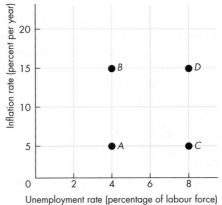

Some events occur that move the economy in a clockwise loop from *A* to *B* to *D* to *C* and back to *A*.

20. Describe the events that could create this sequence. Has the economy experienced demand-pull inflation, cost-push inflation, expected inflation, or none of these?

21. Draw in the figure the sequence of the economy's short-run and long-run Phillips curves.

Use the following news clip to work Problems 22 and 23.

Pause Promises Financial Disaster

The indication is that inflationary expectations have become entrenched and strongly rooted in world markets. As a result, the risk of global stagflation has become significant. A drawn-out inflationary process always precedes stagflation, anathema to the so-called Phillips Curve. Following the attritional effect of inflation, the economy starts to grow below its potential. It experiences a persistent output gap, rising unemployment, and increasingly entrenched inflationary expectations.

Source: *Asia Times Online*, May 20, 2008

22. Evaluate the claim that stagflation is anathema to the Phillips curve.

23. Evaluate the claim made in this article that if "inflationary expectations" become strongly

"entrenched" an economy will experience "a persistent output gap."

Use the following information to work Problems 24 and 25.

In response to a financial crisis, central banks increased the quantity of money and cut interest rates and governments embarked on programs of fiscal stimulus. At the same time, massive changes in the global economy brought the need for massive structural change.

24. Explain how increasing the quantity of money and government fiscal stimulus might influence the short-run and long-run unemployment–inflation tradeoffs. Will the influence come from changes in the expected inflation rate, the natural unemployment rate, or both?

25. Explain how large-scale structural change might influence the short-run and long-run unemployment–inflation tradeoffs. Will the influence come from changes in the expected inflation rate, the natural unemployment rate, or both?

The Business Cycle

Use the following information to work Problems 26 to 28.

Suppose that the business cycle in Canada is best described by RBC theory and that a new technology increases productivity.

26. Draw a graph to show the effect of the new technology in the market for loanable funds.

27. Draw a graph to show the effect of the new technology in the labour market.

28. Explain the when-to-work decision when technology advances.

29. **Real Wages Fail to Match a Rise in Productivity**

For most of the last century, wages and productivity—the key measure of the economy's efficiency—have risen together, increasing rapidly through the 1950s and 1960s and far more slowly in the 1970s and 1980s. But in recent years, the productivity gains have continued while the pay increases have not kept up.

Source: *The New York Times*, August 28, 2006

Explain the relationship between wages and productivity in this news clip in terms of real business cycle theory.

Economics in the News

30. After you have studied *Reading Between the Lines* on pp. 692–693, answer the following questions.

a. What are the main features of the labour force participation rate in Canada and the United States since 2000?

b. What are the main features of the employment rate (employment-to-population ratio) in Canada and the United States since 2000?

c. What are the main features of the unemployment rate in Canada and the United States since 2000?

d. Use the *AS–AD* model to show the changes in aggregate demand and aggregate supply that are consistent with the paths followed by employment in Canada and the United States from 2000 to 2006.

e. Use the *AS–AD* model to show the changes in aggregate demand and aggregate supply that are consistent with the paths followed by employment in Canada and the United States in 2007 to 2011.

31. **Germany Leads Slowdown in Eurozone**

The pace of German economic growth has weakened "markedly," but the reason is the weaker global prospects. Although German policymakers worry about the country's exposure to a fall in demand for its export goods, evidence is growing that the recovery is broadening with real wage rates rising and unemployment falling, which will lead into stronger consumer spending.

Source: *The Financial Times*, September 23, 2010

a. How does "exposure to a fall in demand for its export goods" influence Germany's aggregate demand, aggregate supply, unemployment, and inflation?

b. Use the *AS-AD* model and the the Phillips curve model to illustrate your answer to part (a).

c. What do you think the news clip means by "the recovery is broadening with real wage rates rising and unemployment falling, which will lead into stronger consumer spending"?

d. Use the *AS-AD* model and the Phillips curve model to illustrate your answer to part (c).

Boom and Bust

To cure a disease, doctors must first understand how the disease responds to different treatments. It helps to understand the mechanisms that operate to cause the disease, but sometimes a workable cure can be found even before the full story of the causes has been told.

Curing economic ills is similar to curing our medical ills. We need to understand how the economy responds to the treatments we might prescribe for it. And sometimes, we want to try a cure even though we don't fully understand the reasons for the problem we're trying to control.

You've seen how the pace of capital accumulation and technological change determine the long-term growth trend. You've learned how fluctuations around the long-term trend can be generated by changes in aggregate demand and aggregate supply. And you've learned about the key sources of fluctuations in aggregate demand and aggregate supply.

The *AS-AD* model explains the forces that determine real GDP and the price level in the short run. The model also enables us to see the big picture or grand vision of the different schools of macroeconomic thought concerning the sources of aggregate fluctuations. The Keynesian aggregate expenditure model provides an account of the factors that determine aggregate demand and make it fluctuate.

An alternative real business cycle theory puts all the emphasis on fluctuations in long-run aggregate supply. According to this theory, money changes aggregate demand and the price level but leaves the real economy untouched. Policy actions and economic performance since 2007 will provide a powerful test of this theory.

John Maynard Keynes, *born in England in 1883, was one of the outstanding minds of the twentieth century. He represented Britain at the Versailles peace conference at the end of World War I, was a master speculator on international financial markets (an activity he conducted from bed every morning and which made and lost him several fortunes), and played a prominent role in creating the International Monetary Fund.*

He was a member of the Bloomsbury Group, a circle of outstanding artists and writers that included E.M. Forster, Bertrand Russell, and Virginia Woolf.

Keynes was a controversial and quick-witted figure. A critic once complained that Keynes had changed his opinion on some matter, to which Keynes retorted: "When I discover I am wrong, I change my mind. What do you do?"

Keynes' book, The General Theory of Employment, Interest and Money, *written during the Great Depression and published in 1936, revolutionized macroeconomics.*

> The ideas of economists and political philosophers, both when they are right and when they are wrong, are more powerful than is commonly understood. Indeed the world is ruled by little else.
>
> **JOHN MAYNARD KEYNES**
> *The General Theory of Employment, Interest and Money*

Professor Caballero, why did you decide to become an economist?

Did I decide? I'm convinced that one is either born an economist or not. I began studying business, but as soon as I took the first course in economics, I was captivated by the simple but elegant logic of (good) economic reasoning. Given the complexity of the real world, economic analysis is necessarily abstract. But at the same time, economics is mostly about concrete and important issues that affect the lives of millions of people. Abstraction and relevance—this is a wonderful but strange combination. Not everybody feels comfortable with it, but if you do, economics is for you.

Most of your work has been on business cycles and other high-frequency phenomena. Can we begin by reviewing the costs of recessions? Robert Lucas says that postwar U.S. recessions have cost very little. Do you agree?

No ... but I'm not sure Robert Lucas was really trying to say that. My sense is that he was trying to push the profession to focus a bit more on long-run growth issues. Putting down the costs of recessions was a useful debating device to make his important point.

I believe that the statement that recessions are not costly is incorrect. First, I think his calculation of this magnitude reflects some fundamental flaw in the way the workhorse models we use in economics fail to account for the costs of risk and volatility. This flaw shows up in many different puzzles in economics, including the well-known equity premium puzzle. Economic models underestimate, by an order of magnitude, how unhappy agents are about facing uncertainty. Second, it is highly unlikely that recessions and medium-term growth are completely separable. In particular, the ongoing process of restructuring, which is central to productivity growth, is severely hampered by deep recessions.

Recessions are costly because they waste enormous resources, affect physical and human investment decisions, have large negative distributional consequences, influence political outcomes, and so on.

What about the costs of recessions in other parts of the world, especially Latin America?

The cost of recessions grows exponentially with their size and the country's inability to soften the impact on the most affected. Less developed economies suffer

much larger shocks because their economies are not well diversified, and they experience capital outflows that exacerbate the impact of recessionary shocks. Their domestic financial sectors are small and often become strained during recessions, making it difficult to reallocate scarce resources towards those who need them the most. To make matters worse, the government's ability to use fiscal policy becomes impaired by the capital outflows, and monetary policy is also out of the question when the currency is in free fall and liabilities are dollarized. There are many things that we take for granted in the United States that simply are not feasible for emerging markets in distress. One has to be careful with extrapolating too directly the counter-cyclical recipes used for developed economies to these countries.

> **Recessions are costly because they waste enormous resources [and] affect physical and human investment decisions.**

Your first work, in your M.A. dissertation, was to build a macroeconomic model of the economy of Chile. What do we learn by comparing economies? Does the Chilean economy behave essentially like the U.S. economy or are there fundamental differences?

Ricardo J. Caballero is Ford Professor of International Economics at MIT. He has received many honours, the most notable of which are the Frisch Medal of the Econometric Society (2002) and being named Chile's Economist of the Year (2001). A highly regarded teacher, he is much sought as a special lecturer and in 2005 gave the prestigious Yrjo Jahnsson Lecture at the University of Helsinki.

Professor Caballero earned his B.S. degree in 1982 and M.A. in 1983 at Pontificia Universidad Católica de Chile. He then moved to the United States and obtained his Ph.D. at MIT in 1988.

Michael Parkin and Robin Bade talked with Ricardo Caballero about his work and the progress that economists have made in understanding economic fluctuations.

Chile is a special economy among emerging markets. It began pro-market reforms many years before the rest and has had very prudent macroeconomic management for several decades by now. For that reason, it is a bit more "like the U.S. economy" than most other emerging market economies. However, there are still important differences, of the sort described in my answer to the previous question.

Beyond the specifics of Chile, at some deep level, macroeconomic principles, and economic principles more generally, are the same everywhere. It is all about incentives, tradeoffs, effort, commitment, discipline, transparency, insurance, and so on. But different economies hurt in different places, and hence the practice of economics has plenty of diversity.

During the most recent U.S. expansion, some asset prices—especially house prices—have looked as if they might be experiencing a speculative bubble, and you've done some recent work on bubbles. How can we tell whether we're seeing a bubble or just a rapid increase that is being driven by fundamental market forces?
First things first. I think we need to get used to the presence of speculative bubbles. The reason is that the world today has a massive shortage of financial assets that savers can use to store value. Because of this shortage, "artificial" assets are ready to emerge at all

times. Specific bubbles come and go—from the NASDAQ, to real estate, to commodities—but the total is much more stable.

I do not think the distinction between bubbles and fundamentals is as clear-cut as people describe. Probably outside periods of liquidity crises, all assets have some bubble component in them. The question is how much.

You've studied situations in which capital suddenly stops flowing into an economy from abroad. What are the lessons you've learned from this research?
The most basic lesson for emerging markets is that capital flows are volatile. Sometimes they simply magnify domestic problems, but in many other cases, they are the direct source of volatility. However, the conclusion from this observation is not that capital flows should be limited, just as we do not close the banks in the United States to eliminate the possibility of bank runs. On the contrary, much of the volatility comes from insufficient integration with international capital markets, which makes emerging markets illiquid and the target of specialists and speculators. For the short and medium run, the main policy lesson is that sudden stops to the inflow of capital must be put at the centre of macroeconomic policy design in emerging markets. This has deep implications for the design of monetary and fiscal policy, as well as for international reserves management practices and domestic financial markets regulation.

> The most basic lesson for emerging markets is that capital flows are volatile.

The U.S. current account deficit has been large and increasing for many years, and dollar debt levels around the world have increased. Do you see any danger in this process for either the United States or the rest of the world?
I believe the persistent current account deficits in the United States are not the result of an anomaly that, as such, must go away in a sudden crash, as the conventional view has it. Instead, my view is that these deficits are just the counterpart of large capital inflows resulting from the global shortage of financial assets that I mentioned earlier. Good growth potential in the United States over that of Europe and

Japan and the much better quality of its financial assets over those of emerging Asian and oil-producing countries make the United States very attractive to international private and public investors.

Absent major shocks, this process may still last for quite some time. But of course shocks do happen, and in that sense, leverage is dangerous. However, there isn't much we can or should do, short of implementing structural reforms around the world aimed at improving growth potential in some cases and domestic financial development in others.

You've suggested that an insatiable appetite for safe securities is the root cause of the global financial crisis and that governments must accept a larger responsibility for bearing risk arising from the financial system. Would you explain this idea?
Foreign central banks and investors and U.S. financial institutions have an insatiable demand for safe securities, which puts enormous pressure on the U.S. financial system. The global financial crisis was the result of an interaction between the initial tremors caused by the rise in subprime mortgage defaults and securities created from these mortgages to feed the demand for safe assets.

By 2001, the demand for safe assets began to exceed their supply, and financial institutions searched for ways to create safe assets from previously untapped and riskier ones. Subprime mortgage borrowers were a source of raw material. To convert risky mortgages (and other risky assets, ranging from auto loans to student loans) into safe assets, "banks" created complex securities made from large numbers of risky mortgages broken into tiers of increasing risk.

How did these new complex securities get out of control and lead to the real estate bubble and financial crisis?
A positive feedback loop was created: Supplied with safe assets, funds flowed into banks to finance real estate purchases financed by mortgages. Real estate prices rose rapidly, which reinforced the belief that the securities created from mortgages were indeed safe. But for the banking system and economy, the new-found source of "safe" assets was not safe at all. Combining a large number of risky mortgages to create a safe security works if the risk of default by the initial borrower is uncorrelated with that of others. But in the environment of 2007, the risks were highly correlated. There was one source of default—generally falling home prices.

The triggering event was the crash in the real estate "bubble" and the rise in subprime mortgage defaults that followed it. But this cannot be all of it. The global financial system went into cardiac arrest in response to a relatively small shock which was well within the range of possible scenarios. The real damage came from the unexpected and sudden freezing of the entire securitization industry. Almost instantaneously, confidence vanished and the complexity which made possible the "multiplication of bread" during the boom, turned into a source of counterparty risk, both real and imaginary. Fear fed into more fear, causing reluctance to engage in financial transactions, even among the prime financial institutions. Safe interest rates plummeted to record low levels.

Addressing these issues requires governments to explicitly bear a greater share of systemic risk. There are two prongs within this approach. The first prong is for the countries that demand safe financial assets to rebalance their portfolios towards riskier assets. The second prong is for governments in countries that produce safe assets to provide a greater share of risk-bearing. There are many detailed ways in which this might be done.

What advice do you have for someone who is just beginning to study economics but who wants to become an economist? If they are not in the United States, should they come here for graduate work as you did?
There is no other place in the world like the United States to pursue a Ph.D. and do research in economics. However, this is only the last stage in the process of becoming an economist. There are many superb economists, especially applied ones, all around the world.

I believe the most important step is to learn to think like an economist. I heard Milton Friedman say that he knows many economists who have never gone through a Ph.D. program, and equally many who have completed their Ph.D. but are not really economists. I agree with him on this one. A good undergraduate program and talking about economics is a great first step.

Almost everything in life has an economic angle to it—look for it and discuss it with your friends. It will not improve your social life, but it will make you a better economist.

> Almost everything in life has an economic angle to it—look for it ...

CHAPTER

29

After studying this chapter, you will be able to

◆ Describe the federal budget process and the recent history of outlays, revenues, deficits, and debt

◆ Explain the supply-side effects of fiscal policy

◆ Explain how fiscal stimulus is used to fight a recession

Fiscal Policy

In 2010, the federal government spent 16.5 cents of every dollar that Canadians earned. It raised 14 of those cents in taxes and borrowed the other 2.5 cents. The government had a budget deficit. Does it matter if the government doesn't balance its books? What are the effects of taxes and government spending on the economy? Does a dollar spent by the government have the same effect as a dollar spent by someone else? Does it create jobs, or does it destroy them?

These are the fiscal policy questions that you will study in this chapter. In *Reading Between the Lines* at the end of the chapter, we look at the fiscal policy debate in Canada.

◆ The Federal Budget

The annual statement of the outlays and revenues of the Government of Canada, together with the laws and regulations that approve and support those outlays and revenues, make up the **federal budget**. Similarly, a *provincial budget* is an annual statement of the revenues and outlays of a provincial government, together with the laws and regulations that approve or support those revenues and outlays.

Before World War II, the federal budget had no purpose other than to finance the business of government. But since the late 1940s, the federal budget has assumed a second purpose, which is to pursue the government's fiscal policy. **Fiscal policy** is the use of the federal budget to achieve macroeconomic objectives such as full employment, sustained long-term economic growth, and price level stability. Our focus is this second purpose.

Budget Making

The federal government and Parliament make fiscal policy. The process begins with long, drawn-out consultations between the Minister of Finance and Department of Finance officials and their counterparts in the provincial governments. These discussions deal with programs that are funded and operated jointly by the two levels of government. The Minister also consults with business and consumer groups on a wide range of issues.

After all these consultations, and using economic projections made by Department of Finance economists, the Minister develops a set of proposals, which are discussed in Cabinet and which become government policy. The Minister finally presents a budget plan to Parliament, which debates the plan and enacts the laws necessary to implement it.

Highlights of the 2011 Budget

Table 29.1 shows the main items in the federal budget. The numbers are projected amounts for the fiscal year beginning on April 1, 2011. The three main items shown are

- Revenues
- Outlays
- Budget balance

TABLE 29.1 Federal Budget in 2011–12

Item	Projections (billions of dollars)
Revenues	**249**
Personal income taxes	125
Corporate income taxes	33
Indirect taxes and other taxes	64
Investment income	27
Outlays	**281**
Transfer payments	166
Expenditure on goods and services	85
Debt interest	30
Deficit	**32**

Sources of data: Department of Finance, Budget Plan 2011 and Statistics Canada, CANSIM Table 380–0007.

Revenues Revenues are the federal government's receipts, which in the 2011–12 budget were projected at $249 billion. These revenues come from four sources:

1. Personal income taxes
2. Corporate income taxes
3. Indirect and other taxes
4. Investment income

The largest revenue source is personal income taxes. In 2011–12, personal income taxes were projected to be $125 billion. These are the taxes paid by individuals on their incomes. The second largest source of revenue is indirect taxes, which in 2011–12 were projected to be $64 billion. These taxes include the Harmonized Sales Tax (HST) and taxes on the sale of gasoline, alcoholic drinks, and a few other items. The smallest revenue sources are corporate income taxes, which are the taxes paid by companies on their profits, and investment income, which is the income from government enterprises and investments. In 2011–12, corporate income taxes were projected to raise $33 billion and investment income was projected at $27 billion.

Outlays Total federal government outlays in 2011–12 were projected at $281 billion. Outlays are classified in three categories:

1. Transfer payments
2. Expenditures on goods and services
3. Debt interest

The largest outlay, and by a big margin, is *transfer payments*. Transfer payments are payments to individuals, businesses, other levels of government, and the rest of the world. In 2011–12, this item was $166 billion. It includes unemployment cheques and welfare payments to individuals, farm subsidies, grants to provincial and local governments, aid to developing countries, and dues to international organizations such as the United Nations.

Expenditures on goods and services are expenditures on final goods and services, and in 2011–12 this item totalled $85 billion. These expenditures include those on national defence, computers for the Canada Revenue Agency, government cars, and highways. This component of the federal budget is the government expenditure on goods and services that appears in the circular flow of expenditure and income and in the national income and product accounts (see Chapter 20, pp. 469–470).

Debt interest is the interest on the government debt. In 2011–12, this item was $30 billion. At its peak percentage in 1990, it exceeded government expenditures on goods and services. This interest payment is large because the government has a large debt—$540 billion. This large debt has arisen because, from the mid-1970s to 1997, the federal government had a large and persistent budget deficit.

Budget Balance The government's budget balance is equal to its revenues minus its outlays. That is,

Budget balance = Revenues – Outlays.

If revenues exceed outlays, the government has a **budget surplus**. If outlays exceed revenues, the government has a **budget deficit**. If revenues equal outlays, the government has a **balanced budget**.

In 2011–12, with projected outlays of $281 billion and revenues of $249 billion, the government projected a budget deficit of $32 billion.

How typical is the federal budget of 2011–12? Let's look at its recent history.

The Budget in Historical Perspective

Figure 29.1 shows the government's revenues, outlays, and budget balance from 1961 to 2010. To get a better sense of the magnitudes of these items, they are shown as percentages of GDP. Expressing them in this way lets us see how large the government is relative to the size of the economy, and also helps us to study changes in the scale of government over

FIGURE 29.1   The Budget Surplus and Deficit

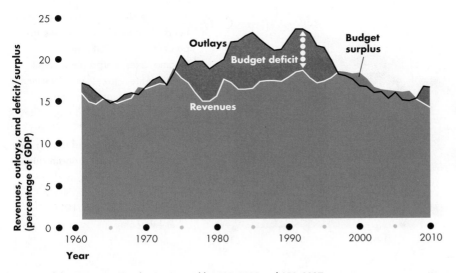

The figure records the federal government's revenues, outlays, and budget balance as percentages of GDP from 1961 to 2010. During the 1960s, outlays and revenues increased. During the late 1970s and through the 1980s, outlays continued to rise but revenues fell and then remained steady, so a large budget deficit arose. During the 1990s, expenditure cuts eliminated the budget deficit, and after 1997, the federal government had a budget surplus. A deficit re-emerged during the 2008–2009 recession.

Source of data: Statistics Canada, CANSIM Tables 380–0002 and 380–0007.

MyEconLab   animation

time. You can think of the percentages of GDP as telling you how many cents of each dollar that Canadians earn get paid to and are spent by the government.

During the 1960s, government expanded but tax revenues and outlays kept pace with each other. But from the mid-1970s through 1996, the federal budget was in deficit, and the average deficit over these years was 4.2 percent of GDP. The deficit climbed to a peak of 6.6 percent of GDP in 1985. It then decreased through the rest of the 1980s. During the recession of 1990–1991, the deficit increased again. The deficit remained above 4 percent of GDP for most of the 1980s and early 1990s.

In 1997, the federal government finally eradicated its deficit. And it did so by cutting outlays, especially transfer payments to provincial governments. But another deficit emerged in the 2008–2009 recession.

Why did the government deficit grow during the early 1980s and remain high through the early 1990s? The immediate answer is that outlays increased while revenues remained relatively constant. But which components of outlays increased? And did all the sources of revenues remain constant?

To answer these questions, we need to examine each of the sources of revenues and outlays in detail. We'll begin by looking at the sources of revenues.

Revenues Figure 29.2 shows the components of government revenues since 1961. Total revenues have no strong trends. They increased through the 1960s and again through the 1980s. But they decreased during the 1970s and the first half of the 2000s. The main source of the fluctuations in revenues was personal income taxes. Indirect taxes also fluctuated but corporate income taxes and investment income were more stable than the other two revenue components.

The increase in personal income taxes during the 1980s resulted from increases in tax rates in successive budgets.

Indirect taxes decreased during the 1990s mainly because an old federal sales tax was replaced by the Goods and Services Tax, or GST. Initially, this switch maintained revenues at a constant level, but gradually, the revenue from indirect taxes (as a percentage of GDP) fell.

Outlays Figure 29.3 shows the components of government outlays since 1961. Total outlays increased steadily from 1971 through 1985, were relatively high through 1993, and then decreased sharply after 1993. The main source of the changing trends in outlays is transfer payments to provincial governments. These payments swelled during the 1980s and were cut drastically during the mid-1990s.

FIGURE 29.2   Federal Government Revenues

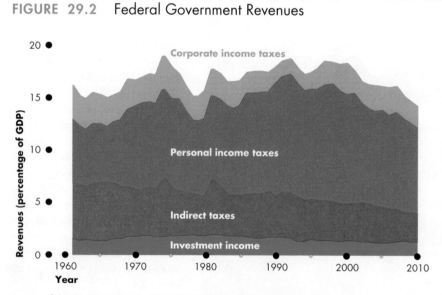

The figure shows four main components of government revenues (as percentages of GDP): personal income taxes, corporate income taxes, indirect taxes, and investment income. Revenues from personal income taxes fluctuated most. They increased during the 1960s and early 1970s, decreased during the late 1970s, increased again during the 1980s and 1990s, and then decreased again during the 2000s. Indirect taxes fell after 1990. The other two components of revenues remained steady.

Source of data: Statistics Canada, CANSIM Tables 380–0002 and 380–0007.

MyEconLab animation

FIGURE 29.3   Federal Government Outlays

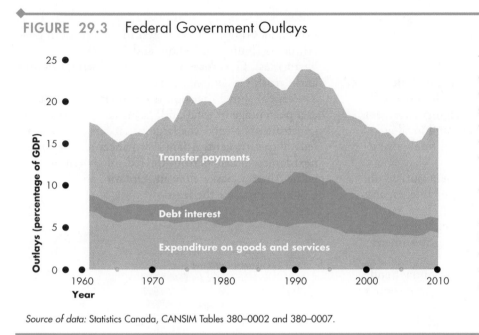

Source of data: Statistics Canada, CANSIM Tables 380–0002 and 380–0007.

The figure shows three components of government outlays (as percentages of GDP): expenditure on goods and services, debt interest, and transfer payments. Expenditure on goods and services have had a downward trend. Transfer payments increased from 1965 to 1990 but decreased sharply during the 1990s. Debt interest increased steadily during the 1980s as the budget deficit fed on itself, but decreased during the late 1990s as surpluses began to lower the government's debt.

MyEconLab   animation ◆

To understand the changes in debt interest, we need to see the connection between the budget deficit and government debt.

Deficit and Debt The government borrows to finance its deficit. And **government debt** is the total amount of government borrowing. It is the sum of past deficits minus the sum of past surpluses.

When the government budget is in deficit, government debt increases, and when the government budget is in surplus, government debt decreases.

A persistent budget deficit emerged during the mid-1970s, and in such a situation, the deficit begins to feed on itself. A budget deficit increases borrowing; increased borrowing leads to larger debt; a larger debt leads to larger interest payments; and larger interest payments lead to a larger deficit and yet larger debt. That is the story of the increasing budget deficit and rising debt of the 1980s.

Similarly, a persistent budget surplus creates a virtuous cycle of falling interest payments, larger surpluses, and falling debt.

Figure 29.4 shows the history of the Government of Canada debt since 1970. In 1970, debt (as a percentage of GDP) was at a low of 5 percent. This almost zero debt resulted from 25 years of surpluses to pay off a huge debt built up during World War II that exceeded 100 percent of GDP.

FIGURE 29.4   The Federal Government Debt

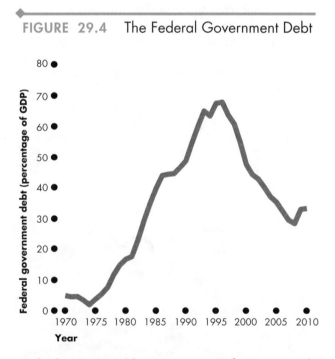

Federal government debt as a percentage of GDP increased from 1974 through 1997 and then began to decrease. It increased slightly during the 2008–2009 recession.

Source of data: Statistics Canada, CANSIM Tables 380–0002 and 380–0010.

MyEconLab   animation ◆

Economics in Action
Provincial and Local Governments

The total government sector of Canada includes provincial and local governments as well as the federal government. In 2010, when federal government outlays were $281 billion, provincial and local government outlays were $413 billion and total government outlays were $694 billion.

Most provincial and local government outlays are on public hospitals and public schools, colleges, and universities.

Figure 1 shows the revenues, outlays, and deficits of the federal government and of total government from 1961 to 2010.

You can see that federal government outlays and revenues and total government outlays and revenues fluctuate in similar ways, but the total government is much larger than the federal government. In other words, the provincial and local governments are a large component of total government. You can also see that total government outlays fluctuate more than federal government outlays.

Both the federal and total government budgets moved into and out of deficit at similar times and both were in surplus from the late 1990s to 2008.

Provincial government outlays and revenue sources vary a great deal across the provinces. Figure 2 shows the range of variation.

Part (a) shows outlays as a percentage of provincial GDP. You can see that outlays as a percentage of

provincial GDP are the greatest in the northern governments (Nunavut, Yukon, and Northwest Territories). Government outlays of Alberta, Ontario, and British Columbia are the least.

Part (b) shows the sources of provincial revenues as a percentage of total outlays. Again, the northern governments receive the largest transfers from the federal government. Atlantic provinces receive the next largest transfers from the federal government, while Alberta, Saskatchewan, Ontario, and British Columbia receive the least.

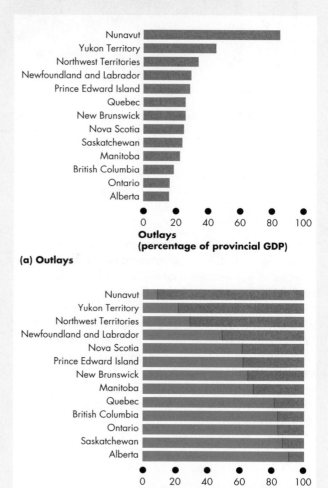

(a) Outlays

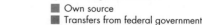

(b) Revenues

Figure 2 Provincial Government Budgets

Source of data: Statistics Canada, CANSIM Tables 380–0002 and 380–0007.

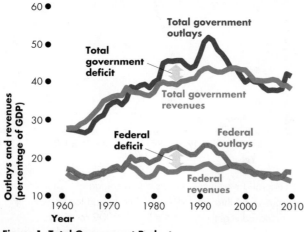

Figure 1 Total Government Budgets

Source of data: Statistics Canada, CANSIM Tables 380–0002 and 380–0007.

Economics in Action

The Canadian Government Budget in Global Perspective

To compare the deficits of governments across countries, we must take into account the differences in local and regional government arrangements. Some countries, and Canada is one of them, have large provincial and local governments. Other countries, and the United Kingdom is one, have larger central government and smaller local governments. These differences make the international comparison more valid at the level of total government. The figure shows the budget balances of all levels of government in Canada and other countries.

Of the countries shown here, the United States has the largest deficit, as a percentage of GDP, and the United Kingdom has the second largest. Japan and some European countries also have large deficits.

The newly industrialized economies of Asia (Hong Kong, South Korea, Singapore, and Taiwan) had small *surpluses* in 2010. A group of other advanced economies, Germany, and Italy had small deficits.

Canada's budget deficit is in the middle of the pack. It is notable that except for the Asian economies, none of the world's major economies had a budget surplus in 2010. Fiscal stimulus to fight recession resulted in deficits everywhere.

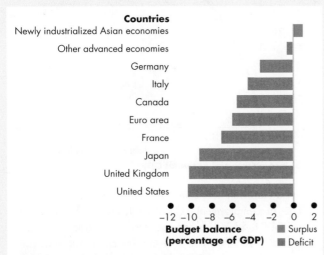

Government Budgets Around the World

Source of data: International Monetary Fund, *World Economic Outlook*, September 2011.

Small budget deficits increased the debt-to-GDP ratio slightly through the 1970s, and large budget deficits increased it dramatically between 1981 and 1986. During the late 1980s, the ratio continued to increase but at a more moderate rate. The debt-to-GDP ratio grew quickly again during the 1990–1991 recession and its growth rate slowed after 1995 and debt interest as a percentage of GDP decreased.

The 2008–2009 recession lowered revenues and increased outlays so the debt-to GDP ratio increased again, but only slightly.

Debt and Capital When individuals and businesses incur debts, they usually do so to buy capital—assets that yield a return. In fact, the main point of debt is to enable people to buy assets that will earn a return that exceeds the interest paid on the debt. The government is similar to individuals and businesses in this regard. Some government expenditure is investment—the purchase of public capital that yields a return. Highways, major irrigation schemes, public schools and universities, public libraries, and the stock of national defence capital all yield a social rate of return that probably far exceeds the interest rate the government pays on its debt.

But Canadian government debt, which is $500 billion, is much larger than the value of the public capital stock. This fact means that some government debt has been incurred to finance public consumption expenditure.

REVIEW QUIZ

1 What are the main items of government revenues and outlays?
2 Under what circumstances does the government have a budget surplus?
3 Explain the connection between a government budget deficit and a government debt.

You can work these questions in Study Plan 29.1 and get instant feedback.

——————————————— MyEconLab ◆

It is now time to study the *effects* of fiscal policy. We'll begin by learning about the effects of taxes on employment, aggregate supply, and potential GDP. Then we'll look at fiscal stimulus and see how it might be used to speed recovery from recession and stabilize the business cycle.

Supply-Side Effects of Fiscal Policy

How do taxes on personal and corporate income affect real GDP and employment? The answer to these questions is controversial. Some economists, known as *supply-siders*, believe these effects to be large and an accumulating body of evidence suggests that they are correct. To see why these effects might be large, we'll begin with a refresher on how full employment and potential GDP are determined in the absence of taxes. Then we'll introduce an income tax and see how it changes the economic outcome.

Full Employment and Potential GDP

You learned in Chapter 22 (pp. 523–525) how the full-employment quantity of labour and potential GDP are determined. At full employment, the real wage rate adjusts to make the quantity of labour demanded equal the quantity of labour supplied. Potential GDP is the real GDP that the full-employment quantity of labour produces.

Figure 29.5 illustrates a full-employment situation. In part (a), the demand for labour curve is *LD*, and the supply of labour curve is *LS*. At a real wage rate of $30 an hour and 25 billion hours of labour a year employed, the economy is at full employment.

In Fig. 29.5(b), the production function is *PF*. When 25 billion hours of labour are employed, real GDP and potential GDP are $1,300 billion.

Let's now see how an income tax changes potential GDP.

The Effects of the Income Tax

The tax on labour income influences potential GDP and aggregate supply by changing the full-employment quantity of labour. The income tax weakens the incentive to work and drives a wedge between the take-home wage of workers and the cost of labour to firms. The result is a smaller quantity of labour and a lower potential GDP.

Figure 29.5 shows this outcome. In the labour market, the income tax has no effect on the demand for labour, which remains at *LD*. The reason is that the quantity of labour that firms plan to hire depends only on how productive labour is and what it costs—its real wage rate.

FIGURE 29.5   The Effects of the Income Tax on Aggregate Supply

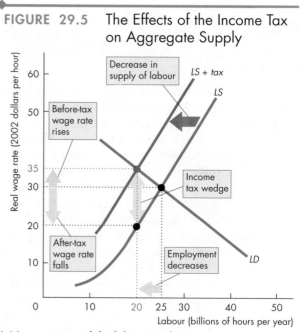

(a) Income tax and the labour market

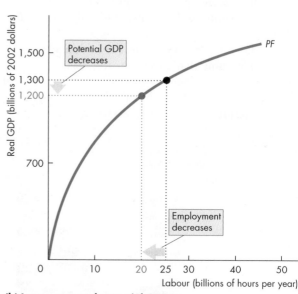

(b) Income tax and potential GDP

In part (a), with no income tax, the real wage rate is $30 an hour and employment is 25 billion hours. In part (b), potential GDP is $1,300 billion. An income tax shifts the supply of labour curve leftward to *LS + tax*. The before-tax wage rate rises to $35 an hour, the after-tax wage rate falls to $20 an hour, and the quantity of labour employed decreases to 20 billion hours. With less labour, potential GDP decreases.

MyEconLab   animation ◆

But the supply of labour *does* change. With no income tax, the real wage rate is $30 an hour and 25 billion hours of labour a year are employed. An income tax weakens the incentive to work and decreases the supply of labour. The reason is that for each dollar of before-tax earnings, workers must pay the government an amount determined by the income tax code. So workers look at the after-tax wage rate when they decide how much labour to supply. An income tax shifts the supply curve leftward to *LS + tax*. The vertical distance between the *LS* curve and the *LS + tax* curve measures the amount of income tax. With the smaller supply of labour, the *before-tax* wage rate rises to $35 an hour but the *after-tax* wage rate falls to $20 an hour. The gap created between the before-tax and after-tax wage rates is called the **tax wedge**.

The new equilibrium quantity of labour employed is 20 billion hours a year—less than in the no-tax case. Because the full-employment quantity of labour decreases, so does potential GDP. And a decrease in potential GDP decreases aggregate supply.

In this example, the tax rate is high—$15 tax on a $35 wage rate is a tax rate of about 43 percent. A lower tax rate would have a smaller effect on employment and potential GDP.

An increase in the tax rate to above 43 percent would decrease the supply of labour by more than the decrease shown in Fig. 29.5. Equilibrium employment and potential GDP would also decrease still further. A tax cut would increase the supply of labour, increase equilibrium employment, and increase potential GDP.

Taxes on Expenditure and the Tax Wedge

The tax wedge that we've just considered is only a part of the wedge that affects labour-supply decisions. Taxes on consumption expenditure add to the wedge. The reason is that a tax on consumption raises the prices paid for consumption goods and services and is equivalent to a cut in the real wage rate.

The incentive to supply labour depends on the goods and services that an hour of labour can buy. The higher the taxes on goods and services and the lower the after-tax wage rate, the less is the incentive to supply labour. If the income tax rate is 25 percent and the tax rate on consumption expenditure is 10 percent, a dollar earned buys only 65 cents worth of goods and services. The tax wedge is 35 percent.

Economics in Action
Some Real World Tax Wedges

Edward C. Prescott of Arizona State University, who shared the 2004 Nobel Prize for Economic Science, has estimated the tax wedges for three countries: the United States, the United Kingdom, and France. We have estimated the tax wedge for Canada.

The wedges are a combination of taxes on labour income and taxes on consumption. They include all taxes on labour, including social insurance taxes. And the wedges are based on marginal tax rates—the tax rates paid on the marginal dollar earned.

The figure shows the tax wedges in these four countries. In the United States, the consumption tax wedge is 13 percent and the income tax wedge is 32 percent. Canada is very similar. In France, the consumption tax wedge is 33 percent and the income tax wedge is 49 percent. The tax wedges in United Kingdom fall between those of France and Canada.

Does the Tax Wedge Matter?

Differences in potential GDP per person arise partly from productivity differences and partly from choices influenced by the tax wedge. Potential GDP (per person) in France is 14 percent below that of the United States and the entire difference is attributed to the difference in the tax wedge in the two countries. Potential GDP in Canada is 16 percent below that of the United States, but this difference is due to different productivities. Potential GDP in the United Kingdom is 41 percent below that of the United States, and about a third of the difference arises from the different tax wedges and two-thirds from productivity difference.

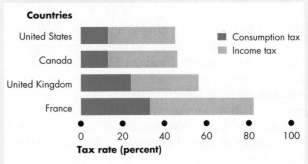

Four Tax Wedges

Source of data: Edward C. Prescott, American Economic Review, 2003.

Taxes and the Incentive to Save and Invest

A tax on interest income weakens the incentive to save and drives a wedge between the after-tax interest rate earned by savers and the interest rate paid by firms. These effects are analogous to those of a tax on labour income. But they are more serious for two reasons.

First, a tax on labour income lowers the quantity of labour employed and lowers potential GDP, while a tax on capital income lowers the quantity of saving and investment and slows the growth rate of real GDP.

Second, the true tax rate on interest income is much higher than that on labour income because of the way in which inflation and taxes on interest income interact. Let's examine this interaction.

Effect of Tax Rate on Real Interest Rate

The interest rate that influences investment and saving plans is the real after-tax interest rate. The real after-tax interest rate subtracts the income tax rate paid on interest income from the real interest rate. But the taxes depend on the nominal interest rate, not the real interest rate. So the higher the inflation rate, the higher is the true tax rate on interest income. Here is an example. Suppose the real interest rate is 4 percent a year and the tax rate is 40 percent.

If there is no inflation, the nominal interest rate equals the real interest rate. The tax on 4 percent interest is 1.6 percent (40 percent of 4 percent), so the real after-tax interest rate is 4 percent minus 1.6 percent, which equals 2.4 percent.

If the inflation rate is 6 percent a year, the nominal interest rate is 10 percent. The tax on 10 percent interest is 4 percent (40 percent of 10 percent), so the real after-tax interest rate is 4 percent minus 4 percent, which equals zero. The true tax rate in this case is not 40 percent but 100 percent!

Effect of Income Tax on Saving and Investment

In Fig. 29.6, initially there are no taxes. Also, the government has a balanced budget. The demand for loanable funds curve, which is also the investment demand curve, is *DLF*. The supply of loanable funds curve, which is also the saving supply curve, is *SLF*. The equilibrium interest rate is 3 percent a year, and the quantity of funds borrowed and lent is $200 billion a year.

A tax on interest income has no effect on the demand for loanable funds. The quantity of investment and borrowing that firms plan to undertake depends only on how productive capital is and what

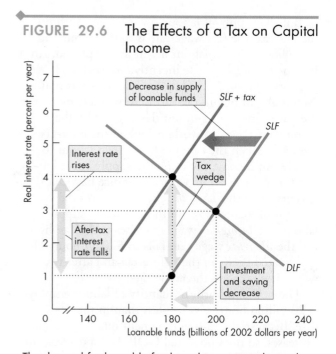

FIGURE 29.6   The Effects of a Tax on Capital Income

The demand for loanable funds and investment demand curve is *DLF*, and the supply of loanable funds and saving supply curve is *SLF*. With no income tax, the real interest rate is 3 percent a year and investment is $200 billion. An income tax shifts the supply curve leftward to *SLF + tax*. The interest rate rises to 4 percent a year, the after-tax interest rate falls to 1 percent a year, and investment decreases to $180 billion. With less investment, the real GDP growth rate decreases.

——— MyEconLab   animation ◆

it costs—its real interest rate. But a tax on interest income weakens the incentive to save and lend and decreases the supply of loanable funds. For each dollar of before-tax interest, savers must pay the government an amount determined by the tax code. So savers look at the after-tax real interest rate when they decide how much to save.

When a tax is imposed, saving decreases and the supply of loanable funds curve shifts leftward to *SLF* + tax. The amount of tax payable is measured by the vertical distance between the *SLF* curve and the *SLF* + tax curve. With this smaller supply of loanable funds, the interest rate rises to 4 percent a year but the after-tax interest rate falls to 1 percent a year. A tax wedge is driven between the interest rate and the after-tax interest rate, and the equilibrium quantity of loanable funds decreases. Saving and investment also decrease.

Tax Revenues and the Laffer Curve

An interesting consequence of the effect of taxes on employment and saving is that a higher tax *rate* does not always bring greater tax *revenue*. A higher tax rate brings in more revenue per dollar earned. But because a higher tax rate decreases the number of dollars earned, two forces operate in opposite directions on the tax revenue collected.

The relationship between the tax rate and the amount of tax revenue collected is called the **Laffer curve**. The curve is so named because Arthur B. Laffer, a member of President Reagan's Economic Policy Advisory Board, drew such a curve on a table napkin and launched the idea that tax cuts could increase tax revenue.

Figure 29.7 shows a Laffer curve. The tax rate is on the *x*-axis, and total tax revenue is on the *y*-axis. For tax rates below T^*, an increase in the tax rate increases tax revenue; at T^*, tax revenue is maximized; and a tax rate increase above T^* decreases tax revenue.

Most people think that Canada is on the upward-sloping part of the Laffer curve; so is the United Kingdom. But France might be close to the maximum point or perhaps even beyond it.

The Supply-Side Debate

Before 1980, few economists paid attention to the supply-side effects of taxes on employment and potential GDP. Then, when Ronald Reagan took office as president, a group of supply-siders began to argue the virtues of cutting taxes. Arthur Laffer was one of them. Laffer and his supporters were not held in high esteem among mainstream economists, but they were influential for a period. They correctly argued that tax cuts would increase employment and increase output. But they incorrectly argued that tax cuts would increase tax revenues and decrease the budget deficit. For this prediction to be correct, the United States would have had to be on the "wrong" side of the Laffer curve. Given that U.S. tax rates are among the lowest in the industrial world, it is unlikely that this condition was met. And when the Reagan administration did cut taxes, the budget deficit increased, a fact that reinforces this view.

Supply-side economics became tarnished because of its association with Laffer and came to be called "voodoo economics." But mainstream economists, including Martin Feldstein, a Harvard professor who was Reagan's chief economic adviser, recognized the

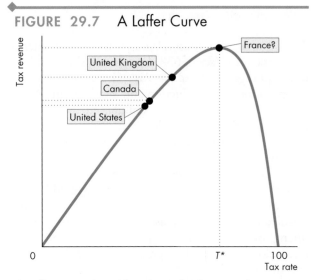

FIGURE 29.7   A Laffer Curve

A Laffer curve shows the relationship between the tax rate and tax revenues. For tax rates below T^*, an increase in the tax rate increases tax revenue. At the tax rate T^*, tax revenue is maximized. For tax rates above T^*, an increase in the tax rate decreases tax revenue.

———————————— MyEconLab animation ◆

power of tax cuts as incentives but took the standard view that tax cuts without spending cuts would swell the budget deficit and bring serious further problems. This view is now widely accepted by economists of all political persuasions.

◢ REVIEW QUIZ

1 How does a tax on labour income influence the equilibrium quantity of employment?
2 How does the tax wedge influence potential GDP?
3 Why are consumption taxes relevant for measuring the tax wedge?
4 Why are income taxes on capital income more powerful than those on labour income?
5 What is the Laffer curve and why is it unlikely that Canada is on the "wrong" side of it?

You can work these questions in Study Plan 29.2 and get instant feedback.

———————————————————— MyEconLab ◆

You now know how taxes influence potential GDP and saving and investment. Next we look at the demand-side effects of fiscal policy.

◆ Fiscal Stimulus

The 2008–2009 recession brought Keynesian macro-economic ideas (see p. 638) back into fashion and put a spotlight on **fiscal stimulus**—the use of fiscal policy to increase production and employment. But whether fiscal policy is truly stimulating, and if so, how stimulating, are questions that generate much discussion and disagreement. You're now going to explore these questions.

Fiscal stimulus can be either *automatic* or *discretionary*. A fiscal policy action that is triggered by the state of the economy with no action by government is called **automatic fiscal policy**. The increase in total unemployment benefits triggered by the rise in the unemployment rate through 2009 is an example of automatic fiscal policy.

A fiscal policy action initiated by an act of Parliament is called **discretionary fiscal policy**. It requires a change in a spending program or in a tax law. A fiscal stimulus act passed by the U.S. government in 2008 (see *Economics in Action* on p. 717) is an example of discretionary fiscal policy.

Whether automatic or discretionary, an increase in government outlays or a decrease in government revenues can stimulate production and jobs. An increase in expenditure on goods and services directly increases aggregate expenditure. And an increase in transfer payments (such as unemployment benefits) or a decrease in tax revenues increases disposable income, which enables people to increase consumption expenditure. Lower taxes also strengthen the incentives to work and invest.

We'll begin by looking at automatic fiscal policy and the interaction between the business cycle and the budget balance.

Automatic Fiscal Policy and Cyclical and Structural Budget Balances

Two items in the government budget change automatically in response to the state of the economy. They are *tax revenues* and *transfer payments*.

Automatic Changes in Tax Revenues The tax laws that Parliament enacts don't legislate the number of tax *dollars* the government will raise. Rather they define the tax rates that people must pay. Tax dollars paid depend on tax rates and incomes. But incomes vary with real GDP, so tax revenues depend on real GDP. When real GDP increases in a business cycle expansion, wages and profits rise, so tax revenues from these incomes rise. When real GDP decreases in a recession, wages and profits fall, so tax revenues fall.

Automatic Changes in Outlays The government creates programs that pay benefits to qualified people and businesses. The spending on these programs results in transfer payments that depend on the economic state of individual citizens and businesses. When the economy expands, unemployment falls and the number of people receiving unemployment benefits decreases, so transfer payments decrease. When the economy is in a recession, unemployment is high and the number of people receiving unemployment benefits increases, so transfer payments increase.

Automatic Stimulus Because government revenues fall and outlays increase in a recession, the budget provides automatic stimulus that helps to shrink the recessionary gap. Similarly, because revenues rise and outlays decrease in a boom, the budget provides automatic restraint to shrink an inflationary gap.

Cyclical and Structural Budget Balances To identify the government budget deficit that arises from the business cycle, we distinguish between the **structural surplus or deficit**, which is the budget balance that would occur if the economy were at full employment, and the **cyclical surplus or deficit**, which is the actual surplus or deficit *minus* the structural surplus or deficit.

Figure 29.8 illustrates these concepts. Outlays *decrease* as real GDP *increases*, so the outlays curve slopes downward; and revenues *increase* as real GDP *increases*, so the revenues curve slopes upward.

In Fig. 29.8(a), potential GDP is $1,200 billion and if real GDP equals potential GDP, the government has a balanced budget. There is no structural surplus or deficit. But there might be a cyclical surplus or deficit. If real GDP is less than potential GDP at $1,100 billion, outlays exceed revenues and there is a cyclical deficit. If real GDP is greater than potential GDP at $1,300 billion, outlays are less than revenues and there is a cyclical surplus.

In Fig. 29.8(b), if potential GDP equals $1,200 billion (line *B*), the *structural balance is zero*. But if potential GDP is $1,100 billion (line *A*), the government budget has a *structural deficit*. And if potential GDP is $1,300 billion (line *C*), the government budget has a structural surplus.

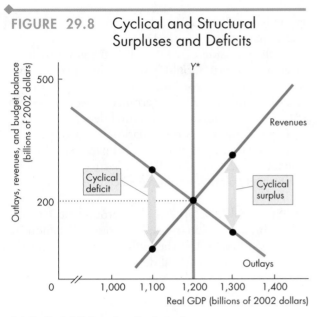

FIGURE 29.8   Cyclical and Structural Surpluses and Deficits

(a) Cyclical deficit and cyclical surplus

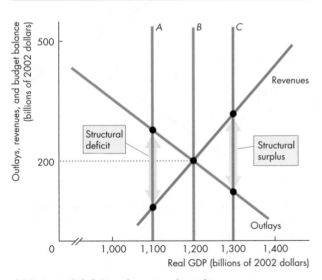

(b) Structural deficit and structural surplus

In part (a), potential GDP is $1,200 billion. When real GDP is $1,100 billion, the budget balance is a *cyclical deficit*. When real GDP is $1,300 billion, the budget balance is a *cyclical surplus*. When real GDP is $1,200 billion, the government has a *balanced budget*.

In part (b), if potential GDP is $1,100 billion, the budget balance is a *structural deficit*. If potential GDP is $1,300 billion, the budget balance is a *structural surplus*. If potential GDP is $1,200 billion, the *structural balance* is zero.

━━━━━━ MyEconLab   animation   ◆

Canadian Structural Budget Balance in 2011   The Canadian federal budget in 2011 was in deficit at $32 billion and the recessionary gap (the gap between real GDP and potential GDP) was estimated by the Bank of Canada to be less than 1 percent of potential GDP or about $10 billion. This recessionary gap is small. With a small recessionary gap and a substantial budget deficit, most of the deficit was structural.

We don't now exactly how much of the deficit was structural and how much was cyclical but *Economics in Action* on the next page provides an illustration and possible breakdown of the deficit into its two parts.

Discretionary Fiscal Stimulus

Most discussion of *discretionary* fiscal stimulus focuses on its effects on aggregate demand. But you've seen (on pp. 710–713) that taxes influence aggregate supply and that the balance of taxes and spending—the government budget deficit—can crowd out investment and slow the pace of economic growth. So discretionary fiscal stimulus has both supply-side and demand-side effects that end up determining its overall effectiveness.

We're going to begin our examination of discretionary fiscal stimulus by looking at its effects on aggregate demand.

Fiscal Stimulus and Aggregate Demand   Changes in government expenditure and changes in taxes change aggregate demand by their influence on spending plans, and they also have multiplier effects.

Let's look at the two main fiscal policy multipliers: the government expenditure and tax multipliers.

The **government expenditure multiplier** is the quantitative effect of a change in government expenditure on real GDP. Because government expenditure is a component of aggregate expenditure, an increase in government spending increases aggregate expenditure and real GDP. But does a $1 billion increase in government expenditure increase real GDP by $1 billion, more than $1 billion, or less than $1 billion?

When an increase in government expenditure increases real GDP, incomes rise and the higher incomes bring an increase in consumption expenditure. If this were the only consequence of increased government expenditure, the government expenditure multiplier would be greater than 1.

But an increase in government expenditure increases government borrowing (or decreases government lending if there is a budget surplus) and

Economics in Action

Canada's 2011 Budget Deficit

Canada's Conservative government places a high priority on maintaining a federal budget surplus for two reasons. First, it believes that the debt created by the long run of deficits during the 1980s and 1990s remains too large and it wants to see that debt lowered every year. Second, it believes that aiming for a surplus places a discipline on a Parliament that can always find reasons to spend ever larger amounts on public projects and social programs.

From 2001 to 2004, we had a negative output gap but the budget balance was a structural surplus. In the recession of 2008–2009, the budget moved into a structural deficit and as the economy

expanded in 2010–2011, the budget deficit increased and remained (see Figure 1).

In the recession of 2008–2009, the government faced a dilemma. Should it stick to its surplus priority or join the call for fiscal stimulus to lessen the recession's impact? The government's decision was to stimulate and move to a structural deficit.

Figure 2 illustrates the situation in Canada in 2011.Potential GDP was (our estimate) $1,360 billion and if actual real GDP had been at that level, the budget balance would have been a structural deficit.

Actual real GDP in 2011 was around $1,350 billion, with a recessionary gap of about $10 billion. At that level of real GDP, the budget had both a structural deficit and a cyclical deficit.

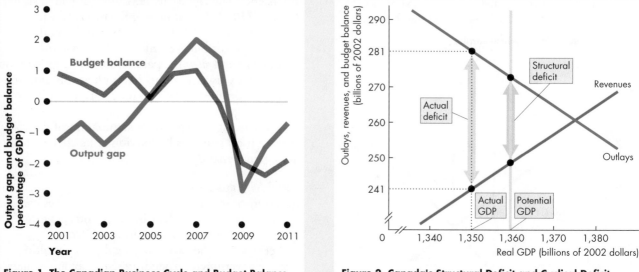

Figure 1 The Canadian Business Cycle and Budget Balance

Figure 2 Canada's Structural Deficit and Cyclical Deficit

Source of data: Statistics Canada, CANSIM Tables 380–0002 and 380–0007 and the Bank of Canada's estimate of the output gap.

raises the real interest rate. With a higher cost of borrowing, investment decreases, which partly offsets the increase in government spending. If this were the only consequence of increased government expenditure, the multiplier would be less than 1.

The actual multiplier depends on which of the above effects is stronger and the consensus is that the crowding-out effect is strong enough to make the government expenditure multiplier less than 1.

The **tax multiplier** is the quantitative effect of a change in taxes on real GDP. The demand-side effects of a tax cut are likely to be smaller than an

equivalent increase in government expenditure. The reason is that a tax cut influences aggregate demand by increasing disposable income, only part of which gets spent. So the initial injection of expenditure from a $1 billion tax cut is less than $1 billion.

A tax cut has similar crowding-out consequences to a spending increase. It increases government borrowing (or decreases government lending), raises the real interest rate, and cuts investment.

The tax multiplier effect on aggregate demand depends on these two opposing effects and is probably quite small.

Graphical Illustration of Fiscal Stimulus Figure 29.9 shows how fiscal stimulus is supposed to work if it is perfectly executed and has its desired effects.

Potential GDP is $1,200 billion and real GDP is below potential at $1,100 billion so the economy has a recessionary gap of $100 billion.

To restore full employment, the government passes a fiscal stimulus package. An increase in government expenditure and a tax cut increase aggregate expenditure by ΔE. If this were the only change in spending plans, the AD curve would shift rightward to become the curve labelled $AD_0 + \Delta E$ in Fig. 29.9. But if fiscal stimulus sets off a multiplier process that increases consumption expenditure, and does not crowd out much investment, aggregate demand increases further and the AD curve shifts rightward to AD_1.

With no change in the price level, the economy would move from point A to point B on AD_1. But

FIGURE 29.9   Expansionary Fiscal Policy

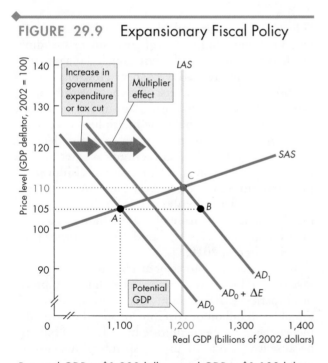

Potential GDP is $1,200 billion, real GDP is $1,100 billion, and there is a $100 billion recessionary gap. An increase in government expenditure and a tax cut increase aggregate expenditure by ΔE. The multiplier increases consumption expenditure and the AD curve shifts rightward to AD_1. The price level rises to 110, real GDP increases to $1,200 billion, and the recessionary gap is eliminated.

Economics in Action
Fiscal Stimulus in the United States

As recession fears grew, the Economic Stimulus Act of 2008, a discretionary fiscal policy, aimed to increase aggregate demand.

Tax rebates were the key component of the package and their effect on aggregate demand depends on the extent to which they are spent and saved.

The last time the U.S. federal government boosted aggregate demand with a tax rebate was in 2001 and a statistical investigation of the effects estimated that 70 percent of the rebates were spent within six months of being received.

The rebates in the 2008 fiscal package were targeted predominantly at low-income individuals and families, so the experience of 2001 would be likely to apply: Most of the rebates would be spent.

The cost of the package in 2008 was about $160 billion, so aggregate demand would be expected to increase by close to this amount and then by a multiplier as the initial spending became someone else's income and so boosted their spending.

The figure illustrates the effects of the package. Before the rebates, aggregate demand was AD_0 and real GDP was $11.7 trillion. The rebates increased aggregate demand to $AD_0 + \Delta E$, and a multiplier increased it to AD_1. Real GDP and the price level increased and the recessionary gap narrowed.

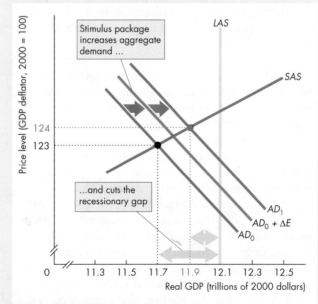

Effects of Fiscal Stimulus

the increase in aggregate demand brings a rise in the price level along the upward-sloping *SAS* curve and the economy moves to point *C*.

At point *C*, the economy returns to full employment and the recessionary gap is eliminated.

When Fiscal Stimulus Is Removed When fiscal stimulus brings a structural budget deficit, government debt grows. Concern about the effect of a deficit on debt often makes governments want to get back to a balanced budget. To do that, government expenditure must be cut and/or taxes must be increased. When these restraining discretionary fiscal policy actions are taken, aggregate demand decreases and a process the reverse of that described and illustrated in Fig. 29.9 kicks in. Care must be taken to try to time this restraint to coincide with an increase in investment and increasing aggregate demand.

Fiscal Stimulus and Aggregate Supply You've seen earlier in this chapter that taxes influence aggregate supply. A tax on labour income (on wages) drives a wedge between the cost of labour and the take-home pay of workers and lowers employment and output (p. 710). A tax on capital income (on interest) drives a wedge between the cost of borrowing and the return to lending and lowers saving and investment (p. 712). With less saving and investment, the real GDP growth rate slows.

These negative effects of taxes on real GDP and its growth rate and on employment mean that a tax *cut* increases real GDP and its growth rate and increases employment.

These supply-side effects of a tax cut occur along with the demand-side effects and are probably much larger than the demand-side effects and make the overall tax multiplier much larger than the government expenditure multiplier—see *Economics in Action*.

An increase in government expenditure financed by borrowing increases the demand for loanable funds and raises the real interest rate, which in turn lowers investment and private saving. This cut in investment is the main reason why the government expenditure multiplier is so small and why a deficit-financed increase in government spending ends up making only a small contribution to job creation. And because government expenditure crowds out investment, it lowers future real GDP.

So a fiscal stimulus package that is heavy on tax cuts and light on government spending works. But an increase in government expenditure alone is not an effective way to stimulate production and create jobs.

The description of the effects of discretionary fiscal stimulus and its graphical illustration in Fig. 29.9 make it look easy: Calculate the recessionary gap and the multipliers, change government expenditure and taxes, and eliminate the gap. In reality, things are not that easy.

Getting the magnitude and the timing right is difficult, and we'll now examine this challenge.

Magnitude of Stimulus Economists have diverging views about the size of the government spending and tax multipliers because there is insufficient empirical evidence on which to pin their size with accuracy. This fact makes it impossible for Parliament to deter-

Economics in Action
How Big Are the Fiscal Stimulus Multipliers?

When a U.S. 2009 fiscal stimulus package cut taxes by $300 billion and increased government spending by almost $500 billion, by how much did aggregate expenditure and real GDP change? How big were the fiscal policy multipliers? Was the government expenditure multiplier larger than the tax multiplier? These questions are about the multiplier effects on *equilibrium real GDP*, not just on aggregate demand.

President Obama's chief economic adviser in 2009, Christina Romer, a University of California, Berkeley, professor, expected the government expenditure multiplier to be about 1.5. So she was expecting the spending increase of $500 billion to go a long way towards closing the $1 trillion output gap by some time in 2010.

Robert Barro, a professor at Harvard University, says this multiplier number is not in line with previous experience. Based on his calculations, an additional $500 billion of government spending would increase aggregate expenditure by only $250 billion because it would lower private spending in a crowding-out effect by $250 billion—the multiplier is 0.5.

Harald Uhlig, a professor at the University of Chicago, says that the government expenditure multiplier on real GDP is even smaller and lies between 0.3 and 0.4, so that a $500 billion increase in government spending increases aggregate expenditure by between $150 billion and $200 billion.

mine the amount of stimulus needed to close a given output gap. Further, the actual output gap is not known and can only be estimated with error. For these two reasons, discretionary fiscal policy is risky.

Time Lags Discretionary fiscal stimulus actions are also seriously hampered by three time lags:

- Recognition lag
- Law-making lag
- Impact lag

Recognition Lag The *recognition lag* is the time it takes to figure out that fiscal policy actions are needed. This process involves assessing the current state of the economy and forecasting its future state.

There is greater agreement about tax multipliers. Because tax cuts strengthen the incentive to work and to invest, they increase aggregate supply as well as aggregate demand.

These multipliers get bigger as more time elapses. Harald Uhlig says that after one year, the tax multiplier is 0.5 so that the $300 billion tax cut would increase real GDP by about $150 billion by early 2010. But with two years of time to respond, real GDP would be $600 billion higher—a multiplier of 2. And after three years, the tax multiplier builds up to more than 6.

The implications of the work of Barro and Uhlig are that tax cuts are a powerful way to stimulate real GDP and employment but spending increases are not effective.

Christina Romer agrees that the economy didn't perform in line with a multiplier of 1.5 but says other factors deteriorated and without the fiscal stimulus, the outcome would have been even worse.

Christina Romer: 1.5

Robert Barro: 0.5

Harald Uhlig: 0.4

Law-Making Lag The *law-making lag* is the time it takes Parliament to pass the laws needed to change taxes or spending. This process takes time because each member of Parliament has a different idea about what is the best tax or spending program to change, so long debates and committee meetings are needed to reconcile conflicting views. The economy might benefit from fiscal stimulation today, but by the time Parliament acts, a different fiscal medicine might be needed.

Impact Lag The *impact lag* is the time it takes from passing a tax or spending change to its effects on real GDP being felt. This lag depends partly on the speed with which government agencies can act and partly on the timing of changes in spending plans by households and businesses. These changes are spread out over a number of quarters and possibly a number of years.

Economic forecasting is steadily improving, but it remains inexact and subject to error. The range of uncertainty about the magnitudes of the spending and tax multipliers make discretionary fiscal stimulus an imprecise tool for boosting production and jobs and the crowding out consequences raise serious questions about its effects on long-term economic growth.

◆ REVIEW QUIZ

1 What is the distinction between automatic and discretionary fiscal policy?
2 How do taxes and transfer payments programs work as automatic fiscal policy to dampen the business cycle?
3 How do we tell whether a budget deficit needs discretionary action to remove it?
4 How can the federal government use discretionary fiscal policy to stimulate the economy?
5 Why might fiscal stimulus crowd out investment?

You can work these questions in Study Plan 29.3 and get instant feedback.

——— MyEconLab ◆

◆ You've now seen the effects of fiscal policy, and *Reading Between the Lines* on pp. 720–721 applies what you've learned to Canadian fiscal policy.

Harper's Fiscal Policy

Economic Woes Bedevil Ottawa

Winnipeg Free Press
September 28, 2011

Prime Minister Stephen Harper met with his finance minister and the Bank of Canada governor Tuesday as opposition parties said the Conservative government's focus on austerity could drive the country into a recession. ...

Harper said the government has one of the best job-creation records "in the entire industrialized world" and won't adopt the NDP's solution—taxes on large corporations that the Conservatives say would kill jobs.

Interim Liberal Leader Bob Rae cited an economist [Sherry Cooper] who has written that Harper's "near-term fiscal tightening" shows he has learned nothing from Hoover's response to the Depression.

Harper again rejected the criticism. "In fact we are running a very expansionary fiscal policy right now. But we are obviously undertaking good management, some modest savings to ensure that as the economy recovers, that we will in fact balance our budget and retain our fiscal advantage."

Under its budget plan, the government will slash $4 billion annually from government programs. The cabinet will spend this autumn deciding where the cuts should occur, and their decisions will be revealed in the 2012 budget. ...

Material reprinted with the express permission of Postmedia News, a division of Postmedia Network Inc.

Economist Says Canada Making Same Mistakes That Led To Great Depression

Financial Post
September 27, 2011

The economic policies advocated by Prime Minister Stephen Harper ... could lead to another global recession and financial crisis, warns BMO Financial Group chief economist Sherry Cooper. ... Mr. Harper's call for reduced government spending ... "shows we have learned nothing from Herbert Hoover's response to the Great Depression." Hoover recommended large tax increases, which were approved in 1932, further exacerbating the rout, Ms. Cooper cautions.

Material reprinted with the express permission of Postmedia News, a division of Postmedia Network Inc.

ESSENCE OF THE STORY

- BMO Financial Group chief economist Sherry Cooper says that fiscal restraint is misplaced and risks creating a major recession or depression.

- Prime Minister Stephen Harper says the government's fiscal policy is sound and economists around the world agree with him.

- Harper says "we are running a very expansionary fiscal policy right now" and it is correct to restrain expenditure to ensure that the budget is balanced when full recovery occurs.

- Under its budget plan, the government will cut $4 billion from government programs annually to balance the budget and retain Canada's fiscal advantage.

ECONOMIC ANALYSIS

- In the fall of 2011, the Canadian economy continued to recover from the 2008–2009 recession but unemployment remained above 7 percent and a recessionary gap remained, although it was small and closing.

- Despite this reasonably healthy economic state, a great deal of fear surrounded the future.

- The sources of concern were "headwinds" into which Canada might be sailing—conditions created by an extremely slow U.S. recovery and the European debt crisis.

- Because of the unfavourable "headwinds," the Bank of Canada has continued to keep interest rates low (for more on this, see Chapter 30) and the Government of Canada continued to maintain strong fiscal stimulus.

- Figure 1 shows the state of the economy as measured by the output gap and the fiscal stimulus. In mid–2011, the output gap was less than 1 percent of potential GDP and the budget deficit, mainly a structural deficit, was 2 percent of GDP.

- Recognizing the danger of a deficit crowding out private investment, the main source of economic growth and jobs growth, the government set out a clear fiscal plan to achieve a balanced budget by 2014–15.

- Figure 1 shows how this return to budget balance might align with a gradual return to a zero output gap and full employment.

- Figure 2 illustrates the situation in the market for real GDP. The aggregate demand curve is AD_0 and the short-run aggregate supply curve is SAS. Equilibrium real GDP is $1,300 billion and the price level is 123. Potential GDP, and long-run aggregate supply (LAS), is $1,350 billion, so the recessionary gap is $50 billion.

- A modest fiscal stimulus is needed to shift the aggregate demand curve to AD^* to close the recessionary gap. Too much stimulus could take the AD curve to AD_1 and open up an inflationary gap.

- The problem facing Canada in 2011 was not too little aggregate demand, but unbalanced sources of aggregate demand. Investment was too low.

- Consumption expenditure remained at 57 percent of GDP and net exports at about –1 percent of GDP, but investment decreased from 20 percent of GDP to 18.4 percent.

- The fiscal stimulus increased government expenditure by the same percentage of GDP as investment fell.

- Two influences on investment need to be considered: the real interest rate, which is the opportunity cost of the funds used to finance investment, and the expected

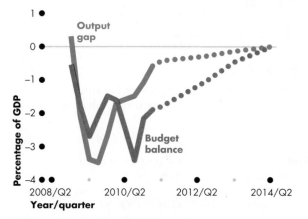

Figure 1 Output Gap and Budget Balance

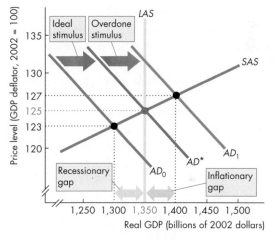

Figure 2 Aggregate Supply and Aggregate Demand

future return from investment, including the degree of uncertainty about that future return.

- More government spending has an adverse effect on both of these influences on investment.

- A larger budget deficit puts upward pressure on the real interest rate and crowds out investment.

- A larger budget deficit also brings uncertainty about what future tax and expenditure changes will be made to eventually bring the budget deficit under control.

- By having a clear budget plan to eliminate the deficit, the government seeks to reduce crowding out and get investment back to its pre-recession percentage of GDP.

SUMMARY

Key Points

The Federal Budget (pp. 704–709)

- The federal budget is used to achieve macroeconomic objectives.
- Revenues can exceed, equal, or fall short of outlays—the budget can be in surplus, balanced, or in deficit.
- Budget deficits create government debt.

Working Problems 1 to 5 will give you a better understanding of the federal budget.

Supply-Side Effects of Fiscal Policy (pp. 710–713)

- Fiscal policy has supply-side effects because taxes weaken the incentive to work and decrease employment and potential GDP.
- The Canadian labour market tax wedge is similar to that in the United States, but smaller than that in France or the United Kingdom.
- Fiscal policy has supply-side effects because taxes weaken the incentive to save and invest, which lowers the growth rate of real GDP.

- The Laffer curve shows the relationship between the tax rate and the amount of tax revenue collected.

Working Problems 6 to 10 will give you a better understanding of the supply-side effects of fiscal policy.

Fiscal Stimulus (pp. 714–719)

- Fiscal policy can be automatic or discretionary.
- Automatic fiscal policy might moderate the business cycle by stimulating demand in recession and restraining demand in a boom.
- Discretionary fiscal stimulus influences aggregate demand *and* aggregate supply.
- Discretionary changes in government expenditure or taxes have multiplier effects of uncertain magnitude, but the tax multiplier is likely the larger one.
- Fiscal stimulus policies are hampered by uncertainty about the multipliers and by time lags (lawmaking lags and the difficulty of correctly diagnosing and forecasting the state of the economy).

Working Problems 11 to 22 will give you a better understanding of fiscal stimulus.

Key Terms

Automatic fiscal policy, 714
Balanced budget, 705
Budget deficit,   705
Budget surplus, 705
Cyclical surplus or deficit, 714
Discretionary fiscal policy, 714
Federal budget, 704
Fiscal policy, 704

Fiscal stimulus, 714
Government debt, 707
Government expenditure
    multiplier, 715
Laffer curve, 713
Structural surplus or deficit, 714
Tax multiplier, 716
Tax wedge, 711

SCAN THIS

STUDY PLAN PROBLEMS AND APPLICATIONS

The Federal Budget (Study Plan 29.1)

1. At the end of 2011, China's government debt was ¥4,700 billion (¥ is yuan, the currency of China). In 2012, the government spent ¥6,000 billion and ended the year with a debt of ¥5,300 billion. How much did the government receive in tax revenue in 2012? How can you tell?

Use the following news clip to work Problems 2 to 4.

The Canadian Debt-Strategy Model

Government debt depends on future interest rates, macroeconomic outcomes, and fiscal policy. The debt managers who are responsible for the government's financing strategy have a complex task. In any given year, a government must borrow to finance any excess of government expenditure over revenues as well as any maturing debt issued in previous periods. This borrowing requirement depends on past decisions regarding debt issuance and on the government's current budget surplus or deficit. The government's budget, in turn, depends on the general performance of the macroeconomy and on fiscal policy.

Source: *Bank of Canada Review*, Summer 2008

2. Explain what factors determine the Government of Canada's budget deficit.
3. Explain what factors determine the Government of Canada's debt.
4. Explain how a persistent budget deficit can feed itself.
5. At the end of 2011, the debt of the Government of Greece was 375 billion euros and Greek GDP was 225 billion euros. The interest rate on Greek government debt was 25 percent a year. How much interest did Greece pay on its debt in 2011? What percentage of Greek GDP did the interest represent?

Supply-Side Effects of Fiscal Policy (Study Plan 29.2)

Use the following information to work Problems 6 and 7.

The government is considering raising the tax rate on labour income and asks you to report on the supply-side effects of such an action. Use appropriate graphs and report *directions* of change, not exact magnitudes.

6. What will happen to
   a. The supply of labour and why?
   b. The demand for labour and why?
   c. The equilibrium before-tax wage rate?
   d. The equilibrium after-tax wage rate?
7. What will happen to
   a. The equilibrium level of employment?
   b. Potential GDP?
8. What fiscal policy action might increase investment and speed economic growth? Explain how the policy action would work.
9. Suppose that instead of taxing *nominal* capital income, the government taxed *real* capital income. Use appropriate graphs to explain and illustrate the effect that this change would have on
   a. The tax rate on capital income.
   b. The supply of and demand for loanable funds.
   c. Investment and the real interest rate.
10. **Did Obama Cause the Weak U.S. Recovery**
    The core of Obama's economic plan is (a) more government spending: $65 billion a year for universal health insurance, $15 billion a year on alternative energy, $20 billion to help homeowners, $60 billion to bolster the nation's infrastructure, $10 billion annually to give students college tuition in exchange for public service, and on and on; and (b) ending the Bush tax cuts on families making more than $250,000 and raising payroll taxes on those same higher-income earners. He would increase the 15 percent capital gains tax rate—probably to 25 percent—raise the tax on dividends, and close $1.3 trillion in "corporate tax loopholes."

    Source: *Fortune*, June 23, 2008

    Explain the potential supply-side effects of the various components of Obama's economic plan. How might these policies change potential GDP and its growth rate?

Fiscal Stimulus (Study Plan 29.3)

11. The economy is in a recession, and the recessionary gap is large.

    a. Describe the discretionary and automatic fiscal policy actions that might occur.

    b. Describe a discretionary fiscal stimulus package that could be used that would not bring an increase in the budget deficit.

    c. Explain the risks of discretionary fiscal policy in this situation.

Use the following news clip to work Problems 12 to 14.

Flaherty Eyes Early Surplus

Jim Flaherty tabled a 2011 budget with a deficit for this fiscal year gradually falling to a surplus in 2015. Mr. Flaherty said the budget aims to find that balance between helping Canadian families and businesses and securing economic growth.

Source: *Financial Post*, March 22, 2011

12. What would be the effect of the budget deficit of 2011 on real GDP and jobs?

13. What would be the effect on real GDP and jobs of the commitment to cut the deficit over the next four years?

14. How does a falling budget deficit "find a balance between helping Canadian families and businesses and securing economic growth"?

15. The economy is in a recession, the recessionary gap is large, and there is a budget deficit.

    a. Do we know whether the budget deficit is structural or cyclical? Explain your answer.

    b. Do we know whether automatic fiscal policy is increasing or decreasing the output gap? Explain your answer.

    c. If a discretionary increase in government expenditure occurs, what happens to the structural deficit or surplus? Explain.

16. **Do Tax Cuts Ever Pay for Themselves?**

    Since even before Arthur Laffer drew his famous curve on a napkin, the political left and right has been having the same fight about taxes and growth. There are but a few cases where tax cuts did pay for themselves.

    Source: *Slate*, June 24, 2011

    a. Explain what is meant by tax cuts paying for themselves. What would this statement imply about the tax multiplier?

    b. In what circumstances would tax cuts pay for themselves?

Use the following news clip to work Problems 17 and 18.

Recession Threat Demands "Immediate Action," NDP Says

The NDP called for immediate action to create jobs by investing in infrastructure and green energy programs to give the economy the kickstart. It needs more than corporate tax cuts, the NDP said.

Source: CBC News, September 29, 2011

17. Is the NDP's proposed infrastructure spending a fiscal stimulus? Would such spending be a discretionary or an automatic fiscal policy?

18. Explain whether, and if so how, "investing in infrastructure and green energy programs" would create jobs.

Use the following news clip to work Problems 19 to 22.

Corporate Tax Cuts to Create 100,000 Jobs

Jack Mintz and Duanjie Chen of the University of Calgary say that fully implementing the Conservative government's corporate tax cut scheme will have "little" impact on budget revenue, and in the medium-term generate an estimated $30-billion in additional business investment and 100,000 new jobs over a seven-year period.

Source: *Financial Post*, January 25, 2011

19. a. Explain how a cut in corporate income taxes would create jobs and have "little" impact on budget revenue. Draw a graph to illustrate the effect.

    b. Explain why the effect of corporate tax cuts would most likely be spread out over a number of years.

20. What would have a larger effect on aggregate demand: corporate tax cuts or an equivalent scale increase in government spending on infrastructure and green energy projects?

21. What would have a larger effect on aggregate supply and potential GDP: corporate tax cuts or an equivalent scale increase in government spending on infrastructure and green energy projects?

22. Compare the impact on equilibrium real GDP of a same-sized decrease in corporate taxes and increase in government infrastructure expenditure.

ADDITIONAL PROBLEMS AND APPLICATIONS

MyEconLab ◆ You can work these problems in MyEconLab if assigned by your instructor.

The Federal Budget

23. **Federal Deficit Narrows to $4.4-billion**

    After the first two months of the current fiscal year, April and May, Canada's deficit sits at $4.4-billion, compared with $7.5-billion in the same period of 2009 when the economy was still in recession. The government projects that the $54-billion budget shortfall it had at the end of the last fiscal year will shrink to just over $49-billion this year.

    Source: *Globe and Mail*, July 29, 2010

    Of the components of government outlays and revenues, which have changed most to contribute to shrinking the deficit during 2009 and 2010?

Supply-Side Effects of Fiscal Policy

Use the following information to work Problems 24 and 25.

Suppose that in Canada, investment is $160 billion, saving is $140 billion, government expenditure on goods and services is $150 billion, exports are $200 billion, and imports are $250 billion.

24. What is the amount of tax revenue? What is the government budget balance?

25. a. Is the government's budget exerting a positive or negative impact on investment?

    b. What fiscal policy action might increase investment and speed economic growth? Explain how the policy action would work.

Use the following information to work Problems 26 and 27.

Suppose that capital income taxes are based (as they are in Canada and most countries) on nominal interest rates. The inflation rate increases by 5 percent.

26. On a graph illustrate the effect of the tax increase on capital income.

27. On a graph of the loanable funds market illustrate the effect of this interest rate change on the supply of loanable funds, the demand for loanable funds, equilibrium investment, and the equilibrium real interest rate.

Use the following news clip to work Problems 28 and 29.

How Did the Global Recession Affect Canada's Economy?

Canada weathered the global financial crisis and recession better than many of its peers, principally as a result of the better policies and regulations already in place. Canada was in a much stronger position going into the recession thanks to its low and declining fiscal debt, budgetary surpluses, and low and well-anchored inflation targets. The design of government policy and the speed of the policy response can make a huge difference in preventing or mitigating the worst of a recession.

Source: Conference Board of Canada, March 2011

28. a. Explain the potential demand-side effects of "low and declining fiscal debt, budgetary surpluses."

    b. Explain the potential supply-side effect of "low and declining fiscal debt, budgetary surpluses."

    c. Draw a graph to illustrate the combined demand-side and supply-side effect of "low and declining fiscal debt, budgetary surpluses."

29. Use the news clips in Problem 17 and Problem 28 to compare the supply-side effect of the Conservative government's budget plan and the alternative proposals of the NDP.

Use the following news clip to work Problems 30 and 31.

Job Creationism

William Watson, an economics professor at McGill University, Montreal, says there's nothing magical, mystical or personal about job creation. It occurs when someone who wants to sell a product or service contracts with someone else to help them do it. It's not rocket science. To create jobs, the most obvious imperative is "Do no harm." Don't complicate, regulate, or over tax it.

Source: *Financial Post*, October 13, 2011

30. Does William Watson think that job creation is primarily a problem that needs an increase in aggregate demand or aggregate supply?

31. How would lowering taxes on employment create jobs?

Fiscal Stimulus

32. The economy is in a boom and the inflationary gap is large.

    a. Describe the discretionary and automatic fiscal policy actions that might occur.

    b. Describe a discretionary fiscal restraint package that could be used that would not produce serious negative supply-side effects.

    c. Explain the risks of discretionary fiscal policy in this situation.

33. The economy is growing slowly, the inflationary gap is large, and there is a budget deficit.

    a. Do we know whether the budget deficit is structural or cyclical? Explain your answer.

    b. Do we know whether automatic fiscal policy is increasing or decreasing aggregate demand? Explain your answer.

    c. If a discretionary decrease in government expenditure occurs, what happens to the structural budget balance? Explain your answer.

Use the following news clip to work Problems 34 to 36.

Juicing the Economy Will Come at a Cost

The $150-billion stimulus plan will bump up the deficit, but not necessarily dollar for dollar. Here's why: If the stimulus works, the increased economic activity will generate federal tax revenue. But it isn't clear what the cost to the economy will be if a stimulus package comes too late—a real concern since legislation could get bogged down by politics.

Source: CNN, January 23, 2008

34. Explain why $150 billion of stimulus won't increase the budget deficit by $150 billion.

35. Is the budget deficit arising from the action described in the news clip structural or cyclical or a combination of the two? Explain.

36. Why might the stimulus package come "too late"? What are the potential consequences of the stimulus package coming "too late"?

Economics in the News

37. After you have studied *Reading Between the Lines* on pp. 720–721, answer the following questions.

    a. What does Stephen Harper say about fiscal stimulus and fiscal policy more generally?

    b. What does Sherry Cooper say about fiscal stimulus and fiscal policy more generally?

    c. Draw graphs to illustrate and contrast the views of Stephen Harper and Sherry Cooper on the need for and role of fiscal stimulus in the Canadian economy in 2011.

38. **U.S. Financial Crisis Over? Not Really**

    Economist Deepak Lal says the U.S. financial crisis is not solved and contains the seeds of a more serious future crisis. For India and China, with no structural deficit, a temporary budget deficit above that resulting from automatic fiscal policy makes sense. But it doesn't make sense for the United States with its large structural deficit.

    Source: rediff.com, October 18, 2010

    More Fiscal Stimulus Needed

    Economist Laura Tyson says there is a strong argument for more fiscal stimulus combined with a multi-year deficit reduction plan.

    Source: marketwatch.com, October 15, 2010

    a. How has the business cycle influenced the U.S. federal budget in the 2008–2009 recession?

    b. With which news clip opinion do you agree and why?

    c. Why might Laura Tyson favour a multi-year deficit reduction plan and would that address the concerns of Deepak Lal?

    d. Why might Laura Tyson and Stephen Harper agree about the role of fiscal policy?

39. **Cameron Urges Swift Eurozone Debt Action**

    U.K. Prime Minister David Cameron on Monday warned that "time was short" for eurozone leaders bidding to solve a debt crisis. Cameron called on Germany to accept the "collective responsibility" of the euro project and beef up the zone's 440-billion-euro ($589-billion) bailout fund.

    Source: AFP, October 11, 2011

    a. How does a large budget deficit that brings a large debt-to-GDP ratio create a "debt crisis"?

    b. What are the alternative ways in which a eurozone nation can address its debt crisis?

    c. What is the dilemma facing a country with a debt crisis and a recession?

CHAPTER 30

Monetary Policy

After studying this chapter, you will be able to

◆ Describe Canada's monetary policy objective and the framework for setting and achieving it

◆ Explain how the Bank of Canada makes its interest rate decision and achieves its interest rate target

◆ Explain the transmission channels through which the Bank of Canada influences real GDP, jobs, and inflation

◆ Explain the Bank of Canada's extraordinary policy actions

How does the Bank of Canada make its interest rate decision? How does a change in the Bank's interest rate influence the economy? Can the Bank speed up economic growth and lower unemployment by lowering the interest rate and can the Bank keep inflation in check by raising the interest rate?

You learned about the functions of the Bank of Canada and its long-run effects on the price level and the inflation rate in Chapter 24. In this chapter, you will learn about the Bank's monetary policy strategy and its influence on the economy. In *Reading Between the Lines* at the end of the chapter, you will see how the Bank of Canada tries to avoid recessionary forces and bring the economy to full employment.

◆ Monetary Policy Objectives and Framework

Canada's monetary policy objective and the framework for setting and achieving that objective stem from the relationship between the Bank of Canada and the Government of Canada.

We'll first discuss the objective of monetary policy and then describe the framework and assignment of responsibility for achieving the objective.

Monetary Policy Objective

The objective of monetary policy is ultimately political, and it stems from the mandate of the Bank, which is set out in the Bank of Canada Act.

Bank of Canada Act The objective of monetary policy as set out in the preamble to the Bank of Canada Act of 1935 is to

> regulate credit and currency in the best interests of the economic life of the nation ... and to mitigate by its influence fluctuations in the general level of production, trade, prices and employment, so far as may be possible within the scope of monetary action ...

In simple language, these words have come to mean that the Bank's job is to control the quantity of money and interest rates in order to avoid inflation and, when possible, prevent excessive swings in real GDP growth and unemployment.

This emphasis on inflation has been made concrete by an agreement between the Bank and the government.

Joint Statement of the Government of Canada and the Bank of Canada In a joint statement (the most recent of which was made in 2011), the Government of Canada and the Bank of Canada agree that

- The target will continue to be defined in terms of the 12-month rate of change in the total CPI.
- The inflation target will continue to be the 2 percent midpoint of the 1 to 3 percent inflation-control range.
- The agreement will run for another five-year period, ending December 31, 2016.

A monetary policy strategy in which the central bank commits to an explicit inflation target and to explaining how its actions will achieve that target is called **inflation rate targeting**.

Interpretation of the Agreement The inflation-control target uses the Consumer Price Index (or CPI) as the measure of inflation. So the Bank has agreed to keep trend CPI inflation at a target of 2 percent a year.

But the Bank also pays close attention to core inflation (see pp. 502–503), which it calls its operational guide. The Bank believes that the core inflation rate provides a better measure of the underlying inflation trend and better predicts future CPI inflation.

Although the Bank watches the core inflation rate closely, it must take into account the possibility that the eight volatile elements that it excludes have a different trend inflation rate from the remaining items. As it turns out, between 1995 and 2000, the core and overall CPI trends were the same. But since 2000, the core rate has run at about 0.5 percent a year below the overall CPI inflation rate.

Actual Inflation The performance of Canada's inflation since the mid-1990s, when the current target was initially set, has been close to target. Figure 30.1 shows just how close.

In part (a), you can see the target range of 1 to 3 percent a year. And you can see that the actual inflation rate has only rarely gone outside the target range. You can also see that the inflation rate has been both above target and below target on occasion, so there is no bias or tendency for inflation to be persistently above or below target.

In part (b), you can see the trend of inflation at the 2 percent target midpoint. The actual path of the CPI was on trend from 1995 through 1998 and again from 2001 through 2007. Between 1999 and 2001, the CPI moved below the 2 percent trend line.

The general message of Fig. 30.1 is that the Bank of Canada has done a remarkable job of holding inflation to its 2 percent target with only small and temporary deviations from that goal.

Rationale for an Inflation-Control Target Two main benefits flow from adopting an inflation-control target. The first benefit is that the purpose of the Bank of Canada's policy actions is more clearly understood by financial market traders. A clearer

FIGURE 30.1   Inflation-Control Target and Outcome

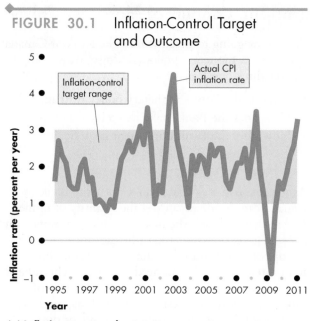

(a) Inflation target and outcome

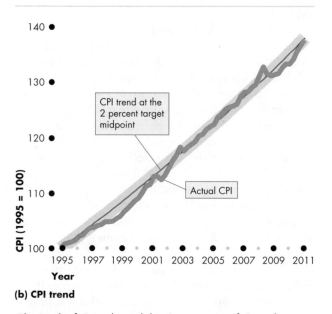

(b) CPI trend

The Bank of Canada and the Government of Canada agree that the inflation-control target range will be 1 percent to 3 percent in part (a) and that policy will aim at keeping the trend of inflation at the 2 percent target midpoint in part (b).

Sources of data: Statistics Canada, CANSIM Table 326-0022 and Bank of Canada, Joint Statement of the Government of Canada and the Bank of Canada on the Renewal of the Inflation-Control Target, November 23, 2006.

———— MyEconLab   animation ◆

understanding leads to fewer surprises and mistakes on the part of savers and investors.

The second benefit is that the target provides an anchor for expectations about future inflation. Firmly held expectations of low inflation make the short-run output-inflation (or unemployment-inflation) tradeoff as favourable as possible. (See Chapter 28, pp. 684–686.) Firmly held (and correct) inflation expectations also help to make better economic decisions, which in turn help to achieve a more efficient allocation of resources and more stable economic growth.

Controversy About the Inflation-Control Target Not everyone agrees that the adoption of an inflation-control target brings benefits. Critics argue that by focusing on inflation, the Bank of Canada sometimes permits the unemployment rate to rise or the real GDP growth rate to suffer.

The fear of these critics is that if the inflation rate begins to edge upward towards and perhaps beyond the upper limit of the target range, the Bank of Canada might rein in aggregate demand and push the economy into recession. Related, the Bank might end up permitting the value of the dollar on the foreign exchange market to rise and making exports suffer.

One response of supporters of inflation targeting is that by keeping inflation low and stable, monetary policy makes its maximum possible contribution towards achieving full employment and sustained economic growth.

Another response is, "Look at the record." The last time the Bank of Canada created a recession was at the beginning of the 1990s when it was faced with the threat of ongoing double-digit inflation. Since that time, monetary policy has been sensitive to the state of employment while maintaining its focus on achieving its inflation target.

Responsibility for Monetary Policy

The Government of Canada and the Bank of Canada jointly agree on the monetary policy target, but the Bank of Canada Act places responsibility for the conduct of monetary policy on the Bank's Governing Council.

Governing Council of the Bank of Canada The members of the Bank's Governing Council are the Governor, Senior Deputy Governor, and four

Deputy Governors. All the members of the Governing Council are experts in monetary economics and monetary policymaking and, normally, they are people who have been promoted from within the ranks of economists working in the Bank's research and policy departments.

The current Governor (appointed in 2008) is Mark Carney, an economist who has had wide experience in private sector banking, government departments, and the Bank of Canada.

Bank of Canada Economists The Bank of Canada employs research economists who write papers on monetary policy and the state of the Canadian and international economies. These economists provide the Governing Council with extensive briefings that guide monetary policy.

Consultations with the Government The Bank of Canada Act requires regular consultations on monetary policy between the Governor and the Minister of Finance. The Act also lays out what must happen if the Governor and the Minister disagree in a profound way.

In such an event, the Minister would direct the Bank in writing to follow a specified course and the Bank would be obliged to accept the directive. The Governor would most likely resign in such a situation. While in the past there have been disagreements between the government and the Bank, no formal directive has ever been issued.

You now know the objective of monetary policy and can describe the framework and assignment of responsibility for achieving that objective. Your next task is to see how the Bank of Canada conducts its monetary policy.

◤ REVIEW QUIZ

1 What is the Bank of Canada's monetary policy objective?
2 What are the two parts of the inflation-control target?
3 How does the core inflation rate differ from the overall CPI inflation rate?
4 What is the Bank of Canada's record in achieving its inflation-control target?

You can work these questions in Study Plan 30.1 and get instant feedback.

———————————————— MyEconLab ◆

◆ The Conduct of Monetary Policy

We're now going to describe how the Bank of Canada conducts its monetary policy. To do so, we're going to answer three questions:

- What is the Bank's monetary policy instrument?
- How does the Bank make its policy decision?
- How does the Bank implement its policy?

The Monetary Policy Instrument

As the sole issuer of Canadian money, the Bank of Canada can decide to control the quantity of money (the monetary base), the price of Canadian money on the foreign exchange market (the exchange rate), or the opportunity cost of holding money (the short-term interest rate). If you need a refresher, check back to Chapter 24, p. 581 to see how the quantity of money affects the interest rate and to Chapter 25, pp. 604–606 to see how the interest rate or direct intervention in the foreign exchange market affects the exchange rate.

While the Bank of Canada can set any one of these three variables, it cannot set all three. The values of two of them are the consequence of the value at which the third one is set. If the Bank decided to decrease the quantity of money, both the interest rate and the exchange rate would rise. If the Bank decided to raise the interest rate, the quantity of money would decrease and the exchange rate would rise. And if the Bank decided to lower the exchange rate, the quantity of money would increase and the interest rate would fall.

So the Bank must decide which of these three instruments to use. It might decide to select one and stick with it. Or it might switch among them.

The Overnight Rate The Bank of Canada's choice of policy instrument (which is the same choice as that made by most other major central banks) is a short-term interest rate. Given this choice, the Bank permits the exchange rate and the quantity of money to find their own equilibrium values and has no preset views about what those values should be.

The specific interest rate that the Bank of Canada targets is the **overnight loans rate**, which is the interest rate on overnight loans that the big banks make to each other.

Figure 30.2 shows the overnight loans rate since 1995. The overnight rate was a bit more than 8 percent a year in 1995 and it was twice increased to

FIGURE 30.2   The Overnight Loans Rate

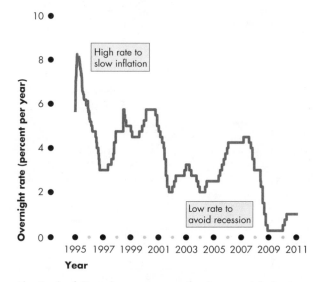

The Bank of Canada sets a target for the overnight loans rate and then takes actions to keep the rate close to its target. When the Bank wants to slow inflation, it raises the overnight loans rate. When inflation is low and the Bank wants to avoid recession, it lowers the overnight loans rate.

Source of data: Statistics Canada CANSIM Table 176–0048.

━━━━━━━━━━ MyEconLab ⬤animation⬤ ◆

around 6 percent and once to 4 percent. These periods with a high overnight rate are ones in which inflation was a concern.

In recent years, the overnight rate has been at historically low levels. The reason is that with inflation well anchored inside its target range, the Bank wanted to lean in the direction of avoiding recession.

Since late 2000, the Bank has established eight fixed dates on which it announces its overnight rate target for the coming period of approximately six weeks. Before 2000, the Bank announced changes in the overnight rate whenever it thought a change was required. And even now, the Bank sometimes acts in an emergency between normal announcement dates.

Although the Bank can change the overnight rate by any (reasonable) amount that it chooses, it normally changes the rate by only a quarter of a percentage point.[1]

How does the Bank decide the appropriate level for the overnight rate?

---

[1] A quarter of a percentage point is also called 25 *basis points*. A basis point is one hundredth of one percentage point.

The Bank's Interest Rate Decision

To make its interest rate decision, the Bank of Canada gathers a large amount of data about the economy, the way it responds to shocks, and the way it responds to policy. It then processes all this data and comes to a judgment about the best level for the overnight loans rate.

The Bank's staff economists use a model of the Canadian economy—a sophisticated version of the aggregate supply–aggregate demand model—to provide the Governor and Governing Council with a baseline forecast. All the available regional, national, and international data on macroeconomic performance, financial markets, and inflation expectations are reviewed, discussed, and weighed in a careful deliberative process that ends with the Governing Council finding a consensus on the interest rate level to set.

After announcing an interest rate decision, the Bank engages in a public communication to explain the reasons for its decision. Twice a year the Bank publishes a highly detailed *Inflation Report* that describes the forces operating on the economy, the outlook for inflation and real GDP growth, and the reasons for the Bank's interest rate decision.

Having made an interest rate decision, how does the Bank ensure that the overnight rate is on target?

Hitting the Overnight Rate Target

Once an interest rate decision is made, the Bank of Canada achieves its target by using two tools: the operating band and open market operation.

The **operating band** is the target overnight rate plus or minus 0.25 percentage points. The Bank creates the operating band by setting two other interest rates: *bank rate* and a rate called the *settlement balances rate*.

Bank rate is the interest rate that the Bank of Canada charges big banks on loans. If a bank is short of reserves, it can always obtain reserves from the Bank of Canada but it must pay bank rate on the amount of borrowed reserves.

The Bank of Canada sets bank rate at the target overnight rate plus 0.25 percentage points. Because the Bank of Canada is willing to lend funds to banks at this interest rate, bank rate acts as a cap on the overnight loans rate. If a bank can borrow from the Bank of Canada at bank rate, it will not borrow from another bank unless the interest rate is lower than or equal to bank rate.

The Bank of Canada pays banks interest on their reserves at the Bank of Canada—called the **settlement**

balances rate—set at the target overnight rate minus 0.25 percentage points. Banks won't make overnight loans to other banks unless they earn a higher interest rate than what the Bank of Canada is paying.

The alternative to lending in the overnight market is to hold reserves. And the alternative to borrowing in the overnight market is to hold smaller reserves. The demand for reserves is the flip side of lending and borrowing in the overnight market.

Figure 30.3 shows the demand curve for reserves as the curve labelled *RD*. If the entire banking system is borrowing from the Bank of Canada, reserves are negative (on the *x*-axis). If the overnight rate (on the *y*-axis) equals bank rate, banks are indifferent between borrowing reserves and lending reserves. The demand curve is horizontal at bank rate. If the overnight rate equals the settlement balances rate, banks are indifferent between holding reserves and lending reserves. The demand curve is horizontal at the settlement balances rate.

You can see that the overnight rate always lies inside the operating band.

The overnight rate cannot exceed bank rate because if it did, a bank could earn a profit by borrowing from the Bank of Canada and lending to another bank. But all banks can borrow from the Bank of Canada at bank rate, so no bank is willing to pay more than bank rate to borrow reserves.

The overnight rate cannot fall below the settlement balances rate because if it did, a bank could earn a profit by borrowing from another bank and increasing its reserves at the Bank of Canada. But all banks can earn the settlement balances rate at the Bank of Canada, so no bank is willing to lend reserves at a rate below the settlement balances rate.

The Bank of Canada's open market operations determine the actual quantity of reserves in the banking system, and equilibrium in the market for reserves determines the actual overnight rate. (We describe how an operation works to change the monetary base in Chapter 24, pp. 573–574.)

If the overnight rate is above target, the Bank buys securities to increase reserves, which increases the supply of overnight funds and lowers the overnight rate. If the overnight rate is below target, the Bank sells securities to decrease reserves, which decreases the supply of overnight funds and raises the overnight rate. If the overnight rate is at the target level, the Bank neither buys nor sells. By using open market operations, the Bank of Canada keeps the overnight rate on target.

FIGURE 30.3   The Market for Reserves

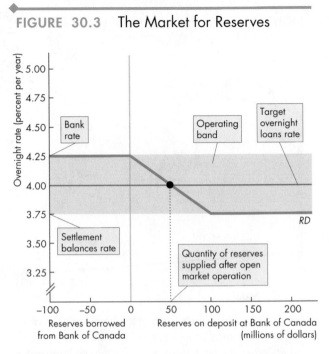

The demand curve for reserves is *RD*. If the overnight rate equals bank rate, banks are indifferent between borrowing reserves and lending reserves. The demand curve is horizontal at bank rate. If the overnight rate equals the settlement balances rate, banks are indifferent between holding reserves and lending reserves. The demand curve is horizontal at the settlement balances rate. Equilibrium, where the quantity of reserves demanded equals the quantity supplied, determines the overnight rate.

MyEconLab   animation ◆

REVIEW QUIZ

1   What is the Bank of Canada's monetary policy instrument?
2   Summarize the Bank of Canada's monetary policy decision-making process.
3   What is the operating band?
4   What happens when the Bank of Canada buys securities in the open market?
5   How is the overnight rate determined in the market for bank reserves?

You can work these questions in Study Plan 30.2 and get instant feedback.

MyEconLab ◆

Monetary Policy Transmission

You've seen that the Bank of Canada's goal is to keep the inflation rate as close as possible to 2 percent a year. And you've seen how the Bank can use its policy tools to keep the overnight loans rate at its desired level.

We're now going to trace the events that follow a change in the overnight loans rate and see how those events lead to the ultimate policy goal—keeping inflation on target.

We'll begin with a quick overview of the transmission process and then look at each step a bit more closely.

Quick Overview

When the Bank of Canada lowers the overnight loans rate, other short-term interest rates and the exchange rate also fall. The quantity of money and the supply of loanable funds increase. The long-term real interest rate falls. The lower real interest rate increases consumption expenditure and investment. And the lower exchange rate makes Canadian exports cheaper and imports more costly, so net exports increase. Easier bank loans reinforce the effect of lower interest rates on aggregate expenditure. Aggregate demand increases, which increases real GDP and the price level relative to what they would have been. Real GDP growth and inflation speed up.

When the Bank raises the overnight loans rate, as the sequence of events that we've just reviewed plays out, the effects are in the opposite directions.

Figure 30.4 provides a schematic summary of these ripple effects for both a cut and a rise in the overnight loans rate.

These ripple effects stretch out over a period of between one and two years. The interest rate and exchange rate effects are immediate. The effects on money and bank loans follow in a few weeks and run for a few months. Real long-term interest rates change quickly and often in anticipation of the short-term interest rate changes. Spending plans change and real GDP growth changes after about one year. The inflation rate changes between one year and two years after the change in the overnight loans rate. But these time lags are not entirely predictable and can be longer or shorter.

We're going to look at each stage in the transmission process, starting with the interest rate effects.

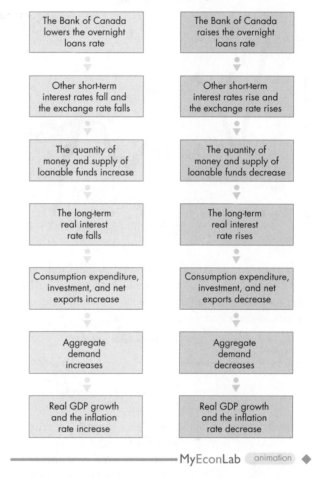

FIGURE 30.4   The Ripple Effects of a Change in the Overnight Loans Rate

MyEconLab   animation

Interest Rate Changes

The first effect of a monetary policy decision by the Bank of Canada is a change in the overnight loans rate. Other interest rates then change. These interest rate effects occur quickly and relatively predictably.

Figure 30.5 shows the fluctuations in three interest rates: the overnight loans rate, the short-term bill rate, and the long-term bond rate.

Overnight Loans Rate As soon as the Bank of Canada announces a new setting for the overnight loans rate, it undertakes the necessary open market operations to hit the target. There is no doubt about where the interest rate changes shown in Fig. 30.5 are generated. They are driven by the Bank of Canada's monetary policy.

FIGURE 30.5 Three Interest Rates

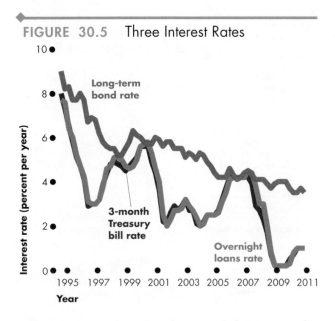

The short-term interest rates—the overnight loans rate and the 3-month Treasury bill rate—move closely together. The long-term bond rate is higher than the short-term rates, and it fluctuates less than the short-term rates.

Source of data: Statistics Canada, CANSIM Table 176–0043.

MyEconLab animation ◆

3-Month Treasury Bill Rate The 3-month Treasury bill rate is the interest rate paid by the Government of Canada on 3-month debt. It is similar to the interest rate paid by Canadian businesses on short-term loans. Notice how closely the 3-month Treasury bill rate follows the overnight loans rate. The two rates are almost identical.

A *powerful substitution effect* keeps these two interest rates close. Chartered banks have a choice about how to hold their short-term liquid assets, and an overnight loan to another bank is a close substitute for short-term securities such as Treasury bills. If the interest rate on Treasury bills is higher than the overnight loans rate, the quantity of overnight loans supplied decreases and the demand for Treasury bills increases. The price of Treasury bills rises and the interest rate falls.

Similarly, if the interest rate on Treasury bills is lower than the overnight loans rate, the quantity of overnight loans supplied increases and the demand for Treasury bills decreases. The price of Treasury bills falls and the interest rate rises.

When the interest rate on Treasury bills is close to the overnight loans rate, there is no incentive for a bank to switch between making an overnight loan and buying Treasury bills. Both the Treasury bill market and the overnight loans market are in equilibrium.

The Long-Term Bond Rate The long-term bond rate is the interest rate paid on bonds issued by large corporations. It is this interest rate that businesses pay on the loans that finance their purchase of new capital and that influences their investment decisions. Two features of the long-term bond rate stand out: It is higher than the short-term rates, and it fluctuates less than the short-term rates.

The long-term interest rate is higher than the two short-term rates because long-term loans are riskier than short-term loans. To provide the incentive that brings forth a supply of long-term loans, lenders must be compensated for the additional risk. Without compensation for the additional risk, only short-term loans would be supplied.

The long-term interest rate fluctuates less than the short-term rates because it is influenced by expectations about future short-term interest rates as well as current short-term interest rates. The alternative to borrowing or lending long term is to borrow or lend using a sequence of short-term securities. If the long-term interest rate exceeds the expected average of future short-term interest rates, people will lend long term and borrow short term. The long-term interest rate will fall. And if the long-term interest rate is below the expected average of future short-term interest rates, people will borrow long term and lend short term. The long-term interest rate will rise.

These market forces keep the long-term interest rate close to the expected average of future short-term interest rates (plus a premium for the extra risk associated with long-term loans). The expected average future short-term interest rate fluctuates less than the current short-term interest rate.

Exchange Rate Fluctuations

The exchange rate responds to changes in the interest rate in Canada relative to the interest rates in other countries—*the Canadian interest rate differential*. We explain this influence in Chapter 25 (see pp. 596–597).

When the Bank of Canada raises the overnight loans rate, the Canadian interest rate differential rises and, other things remaining the same, the Canadian dollar appreciates, and when the Bank lowers the overnight loans rate, the Canadian interest rate differential falls and, other things remaining the same, the Canadian dollar depreciates.

Many factors other than the Canadian interest rate differential influence the exchange rate, so when the Bank changes the overnight loans rate, the exchange rate does not usually change in exactly the way it would with other things remaining the same. So while monetary policy influences the exchange rate, many other factors also make the exchange rate change.

Money and Bank Loans

The quantity of money and bank loans change when the Bank changes the overnight loans rate target. A rise in the overnight loans rate decreases the quantity of money and bank loans, and a fall in the overnight loans rate increases the quantity of money and bank loans. These changes occur for two reasons: The quantity of deposits and loans created by the banking system changes and the quantity of money demanded changes.

You've seen that to change the overnight loans rate, the quantity of bank reserves must change. A change in the quantity of bank reserves changes the monetary base, which in turn changes the quantity of deposits and loans that the banking system can create. A rise in the overnight loans rate decreases reserves and decreases the quantity of deposits and bank loans created; and a fall in the overnight loans rate increases reserves and increases the quantity of deposits and bank loans created.

The quantity of money created by the banking system must be held by households and firms. The change in the interest rate changes the quantity of money demanded. A fall in the interest rate increases the quantity of money demanded; and a rise in the interest rate decreases the quantity of money demanded.

A change in the quantity of money and the supply of bank loans directly affects consumption and investment plans. With more money and easier access to loans, consumers and firms spend more; with less money and loans harder to get, consumers and firms spend less.

The Long-Term Real Interest Rate

Demand and supply in the loanable funds market determine the long-term *real interest rate*, which equals the long-term *nominal* interest rate minus the expected inflation rate. The long-term real interest rate influences expenditure decisions.

In the long run, demand and supply in the loanable funds market depend only on real forces—on saving and investment decisions. But in the short run, when the price level is not fully flexible, the supply of loanable funds is influenced by the supply of bank loans. Changes in the overnight loans rate change the supply of bank loans, which changes the supply of loanable funds and changes the interest rate in the loanable funds market.

A fall in the overnight loans rate that increases the supply of bank loans increases the supply of loanable funds and lowers the equilibrium real interest rate. A rise in the overnight loans rate that decreases the supply of bank loans decreases the supply of loanable funds and raises the equilibrium real interest rate.

These changes in the real interest rate, along with the other factors we've just described, change expenditure plans.

Expenditure Plans

The ripple effects that follow a change in the overnight loans rate change three components of aggregate expenditure:

- Consumption expenditure
- Investment
- Net exports

Consumption Expenditure   Other things remaining the same, the lower the real interest rate, the greater is the amount of consumption expenditure and the smaller is the amount of saving.

Investment   Other things remaining the same, the lower the real interest rate, the greater is the amount of investment.

Net Exports   Other things remaining the same, the lower the interest rate, the lower is the exchange rate and the greater are exports and the smaller are imports.

So eventually, a cut in the overnight loans rate increases aggregate expenditure and a rise in the overnight loans rate curtails aggregate expenditure. These changes in aggregate expenditure plans change aggregate demand, real GDP, and the price level.

The Change in Aggregate Demand, Real GDP, and the Price Level

The final link in the transmission chain is a change in aggregate demand and a resulting change in real GDP and the price level. By changing real GDP and the price level relative to what they would have been without a change in the overnight loans rate, the Bank of Canada influences its ultimate goals: the inflation rate and the output gap.

The Bank of Canada Fights Recession

If inflation is low and real GDP is below potential GDP, the Bank acts to restore full employment. Figure 30.6 shows the effects of the Bank's actions, starting in the market for bank reserves and ending in the market for real GDP.

Market for Bank Reserves In Fig. 30.6(a), which shows the market for bank reserves, the Bank lowers the target overnight loans rate from 5 percent to 4 percent a year. To achieve the new target, the Bank

buys securities and increases the supply of reserves of the banking system from RS_0 to RS_1.

Money Market With increased reserves, the banks create deposits by making loans and the supply of money increases. The short-term interest rate falls and the quantity of money demanded increases.

In Fig. 30.6(b), the supply of money increases from MS_0 to MS_1, the interest rate falls from 5 percent to 4 percent a year, and the quantity of money increases from $800 billion to $900 billion. The interest rate in the money market and the overnight loans rate are kept close to each other by the powerful substitution effect described on p. 734.

Loanable Funds Market Banks create money by making loans. In the long run, an increase in the supply of bank loans is matched by a rise in the price level and the quantity of *real* loans is unchanged. But in the short run, with a sticky price level, an increase in the supply of bank loans increases the supply of (real) loanable funds.

FIGURE 30.6   The Bank of Canada Fights Recession

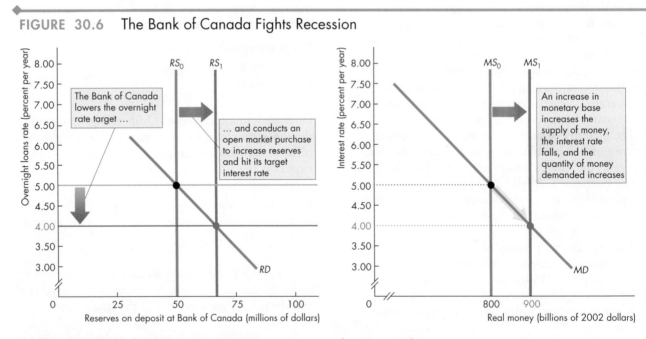

(a) The market for bank reserves

In part (a), the Bank of Canada lowers the overnight loans rate target from 5 percent to 4 percent. The Bank buys securities in an open market operation and increases the supply of reserves from RS_0 to RS_1 to hit the new overnight loans rate target.

(b) Money market

In part (b), the supply of money increases from MS_0 to MS_1, the short-term interest rate falls, and the quantity of money demanded increases. The short-term interest rate and the overnight loans rate change by similar amounts.

In Fig. 30.6(c), the supply of loanable funds curve shifts rightward from SLF_0 to SLF_1. With the demand for loanable funds at DLF, the real interest rate falls from 6 percent to 5.5 percent a year. (We're assuming a zero inflation rate so that the real interest rate equals the nominal interest rate.) The long-term interest rate changes by a smaller amount than the change in the short-term interest rate for the reason explained on p. 734.

The Market for Real GDP Figure 30.6(d) shows aggregate demand and aggregate supply—the demand for and supply of real GDP. Potential GDP is $1,200 billion, where LAS is located. The short-run aggregate supply curve is SAS, and initially, the aggregate demand curve is AD_0. Real GDP is $1,180 billion, which is less than potential GDP, so there is a recessionary gap. The Bank of Canada is reacting to this recessionary gap.

The increase in the supply of loans and the decrease in the real interest rate increase aggregate planned expenditure. (Not shown in the figure, a fall

in the interest rate lowers the exchange rate, which increases net exports and aggregate planned expenditure.) The increase in aggregate expenditure, ΔE, increases aggregate demand and shifts the aggregate demand curve rightward to $AD_0 + \Delta E$. A multiplier process begins. The increase in expenditure increases income, which induces an increase in consumption expenditure. Aggregate demand increases further, and the aggregate demand curve eventually shifts rightward to AD_1.

The new equilibrium is at full employment. Real GDP is equal to potential GDP. The price level rises to 115 and then becomes stable at that level. So after a one-time adjustment, there is price stability.

In this example, the Bank of Canada makes a perfect hit, achieving full employment and a stable price level. It is unlikely that the Bank would be able to achieve the precision of this example. If the Bank stimulated demand by too little and too late, the economy would experience a recession. And if the Bank hit the gas pedal too hard, it would push the economy from recession to inflation.

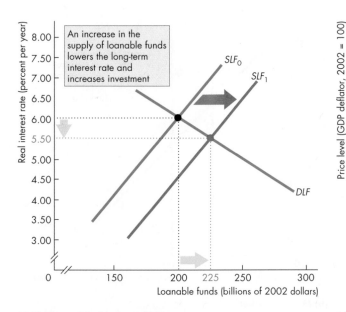

(c) The loanable funds market

In part (c), an increase in the supply of bank loans increases the supply of loanable funds and shifts the supply curve from SLF_0 to SLF_1. The real interest rate falls and investment increases.

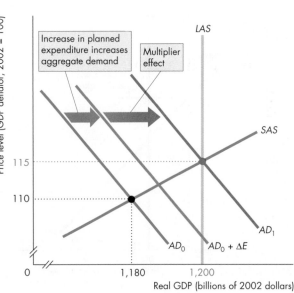

(d) Real GDP and the price level

In part (d), the increase in investment increases aggregate planned expenditure. The aggregate demand curve shifts to $AD_0 + \Delta E$ and eventually it shifts rightward to AD_1. Real GDP increases to potential GDP, and the price level rises.

The Bank of Canada Fights Inflation

If the inflation rate is too high and real GDP is above potential GDP, the Bank takes actions that are designed to lower the inflation rate and restore price stability. Figure 30.7 shows the effects of the Bank's actions starting in the market for reserves and ending in the market for real GDP.

Market for Bank Reserves　In Fig. 30.7(a), which shows the market for bank reserves, the Bank raises the target overnight loans rate from 5 percent to 6 percent a year. To achieve the new target, the Bank sells securities and decreases the supply of reserves of the banking system from RS_0 to RS_1.

Money Market　With decreased reserves, the banks shrink deposits by decreasing loans and the supply of money decreases. The short-term interest rate rises and the quantity of money demanded decreases. In Fig. 30.7(b), the supply of money decreases from MS_0 to MS_1, the interest rate rises from 5 percent to

6 percent a year, and the quantity of money decreases from $800 billion to $700 billion.

Loanable Funds Market　With a decrease in reserves, banks must decrease the supply of loans. The supply of (real) loanable funds decreases, and the supply of loanable funds curve shifts leftward in Fig. 30.7(c) from SLF_0 to SLF_1. With the demand for loanable funds at DLF, the real interest rate rises from 6 percent to 6.5 percent a year. (Again, we're assuming a zero inflation rate so that the real interest rate equals the nominal interest rate.)

The Market for Real GDP　Figure 30.7(d) shows aggregate demand and aggregate supply in the market for real GDP. Potential GDP is $1,200 billion where LAS is located. The short-run aggregate supply curve is SAS and initially the aggregate demand curve is AD_0. Now, real GDP is $1,220 billion, which is greater than potential GDP, so there is an inflationary gap. The Bank is reacting to this inflationary gap.

FIGURE 30.7　The Bank of Canada Fights Inflation

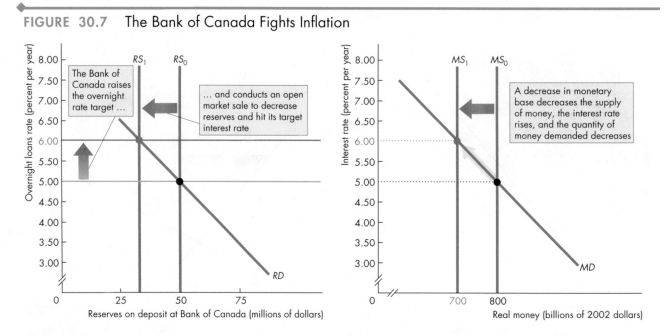

(a) The market for bank reserves

In part (a), the Bank of Canada raises the overnight loans rate from 5 percent to 6 percent. The Bank sells securities in an open market operation to decrease the supply of reserves from RS_0 to RS_1 and hit the new overnight loans rate target.

(b) Money market

In part (b), the supply of money decreases from MS_0 to MS_1, the short-term interest rate rises, and the quantity of money demanded decreases. The short-term interest rate and the overnight loans rate change by similar amounts.

The increase in the short-term interest rate, the decrease in the supply of bank loans, and the increase in the real interest rate decrease aggregate planned expenditure. (Not shown in the figures, a rise in the interest rate raises the exchange rate, which decreases net exports and aggregate planned expenditure.)

The decrease in aggregate expenditure, ΔE, decreases aggregate demand and shifts the aggregate demand curve to $AD_0 - \Delta E$. A multiplier process begins. The decrease in expenditure decreases income, which induces a decrease in consumption expenditure. Aggregate demand decreases further, and the aggregate demand curve eventually shifts leftward to AD_1.

The economy returns to full employment. Real GDP is equal to potential GDP. The price level falls to 115 and then becomes stable at that level. So after a one-time adjustment, there is price stability.

Again, in this example, we have given the Bank a perfect hit at achieving full employment and keeping the price level stable. If the Bank decreased aggregate demand by too little and too late, the economy would have remained with an inflationary gap and the inflation rate would have moved above the rate that is consistent with price stability. And if the Bank hit the brakes too hard, it would push the economy from inflation to recession.

Loose Links and Long and Variable Lags

The ripple effects of monetary policy that we've just analyzed with the precision of an economic model are, in reality, very hard to predict and anticipate.

To achieve price stability and full employment, the Bank needs a combination of good judgment and good luck. Too large an interest rate cut in an under-employed economy can bring inflation, as it did during the 1970s. And too large an interest rate rise in an inflationary economy can create unemployment, as it did in 1981 and 1991. Loose links between the overnight loans rate and the ultimate policy goals make unwanted outcomes inevitable, and long and variable time lags add to the Bank's challenges.

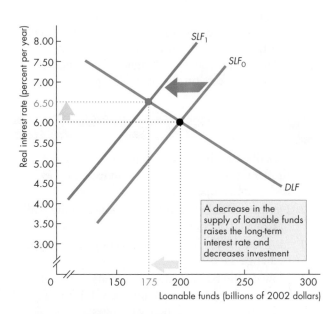

(c) The loanable funds market

In part (c), a decrease in the supply of bank loans decreases the supply of loanable funds and the supply curve shifts from SLF_0 to SLF_1. The real interest rate rises and investment decreases.

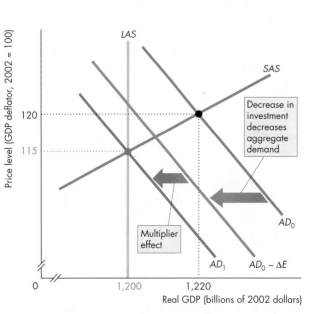

(d) Real GDP and the price level

In part (d), the decrease in investment decreases aggregate planned expenditure. Aggregate demand decreases and the AD curve shifts leftward from AD_0 to AD_1. Real GDP decreases to potential GDP and the price level falls.

MyEconLab animation ◆

Economics in Action
A View of the Long and Variable Lag

You've studied the theory of monetary policy. Does it really work in the way we've described? It does, and the figure opposite provides some evidence to support this claim.

The blue line in the figure is the overnight loans rate that the Bank of Canada targets *minus* the long-term bond rate. (When the long-term bond rate exceeds the overnight loans rate, this gap is negative.)

We can view the gap between the overnight loans rate and the long-term bond rate as a measure of how hard the Bank is trying to steer a change in the economy's course.

When the Bank is more concerned about recession than inflation and is trying to stimulate real GDP growth, it cuts the overnight loans rate target and the overnight loans rate minus the long-term bond rate falls.

When the Bank is more concerned about inflation than recession and is trying to restrain real GDP growth, it raises the overnight loans rate target and the the overnight loans rate minus the long-term bond rate rises.

The red line in the figure is the real GDP growth rate *one year later*. You can see that when the Bank of Canada raises the overnight loans rate, the real GDP growth rate slows one year later. And when the Bank

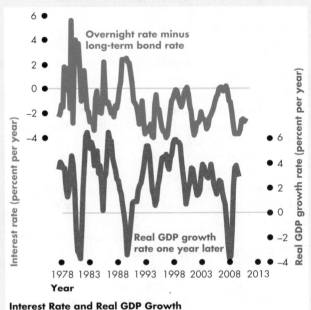

Interest Rate and Real GDP Growth

Source of data: Statistics Canada, CANSIM Tables 176-0043 and 380-0002.

lowers the overnight loans rate, the real GDP growth rate speeds up one year later.

Not shown in the figure, the inflation rate increases and decreases corresponding to the fluctuations in the real GDP growth rate. But the effects on the inflation rate take even longer and are not as strong as the effects on the real GDP growth rate.

Loose Link from Overnight Rate to Spending The real long-term interest rate that influences spending plans is linked only loosely to the overnight loans rate. Also, the response of the *real* long-term interest rate to a change in the nominal interest rate depends on how inflation expectations change. And the response of expenditure plans to changes in the real interest rate depend on many factors that make the response hard to predict.

Time Lags in the Adjustment Process The Bank of Canada is especially handicapped by the fact that the monetary policy transmission process is long and drawn out. Also, the economy does not always respond in exactly the same way to a policy change. Further, many factors other than policy are constantly changing and bringing new situations to which policy must respond.

REVIEW QUIZ

1 Describe the channels by which monetary policy ripples through the economy and explain how each channel operates.
2 Do interest rates fluctuate in response to the Bank of Canada's actions?
3 How do the Bank of Canada's actions change the exchange rate?
4 How do the Bank's actions influence real GDP and how long does it take for real GDP to respond to the Bank's policy changes?
5 How do the Bank's actions influence the inflation rate and how long does it take for inflation to respond to the Bank's policy changes?

You can work these questions in Study Plan 30.3 and get instant feedback.

MyEconLab ◆

Extraordinary Monetary Stimulus

During the financial crisis and recession of 2008–2009, the Bank of Canada, the U.S. Federal Reserve, and other central banks lowered their overnight loans rate targets to the floor. The overnight rate can't go below zero, so what can a central bank do to stimulate the economy when it can't lower the interest rate?

Central banks answered this question with some extraordinary policy actions, and none more extraordinary than those of the U.S. Federal Reserve (the Fed). To understand those actions, we need to dig a bit into the anatomy of the financial crisis to which central banks responded. That's what we'll now do. We'll look at the key elements in the financial crisis and then look at the U.S. Fed's response and the responses of some other central banks.

The Key Elements of the Crisis

We can describe the crisis by identifying the events that changed the values of the assets and liabilities of banks and other financial institutions. Canada's banks were in better shape to ride the storm than the U.S and European banks, so we focus here on the regions hit hardest.

Figure 30.8 shows the stylized balance sheet of a bank: Deposits plus equity equals reserves plus loans and securities (see Chapter 24, p. 572). Deposits and owners' capital—equity—are the bank's source of funds (other borrowing by banks is ignored here). Deposits are the funds loaned to the bank by households and firms. Equity is the capital provided by the bank's stockholders and includes the bank's undistributed profits (and losses). The bank's reserves are currency and deposits at the central bank. The bank's loans and securities are the loans made by the bank and government bonds, private bonds, asset-backed bonds, and other securities that the bank holds.

Three main events can put a bank under stress:

1. Widespread fall in asset prices
2. A significant currency drain
3. A run on the bank

Figure 30.8 summarizes the problems that each event presents to a bank. A widespread fall in asset prices—a *capital loss*—means a bank must write down the value of its assets so the value of the bank's equity decreases by the same amount as the fall in the value of its assets. If the fall in asset prices is large enough, the bank's equity might fall to zero, in which case the bank is insolvent. It fails.

A significant currency drain means that depositors withdraw funds and the bank loses reserves. This event puts the bank in a liquidity crisis. It is short of cash reserves.

A run on the bank occurs when depositors lose confidence and withdraw their deposits. The bank loses reserves and must call in loans and sell off securities at unfavourable prices. Its equity shrinks.

The red arrows in Fig. 30.8 summarize the effects of these events and the problems they brought in the 2007–2008 financial crisis. A widespread fall in asset prices was triggered by the bursting of a house-price bubble that saw house prices switch from rapidly rising to falling. With falling house prices, sub-prime mortgage defaults occurred and the prices of mortgage-backed securities and derivatives whose values are based on these securities began to fall.

People with money market mutual fund deposits began to withdraw them, which created a fear of a massive withdrawal of these funds analagous to a run on a bank. In the United Kingdom, one bank, Northern Rock, experienced a bank run.

With low reserves and even lower equity, banks turned their attention to securing their balance sheets and called in loans. The loanable funds market and money market dried up.

FIGURE 30.8   The Ingredients of a Financial and Banking Crisis

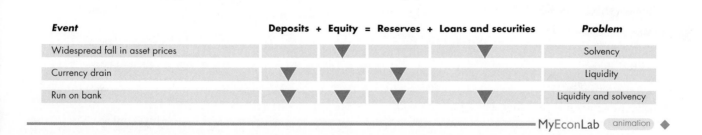

Event	Deposits	+	Equity	=	Reserves	+	Loans and securities	Problem
Widespread fall in asset prices			▼				▼	Solvency
Currency drain	▼				▼			Liquidity
Run on bank	▼		▼		▼		▼	Liquidity and solvency

Because the loanable funds market is global, the same problems quickly spread to all economies, and foreign exchange markets became highly volatile.

Hard-to-get loans, market volatility, and increased uncertainty transmitted the financial and monetary crisis to real expenditure decisions.

The Policy Actions

Five types of policy action dribbled out over a period of more than a year. They were

1. Open market operations
2. Extension of deposit insurance
3. Central bank and government swapping government securities for toxic assets
4. Government buying bank shares
5. Fair value accounting

Figure 30.9 summarizes these actions, their effects on a bank's balance sheet (red and blue arrows), and the problem that each action sought to address.

An open market operation is the classic policy (described on pp. 573–574) for providing liquidity and enabling a central bank to hit its overnight rate target. With substantial interest rate cuts, heavy open market operations were used to keep the banks well supplied with reserves. This action lowered bank holdings of securities and increased their reserves.

By extending deposit insurance, people with bank deposits had less incentive to withdraw them. Both deposits and bank reserves increased.

Some central banks bought troubled assets that no one could sell (so-called toxic assets) and sold good quality government securities in their place. These actions swapped bad loans and securities for good ones and addressed the liquidity problem.

Some governments bought shares in banks. This action boosted bank capital and addressed the insolvency problem.

The final action is not a monetary policy but a change in accounting standards. It relaxed the requirement for institutions to value their assets at current market value—called "mark-to-market"—and permitted them, in rare conditions, to use a model to assess "fair market value."

Taken as a whole, a huge amount of relief was thrown at the financial crisis.

Painfully Slow Recovery

Despite extraordinary monetary (and fiscal) stimulus, at the end of 2011, three years after the first extraordinary stimulus was undertaken, the U.S. economy remained stuck with slow real GDP growth and an unemployment rate greater than 9 percent. Why?

No one knows for sure, but the Fed's critics say that the Fed itself contributed to the problem more than to the solution. That problem is extreme uncertainty about the future that is keeping business investment low. Critics emphasize the need for greater clarity about monetary policy *strategy*. We'll conclude this review of monetary policy by looking at two suggested policy strategies that do bring clarity.

Policy Strategies and Clarity

Unlike the Bank of Canada, with its clear *inflation rate targeting* strategy, the U.S. Fed pursues what is called a *dual mandate*, which is to keep *both* the inflation rate and the unemployment rate low. The pursuit of this dual mandate is a source of confusion and uncertainty about monetary policy. The central problem with the U.S. dual mandate is that it seeks to

---

FIGURE 30.9   Policy Actions in a Financial and Banking Crisis

Action	Deposits	+ Equity	= Reserves	+ Loans and securities	Problem addressed
Open market operation			▲	▼	Liquidity
Extension of deposit insurance	▲		▲		Liquidity
Swap government securities for toxic assets			▲	▼	Liquidity
Buy bank shares		▲	▲		Solvency
Fair value accounting		▲		▲	Solvency

acheive the impossible. You've seen in Chapter 28 (pp. 684–686) that stabilization policy faces a *tradeoff* between inflation and unemployment in the short run. If policy seeks to lower the inflation rate, the unemployment rate rises in the short run. If policy seeks to lower the unemployment rate, the inflation rate rises in the short run.

In the *long run*, monetary policy influences the inflation rate but has no effect on the unemployment rate, which is determined by the natural unemployment rate.

It is because monetary policy influences only the inflation rate in the long run that inflation rate targeting is an attractive monetary policy strategy. This approach is now used not only by Canada but also by Australia, New Zealand, Sweden, the United Kingdom, and the European Union.

Inflation targeting focuses the public debate on what monetary policy can achieve and the best contribution it can make to attaining full employment and sustained growth. The central fact is that monetary policy is about managing inflation expectations. An explicit inflation target that is taken seriously and towards which policy actions are aimed and explained is a sensible way to manage those expectations.

It is when the going gets tough that inflation targeting has the greatest benefit. It is difficult to imagine a serious inflation-targeting central bank permitting inflation to take off in the way that it did during the 1970s. And it is difficult to imagine deflation and ongoing recession such as Japan has endured for the past 10 years if monetary policy is guided by an explicit inflation target.

One way to pursue an inflation target is to set the policy interest rate (for the Bank of Canada, the overnight loans rate) by using a rule or formula. The most famous and most studied interest rate rule is the *Taylor rule* described in *Economics in Action.*

Supporters of the Taylor rule argue that in computer simulations, the rule works well and limits fluctuations in inflation and output. By using such a rule, monetary policy contributes towards lessening uncertainty—the opposite of current U.S. monetary policy. In financial markets, labour markets, and markets for goods and services, people make long-term commitments. So markets work best when plans are based on correctly anticipated inflation. A well-understood monetary policy helps to create an environment in which inflation is easier to forecast and manage.

The debates on inflation targeting and the Taylor rule will continue!

Economics in Action
The Taylor Rule

The idea of setting the overnight loans rate based on a rule was suggested by Stanford University economist John B. Taylor, and the rule bears his name.

The Taylor rule is a formula for setting the overnight loans rate. Calling the overnight loans rate R, the inflation rate INF, and the output gap GAP (all percentages), the Taylor rule formula is

$$R = 2 + INF + 0.5(INF - 2) + 0.5\,GAP.$$

In words, the Taylor rule sets the overnight loans rate at 2 percent plus the inflation rate plus one half of the deviation of inflation from 2 percent, plus one half of the output gap.

If the Bank of Canada had followed the Taylor rule, the overnight loans rate would have been higher on some occasions and lower on others. During 2008, when the overnight loans rate was 1.5 percent, the Taylor Rule would have kept it close to 4 percent.

The Bank believes that because it uses more information than just the current inflation rate and the output gap, it is able to set the overnight loans rate more intelligently than the Taylor rule would set it.

◤ REVIEW QUIZ

1 What are the three ingredients of a financial and banking crisis?
2 What are the policy actions taken by central banks in response to the financial crisis?
3 Why was the U.S. recovery from the 2008–2009 recession so slow?
4 How might inflation targeting improve U.S. monetary policy?
5 How might using the Taylor rule improve the Fed's monetary policy?

You can work these questions in Study Plan 30.4 and get instant feedback.

──────────────────────────── MyEconLab ◆

◆ To complete your study of monetary policy, take a look at *Reading Between the Lines* on pages 744–745, which examines the Bank of Canada's monetary stimulus in 2011.

The Bank of Canada Fights Recession in 2011

Bank of Canada Holds Rates at 1%

Financial Post
September 7, 2011

Amid an environment of growing economic uncertainty at home and abroad, Governor Mark Carney and the Bank of Canada decided Wednesday to maintain the key lending rate at 1% while declaring the need for rate hikes has "diminished."

In a sharp turnaround from July when the bank actually said monetary policy stimulus "will be withdrawn," the Bank of Canada has now changed its tune.

"In light of slowing global economic momentum and heightened financial uncertainty, the need to withdraw monetary policy stimulus has diminished," the bank said. "The bank will continue to monitor carefully economic and financial developments in the Canadian and global economies, together with the evolution of risks, and set monetary policy consistent with achieving the 2% inflation target over the medium term." ...

"Net exports are now expected to remain a major source of weakness, reflecting more modest global demand and ongoing competitiveness challenges, in particular the persistent strength of the Canadian dollar," the bank said.

... The recession of Canada's biggest trading partner "was deeper and its recovery has been shallower than previously reported," the bank said of the United States. The bank warns that this means growth "will be weaker than previously anticipated." The bank now expects U.S. household spending to be "even more subdued" due to high debt, widespread declines in wealth and a tough job market.

ESSENCE OF THE STORY

- The Bank of Canada held the overnight rate steady at 1 percent in September 2011.

- In July 2011, the Bank expected to soon begin withdrawing monetary stimulus but events between July and September changed the outlook.

- Global economic growth slowed.

- Financial uncertainty increased.

- Net exports were expected to remain weak with a strong Canadian dollar.

- U.S. economic growth was expected to be very slow.

ECONOMIC ANALYSIS

- In September 2011, the Bank of Canada decided to hold the overnight rate at 1 percent.

- The Bank also signalled that it would not be raising the overnight rate in the immediate future.

- In a normal period, with inflation on target and with real GDP equal to potential GDP at full employment, the overnight rate would be between 3 percent and 4 percent.

- An overnight rate of 1 percent means that the Bank is boosting aggregate demand with monetary stimulus. If the Bank raised the overnight rate in stages to 3 percent, it would be withdrawing monetary stimulus and making monetary policy neutral.

- In 2011, the economy was close to full employment and although CPI inflation was greater than 3 percent, the Bank expected a return to 2 percent inflation and feared strong recessionary forces from the global and U.S. economies.

- Figure 1 illustrates the economy in 2011 according to the Bank of Canada's estimate of the output gap (a recessionary gap) and Statistics Canada's GDP data.

- Figure 2 shows what the Bank of Canada was forecasting by 2013 in the absence of continued monetary stimulus.

- Potential GDP was expected to grow by about 3 percent per year but aggregate demand was expected to grow more slowly so that, without monetary stimulus, the output gap would widen and the inflation rate would fall below 2 percent per year.

- Figure 3 shows the outcome in 2013 that the Bank wants to achieve and that it says will be achieved by maintaing the overnight rate at 1 percent and thereby maintaining substantial monetary stimulus.

- If the Bank gets it right, the price level rises to 130. Inflation at 2 percent per year takes the price level from 125 in 2011 to 130 in 2013. And real GDP rises to equal potential GDP.

- If the Bank gets it wrong by overstimulating aggregate demand, by 2013, the price level will have risen to more than 130—the inflation rate will exceed 2 percent per year—and there will be an inflationary gap.

- If the global economy and U.S. economy slow even more than forecast and the Bank gets it wrong by stimulating aggregate demand too little, by 2013, the price level will have risen to less than 130—the inflation rate will be less than 2 percent per year—and a recessionary gap will remain.

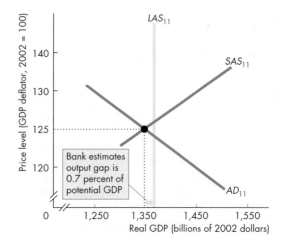

Figure 1 The Economy in 2011

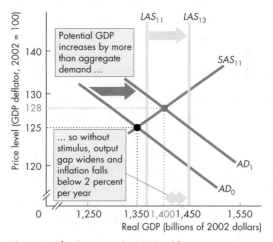

Figure 2 The Economy in 2013 without Monetary Stimulus

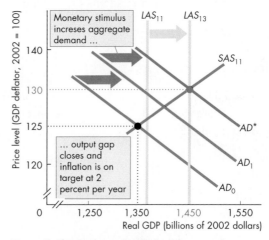

Figure 3 The Economy in 2013 with Monetary Stimulus

SUMMARY

Key Points

Monetary Policy Objectives and Framework
(pp. 728–730)

- The Bank of Canada Act requires the Bank to use monetary policy to avoid inflation and moderate cycles in real GDP and employment.
- The Government of Canada and the Bank of Canada have jointly agreed that the Bank will seek to keep CPI inflation between 1 percent and 3 percent a year and will aim for the 2 percent midpoint.
- The Bank has successfully achieved its inflation-control target.
- The Bank's Governing Council has the responsibility for the conduct of monetary policy, but the Bank and the government must consult regularly.

Working Problems 1 to 4 will give you a better understanding of monetary policy objectives and framework.

The Conduct of Monetary Policy (pp. 730–732)

- The Bank of Canada's monetary policy instrument is the overnight loans rate.
- The Bank sets the overnight loans rate target and announces changes on eight dates each year.
- To decide on the appropriate level of the overnight loans rate target, the Bank monitors the inflation rate and all the factors that influence inflation.
- The Bank sets the overnight loans rate at the level expected to keep inflation inside its target range and, on average, to hit the middle of the target range.
- The Bank achieves its overnight loans rate target by using open market operations.

Working Problems 5 to 10 will give you a better understanding of the conduct of monetary policy.

Monetary Policy Transmission (pp. 733–740)

- A change in the overnight loans rate changes other interest rates, the exchange rate, the quantity of money and loans, aggregate demand, and eventually real GDP and the price level.
- Changes in the overnight loans rate change real GDP about one year later and change the inflation rate with an even longer time lag.

Working Problems 11 to 20 will give you a better understanding of monetary policy transmission.

Extraordinary Monetary Stimulus (pp. 741–743)

- A financial crisis has three ingredients: a widespread fall in asset prices, a currency drain, and a run on banks.
- Central banks responded to financial crisis with classic open market operations and by several other unconventional measures.
- Inflation targeting and the Taylor rule are monetary policy strategies designed to enable the central bank to manage inflation expectations and reduce uncertainty.

Working Problems 21 to 25 will give you a better understanding of extraordinary monetary stimulus.

Key Terms

Bank rate, 731
Inflation rate targeting, 728
Operating band, 731

Overnight loans rate, 730
Settlements balances rate, 731

SCAN THIS

STUDY PLAN PROBLEMS AND APPLICATIONS

MyEconLab ◆ You can work Problems 1 to 25 in Chapter 30 Study Plan and get instant feedback.

Monetary Policy Objectives and Framework
(Study Plan 30.1)

1. "Unemployment is a more serious economic problem than inflation and it should be the focus of the Bank of Canada's monetary policy." Evaluate this statement and explain why the Bank's policy goal is a target inflation rate.

2. "Because the inflation rate includes the prices of food and fuel, which fluctuate a great deal, the Bank of Canada should pay little attention to short-term fluctuations in inflation and be more concerned with long-term trends." Explain why the Bank of Canada has been concerned with long-term trends.

3. "Monetary policy is too important to be left to the Bank of Canada. The government should be responsible for it." How is responsibility for monetary policy allocated between the the Bank of Canada and the government?

4. **Inflation Control Target Renewal**

   The 2006 inflation control target agreement between the government of Canada and the Bank of Canada runs to the end of 2011.

   Source: *Bank of Canada*, November 5, 2006

   a. What role does the Government of Canada play in the inflation control agreement?

   b. What role does the Bank of Canada play in the inflation control agreement?

   c. Why is it important that the agreement be renewed in 2011 and what might be some obstacles to its renewal?

The Conduct of Monetary Policy (Study Plan 30.2)

5. What are the two possible monetary policy instruments, which one does the Bank of Canada use, and how has its value behaved since 2000?

6. How does the Bank of Canada hit its overnight loans rate target?

7. What does the Bank of Canada do to determine whether the overnight loans rate should be raised, lowered, or left unchanged?

Use the following news clip to work Problems 8 and 9.

Carney Says Headwinds May Keep Interest Rates Low

Canada is in an environment of substantial headwinds from Europe and the United States and monetary policy may need to maintain stimulus to achieve the inflation target at full employment.

Source: Bloomberg, June 24, 2011

8. Explain the situation faced by the Bank of Canada in 2011.

9. a. How would the Bank of Canada "maintain stimulus"?

   b. Why might the Bank of Canada decide to lower the interest rate in the face of "headwinds"?

10. **Fed's $2 trillion Boost for Bank Reserves**

    The Fed has boosted bank reserves and the monetary base by $2 trillion.

    Source: Bloomberg, October 7, 2010

    Explain the actions that the Fed (the U.S. central bank) must have taken to boost bank reserves.

Monetary Policy Transmission (Study Plan 30.3)

Use the following news clip to work Problems 11 and 12.

Sorry Ben, You Don't Control Long-Term Rates

Perhaps Ben Bernanke (Chairman of the U.S. Fed) didn't learn in school that long-term interest rates are set by the market, but he is about to learn this lesson. Long-term interest rates cannot be manipulated lower by the central bank for a great length of time.

Source: safehaven.com, May 5, 2009

11. What is the role of the long-term interest rate in the monetary policy transmission process?

12. a. Is it the long-term nominal interest rate or the long-term real interest rate that influences spending decisions? Explain why.

    b. How does the market determine the long-term nominal interest rate and why doesn't it move as much as the short-term interest rates?

Use the following news clip to work Problems 13 and 14.

Loonie Down Amid Soft Chinese Economic Data

The Canadian dollar was down to 98 cents US on news that China's international trade growth slowed.

Source: Sympatico.ca, October 15, 2011

13. How does a lower Canadian dollar exchange rate influence monetary policy transmission?

14. Would a fall in the exchange rate mainly influence unemployment or inflation?

Use the following news clip to work Problems 15 to 17.

Economists' Growth Forecasts Through 2011

Economists surveyed boosted their forecasts for business investment in 2011.

Source: Bloomberg, October 11, 2010

15. Explain the effects of the Bank of Canada's low interest rates on business investment. Draw a graph to illustrate your explanation.

16. Explain the effects of business investment on aggregate demand. Would you expect it to have a multiplier effect? Why or why not?

17. What actions might the Bank of Canada take to stimulate business investment further?

Use the following news clip to work Problems 18 to 20.

Canada to Lead in Growth: OECD

The Organization for Economic Co-operation and Development predicted Tuesday that Canada will lead industrialized countries in economic growth during the first half of this year.

The think tank also said the economic outlook has brightened for all G7 countries since its last forecast in November, with the exception of Japan.

When the numbers are final, Canada is expected to have grown by 5.2 per cent in the first three months of 2011, and 3.8 per cent in the second quarter.

Source: CBC News, April 5, 2011

18. If the OECD forecasts turn out to be correct, what would most likely happen to the output gap and unemployment in 2011 and 2012?

19. a. What actions taken by the Bank of Canada in 2009 and 2010 would you expect to influence Canadian real GDP growth in 2011 and 2012? Explain how those policy actions would transmit to real GDP.
    b. Draw a graph of aggregate demand and aggregate supply to illustrate your answer to part (a).

20. What further actions might the Bank of Canada take in 2012 to influence the real GDP growth rate in 2012? (Remember the time lags in the operation of monetary policy.)

Extraordinary Monetary Stimulus (Study Plan 30.4)

Use the following news clip to work Problems 21 to 23.

Dollar Under Pressure Amid QE2 Speculation

Persistent speculation that the Federal Reserve would soon embark on a fresh program of long-term asset purchases—a second round of quantitative easing or QE2—kept the U.S. dollar under pressure in the foreign exchange market ahead of crucial U.S. employment data.

Source: ft.com, October 7, 2010

21. What is the connection between actions that the Fed might take and U.S. employment data?

22. What does the news clip mean by "the U.S. dollar under pressure"?

23. Why was the Fed contemplating QE2? What were the arguments for and against further quantitative easing in the fall of 2010?

24. **Prospects Rise for Fed Easing Policy**

    William Dudley, president of the New York Fed, raised the prospect of the Fed becoming more explicit about its inflation goal to "help anchor inflation expectations at the desired rate."

    Source: ft.com, October 1, 2010

    a. What monetary policy strategy is William Dudley raising?
    b. How does inflation rate targeting work and why might it "help anchor inflation expectations at the desired rate"?

25. Suppose that the Bank of England decides to follow the Taylor rule. In 2005, the United Kingdom had an inflation rate of 2.1 percent a year and its output gap was −0.3 percent. At what level would the Bank of England have set the repo rate (the U.K. equivalent of the overnight loans rate)?

ADDITIONAL PROBLEMS AND APPLICATIONS

MyEconLab ◆ You can work these problems in MyEconLab if assigned by your instructor.

Monetary Policy Objectives and Framework

Use the following information to work Problems 26 to 28.

The Bank of Canada and the Government of Canada have agreed that the Bank will achieve an inflation rate target.

26. Explain how inflation targeting promotes full employment in the long run.

27. Explain the conflict between inflation targeting and unemployment targeting in the short run.

28. Based on the performance of Canadian inflation and unemployment, has the Bank's inflation targeting been successful?

29. Suppose Parliament decided to strip the Bank of Canada of its monetary policy powers and decided to legislate interest rate changes. How would you expect the policy choices to change? Which arrangement would most likely provide price stability?

Use the following news clip to work Problems 30 to 32.

A World Awash in Government Debt

In the 1980s, it was Argentina, Mexico, and the Philippines that struggled with unsustainable debt loads. In the 1990s it was Russia and the go-go economies of East Asia. Today, it is the United States, Japan, and Europe.

Source: globalpost.com, August 2, 2011

30. How does a government get funds to cover a budget deficit? How does financing a budget deficit affect the the central bank's monetary policy?

31. How was Canada's budget deficit of 2011 influenced by the Bank of Canada's low interest rate policy?

32. a. How would the budget deficit change in 2012 and 2013 if the Bank of Canada moved interest rates up?
    b. How would the budget deficit change in 2012 and 2013 if the Bank of Canada's monetary policy led to a rapid appreciation of the dollar?

33. The U.S. Federal Reserve Act of 2000 instructs the Fed to pursue its goals by "maintain[ing] long-run growth of the monetary and credit aggregates commensurate with the economy's long-run potential to increase production."
    a. How would following this instruction make the U.S. monetary policy instrument different from Canada's monetary policy instrument?
    b. Why might a central bank increase the quantity of money by more than the increase in potential GDP?

The Conduct of Monetary Policy

34. Looking at the overnight loans rate since 2000, identify periods during which, with the benefit of hindsight, the rate might have been kept too low. Identify periods during which it might have been too high.

Use the following information to work Problems 35 to 39.

At the end of 2009, the unemployment rate was 8.3 percent, the inflation rate was 0.8 percent, and the overnight rate target was 0.25 percent. In mid-2011, the unemployment rate was 7.6 percent, the inflation rate was 3.3 percent, and the overnight rate target was 1 percent.

35. How might the Bank of Canada's decisions that raised the overnight rate from 0.25 percent to 1 percent have been influenced by the unemployment rate and the inflation rate?

36. Explain the dilemma that rising inflation and high unemployment poses for the Bank of Canada.

37. Why might the Bank of Canada decide to keep the overnight rate at 1 percent in 2012?

38. Why might the Bank of Canada decide to raise the overnight rate in 2012?

39. Why might the Bank of Canada decide to lower the overnight rate in 2012?

Monetary Policy Transmission

Use the following information to work Problems 40 to 42.

From 2007 to 2009, the long-term *real* interest rate paid by the safest corporations increased from 2.3 percent to 3.8 percent. During that same period, the overnight loans rate fell from 4.5 percent to 0.25 percent a year.

40. What role does the long-term real interest rate play in the monetary policy transmission process?

41. How does the overnight loans rate influence the long-term real interest rate?

42. What do you think happened to inflation expectations between 2007 and 2009 and why?

43. **U.S. Dollar Tumbles to 15-Year Low Against Yen**

    The U.S. dollar tumbled to a fresh 15-year low on persistent fears over the U.S. economic outlook.

    Source: yahoo.com, October 7, 2010

    a. How do "fears over the U.S. economic outlook" influence the exchange rate?

    b. How does monetary policy influence the exchange rate?

Use the following news clip to work Problems 44 and 45.

Top Economist Says America Could Plunge into Recession

Robert Shiller, Professor of Economics at Yale University, predicted that there was a very real possibility that the United States would be plunged into a Japan-style slump, with house prices declining for years.

Source: timesonline.co.uk, December 31, 2007

44. If the Fed had agreed with Robert Shiller in December 2007, what actions might it have taken differently from those it did take? How could monetary policy prevent house prices from falling?

45. Describe the time lags in the response of output and inflation to the policy actions you have prescribed.

Use the following news clip to work Problem 46.

Greenspan Says Economy Strong

The central bank chairman, Alan Greenspan, said inflation was low, consumer spending had held up well through the downturn, housing-market strength was likely to continue, and businesses appeared to have unloaded their glut of inventories, setting the stage for a rebound in production.

Source: cnn.com, July 16, 2002

46. What monetary policy actions would you expect the Fed to take in the situation described by Alan Greenspan?

Extraordinary Monetary Stimulus

47. **Fed's Plosser: Doesn't Currently Support Further Asset Buying**

    Further Federal Reserve asset purchases will not speed up the labour market recovery and could damage the Fed's credibility, said Federal Reserve Bank of Philadelphia President Charles Plosser, who is opposed to further asset buying of any size at this time.

    Source: nasdaq.com, October 12, 2010

    a. Describe the asset purchases that caused Charles Plosser concern.

    b. How might asset purchases damage the Fed's credibility?

48. Suppose that the Reserve Bank of New Zealand is following the Taylor rule. In 2009, it sets the official cash rate (its equivalent of the overnight loans rate) at 4 percent a year. If the inflation rate in New Zealand is 2 percent a year, what is its output gap?

Economics in the News

49. After you have studied *Reading Between the Lines* on pp. 744–745, answer the following questions.

    a. What was the state of the Canadian economy in 2011?

    b. What was the Bank of Canda's expectation about future real GDP growth and inflation in September 2011?

    c. How would maintaining the overnight rate at 1 percent influence the market for bank reserves, the loanable funds market, and aggregate demand and aggregate supply?

    d. How would you expect the Canadian dollar exchange rate to feature in the transmission of monetary policy to real GDP and the price level?

International Trade Policy

After studying this chapter, you will be able to

◆ Explain how markets work with international trade and identify its winners and losers

◆ Explain the effects of international trade barriers

◆ Explain and evaluate arguments used to justify restricting international trade

iPods, Wii Games, and Nike shoes are just three of the items you might buy that are not produced in Canada. In fact, most of the things that you buy are produced abroad, often in Asia, and transported here in container ships and FedEx cargo jets. International trade is part of the sometimes controversial globalization process that is having a profound effect on our lives.

Why do we go to such lengths to trade and communicate with others in faraway places? You will find some answers in this chapter. And in *Reading Between the Lines* at the end of the chapter, you can apply what you've learned and examine the effects of a Canadian tariff on ski jackets imported from China.

◆ How Global Markets Work

Because we trade with people in other countries, the goods and services that we can buy and consume are not limited by what we can produce. The goods and services that we buy from other countries are our **imports**; and the goods and services that we sell to people in other countries are our **exports**.

International Trade Today

Global trade today is enormous. In 2010, global exports and imports were $37 trillion, which is 58 percent of the value of global production. The United States is the world's largest international trader and accounts for 10 percent of world exports and 13 percent of world imports. Germany and China, which rank 2 and 3 behind the United States, lag by a large margin.

In 2010, total Canadian exports were $478 billion, which is about 30 percent of the value of Canadian production. Total Canadian imports were $509 billion, which is about 31 percent of total expenditure in Canada.

We trade both goods and services. In 2010, exports of services were about 17 percent of total exports and imports of services were about 21 percent of total imports.

What Drives International Trade?

Comparative advantage is the fundamental force that drives international trade. Comparative advantage (see Chapter 2, p. 38) is a situation in which a person can perform an activity or produce a good or service at a lower opportunity cost than anyone else. This same idea applies to nations. We can define *national comparative advantage* as a situation in which a nation can perform an activity or produce a good or service at a lower opportunity cost than any other nation.

The opportunity cost of producing a T-shirt is lower in China than in Canada, so China has a comparative advantage in producing T-shirts. The opportunity cost of producing a regional jet is lower in Canada than in China, so Canada has a comparative advantage in producing these airplanes.

You saw in Chapter 2 how Liz and Joe reap gains from trade by specializing in the production of the good at which they have a comparative advantage and then trading with each other. Both are better off.

This same principle applies to trade among

Economics in Action
Canada's Most Traded Items

The figure shows Canada's four largest exports and imports by value. Crude oil is our biggest export and machinery and equipment as well as consumer goods are our biggest imports. Trade in automobiles—both exports and imports—has slipped from the top spot it occupied in earlier years.

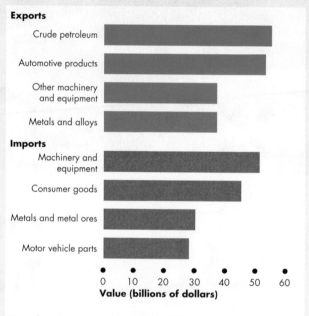

Canadian Exports and Imports in 2011

Source of data: Statistics Canada.

nations. Because China has a comparative advantage at producing T-shirts and Canada has a comparative advantage at producing regional jets, the people of both countries can gain from specialization and trade. China can buy airplanes from Canada at a lower opportunity cost than that at which Chinese firms can produce them. And Canadians can buy T-shirts from China for a lower opportunity cost than that at which Canadian firms can produce them. Also, through international trade, Chinese producers can get higher prices for their T-shirts and Bombardier can sell its regional jets for a higher price. Both countries gain from international trade.

Let's now illustrate the gains from trade that we've just described by studying demand and supply in the global markets for T-shirts and regional jets.

Why Canada Imports T-Shirts

Canada imports T-shirts because the rest of the world has a comparative advantage in producing them. Figure 31.1 illustrates how this comparative advantage generates international trade and how trade affects the price of a T-shirt and the quantities produced and bought.

The demand curve D_{Can} and the supply curve S_{Can} show the demand and supply in the Canadian domestic market only. The demand curve tells us the quantity of T-shirts that Canadians are willing to buy at various prices. The supply curve tells us the quantity of T-shirts that Canadian garment makers are willing to sell at various prices—that is, the quantity supplied at each price when all T-shirts sold in Canada are produced in Canada.

Figure 31.1(a) shows what the Canadian T-shirt market would be like with no international trade.

The price of a shirt would be $8 and 4 million shirts a year would be produced by Canadian garment makers and bought by Canadian consumers.

Figure 31.1(b) shows the market for T-shirts with international trade. Now the price of a T-shirt is determined in the world market, not the Canadian domestic market. The world price of a T-shirt is less than $8, which means that the rest of the world has a comparative advantage in producing T-shirts. The world price line shows the world price at $5 a shirt.

The Canadian demand curve, D_{Can}, tells us that at $5 a shirt, Canadians buy 6 million shirts a year. The Canadian supply curve, S_{Can}, tells us that at $5 a shirt, Canadian garment makers produce 2 million T-shirts a year. To buy 6 million T-shirts when only 2 million are produced in Canada, we must import T-shirts from the rest of the world. The quantity of T-shirts imported is 4 million a year.

FIGURE 31.1   A Market with Imports

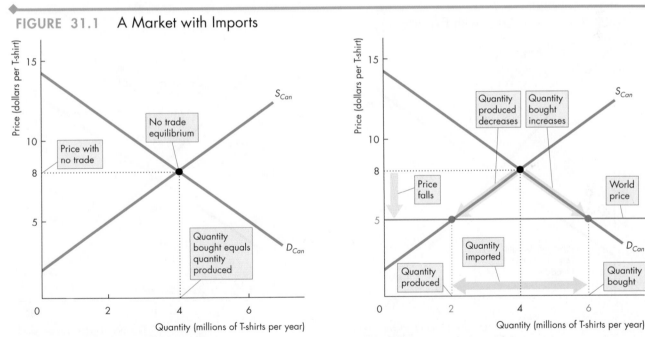

(a) Equilibrium with no international trade

(b) Equilibrium in a market with imports

Part (a) shows the Canadian market for T-shirts with no international trade. The Canadian domestic demand curve D_{Can} and Canadian domestic supply curve S_{Can} determine the price of a T-shirt at $8 and the quantity of T-shirts produced and bought in Canada at 4 million a year.

Part (b) shows the Canadian market for T-shirts with

international trade. World demand and world supply determine the world price of a T-shirt, which is $5. The price in the Canadian market falls to $5 a shirt. Canadian purchases of T-shirts increase to 6 million a year, and Canadian production of T-shirts decreases to 2 million a year. Canada imports 4 million T-shirts a year.

MyEconLab animation

Why Canada Exports Regional Jets

Canada exports regional jets because it has a comparative advantage in producing them. Figure 31.2 illustrates how this comparative advantage generates international trade in regional jets and how this trade affects the price of a regional jet and the quantities produced and bought.

Figure 31.2 illustrates international trade in regional jets. The demand curve D_{Can} and the supply curve S_{Can} show the demand and supply in the Canadian domestic market only. The demand curve tells us the quantity of regional jets that Canadian airlines are willing to buy at various prices. The supply curve tells us the quantity of regional jets that Canadian aircraft makers are willing to sell at various prices.

Figure 31.2(a) shows what the Canadian market for regional jets would be like with no international

trade. The price of a regional jet would be $100 million and 40 a year would be produced by Bombardier and bought by Canadian airlines.

Figure 31.2(b) shows the Canadian market for regional jets with international trade. Now the price of a regional jet is determined in the world market and the world price is higher than $100 million, which means that Canada has a comparative advantage in producing regional jets. The world price line shows the world price at $150 million.

The Canadian demand curve, D_{Can}, tells us that at $150 million each, Canadian airlines buy 20 regional jets a year. The Canadian supply curve, S_{Can}, tells us that at $150 million each, Bombardier produces 70 regional jets a year. The quantity produced in Canada (70 a year) minus the quantity purchased by Canadian airlines (20 a year) is the quantity exported, which is 50 regional jets a year.

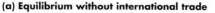

FIGURE 31.2   A Market with Exports

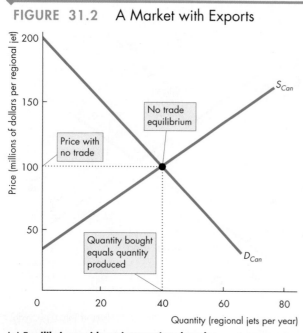

(a) Equilibrium without international trade

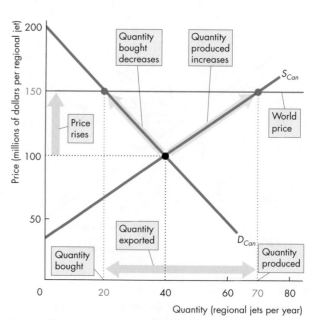

(b) Equilibrium in a market with exports

In part (a), the Canadian market with no international trade, the domestic demand curve D_{Can} and domestic supply curve S_{Can} determine the price of a regional jet at $100 million and 40 regional jets are produced and bought each year.

In part (b), with international trade, world demand

and world supply determine the world price of a regional jet, which is $150 million. The price in Canada rises to the world price. Canadian production increases to 70 a year, and Canadian purchases decrease to 20 a year. Canada exports 50 regional jets a year.

MyEconLab   animation   ◆

Winners and Losers from International Trade

International trade has winners and it has losers. It is because some people lose that we often hear complaints about international competition. We're now going to see who wins and who loses from international trade. Then you will be able to understand why we hear producers complaining about cheap foreign imports. You will also understand why we never hear consumers of imported goods and services complaining and why we never hear exporters complaining except when they want greater access to foreign markets.

Gains and Losses from Imports   We can measure the gains and losses from imports by examining their effect on the price paid and quantity consumed by domestic consumers and their effect on the price received and quantity sold by domestic producers.

Domestic Consumers Gain from Imports   When a country freely imports something from the rest of the world, it is because the rest of the world has a comparative advantage at producing that item. Compared to a situation with no international trade, the price paid by the consumer falls and the quantity consumed increases. It is clear that the consumer gains. The greater the fall in price and increase in quantity consumed, the greater is the gain to the consumer.

Domestic Producers Lose from Imports   Compared to a situation with no international trade, the price received by a domestic producer of an item that is imported falls. Also, the quantity sold by the domestic producer of a good or service that is imported decreases. Because the domestic producer of such an item sells a smaller quantity and for a lower price, this producer loses from international trade. Import-competing industries shrink in the face of competition from cheaper foreign-produced goods.

The profits of firms that produce import-competing goods and services fall. As these firms cut their workforces, unemployment in these industries increases and wages fall. When these industries have a geographical concentration, such as steel production around Sydney, Nova Scotia, an entire region can suffer economic decline.

Gains and Losses from Exports   Just as we did for imports, we can measure the gains and losses from exports by looking at their effect on the price paid and quantity consumed by domestic consumers and

their effect on the price received and quantity sold by domestic producers.

Domestic Consumers Lose from Exports   When a country exports something to the rest of the world, it is because the country has a comparative advantage at producing that item. Compared to a situation with no international trade, the price paid by the consumer rises and the quantity consumed in the domestic economy decreases. The domestic consumer loses. The greater the rise in price and decrease in quantity consumed, the greater is the loss to the consumer.

Domestic Producers Gain from Exports   Compared to a situation with no international trade, the price received by a domestic producer of an item that is exported rises. Also, the quantity sold by the domestic producer of a good or service that is exported increases. Because the domestic producer of an item that is exported sells a larger quantity and for a higher price, this producer gains from international trade. Export industries expand in the face of global demand for their product.

The profits of firms that produce exports rise. As these firms expand their workforces, unemployment in these industries decreases and wages rise. When these industries have a geographical concentration, an entire region can boom.

Net Gain   Export producers and import consumers gain, export consumers and import producers lose, but the gains are greater than the losses. In the case of imports, the consumer gains what the producer loses and then gains even more on the cheaper imports. In the case of exports, the producer gains what the consumer loses and then gains even more on the items it exports. So international trade provides a net gain for a country.

◤ REVIEW QUIZ

1 Explain the effects of imports on the domestic price and quantity, and the gains and losses of consumers and producers.
2 Explain the effects of exports on the domestic price and quantity, and the gains and losses of consumers and producers.

You can work these questions in Study Plan 31.1 and get instant feedback.

MyEconLab ◆

International Trade Restrictions

Governments use four sets of tools to influence international trade and protect domestic industries from foreign competition. They are

- Tariffs
- Import quotas
- Other import barriers
- Export subsidies

Tariffs

A **tariff** is a tax on a good that is imposed by the importing country when an imported good crosses its international boundary. For example, the government of India imposes a 100 percent tariff on wine imported from Ontario. So when an Indian imports a $10 bottle of Ontario wine, he pays the Indian government a $10 import duty.

Tariffs raise revenue for governments and serve the self-interest of people who earn their incomes in import-competing industries. But as you will see, restrictions on free international trade decrease the gains from trade and are not in the social interest.

The Effects of a Tariff To see the effects of a tariff, let's return to the example in which Canada imports T-shirts. With free trade, the T-shirts are imported and sold at the world price. Then, under pressure from Canadian garment makers, the Canadian government imposes a tariff on imported T-shirts. Buyers of T-shirts must now pay the world price plus the tariff. Several consequences follow and Fig. 31.3 illustrates them.

Figure 31.3(a) shows the situation with free international trade. At the world price of $5 a shirt, Canada produces 2 million T-shirts a year and imports 4 million a year. Figure 31.3(b) shows what happens with a tariff set at $2 per T-shirt.

FIGURE 31.3   The Effects of a Tariff

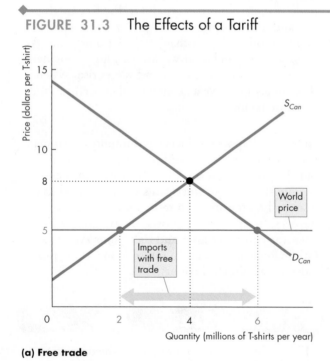

(a) Free trade

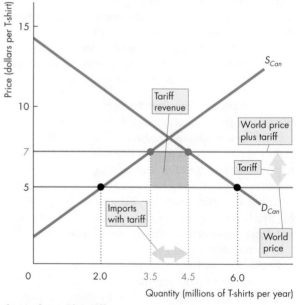

(b) Market with tariff

The world price of a T-shirt is $5. With free trade in part (a), Canadians buy 6 million T-shirts a year. Canadian garment makers produce 2 million T-shirts a year and Canada imports 4 million a year.

With a tariff of $2 per T-shirt in part (b), the price in

the Canadian market rises to $7 a T-shirt. Canadian production increases, Canadian purchases decrease, and the quantity imported decreases. The Canadian government collects a tariff revenue of $2 on each T-shirt imported, which is shown by the purple rectangle.

The following changes occur in the market for T-shirts:

- The price of a T-shirt in Canada rises by $2.
- The quantity of T-shirts bought in Canada decreases.
- The quantity of T-shirts produced in Canada increases.
- The quantity of T-shirts imported into Canada decreases.
- The Canadian government collects a tariff revenue.

Rise in Price of a T-Shirt To buy a T-shirt, Canadians must pay the world price plus the tariff, so the price of a T-shirt rises by the $2 tariff to $7. Figure 31.3(b) shows the new domestic price line, which lies $2 above the world price line. The price rises by the full amount of the tariff.

Decrease in Purchases The higher price of a T-shirt brings a decrease in the quantity demanded along the demand curve. Figure 31.3(b) shows the decrease from 6 million T-shirts a year at $5 a shirt to 4.5 million a year at $7 a shirt.

Increase in Domestic Production The higher price of a T-shirt stimulates domestic production, and Canadian garment makers increase the quantity

supplied along the supply curve. Figure 31.3(b) shows the increase from 2 million T-shirts at $5 a shirt to 3.5 million a year at $7 a shirt.

Decrease in Imports T-shirt imports decrease by 3 million, from 4 million to 1 million a year. Both the decrease in Canadian purchases and the increase in domestic production contribute to this decrease in Canadian imports.

Tariff Revenue The government's tariff revenue is $2 million—$2 per shirt on 1 million imported shirts—shown by the purple rectangle.

Winners, Losers, and the Social Loss from a Tariff

A tariff on an imported good creates winners and losers and a social loss. When the Canadian government imposes a tariff on an imported good,

- Canadian consumers of the good lose.
- Canadian producers of the good gain.
- Canadian consumers lose more than Canadian producers gain.
- Society loses.

Canadian Consumers of the Good Lose Because the price of a T-shirt in Canada rises, the quantity of T-shirts demanded decreases. The combination of a

Economics in Action
Tariffs Almost Gone

Canadian tariffs were in place before Confederation. They increased sharply in the 1870s and remained high until the 1930s. Since the **General Agreement on Tariffs and Trade (GATT)** was established in 1947, tariffs have fallen in a series of negotiating rounds, the most significant of which are identified in the figure. Tariffs have almost gone, but import quotas and other trade barriers persist.

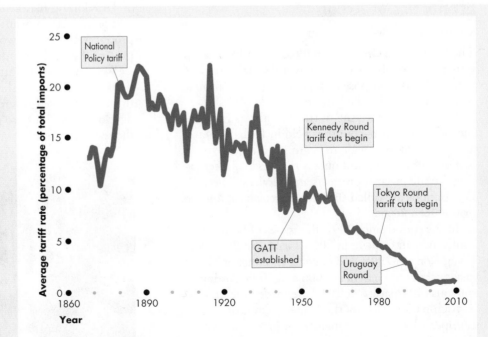

Canadian Tariffs: 1867–2010

Sources of data: Statistics Canada Historical Statistics of Canada, Catalogue 11-516, July 1999, and CANSIM Tables 380-0002 and 380-0034.

higher price and smaller quantity bought brings a loss to Canadian consumers from a tariff.

Canadian Producers of the Good Gain Because the price of an imported T-shirt rises by the amount of the tariff, Canadian T-shirt producers are now able to sell their T-shirts for the world price plus the tariff so the quantity of T-shirts supplied by Canadian producers increases. The combination of a higher price and larger quantity produced increases producers' profits—the gain to Canadian producers from the tariff.

Canadian Consumers Lose More Than Canadian Producers Gain Consumers lose from a tariff for three reasons:

1. They pay a higher price to domestic producers.
2. They consume a smaller quantity of the good.
3. They pay tariff revenue to the government.

The tariff revenue is a loss to consumers but is not a social loss. The government can use the tax revenue to buy public services that consumers value. But the other two sources of consumer loss include some social losses.

Society Loses There is a social loss because part of the higher price paid to domestic producers pays for the higher cost of domestic production. The tariff increases domestic production, but this increase in the quantity available in the domestic economy could have been obtained at lower cost by importing the good. There is also a social loss from the decreased quantity of the good consumed at the higher price.

Import Quotas

We now look at the second tool for restricting trade: import quotas. An **import quota** is a restriction that limits the maximum quantity of a good that may be imported in a given period. Most countries impose import quotas on a wide range of items. Canada imposes them on food products such as meat, eggs, and dairy and manufactured goods such as textiles and steel.

Import quotas enable the government to satisfy the self-interest of the people who earn their incomes in the import-competing industries. But you will discover that like a tariff, an import quota decreases the gains from trade and is not in the social interest.

Economics in Action
Self-Interest Beats the Social Interest

The **World Trade Organization (WTO)** is an international body established by the world's major trading nations for the purpose of supervising international trade and lowering the barriers to trade.

In 2001, at a meeting of trade ministers from all the WTO member-countries held in Doha, Qatar, an agreement was made to begin negotiations to lower tariff barriers and quotas that restrict international trade in farm products and services. These negotiations are called the **Doha Development Agenda** or the **Doha Round**.

In the period since 2001, thousands of hours of conferences in Cancún in 2003, Geneva in 2004, and Hong Kong in 2005, and ongoing meetings at WTO headquarters in Geneva in 2006 and 2008, costing millions of taxpayers' dollars, have made little progress.

Rich nations, led by the United States, the European Union, and Japan, want greater access to the markets of developing nations in exchange for allowing those nations greater access to the markets of the rich world, especially those for farm products.

Developing nations, led by Brazil, China, India, and South Africa, want access to the markets of farm products of the rich world, but they also want to protect their infant industries.

With two incompatible positions, these negotiations are stalled and show no signs of a breakthrough. The self-interests of rich nations and developing nations are preventing the achievement of the social interest.

The Effects of an Import Quota The effects of an import quota are similar to those of a tariff. The price rises, the quantity bought decreases, and the quantity produced in Canada increases. Figure 31.4 illustrates the effects.

Figure 31.4(a) shows the situation with free international trade. Figure 31.4(b) shows what happens with an import quota of 1 million T-shirts a year. The Canadian supply curve of T-shirts becomes the domestic supply curve, S_{Can}, plus the quantity that the import quota permits. So the Canadian supply curve becomes S_{Can} + *quota*. The price of a T-shirt rises to $7, the quantity of T-shirts bought in Canada decreases to 4.5 million a year, the quantity of T-shirts produced in Canada increases to 3.5 million a year, and the quantity of T-shirts imported into Canada decreases to the quota quantity of 1 million a year. All the effects of this quota are identical to the effects of a tariff of $2 per T-shirt, as you can check in Fig. 31.3(b).

Winners, Losers, and the Social Loss from an Import Quota An import quota creates winners and losers that are similar to those of a tariff but with an interesting difference.

When the government imposes an import quota,

- Canadian consumers of the good lose.
- Canadian producers of the good gain.
- Importers of the good gain.
- Society loses.

Canadian Consumers of the Good Lose Because the price of a T-shirt in Canada rises, the quantity of T-shirts demanded decreases. The combination of a higher price and smaller quantity bought makes the Canadian consumers worse off. So Canadian consumers lose when an import quota is imposed.

Canadian Producers of the Good Gain Because the price of an imported T-shirt rises, Canadian T-shirt producers increase production. The combination of a

---

FIGURE 31.4   The Effects of an Import Quota

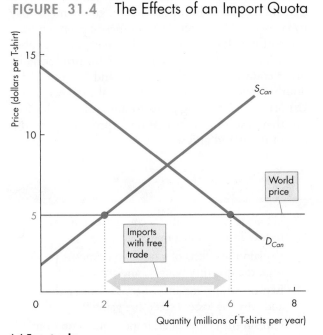

(a) Free trade

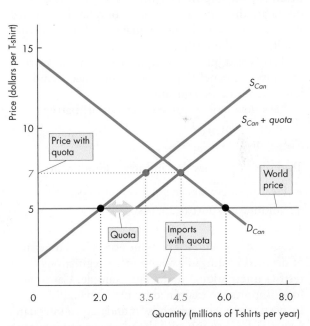

(b) Market with import quota

With free international trade, in part (a), Canadians buy 6 million T-shirts at the world price. Canada produces 2 million T-shirts and imports 4 million a year. With an import quota of 1 million T-shirts a year, in part (b), the supply of

T-shirts in Canada is shown by the curve S_{Can} + *quota*. The price in Canada rises to $7 a T-shirt. Canadian production increases, Canadian purchases decrease, and the quantity of T-shirts imported decreases.

higher price and a larger quantity produced increases producers' profit. So Canadian producers gain from the quota.

Importers of the Good Gain The importer is able to buy the good on the world market at the world market price, and sell the good in the domestic market at the domestic price. Because the domestic price exceeds the world price, the importer gains.

Society Loses Society loses because the loss to consumers exceeds the gains of domestic producers and importers. Just like the social losses from a tariff, there is a social loss from the quota because part of the higher price paid to domestic producers pays the higher cost of domestic production. There is a social loss from the decreased quantity of the good consumed at the higher price.

Tariff and Quota Compared You've looked at the effects of a tariff and a quota and can now see the essential differences between them. A tariff brings in revenue for the government while a quota brings a profit for the importers. All the other effects of a quota are the same as the effects of a tariff, provided the quota is set at the same quantity of imports that results from the tariff.

Tariffs and quotas are equivalent ways of restricting imports, benefiting domestic producers, and harming domestic consumers.

Let's now look at some other import barriers.

Other Import Barriers

Two sets of policies that influence imports are

- Health, safety, and regulation barriers
- Voluntary export restraints

Health, Safety, and Regulation Barriers Thousands of detailed health, safety, and other regulations restrict international trade. For example, Canadian food imports are examined by the Canadian Food Inspection Agency, which is "mandated to safeguard Canada's food supply and the plants and animals upon which safe and high-quality food depends." The discovery of BSE (mad cow disease) in just one cow in 2003 was enough to close down international trade in Canadian beef. The European Union bans imports of most genetically modified foods, such as Canadian-produced soybeans. Although regulations

of the type we've just described are not designed to limit international trade, they have that effect.

Voluntary Export Restraints A *voluntary export restraint* is like a quota allocated to a foreign exporter of a good. This type of trade barrier isn't common. It was initially used during the 1980s when Japan voluntarily limited its exports of car parts to Canada and the United States.

Export Subsidies

A *subsidy* is a payment by the government to a producer. When the government pays a subsidy, the cost of production falls by the amount of the subsidy, so supply of the subsidized good increases.

An *export subsidy* is a payment by the government to the producer of an exported good. Export subsidies are illegal under a number of international agreements, including the North American Free Trade Agreement (NAFTA), and the rules of the World Trade Organization (WTO).

Although export subsidies are illegal, the subsidies that the U.S. and European Union governments pay to farmers end up increasing domestic production, some of which gets exported. These exports of subsidized farm products make it harder for producers in other countries, notably in Africa and Central and South America, to compete in global markets. Export subsidies bring gains to domestic producers, but they result in inefficient underproduction in the rest of the world and society loses.

◆ REVIEW QUIZ

1 What are the tools that a country can use to restrict international trade?
2 Explain the effects of a tariff on domestic production, the quantity bought, and the price.
3 Explain who gains and who loses from a tariff and why the losses exceed the gains.
4 Explain the effects of an import quota on domestic production, consumption, and price.
5 Explain who gains and who loses from an import quota and why the losses exceed the gains.

You can work these questions in Study Plan 31.2 and get instant feedback.

MyEconLab ◆

The Case Against Protection

For as long as nations and international trade have existed, people have debated whether a country is better off with free international trade or with protection from foreign competition. The debate continues, but for most economists, a verdict has been delivered and is the one you have just seen. Free trade promotes prosperity for all countries; protection is inefficient. We've seen the most powerful case for free trade—it brings gains for consumers that exceed any losses incurred by producers, so there is a net gain for society.

But there is a broader range of issues in the free trade versus protection debate. Let's review these issues.

Two classical arguments for restricting international trade are

- The infant-industry argument
- The dumping argument

The Infant-Industry Argument

The **infant-industry argument** for protection is that it is necessary to protect a new industry to enable it to grow into a mature industry that can compete in world markets. The argument is based on the idea that comparative advantage changes or is dynamic and that on-the-job experience—*learning-by-doing*—is an important source of changes in comparative advantage. The fact that learning-by-doing can change comparative advantage doesn't justify protecting an infant industry.

First, the infant-industry argument is not valid if the benefits of learning-by-doing accrue *only* to the firms in the infant industry. The reason is that these firms will anticipate and reap the benefits of learning-by-doing without the additional incentive of protection from foreign competition.

For example, there are huge productivity gains from learning-by-doing in the manufacture of aircraft, but these gains benefit Bombardier and other aircraft producers. Because the people making the decisions are the ones who benefit, they take the future gains into account when they decide on the scale of their activities. No benefits accrue to firms in other industries or other parts of the economy, so there is no need for government assistance to achieve an efficient outcome.

Second, even if the case is made for protecting an infant industry, it is more efficient to do so by giving the firms in the industry a subsidy, which is financed out of taxes. Such a subsidy would encourage the industry to mature and to compete with efficient world producers and keep the price faced by consumers at the world price.

The Dumping Argument

Dumping occurs when a foreign firm sells its exports at a lower price than its cost of production. Dumping might be used by a firm that wants to gain a global monopoly. In this case, the foreign firm sells its output at a price below its cost to drive domestic firms out of business. When the domestic firms have gone, the foreign firm takes advantage of its monopoly position and charges a higher price for its product. Dumping is illegal under the rules of the WTO and is usually regarded as a justification for temporary tariffs, which are called *countervailing duties*.

But there are powerful reasons to resist the dumping argument for protection. First, it is virtually impossible to detect dumping because it is hard to determine a firm's costs. As a result, the test for dumping is whether a firm's export price is below its domestic price. But this test is a weak one because it can be rational for a firm to charge a low price in a market in which the quantity demanded is highly sensitive to price and a higher price in a market in which demand is less price-sensitive.

Second, it is hard to think of a good that is produced by a *global* monopoly. So even if all the domestic firms in some industry were driven out of business, it would always be possible to find alternative foreign sources of supply and to buy the good at a price determined in a competitive market.

Third, if a good or service were a truly global monopoly, the best way of dealing with it would be by regulation—just as in the case of domestic monopolies. Such regulation would require international cooperation.

The two arguments for protection that we've just examined have an element of credibility. The counterarguments are in general stronger, so these arguments do not make the case for protection. But they are not the only arguments that you might encounter. There are many other new arguments against globalization and for protection.

The most common ones are that protection

- Saves jobs
- Allows us to compete with cheap foreign labour
- Penalizes lax environmental standards
- Prevents rich countries from exploiting developing countries

Saves Jobs

First, free trade does cost some jobs, but it also creates other jobs. It brings about a global rationalization of labour and allocates labour resources to their highest-valued activities. International trade in textiles has cost tens of thousands of jobs in Canada as textile mills and other factories closed. But tens of thousands of jobs have been created in other countries as textile mills opened. And many thousands of Canadian workers got better-paying jobs than as textile workers because Canadian export industries expanded and created new jobs. More jobs have been created than destroyed.

Although protection does save particular jobs, it does so at a high cost. For example, until 2005, U.S. textile jobs were protected by an international agreement called the Multifibre Arrangement. The U.S. International Trade Commission (ITC) has estimated that because of import quotas, 72,000 jobs existed in the textile industry that would otherwise have disappeared and that the annual clothing expenditure in the United States was $15.9 billion ($160 per family) higher than it would have been with free trade. Equivalently, the ITC estimated that each textile job saved cost $221,000 a year.

Imports don't only destroy jobs. They create jobs for retailers that sell imported goods and for firms that service those goods. Imports also create jobs by creating income in the rest of the world, some of which is spent on Canadian-made goods and services.

Allows Us to Compete with Cheap Foreign Labour

With the removal of tariffs on trade between Canada, the United States, and Mexico, people said we would hear a "giant sucking sound" as jobs rushed to Mexico. Let's see what's wrong with this view.

The labour cost of a unit of output equals the wage rate divided by labour productivity. For example, if a Canadian autoworker earns $40 an hour and produces 20 units of output an hour, the average labour cost of a unit of output is $2. If a Mexican auto assembly worker earns $4 an hour and produces 1 unit of output an hour, the average labour cost of a unit of output is $4. Other things remaining the same, the higher a worker's productivity, the higher is the worker's wage rate. High-wage workers have high productivity; low-wage workers have low productivity.

Although high-wage Canadian workers are more productive than low-wage Mexican workers, there are differences across industries. Canadian labour is relatively more productive in some activities than in others. For example, the productivity of Canadian workers in producing movies, financial services, and customized computer chips is relatively higher than their productivity in the production of metals and some standardized machine parts. The activities in which Canadian workers are *relatively* more productive than their Mexican counterparts are those in which Canada has a *comparative advantage.*

By engaging in free trade, increasing our production and exports of the goods and services in which we have a comparative advantage, and decreasing our production and increasing our imports of the goods and services in which our trading partners have a comparative advantage, we can make ourselves and the citizens of other countries better off.

Penalizes Lax Environmental Standards

Another argument for protection is that many poorer countries, such as China and Mexico, do not have the same environmental policies that we have and, because they are willing to pollute and we are not, we cannot compete with them without tariffs. So if poorer countries want free trade with the richer and "greener" countries, they must raise their environmental standards.

This argument for protection is weak. First, a poor country cannot afford to be as concerned about its environmental standard as a rich country can. Today, some of the worst air and water pollution is found in China, Mexico, and Eastern Europe. But only a few decades ago, London and Los Angeles topped the pollution league chart. The best hope for cleaner air in Beijing and Mexico City is rapid income growth. And free trade contributes to that growth. As incomes in developing countries grow, they will have the *means* to match their desires to improve their environment.

Second, a poor country may have a comparative advantage at doing "dirty" work, which helps it to raise its income and at the same time enables the global economy to achieve higher environmental standards than would otherwise be possible.

Prevents Rich Countries from Exploiting Developing Countries

Another argument for protection is that international trade must be restricted to prevent the people of the rich industrial world from exploiting the poorer people of the developing countries and forcing them to work for slave wages.

Child labour and near-slave labour are serious problems that are rightly condemned. But by trading with poor countries, we increase the demand for the goods that these countries produce and, more significantly, we increase the demand for their labour. When the demand for labour in developing countries increases, the wage rate also increases. So, rather than exploiting people in developing countries, trade can improve their opportunities and increase their wages.

All these arguments for protection leave free trade unscathed, but a new phenomenon is at work: *offshore outsourcing*. Surely we need protection from this new source of foreign competition. Let's investigate.

Offshore Outsourcing

Roots, Canadian Tire, and BlackBerry: What do these Canadian icons have in common? They all send jobs that could be done in Canada to China, India, Thailand, or even the United States—they are offshoring. What exactly is offshoring?

What Is Offshoring? A firm in Canada can obtain the goods and services that it sells in any of four ways:

1. Hire Canadian labour and produce in Canada.
2. Hire foreign labour and produce in other countries.
3. Buy finished goods, components, or services from other firms in Canada.
4. Buy finished goods, components, or services from other firms in other countries.

Activities 3 and 4 are **outsourcing**, and activities 2 and 4 are **offshoring**. Activity 4 is **offshore outsourcing**. Notice that offshoring includes activities that take place inside Canadian firms. If a Canadian firm opens its own facilities in another country, then it is offshoring.

Offshoring has been going on for hundreds of years, but it expanded rapidly and became a source of concern during the 1990s as many Canadian firms moved information technology services and general office services such as finance, accounting, and human resources management overseas.

Why Did Offshoring of Services Boom During the 1990s? The gains from specialization and trade that you saw in the previous section must be large enough to make it worth incurring the costs of communication and transportation. If the cost of producing a T-shirt in China isn't lower than the cost of producing the T-shirt in Canada by more than the cost of transporting the shirt from China to Canada, then it is more efficient to produce shirts in Canada and avoid the transportation costs.

The same considerations apply to trade in services. If services are to be produced offshore, then the cost of delivering those services must be low enough to leave the buyer with an overall lower price. Before the 1990s, the cost of communicating across large distances was too high to make the offshoring of business services efficient. But during the 1990s, when satellites, fibre-optic cables, and computers cut the price of a phone call between Canada and India to less than a dollar an hour, a huge base of offshore resources became competitive with similar resources in Canada.

What Are the Benefits of Offshoring? Offshoring brings gains from trade identical to those of any other type of trade. We could easily change the names of the items traded from T-shirts and airplanes (the examples in the previous sections of this chapter) to banking services and call centre services (or any other pair of services). A Canadian bank might export banking services to Indian firms, and Indians might provide call centre services to Canadian firms. This type of trade would benefit both Canadians and Indians provided Canada has a comparative advantage in banking services and India has a comparative advantage in call centre services.

Comparative advantages like these emerged during the 1990s. India has the world's largest educated English-speaking population and is located in a time zone half a day ahead of the Canadian east coast and midway between Asia and Europe, which facilitates 24/7 operations. When the cost of communicating with a worker in India was several dollars a minute, as it was before the 1990s, tapping these vast resources was just too expensive. But at today's price of a long-distance telephone call or Internet connection, resources in India can be used to produce services for Canadians at a lower cost than those services can be produced by using resources located in Canada. And with the incomes that Indians earn from exporting services, some of the services (and goods) that Indians buy are produced in Canada.

Why Is Offshoring a Concern?

Despite the gain from specialization and trade that offshoring brings, many people believe that it also brings costs that eat up the gains. Why?

A major reason is that offshoring is taking jobs in services. The loss of manufacturing jobs to other countries has been going on for decades, but the Canadian service sector has always expanded by enough to create new jobs to replace the lost manufacturing jobs. Now that service jobs are also going overseas, the fear is that there will not be enough jobs for Canadians. This fear is misplaced.

Some service jobs are going overseas, while others are expanding at home. Canada imports call centre services, but it exports education, health care, legal, financial, and a host of other types of services. Jobs in these service sectors are expanding and will continue to do so.

The exact number of jobs that have moved to lower-cost offshore locations is not known, and estimates vary. But even the highest estimate is a tiny number compared to the normal rate of job creation.

Winners and Losers

Gains from trade do not bring gains for every single person. Canadians, on average, gain from offshore outsourcing, but some people lose. The losers are those who have invested in the human capital to do a specific job that has now gone offshore.

Unemployment benefits provide short-term temporary relief for these displaced workers. But the long-term solution requires retraining and the acquisition of new skills.

Beyond providing short-term relief through unemployment benefits, there is a large role for government in the provision of education and training to enable the labour force of the twenty-first century to be capable of ongoing learning and rapid retooling to take on new jobs that today we can't foresee.

Schools, colleges, and universities will expand and get better at doing their jobs of producing a highly educated and flexible labour force.

Avoiding Trade Wars

We have reviewed the arguments commonly heard in favour of protection and the counterarguments against them. There is one counterargument to protection that is general and quite overwhelming: Protection invites retaliation and can trigger a trade war.

The best example of a trade war occurred during the Great Depression of the 1930s when the United States introduced the Smoot-Hawley tariff. Country after country retaliated with its own tariff, and in a short period, world trade had almost disappeared. The costs to all countries were large and led to a renewed international resolve to avoid such self-defeating moves in the future. The costs also led to the creation of GATT and are the impetus behind current attempts to liberalize trade.

Why Is International Trade Restricted?

Why, despite all the arguments against protection, is trade restricted? There are two key reasons:

- Tariff revenue
- Rent seeking

Tariff Revenue   Government revenue is costly to collect. In developed countries such as Canada, a well-organized tax collection system is in place that can generate billions of dollars of income and sales tax revenues. This tax collection system is made possible by the fact that most economic transactions are done by firms that must keep properly audited financial records. Without such records, revenue collection agencies (such as Canada Revenue Agency) would be severely hampered in their work. Even with audited financial accounts, some potential tax revenue is lost. So for industrialized countries, the income and sales taxes are the major sources of revenue and tariffs play a very small role.

But governments in developing countries have a difficult time collecting taxes from their citizens. Much economic activity takes place in an informal economy with few financial records, so only a small amount of revenue is collected from income taxes and sales taxes. The one area in which economic transactions are well recorded and audited is international trade. So this activity is an attractive base for tax collection in these countries and is used much more extensively than it is in developed countries.

Rent Seeking Rent seeking is the major reason why international trade is restricted. **Rent seeking** is lobbying for special treatment by the government to create economic profit or to divert trade away from others. Free trade increases consumption possibilities *on average*, but not everyone shares in the gain and some people even lose. Free trade brings benefits to some and imposes costs on others, with total benefits exceeding total costs. The uneven distribution of costs and benefits is the principal obstacle to achieving more liberal international trade.

Returning to the example of trade in T-shirts and regional jets, the benefits from free trade accrue to the producers of jets and to the consumers of T-shirts. The domestic producers of T-shirts have to bear the costs of adjusting to a smaller garment industry. These costs are transition costs, not permanent costs. The costs of moving to free trade are borne by the garment producers and their employees who must become producers of other goods and services in which Canada has a comparative advantage.

The number of winners from free trade is large, but because the gains are spread thinly over a large number of people, the gain per person is small. The winners could organize and become a political force lobbying for free trade. But political activity is costly. It uses time and other scarce resources and the gains per person are too small to make the cost of political activity worth bearing.

In contrast, the number of losers from free trade is small, but the loss per person is large. Because the loss per person is large, the people who lose *are* willing to incur considerable expense to lobby against free trade.

Both the winners and losers weigh the benefits and costs. Those who gain from free trade weigh the benefit it brings against the cost of achieving it. Those who lose from free trade and gain from protection weigh the benefit of protection against the cost of maintaining it. Because protectionists have more at stake, they undertake a larger quantity of political lobbying than do the free traders.

Compensating Losers

If, in total, the gains from free international trade exceed the losses, why don't those who gain compensate those who lose so that everyone is in favour of free trade?

Some compensation does take place. When the North American Free Trade Agreement (NAFTA) was entered into with the United States and Mexico, the United States created a fund to support and retrain U.S. workers who lost their jobs as a result of the new trade agreement. During NAFTA's first six months, only 5,000 workers applied for benefits under this scheme. The losers from international trade are also compensated indirectly through the normal unemployment compensation arrangements. But only limited attempts are made to compensate those who lose.

The main reason why full compensation is not attempted is that the costs of identifying all the losers and estimating the value of their losses would be enormous. Also, it would never be clear whether a person who has fallen on hard times is suffering because of free trade or for other reasons that might be largely under her or his control. Furthermore, some people who look like losers at one point in time might, in fact, end up gaining. The young autoworker who loses his job in Windsor and gets a job on Alberta's oil patch might resent the loss of work and the need to move. But a year later, looking back on events, he counts himself fortunate. And his kids are delighted to be living in Calgary.

Because we don't in general compensate the losers from free international trade, protectionism is a popular and permanent feature of our national economic and political life and discussion.

◢ ◼ REVIEW QUIZ

1 What are the infant-industry and dumping arguments for protection? Are they correct?

2 Can protection save jobs and the environment and prevent workers in developing countries from being exploited?

3 What is offshore outsourcing? Who benefits from it and who loses?

4 What are the main reasons for imposing a tariff?

5 Why don't the winners from free trade win the political argument?

You can work these questions in Study Plan 31.3 and get instant feedback.

———————————————— MyEconLab ◆

◆ We end this chapter with *Reading Between the Lines* on pp. 766–767, where we apply what you've learned by looking at the effects of a Canadian tariff on imports of ski jackets from China.

A Tariff on Ski Jackets

Why This Ski Jacket Still Costs More Here

Toronto Star
January 22, 2011

A Karbon brand ski jacket made in China for a company in Toronto costs more to buy in Canada than in the United States. ...

The gap has closed in the three years since the dollar first hit parity with its U.S. counterpart, but only by about 10 percent, says Hugh Schure, president of Schure Sports, the Toronto-based designer of Karbon brand skiwear. ...

A Karbon ski jacket from its Graphite Alpha Stretch collection that will retail next fall for $550 in Canada will be priced at just $450 in the United States, a $100 difference.

Schure blames Canada's higher tariffs, which can add as much as 16 percent to the cost of importing an outwear item into Canada compared to the United States.

That additional cost gets magnified as the jacket makes its way through the supply chain, as first the wholesaler and then the retailer add their markups, he explained.

"An item with a $50 price difference at wholesale is going to have a $100 difference at retail," he said.

On items with lower tariffs, such as inner layers worn under jackets, cross-border prices are closer to parity, he says.

His manufacturer's suggested retail price on a Karbon brand mid-layer jacket, called the Force, will be $110 in Canada this fall and $100 in the United States, he said. ...

Reprinted with permission—Torstar Syndication Services.

ESSENCE OF THE STORY

- Canada's tariff on outwear is 16 percent higher than the equivalent U.S. tariff.

- The additional cost gets magnified by higher wholesale and retail costs in Canada.

- A Karbon brand Graphite Alpha Stretch ski jacket made in China for a Toronto company costs $550 in Canada and $450 in the United States.

- A Karbon brand mid-layer Force ski jacket costs $110 in Canada and $100 in the United States.

ECONOMIC ANALYSIS

- This news article illustrates the effects of a tariff on a Canadian import and also illustrates the distinction between the importer–manufacturer market for a good and the retail market for the good.

- The tariff on imports of ski jackets into Canada is 18 percent of the value imported.

- We don't know the price that Schure Sports pays the Chinese manufacturer, but it is probably about $140, in which case, the import duty is 18 percent of this price—a tariff of approximately $25—and the supply price of a jacket to Canada is $165.

- If you buy the same jacket from a Canadian retailer, you pay $450.

- To buy the same jacket from a U.S. retailer, you'd pay $450 to the store and an import duty of 18 percent on this price—a tariff of $81—a total of $531.

- How does a $140 jacket become a $450 jacket in the United States and a $550 jacket in Canada?

- The answer is that a jacket in a store is a combination of a jacket and the retail (and wholesale and transportation) services that make it available to the final buyer. The retail price includes the costs of these additional services (and the profit on them).

- Figure 1 shows the market for Karbon Graphite Alpha Stretch ski jackets in Canada. Without the tariff, the jacket would be retailed for $525. With the tariff, the price is $550.

- Figure 2 shows the market for Karbon Graphite Alpha Stretch ski jackets if they are bought by Canadians from U.S. stores. The jacket is supplied in retail stores for $450 and at that price, quantity C would be bought. But with a tariff of $81 per jacket, the quantity bought is B.

- The retail (and wholesale and transportation) markets in the United States are more competitive than those in Canada, and this fact accounts for most of the lower price in the United States.

- Would Canadians buy their jackets in Canada or the United States? Most likely the answer is in Canada. The price difference of $19 per jacket is probably not enough to justify the additional time and effort needed to make a purchase in the United States.

- A Canadian importer might decide to smuggle (avoid paying customs duty), but that illegal transaction incurs the cost of breaking the law.

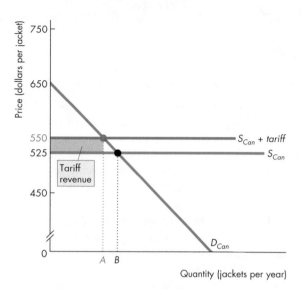

Figure 1 Canadians Buy Ski Jackets in Canada

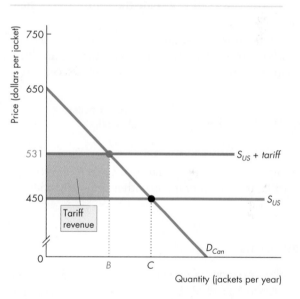

- Notice that the price to a Canadian buyer is similar regardless of where the jacket is bought. Hugh Schure's suggestion that "additional cost gets magnified as the jacket makes its way through the supply chain, as first the wholesaler and then the retailer add their markups" isn't convincing because it doesn't explain why the costs get magnified. Market forces and the $81 tariff on an imported ski jacket by a Canadian consumer is what drives the Canadian retail price to $550.

◆◼ SUMMARY

Key Points

How Global Markets Work (pp. 752–755)

- Comparative advantage drives international trade.
- If the world price of a good is lower than the domestic price, the rest of the world has a comparative advantage in producing that good and the domestic country gains by producing less, consuming more, and importing the good.
- If the world price of a good is higher than the domestic price, the domestic country has a comparative advantage in producing that good and gains by producing more, consuming less, and exporting the good.
- Compared to a no-trade situation, in a market with imports, consumers gain, producers lose, but with free international trade the gains exceed the losses.
- Compared to a no-trade situation, in a market with exports, consumers lose, producers gain, but with free international trade the gains exceed the losses.

Working Problems 1 to 11 will give you a better understanding of how global markets work.

International Trade Restrictions (pp. 756–760)

- Countries restrict international trade by imposing tariffs, import quotas, and other import barriers.

- Trade restrictions raise the domestic price of imported goods, lower the quantity imported, make consumers worse off, make producers better off, and damage the social interest.

Working Problems 12 to 21 will give you a better understanding of international trade restrictions.

The Case Against Protection (pp. 761–765)

- Arguments that protection is necessary for infant industries and to prevent dumping are weak.
- Arguments that protection saves jobs, allows us to compete with cheap foreign labour, is needed to penalize lax environmental standards, and prevents exploitation of developing countries are flawed.
- Offshore outsourcing is just a new way of reaping gains from trade and does not justify protection.
- Trade restrictions are popular because protection brings a small loss per person to a large number of people and a large gain per person to a small number of people. Those who gain have a stronger political voice than those who lose and it is too costly to identify and compensate losers.

Working Problem 22 will give you a better understanding of the case against protection.

Key Terms

Doha Development Agenda (Doha Round), 758
Dumping, 761
Exports, 752
General Agreement on Tariffs and Trade (GATT), 757
Import quota, 758
Imports, 752

Infant-industry argument, 761
Offshore outsourcing, 763
Offshoring, 763
Outsourcing, 763
Rent seeking, 765
Tariff, 756
World Trade Organization (WTO), 758

SCAN THIS

STUDY PLAN PROBLEMS AND APPLICATIONS

MyEconLab ◆ You can work Problems 1 to 22 in Chapter 31 Study Plan and get instant feedback.

How Global Markets Work (Study Plan 31.1)

Use the following information to work Problems 1 to 3.

Canada produces both lumber and wine, it exports lumber, and it imports wine. The rest of the world imports Canadian lumber and exports wine to Canada.

1. a. If Canada did not trade with the rest of the world, compare the equilibrium prices of lumber and wine in Canada with the world prices of lumber and wine.
   b. Does Canada or the rest of the world have a comparative advantage in producing lumber? Does Canada or the rest of the world have a comparative advantage in producing wine?

2. a. Compare the quantities of wine that Canadian wineries produce and that Canadians buy with and without trade with the rest of the world.
   b. Compare the quantities of lumber that the rest of the world produces and that it buys with and without trade with Canada.

3. What are the gains from the trade in lumber and wine between Canada and the rest of the world?

Use the following information to work Problems 4 to 6.

Wholesalers of roses (the firms that supply your local flower shop with roses for Valentine's Day) buy and sell roses in containers that hold 120 stems. The table provides information about the North American wholesale market for roses. The demand schedule is the wholesalers' demand and the supply schedule is the North American rose growers' supply.

Price (dollars per container)	Quantity demanded	Quantity supplied
	(millions of containers per year)	
100	15	0
125	12	2
150	9	4
175	6	6
200	3	8
225	0	10

Wholesalers can buy roses at auction in Aalsmeer, Holland, for $125 per container.

4. a. Without international trade, what would be the price of a container of roses and how many containers of roses a year would be bought and sold in North America?
   b. At the price in your answer to part (a), does North America or the rest of the world have a comparative advantage in producing roses?

5. If North American wholesalers buy roses at the lowest possible price, how many do they buy from local growers and how many do they import?

6. Draw a graph to illustrate the North American wholesale market for roses. Show the market equilibrium with no international trade and the market equilibrium with free trade. Mark the quantity of roses produced by local growers, the quantity imported, and the total quantity bought.

Use the following news clip to work Problems 7 and 8.

Underwater Oil Discovery to Transform Brazil into a Major Exporter

A huge underwater oil field discovered late last year has the potential to transform Brazil into a sizable exporter. Fifty years ago, Petrobras was formed as a trading company to import oil to support Brazil's growing economy. Two years ago, Brazil reached its long-sought goal of energy self-sufficiency.

Source: *International Herald Tribune*, January 11, 2008

7. Describe Brazil's comparative advantage in producing oil and explain why its comparative advantage has changed.

8. a. Draw a graph to illustrate the Brazilian market for oil and explain why Brazil was an importer of oil until a few years ago.
   b. Draw a graph to illustrate the Brazilian market for oil and explain why Brazil may become an exporter of oil in the near future.

Use the following news clip to work Problems 9 and 10.

Postcard: Bangalore. Hearts Set on Joining the Global Economy, Indian IT Workers Are Brushing Up on Their Interpersonal Skills

The huge number of Indian workers staffing the world's tech firms and call centres possess cutting-edge technical knowledge, but their interpersonal and communication skills lag far behind. Enter Bangalore's finishing schools.

Source: *Time*, May 5, 2008

9. a. What comparative advantages does this news clip identify?

   b. Using the information in this news clip, what services do you predict Bangalore (India) exports and what services do you predict it imports?

10. Who will gain and who will lose from the trade in services predicted in the news clip?

11. Use the information on the North American wholesale market for roses in Problem 4 to

   a. Explain who gains and who loses from free international trade in roses compared to a situation in which North Americans buy only roses grown locally.

   b. Explain why there is a net gain from international trade.

International Trade Restrictions (Study Plan 31.2)

Use the information on the North American wholesale market for roses in Problem 4 to work Problems 12 to 17.

12. If a tariff of $25 per container is imposed on imports of roses, what happens to the price of roses in North America, the quantity of roses bought, the quantity produced locally, and the quantity imported?

13. If a tariff of $25 per container is imposed on imports of roses, explain who gains and who loses from this tariff.

14. Draw a graph to illustrate the effect of the tariff on domestic consumers and producers and the tariff revenue collected by the government.

15. If an import quota of 5 million containers is imposed on roses, what happens to the price of roses in North America, the quantity of roses bought, the quantity produced locally, and the quantity imported?

16. If an import quota of 5 million containers is imposed on roses, explain who gains and who loses from the import quota.

17. If an import quota of 5 million containers is imposed on roses, explain why society loses.

Use the following news clip to work Problems 18 and 19.

Car Sales Go Up as Prices Tumble

Car affordability in Australia is now at its best in 20 years, fuelling a surge in sales as prices tumble. In 2000, Australia cut the tariff to 15 percent and on January 1, 2005, it cut the tariff to 10 percent.

Source: *Courier Mail*, February 26, 2005

18. Explain who gains and who loses from the lower tariff on imported cars.

19. Draw a graph to show how the price of a car, the quantity of cars bought, the quantity of cars produced in Australia, and the quantity of cars imported into Australia changed.

Use the following news clip to work Problems 20 and 21.

Why the World Can't Afford Food

As [food] stocks dwindled, some countries placed export restrictions on food to protect their own supplies. This in turn drove up prices, punishing countries—especially poor ones—that depend on imports for much of their food.

Source: *Time*, May 19, 2008

20. a. What are the benefits to a country from importing food?

   b. What costs might arise from relying on imported food?

21. If a country restricts food exports, what effect does this restriction have in that country on the price of food, the quantity of food it produces, the quantity of food it consumes, and the quantity of food it exports?

The Case Against Protection (Study Plan 31.3)

22. **Chinese Tire Maker Rejects U.S. Charge of Defects**

   U.S. regulators ordered the recall of more than 450,000 faulty tires. The Chinese tire producer disputed the allegations and hinted that the recall might be an effort by foreign competitors to hamper Chinese exports to the United States. Mounting scrutiny of Chinese-made goods has fuelled worries among U.S. regulators, corporations, and consumers about the risks associated with many products imported from China.

   Source: *International Herald Tribune*, June 26, 2007

   a. What does the information in the news clip imply about the comparative advantage of producing tires in the United States and China?

   b. Could product quality be a valid argument against free trade?

   c. How would the product-quality argument against free trade be open to abuse by domestic producers of the imported good?

ADDITIONAL PROBLEMS AND APPLICATIONS

MyEconLab ◆ You can work these problems in MyEconLab if assigned by your instructor.

These problems can be worked in MyEconLab if assigned by your instructor.

How Global Markets Work

23. Suppose that the world price of eggs is $1 a dozen, Canada does not trade internationally, and the equilibrium price of eggs in Canada is $3 a dozen. Canada then begins to trade internationally.
    a. How does the price of eggs in Canada change?
    b. Do Canadians buy more or fewer eggs?
    c. Do Canadian egg farmers produce more or fewer eggs?
    d. Does Canada export or import eggs and why?
    e. Would employment in the Canadian egg industry change? If so, how?

24. Suppose that the world price of steel is $100 a tonne, India does not trade internationally, and the equilibrium price of steel in India is $60 a tonne. India then begins to trade internationally.
    a. How does the price of steel in India change?
    b. How does the quantity of steel produced in India change?
    c. How does the quantity of steel bought by India change?
    d. Does India export or import steel and why?

25. A semiconductor is a key component in your laptop, cell phone, and iPod. The table provides information about the market for semiconductors in Canada.

Price (dollars per unit)	Quantity demanded	Quantity supplied
	(billions of units per year)	
10	25	0
12	20	20
14	15	40
16	10	60
18	5	80
20	0	100

Producers of semiconductors can get $18 a unit on the world market.

a. With no international trade, what would be the price of a semiconductor and how many semiconductors a year would be bought and sold in Canada?
b. Does Canada have a comparative advantage in producing semiconductors?

26. **Act Now, Eat Later**

The hunger crisis in poor countries has its roots in U.S. and European policies of subsidizing the diversion of food crops to produce biofuels such as corn-based ethanol. That is, doling out subsidies to put the world's dinner into the gas tank.

Source: *Time*, May 5, 2008

a. What is the effect on the world price of corn of the increased use of corn to produce ethanol in the United States and Europe?
b. How does the change in the world price of corn affect the quantity of corn produced in a poor developing country with a comparative advantage in producing corn, the quantity it consumes, and the quantity that it either exports or imports?

Use the following news clip to work Problems 27 and 28.

South Korea Agrees on Terms to Lift Eight-Year Ban on Canada Beef Imports

South Korea agrees to lift the ban on beef imports from Canada, which was imposed after the outbreak of mad-cow disease in 2003. Before the ban, South Korea was the fourth-biggest market for Canadian beef, with exports valued at C$50 million a year.

Source: Bloomberg, June 28, 2011

27. a. Explain how South Korea's import ban on Canadian beef affected beef producers and consumers in South Korea.
    b. Draw a graph of the market for beef in South Korea to illustrate your answer to part (a).

28. a. Assuming that South Korea is the only importer of Canadian beef, explain how South Korea's import ban affected Canadian beef producers and consumers.
    b. Draw a graph of the Canadian market for beef to illustrate your answer to part (a).

International Trade Restrictions

Use the following information to work Problems 29 to 31.

Before 1995, trade between Canada and Mexico was subject to tariffs. In 1995, Mexico joined NAFTA and all Canadian and Mexican tariffs have gradually been removed.

29. Explain how the price that Canadians pay for goods from Mexico and the quantity of Canadian imports from Mexico have changed. Who are the winners and who are the losers from this free trade?

30. Explain how the quantity of Canadian exports to Mexico and the Canadian government's tariff revenue from trade with Mexico have changed.

31. Suppose that in 2008, tomato growers in Ontario lobby the Canadian government to impose an import quota on Mexican tomatoes. Explain who in Canada would gain and who would lose from such a quota.

Use the following information to work Problems 32 and 33.

Suppose that in response to huge job losses in the Canadian textile industry, the Government of Canada imposes a 100 percent tariff on imports of textiles from China.

32. Explain how the tariff on textiles will change the price that Canadians pay for textiles, the quantity of textiles imported, and the quantity of textiles produced in Canada.

33. Explain how the Canadian and Chinese gains from trade will change. Who in Canada will lose and who will gain?

Use the following information to work Problems 34 and 35.

With free trade between Australia and Canada, Australia would export beef to Canada. But Canada imposes an import quota on Australian beef.

34. Explain how this quota influences the price that Canadian consumers pay for beef, the quantity of beef produced in Canada, and the Canadian and the Australian gains from trade.

35. Explain who in Canada gains from the quota on beef imports and who loses.

The Case Against Protection

36. **Trading Up**

    The cost of protecting jobs in uncompetitive sectors through tariffs is high: Saving a job in the sugar industry costs American consumers $826,000 in higher prices a year; saving a dairy industry job costs $685,000 per year; and saving a job in the manufacturing of women's handbags costs $263,000.

    Source: *The New York Times*, June 26, 2006

    a. What are the arguments for saving the jobs mentioned in this news clip?

    b. Explain why these arguments are faulty.

    c. Is there any merit to saving these jobs?

Economics in the News

37. After you have studied *Reading Between the Lines* on pp. 766–767, answer the following questions.

    a. What is the distinction between a good (such as a ski jacket) and wholesale and retail services?

    b. When an imported good has a tariff imposed on it, does the tariff apply to the manufacturer's price, the wholesale price, or the retail price of the item?

    c. Why are Canadian retail services less efficient than U.S. retail services? Can these services be traded internationally?

    d. Draw a graph to illustrate the effects of removing the tariff on ski jackets.

    e. What is Mr. Schure's explanation for the price gap between Canada and the United States?

    f. Draw a graph to illustrate the effects of removing the tariff on ski jackets if Mr. Schure's explanation for the price gap between Canada and the United States is correct.

38. **E.U. Agrees Trade Deal with South Korea**

    Italy has dropped its resistance to a E.U. trade agreement with South Korea, which will wipe out $2 billion in annual duties on E.U. exports. Italians argued that the agreement, which eliminates E.U. duties on South Korean cars, would put undue pressure on its own automakers.

    Source: *The Financial Times*, September 16, 2010

    a. What is a free-trade agreement? What is its aim?

    b. Explain how a tariff on E.U. car imports changes E.U. production of cars, purchases of cars, and imports of cars.

    c. Illustrate your answer to part (b) with an appropriate graphical analysis.

    d. Explain who wins and who loses from the move to free trade in cars.

    e. Explain why Italian automakers opposed cuts in car import tariffs.

Tradeoffs and Free Lunches

A policy tradeoff arises if, in taking an action to achieve one goal, some other goal must be forgone. The Bank of Canada wants to avoid a rise in the inflation rate and a rise in the unemployment rate. But if the Bank of Canada raises the interest rate to curb inflation, it might lower expenditure and increase unemployment. The Bank of Canada faces a short-run tradeoff between inflation and unemployment.

A policy free lunch arises if in taking actions to pursue one goal, some other (intended or unintended) goal is also achieved. The Bank of Canada wants to keep inflation in check and, at the same time, to boost the economic growth rate. If lower inflation brings greater certainty about the future and stimulates saving and investment, the Bank of Canada gets both lower inflation and faster real GDP growth. It enjoys a free lunch.

The first two chapters in this part have described the institutional framework in which fiscal policy (Chapter 29) and monetary policy (Chapter 30) are made, described the instruments of policy, and analyzed the effects of policy. The final chapter (Chapter 31) has explained international trade policy. This exploration of economic policy draws on almost everything that you learned in previous chapters.

These policy chapters serve as a capstone on your knowledge of macroeconomics and draw together all the strands in your study of the previous chapters.

Milton Friedman, whom you meet below, has profoundly influenced our understanding of macroeconomic policy, especially monetary policy.

Milton Friedman *was born into a poor immigrant family in New York City in 1912. He was an undergraduate at Rutgers and a graduate student at Columbia University during the Great Depression. From 1977 until his death in 2006, Professor Friedman was a Senior Fellow at the Hoover Institution at Stanford University. But his reputation was built between 1946 and 1983, when he was a leading member of the "Chicago School," an approach to economics developed at the University of Chicago and based on the views that free markets allocate resources efficiently and that stable and low money supply growth delivers macroeconomic stability.*

Friedman has advanced our understanding of the forces that determine macroeconomic performance and clarified the effects of the quantity of money. For this work, he was awarded the 1977 Nobel Prize for Economic Science.

By reasoning from basic economic principles, Friedman (along with Edmund S. Phelps, the 2006

Inflation is always and everywhere a monetary phenomenon.

MILTON FRIEDMAN
The Counter-Revolution in Monetary Theory

Economics Nobel Laureate) predicted that persistent demand stimulation would not increase output but would cause inflation.

When output growth slowed and inflation broke out in the 1970s, Friedman seemed like a prophet, and for a time, his policy prescription, known as monetarism, was embraced around the world.

Pierre, why did you become an economist and what attracted you to macroeconomics?

As an undergraduate at McGill University in Montreal I was majoring in mathematics. I was especially interested in statistics and I enrolled in an econometrics course. The econometrics lecturer emphasized how statistical tools could be used to help us understand economic phenomena. I became fascinated by the sheer breadth and scope of the economic phenomena that could be studied with econometric tools. I was particulary impressed by that range of macroeconomic questions that could be studied. After taking that econometrics course, I was hooked and I resolved to take economics in graduate school.

You've specialized in the study of monetary policy: How would you describe the most important principles that you and other economists have discovered for the conduct of monetary policy?

After much research I have come to the conclusion that monetary policy can help smooth business cycle fluctuations in the short to medium term (say around 2–3 years) but not beyond.

Consistently good monetary policy can lead to desirable economic outcomes with low and predictable inflation. Canada's monetary policy during the period of inflation targeting is an example of the achievemment of good outcomes with good policy.

> **The clear and convincing communication of monetary policy decisions [is] vital.**

Similarly, consistently bad monetary policy can lead to disastrous economic outcomes with hyperinflation, perhaps, the single best example of monetary policy that has utterly failed.

The clear and convincing communication of monetary policy decisions plays an important role in the achievement of good policy outcomes, although its vital importance is difficult to demonstrate.

The past few years have been extraordinary for macroeconomic performance and policy. What do we know right now [in October 2011] about the causes of the global financial crisis of 2007 and 2008?

Four failings led to the global financial crisis. First, there is little doubt that policymakers failed to properly supervise the financial sector, so many large banks were permitted to operate with more risk and

leverage than was safe. Second, the enormous growth of the so-called shadow banks was ignored. Third, beyond these two primary sources, there is some truth to the argument that both policymakers and the public more generally became complacent about underlying imbalances—large debts both inside and among nations—that were building around the world. Finally, fundamental flaws in the design of some institutions were ignored.

Can you provide an example of institution design flaws?

The European Central Bank comes to mind. It was not designed to act as a lender of last resort to member countries about to default on their sovereign debt. But with the serious debt situation in Greece and the threat of more countries following

> **The European Central Bank ... not designed to act as lender of last resort to member countries about to default on their sovereign debt.**

Pierre Siklos is Professor of Economics and Director of the Viessmann European Research Centre at Wilfrid Laurier University in Waterloo, Ontario. He was an undergraduate at McGill University in Montreal, where he was born, and a graduate student at the University of Western Ontario and Carleton University, where he received his PhD in 1981.

Professor Siklos is a macroeconomist who studies inflation, central banks, and financial markets. His work is data driven and he uses statistical methods to uncover the mechanisms at work. His research is published in a variety of international journals.

He has been a visiting scholar at universities around Europe and North America, Australia, and New Zealand. Pierre is a member of the C.D. Howe Institute's Monetary Policy Council.

Michael Parkin and Robin Bade talked with Pierre Siklos about his work and about the problems facing Canada today.

the same path, the European Central Bank has been placed in the uncomfortable position of having to hold the debt of euro area countries that may well default.

The failure of the European Stability and Growth Pact, which aimed at preventing euro area members from engaging in excessively loose fiscal policy, is a prime culprit for this state of affairs.

Why did the global financial crisis lead to a global recession and a particularly severe recession in the United States?

What translated a financial crisis into a recession was the collapse of asset prices, particularly house prices. Unlike earlier crises, a significant correction in asset prices, especially in the area of housing, is leading to a slow recovery that can take years to show results.

However, it is unclear whether the public, or even financial markets, have the patience to wait out the necessary adjustments until normal economic growth resumes.

What have we learned as a consequence of the recent crisis about stabilization policy?

A successful stabilization policy must have clearly laid out objectives, it has to be credible, and monetary and fiscal policies must act in concert with each other. It is far from obvious that all of these objectives have been met. Indeed, while fiscal stimulus on a global scale may well have avoided a much worse outcome—say a second Great Depression—a sensible plan to return fiscal policy to a more neutral state is one that seems to have eluded politicians.

This failure of fiscal policy planning is the source of Europe's current problems and could become an even bigger problem for the United States.

Canada's size and openness to international trade and investment make us vulnerable to shocks emanating from the global economy and more particularly from the United States. Can Canada do anything to insulate its real GDP growth rate from that of the United States?

In the short term I believe the answer is yes. Indeed, we have continued to outperform the United States along many macroeconomic indicators. In the medium to long term it is difficult to see how Canada, or most countries for that matter, can escape the effects of a struggling U.S. economy.

> ... sound fiscal and monetary policies are the key to achieving maximum insulation from U.S. economic fluctuations.

Our robust resources sector and sound fiscal and monetary policies are the key to achieving maximum insulation from U.S. economic fluctuations.

We have pursued a successful inflation targeting regime for several years and have achieved remarkably steady and predictable inflation. Our larger neighbour has not adopted inflation targeting and instead pursues a so-called dual mandate of stabilizing inflation and unemployment. Can Canada count on continuing to insulate its inflation rate from that of the United States?

If one believes in the insulating properties of a flexible exchange rate, the answer is a resounding yes. However, it also helps to have all of the macroeconomic fundamentals in good order—namely an appropriate monetary policy, a fiscal policy that is unlikely to shake individual or investor confidence, and regulatory institutions that adequately supervise the financial sector. It is no accident that Canada has adopted a flexible exchange rate strategy for much of its existence. Less than flexible exchange rates have been the exception rather than the rule since Confederation. It has proven to be the right exchange rate regime for our small, open economy.

If you were Mark Carney, what would you now [in October 2011] be doing to sustain recovery and sustain low inflation?
If the financial crisis of 2008–2009 signals a fundamental structural shift in the economy, there is little that monetary policy can do to improve the macroeconomic situation. Rather it is the task of the fiscal authorities to create an environment to sustain adequate economic growth.

> **What Carney can do to restore confidence is to explain … the circumstance under which interest rates will return to normal …**

What Carney can do to restore confidence is to explain as clearly as possible the circumstance under which interest rates will return to normal as well as stress that low and stable inflation remains a goal that both the Bank of Canada and the federal government aspire to.

The global financial crisis has created another policy objective for central banks: financial system stability. So far, no consensus has emerged about the policies that might achieve this goal.

Carney might also consider trying to exert a little more influence abroad—after all, he is Chairman of the Bank for International Settlements' Committee on the Global Financial System (CGFS)—to ensure that the authorities of other countries enact sensible policies, something that, as of October 2011, appears to be lacking.

If you were Stephen Harper, what would you now be doing to sustain recovery and create more jobs?
Ensure that the fiscal policy in place is adequate, that the tax system encourages innovation and investment, and that the federal government and the provinces pay more than lip service in their attempts to coordinate policies. Too much reliance on so-called tax expenditures, a politician's favourite tool, may help with re-election prospects but they likely do little to encourage economic growth on a consistent basis.

> **Ensure that … the tax system encourages innovation and investment …**

Since a form of autonomy has proved successful in improving the quality of monetary policy, perhaps the Prime Minister could ask whether certain elements of fiscal policy could be decided by an autonomous fiscal council. This might be a way of dealing with the tensions that currently exist between the Parliamentary Budget Officer and the government. Several noted academics have proposed several interesting variants on the idea of a fiscal council.

More generally, as the Canadian economy undergoes yet another structural shift, it may be time to rethink the balance between individual and corporate tax burdens as well as how tax revenues are raised between income and wealth taxes versus taxes on goods and services. Just as imbalances have built up in the world economy, incentives become easily misplaced in a tax system that is static and does not reflect changes in economic structure.

What advice do you have for a student who is just starting to study economics? Is it a good choice of major? What subjects go well with it?
Remember that the technical aspects of economics that scare away many potential students interested in the subject represent a means to an end and not an end in itself. Ultimately, a successful economist must remain curious about the world around him or her, and the mathematical and graphical devices favoured by most economists are designed to focus on the critical aspects of an economic problem that requires some explanation. By all means, read the quality financial press as the study of economics will eventually permit you to critically assess good from bad economic advice or opinion. Also keep in mind that macroeconomics especially will undergo some profound changes in the coming years as economists and policymakers attempt to draw the correct lessons from recent events.

Above full-employment equilibrium A macroeconomic equilibrium in which real GDP exceeds potential GDP. (p. 634)

Absolute advantage A person has an absolute advantage if that person is more productive than another person. (p. 38)

Aggregate demand The relationship between the quantity of real GDP demanded and the price level. (p. 628)

Aggregate planned expenditure The sum of planned consumption expenditure, planned investment, planned government expenditure on goods and services, and planned exports minus planned imports. (p. 648)

Aggregate production function The relationship between real GDP and the quantity of labour when all other influences on production remain the same. (p. 523)

Allocative efficiency A situation in which goods and services are produced at the lowest possible cost and in the quantities that provide the greatest possible benefit. We cannot produce more of any good without giving up some of another good that we *value more highly*. (p. 33)

Automatic fiscal policy A fiscal policy action that is triggered by the state of the economy with no action by the government. (p. 714)

Autonomous expenditure The sum of those components of aggregate planned expenditure that are not influenced by real GDP. Autonomous expenditure equals the sum of investment, government expenditure, exports, and the autonomous parts of consumption expenditure and imports. (p. 652)

Autonomous tax multiplier The change in equilibrium expenditure and real GDP that results from a change in autonomous taxes divided by the change in autonomous taxes. (p. 670)

Balanced budget A government budget in which receipts and outlays are equal. (p. 705)

Balanced budget multiplier The change in equilibrium expenditure and real GDP that results from equal changes in government expenditure and lump-sum taxes divided by the change in government expenditure. (p. 671)

Balance of payments accounts A country's record of international trading, borrowing, and lending. (p. 607)

Bank rate The interest rate that the Bank of Canada charges big banks on loans. (p. 731)

Below full-employment equilibrium A macroeconomic equilibrium in which potential GDP exceeds real GDP. (p. 635)

Benefit The benefit of something is the gain or pleasure that it brings and is determined by preferences. (p. 8)

Bond A promise to make specified payments on specified dates. (p. 545)

Bond market The market in which bonds issued by firms and governments are traded. (p. 545)

Budget deficit A government's budget balance that is negative—outlays exceed receipts. (p. 705)

Budget surplus A government's budget balance that is positive—receipts exceed outlays. (p. 705)

Business cycle The periodic but irregular up-and-down movement of total production and other measures of economic activity. (p. 475)

Canadian interest rate differential The Canadian interest rate minus the foreign interest rate. (p. 599)

Canadian official reserves The government's holding of foreign currency. (p. 607)

Capital The tools, equipment, buildings, and other constructions that businesses use to produce goods and services. (p. 4)

Capital accumulation The growth of capital resources, including *human capital*. (p. 36)

Capital and financial account A record of foreign investment in a coun-

try minus its investment abroad. (p. 607)

Central bank A bank's bank and a public authority that regulates the nation's depository institutions and conducts monetary policy, which means it adjusts the quantity of money in circulation and influences interest rates. (p. 572)

Ceteris paribus Other things being equal—all other relevant things remaining the same. (p. 22)

Chained-dollar real GDP A measure of real GDP derived by valuing production at the prices of both the current year and previous year and linking (chaining) those prices back to the prices of the reference base year. (p. 484)

Chained price index for consumption (CPIC) An index of the prices of all the items included in consumption expenditure in GDP. It is the ratio of nominal consumption expenditure to real consumption expenditure. (p. 504)

Change in demand A change in buyers' plans that occurs when some influence on those plans other than the price of the good changes. It is illustrated by a shift of the demand curve. (p. 58)

Change in supply A change in sellers' plans that occurs when some influence on those plans other than the price of the good changes. It is illustrated by a shift of the supply curve. (p. 63)

Change in the quantity demanded A change in buyers' plans that occurs when the price of a good changes but all other influences on buyers' plans remain unchanged. It is illustrated by a movement along the demand curve. (p. 61)

Change in the quantity supplied A change in sellers' plans that occurs when the price of a good changes but all other influences on sellers' plans remain unchanged. It is illustrated by a movement along the supply curve. (p. 64)

Chartered bank A private firm, chartered under the Bank Act of 1992 to receive deposits and make loans. (p. 571)

Classical The description of a macro-economist who believes that the economy is self-regulating and always at full employment. (p. 638)

Classical growth theory A theory of economic growth based on the view that the growth of real GDP per person is temporary and that when it rises above subsistence level, a population explosion eventually brings it back to subsistence level. (p. 531)

Comparative advantage A person or country has a comparative advantage in an activity if that person or country can perform the activity at a lower opportunity cost than anyone else or any other country. (p. 38)

Competitive market A market that has many buyers and many sellers, so no single buyer or seller can influence the price. (p. 56)

Complement A good that is used in conjunction with another good. (p. 59)

Consumer Price Index (CPI) An index that measures the average of the prices paid by urban consumers for a fixed basket of consumer goods and services. (p. 501)

Consumption expenditure The total payment for consumer goods and services. (p. 469)

Consumption function The relationship between consumption expenditure and disposable income, other things remaining the same. (p. 648)

Core inflation rate The inflation rate excluding volatile elements (food and fuel). (p. 504)

Cost-push inflation An inflation that results from an initial increase in costs. (p. 680)

Crawling peg An exchange rate that follows a path determined by a decision of the government or the central bank and is achieved in a similar way to a fixed exchange rate. (p. 605)

Creditor nation A country that during its entire history has invested more in the rest of the world than other countries have invested in it. (p. 609)

Crowding-out effect The tendency for a government budget deficit to raise the real interest rate and decrease investment. (p. 556)

Currency The notes and coins held by individuals and businesses. (p. 569)

Currency drain ratio The ratio of currency to deposits. (p. 576)

Current account A record of receipts from exports of goods and services, payments for imports of goods and services, net interest income paid abroad, and net transfers received from abroad. (p. 607)

Cycle The tendency for a variable to alternate between upward and downward movements. (p. 483)

Cyclical surplus or deficit The actual surplus or deficit minus the structural surplus or deficit. (p. 714)

Cyclical unemployment The higher than normal unemployment at a business cycle trough and the lower than normal unemployment at a business cycle peak. (p. 497)

Debtor nation A country that during its entire history has borrowed more from the rest of the world than other countries have lent it. (p. 609)

Deflation A persistently falling price level. (p. 500)

Demand The entire relationship between the price of the good and the quantity demanded of it when all other influences on buyers' plans remain the same. It is illustrated by a demand curve and described by a demand schedule. (p. 57)

Demand curve A curve that shows the relationship between the quantity demanded of a good and its price when all other influences on consumers' planned purchases remain the same. (p. 58)

Demand for loanable funds The relationship between the quantity of loanable funds demanded and the real interest rate when all other influences on borrowing plans remain the same. (p. 550)

Demand for money The relationship between the quantity of real money demanded and the nominal interest rate when all other influences on the amount of money that people wish to hold remain the same. (p. 579)

Demand-pull inflation An inflation that starts because aggregate demand increases. (p. 678)

Depository institution A financial firm that takes deposits from households and firms. (p. 571)

Depreciation The decrease in the value of a firm's capital that results from wear and tear and obsolescence. (p. 470)

Desired reserve ratio The ratio of reserves to deposits that banks *plan* to hold. (p. 576)

Direct relationship A relationship between two variables that move in the same direction. (p. 16)

Discounting The calculation we use to convert a future amount of money to its present value. (p. 432)

Discouraged worker A marginally attached worker who has stopped looking for a job because of repeated failure to find one. (p. 495)

Discretionary fiscal policy A fiscal action that is initiated by an act of Parliament. (p. 714)

Disposable income Aggregate income minus taxes plus transfer payments. (pp. 630, 648)

Doha Development Agenda (Doha Round) Negotiations held in Doha, Qatar, to lower tariff barriers and quotas that restrict international trade in farm products and services. (p. 758)

Dumping The sale by a foreign firm of exports at a lower price than the cost of production. (p. 761)

Economic growth The expansion of production possibilities. (p. 36)

Economic growth rate The annual percentage change in real GDP. (p. 518)

Economic model A description of some aspect of the economic world that includes only those features of the world that are needed for the purpose at hand. (p. 10)

Economics The social science that studies the *choices* that individuals, businesses, governments, and entire societies make as they cope with *scarcity* and the *incentives* that influence and reconcile those choices. (p. 2)

Efficiency A situation in which the available resources are used to produce goods and services at the lowest possible cost and in quantities that give the greatest value or benefit. (p. 5)

Employment-to-population ratio The percentage of people of working age who have jobs. (p. 495)

Entrepreneurship The human resource that organizes the other three factors of production: labour, land, and capital. (p. 4)

Equilibrium expenditure The level of aggregate expenditure that occurs when aggregate *planned* expenditure equals real GDP. (p. 654)

Equilibrium price The price at which the quantity demanded equals the quantity supplied. (p. 66)

Equilibrium quantity The quantity bought and sold at the equilibrium price. (p. 66)

Excess reserves A bank's actual reserves minus its desired reserves. (p. 576)

Exchange rate The price at which one currency exchanges for another in the foreign exchange market. (p. 594)

Expansion A business cycle phase between a trough and a peak—a period in which real GDP increases. (p. 475)

Exports The goods and services that we sell to people in other countries. (pp. 470, 752)

Factors of production The productive resources used to produce goods and services. (p. 3)

Federal budget The annual statement of the outlays and revenues of the Government of Canada, together with the laws and regulations that approve and support those outlays and revenues. (p. 704)

Final good An item that is bought by its final user during the specified time period. (p. 468)

Financial capital The funds that firms use to buy physical capital. (p. 544)

Financial institution A firm that operates on both sides of the market for financial capital. It borrows in one market and lends in another. (p. 546)

Firm An economic unit that hires factors of production and organizes those factors to produce and sell goods and services. (p. 41)

Fiscal policy The use of the federal budget, by setting and changing tax rates, making transfer payments, and purchasing goods and services, to achieve macroeconomic objectives such as full employment, sustained economic growth, and price level stability. (pp. 630, 704)

Fiscal stimulus The use of fiscal policy to increase production and employment. (p. 714)

Fixed exchange rate An exchange rate the value of which is determined by a decision of the government or the central bank and is achieved by central bank intervention in the foreign exchange market to block the unregulated forces of demand and supply. (p. 604)

Flexible exchange rate An exchange rate that is determined by demand and supply in the foreign exchange market with no direct intervention by the central bank. (p. 604)

Foreign currency The money of other countries, regardless of whether that money is in the form of notes, coins, or bank deposits. (p. 594)

Foreign exchange market The market in which the currency of one country is exchanged for the currency of another. (p. 594)

Frictional unemployment The unemployment that arises from normal labour turnover—from people entering and leaving the labour force and from the ongoing creation and destruction of jobs. (p. 497)

Full employment A situation in which the unemployment rate equals the natural unemployment rate. At full employment, there is no cyclical unemployment—all unemployment is frictional and structural. (p. 497)

Full-employment equilibrium A macroeconomic equilibrium in which real GDP equals potential GDP. (p. 635)

GDP deflator An index of the prices of all the items included in GDP. It is the ratio of nominal GDP to real GDP. (p. 504)

General Agreement on Tariffs and Trade (GATT) An international agreement signed in 1947 to reduce tariffs on international trade. (p. 757)

Goods and services The objects that people value and produce to satisfy human wants. (p. 3)

Government debt The total amount that the government has borrowed. It equals the sum of past budget deficits minus the sum of past budget surpluses. (p. 707)

Government expenditure Goods and services bought by government. (p. 470)

Government expenditure multiplier The quantitative effect of a change in government expenditure on real GDP. It is calculated as the change in real GDP that results from a change in government expenditure divided by the change in government expenditure. (pp. 670, 715)

Government sector balance An amount equal to net taxes minus government expenditure on goods and services. (p. 610)

Gross domestic product (GDP) The market value of all final goods and services produced within a country during a given time period. (p. 468)

Gross investment The total amount spent on purchases of new capital and on replacing depreciated capital. (pp. 470, 544)

Human capital The knowledge and skill that people obtain from education, on-the-job training, and work experience. (p. 3)

Hyperinflation An inflation rate of 50 percent a month or higher that grinds the economy to a halt and causes a society to collapse. (p. 500)

Implicit rental rate The firm's opportunity cost of using its own capital. (p. 228)

Import quota A restriction that limits the maximum quantity of a good that may be imported in a given period. (p. 1758)

Imports The goods and services that we buy from people in other countries. (pp. 470, 752)

Incentive A reward that encourages an action or a penalty that discourages one. (p. 2)

Incentive system A method of organizing production that uses a market-like mechanism inside the firm. (p. 233)

Income effect The effect of a change in income on buying plans, other things remaining the same. (p. 213)

Income elasticity of demand The responsiveness of demand to a change in income, other things remaining the same. It is calculated as the percentage change in the quantity demanded divided by the percentage change in income. (p. 92)

Indifference curve A line that shows combinations of goods among which a consumer is *indifferent*. (p. 207)

Individual transferable quota (ITQ) A production limit that is assigned to an individual who is free to transfer (sell) the quota to someone else. (p. 402)

Induced expenditure The sum of the components of aggregate planned expenditure that vary with real GDP. Induced expenditure equals consumption expenditure minus imports. (p. 652)

Inelastic demand A demand with a price elasticity between 0 and 1; the percentage change in the quantity demanded is less than the percentage change in price. (p. 86)

Infant-industry argument The argument that it is necessary to protect a new industry to enable it to grow into a mature industry that can compete in world markets. (p. 761)

Inferior good A good for which demand decreases as income increases. (p. 60)

Inflation A persistently rising price level. (p. 500)

Inflationary gap An output gap in which real GDP exceeds potential GDP. (p. 634)

Inflation rate targeting A monetary policy strategy in which the central bank makes a public commitment to achieve an explicit inflation rate and to explain how its policy actions will achieve that target. (p. 728)

Interest The income that capital earns. (p. 4)

Interest rate parity A situation in which the rates of return on assets in different currencies are equal. (p. 602)

Intermediate good An item that is produced by one firm, bought by another firm, and used as a component of a final good or service. (p. 468)

Inverse relationship A relationship between variables that move in opposite directions. (p. 17)

Investment The purchase of new plant, equipment, and buildings, and additions to inventories. (p. 470)

Job A contract for the trade of labour services. (p. 416)

Keynesian A macroeconomist who believes that left alone, the economy would rarely operate at full employment and that to achieve full employment, active help from fiscal policy and monetary policy is required. (p. 638)

Keynesian cycle theory A theory that fluctuations in investment driven by fluctuations in business confidence—summarized by the phrase "animal spirits"—are the main source of fluctuations in aggregate demand. (p. 688)

Labour The work time and work effort that people devote to producing goods and services. (p. 3)

Labour force The sum of the people who are employed and who are unemployed. (p. 493)

Labour force participation rate The percentage of the working-age population who are members of the labour force. (p. 494)

Labour productivity The quantity of real GDP produced by an hour of labour. (p. 527)

Labour union An organized group of workers that aims to increase the wage rate and influence other job conditions. (p. 422)

Laffer curve The relationship between the tax rate and the amount of tax revenue collected. (p. 713)

Land The "gifts of nature" that we use to produce goods and services. (p. 3)

Law of demand Other things remaining the same, the higher the price of a good, the smaller is the quantity demanded of it; the lower the price of a good, the larger is the quantity demanded of it. (p. 57)

Law of diminishing returns As a firm uses more of a variable factor of production with a given quantity of the fixed factor of production, the marginal product of the variable factor of production eventually diminishes. (p. 255)

Law of supply Other things remaining the same, the higher the price of a good, the greater is the quantity supplied of it. (p. 62)

Legal monopoly A market in which competition and entry are restricted by the granting of a public franchise, government license, patent, or copyright. (p. 300)

Lender of last resort The Bank of Canada is the lender of last resort—depository institutions that are short of reserves can borrow from the Bank of Canada. (p. 572)

Limit pricing The practice of setting the price at the highest level that inflicts a loss on an entrant. (p. 355)

Linear relationship A relationship between two variables that is illustrated by a straight line. (p. 16)

Loanable funds market The aggregate of all the individual markets in which households, firms, governments, banks, and other financial institutions borrow and lend. (p. 548)

Long run The time frame in which the quantities of *all* factors of production can be varied. (p. 252)

Long-run aggregate supply The relationship between the quantity of real GDP supplied and the price level when the money wage rate changes in step with the price level to maintain full employment. (p. 624)

Long-run average cost curve The relationship between the lowest attainable average total cost and output when the firm can change both the plant it uses and the quantity of labour it employs. (p. 263)

Long-run macroeconomic equilibrium A situation that occurs when real GDP equals potential GDP—the economy is on its long-run aggregate supply curve. (p. 632)

Long-run market supply curve A curve that shows how the quantity supplied in a market varies as the market price varies after all the possible adjustments have been made, including changes in each firm's plant and the number of firms in the market. (p. 287)

Long-run Phillips curve A curve that shows the relationship between inflation and unemployment when the actual inflation rate equals the expected inflation rate. (p. 685)

Lorenz curve A curve that graphs the cumulative percentage of income or wealth against the cumulative percentage of households. (p. 441)

Low-income cut-off The income level below which a family normally spends 63.6 percent or more of its income on food, shelter, and clothing. (p. 445)

M1 A measure of money that consists of currency held by individuals and businesses plus chequable deposits owned by individuals and businesses. (p. 569)

M2 A measure of money that consists of M1 plus all other deposits—non-chequable deposits and fixed time deposits. (p. 569)

Macroeconomics The study of the performance of the national economy and the global economy. (p. 2)

Margin When a choice is made by comparing a little more of something with its cost, the choice is made at the margin. (p. 9)

Marginal benefit The benefit that a person receives from consuming one more unit of a good or service. It is measured as the maximum amount that a person is willing to pay for one more unit of the good or service. (pp. 9, 34)

Marginal benefit curve A curve that shows the relationship between the marginal benefit of a good and the quantity of that good consumed. (p. 34)

Marginal cost The *opportunity cost* of producing *one* more unit of a good or service. It is the best alternative forgone. It is calculated as the increase in total cost divided by the increase in output. (pp. 9, 33, 258)

Marginal cost pricing rule A rule that sets the price of a good or service equal to the marginal cost of producing it. (p. 313)

Marginal external benefit The benefit from an additional unit of a good or service that people other than the consumer enjoy. (p. 379)

Marginal external cost The cost of producing an additional unit of a good or service that falls on people other than the producer. (p. 375)

Marginal private benefit The benefit from an additional unit of a good or service that the consumer of that good or service receives. (p. 379)

Marginal private cost The cost of producing an additional unit of a good or service that is borne by the producer of that good or service. (p. 375)

Marginal product The increase in total product that results from a one-unit increase in the variable input, with all other inputs remaining the same. It is calculated as the increase in total product divided by the increase in the variable input employed, when the quantities of all other inputs remain the same. (p. 253)

Marginal propensity to consume The fraction of a *change* in disposable income that is spent on consumption. It is calculated as the *change* in consumption expenditure divided by the *change* in disposable income. (p. 650)

Marginal propensity to import The fraction of an increase in real GDP that is spent on imports. It is calculated as the *change* in imports divided by the *change* in real GDP, other things remaining the same. (p. 651)

Marginal propensity to save The fraction of a *change* in disposable income that is saved. It is calculated as the *change* in saving divided by the *change* in disposable income. (p. 650)

Marginal rate of substitution The rate at which a person will give up good *y* (the good measured on the *y*-axis) to get an additional unit of good *x* (the good measured on the *x*-axis) while at the same time remaining indifferent (remaining on the same indifference curve) as the quantity of *x* increases. (p. 208)

Marginal revenue The change in total revenue that results from a one-unit increase in the quantity sold. It is calculated as the change in total revenue divided by the change in quantity sold. (p. 274)

Marginal social benefit The marginal benefit enjoyed by society—by the consumer of a good or service (marginal private benefit) plus the marginal benefit enjoyed by others (marginal external benefit). (p. 379)

Marginal social cost The marginal cost incurred by the producer and by everyone else on whom the cost falls—by society. It is the sum of marginal private cost and marginal external cost. (p. 375)

Marginal utility The *change* in total utility resulting from a one-unit increase in the quantity of a good consumed. (p. 181)

Marginal utility per dollar The marginal utility from a good that results from spending one more dollar on it. It is calculated as the marginal utility from the good divided by its price. (p. 184)

Marginally attached worker A person who currently is neither working nor looking for work but has indicated that he or she wants and is available for a job and has looked for work some time in the recent past. (p. 495)

Market Any arrangement that enables buyers and sellers to get information and to do business with each other. (p. 42)

Means of payment A method of settling a debt. (p. 568)

Microeconomics The study of the choices that individuals and businesses make, the way these choices interact in markets, and the influence of governments. (p. 2)

Monetarist A macroeconomist who believes that the economy is self-regulating and that it will normally operate at full employment, provided that monetary policy is not erratic and that the pace of money growth is kept steady. (p. 639)

Monetarist cycle theory A theory that fluctuations in both investment and consumption expenditure, driven by fluctuations in the growth rate of the quantity of money, are the main source of fluctuations in aggregate demand. (p. 688)

Monetary base The sum of Bank of Canada notes, coins, and depository institution deposits at the Bank of Canada. (p. 573)

Monetary policy The Bank of Canada conducts the nation's monetary policy by changing interest rates and adjusting the quantity of money. (p. 630)

Money Any commodity or token that is generally acceptable as a means of payment. (pp. 42, 568)

Money multiplier The ratio of the change in the quantity of money to the change in the monetary base. (p. 577)

Money price The number of dollars that must be given up in exchange for a good or service. (p. 56)

Mortgage A legal contract that gives ownership of a home to the lender in the event that the borrower fails to meet the agreed loan payments (repayments and interest). (p. 545)

Mortgage-backed security A type of bond that entitles its holder to the income from a package of mortgages. (p. 546)

Multiplier The amount by which a change in autonomous expenditure is magnified or multiplied to determine the change in equilibrium expenditure and real GDP. (p. 656)

National saving The sum of private saving (saving by households and businesses) and government saving. (p. 549)

Natural unemployment rate The unemployment rate when the economy is at full employment—natural unemployment as a percentage of the labour force. (p. 497)

Negative relationship A relationship between variables that move in opposite directions. (p. 17)

Neoclassical growth theory A theory of economic growth that proposes that real GDP per person grows because technological change induces an amount of saving and investment that makes capital per hour of labour grow. (p. 531)

Net borrower A country that is borrowing more from the rest of the world than it is lending to it. (p. 609)

Net exports The value of exports of goods and services minus the value of imports of goods and services. (pp. 470, 610)

Net investment The amount by which the value of capital increases—gross investment minus depreciation. (pp. 470, 544)

Net lender A country that is lending more to the rest of the world than it is borrowing from it. (p. 609)

Net taxes Taxes paid to governments minus cash transfers received from governments. (p. 548)

Net worth The market value of what a financial institution has lent minus the market value of what it has borrowed. (p. 547)

New classical A description of a macroeconomist who holds the view that business cycle fluctuations are the efficient responses of a well-functioning market economy bombarded by shocks that arise from the uneven pace of technological change. (p. 638)

New classical cycle theory A rational expectations theory of the business cycle in which the rational expectation of the price level, which is determined by potential GDP and *expected* aggregate demand, determines the money wage rate and the position of the *SAS* curve. (p. 688)

New growth theory A theory of economic growth based on the idea that real GDP per person grows because of the choices that people make in the pursuit of profit and that growth will persist indefinitely. (p. 532)

New Keynesian A macroeconomist who holds the view that not only is the money wage rate sticky but also that the prices of goods and services are sticky. (p. 639)

New Keynesian cycle theory A rational expectations theory of the business cycle that emphasizes the fact that today's money wage rates were negotiated at many past dates, which means that *past* rational expectations of the current price level influence the money wage rate and the position of the *SAS* curve. (p. 688)

Nominal GDP The value of the final goods and services produced in a given year valued at the prices that prevailed in that same year. It is a more precise name for GDP. (p. 473)

Nominal interest rate The number of dollars that a borrower pays and a lender receives in interest in a year expressed as a percentage of the number of dollars borrowed and lent. (p. 549)

Normal good A good for which demand increases as income increases. (p. 60)

Official settlements account A record of the change in official reserves, which are the government's holdings of foreign currency. (p. 607)

Offshore outsourcing A Canadian firm buys finished goods, components, or services from other firms in other countries. (p. 763)

Offshoring A Canadian firm hires foreign labour and produces in a foreign country or a Canadian firm buys finished goods, components, or services from firms in other countries. (p. 763)

Open market operation The purchase or sale of government securities—Treasury bills and bonds—by the Bank of Canada in the loanable funds market. (p. 573)

Operating band The target overnight loans rate plus or minus 0.25 percentage points. (p. 731)

Opportunity cost The highest-valued alternative that we must give up to get something. (pp. 8, 31)

Output gap The gap between real GDP and potential GDP. (pp. 498, 634)

Outsourcing A Canadian firm buys finished goods, components, or services from other firms in Canada or from firms in other countries. (p. 763)

Overnight loans rate The interest rate on overnight loans that the big banks make to each other. (p. 730)

Phillips curve A curve that shows a relationship between inflation and unemployment. (p. 684)

Positive relationship A relationship between two variables that move in the same direction. (p. 16)

Potential GDP The value of production when all the economy's labour, capital, land, and entrepreneurial ability are fully employed; the quantity of real GDP at full employment. (p. 474)

Preferences A description of a person's likes and dislikes and the intensity of those feelings. (pp. 8, 34)

Present value The amount of money that, if invested today, will grow to be as large as a given future amount when the interest that it will earn is taken into account. (p. 432)

Price level The average level of prices. (p. 500)

Private sector balance An amount equal to saving minus investment. (p. 610)

Production efficiency A situation in which goods and services are produced at the lowest possible cost. (p. 31)

Production possibilities frontier The boundary between the combinations of goods and services that can be produced and the combinations that cannot. (p. 30)

Purchasing power parity A situation in which the prices in two countries are equal when converted at the exchange rate. (p. 602)

Quantity demanded The amount of a good or service that consumers plan to buy during a given time period at a particular price. (p. 57)

Quantity supplied The amount of a good or service that producers plan to sell during a given time period at a particular price. (p. 62)

Quantity theory of money The proposition that in the long run, an increase in the quantity of money brings an equal percentage increase in the price level. (p. 582)

Rational choice A choice that compares costs and benefits and achieves the greatest benefit over cost for the person making the choice. (p. 8)

Rational expectation The best forecast possible, a forecast that uses all the available information. (p. 683)

Real business cycle theory A theory of the business cycle that regards random fluctuations in productivity as the main source of economic fluctuations. (p. 688)

Real exchange rate The relative price of Canadian-produced goods and services to foreign-produced goods and services. (p. 603)

Real GDP The value of final goods and services produced in a given year when valued at the prices of a reference base year. (p. 473)

Real GDP per person Real GDP divided by the population. (pp. 474, 518)

Real income A household's income expressed as a quantity of goods that the household can afford to buy. (p. 205)

Real interest rate The nominal interest rate adjusted to remove the effects of inflation on the buying power of money. It is approximately equal to the nominal interest rate minus the inflation rate. (p. 549)

Real wage rate The money (or nominal) wage rate divided by the price level. The real wage rate is the quantity of goods and services that an hour of labour earns. (p. 524)

Recession A business cycle phase in which real GDP decreases for at least two successive quarters. (p. 475)

Recessionary gap An output gap in which potential GDP exceeds real GDP. (p. 635)

Relative price The ratio of the price of one good or service to the price of another good or service. A relative price is an opportunity cost. (p. 56)

Rent The income that land earns. (p. 4)

Rent seeking The lobbying for special treatment by the government to create economic profit or to divert consumer surplus or producer surplus away from others. The pursuit of wealth by capturing economic rent. (p. 765)

Reserves A bank's reserves consist of notes and coins in its vaults plus its deposit at the Bank of Canada. (p. 571)

Ricardo-Barro effect The government budget, whether in surplus or deficit, has no effect on either the real interest rate or investment. (p. 556)

Rule of 70 A rule that states that the number of years it takes for the level of any variable to double is approximately 70 divided by the annual percentage growth rate of the variable. (p. 518)

Saving The amount of income that is not paid in taxes or spent on consumption goods and services. (p. 544)

Saving function The relationship between saving and disposable income, other things remaining the same. (p. 648)

Scarcity Our inability to satisfy all our wants. (p. 2)

Scatter diagram A graph that plots the value of one variable against the value of another variable for a number of different values of each variable. (p. 14)

Self-interest The choices that you think are the best ones available for you are choices made in your self-interest. (p. 5)

Settlements balances rate The target overnight loans rate minus 0.25 percentage points. (p. 731)

Short-run aggregate supply The relationship between the quantity of real GDP supplied and the price level when the money wage rate, the prices of other resources, and potential GDP remain constant. (p. 625)

Short-run macroeconomic equilibrium A situation that occurs when the quantity of real GDP demanded equals the quantity of real GDP supplied—at the point of intersection of the *AD* curve and the *SAS* curve. (p. 632)

Short-run Phillips curve A curve that shows the tradeoff between inflation and unemployment when the expected inflation rate and the natural unemployment rate are held constant. (p. 684)

Slope The change in the value of the variable measured on the *y*-axis divided by the change in the value of the variable measured on the *x*-axis. (p. 20)

Social interest Choices that are the best ones for society as a whole. (p. 5)

Stagflation The combination of inflation and recession. (pp. 637, 681)

Stock A certificate of ownership and claim to the firm's profits. (p. 546)

Stock market A financial market in which shares of stocks of corporations are traded. (p. 546)

Structural surplus or deficit The budget balance that would occur if the economy were at full employment and real GDP were equal to potential GDP. (p. 714)

Structural unemployment The unemployment that arises when changes in technology or international competition change the skills needed to perform jobs or change the locations of jobs. (p. 497)

Substitute A good that can be used in place of another good. (p. 59)

Supply The entire relationship between the price of a good and the quantity supplied of it when all other influences on producers' planned sales remain the same. It is described by a supply schedule and illustrated by a supply curve. (p. 62)

Supply curve A curve that shows the relationship between the quantity supplied of a good and its price when all other influences on producers' planned sales remain the same.(p. 62)

Supply of loanable funds The relationship between the quantity of loanable funds supplied and the real interest rate when all other influences on lending plans remain the same. (p. 551)

Tariff A tax that is imposed by the importing country when an imported good crosses its international boundary. (p. 756)

Tax multiplier The quantitative effect of a change in taxes on real GDP. It is calculated as the change in real GDP that results from a change in taxes divided by the change in taxes. (p. 716)

Tax wedge The gap between the before-tax and after-tax wage rates. (p. 711)

Technological change The development of new goods and of better ways of producing goods and services. (p. 36)

Time-series graph A graph that measures time (for example, years, quarters, or months) on the *x*-axis and the variable or variables in which we are interested on the *y*-axis. (p. 482)

Tradeoff A constraint that involves giving up one thing to get something else. (p. 8)

Trend The tendency for a variable to move in one general direction. (p. 483)

Unemployment rate The percentage of the people in the labour force who are unemployed. (p. 494)

Velocity of circulation The average number of times a dollar of money is used annually to buy the goods and services that make up GDP. (p. 582)

Wages The income that labour earns. (p. 4)

Wealth The value of all the things that people own—the market value of their assets—at a point in time. (pp. 442, 544)

Working-age population The total number of people aged 15 years and over. (p. 493)

World Trade Organization (WTO) An international organization that places obligations on its member countries to observe the GATT rules. (p. 758)

Note: Key terms and the pages on which they are defined are **bolded.** References to "*f*" denote a figure and "*t*" denote a table.

A

ability to pay, 58
above full-employment equilibrium, 634
absolute advantage, 38–39
Africa, 479, 521, 622, 760
age distribution of population, 497
aggregate demand, 628, 628–631, 628*f*
 see also AS-AD model
 changes in, 629–631, 631*f,* 662–663, 663*f*
 cost-push inflation, 681
 curve, 628
 demand-pull inflation, 678
 equilibrium expenditure, 662*f*
 expectations, 629–630
 fiscal policy, 630
 and fiscal stimulus, 715–716
 fluctuations in, 636–637, 636*f,* 638, 639
 long-run increase, 664–665
 monetary policy, 630
 overnight loans rate, change in, 736
 quantity of real GDP demanded, 628
 and real GDP, 648
 shifts of aggregate demand curve, 631
 short-run increase, 664
 substitution effects, 629
 wealth effect, 628–629
 world economy, 630–631
aggregate demand curve, 661–662
aggregate demand schedule, 628
aggregate expenditure, 470, 471, 471*f*
 algebra of, 668
 changes in, 662–663
 overnight loans rate, change in, 735
 and real GDP, 648, 651
aggregate expenditure curve, 653*f,* 658, 658*f,* 661, 668, 668*f*
aggregate income, 470, 472, 472*f*
aggregate labour market, 523–525
aggregate planned expenditure, 648, 652, 653*f*
aggregate production function, 523, 523*f,* 544
aggregate supply, 624–627
 see also AS-AD model
 changes in aggregate supply, 626–627
 cost-push inflation, 680

fiscal stimulus, 718
fluctuations in, 637, 637*f*
income taxes, effects of, 710–711, 710*f*
long-run aggregate supply, 624, 625*f*
money wage rate, changes in, 627, 627*f*
potential GDP, changes in, 626, 626*f*
quantity of real GDP supplied and price level, 624
response to fluctuations in aggregate demand, 638, 639
short-run aggregate supply, 625, 625*f*
aggregate supply-aggregate demand *(AS-AD)* model. *See AS-AD* model
Agricultural Revolution, 51
agriculture, 3, 3*f*
AIG, 547
allocative efficiency, 33–35
animal spirits, 551
appreciation of the dollar, 594, 601
arbitrage, 602
AS-AD model
 aggregate demand, 628–631, 636–637, 636*f*
 aggregate supply, 624–627, 637, 637*f*
 business cycle, 634–635, 635*f*
 economic growth, 633–634
 fluctuations in aggregate demand, 636–637, 636*f*
 fluctuations in aggregate supply, 637, 637*f*
 inflation, 633–634
 long-run macroeconomic equilibrium, 632–633, 633*f*
 macroeconomic schools of thought, 638–639
 macroeconomic trends and fluctuations, 632–637
 purpose of, 624, 632
 short-run macroeconomic equilibrium, 632, 632*f*
Asia, 522
Asian financial crisis, 7
Athey, Susan, 84–86
auction-based marketplace, 84–86
Australia, 479, 745
automatic fiscal policy, 714–715
automatic stimulus, 714
autonomous consumption, 648
autonomous expenditure, 652, 656
autonomous tax multiplier, 670, 670*f*
axes, 13

B

bailout loans, 7
balance of payments accounts, 607–609, **607**–609, 607*t*
 and exchange rates, 611
 individual's balance of payments account, 608–609
balance sheet of Bank of Canada, 573, 574
balanced budget, 705
balanced budget multiplier, 671, 671*f*
bank bailouts, 7
bank loans, 735
bank notes, 573
Bank of America, 547
Bank of Canada, 7, 516, 572–574, 630, 744–745
 see also central bank; monetary policy
 assets, 573
 balance sheet, 573, 574
 bank notes, issuer of, 573
 bank rate, 731
 banker to banks and government, 572
 consultations with government, 730
 economists, 730
 Governing Council, 729–730
 inflation fighting, 738–739
 inflation rate targeting, 728, 743, 775–776
 interest rate decision, 731
 joint statement with Government of Canada, 728
 lender of last resort, 572–573
 liabilities, 573
 monetary base, 573, 573*t,* 576
 monetary policy, responsibility for, 729–730
 monetary policy transmission, 733–740
 open market operation, 573–574, 574*f,* 580
 open market purchase, 573–574
 open market sale, 574–575, 576
 overnight loans rate, 730–731, 731*f,* 733–735
 recession, 729, 736–737, 736*f*
 settlement balances rate, 731–732
 Taylor rule, 743
Bank of Canada Act, 728, 730
Bank of England, 630
Bank of Montreal, 571
Bank of Nova Scotia, 571, 692
bank rate, 731

bank reserves. *See* reserves
bank runs, 741
banking system, 571–574
banks, 546
    see also depository institution
    bank bailouts, 7
    bank runs, 741
    banking system, 571–574
    in Canada, 571
    central bank, 572
    chartered bank, 571
        see also chartered bank
    deposit creation, 575–576
    desired currency holding, 576
    desired reserve ratio, 576, 586
    excess reserves, 576
    loans, 575–576
    monetary base, 576
    money creation, 575–577, 577*f*
Barro, Robert, 718, 719*f*
barter, 568
base year, 485
basis points, 731*n*
Bear Stearns, 492, 547
below full-employment equilibrium,
    635
benefit, 8
Bennenbroek, Nick, 560
Bernanke, Ben, 492, 584
Bhagwati, Jagdish, 10, 52–53
biased CPI, 503–504
bilateral free trade areas, 53–54
Billes, Alfred J., 42
Billes, John W., 42
Blas, Javier, 74*n*
Bombardier, 5, 761
bond, 545
bond market, 545–546
bond rate, 734
Boorstin, Daniel J., 83
borrowing, 557, 558*f*
borrowing costs, 572
Brazil, 45, 758
budget deficit, 555–556, 556*f,* **705,**
    705*f,* 707, 716
budget surplus, 555, 555*f,* **705,** 705*f,*
    707
business cycle, 475, 475*f,* 687–691
    AS-AD model, 634–635, 635*f*
    Canada, 634
    and growth, 691
    and inflation, 683
    Keynesian cycle theory, 688
    mainstream business cycle theory,
        687–688
    monetarist cycle theory, 688
    new classical cycle theory, 688
    new Keynesian cycle theory, 688
    real business cycle theory, 688–691,
        689*f,* 690*f*
    real GDP and unemployment,
        498–499
    turning points, 660
business inventories, 666–667
business investment, 666–667
buyers, 56

C

Caballero, Ricardo J., 700–702
caisses populaires, 546, 571
California, 71
Canada
    balance of payments accounts, 607*t*
    banks, 546
    budget deficit, 2011, 716
    business cycle, 634
    Canadian economy contracts, 640–641
    and China, gains from trade, 41
    consumption function, 651
    cost-push inflation, 682
    debtor nation, 609
    demand-pull inflation, 680
    economic growth, 520, 520*f,* 633
    economy, 480–481, 492
    ethanol production, 45
    exporting regional jets, 754
    farm products and services, 758
    federal budget. *See* federal budget
    global trade, 752
    health and safety regulations, 760
    Human Development Index (HDI),
        479
    importing T-shirts, 753
    income and expenditure, 2001-2010,
        14, 15*f*
    inflation, 633
    inflation rate targeting, 745
    investment, 549
    jobs growth, 506–507, 692–693
    money, 569–570
    money multiplier, 587
    most traded items, 752
    net borrower, 609
    net ;lender, 609
    pollution, 478
    production possibilities per person, 37
    real GDP per person, 520, 521
    recession, 475
    standard of living, 474*f*
    structural budget balance, 2011, 715
    structural unemployment, 498
    tariffs, 757
    unemployment benefits, 498
    unemployment rate, 515
    women in the work force, 477
Canadian dollar
    appreciation, 601
    change in demand, 599
    change in supply, 600, 600*f*
    demand curve, 596, 596*f*
    depreciation, 601
    exchange rate, 594, 595
    supply curve, 597, 597*f*
Canadian Food Inspection Agency, 760
Canadian interest rate differential, 599,
    600
Canadian official reserves, 607, 608
Canadian Tire, 41
capital, 4
    financial capital, 4, 544
    international capital mobility, 557
    and investment, 544, 545*f*
    physical capital, 544
    quantity of capital, 626
capital accumulation, 36
capital and financial account, 607, 608
capital gains, 544
capital losses, 544, 741
Carney, Mark, 480, 730, 744, 776
causation, 16
cause and effect, 10
Central America, 521, 700, 760
central bank, 572
    see also Bank of Canada; U.S. Federal
        Reserve
    extraordinary monetary stimulus,
        741–743
    foreign exchange market equilibrium,
        598
central planning, 41
ceteris paribus, **22**–23
chained-dollar real GDP, 484–485
chained price index for consumption
    (CPIC), 504
change in demand, 58–60, 59*f,* 60*t*
    aggregate demand, 629–631, 631*f*
    all possible changes, 72, 73*f*
    Canadian dollars, 599
    vs. change in quantity demanded,
        60–61, 61*f*
    credit, 60
    decrease in both demand and supply,
        72, 73*f*
    decrease in demand, 68

decrease in demand and increase in supply, 72, 73*f*
effects of, 68, 68*f*
expected future income, 60
expected future prices, 59–60
financial markets, 552–553, 553*f*
global loanable funds market, 558
income, 60
increase in both demand and supply, 72, 73*f*
increase in demand, 68
increase in demand and decrease in supply, 72, 73*f*
loanable funds, 550–551
money, 579, 579*f*
with no change in supply, 72, 73*f*
population, 60
preferences, 60
related goods, price of, 59
shift in demand curve, 61
change in supply, 63–64, 64*f*, 65*t*
aggregate supply, 626–627
all possible changes, 72, 73*f*
Canadian dollars, 600, 600*f*
vs. change in the quantity supplied, 64–65, 65*f*
decrease in both demand and supply, 72, 73*f*
decrease in supply, 70
decrease in supply and increase in demand, 72, 73*f*
effects of, 70, 70*f*
expected future prices, 64
financial markets, 552–553, 553*f*
global loanable funds market, 558
increase in both demand and supply, 72, 73*f*
increase in supply, 70
increase in supply and decrease in demand, 72, 73*f*
loanable funds, 551–552
with no change in demand, 72, 73*f*
prices of factors of production, 63
related goods, prices of, 63
shift in supply curve, 64
state of nature, 64
suppliers, number of, 64
technology, 64
change in the quantity demanded, 60–61, 61*f*
change in the quantity supplied, 64–65, 65*f*
chartered bank, 571
see also banks
liquid assets, 571

loans, 571–572
reserves, 571
securities, 571
sources and uses of funds, 572*t*
cheques, 570
Chicago School, 773
Chile, 700–701
China
and Canada, gains from trade, 41
carbon emissions, 6
central planning, 41
as developing nation, 536–537
Doha Round, 758
economic growth, 522
environmental standards, 762
exchange rate management, 605–606
fixed exchange rate, 604
global trade, 752
People's Bank of China, 605–606, 612–613
political freedom, 478
pollution, 478
purchasing power parity (PPP), 476
real GDP, 476, 476*f*
choice
benefit, 8
choosing at the margin, 9
and incentives, 9
making choices, 2
opportunity cost, 8–9
rational choice, 8
as tradeoff, 8
Chomsky, Noam, 53
CIBC, 571
circular flows
expenditure and income, 469–470, 469*f*, 549*f*
through markets, 42
Citigroup, 547
classical, 638
classical growth theory, 531
climate change, 6
coffee prices, 74–75
Colombia, 74
commodity substitution bias, 503
comparative advantage, 38–39, 752–754, 762
learning-by-doing, 761
national comparative advantage, 752
competitive market, 56
complement, 59, 63
compound interest, 518–519
conditional convergence, 620–621
consumer choice. *See* choice
consumer expenditure, 666–667

Consumer Price Index (CPI), 501–502, 501*f*, 502*t*
biased CPI, 503–504
commodity substitution bias, 503
core inflation rate, 504–505
CPI basket, 501–502, 501*f*
as inflation measure, 728
and inflation rate, 503*f*
new goods bias, 503
outlet substitution bias, 504
quality change bias, 503
consumption
autonomous consumption, 648
as function of real GDP, 651
induced consumption, 648
marginal propensity to consume, 650, 650*f*, 659
consumption expenditure, 469, 471, 648–649, 735
consumption function, 648–649, 649*f*, 651, 668
convergence to equilibrium, 655
Cooper, Sherry, 720
coordinates, 13
core inflation, 504–505, 505*f*
core inflation rate, 504–505
correlation, 16
cost-push inflation, 680–682, 681*f*, 682*f*
costs
borrowing costs, 572
marginal cost. *See* marginal cost
recession, 700
countervailing duties, 761
CPI basket, 501–502, 501*f*
crawling peg, 605–606
credit, 60
credit cards, 570
credit unions, 546, 571
creditor nation, 609
crowding-out effect, 556
crude oil, 69
Cuba, 41
currency, 569
currency drain ratio, 576, 741
current account, 607, 608
current account balance, 610
current account deficits, 608, 701–702
curve, 16
curved line, slope of, 21–22
cycle, 483
cyclical deficit, 714, 715*f*
cyclical surplus, 714, 715*f*
cyclical unemployment, 497

D

Darwin, Charles, 531
debt interest, 705
debtor nation, 609
decentralized coordination, 41–43
default risk, 552
deficits
    budget deficit, 555–556, 556f, 716
    current account deficits, 608
    cyclical deficit, 714, 715f
    structural deficit, 714, 715f
deflation, 500
demand, 57–61
    see also demand and supply model
    aggregate demand. *See* aggregate
        demand; *AS-AD* model
    for Canadian exports, 599
    change in demand. *See* change in
        demand
    change in quantity demanded, 60–61
    demand curve, 57–58, 58f
    demand schedule, 58, 58f
    in foreign exchange market, 595–596
    funds in global markets, 557–558
    global loanable funds market, 557–558
    for imports, 600
    law of demand, 57, 60t, 595–596
    for loanable funds, 550–551, 550f
    for money, 579
    quantity demanded, 57
demand and supply model
    all possible changes in demand and
        supply, 72, 73f
    coffee prices, 74–75
    demand. *See* demand
    market equilibrium, 66–67
    price, predicting changes in, 68–72
    quantity, predicting changes in, 68–72
    strawberry market, 71
    supply. *See* supply
demand curve, 57–58, 58f, 76
    Canadian dollars, 596, 596f
    movement along, 61, 61f
    shift of, 61
demand for loanable funds, 550–551,
    550f
demand for money, 579, 579f
demand-pull inflation, 678–680, 678f,
    679f
demand schedule, 58, 58f
depository institution, 571–572
    borrowing costs, 572
    borrowing short and lending long, 572
    economic benefits, 572
    functions of, 571–572

    liquidity, 572
    monitoring borrowers, cost of, 572
    pooled risk, 572
deposits, 569, 570, 575–576
depreciation, 470, 472
depreciation of the dollar, 594, 601
desired currency holding, 576
desired reserve ratio, 576, 586
developing countries
    environmental standards, 762–763
    exploitation of, 763
    international aid, 535
diminishing returns, 526, 531–532
direct relationship, 16, 17f
discouraged worker, 495
The Discoverers (Boorstin), 83
discretionary fiscal policy, 714
discretionary fiscal stimulus, 715–719
disposable income, 551, 630, 648
dissaving, 649
distribution of income. *See* income
    distribution
Doha Development Agenda (Doha
    Round), 54, 758
double coincidence of wants, 568
double counting, 468
double-dip recession, 480–481
dual mandate, 742–743
dumping, 761

E

Easterly, William, 622n
Eastern Europe, 521, 762
economic coordination, 41–43
economic data, graphs of, 13–16, 14f
economic forecasting, 719
economic growth, 36–37, 36f
    AS-AD model, 633–634
    basics of, 518–519
    Canada, 520, 520f, 633
    classical growth theory, 531
    cost of, 36
    empirical evidence on causes of, 534
    growth theories, 531–534
    influence son, 535t
    intellectual property rights, 528–529
    labour productivity, growth of,
        528–530
    Malthusian theory, 531, 534
    nation's economic growth, 37
    neoclassical growth theory, 531–532,
        620–621
    new growth theory, 532–534
    and opportunity cost, 36
    policies for faster growth, 534–535

    potential GDP, 523–528
    Rule of 70, 518–519, 519f
    sources of, 530f
    sustained growth, 518–519
    trends, 520–522
    world economy, 521–522, 521f
economic growth rate, 518
Economic Growth (Sala-i-Martin and
    Barro), 621
economic inequality, 622
economic instability, 7
economic model, 10, 16–19
economic revolution, 51–54
economic way of thinking, 8–9
economics, 2
    economic way of thinking, 8–9
    macroeconomics, 2
    microeconomics, 2
    as policy tool, 10
    scope of economics, 8, 51–54
    self interest *vs.* social interest, 5–7
    as social science tool, 10
    supply-side economics, 710–713
    two big economic questions, 3–7
    what, how and for whom, 3–4
education, quality of, 535
efficiency, 5
efficiency wage, 498
empirical evidence, 534
employment
    full employment, 497, 624
    full-employment equilibrium, 635
    inflation and deflation, 500
employment-to-population ratio, 495
entrepreneurship, 4
environmental issues
    climate change, 6
    environmental quality, 478
    global warming, 6
    greenhouse gas emissions, 6
    lax environmental standards, 762–763
    pollution, 478
environmental quality, 478
equal risk, 557
equations of straight lines, 24–25
equilibrium, 66, 66f
    above full-employment equilibrium,
        634
    below full-employment equilibrium,
        635
    convergence to equilibrium, 655
    equilibrium expenditure, 654–655,
        654f
    exchange rates, 598, 598f
    foreign exchange market, 598, 598f

full-employment equilibrium, 635
labour market equilibrium, 524–525, 524*f*
loanable funds market, 552, 552*f*
long-run macroeconomic equilibrium, 632–633, 633*f*
market equilibrium, 66–67, 77
in market with exports, 754*f*
in market with imports, 753*f*
money market, 580–581, 580*f*
with no international trade, 753*f*, 754*f*
price adjustments, 67
price as regulator, 66–67
real GDP, 663–665, 718
short-run macroeconomic equilibrium, 632, 632*f*
equilibrium expenditure, 654–655, 654*f*, 662*f*, 669, 669*f*
equilibrium price, 66
equilibrium quantity, 66, 86
equity, 5
see also fairness
Essays, Moral and Political (Hume), 513
ethanol production, 45, 45*f*
European Central Bank, 630, 774–775
European Stability and Growth Pact, 775
European Union, 53–54
carbon emissions, 6
Doha Round, 758
farm products and services, 758
financial markets, 560
health and safety regulations, 760
inflation rate targeting, 743
real GDP per person, 521
excess reserves, 576
exchange rate policy, 604–606
exchange rates, 594
and balance of payments, 611
Canadian interest rate differential, 599
change in demand for Canadian dollars, 599
change in supply of Canadian dollars, 600, 600*f*
changes in, 600
crawling peg, 605–606
equilibrium, 598, 598*f*
exchange rate policy, 604–606
expectations, 602
expected future exchange rate, 599, 600
fixed exchange rate, 604–605
flexible exchange rate, 604
fluctuations, 599–603, 734–735
fundamental influences, 602
as price, 594–595

purchasing power parity (PPP), 602
real exchange rate, 603
expansion, 475
expectations, 629–630
expected future exchange rate, 599, 600
expected future income, 60, 551
expected future prices, 59–60, 64
expected inflation, 682–683, 683*f*
expected profit effect, 596, 597
expected return, 602
expenditure
actual expenditure, planned expenditure, and real GDP, 653
aggregate expenditure, 470, 471, 471*f*
aggregate planned expenditure, 652
autonomous expenditure, 652, 656
circular flow of expenditure and income, 469–470, 469*f*, 549*f*
consumer expenditure, 666–667
consumption expenditure, 469, 471, 648–649
government expenditure, 470
induced expenditure, 652, 656
taxes on expenditure, 711
expenditure approach, 471, 471*f*, 471*t*
expenditure plans, 648
export subsidies, 760
exports, 470, 752
decrease in, 666–667
gains and losses from, 755
market with exports, 754*f*
net exports, 470, 471, 610–611, 610*t*, 735
world demand for Canadian exports, 599
exports effect, 596
extraordinary monetary stimulus, 741–743

F

factors of production, 3
capital, 4
entrepreneurship, 4
labour, 3
land, 3
market for, 56
prices of, 63
selling services of, 4
fair trade, 53
fairness, 5
Fannie Mae, 492, 547
farm inventories, 666–667
federal budget, 704–709, 704*t*
balanced budget, 705
budget balance, 705

budget deficit, 555–556, 556*f*, 705, 705*f*, 707
budget making, 704
budget surplus, 555, 555*f*, 705, 705*f*, 707
capital, 709
global perspective, 709
government debt, 707, 707*f*, 709
highlights of 2011 budget, 704–705, 704*t*
historical perspective, 705–707
final good, 468
finance, 544
financial assets, 548
financial capital, 4, 544
financial crises, 7, 702, 741–743, 741*t*, 775
financial innovation, 578
financial institutions, 546–548
banks, 546
caisses populaires, 546
credit unions, 546
depository institutions, 571–572
illiquidity, 547
insolvency, 547
insurance companies, 546–547
net worth, 547
pension funds, 546
trust and loan companies, 546
financial markets, 545–548
see also loanable funds market
bond market, 545–546
changes in demand and supply, 552–553, 553*f*
loan markets, 545
stock market, 546
financial property, 42
financing, 545
firm, 41
circular flow of expenditure and income, 469–470, 469*f*
and economic coordination, 41–42
fiscal policy, 630, 704
automatic fiscal policy, 714–715
discretionary fiscal policy, 714
expansionary fiscal policy, 717*f*
fiscal stimulus, 714–719
full employment and potential GDP, 710
income tax, effects of, 710–711, 710*f*
Laffer curve, 713, 713*f*
recessions, 630
Stephen Harper, 720–721
supply-side effects, 710–713, 718
tax wedge, 711

taxes and incentive to save and invest, 712
taxes on expenditure, 711
fiscal stimulus, 714–719
    and aggregate demand, 715–716
    and aggregate supply, 718
    discretionary fiscal stimulus, 715–719
    graphical illustration, 717–718
    magnitude of stimulus, 715
    multipliers, 718
    removal of, 718
    time lags, 719
    United States, 717
fixed exchange rate, 604–605
fixed prices, 648–651
Flaherty, Jim, 480
flexible exchange rate, 604
Florida, 71
food, opportunity cost of, 44–45
for whom (economic question), 4
forecasting
    economic forecasting, 719
    inflation, 683
foreign currency, 594
foreign exchange brokers, 594
foreign exchange market, 594–598
    Canadian dollar exchange rate, 594
    change in demand for Canadian dollars, 599
    change in supply of Canadian dollars, 600, 600*f*
    competitive market, 595, 601
    demand, 595–596
    demand curve for Canadian dollars, 596, 596*f*
    exchange rates. *See* exchange rates
    expected profit effect, 596, 597
    exports effect, 596
    imports effect, 597
    intervention, 605*f*
    law of demand, 595–596
    law of supply, 597
    market equilibrium, 598, 598*f*
    supply, 595, 597
    supply curve for Canadian dollars, 597, 597*f*
    trading currencies, 594
France, 521, 711
Freddie Mac, 492, 547
free lunches, 773
free trade, 53
frictional unemployment, 497
Friedman, Milton, 584, 773
fringe benefits, 4
full employment, 497, 624, 710

full-employment equilibrium, 635
full-employment quantity of labour, 626

G
G7 nations, 521
gains from trade, 38–40, 40*f*
    absolute advantage, 38–39
    achieving, 39–40
    comparative advantage, 38–39, 752–754
    international trade, 41
    net gain from trade, 755
Gates, Bill, 6
GDP. *See* gross domestic product (GDP)
GDP deflator, 504
General Agreement on Tariffs and Trade (GATT), 53, **757**
General Motors, 7, 41
General Theory of Employment, Interest, and Money (Keynes), 492, 699
genuine progress index (GPI), 479
Germany, 521, 560, 752
global loanable funds market, 557–559
    changes in demand and supply, 558
    demand and supply, 557–558
    international borrowing and lending, 557, 558*f*
    international capital mobility, 557
    real interest rates, 559
global markets
    see also international trade
    and aggregate demand, 630–631
    case against protection, 761–765
    how global markets work, 752–754, 752–755
    losers, 755
    net gain from trade, 755
    trade restrictions. *See* trade restrictions
    winners, 755
global monopoly, 761
global oil market, 69
global warming, 6
globalization, 5
goods
    complement, 59
    final good, 468
    inferior good, 60
    intermediate good, 468
    market for, 56
    normal good, 60
    public good, 532
    related goods, 59, 63
    substitute, 59
goods and services, 3
    see also goods

government
    banker to, 572
    budget deficit, 555–556, 556*f*
    budget surplus, 555, 555*f*
    circular flow of expenditure and income, 470
    debt interest, 705
    intervention. *See* government intervention
    in loanable funds market, 555–556
    local governments, 708
    outlays, 705, 706–707, 707*f*
    provincial governments, 708
    revenues, 704, 706, 706*f*
    transfer payments, 471, 705
government debt, 707, 707*f*
government expenditure, 470, 471, 705
government expenditure multiplier, 670, 670*f,* **715**
government intervention
    foreign exchange market, 605*f*
    international trade restrictions, 756–760
    tariffs, 756–758
    taxes. *See* taxes
Government of Canada, 546, 728, 729
government policies
    classical view of policy, 638
    economic growth, 534–535
    exchange rate policy, 604–606
    fiscal policy. *See* fiscal policy
    Keynesian view, 639
    monetarist policy, 639
    monetary policy. *See* monetary policy
    policy free lunches, 773
    policy tradeoff, 773
    stabilization policy, 775
government sector balance, 610, 611
graphs
    axes, 13
    breaks in the axes, 16
    causation, 16
    ceteris paribus, 22–23
    coordinates, 13
    correlation, 16
    curve, 16
    curved line, slope of, 21–22
    data, 13–16, 14*f*
    economic models, 16–19
    macroeconomics, 482–483
    making a graph, 13*f*
    misleading graphs, 16
    more than two variables, 22–23, 23*f*
    origin, 13
    ratio scale, 483, 483*f*

scatter diagram, 14–16, 15*f*
slope of a relationship, 20–22
straight line, slope of, 20–21, 20*f*
time-series graph, 482–483, 482*f*
unrelated variables, 19, 19*f*
variables moving in opposite
    directions, 17–18
variables moving in same direction,
    16–17
variables with maximum or minimum,
    18, 19*f*
when other things change, 23
x-axis, 13
x-coordinate, 13
y-axis, 13
y-coordinate, 13
Great Depression, 7, 492, 660, 720, 764
Great Moderation, 7
Greece, 560–561, 752
greenhouse gas emissions, 6
Greenspan, Alan, 551, 559
gross domestic product (GDP), 468
    aggregate expenditure, 470
    aggregate income, 470
    circular flow of expenditure and
        income, 469–470, 469*f*
    environmental quality, 478
    expenditure approach, 471, 471*f*, 471*t*
    final goods and services, 468
    in a given time period, 468
    "gross," meaning of, 470
    health and life expectancy, 478
    and household production, 477
    income approach, 472, 472*f*, 472*t*
    leisure time, 478
    limitations, 477–479
    market value, 468
    measurement of, 470, 471–473
    nominal GDP, 473
    political freedom, 478
    potential GDP, 474, 523–528
    produced within a country, 468
    real GDP. *See* real GDP
    security, 478
    social justice, 478
    statistical discrepancy, 472
    and underground economy, 477–478
gross investment, 470, 472, 544
gross profit, 470
growth theories, 531–534
    classical growth theory, 531
    Malthusian theory, 531, 534
    neoclassical growth theory, 531–532
    new growth theory, 532–534

H
Harper, Stephen, 720–721, 776
health, 478
health regulations, 760
Holt, Derek, 692
Hong Kong, 37, 522, 604
Hoover, Herbert, 720
household
    circular flow of expenditure and
        income, 469–470, 469*f*
    production, 477
housing market bubble, 554
how (economic question), 3–4
Howitt, Peter, 514–516
human capital, 3, 4*f*, 626
    capital accumulation, 36
    growth, 529
    lost human capital, 492–493
Human Development Index (HDI), 479
Hume, David, 513
Hydro One, 32
hyperinflation, 500

I
illiquidity, 547
impact lag, 719
import function, 651, 668
import quota, 758–760, 759*f*
imports, 470, 752
    Canadian demand for, 600
    gains and losses from, 755
    marginal propensity to import, 651,
        659
    market with imports, 753*f*
    multiplier, 659
imports effect, 597
incentive, 2, 9
income
    aggregate income, 470
    and change in demand, 60
    circular flow of expenditure and
        income, 469–470, 469*f*, 549*f*
    disposable income, 551, 630
    expected future income, 60, 551
    income effect, 57
    lost incomes, 492
    supplementary labour income, 472
income approach, 472, 472*f*, 472*t*
income distribution, 621
income effect, 57
income inequality. *See* economic
    inequality
income redistribution, 500
income taxes, 659, 710–711, 710*f*, 712
India, 6, 758

indirect tax, 472
individual's balance of payments account,
    608–609
induced consumption, 648
induced expenditure, 652, 656
Industrial Revolution, 51, 528
inequality. *See* economic inequality
infant-industry argument, 761
inferior good, 60
inflation, 500
    actual inflation, Canada, 728, 729*f*
    AS-AD model, 633–634
    Bank of Canada, role of, 738–739
    and business cycle, 683
    in Canada, 633
    core inflation, 504–505, 505*f*
    cost-push inflation, 680–682, 681*f*,
        682*f*
    demand-pull inflation, 678–680, 678*f*,
        679*f*
    expected inflation, 682–683, 683*f*
    forecasting inflation, 683
    high inflation *vs.* high price level, 503
    hyperinflation, 500
    inflation cycles, 678–683
    low inflation, pursuit of, 516
    money, effect on, 569
    Phillips curve, 684–686, 684*f*, 685*f*
    problem of, 500
    stagflation, 637, 681
    and unemployment, 684–686, 684*f*,
        685*f*
inflation cycles, 678–683
inflation rate
    and Consumer Price Index (CPI), 503*f*
    core inflation rate, 504–505
    measurement of, 502
inflation rate targeting, 728, 743,
    775–776
inflationary gap, 634
information-age economy, 6
Information Revolution, 6, 51
inputs, market for, 56
insolvency, 547
insurance companies, 546–547
Intel Corporation, 6
intellectual property, 42
intellectual property rights, 528–529
interest, 4
interest rate
    and asset prices, 548
    Bank of Canada's interest rate decision,
        731
    bank rate, 731

Canadian interest rate differential, 599, 600

changes in, 733–734

long-term bond rate, 734

long-term real interest rate, 735

nominal interest rate, 549, 578

overnight loans rate, 730–731, 731*f*, 733–735

real interest rate, 505, 549–550, 557, 712, 735

3-month Treasury bill rate, 734

interest rate parity, 602

intermediate good, 468

international aid, 535

international borrower, 557–558

international borrowing and lending, 557

international capital mobility, 557

International Coffee Organization, 74

international lender, 558

International Monetary Fund, 537, 560

international substitution effect, 661

international trade

see also global markets

comparative advantage, 752–754

drivers of, 752

and economic growth, 535

financing international trade, 607–611

today, 752

trade restrictions. *See* trade restrictions

trade wars, 764

intertemporal substitution effect, 629, 661

inventory investment, 666–667

inverse relationship, 17–18, 18*f*

investment, 470, 471

business investment, 666–667

Canada, 549

and capital, 544, 545*f*

gross investment, 470, 472, 544

income taxes, 712

inventory investment, 666–667

net investment, 470, 544

overnight loans rate, change in, 735

taxes and incentive to save and invest, 712

involuntary part-time rate, 494

Ireland, 573

irrational exuberance, 551

Italy, 521

J

Japan, 521, 536–537, 758

jobs growth, 506–507

Johnson, Harry, 52

JPMorgan Chase, 547

K

Keynes, John Maynard, 492, 551, 699

Keynesian, 638–639

Keynesian cycle theory, 688

Keynesian model

actual expenditure, planned expenditure, and real GDP, 653

aggregate planned expenditure, 652

algebra of, 668–671

consumption as function of real GDP, 651

consumption expenditure, 648–649

convergence to equilibrium, 655

equilibrium expenditure, 654–655, 654*f*

expenditure plans, 648

fixed prices, 648–651

import function, 651

marginal propensity to consume, 650, 650*f*

marginal propensity to save, 650, 650*f*

multiplier. *See* multiplier

real GDP with fixed price level, 652–655

saving plans, 648–649

slope and marginal propensities, 650

knowledge, 532

Korea, 522

Kowalczyk, Dariusz, 612

L

labour, 3

full-employment quantity of labour, 626

income from, 4

market for. *See* labour market

quality of labour, 3

supplementary labour income, 472

labour demand, 523–524

labour force, 493, 493*t*

labour force participation rate, 494–495, 495*f*

Labour Force Survey, 493

labour market

aggregate labour market, 523–525

equilibrium. *See* labour market equilibrium

indicators, 493–495

and potential GDP, 525*f*

real business cycle, 690*f*

slow recovery, 692–693

state of, 624

labour market equilibrium, 524–525, 524*f*

labour productivity, 527

growth of, 527–528, 527*f*

human capital growth, 529

physical capital growth, 529

preconditions for growth, 528–529

and real GDP, 527–528, 527*f*

technological advances, 529–530

labour supply, 524

growth, 525–526

income taxes, effect of, 711

Laffer, Arthur B., 713

Laffer curve, 713, 713*f*

Laidler, David, 10

land, 3

law-making lag, 719

law of demand, 57, 60*t*, 595–596

law of diminishing returns, 524

law of supply, 62, 65*t*, 597

Lazaridis, Mike, 4

learning-by-doing, 761

Lehman Brothers, 547

leisure time, 478

lender of last resort, 572–573

lending, 557, 558*f*

level playing field, 53

life expectancy, 478

linear equations, 24–25

linear relationship, 16–17

liquid assets, 571

liquidity, 572

loan markets, 545

loanable funds market, 548–553

see also financial markets

Bank of Canada and inflation, 738, 739*f*

Bank of Canada and recessions, 736–737, 737*f*

changes in demand and supply, 552–553, 553*f*

demand for loanable funds, 550–551, 550*f*

equilibrium, 552, 552*f*

funds that finance investment, 548–549

global loanable funds market, 557–559

government in, 555–556

housing bubble, 554

long-run growth of demand and supply, 553

real business cycle, 690*f*

real interest rate, 549–550

supply of loanable funds, 551–552, 551*f*

loans, 571–572, 575–576

local governments, 708

long and variable lags, 739–740

long run
    monetary policy, 745
    money market equilibrium, 580–581
    multiplier, 665*f*
    real exchange rate, 603
    transition from short run, 581
long-run aggregate supply, 624, 625*f*
long-run macroeconomic equilibrium,
    632–633, 633*f*
long-run Phillips curve, 685, 685*f*
long-term bond rate, 734
long-term real interest rate, 735
long-term unemployment, 496, 496*f*
Lucas, Robert E. Jr., 474, 700
Lucas wedge, 474, 475*f*

M
M1, 569–570
M2, 569–570
M1 multiplier, 577
M2 multiplier, 577
macroeconomics, 2
    classical view, 638
    fluctuations, 632–637, 699–702
    graphs, 482–483
    Keynesian view, 638–639
    monetarist, 639
    monitoring macroeconomic
        performance, 513–516
    new classical view, 638
    new Keynesian view, 639
    real variables, 505
    schools of thought, 638–639
    trends, 619–622, 632–637
mad cow disease (BSE), 760
mainstream business cycle theory,
    687–688
Malthus, Thomas Robert, 531
Malthusian theory, 531, 534
manufacturing, 3, 3*f*
margin, 9
marginal benefit, 9, 34, 34*f*
    ability to pay, 58
    and marginal cost, 35*f*
    and preferences, 34
    principle of decreasing marginal
        benefit, 34
    willingness to pay, 58
marginal benefit curve, 34, 34*f*
marginal cost, 9, 33
    and marginal benefit, 35*f*
    and production possibilities frontier,
        33, 33*f*
marginal propensity to consume, 650,
    650*f,* 659

marginal propensity to import, 651,
    659
marginal propensity to save, 650, 650*f*
marginally attached worker, 495
Maritimes, 498
market, 42
    buyers and sellers, 56
    circular flows, 42, 43*f*
    competitive market. *See* competitive
        market
    coordinating decisions, 42
    and economic coordination, 42
    with exports, 754*f*
    for factors of production, 56
    financial markets, 545–548
    global markets. *See* global markets
    for goods and services, 56
    with imports, 753*f*
    for inputs, 56
    money market, 578–581, 736, 738,
        738*f*
    and prices, 56
    for real GDP, 737, 737*f,* 738–739,
        739*f*
    for reserves, 732*f,* 736, 736*f,* 738,
        738*f*
market equilibrium, 66–67, 77
    see also equilibrium
market exchange rate, 476
market price, 472
market value, 468
Marshall, Alfred, 83
Marshall, Bob, 83
Marshall, Mary Paley, 83
maximum points, 18, 19*f*
means of payment, 568
medium of exchange, 568
Merrill Lynch, 547
Mexico, 762
microeconomics, 2
microloans, 530
Microsoft Corp., 6
minimum points, 18, 19*f*
minimum wage, and unemployment, 498
misallocated resources, 31
misleading graphs, 16
Mitsubishi, 547
model economy, 30
monetarist, 639
monetarist cycle theory, 688
monetary base, 573, 573*t,* 576
monetary policy, 630
    see also Bank of Canada
    aggregate demand, change in, 736
    bank loans, changes in, 735

    conduct of, 730–732
    effects of, 733–740
    exchange rate fluctuations, 734–735
    expenditure plans, 735
    extraordinary monetary stimulus,
        741–743
    inflation-control target, 728–729, 729*f*
    interest rate changes, 733–734
    long and variable lags, 739–740
    in long run, 745
    long-term real interest rate, 735
    loose links and unwanted outcomes,
        739–740
    monetary policy instrument, 730–731
    money, quantity of, 735
    objectives, 728–729
    operating band, 731
    overnight loans rate, 730–731, 731*f,*
        733–735
    overnight rate target, 731–732
    price level, change in, 736
    real GDP, change in, 736
    recessions, 630
    responsibility for, 729–730
    study of, 774
    transmission, 733–740
money, 42, 544, 568
    in Canada today, 569–570
    changes in demand for money, 579,
        579*f*
    changes in quantity, 735
    creation of, 575–577, 577*f*
    currency, 569
    demand for money, 579, 579*f*
    deposits, 569, 570
    and economic coordination, 42
    functions of, 568–569
    and inflation, 569
    M1, 569–570
    M2, 569–570
    medium of exchange, 568
    money multiplier, 577, 586–587
    official measures of money, 569–570
    quantity theory of money, 582–583
    in real business cycle theory, 691
    store of value, 569
    unit of account, 568–569, 568*t*
    velocity of circulation, 582
money market, 578–581
    Bank of Canada and inflation, 738,
        738*f*
    Bank of Canada and recessions, 736,
        736*f*
    changes in demand for money, 579,
        579*f*

demand for money, 579, 579*f*
equilibrium, 580–581, 580*f*
financial innovation, 578
influences on money holding, 578
long-run equilibrium, 580–581
nominal interest rate, 578
price level, 578
real GDP, 578
short-run equilibrium, 580
transition from short-run to long-run, 581
money multiplier, 577, 586–587
money price, 56
money wage rate, 627, 679
monopoly, global, 761
Moore, Gordon, 6
Morgan Stanley, 547
mortgage, 545
mortgage-backed security, 546, 547, 571
Multifibre Arrangement, 762
multiplier, 656, 657*f*
aggregate demand, 662–663
aggregate demand curve, 661–662
aggregate expenditure, 662–663
aggregate expenditure curve, 661
algebra of, 669, 669*f*
autonomous tax multiplier, 670, 670*f*
balanced budget multiplier, 671, 671*f*
basic idea of, 656
business cycle turning points, 660
equilibrium real GDP and price level, 663–665
fiscal stimulus, 718
government expenditure multiplier, 670, 670*f,* 715
in Great Depression, 660
greater than 1, 657
imports, 659
income taxes, 659
long run, 665*f*
money multiplier, 577, 586–587
multiplier effect, 656–657
multiplier process, 659, 659*f*
and price level, 661–665
short run, 664*f*
size of, 657
and slope of *AE* curve, 658, 658*f*
tax multiplier, 716
multiplier effect, 656–657

N

National Bank of Canada, 571
national comparative advantage, 752
National Income and Expenditure Accounts, 471, 472

national saving, 545, 549
national wealth, 545
natural resources, 3
see also land
natural selection, 531
natural unemployment rate, 497–498, 685–686, 685*f*
negative relationship, 17–18, 18*f,* 25, 25*f*
negative slope, 20*f*
neoclassical growth theory, 531–532, 620–621
net borrower, 609
net domestic income at market prices, 472
net exports, 470, 471, **610**–611, 610*t,* 735
net investment, 470, 544
net lender, 609
net taxes, 548
net worth, 547
new classical, 638
new classical cycle theory, 688
New Deal, 492
new goods bias, 503
new growth theory, 532–534
new Keynesian, 639
new Keynesian cycle theory, 688
New Zealand, 743
Newfoundland and Labrador, 498
Nike, 5
nominal GDP, 473, 473*t*
nominal interest rate, 549, 578
normal good, 60
normative statements, 10
North American Free Trade Agreement (NAFTA), 53–54, 760, 765
North Korea, 41
Northern Rock, 741
Norway, 479

O

Obama, Barack, 54, 718
off-shore outsourcing, 763–764
official settlements account, 607
offshoring, 763–764
oil, 69, 680*n*
Ontario, 498
open market operation, 573–574, 574*f,* 580
operating band, 731
opportunity cost, 8–9, **31**
and economic growth, 36
food, 44–45
highest-valued alternative foregone, 56
of increase in activity, 9

increasing, 32
and production possibilities, 31–32, 33*f*
ratio, 31
relative price, 56
Organization of Petroleum Exporting Countries (OPEC), 69
other factor incomes, 472
outlet substitution bias, 504
output gap, 498, 499*f,* **634**
outsourcing, 763
overnight loans rate, 730–731, 731*f,* 733–735

P

peak, 475
pension funds, 546
People's Bank of China, 605–606, 612–613
perpetual motion economy, 533, 533*f*
Petramala, Diana, 640
Petro-Canada, 546
Phelps, Edmund S., 773
Phillips, A.W., 684
Phillips curve, 684–686, 684*f,* 685*f*
long-run Phillips curve, 685, 685*f*
natural unemployment rate, changes in, 685–686, 685*f*
shifting short-run tradeoff, 686
short-run Phillips curve, 684, 684*f*
physical capital, 544
physical capital growth, 529
Poland, 478
policy advice, 10
policy goal, 10
political freedom, 478
pollution, and environmental quality, 478
pooled risk, 572
population, and change in demand, 60
population growth, 526, 526*f*
Malthusian theory, 531, 534
neoclassical theory, 531
Porter, Doug, 506
positive relationship, 16, 17*f,* 25
positive statements, 10
potential GDP, 474
aggregate labour market, 523–525
aggregate production function, 523, 523*f*
change in, 626, 626*f*
determination of, 523–525
and full employment, 710
growth of, 523–528
and labour market, 525*f*
labour productivity, 527–528, 527*f*

labour supply growth, 525–526
population growth, 526, 526*f*
tax wedge, 711
preferences, 8, 34, 34*f*
and change in demand, 60
and marginal benefit, 34
Prescott, Edward C., 711
price
adjustments, 67, 661
change in demand, effects of, 68, 68*f*
change in supply, effects of, 70, 70*f*
coffee prices, 74–75
equilibrium price. *See* equilibrium price
exchange rates as price, 594–595
expected future prices, 59–60, 64
factors of production, 63
fixed prices, 648–651
market price, 472
and markets, 56
minimum supply price, 63
money price, 56
predicting changes in, 68–72
as regulator, 66–67
related goods, 59
relative price, 56, 57
and shortage, 67
and surplus, 67
price indexes, 504
see also Consumer Price Index (CPI)
price level, 500
cost-push rise in, 681*f*
demand-pull rise in, 678*f*
and equilibrium real GDP, 663–665
fixed price level, 648, 652–655
high inflation *vs.* high price level, 503
and money holding, 578
multiplier, 661–665
overnight loans rate, change in, 736
and quantity of real GDP supplied, 624
real GDP with fixed price level, 652–655
substitution effect, 629
wealth effect, 628
principle of decreasing marginal benefit, 34
The Principles of Economics (Marshall), 83
private sector balance, 610, 611
production
household, 477
lost production, 492
production efficiency, 31
production possibilities frontier, 30, 30*f*, 523

allocative efficiency, 33–35
economic coordination, 41–43
economic growth, 36–37
gains from trade, 38–40, 40*f*
marginal benefit, 34, 34*f*
marginal cost, 33, 33*f*
and opportunity cost, 31–32, 33*f*
preferences, 34, 34*f*
production efficiency, 31
scarcity, 30–31
tradeoff, 31
productivity growth slowdown, 474–475
profit, 4
expected profit effect, 596
gross profit, 470
and technological change, 532
property rights, 42
and economic coordination, 42
financial property, 42
intellectual property, 42
real property, 42
prosperity, 532
protectionism. *See* trade restrictions
provincial governments, 708
public good, 532
purchasing power parity (PPP), 476, **602**

Q

quality change bias, 503
quantitative easing, 584
quantity
adjustments, 661
of capital, 626
equilibrium quantity, 66
full-employment quantity of labour, 626
predicting changes in, 68–72
quantity demanded, 57, 60–61, 61*f*
quantity supplied, 62, 624
quantity theory of money, 582–583
Quebec, 498
quota, import, 758–760, 759*f*

R

Rae, Bob, 720
Ragan, Christopher, 10
ratio scale, 483, 483*f*
rational choice, 8
rational expectation, 683
Reading Between the Lines
The Rising Opportunity Cost of Food, 44
Demand and Supply: The Price of Coffee, 74

Real GDP Forecasts in the Uncertain Economy of 2011, 480
Jobs Growth Lags Recovery, 506
Economic Growth in China, 536
Euro Crisis and the Global Market, 560
Can More Money Keep a Recovery Going?, 584
China's Exchange Rate Policy, 612
Aggregate Supply and Aggregate Demand in Action, 640
Inventory Investment in a 2011 Contraction, 666
Labour Markets in Slow Recovery, 692
Harper's Fiscal Policy, 720
The Bank of Canada Fights Recession in 2011, 744
A Tariff on Ski Jackets, 766
RBC theory, 688–691*f*, 690*f*
Reagan, Ronald, 713
real business cycle theory, 688–691, 689*f*, 690*f*
real estate bubble, 702
real exchange rate, 603
real GDP, 473, 485*t*
and actual expenditure and planned expenditure, 653
and aggregate demand, 648
and aggregate expenditure, 648, 651
calculation of, 473, 473*t*, 484*t*
chained-dollar real GDP, 484–485
China, 476, 476*f*
consumption as function of, 651
decrease in, 666–667
equilibrium real GDP, 663–665, 718
with fixed price level, 652–655
fluctuations of, 474, 475
forecasts, 480–481
growth in world economy, 521–522
inflation and deflation, 500
limitations, 477–479
market for, 737, 737*f*, 738–739, 739*f*
and money holding, 578
overnight loans rate, change in, 736
quantity demanded, 628
quantity supplied, 624
real GDP per person. *See* real GDP per person
standard of living across countries, 476
standard of living over time, 474–475
and unemployment, 498–499
United States, 476
uses and limitations, 474–479
real GDP per person, 474–475, 479, **518**

Canada, 520
sustained growth of, 518–519
world economy, 521–522
real interest rate, 505, **549**–550, 557,
    559, 712, 735
real property, 42
real wage rate, 498, **524,** 624
recession, 475
    Bank of Canada, role of, 736–737,
        736*f*
    costs of, 700
    double-dip recession, 480–481
    fiscal policy, 630
    monetary policy, 630
    stagflation, 637, 681
recessionary gap, 635
recognition lag, 719
recovery, 742
redistribution of income, 500
reference base year, 485
Registered Retirement Saving Plans
    (RRSPs), 534
regulatory barriers, 760
related goods, 59, 63
relationship
    direct relationship, 16, 17*f*
    inverse relationship, 17–18, 18*f*
    negative relationship, 17–18, 18*f,* 25,
        25*f*
    positive relationship, 16, 17*f,* 25
    slope of a relationship, 20–22
relative price, 56, 57
rent, 4
rent seeking, 765
research and development, 535
reserves, 571, 732*f,* 736, 736*f,* 738, 738*f*
resources
    inflation and deflation, 500
    misallocated resources, 31
    natural resources. *See* natural resources
    unused resources, 31
revenue, government, 704, 706, 706*f*
Ricardo, David, 531
Ricardo-Barro effect, 556, 556*f*
RIM, 4
risk premium, 557
Romer, Christina, 718, 719*f*
Romer, Paul, 532
Roosevelt, Franklin D., 492
Royal Bank of Canada, 571, 692
Rule of 70, 518–519, 519*f*
Russia, 6, 41, 44

S
safe securities, 702

safety regulations, 760
Sala-i-Martin, Xavier, 620–622
salaries, 472
Samuelson, Paul, 53
Saskatchewan, 498
saving, 534, **544**
    dissaving, 649
    income taxes, 712
    national saving, 545, 549
    taxes and incentive to save and invest,
        712
saving function, 648, 649, 649*f*
saving plans, 648–649
scarcity, 2, 30–31
scatter diagram, 14–16, 15*f,* 633
Schumpeter, Joseph, 532, 619
Scotiabank. *See* Bank of Nova Scotia
Scotland, 573
sealed-bid auction, 85–86
securities, 571
security, 478
self-interest, 5
    vs. selfish actions, 9
    and social interest, 5–7, 9
    vs. social interest, 758
selfish actions, 9
sellers, 56
services. *See* goods and services
settlement balances rate, 731–732
short run
    money market equilibrium, 580
    multiplier, 664*f*
    real exchange rate, 603
    transition to long run, 581
short-run aggregate supply, 625, 625*f*
**short-run macroeconomic equilibrium,
    632,** 632*f*
short-run Phillips curve, 684, 684*f*
short-term unemployment, 496*f*
shortage, 67
Siklos, Pierre, 774–776
Singapore, 522
slope, 20
    across an arc, 21–22, 22*f*
    aggregate expenditure curve, 658, 658*f*
    of curved line, 21–22
    and marginal propensities, 650
    negative slope, 20*f*
    at a point (in curved line), 21, 21*f*
    positive slope, 20*f*
    of a relationship, 20–22
    of straight line, 20–21, 20*f,* 24–25
Smith, Adam, 51, 53, 531, 534
Smoot-Hawley tariff, 764
social interest, 5, 9, 758

social justice, 478
social loss
    import quota, 759–760
    tariff, 757–758
social science, 10
Solow, Robert, 531
South Africa, 534, 758
South America, 521, 700, 760
"spaghetti bowl" problem, 54
specialization, 38
stabilization policy, 775
stagflation, 637, 681
standard of living
    across countries, 476
    and economic growth, 36
    over time, 474–475
    rising, in Canada, 474*f*
state of nature, 64
statistical discrepancy, 472
Statistics Canada, 471, 485, 493, 501,
    640
stock, 546
stock market, 546
store of value, 569
straight line
    equations of straight lines, 24–25
    negative relationship, 25, 25*f*
    position of, 25
    positive relationships, 25
    slope of, 20–21, 20*f,* 24–25
strawberries, 71
structural change, 497–498
structural deficit, 714, 715*f*
structural surplus, 714, 715*f*
structural unemployment, 497, 498
subsidy, export, 760
substitutes, 57, 59, 63
substitution effect, 57
    aggregate demand, 629
    aggregate demand curve, 661–662
    international substitution effect, 661
    intertemporal substitution effect, 629,
        661
Sumner, Scott, 584
supplementary labour income, 472
suppliers, number of, 64
supply, 62–65
    see also demand and supply model
    aggregate supply. *See* aggregate supply;
        AS-AD model
    change in supply. *See* change in supply
    foreign exchange market, 595, 597
    funds in global markets, 557–558
    global loanable funds market, 557–558
    law of supply, 62, 65*t*

of loanable funds, 551–552, 551*f*
minimum supply price, 63
quantity supplied, 62
supply curve, 62–63, 63*f*
supply curve, 62–63, 63*f,* 76
Canadian dollars, 597, 597*f*
shift in, 64
supply of loanable funds, 551–552, 551*f*
supply of loanable funds curve, 551–552, 551*f*
supply-side economics, 710–713, 718
surplus
budget surplus, 555, 555*f,* 705, 705*f,* 707
cyclical surplus, 714, 715*f*
and prices, 67
structural surplus, 714, 715*f*
Sweden, 743

T
tariff revenue, 764
tariffs, 756–758, 756*f,* 760, 766–767
tax multiplier, 716
tax wedge, 711
taxes
automatic changes in tax revenues, 714
on expenditure, 711
incentive to save and invest, 712
income taxes, 659, 710–711, 710*f,* 712
indirect tax, 472
Laffer curve, 713, 713*f*
net taxes, 548
saving, incentives for, 534
tax rate, and real interest rate, 712
Taylor rule, 743
TD Canada Trust, 571
technological change, 36
and diminishing returns, 531–532
financial innovation, 578
and labour productivity, 529–530
and population growth, 531
potential GDP, 627
and profit, 532
technology, and change in supply, 64
3-month Treasury bill rate, 734
Tim Hortons, 41
time lags, 719, 739–740
time-series graph, 482–483, 482*f*
trade restrictions, 756–760
case against protection, 761–765
cheap labour, competition with, 762
dumping, 761

exploitation of developing countries, 763
export subsidies, 760
health, safety, and regulation barriers, 760
import quota, 758–760, 759*f*
infant-industry argument, 761
and jobs, 762
lax environmental standards, 762–763
and off-shore outsourcing, 763–764
rent seeking, 765
tariff revenue, 764
tariffs, 756–758, 756*f,* 766–767
trade wars, 764
voluntary export restraint, 760
trade wars, 764
tradeoff, 8
along production possibilities frontier, 31
policy tradeoff, 773
shifting short-run Phillips curve, 686
transfer payments, 471, 705
Treasury bills, 546, 571, 573
trend, 483
trough, 475
trust and mortgage loan companies, 546, 571

U
Uhlig, Harald, 718, 719*f*
Ukraine, 478
underground economy, 477–478
unemployment
cyclical unemployment, 497
duration of unemployment spells, 496*f*
employment-to-population ratio, 495
frictional unemployment, 497
and inflation, 684–686, 684*f,* 685*f*
involuntary part-time rate, 494
labour force participation rate, 494–495, 495*f*
long-term unemployment, 496, 496*f*
lost human capital, 492–493
lost incomes and production, 492
most costly unemployment, 496
natural unemployment, 497
official measure of, 495–496
other definitions, 495–496
Phillips curve, 684–686, 684*f,* 685*f*
problem of, 492–495
and real GDP, 498–499
short-term unemployment, 496*f*
structural unemployment, 497, 498
unemployment rate, 494
unemployment benefits, 498

unemployment rate, 494, 494*f*
Canada, 515
natural unemployment rate, 497–498, 685–686, 685*f*
and output gap, 499*f*
unit of account, 568–569, 568*t*
United Kingdom, 521, 711, 743
United Nations, 479
United Nations' Food and Agriculture Organization, 44
United States
bank bailouts, 7
carbon emissions, 6
current account deficit, 701–702
debtor nation, 609
Doha Round, 758
double-dip recession, 480–481
dual mandate, 742–743
Employ American Workers Act (EAWA), 54
ethanol production, 45
fiscal stimulus, 717
global trade, 752
housing market bubble, 554
Human Development Index (HDI), 479
international borrowing, issue of, 609
purchasing power parity (PPP), 476
real GDP, 476
real GDP per person, 521
recession, 775
recovery, 584–585
tax wedge, 711
unemployment benefits, 498
unemployment in, 506–507
unrelated variables, 19, 19*f*
unused resources, 31
U.S. Commerce Department, 54
U.S. Department of Agriculture, 44
U.S. Federal Reserve, 7, 492, 515, 547, 554, 559, 574, 584–585, 630, 741–743
see also central bank
U.S. International Trade Commission (ITC), 762
U.S. National Bureau of Economic Research, 475

V
variables
cycle, 483
direct relationship, 16, 17*f*
inverse relationship, 17–18, 18*f*
with maximum or minimum, 18, 19*f*
more than two variables, 22–23, 23*f*

moving in opposite directions, 17–18
moving in same direction, 16–17
negative relationship, 17–18, 18*f*
positive relationship, 16, 17*f*
real variables, 505
time-series graphs, 482
trend, 483
unrelated variables, 19, 19*f*
velocity of circulation, 582
voluntary export restraint, 760

W

Wachovia, 547
wages, 4, 472
 efficiency wage, 498
 minimum wage, 498
 money wage rate, 627, 627*f,* 679

real wage rate, 498, 524, 624
wants, 57
Washington Mutual, 547
wealth, 544
 national wealth, 545
 redistribution, and inflation, 500
 and saving, 551
wealth effect, 628–629, 661
Wealth of Nations (Smith), 51, 534
Wells Fargo Bank, 560
what (economic question), 3
willingness to pay, 34, 58
women
 microloans, 530
 in the work force, 477
Woods, Karen Cordes, 692
working-age population, 493

World Trade Organization (WTO), 53,
 758, 761
Wright, Craig, 692

X

x-axis, 13
x-coordinate, 13

Y

y-axis, 13
y-coordinate, 13
Yao Jian, 536

Z

Zimbabwe, 479

College students (p. 1) Adresr/ Shutterstock

Nike factory (p. 5) Adek Berry/AFP/ Getty Images

Intel chip (p. 6) Christian Prand/ Imagebroker/Alamy

Smokestacks (p. 6) Don B. Stevenson/ Alamy

House for sale sign (p. 7) Toronto Star/ GetStock

Grown for biofuel sign (p. 29) Dave Reede/All Canada Photos

Jet factory (p. 41) Bloomberg/ Getty Images

Garment worker (p. 41) David R. Frazier Photolibrary Inc./Alamy

Adam Smith (p. 51) John Kay/ Bettmann/Corbis

Jagdish Bhagwati (p. 52) Courtesy of Michael Parkin

Coffee shop (p. 55) Image Source/ Getty Images

Ocean oil platform (p. 69) Alberto Incrocci/Riser/Getty Images

Strawberry picker (p. 71) Chris O'Meara/AP Images

Alfred Marshall (p. 83) Public Domain/ Wikipedia

Susan Athey (p. 84) Courtesy of Susan Athey

Financial analyst (p. 467) Michael Pearcy/Alamy

McDonald's (p. 476) Scott Olson/ Getty Images

Restaurant chefs (p. 477) Philippe Lopez/AFP/Getty Images

Woman in home kitchen (p. 477) Elise Manand Rus/AFP/Getty Images

Smiling woman (p. 491) Dmitry Shironosov/Alamy

Great Depression (p. 492) George Grantham Bain Collection/Library of Congress

David Hume (p. 513) Library of Congress

Peter Howitt (p. 514) Courtesy of Peter Howitt

Cityscape (p. 517) JLImages/Alamy

Steam engine (p. 529) National Railway Museum/SSPL/The Image Works

Outdoor market (p. 530) Jose Silva Pinto/AP Images

TMX board (p. 543) Malcolm Taylor/ Getty Images

Fannie Mae (p. 547) Karen Bleirer/ AFP/Getty Images

Freddie Mac (p. 547) Paul J. Richards/ AFP/Getty Images

Alan Greenspan (p. 559) Scott J. Ferrell/CQ-Roll Call Group/Getty Images

Wallet with money (p. 567) Denis Pepin/Fotolia

Currency exchange kiosk (p. 593) Greg Balfour Evans/Alamy

Yuan and U.S. dollars (p. 612) Reuters

Joseph Schumpeter (p. 619) Bettmann/Corbis

Xavier Sala i Martín (p. 620) Courtesy of Michael Parkin

Construction site (p. 623) Mike Dobel/ Alamy

Jim Flaherty (p. 630) Toronto Star/ GetStock

John McCallum (p. 630) Tom Hanson/ CP Images

Ben Bernanke (p. 630) Susan Walsh/ AP Images

Mervyn King (p. 630) Martin Rickett/ PA Wire/AP Images

Jean-Claude Trichet (p. 630) Bernd Kammerer/dapd/AP Images

Mark Carney (p. 630) Adrian Wyld/CP Images/AP Images

Shipping containers (p. 647) Photo Bliss/Alamy

Couple looking at bills (p. 677) WavebreakMediaMicro/Fotolia

John Maynard Keynes (p. 699) Stock Montage

Ricardo J. Caballero (p. 700) Courtesy of Michael Parkin

Parliament Hill (p. 703) Denis Roger/Shutterstock

Christina Romer (p. 719) Tom Williams/CQ-Roll Call Group/ Getty Images

Robert Barro (p. 719) Courtesy of Robert Barro

Harald Uhlig (p. 719) Courtesy of Harald Uhlig

Bank of Canada (p. 727) Bloomberg/ Getty Images

FedEx plane (p. 751) Oliver Berg/dpa/ Corbis

WTO meeting (p. 758) Fabrice Coffrini/AFP/Getty Images

Milton Friedman (p. 773) Marshall Heinrichs/Addison Wesley

Pierre Siklos (p. 774) Courtesy of Bill Todd and Pierre Siklos

NOTES

NOTES

NOTES

NOTES

READING BETWEEN THE LINES

2 The Rising Opportunity Cost of Food   44

3 Demand and Supply: The Price of Coffee   74

20 Real GDP Forecasts in the Uncertain Economy of 2011   480

21 Jobs Growth Lags Recovery   506

22 Economic Growth in China   536

23 Euro Crisis and the Global Market   560

24 Can More Money Keep a Recovery Going?   584

25 China's Exchange Rate Policy   612

26 Aggregate Supply and Aggregate Demand in Action   640

27 Inventory Investment in a 2011 Contraction   666

28 Labour Markets in Slow Recovery   692

29 Harper's Fiscal Policy   720

30 The Bank of Canada Fights Recession in 2011   744

31 A Tariff on Ski Jackets   766